History Of The Town Of Peterborough, Hillsborough County, New Hampshire

Albert Smith

HISTORY

OF THE

TOWN OF PETERBOROUGH,

HILLSBOROUGH COUNTY,

NEW HAMPSHIRE,

WITH THE

REPORT OF THE PROCEEDINGS AT THE CENTENNIAL CELEBRATION
IN 1839; AN APPENDIX CONTAINING THE RECORDS OF THE
ORIGINAL PROPRIETORS; AND A GENEALOGICAL
AND HISTORICAL REGISTER.

By ALBERT SMITH, M. D., LL. D.

"Memor esto majorum."

BOSTON:

PRESS OF GEORGE H. ELLIS,

No. 7 TREMONT PLACE.

1876.

James Miller

PREFACE.

THIS history is given to the public as it is. That it would have been better with more research and a longer time devoted to its preparation, there can be no doubt; but the hastening years and the attendant infirmities of age admonished the writer (now past seventy-five years) that the work must soon be completed, if ever.

The work was undertaken at the earnest solicitation of friends who thought it might prove an agreeable and useful occupation, as I withdrew from the labors of an active profession; and it has now for five years engaged almost my entire attention. It has proved a work of great labor. Till I commenced my researches, I did not realize my own ignorance, nor the ignorance of others of my own age, of the early history of the town. The old men of the second generation, so familiar with all the early affairs of the town, were gone. Every succeeding generation knows less of its predecessors, and the men of the third generation were found to be sadly deficient in any definite knowledge of their ancestors; so there has been little or nothing to my hand for this history. Mr. Dunbar's history is barely a sketch, which it purports to be, and is of very little value in an extended history like this. The town records have gone on uninterruptedly to the present time, but they furnish little material for history; they do little else than furnish the dates of certain events. No town papers of any kind are found preserved, till near the beginning of the present century. The invoice is not found till 1792, but can then be traced down to the present time. All these sources of information have been carefully explored and used.

This history was begun too late,—not till the second generation had all passed away, and the third had become old men. It is unfortunate that the second generation was suffered to pass away before any one had been found to put in a permanent form the large knowledge which it possessed relating to the men and events in the early history of Peterborough. I have found many descendants of the early settlers of the town lamentably deficient in the history of their own families, being able to go no farther back than their grandfathers. I have had, in numerous instances, to make up the first and often the second generations of these families as I could from other sources.

At the present time, tradition seems to have died out. Many large families have become extinct, strangers having come into their places, who knew not the fathers; while other families have been greatly reduced by emigration and removal. Altogether, such changes have taken place that it becomes almost impossible to trace back the history of the early times.

A great loss was experienced in the destruction of the church records in the conflagration of Dea. Morison's house, in 1791. We can never know much concerning the establishing of the church, or of the ministries of Messrs. Morrison and Annan. This has been a great misfortune, as the history of the church in those times was the history of the town. No private diaries and no other written record of individuals have come down to us as they have done in many other towns, to throw light on these times. The fathers were men to *act* rather than write, and so our record comes short, no one having recorded their deeds.

Much aid has been afforded by Mr. Dunbar's "Church Book of the Congregational Society," which he kept faithfully through his ministry of twenty-seven years,—from 1799 to 1827. All his facts and items have been found to be correct, and have greatly helped to correct dates and determine events in the town history.

But with all the sources of information furnished, and with the helps and aids from every quarter, we must yet ask, Who is there to tell us of the habits, customs, manners, modes of life, amusements, etc., of the fathers ? The third generation, now on the stage, is small and profoundly ignorant of these matters, and we can hardly go beyond conjecture on these topics.

I am especially indebted to George W. Moore, Esq., of Medina, Mich., for much information in relation to the early inhabitants of the town, and for some of the most interesting sketches of the book. His interest and help have encouraged me in every stage of my work. N. H. Morison, LL. D., Provost of the Peabody Institute, Baltimore, Md., has made many researches, and examined much historical record out of my reach, and kindly looked over my manuscript before publishing. I wish gratefully to acknowledge his continued interest and encouragement in all stages of my labors. I am also not less indebted to John H. Morison, D. D., for substantial aid to the book, as well as an encouraging word to the writer amid the perplexity of his researches.

I am also especially indebted to Dr. David Youngman, of Boston, for the very efficient aid he has rendered me in the various stages of my labor. During the past winter, and through a long indisposition in the spring, he has been my agent and manager in all matters relating to this history. He has not only furnished important facts and items, but very largely assisted in correcting proofs.

He also had the entire charge of the lithographic engravings, some of which were obtained by his own exertions, and all of them received his personal oversight. Although a few were obtained from old, faded pictures, they reflect great credit on him and the Messrs. Bufford, the gentlemanly and accomplished artists.

The author and readers of this history are also indebted to Dr. Youngman for the very full and well-arranged index at the close of the volume.

I have also been indebted to many others for genealogical records, whose aid I have acknowledged in its proper place in the book.

But for the interest and encouragement of a few friends, being left generally to work out the history as I could, I should have faltered and failed in my enterprise, so great and complicated were the difficulties that environed me.

The book now goes forth in the Centennial year, as the last and only tribute we can pay to the fathers who were on the stage a century ago. It is with regret we say that perhaps the best part of their history is unrelated, having passed out of the recollection of any one living; yet what little we have saved is now put into a permanent form for another century.

ALBERT SMITH.

PETERBOROUGH, N. H., Sept. 1, 1876.

CONTENTS.

CHAPTER I.

The Objects of History. — Characters of the First Set-
tlers. — Use of Town Histories. — Scanty Materials for
the Same. — Decrease of the Early Families. — Town
had its Origin in a Spirit of Speculation. — Petition to
Massachusetts Legislature. — Petition Granted. — Act
became a Law in 1738. — Grantees Admitted, Survey
Made, 1738. — East Mountain not Included. — Starting
Point. — Report of Surveyor. — Accepted and Town
Granted. — Grantees Selected. — All Falls into the
Hands of Four. — Their Character and Object. — First
Meeting and Drawing Lots. — Proprietors' Meeting in
Town, 1753. — Surveys in Town, 1738. — A Farm to each
Proprietor of 500 Acres. — Masonian Proprietors Quit-
claim their Right, 1748, by Agreement. — Conditions. —
Early Surveys of Little Value.

CHAPTER II.

Character of Early Settlers. — Intelligent. — Stern Presbyterians. — Persecutions. — Emigration to Ireland. — Their
Hardships. — History of the Scotch-Irish. — Irish Rebellion and Confiscation. — Second Rebellion. — Repeopling
from Scotland. — Principally about 1610. — One Company from London. — Prosperity. — Persecution of Pres-

byterians in Scotland. — Claverhouse sent against them.
— Contest from 1670 to 1688. — Presbyterians Rush to
Ireland. — Ulster County Prosperous. — Exactions of
Government. — Advance of Rents. — Emigrate in great
Numbers. — Beginning Eighteenth Century. — Landlords
Alarmed. — First and Second Emigration. — Settled in
Pennsylvania, Virginia, Tennessee, &c. — Character of
these Men. — Number of Descendants. — Service in the
Revolution. — All Loyal. — Their Perseverance.

CHAPTER III.

Uncertainty as to the Early Settlers. — Names. — All
came to Town. — Time of Settlement. — How Fixed. —
Petition. — Time of Centennial. — Small Party, 1742. —
Morison and Russell, 1743. — Visit of Indians to their
Camp. — Their Theft. — Return to Townsend. — Frontier
Line. — Danger of Settlement. — Causes that Retarded
the Settlement of the Town. — No Permanent Settle-
ments till 1749. — After Close of War of 1744 and the
Quitclaim of the Masonian Proprietors. — Tardiness to
Comply with it. — Causes.

CHAPTER IV.

Name of the Town. — How Obtained. — Early Method
Naming Towns. — Account of Earl Peterborough. — Not
on Proprietors' Records till 1753. — Petition for Incorporation. — Town Charter. — First Meeting. — Record of
Town Meetings. — Entire Loss of Town Papers. — Materials for Early History Sparse.

CHAPTER V.

No Permanent Settlements till 1749. — All Residences
before Temporary. — Great Increase from 1749 to 1759.
— Causes. — Not Checked by the War of 1754. — Reasons. — Loyalty of the First Settlers, and Disasters to
· them. — The First Settlers of the Town.

CHAPTER VI.

Home Life. — Apparent Austerity. — Fun and Humor. — Daily Family Worship. — Industry of all. — Hard Condition of Women. — Effects of Bible. — Intelligence of Settlers. — How Obtained. — Diet. — Wild Game. — Fish. — No Luxuries. — Articles Used. — Abundant. — Mode of Dressing. — Probably Insufficient. — Poor Dwellings. — All Attended Meeting. — Inconveniences.

CHAPTER VII.

Home Manufactures. — Flax preceded Wool. — Wolves Common. — Process of Preparing Wool. — Articles Manufactured. — No Machinery but Home-made, Cheap, and Rude. — Was a Business. — Prices. — Flax Culture a Great Business. — Flax Crop Profitable. — Process of Preparing Flax. — Great Skill. — All Families Engaged in Manufacture. — Decline after Revolution. — All now Passed Away.

CHAPTER VIII.

Difficulties of the Subject. — The Use of Spirit. — Its Dangers not known. — Its Excess an Abuse. — Wrestling an Amusement. — Quoits. — Social Gatherings. — Mode of Recreation. — Spirits used Freely. — Conversation Useful and Instructive. — Various kinds of Recreations. — Raisings, Huskings, Log-rollings, Quiltings, Appleparings, and Parties to Destroy Wild Game. — Trainings and Musters. — Election Days. — Horse Racing and the Horse Jockeys. — Bowling Alleys.

CHAPTER IX.

First Meeting-houses. — Rev. John Morrison. — His Scandalous Ministry according to a Petition from Inhabitants

2

CHAPTER XII.

CHAPTER XIII.

CHAPTER XIV.

CHAPTER XV.

CHAPTER XVI.

Legislation on Roads in Town Meeting. — Roads Poor
before Incorporation. — A Road Cut and Cleared by Proprietors from Meeting-House to New Ipswich in 1738. —
Object of Incorporation to Improve the Roads. — The
Roads in Town.

CHAPTER XVII.

Bell Factory. — Phœnix. — Eagle. — South. — North. —
Union Manufacturing Co. — Paper Manufacture. — Wool-
len Manufacture. — Peg Mill. — Stone Grist Mill. — Bas-
ket Shop. — Manufacture of Barometers and Thermome-
ters. — Manufacture of Hand-Cards for Cotton and Wool.
— Machine Shop and Foundry. — Marble and Granite
Works. — Briggs' Manufactory of Portable and Patent
Piano-Stools.

CHAPTER XVIII.

Situation of the Town, etc.— Village.— Little Waste Land
at First.— East Mountain Added. — Uneven in its Surface. — Best Portions of It.— Forests. — Letter of S. J.
Todd, Esq. — Forests Destroyed and Land Deteriorated.
— Small Growth of Wood now. — Game has all Disappeared. — Climate not Materially Changed. — Salubrious.
— Longevity Increased. — Causes. — Rivers. — Contoocook. — Nubanusit. — Brooks. — Arboreal Products. —
Wild Fruit. — Wild Animals. — Insects Injurious to Vegetation.'— Putnam's Grove.

CHAPTER XIX.

Three Cemeteries in Town. — The Little Cemetery. —
Old Cemetery. — First Burials in It. — Gravestones

ILLUSTRATIONS.

IN THE GENEALOGY.

Albert Smith.

HISTORY OF PETERBOROUGH.

CHAPTER I.

GRANT AND LAYING OUT OF THE TOWN IN 1738.

The Objects of History.—Characters of the First Settlers.—Use of Town Histories.—Scanty Materials for the Same.—Decrease of the Early Families.—Town had its Origin in a Spirit of Speculation.—Petition to Massachusetts Legislature.—Petition Granted.—Act became a Law in 1738.—Grantees Admitted, Survey Made, 1738.—East Mountain not Included.—Starting Point.—Report of Surveyor.—Accepted and Town Granted.—Grantees Selected.—All Falls into the Hands of Four.—Their Character and Object.—First Meeting and Drawing Lots.—Proprietors' Meeting in Town, 1753.—Surveys in Town, 1738.—A Farm to each Proprietor of 500 Acres.—Masonian Proprietors Quitclaim their Right, 1748, by Agreement.—Conditions.—Early Surveys of Little Value.

THE object of history is to develop the causes, the first germs or movement of things, as well as to relate the events themselves, that occur in consequence. Local history is perhaps, in many respects, much less important than general, but nevertheless it is of great value to the localities to which it pertains, and to the *descendants* of those concerned in the historical record.

It can never cease to be a matter of surprise and wonder how the early pioneers of the forbidding soil and climate of New Hampshire rushed upon their lands and beat their way amid all the difficulties and privations of such an adventure, and finally, surmounting all obstacles, attained an eminent

3

success. It is to be remembered that the soil was then in its virgin state, and was very productive, even with inadequate cultivation, when to us now it requires vigorous muscular power and strong fertilizers to yield much return. Yet very much of this success was due to the men, to their persevering spirit, and enlightened will. History must tell us of these men. They were not an ordinary race, not men of grovelling appetites, of low, mean aspirations, or narrow-minded views; but they were strong-minded, earnest, cheerful and hopeful. And then they were religious in the best sense of the word, — and that made good moral, conscientious men. If they knew little of other books, they knew their Bible well. Such men were adequate to anything. They boldly plunged into the dense forests, sat down with their families, almost isolated from the world, and there worked with patience and perseverance for a good home and a good inheritance, with all the comforts of life. And how fortunate for us and our country that our fathers possessed this bold enterprise and courage, even if it often impelled them, as it did, to very frequent changes from one place to another.

Town histories are not generally of much interest, except to the descendants of the early inhabitants and those concerned in its present administration; yet there are points in all these productions that are of great value in making up the rise and progress of the country, and in accounting for the opinions and conduct of the inhabitants. It has its difficulties equal to any other history, if not even more. The early settlers were unlettered men, little accustomed to commit their thoughts to written language, with only enough of the rudiments of learning to transact their business; and it was not to be expected that any written record of them should come down to us. We have hardly anything for a long series of years but the scanty and unsatisfactory record of the town-meetings. We have not been so fortunate as to find a diary of a single individual in all this region, and only one thing of value has come to us; viz., the Church Records of Rev. E. Dunbar, during his ministry from 1799 to 1827. This has been of great value, as to dates of deaths and marriages, and has been found to be perfectly correct and reliable, as compared with other sources of information. Perhaps we should not omit to mention that the old Cemetery has often been almost the only history that could be obtained of a few individuals. So imperfect and scanty are the materials of history in the town that, in many instances, we cannot tell where the early settlers lived, where at the time of their death, or what became of their families. Tradition can help us but little. Many of the old and influential families have faded out so entirely as not to leave a trace behind them; and others, that have left descendants, are no better, as they know little or nothing of their ancestors. Of the large and influential families of Todd, Templeton, Swan, Alld, Stuart, Cunningham, Mitchell, Ritchie, Ferguson, and many more, not a single individual of their name remains in the town; and of the large families of Steele Robbe, Smith, Holmes, Moore, and Morison, their numbers are greatly lessened, and they are growing less every year. This presents an unfavorable prospect to an historian of the town, for he has, in many cases, neither written nor traditional aid on which he can rely. But this history, such as it is, is presented to the public with all its imperfections.

We have every reason to believe that the first conception of the township, which afterwards took the name of Peterborough, had its entire origin in the speculative spirit of the petitioners to the Massachusetts Legislature, which was then supposed to have jurisdiction over this unappropriated territory. Not one of these petitioners or of the proprietors ever settled on this soil. It might have been a mode of proceeding suited to the times, and was encouraged, though urged on false pretences, as a means of more rapidly increasing the settlement.

At a meeting of the Great and General Court of Massachusetts, assembled Dec. 5, 1737, Samuel Heywood and others urge their petition as follows: "That in the year 1721 they humbly preferred their petition to the Great and General Court then sitting, praying, for the reasons then mentioned, they might be granted a tract of land on Souhegan River for a township, being without land for their posterity, and desirous they should not remove from out of the province, but settle together under the laws and liberties of this government, where they were born; that the honorable House of Representatives then passed a vote in favor of them, but, the Indian War then breaking out, they dropped their petition, and that ever since they have held together, and have often petitioned this honorable Court for a tract of unappropriated land for a township."

They go on to say, " that, although they received much encouragement, but by the carelessness and indiscretion of those who appeared for the petitioners, their petition never passed this honorable Court till the year 1735, when they voted them a township of six miles square, but voted that they should be grantees of one of the line towns, and having made choice of one, the honorable Committee of the General Court assigned that township to the Hopkinton petitioners, which, although they do not doubt the justice of it, so far broke our Committee measures, and discouraged them, that they left their trust and companions, and most of them were admitted grantees in other townships. But, however, the far greater number of the petitioners kept to their first intention of settling together, though this accident made them quite irresolute for a season, and was the occasion that, hitherto, they have unhappily failed of it. Whereupon, the petitioners would humbly represent to your Excellency and honors that their design of settling together was, as they conceive, laudable in itself, and conducing to the public good, in cultivating the waste land of the Province, that they have a long while persevered in this design from the year 1721." The above petition was signed by forty-nine persons, and a grant of unappropriated land for a township six miles square, situated on what was commonly called the line of towns, was made, on the supposition that this territory was in the Province of Massachusetts. The following are the proceedings : —

In the House of Representatives, Dec. 8, 1737.

Read and ordered that the petition be granted, and the petitioners and their associates be, and are hereby empowered by a Surveyor and Chainmen on oath, to survey and lay out a township of the contents of six miles square, in some part of the unappropriated lands of the Province suitable for a township, and that they return a plat thereof to this Court within twelve months for confirmation. And for the more effectual bringing forward the settlement of said new town, ordered, "that there be sixty-three house lots laid out in a suitable and defensible manner, one of which to be for the first settled minister, and one for the second settled minister, and one for the school ; each of said three lots to draw equal divisions with the other grantees of the said sixty lots. That the grantees do, within three years from the confirmation of the plan, have settled on each home lot a good family, and in order thereto, that they build thereon a dwelling-house of eighteen feet square and seven feet studs at least, and finish the same, and have well fenced and brought to hay, grain, or ploughed, six acres to each home lot. That they settle an orthodox minister and build a decent convenient meeting-house for the public worship of God ; and that Col. Josiah Willard and Capt. John Hobson, with such as shall be appointed by the honorable board, be a Committee for admitting the grantees or settlers, and that they take effectual care that no persons are admitted as such who have had any grants for the space of three years, and that each grantee give bonds to the Province Treasurer or his successor in the sum of forty pounds for his fulfilling or complying with the terms or conditions of the grant ; and if any of the settlers fail of performing the said conditions, then his or their right or share to revert to and be at the disposition of the Province."

The above Act having become a law by the signature of Gov. Belcher, January 16, 1738, the Committee appointed to admit the grantees or settlers into a township granted the petitioners and other associates, whose names are entered on a petition of Samuel Heywood and others; *viz.*, William Dudley, Josiah Willard, and John Hobson, Esq., met at Woburn, March 17, 1738, and admitted sixty grantees of such as had not had any land grants for the three years last past. Not one of all this number ever settled on the land, or probably ever saw it. A majority of them belonged to Concord, as we learn by a vote, in regard to notifying meetings, August 12, 1738, "that the clerk be empowered to call meetings of the future by posting up notifications at Concord, &c., where great numbers of the proprietors dwell." It was now past

the middle of March, and no time was lost by the proprietors
in preparing to select and survey the township of unappropriated land granted them by the Legislature. They accordingly
employed one Joseph Wilder as Surveyor, and Joseph Richardson and Zacheus Lovell as Chainmen, to run the lines
round their grant, who were required to make oath to the
same. We see that the work was hurried as soon as the
spring should open and admit of an examination and survey
through the trackless wilds of this region, for by the 21st of
May succeeding the selection had been made, a plat laid out
and surveyed of a township six miles square.

We can form no idea of what governed the Surveyor in the
location of the town. It is to be supposed that he was aided
by some of the proprietors interested in the grant in selecting
the spot he did. After passing the mountain, no surveyor's
lines had ever been run; on the north to Hillsborough, and
perhaps even farther north, and on the west to Keene and
Hinsdale, a large amount of unappropriated land lay before
him. We suppose that he could go anywhere in this region
and lay out his six miles square. It was a rough country, and
contained a vast amount of waste land; the object would be
to select a plat that should be as free from these natural obstructions as possible.

We can imagine that, in search for this location, he came
through what was afterwards Temple, up to the Notch of the
Mountain, so called, where the great travelled road now runs.
Of course he desired to include as little of the East Mountains in his township as possible ; so he passed west of the
mountain somewhat, on very high land, where he could look
over a great portion of all the territory that would be included
in the new town. Here was spread out before him the Monadnock, in all its grandeur and beauty, which he was satisfied
that his survey would not reach ; also a large amphitheatre of
land, unbroken with any mountainous ridges or precipitous
hills, with a considerable river running through its midst.
With such a view before him, he no doubt determined to
carve his new township out of this particular region. All this
would be north-east from the great Monadnock Hill, as it is

called in the survey. These suppositions may account in some degree for what has seemed the fortunate location of Peterborough beyond that of any town in this part of the State.

The next proceeding of the Surveyor was to determine where he should make his starting point. He was now over the mountains, or sufficiently so as to leave them principally on the east, and so he commenced his survey at the southeast corner of the town, which must have been quite high on the mountain's side; nevertheless, sufficiently west to shun the East Mountains in the survey. It was determined to lay out the town in a square, each side being six miles in length, and exactly in the points of the compass. We have no vestige of this survey, except the following sworn report of the Surveyor and Chainmen, made to the Legislature: —

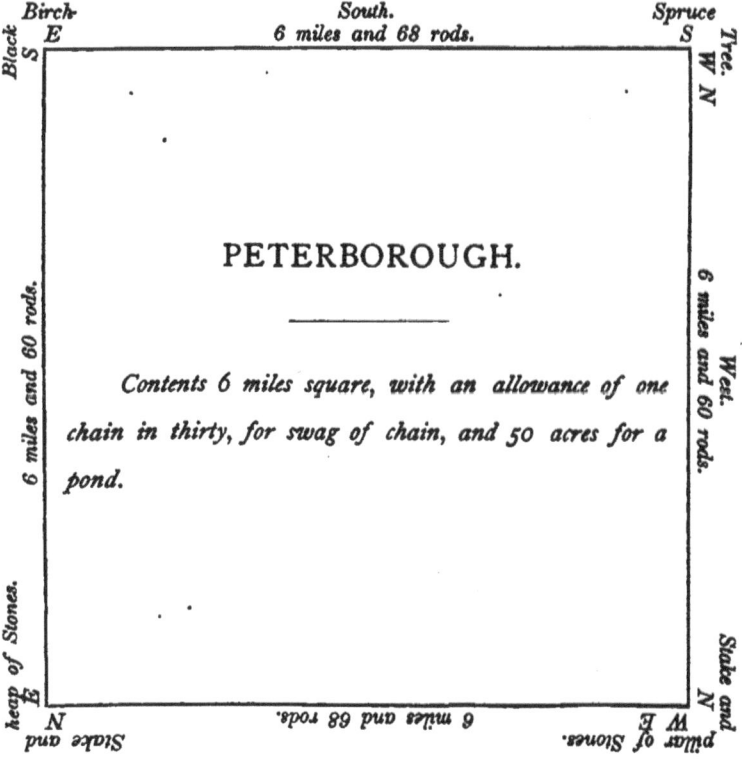

Birch. **South.** **Spruce**

6 miles and 68 rods.

PETERBOROUGH.

Contents 6 miles square, with an allowance of one chain in thirty, for swag of chain, and 50 acres for a pond.

Report of the Surveyors : —

May 21st, 1738.   Then finished the surveying and laying out of
a township, of the contents of six miles square, to satisfy a grant
of the Great and General Court of the Province of Massachusetts
Bay, made the 16th day of January, 1737, on the petition of
Samuel Heywood and others, and their associates, lying on the
easterly side of a great hill, called Monadnock Hill, between said
hill and a township laid out to the inhabitants of Salem and others
(Amherst), who served in the expedition to Canada in 1690, and
lyeth on a southerly branch of the Contoocook River, near the
head thereof, said branch running through it.   It began at a black
Birch Tree, the south-east corner, and from thence it ran west six
miles and sixty-eight rods by a line of marked trees to a spruce.
tree marked for the south-west corner ; from thence, it ran north
by a line of marked trees six miles and sixty rods to a stake and
pillar of stones, the northwest corner; and from thence it ran east
by a line of marked trees six miles and sixty-eight rods to a stake
and heap of stones, the north-east corner ; and from thence straight
to where it began, six miles and sixty rods.   The lines above said
did contain the contents of six miles square, with the allowance of
one chain in thirty for swag of chain, and fifty acres for a pond.

JOSEPH WILDER, *Surveyor.*

Then follows, June 8, 1738, the certificate of the oath of
the above of Joseph Wilder, the Surveyor, and of Joseph
Richardson and Zacheus Lovell, Chainmen, before William
Dudley, Justice of the Peace, of Boston.

The Act confirming the land to the grantees was as follows:

In House of Representatives, June 14, 1738.

Read and ordered that the plat be accepted, and the land therein
delineated and described be and hereby are confirmed to the
Grantees, the Petitioners mentioned in the petition of Samuel
Heywood and others and their associates, agreeable to the grant
of this Court of said Township made them at the settling, begun
and held the thirtieth of November last past, and to their heirs and
assigns respectfully forever, they effectually complying with and
fulfilling the conditions of the grant.   Provided the Plat exceed
not the quantity of six miles square of land and does not inter-
fere with any former grant.

The grant of the township having been confirmed by the General Court, the sixty grantees or proprietors having been selected by the Committee of the Legislature, and Jonathan Prescott, by a subsequent Act of June 28, 1738, having been authorized to call the first meeting, they were now in order to begin their new enterprise. Singular as it may seem, in all this array of the names of sixty proprietors, only four are found to be really concerned in the settlement; *viz.*, John Hill, John Fowle, Jr., Jeremiah Gridley, and Peter Prescott, not one of whom was among the original petitioners.

These men seem to have been purely speculators, who bought out the original grantees for their own profit. What must we think of those disinterested petitioners, whose zeal for the public good was so great that they were only anxious for permission to redeem some of the waste lands of the Province from the wilderness; and whose desire to form a community by themselves was so strong that they had wearied the General Court for seventeen years with importunate petitions for a township of land, where they might settle in a body, and enjoy that pleasant social intercourse with each other which they so much coveted? Many of them must have disposed of their rights before the grant was finally made, on the 14th of June, 1738, and in six months from that time only two of the proprietors, and they not among the petitioners, retained theirs. Every man and one woman who signed that petition of Dec. 7, 1737, forgetting the fervent zeal which, in it, he had professed for the improvement of the Province, forgetting the brotherly love which he said had bound him to his fellow-petitioners for seventeen years of earnest longing and waiting, of trial and disappointment, and just when success had crowned his efforts and made the end sure, sold out, pocketed the profits, and was ready, it is supposed, for another adventure.

Jonathan Prescott, as empowered by the General Court, issued his mandate for a meeting of the proprietors on the 25th of July, 1738, the meeting to take place the same day, at the public house, or tavern, of Luke Verdy, in Boston. The ease with which a meeting could be called in a single day of

4

sixty proprietors, a majority of whom lived twenty miles distant, shows conclusively that the rights of the other proprietors had been already gathered into a few hands in the immediate vicinity. The changes which had taken place among the proprietors were shown in the meeting, as John Hill, a new name, was chosen moderator, and Peter Prescott, another new name, was made proprietors' clerk. At an adjourned meeting, a committee of five (any three of them to act) was appointed to "view" the township, and to lay out "the town lots" required as a condition of the grant. This committee consisted of Hill, Fowle, Gridley, Jonathan and Peter Prescott; none but Jonathan Prescott among the original proprietors. This meeting also appointed John Hill treasurer, levied a tax of ten pounds on each right, to defray the expenses of the survey, etc., and empowered the committee, or any three of them, to agree with some person to build a saw-mill, and fix the price of sawing.

It is evident, from the officers chosen, from the committee appointed, and from the whole proceeding, that the four associates, Hill, Fowle, Gridley, and Prescott, had the management entirely in their own hands. It is not known how many of the original proprietors still retained their rights; but on the 29th of November, when the first division of the lots took place, these four men had become proprietors of all but two lots in the township. Each of the four represented himself as the assignee of fourteen proprietors, but Hill actually obtained the portion of sixteen proprietors, we suppose, to make up the sixty required in the grant. After Nov. 29, 1738, when this drawing took place, the two original proprietors, Hubbard and Jonathan Prescott, disappear from the record, and the other four act as sole proprietors of the township.

We can only briefly allude to the proceedings of the proprietors up to 1756, by relating all their important acts. The proprietors usually met at a tavern in Boston, but sometimes at Mr. Foster's in Woburn, and once at Peterborough, Sept. 26, 27, 1753, where, for the first time on their record, the name of the town, Peterborough, is recorded as the place of meeting. Mr. Gridley usually acted as moderator. The following are some of their proceedings, related without the particular dates. They ordered the town to be surveyed by Joseph Wilder, who laid out the sixty-three home lots (each home lot containing fifty acres, being united with a proprietor's lot of fifty acres). He laid out the rest of the town in lots not exceeding two hundred acres, nor less than one hundred acres each. They cut and cleared a road, five rods wide, from New Ipswich to the meeting-house (the present street road is part of the same) ; presented a lot of fifty acres to the school ; two lots of fifty acres each to the first and the second minister, reserving ten acres for the meeting-house, burying-ground, and training-field ; they presented fifty acres to John Ritchie, the first child born in the town ; sent a gun to Rev. Mr. Harvey ; in 1750, sent ten pounds of powder, and twenty pounds of lead ; and in 1754, at the beginning of the French and Indian War, sent half a barrel of powder, one hundred pounds of lead, and two hundred flints to the settlers.

The first survey of lots by Wilder must have been made in the summer and autumn of 1738, as the plat was ready and the division made among the proprietors on the 29th of November. It is well known that the first attempt at settlement was made in 1739. As all the lots surveyed had been divided among the proprietors, each one must have undertaken to provide settlers for his own lands. The plat in the records, though undoubtedly made to be presented to the Masonian proprietors, is especially useful, as showing the position of farms occupied by all the original settlers. In addition to the lands divided according to the Wilder survey, each proprietor received a farm containing five hundred acres of land not surveyed in the previous surveys. Farm A, the most valuable of them all, situated just above, and taking in the upper portion of the village, and embracing the farms now occupied by Cyrus Frost and son, Stephen D. Robbe, Charles McCoy, and W. Hiram Longley, and eighty acres east of the River Nubunusit, was assigned to Gridley ; Farm B to Hill ; C to Prescott ; D to Fowle ; these farms lying on the Contoocook River, extending from Hancock line nearly to the North Factory.

In the meantime, before any settlements were permanently made, the proprietors had discovered that the township was not under the jurisdiction of Massachusetts; and that the assignees of John Tufton Mason claimed the territory, under the Masonian grant, of a large portion of southern New Hampshire. We have no means of telling how this discovery was made, or what its influence was upon the proprietors and settlers of the town, or whether it either accelerated or retarded the final settlement of the town. We are equally ignorant of all the discussions between the parties, their propositions and counter-propositions on this subject. There must have been room for much diplomacy,—for much recrimination and hard feeling, in the few years that intervened between the discovery and the final settlement in 1748. There was hardly a single settler in town at this time. The records are silent on all these points, but they give a document dated January 26, 1748, in which the Masonian proprietors grant and quitclaim the whole town to Hill, Fowle, Gridley, and the heirs of John Vassal, on certain conditions, only reserving to themselves thirty-four hundred acres of land, which was not to be taxed until improved, and all the "trees fit for masting his Majesty's navy." This is the only legal document by which the proprietors ever held the town. It will be observed that Prescott was not one of the grantees. It is probable that he had not the means of meeting the expenses of the settlement, and had sold out to his associates at the time of his resignation of the clerkship, in 1754. Under the Masonian grant, the failure of any proprietor to meet his share of the expenses, wrought a total forfeiture of his rights to the other proprietors. Under this provision the heirs of John Vassal forfeited their interest in the grant. The conditions of the grant required that the "grantees shall settle forty families on said tract of land within four years, and each family shall have fifteen acres of land cleared and fitted for tillage,—have a meeting-house built there, and preaching in the same constantly supported. The time of the Indian war was not to count as a part of the four years."

The Masonian grant annulled the Massachusetts grant, and

all the conditions contained in it. All could have been begun anew, had the proprietors so chosen; but they did not. The old division of lots was retained, and all their previous acts were assumed to be valid in all their subsequent proceedings.

We have no further demonstration of any acts of the Masonian proprietors, who owned all the lands adjoining the town, except that, under their direction and instruction, at such a time as they had authority so to do, for the purpose of improving the townships of Jaffrey and Dublin, Colonel Blanchard run the west line of the town one entire range and half of another, farther east than the original line, and added the same amount, three-fourths of a mile, on the east line, — of course including most of the largest of the East Mountains, which the first survey had so adroitly avoided; of which act the proprietors say, — " which was a great damage to the settlers, and expense as well as damage to the proprietors." We know not whether it was in the spirit of injury, that the thirty-four hundred acres, reserved by the Masonian proprietors, were assigned to them of this very portion added by the Blanchard survey, which being situated on the East Mountains was almost worthless for any purpose, the little that could be settled being very undesirable and unsalable. This controversy probably bred a good deal of ill-feeling, ·for it continued to linger along for twenty years, till May 22, 1767, when John Hill, the clerk, sent them a plat of the town, with the Mason lots laid out, and the alterations made in its position by the Blanchard survey, marked upon it; and thus the subject was finally disposed of. This act of Hill's is the last transaction recorded in the proprietors' book.

It must be acknowledged that the Masonian proprietors were very lenient to these intruders upon their premises. They had come in and carved out the only six miles square that could be found in this region, so free from mountains or ponds, and embracing so many advantages for a successful settlement. It is perfectly natural that they should insist upon a change of bounds, so as to render the adjoining towns — all owned by them — better adapted to settlement. They cut off from the west line of the town about three-fourths of a mile in width, and added the same amount on the east side, — throwing the town so far east. It was a damage to the town, as it threw the Contoocook River to the west of the centre of the town, when by the original survey it run nearly through the middle of it; and it substituted an almost worthless tract of land for what was well adapted to settlement. It must have been a poor remuneration for their property, which the Masonian proprietors derived from this town. The thirty-four hundred acres set off in the plan, was, a good part of it, entirely worthless, being situated on the mountain, and the rest too poor to be of much value.

These surveys were all that have come down to us from the beginning of the town to the present time. The lots are so irregular in form, so unequal in size, and laid out in such a manner that they cannot be recognized by number of lot or range, and we cannot rely upon them to designate the localities of the early settlers.

We have thus given as brief an account as we could of the early starting, of the situation, of the territory, of the survey, and of the laying out in lots, of the town; all of which constitutes a part of the historical record that could by no means be omitted.

CHAPTER II.

ACCOUNT OF THE SCOTCH-IRISH.

Character of Early Settlers.— Intelligent.— Stern Presbyterians. — Perse-
cutions. — Emigrtion to Ireland. — Their Hardships. — History of the
Scotch-Irish. — Irish Rebellion and Confiscation. — Second Rebellion.
—Re-peopling from Scotland. — Principally about 1610. — One Com-
pany from London. — Prosperity. — Persecution of Presbyterians in
Scotland. — Claverhouse sent against them. — Contest from 1670 to
1688. — Presbyterians Rush to Ireland. — Ulster County Prosperous.
— Exactions of Government.— Advance of Rents.— Emigrate in great
Numbers.— Beginning Eighteenth Century.—Landlords Alarmed. —
First and Second Emigration. — Settled in Pennsylvania, Virginia,
Tennessee, &c.— Character of these Men. — Number of Descend-
ants.— Service in the Revolution.— All Loyal.— Their Perseverance.

THE town of Peterborough was uncommonly fortunate in
the character of its early settlers. They were not a mixture
of all nationalities and languages and habits, as in all our new
settlements at the present time, but consisted principally of
Scotch-Irish, who themselves emigrated from Ireland, or were
the immediate descendants of the same. They were not of
the lower order of the European population, but were of the
middling class, men considerably educated, so that they were
well qualified to understand the tyrannical and exacting course
pursued by their government towards them, and fully to ap-
preciate their civil and religious rights.

When a colony contemplated a settlement in America, induced by the favorable representation of a young man by the
name of Holmes, who had visited this country, they previously sent an agent with a petition to Gov. Shute, of Massachusetts, signed by two hundred and seventeen, all but seven

of whom signed it in a fair and legible hand. This circumstance shows that a large proportion of them had learned to
write, and were superior to the common class of emigrants.
This occurred March 26, 1718. These men were rigid Presbyterians, and felt that they could not endure the exactions of
Protestant England in regard to the Episcopal Church. They
were not only heavily taxed, but they were often involved in
difficulties from their determination never to conform to their
Book of Common Prayer. Besides, they could hold land only
on lease, and were subject to such exactions as their landlords
pleased. They could not endure such a state of things, and
they resolved, at all hazards, to try their fortunes in a new
country. They were fully aware of all the dangers and perils
of an emigration to a new country, where they knew they were
to meet an inhospitable climate, a hard soil, and, still more, and
worse than all, where they were to encounter a savage foe.
It required no small strength of character to carry out such a
resolution, to brave the perils of the ocean, and all the dangers
incident to planting a new colony, with such slender means as
they possessed. This race of men held such a prominent
rank among the first settlers of the town, it so impressed its
peculiar habits and modes of thinking and of action upon
them and their descendants, that I shall be pardoned if I more
fully detail its previous history. I do this the more readily
because I have found that many of the descendants of the
Scotch-Irish know little else of them, except that they emigrated from the north of Ireland, and were their worthy ancestors.*

During the Irish rebellion, in the reign of Elizabeth, the Province of Ulster, embracing the northern counties of Ireland,
was reduced to the lowest extremity of poverty and wretchedness; and its moral and religious state was scarcely less deplo-
rable than its civil. Soon after the ascension of James I., his
quarrels with the Roman Catholics of that province led to a conspiracy against the British authority. O'Neill and O'Donnell,

---

* For what follows in relation to the Scotch-Irish, we are chiefly indebted to a historical
discourse delivered by J. Smith Futhey at the one hundred and fiftieth anniversary of the Octorara
Church, Chester County, Pennsylvania, page 27.

two Irish lords, who had been created earls by the English government, arranged a plot against the government.   Its detection led these chief conspirators to flee the country, leaving
their extensive estates, about 500,000 acres, at the mercy of
the king, who only wanted a pretext for taking possession.
A second insurrection soon gave occasion for another large
forfeiture, and nearly six entire counties in the Province of
Ulster were confiscated, and subjected to the disposal of the
crown.   But it was a territory which showed the effects of a
long series of lawless disturbances.   It was almost depopu-
lated, its resources wasted, and the cultivation of the soil in a
great measure abandoned.

"It became a favorite project with the King to re-people
these counties with a Protestant population, who would be disposed to cultivate the arts of peace and industry, the better to
preserve order, to establish more firmly the British rule, and to
introduce a higher state of cultivation into that portion of his
domains."   To promote this object, liberal offers of land were
made, and other inducements held out in England and Scotland for colonists to occupy this wide and vacant territory.
This was about the year 1610.   The project was eagerly embraced, companies and colonies were formed, and individuals
without organization were tempted to partake of the advantageous offers of the government.   A London company, among
the first to enter upon this new acquisition, established itself
at Derry, and gave such character to the place as to cause it
to be known and called the city of Londonderry.

"The principal emigration, however, was from Scotland.   It
consisted of a population distinguished for thrift, industry, and
endurance, and also bringing with them their Presbyterianism, with a rigid adherence to the Westminster standards.
They settled principally in the counties of Down, Londonderry, and Antrim, which has given a peculiar character to
this portion of the Emerald Isle."

It is said that the Presbyterians of Scotland, who furnished
the largest element of this population, have maintained their
ascendency to the present day, though assailed on the one
side by the persevering efforts of the government Church, and

5

on the other by the Romanists. The Presbyterian Church was established in the County of Antrim, Ireland, in 1613.

The province had great prosperity for some years in consequence of this large influx of population; but such was the bigotry and despotism of the British government at that time, that this prosperity was not destined to continue. A persecution of the most oppressive kind was begun in Ulster in 1661, and every expedient, short of extermination, was resorted to to break the attachment of the people to their Presbyterian polity, and to alienate them from it. But, as is always the case, these persecutions made them more strongly adhere to their faith.

After a while, the persecution ceased in Ireland and was transferred to Scotland. Charles II. and James II., blind to the dictates of justice and humanity, pursued a course of measures tending to wean from their support their Presbyterian subjects, who had been among the most loyal, and to whose assistance Charles II. owed his restoration to the throne. Col. James Graham, better known as Claverhouse, of infamous memory to this day among the Presbyterians, and graphically exhibited in Scott's novel of " The Heart of Midlothian," was sent with his dragoons upon a mistaken mission of compelling the Presbyterians to conform in their religious worship to the Establishment; and from 1670 to the accession of William and Mary in 1688, they had no open worship, nor any hidden, but at the peril of their lives.

The attempts to establish the Church of England in Scotland, and to destroy the prevailing religious systems so dear to the people, were persistently pursued by the Charleses and James II., and to accomplish their purpose they were guilty of persecutions as mean, cruel, and savage as any which have disgraced the annals of religious bigotry and crime. "Many were treacherously and ruthlessly butchered, and the ministers were prohibited, under severe penalties, from preaching, baptizing, or ministering in any way for their flocks."

Having suffered every extreme of cruelty and oppression, and being tired out in such an unequal contest, these unconquerable and enduring Presbyterians abandoned their homes and the land of their birth, and, fleeing to Ireland, found an asylum among their countrymen, who had preceded them there.

They took up their residence in Ulster, reaching there as they could, even crossing the narrow sea in open boats. But they carried with them all their religious peculiarities, which became even more dear to them in this land of their exile, for the dangers and sorrows they had endured in their behalf.

" This is the race, composed of various tribes, flowing from different parts of Scotland, which furnished the population in the north of Ireland, familiarly known as Scotch-Irish. This term, Scotch-Irish, does not denote admixture of the Scotch and Irish races. The one did not intermarry with the other. The Scotch were principally Saxon in blood and Presbyterian in religion; the native Irish, Celtic in blood and Roman Catholic in religion; and these were elements which could not very readily coalesce. Hence the races are as distinct in Ireland at the present day, after a lapse of two centuries and a half, as when the Scotch first took up their abode in that island. They were called Scotch-Irish simply from the circumstance that they were the descendants of Scots who had taken up their residence in the north of Ireland."

In their new country, these people, by their frugality, industry, and skill, soon became prosperous, and made the region into which they had removed rich and flourishing. They improved agriculture, introduced manufactures, were noted for the excellence and great reputation of their productions, and attracted trade and commerce to their markets. But the government of that day, never wise in their commercial relations or their governmental affairs, began to recognize them only in the shape of taxes and embarrassing regulations upon their industry and trade. In addition to these restrictions, the landlords (for the people did not own land, they only rented it), whose long leases had now expired, occasioned much distress by an extravagant advance upon the rents, which brought the people to a degrading subjection to England; and many of them were reduced to comparative poverty.

By their grievances, their patience at length became exhausted; and these self-willed Scotch-Irish, animated by the same spirit that moved the American mind in the days of the Revolution, resolved to submit to these oppressive measures no longer; and, by another change of residence, they sought a freer field for the exercise of their industry, and for the enjoyment of their religion.

"Ireland was not the home of their ancestors; it was endeared to them by no traditions; and numbers determined to quit it, and seek in the American wilds a better home than they had in the Old World."

About the beginning of the eighteenth century they began to emigrate to America in large numbers. So great was the emigration of this period that it threatened almost a depopulation of the Old Country. Such multitudes of husbandmen, laborers, tradesmen, and manufacturers flocked over the Atlantic that the landlords became alarmed, and began to concert measures to prevent the growing evil. At this time scarcely a vessel sailed for the colonies that was not crowded with men, women, and children. "They came principally to Pennsylvania, though some settled in New England, and others found their way to the Carolinas. It is stated by Proud, in his history of Pennsylvania, that by the year 1729, six thousand Scotch-Irish had come to that colony, and that before the middle of the century nearly twelve thousand arrived annually for several years. In September, 1736, one thousand families sailed from Belfast, on account of the difficulty of renewing their leases."

All these emigrants at this period were Protestants, and principally Presbyterian, few or none of the Catholic Irish coming till after the Revolution.

"Extensive emigration from the northern counties of Ireland was principally made at two distinct periods of time. The first, of which we have been speaking, from about the year 1718, to the middle of the century; the second, from about 1771 to 1773, although there was a gentle current westward between these two eras."

The causes of this second extensive emigration were somewhat similar to that of the first. It is well known that the greater portion of the lands in Ireland are owned by a comparatively small number of proprietors, who rent them to the farming-classes on long leases. In 1771, the leases on an estate in the County of Antrim, the property of the Marquis of Donegal, having expired, the rents were so largely advanced that many of the tenants could not comply with the demands, and were deprived of the farms they had occupied. This aroused a spirit of resentment at the oppression of the landed proprietors; and an immediate and extensive emigration to America was the consequence. From 1771 to 1773 there sailed from the ports of the north of Ireland nearly one hundred vessels, carrying as many as twenty-five thousand passengers, all Presbyterians. This was shortly before the breaking out of the Revolutionary war; and these people, leaving the Old World in such a temper, became a powerful contribution to the cause of liberty, and to the separation of the colonies from the mother country. Most of these Scotch-Irish emigrants landed at New Castle and Philadelphia, and from these places made their way northward and westward. One stream followed the great Cumberland Valley into Virginia and North Carolina; and from there colonies passed into Kentucky and Tennessee. Another large body went into western Pennsylvania, and settled on the head waters of the Ohio, in the vicinity of Pittsburg, and became famous in both civil and ecclesiastical history.

Such is a brief history of the people known as Scotch-Irish, and their emigration to this country. This race, "in energy, enterprise, intelligence, education, patriotism, religious and moral character, the maintenance of civil and religious liberty, and inflexible resistance to all usurpation in Church and State, was not surpassed by any class of settlers in the American colonies."

Pennsylvania owes much of what she is to-day to the fact, that so many of this race settled within her borders. It is supposed that not less than five millions of the people of America have the blood of these Scotch-Irish in their veins; and there is not one of them, man or woman, that is not proud of it, or would exchange it for any other lineage.   This race has already furnished five Presidents of the United States, seven governors of Pennsylvania, besides many impor- tant officers of trust and honor in many of the other States.

" The first public voice in America for dissolving all con- nection with Great Britain," says Bancroft, " came from the Scotch-Irish Presbyterian."   A large number of them were signers of the Declaration of Independence ; and throughout the Revolution, they were devoted to the cause of the coun- try.   The cause might have failed but for this timely help. Such a thing as a Scotch-Irish tory was unheard of ; the race never produced one.

"The race is noted," says our author, "for its firmness, per- severance, and undaunted energy in whatever it undertakes ; and those characteristics have aided in carrying it success- fully through many a conflict.   Whatever an individual with Scotch-Irish blood predominating in his veins undertakes, he generally performs, if in his power."

CHAPTER III.

SETTLEMENT.

Uncertainty as to the Early Settlers. — Names. — All came to Town. — Time of Settlement. — How Fixed. — Petition. — Time of Centennial. — Small Party, 1742. — Morison and Russell, 1743. — Visit of Indians to their Camp. — Their Theft. — Return to Townsend. — Frontier Line. — Danger of Settlement. — Causes that Retarded the Settlement of the Town. — No Permanent Settlements till, 1749. — After Close of War of 1744 and the Quitclaim of the Masonian Proprietors. — Tardiness to Comply with it. — Causes.

THERE is great uncertainty as to the first settlement in Peterborough, and also as to the first settlers. The names of these persons, according to Mr. Dunbar's "Sketch of Peterborough," * were William Robbe, Alexander Scott, Hugh Gregg, William Gregg, and Samuel Stinson ; but John Todd, Sen., who was high authority in the antiquities of the town, says they were William Scott, William Robbe, William Wallace, William Mitchell, and Samuel Stinson. It is probable that all the men mentioned by each of the above authorities were the first settlers of the town. Of many of them we know nothing, — tradition has only handed down their names. We have no genealogy of their families, and have not been able to obtain the least trace of Hugh Gregg, William Gregg, William Wallace, William Mitchell, and Samuel Stinson.

The time of the first settlement was supposed to be determined by an expression in a petition for an Act of Incorpora-

---

* See N. H. Historical Collections, Vol. I. p. 129.

tion Oct. 31, 1759, signed by Thomas Morison, Jonathan Morison, and Thomas Cunningham, which says:—

"That about the year of our Lord 1739 a number of Persons, in consequence of a Grant of a tract of land, had and obtained from the Great and General Court or Assembly of the Province of the Massachusetts Bay, by Samuel Haywood and others his associates, granting to them the said tract of land on certain conditions of settlement. And in pursuance whereof a number of People immediately went on to said tract of land and began a settlement (tho then very far from any other inhabitants) which we have continued increasing ever since the year 1739, except sometimes when we left said Township for fear of being destroyed by the enemy, who several times drove us from our Settlement soon after we began, and almost ruined many of us. Yet what little we had in the World lay there, we, having no whither else to go, returned to our settlement as soon as prudence wood addmitt where we have continued since and have cultivated a rough part of the Wilderness to a fruitful field — the Inhabitants of said tract of land are increased to the number of forty-five or fifty familys and our situation with respect to terms we at first settled on are such that we cannot hold any Provincial meetings at all, to pass any vote or votes that will be sufficient to oblige any person to do any part towards supporting the Gospel, building a Meeting-house and Bridges, Clereing and repairing Roads and all which would not only be beneficial to us settlers to have it in our power to do, but a great benefit to people travelling to Connecticut river and those towns settling beyond us." To which the following is added: "Your petitioners beg leave to add, as a matter of considerable importance, that the only road from Portsmouth thro' this Province to number four is through said township of Peterborough, and which makes it more necessary to repair said Road within said Township, and to make many bridges which they cannot do unless incorporated, and enabled to raise taxes, &c."

This is almost all the history we have of the earliest settlement of the town. The time for holding the Centennial was fixed from this document, though no permanent settlements took place till 1749. It is probable that after a partial survey and a distribution of the lots among the original proprietors that each one of them made efforts to sell lots as he could, and

that these lots were sold to those who intended and, afterwards, actually did make the settlement. It is plain that none
of the early settlers had removed their families to town before
the year 1749; but it may be that much work had been done
in clearing up the land purchased, and preparing it for culture,
by a temporary residence of the owners.

Of the party that came in 1739, all were probably driven
away, by fear of the Indians, before any considerable clearing
had been made. In 1742,* a party of five, with their axes
and provisions on their shoulders, came from Lunenburg and
cleared a small patch of land near the old meeting-house.
"They abandoned the settlement at, or more probably considerably before, the alarm* of the war in 1744." Another
attempt was made, some time before 1744, by William Mcnee,
John Taggart, and William Ritchie, which was confined to the
Ritchie hill, on the very south border of the town. Before
leaving the settlement † they cut a strip of land on the end of
their lots, about twenty rods wide, also all the underbrush,
and girdled the large trees. When they returned in 1749 or
1750, with their families, this chopping had been burned by
hunters, or the Indians, and was in good order for a crop of
corn or rye. They had abundant crops the first year.

No other attempts at settlement were made after this, except the following, the account of which has been derived
principally from the manuscript notes of Samuel Smith. He
says that Capt. Thomas Morison, accompanied by a Mr.
Russell, came to town as early as 1744, but more probably in
1743. Their camp was about twenty rods north of where the
large barn was built, — about north-east of the Thomas
Morison house. This camp, by other authority,‡ is said to
have been made by the side of a great boulder, about in the
position indicated above, having a perpendicular side six or
seven feet high, against which the camp-fire was built. They
selected for their encampment the beautiful spot indicated,
which was near the banks of the "Great River," and between

---

* Centennial Address.
† Manuscript Notes of Samuel Smith.
‡ P. Transcript, Sept. 18, 1873, N. H. M.

two sheltering hills, with a pleasant valley widening southward
into a broad, level plain, now one of the smoothest and most
fertile fields in town. A gushing spring of pure water was
close at hand, long after much used for purposes of washing.
No spot in the neighborhood can compare with this for the
shelter and convenience which it affords for a camp. After
building a camp of green poles and hemlock boughs, in which
they deposited their few provisions, consisting of salt pork
and corn meal, which they had brought on their backs from
Townsend. It is supposed that they spent but one night
under its sheltering roof.

When Morison and Russell went out in the morning, they
perceived two Indian men, a squaw, and a small Indian. They
intended to be friendly to them, and spoke to them, and invited them to come in and take breakfast, which they did.
The Indians certainly manifested no hostile intentions. They
were probably fishing up the Contoocook River, as the smoke
of their encampment was seen on the opposite side of the
river, about where John Upton's house now stands. When
they returned to camp at noon, after a hard morning's work
at chopping, expecting to find the pork, which they had put
into the pot, cooked and ready for their dinner, they found the
pot empty, and every article of food which they had brought
with them gone. The Indians across the river had visited
their vacant camp, and stolen every edible thing which it
contained, even taking the pork from the boiling pot, and
probably the pot with it. The hungry men were obliged to
thread their backward steps through the forests for more than
twenty miles to Townsend, before they could get a morsel of
food, or a substitute for their stolen dinner.

This incident is of more than common interest in the history of the town, as being the only well-authenticated account
of any Indians coming near our early settlements, and then
with no hostile intentions, although they were so terribly
dreaded and feared by the people. We do not wonder at the
great fear of the Indians in those times, as the Indian warfare
had heretofore been of the most cruel character. No mercy
was expected from them ; no faith could be put in their prom-

ises; towards captive enemies they exhibited nothing but the cruelty and ferocity of the tiger. Besides, Peterborough was at this time a frontier town, and far from any other on which it could call for aid. At this time (about 1746 *), "a line drawn from Rochester and Barrington to Boscawen and Concord, thence through Hopkinton, Hillsborough, and Peterborough, to Keene, Swanzey, Winchester, and Hinsdale, constituted the frontier line. The whole region north of it, with the exception of small openings at Westmoreland and Charlestown, occupied by a few families, was a gloomy forest, — a fit lurking-place for savages." Peterborough, though so much exposed to Indian depredations, escaped wonderfully, never having been once molested, while most of the other frontier towns suffered largely.†

During the French war with Great Britain, the Indians in the employ of the French were lurking on all the frontiers of the settlements, and ready at any time to make assaults upon the most defenceless and helpless. This was especially the case in the French war from 1744 to 1748. In the later warfare with the Indians, there was less of cruelty and murder than ever before. The Indians were paid by the French so much a head for all the captives they could bring into Canada, which made them more humane in their treatment of captives. "So there were no instances of deliberate murder, nor torture exercised on those who fell into their hands. And even the old custom of making them run the gauntlet was in most instances omitted. When feeble, they assisted them in travelling; and in cases of distress from want of provision, they shared with them in equal proportions." During the war (1744–8), the French "kept out small parties engaged continually in killing, scalping, and taking prisoners. These prisoners were sold in Canada, and redeemed by their friends at a great expense. By this mode of conduct, the French made their enemies pay the whole charge of their predatory excursions, besides reaping a handsome profit for themselves."

There were other causes beside these that retarded the

* Whiton's History of New Hampshire, p. 89.
† Belknap's History of New Hampshire, pp. 287, 296.

settlement.*   The boundary line between New Hampshire and Massachusetts was a long time in controversy, and the uncertainty that hung over their titles, their grant coming from the Massachusetts Legislature, which had no jurisdiction over the territory, and no rights in it to dispense, seemed to unsettle everything in relation to the new township.

The dispute with New Hampshire about boundaries had much to do with the grant of the town of Peterborough. This dispute had lasted seventy years. Massachusetts claimed all lands lying south and west of the Merrimack River, — claimed that her line started three miles north of the mouth of the stream, and run at that distance from the stream along its northern and eastern bank up to the Pemigewasset, where the river forks and where the town of Franklin now is, and thence due west to the south sea. Her boundary, according to her charter, was to run "everwhere" three miles north of, and parallel to, the Merrimack, to its head, and from a point three miles north of its head due west to the south sea. New Hampshire maintained that it was impossible to run a line "everwhere" three miles north of a stream flowing mostly southward; that in 1629 when the Charter of Massachusetts was given, the river was supposed to come from the west, and was not known to turn north; that the line could not be drawn according to the Massachusetts Charter, and, therefore, it ought to be drawn as near as possible to what was supposed to be the fact when the charter was given; *viz.*, that the river came from the west. She therefore claimed that the line should start from a point three miles north of the middle of the stream at its mouth and run due west to the south sea, or to other provinces. In 1731 commissioners appointed by the two provinces met at Newbury, disputed, and separated without deciding.

From 1732 to 1737 the discussion was particularly hot and bitter, the New Hampshire men being determined to have the question settled; and they finally referred it to the king for

---

* For the following in relation to the boundary of the State derived from the Massachusetts collection, Palfrey's " New England," and Belknap's and Sanborn's " New Hampshire," I am indebted to N. H. Morison, LL. D., of Baltimore, Md.

decision, who passed it over to the lords of trade. They referred it to twenty commissioners, to be taken from four other colonies not interested; *viz.*, Nova Scotia, Rhode Island, New York, and New Jersey, who met at Hampton August 1, 1737. Meantime, Massachusetts perceived that she was playing a losing game, and hastened to assert her authority by laying out numerous towns in the disputed territory before the decision should be made. She would thus secure much land to her own people. Among the grants thus hurried through at this time were nine townships, called Canada towns, because granted to Massachusetts towns for service rendered in the expedition to Quebec in 1690, six of which towns were in New Hampshire; among them was Rindge granted to Rowley, and Lyndeborough granted to Salem. We have not traced the other four. She at the same time granted seven townships to the officers and soldiers who served in the Indian war of 1675, called King Philip's war. Among these last were Amherst, then called Souhegan West, and Merrimack, called Souhegan East. Under spur of the same feeling, she now listened favorably to the petitioners, who, since 1722, according to their own account, had sought in vain for a township of land on which to settle, and granted their request without further delay.

The commissioners which met at Hampton, Aug. 1, 1737, agreed upon the northern, which is really the eastern, boundary of the State, admitting in full the New Hampshire claim, and greatly enlarging the province on that side; but they referred the southern boundary back to the king for decision. In 1740, the king in council confirmed the northern boundary as fixed by the commissioners, and decided that the southern boundary should run three miles north of and parallel to the Merrimack to a point north of Pawtucket Falls when the river turns north, and from that point should run due west. That is, like sensible men, they decided to execute the charter, so far as it could be executed, by following the north bank of the river; and when the river turned so as to have no north bank, they took a straight line. Had the river turned to the south, they said, instead of the north.

Massachusetts would have justly complained of a loss of territory by following the stream, and the same rule ought to hold now that the stream is found to come from the north. The course of the stream from Lowell to Newburyport is considerable north of east; so that by following the stream up three miles from its bank, the point from which the line was to run due west was carried fourteen miles south of the starting point claimed by New Hampshire at the mouth of the stream. This in fact gave to New Hampshire a strip of land fourteen miles wide, extending from the Merrimack to the Connecticut (fifty miles), and containing twenty-eight townships, more than she had ever claimed! In 1741, the new line was run by New Hampshire surveyors, Massachusetts refusing to take any part in it. This decision of the Privy Council transferred a large part, if not the whole town, of Peterborough from the jurisdiction of Massachusetts to that of New Hampshire. Had the line been run as New Hampshire claimed it should be, due west from a point three miles north of the middle of the Merrimack at its mouth, the State line must have passed through or near the northern part of the town.

This dispute about boundaries, the jealousy of Massachusetts, and, it is said, the direct promptings of her magistrates, aroused John Tufton Mason, the heir of the Masons, to assert and finally to establish his claim to the proprietorship of the soil extending sixty miles from the sea, which claim had been illegally sold in 1691 to Samuel Allen; and he offered to sell his claim to the province, through Tomlinson, the New Hampshire agent in London, for £1,000; but the long and bitter dispute with Massachusetts, the Indian war of 1744, and the expedition to Louisburg, in which Mason took part, so engrossed the attention of the province, that this offer was not accepted till it was too late. Wearied out by the long delay, Mason sold his claim, in 1746, to twelve proprietors of New Hampshire, men living in Portsmouth, for £1,500.

The property was conveyed by deed on the very day that the Assembly agreed to accept the proposition made to Tomlinson; and this gave rise to an angry discussion between the government of the province and the new proprietors. This claim had always been an odious one to the settlers, seriously impairing the value of their land, and threatening some day to dispossess them of it entirely. To forestall the outcry which was sure to follow the purchase of this claim, the proprietors voluntarily and at once sent a quitclaim deed to all the towns that had been actually settled under a grant from either Massachusetts or New Hampshire; and to the proprietors of townships which had been granted but not yet settled they were extremely liberal. Their claim had been divided into fifteen shares; and their settlements with the townships was uniformly made by reserving one portion of land for each of their fifteen shares and one for each of their two secretaries, making seventeen portions of land in each township reserved to themselves. In the case of Peterborough, each one of these portions contained two hundred acres, making the thirty-four hundred acres reserved on the East Mountain.

In these very years, in which no permanent occupation of Peterborough was made, from 1739 to 1749, there arose a still more serious obstacle to the success of the settlement, — the claims of the Masonian Proprietors. We know not how much this claim retarded the settlement, but probably a good deal. The lots offered for sale with a doubtful title could not be sold; and it is significant that immediately after the quitclaim deed of the Masonian Proprietors was made, in 1748, the settlement went on with great success. The following is a copy of the quitclaim of the Masonian Proprietors : —

PROVINCE OF NEW HAMPSHIRE.

At a meeting of the Proprietors of the lands purchased of John Tufton Mason Esq, lying within the province of New Hampshire, held by adjournment at the dwelling-house of Sarah Priest widow in Portsmouth in said Province on Thursday the twenty-sixth day of January Anno Domini 1748.

Upon reading and considering the petition of John Hill & John Fowle Esqs to have a grant of the said Proprietors of their right in that tract of land called & known by the name of Peterborough made to them and Jeremiah Gridley Esq and the heirs of John Vassall Esq, deceased, for the reasons set forth in the said petition on file —

Voted, that for the said reasons, first reserving to the said Proprietors their heirs and assigns, the quantity of thirty-four hundred acres of the said tract of land to be laid as the said Petitioners & others interested as aforesaid shall think most convenient for promoting the said settlement, (but not be subject to any charge or Tax, until improved by the said Proprietors or those who hold under them or any of them) they have and hereby do grant on the terms and conditions hereafter mentioned, All their right title estate interest & property of in and unto the said tract of land, and quit their claim unto the said John Hill John Fowle Jeremiah Gridley and the heirs of the said John Vassall their heirs and assigns in equal shares, that is to say, the share of the said Heirs of the said John Vassall being equal to one of the other shares of the said Grantees they the said Grantees making a plan of the whole township and the lots therein and how the said reserved lands are laid out, and returning the same to the said Proprietors, —

Provided that in case either of the said Grantees of the said Shares shall neglect to perform & pay a proportionable part of all the duty and charge of making the settlement, then such delinquent Grantee shall forfeit his right and Share in said lands, to the owners or owner of the other Shares, who shall perform and pay the same.

Provided, also that the said Grantees settle forty families on said tract of land within four years from this time, and each family have fifteen acres of land cleared and fitted for tillage, — have a meeting-house built there, and preaching in the same constantly supported thence forward, but in case of an Indian war within the said term, the same time to be allowed after that impediment shall be removed.

Provided, also that all trees fit for his majesty's use for masting the royal navy be kept reserved and spared from waste and destruction, which are hereby reserved for and granted to the use of his majesty, his heirs and successors for the use aforesaid.

Copy of Record

Attest   GEO: JAFFREY Junr Pro. Clerk.

Though this quitclaim seemed to be the end of the controversy, yet the matter hung on the proprietors for nearly twenty years, till John Hill, the clerk, sent to the Masonian Proprietors the following letter, and plan of the town, which is found in a good state of preservation among the Masonian records in the possession of Robert E. Pierce, of Portsmouth:

BOSTON, May 22, 1765.

Sir, — I here enclose a plan of Peterborough and a plan of Hillsborough the reservations of the grant of the Proprietors of the lands purchased of John Tufton Mason Esqr are marked and described on each plan, which please to present said Proprietors with my compliments and dutiful regards to said Proprietors and you'l very much oblige your humble servant

JOHN HILL.

P. S.   Please to acquaint me with the receipt of the same.
To Geo: Jaffrey Esqr at Portsmouth New Hampshire.

The following is the last recorded act of the proprietors:*

Sent the plan of Peterborough to Mason's Proprietors and wrote on it thus;

This is a plat of Peterborough town and the lots marked Mason are numbered from one to thirty-four inclusive are laid out by the Grantees of said town of Peterborough agreeable to the grant of the Proprietors of the lands purchased of John Tufton Mason Esq; the said lots contain thirty-four hundred acres, they are laid out where the said Grantees think it most convenient for promoting the settlement of said town, as by the said Proprietors quitclaim to the Grantees will appear.   The prict lines and the numbered lots show so much of said town, that Col Blanchard left out on the west side of said town, and throw'd the town so much farther to the east, which was a great damage to the settlers and expense as well as damage to the Proprietors.

It is probable that this tardy settlement with the Masonian Proprietors was occasioned by an unwillingness on the part of the Peterborough Proprietors to comply with this condition of the quitclaim; *viz.,* "making a plan of the whole township, and the lots therein, and how the said reserved

---

* Copied from an attested copy from Proprietors' records by Judge Smith in 1787, which original records cannot be found.

7

lands are laid out, and returning the same to the said Proprietors," for this would admit the right of Col. Blanchard in
cutting off a valuable strip of land on the west side of the
town, and adding the same quantity of mountainous and
worthless land on the east. It was finally thought best to
comply with all the conditions of the Masonian Proprietors, —
and thus ended this long controversy. It must, however, be
acknowledged that the Masonian Proprietors dealt with great
leniency with all the townships started under a false jurisdiction, and quite relieved their fears by assurances of their not
being molested by complying with very mild and easy terms,
which they carried out in good faith.

As far as we can ascertain, it would appear that from 1744
to 1749 the town was entirely deserted, not a single person
having been here for the purpose of making improvements on
the land, or even for a temporary residence.

It is probable that before this a number of persons had
bought lots of land, and had made some improvement on the
same; but during this cruel war of 1744 a strict non-inter-
course was observed. It is hardly possible to conceive what
a change has taken place in this region since that time. It
was then a frontier town, and so continued for many years,
and nothing but a wilderness lay between it and the Canadas.
At home, it had no nearer neighbors than Townsend and
Lunenburg. How rapidly has all this changed; what towns,
villages, cities, manufactures, and business of all kinds have
sprung up around and among us, — leaving us to wonder if,
within so short a period, all these changes could have taken
place. Never was there a more restless spirit than that in
our ancestors; they pushed on fearlessly to take up land, and
bravely endured the hardships of such a life. Belknap says,
very justly p. 325, "The passion for occupying new lands
rose to a great height. These tracts were filled with emigrants from Massachusetts and Connecticut. Population and
cultivation began to increase with a rapidity hitherto unknown;
and from this time may be dated the flourishing State of New
Hampshire, which before had been circumscribed and stinted
in its growth by the continued danger of a savage enemy."

CHAPTER IV.

PETITION FOR INCORPORATION, 1759.

Name of the Town. — How Obtained. — Early Method Naming Towns.
— Account of Earl Peterborough. — Not on Proprietors' Records till
1753. — Petition for Incorporation. — Town Charter. — First Meeting. — Record of Town Meetings. — Entire Loss of Town Papers. —
Materials for Early History Sparse.

WE know nothing in what manner Peterborough received
its name. The author has heard his father (the late Hon.
Samuel Smith) say that it was given in honor of the Earl of
Peterborough, but by whom or how he did not know. This
town, probably, like many of its neighboring towns, was not
named till sometime after its settlement. The towns near
Peterborough were known for a considerable time after their
settlement as Monadnocks No. 1, 2, 3, and 4, and so continued till a name was selected. It is significant that in a certain deed to Lieut. John Gregg, of the farm C, by John Hill,
Dec. 6, 1743, it is described as in "East Monadnick." It
may be that this was at first the designation of the town,
which it so well represents in location, till near 1750. Previous to this the proprietors had called it the "township." It
is first recognized in their records by the name of Peterborough, at their meeting held at Peterborough, Sept. 22,
1753.*

---

* For many of the following facts I am indebted to Nathaniel H. Morison, LL. D., Provost
Peabody Institute, Baltimore, prepared from the " Proceedings of the Massachusetts Historical
Society," February, 1873, in a paper by Wm. H. Whitmore.

Many of the early towns in Massachusetts were named from English towns, often obscure ones, from which some one of the early settlers had emigrated. These early towns were all named in the act of incorporation, and not till 1732 was a town incorporated in blank. During that year Harvard and Townsend were so incorporated, the names being fitted in afterwards. This practice of incorporating towns in blank became more frequent from 1732 to 1760, when Bernard became governor. During his administration most of the towns were so incorporated, and the name filled in by him. This practice continued down to the Revolution. The first towns named from distinguished Englishmen were Berwick (1713) and Georgetown (1716). After this it became more common to give the names of persons, especially of noblemen, ministers of state, and other distinguished personages, to the new towns. From 1730 to 1774 most of the towns incorporated received the names of persons, English or American, as Amherst, Temple, Townsend, Mason, Fitchburg, Jaffrey, Fitzwilliam, Marlborough, Keene, Hancock, etc. It must be remembered that at the time Peterborough was settled these towns were supposed to be in Massachusetts.

There can be no doubt that the statement of Hon. S. Smith, that the town was named from the Earl of Peterborough, is entirely correct. It is in strict accordance with what had become a common custom in Massachusetts; and the proprietors, all of whom lived in that State, in so naming the town would but follow the general practice of their time. And there were ample reasons for selecting the Earl of Peterborough for this honor. That brilliant but eccentric nobleman, "the most extraordinary character of that age, not excepting the king of Sweden," says Lord Macaulay, was born in 1658, and died in 1735. His daring and brilliant exploits in Spain, during the war of the Spanish succession, where, landing with a small army of five thousand men, he maintained himself for two years against all the efforts of Spain and France to dislodge him, gaining victories over vastly superior forces, capturing important cities, raising in a single day the siege of Barcelona, then in a desperate condition, by passing through the allied fleet, in a dark night, in a small boat with a single companion, and leading the English squadron to victory the next day, had captivated the imagination of Englishmen all the world over.   He possessed in the highest degree many of those qualities which create and adorn a popular hero,—wit, courtesy, generosity, and reckless daring.   Some of the settlers are known to have admired him, and it would be strange if the proprietors did not share in the general feeling of their countrymen.   I think there can be little doubt, therefore, that admiration for the heroic deeds of Charles Mordaunt, Earl of Peterborough, who had died eighteen years before, caused the title by which he was universally known to be selected as the name of the town.

In regard to the names of the towns in New England, it seems a great misfortune that many of the beautiful Indian names of the new territory were not adopted, and that the early settlers almost uniformly selected the English, Scottish, or Irish names, which are kept up even to the present time. In all the region of the Monadnock Mountain not one town received this beautiful name; and it is but recently that it has been applied to the railroad and to the East Jaffrey bank. Not one town on its borders received the euphonious name of Souhegan; and but one town in all the course of the Contoocook River received anything like its name; i. e., Contoocookville.

The settlement went on prosperously up to 1759; but great inconveniences were experienced in the management of the common finances, and of all subjects of general improvement, as to roads, support of public worship, bridges, etc., and the settlers felt the need of being incorporated, so they could act for themselves, instead of being entirely dependent upon the proprietors.   A petition was sent to the provincial legislature, signed by Thomas Morison, Jonathan Morison, and Thomas Cunningham, an authorized committee for this purpose, as seen in a preceding chapter.

Agreeably to this petition, the following act of incorporation was granted Jan. 17, 1760:—

PROVINCE OF NEW HAMPSHIRE.

{P. S.} George the Second By the Grace of God of Great Brittain France & Ireland, King Defenderof the Faith &c.

To all to whom these Presents shall come,   Greeting :

Whereas our loyal subjects, Inhabitants of a Tract of Land within our Province of New Hampshire, known by the name of Peterborough have humbly Petitioned & Requested us that they may be erected & incorporated into a Township & enfranchised with the same Powers & Privileges which other Towns within our said Province, by Law, have & Enjoy, and it appearing to us to be conducive to the general good of our said Province, as well as to the said Inhabitants in particular by maintaining good order & Encouraging the coulture of the Land that the same should be done.

Know ye therefore, that we of our special Grace, certain Knowledge & for the Encouragement & Promoting the good Ends & Purposes aforesaid by & with the advice of our Trusty & well beloved Benning Wentworth Esqr our Governour & Commander in chief & of our Council for said Province of New Hampshire, Have Erected & ordained & by these Presents for us our Heirs & Successors, Do will & ordain that the Inhabitants of the Tract of Land aforesaid or that shall Inhabit or improve thereon the same being Limited & Bounded as follows, beginning at a Burch Tree marked, standing at the South East Corner of the Premises, thence Running west six miles by the North Line of a Tract of Land, called Peterborough Slip, to a Beach Tree marked, thence North by the East line of two Tracts of Land, called the Middle and North Menadnock six miles to a Red Oak Tree marked, from thence East, six miles by Land claimed by Mark Hunking Wenthforth Esq and by Land claimed by the Heirs of Joseph Blanchard Esq deceased to a Hemlock Tree marked and from thence South Six miles to the Tree first mentioned Shall be & by these Presents are Declared & ordained to be a Town corporate and are hereby erected and Incorporated into a Body Politic & corporate to have a continuance two years only by the Name of Peterborough, with all the Powers & Authorities Privileges Immunities & Franchises which any other Town, in said Province by law hold & enjoy, — allways Reserving to us our Heirs & Successors all which Pine Trees that are or shall be found growing & being on said Tract of Land fit for the use of our Royal Navy, Reserving to us, our Heirs and successors the Power & Right of Dividing said Town when it Shall appear Necessary & Convenient for the Benefit of the Inhabitants thereof — Provided, Nevertheless and it is hereby Declared, that this our Charter and Grant is not intended, or shall in any manner be construed to extend to or effect the Private Property of the Soil within the Limits aforesaid, and as the several Towns within our said Province of New Hampshire are by the Laws thereof Enabled & authorized to assemble & by the majority of the votes Present to choose all such officers and transact such affairs as by the said Laws are Declared. We do by these Presents Nominate & appoint Mr Hugh Willson to call the First Meeting of said Inhabitants to be held within the said Town at any time within Sixty Days from the date hereof giving Legal Notice of the time & design of Holding such meeting, after which the annual meeting of said Town for the choice of such officers & management of the affairs aforesaid, shall be held within the same, on the first Tuesday of January annually. In testimony whereof we have caused the Seal of our said Province to be hereunto affixed.

Witness Benning Wentworth Esq our Governour & Commander in chief of our said Province of New Hampshire the 17th Day of Jany in the 33^d year of our reign & in the year of our Lord Christ 1760.

B. WENTWORTH.

By His Excellency's command with advice of Council.

THEODORE ATKINSON Sec.

Province of New Hampshire Feb. 5th 1760.

Recorded according to the original charter under the Province Seal.

THEODORE ATKINSON Sec.

STATE OF NEW HAMPSHIRE.

Secretary's Office, Concord, Oct. 4, 1875.

I certify that the above is a true copy of the original record of the Charter of Peterborough.

A. B. THOMPSON,
Dep'y Secretary of State.

The following is a copy *verbatim et literatim* of the first meeting of the town : —

1760

Pursuant To an order from His Excelency Benning Wintworth Esqr Governer of his majasties Province of newhampshire the honourable his majasties Counsill of s^d Province by their Charter incorporateing of a tract of Land lying in s^d Province of the contents of about Six miles Square commonly called and known by the name of Peterborough authorizing and Directing me the Subcriber to call the first meeting of s^d Inhabitants to chuse town officers for the year insuing : These are thereforeto Give notice to s^d Inhabitants that they assemble & meet at the meetinghouse in s^d Peterborough on munday the Seventeenth day of march Instant at ten o' the clock in ye forenoon. first to hear the Charter of said township read & then to Proceed in chusing a town clerk and Select men & all other necessary town officers for the year Ensuing :

Given under my han and seal this ye First Day of {
     march A. D. 1760. Hugh Willson. {

all the freeholders and other Inhabitants Being met on s^d day according to the time appointed in the warrant : the Charter being read and the meeting being opened John Fargusson was chosen town clerk and then the select men which were as followeth Hugh Willson thomas morison Jonathan morison Gentⁿ Joseph Caldwell & John Swan jun^r were the Select men that weare Chosen by vote. it was also voted that Hugh willson Thomas morison & Jonathan morison Gentⁿ John Smith Thos Cuningham & John Robbe, Should be Surveyrs of the high ways this year. William Robbe Junr Constable James Robbe & Hugh Dunlap tithingmen. Thos archable & John Robbe Hogg Reifs fence viewers and Prisers. voted that Saml mitchel Alexander Robbe & William Smith be a Commitee to recken with the old Commitee. voted under the same head that William m^cnee william Smith and John Robbe be a commitee to invite regular minisers to Preach this year, &c.

The town started off with this meeting in a course of town legislation that has continued in uninterrupted succession, and with a fair record of the same, with two exceptions, to the present time. The proceedings of the first meeting that failed to be recorded occurred in 1770, while Dea. Samuel Mitchell was town clerk; the second, under the clerkship of A. C. Blodgett, being the Presidential meeting of 1840. The early records are in a tolerable state of preservation, but they will have to be copied soon for more ready examination, if they are to be transmitted to succeeding centuries. This record of the town meetings is all the record of town proceedings that is preserved down to near 1790. Not a paper or tax-list of any kind can be found. It is supposed that these papers were accidentally destroyed or lost; or it may be that they were ·deliberately burned, as was done in a neighboring town, after the settlement had been completed.

Of course, with such sparse materials, it cannot be expected that a very extended history of the town can be made during this period; too much must rest on conjecture or surmise, or in inferences drawn from coincident events; and though, in the main it may be correct, the exact dates must be in a good degree conjectural.

8

CHAPTER V.

THERE were no permanent settlements made in town till
1749, after the cessation of hostilities between Great Britain
and France in 1748, and the settlement of the claims of the
Masonian Proprietors. The settlers had had only a temporary
residence in town in preparing their farms for the support of
their families. After all danger of Indian depredations was
removed, and their titles made sure, they came with their
families, and the emigration for the next ten years was large,
amounting to forty-five or fifty families, or nearly three hundred persons. Though another French war occurred in 1754,
it did not seem to check the emigration; it is probable that
they felt a greater security in their numbers, and also in the
brave men who constituted the settlement. The early settlers
grew wonderfully sagacious as to the arts and manœuvres of
the Indians, and were able to meet them with a superior
sagacity, with a superior use of fire-arms, and with all the arts
and cunning the savage could exercise. Men who had, in
part, to subsist by wild game became expert marksmen and
were already most effective soldiers in any warfare. They
rendered very efficient service in all the early French and
Indian wars, though always reluctant to be amenable to mili-

tary discipline. These men were loyal to their government, and from this infant colony fourteen men were lost in the war of 1754. Of this number, seven fell in one disastrous moment by an Indian ambuscade near Lake George, Sept. 13, 1758, in Rodgers' Rangers; *viz.*, John Stewart, Robert McNee, John Dinsmore, Charles McCoy, David Wallace, William Wilson, and John Kelly.

As far as we can ascertain, the first settlers, who took up their permanent residence in town with their families from 1749, were as follows : —

William Ritchie came from Lunenburg, Mass., where he paid a poll tax in 1746, to Peterborough with his family, probably in 1749, and settled on the Ritchie farm, so called, in the south part of the town. His son John was born Feb. 11, 1750,* the first child born in town.

Dea. William McNee moved his family here May 1, 1752.† He occupied the place now owned by George Shedd, in the south part of the town, reaching to the south line of the same. He removed from Roxbury in Massachusetts. *Vide Gen.*

Dea. William McNee, Jr., was twelve years of age when his father removed to Peterborough. He removed to Dublin in 1760, and occupied the farm afterwards owned by Cyrus Piper; and after remaining there a few years, he returned to Peterborough, where he died. His oldest child Robert was the first male child born in Dublin.‡ He lived on the Pitman Nay place, begun by Ensign Joseph Caldwell, and lately owned and occupied by Joseph Upton. *Vide Gen.*

Joseph Caldwell (called Ensign), supposed to have occupied the Pitman Nay farm,§ which he sold, and which passed into the hands of Dea. William McNee, Jr., about 1765 or 1766. He built the first buildings on this farm. He removed from town about 1770. *Vide Gen.*

John Taggart came to town with his family about May 1, 1752, from Roxbury, Mass., having bought a framed house

---

that had been built on the Caldwell place, and removed it to his lot in 1751. His lot was probably the south part of the present George Shedd farm. He is represented in the "History of Dublin" as residing in Peterborough and Sharon till 1797, when he removed to Dublin, where he died Nov. 15, 1832, aged 82 yrs. *Vide Gen.*

Gustavus Swan begun the Samuel Morison place, in the south part of the town, and came to town from Lunenburg about the year 1750, before the birth of his second child, Robert, in 1752. He went early to New York to make brick, and his father, "old John Swan," came from Lunenburg, and lived and died on that place. He was the progenitor of all the Swans in town. The place was sold by his son, Lieut. John Swan, to Aaron Brown and a Mr. Stowell in 1774. Brown lived on it before the Revolution.* He was one of the selectmen in 1776, but after this we have no record of the man. The same place was occupied a few years by Mathew Wallace, and then sold to Samuel Morison in 1789. *Vide Gen.*

William Stuart came to town from Lunenburg about 1750, and occupied a farm just south of the William Smith farm. He was the father of Thomas and Charles Stuart. He died March 15, 1753, aged 53. He was the first man who died in town. He was buried in the little cemetery on Meeting-house Hill.

William Smith, son of Robert Smith, of Lunenburg, *vide Gen.*, settled on the west side of the street road in the south part of the town in 1751, or possibly in 1750, as he was married Dec. 31, 1751, and at that time began life with his wife on this place. The estate remained in the family till 1873. *Vide Gen.*

Samuel Miller, spelt formerly Millow, a race entirely distinct from the other race of the same name in town, though both came from Londonderry, removed to town in 1753, before the birth of his daughter Ann in 1754. He settled on a lot directly opposite William Smith's place on the east side

---

* S. S. Manuscript Notes.

of the street road. He had twelve children, the first eight of whom were born in Londonderry. *Vide Gen.*

Thomas Cuningham emigrated from the north of Ireland, and was of Scotch-Irish descent. It is somewhat uncertain when he came to Peterborough, but probably about 1750. He removed directly from Townsend, and settled on a lot north of the Dea. John Field place, on the east side of the street road. He left a family of eight children He died in Peterborough, Sept. 23, 1790, aged 84. The name of Cuningham was originally pronounced in Peterborough *Kinnacum.* *Vide Gen.*

Alexander Scott was among the five who made the first attempt at settlement in town in 1739 as represented in the petition for the act of incorporation. He, and probably the others, came from Lunenburg or Townsend. Little else was done except to purchase the land, and make a beginning. He settled on the west side of the street road, south of the Capt. Wilson farm, in 1750 or '51, and kept a tavern, as it was called in those days. The proprietors of the town met at his house, Sept. 26, 1753. He was a relative of William ·Scott, who came to Peterborough from Hopkinton. We know little of the man. He afterwards lived east of the old cemetery, and about 1760 removed to Dublin, and occupied the place where Thaddeus Morse now lives, on the borders of Monadnock Lake. He was the father of Maj. William Scott (long). *Vide Gen.*

*James Robbe,** supposed a son of William and Agnes Patterson Robbe, settled the Thomas Caldwell place where Charles F. Bruce now lives. After 1774 his name does not appear on the town records, nor is anything known of him after this. He has the births of three children recorded, in 1760, '62, '64. *Vide Gen.*

John White came to town about 1760. His first seven children were born in Lunenburg, — date of the last birth, Nov. 4, 1759. Two children were born after his removal to Peterborough; *viz,* Susan, m. David Grimes, and Dr. Jona-

* S. S. Manuscript Notes.

than White. Jeremiah Gridley and John Hill deeded to him the lot on which he settled of two hundred and sixty-eight acres, May 5, 1762. It is the same place afterwards occupied by Robert White, and now owned by Nathaniel H. Morison, Esq., of Baltimore, Md., and used as a summer residence. *Vide Gen.*

John Morison, the progenitor of the Peterborough Morisons, came to town quite early, somewhere from 1749 to '51, and occupied the place afterwards owned by Dea. Robert Morison, and now in possession of the heirs of the late Horace Morison. He was one of the first settlers of Londonderry, and resided there about thirty years before his removal to Peterborough, and then became one of the first settlers of this town, and lived here twenty-six or twenty-seven years before his death, 1776, aged ninety-eight. *Vide Gen.*

Jonathan Morison, his son, probably came at the time his father did. He was a great mechanic. He built the first grist-mill in town, on the site of the "Peterborough First Factory," in 1751, and was for a time the owner of the "Mill lot," * so called, which he purchased of —— Gordon, of Dunstable, containing sixty-eight acres, which he sold to James and Thomas Archibald, saddled with a mortgage to —— Gordon and Hugh Wilson. He was the first male child born in Londonderry. He left Peterborough late in life, and nothing is known of the time or place of his death. Supposed to have died somewhere in Vermont, about 1778. *Vide Gen.*

Capt. Thomas Morison came to town from Lunenburg in 1749, and built a house made of hard-pine logs ten inches square,† and moved his family in the fall of 1750, and his son Thomas was born in town April 20, 1751. He occupied what was called the "Mill farm," the same now occupied by Samuel McCoy, South Peterborough, and besides much adjacent land now detached from it. *Vide Gen.*

John Smith, son of Robert Smith, came to town from Lunenburg in 1753, and settled on the place so long occupied

---

* S. S. Manuscript Notes, p. 157.   † S. S. Manuscript Notes, p. 50.

MORISON HOMESTEAD.

by William Smith, his son, in the south part of the town. He raised a large family. *Vide Gen.*

Dea. Thomas Davison * was born in Ireland, and first settled in Londonderry on his emigration, but removed to Peterborough about 1757, soon after his marriage. His first child was born Dec. 20, 1758. He settled a lot in the south-west part of the town, and owned a large tract of land bordering on Jaffrey. He had a large family; was a deacon in the Presbyterian church. *Vide Gen.*

Thomas Turner was born in Ireland in 1725, and was accompanied by his parents when he emigrated to America, both of whom died in town. He came to town quite early probably in 1751 or '52. When the proprietors of Peterborough met in town, September, 1753, they granted him fifty acres, or lot 92, adjóining his lot, No. 29, in consideration of his relinquishing to them lot No. 7, of fifty acres.

Dea. Samuel Mitchell came to town in 1759.† He bought, of James and Thomas Archibald, the "Mill farm," so called, of sixty-eight acres, on which had been built some years before, by Jonathan Morison, the first grist-mill in town. Dea. Mitchell deeded to Dr. John Young that part lying on the east side of the Contoocook, extending north as far as the Payson place, from Carter's Corner. He also sold a piece to Rev. Mr. Morison (supposed Rev. John M.), on the east side of the river, where the old town-house stood, — the present site of John N. Thayer's house. Having reserved to himself twenty-five acres, the part that was ultimately owned by Daniel Abbot, he sold all the lot to Asa Evans, about 1784, except ten acres before sold to John White, and what had been sold to Dr. John Young east of the River Contoocook. *Vide Gen.*

William Scott emigrated to America, accompanied by his father's family, in 1736, and first lived in Hopkinton, and is represented as one of the very first settlers of Peterborough. He took up his lot on the north side of the road, and between

---

* Letter of G. W. Moore, Esq.   † S. S. Manuscript Notes, p. 159.

the Carter and Hunt Corners. He left a large family. He lived and died on this place. *Vide Gen.*

William Mitchell, father to Isaac Mitchell, began the James Wilson place. Isaac succeeded his father, and next followed James Wilson.

. *Rev. Mr. Harvey,* called old Mr. Harvey, probably began what was afterwards known as the Hunt farm. He was succeeded by James Houston, blacksmith.

Samuel Stinson. We know little of his genealogy except what is told by his gravestones. Four children are laid in the old cemetery,—died young; and one daughter married Thomas Stuart. He died in town, Sept. 3, 1771, aged seventy; his wife Feb. 18, 1784, aged ninety. He was one of the first settlers in town, and probably took up his permanent residence in 1749, with his family. · He settled on the John Little place, north of the Meeting-house Hill. We have no means of knowing where he came from. Samuel Stinson never held any office in town. Moor Stinson was surveyor in 1767, and James Stinson in 1773. These are the only notices of the name on the town records.

William Robbe came from Lunenburg in 1739, but probably did little else but prepare for the settlement. He is the progenitor of all the Robbes in town. He was driven away by fear of the Indians, and did not return for a permanent residence with his family till 1749, '50. He settled on land west and north of the John Little place, afterwards called the "Mitchell farm." *Vide Gen.*

Samuel Todd, son of Col. Andrew Todd, of Londonderry, began the Todd place, so called. It was the first improvement made in this part of the town. About 1751 or '52, Samuel Todd and Dea. Samuel Moore came to town and purchased a lot of land, at a crown an acre, of the proprietors, John Fowle, John Hill, and Jeremiah Gridley, for four hundred and thirty-nine acres, comprising lots Nos. 57, 58, 66, 67, 68, according to a deed dated Nov. 15, 1753. This lot was in the north-west part of the town, and comprised the Todd and Spring farms. They held it in common about ten years, but divided it a short time before Samuel Todd was killed by the falling of a tree. In the division Moore took the westerly part, while Todd improved the easterly. *Vide Gen.*

Dea. Samuel Moore came to town in company with Samuel Todd, and purchased land as related above. Dea. Moore, on account of the Indian war, returned with his family to Londonderry in 1754, and remained there till about 1762 or '63. He lived on the westerly part of the lot originally purchased, —the "Spring place," long since abandoned, on which he built a house. In 1779 he swapped this place with Dr. Marshall Spring, and began the farm where Benjamin and Jona. Mitchell lived and died there. *Vide Gen.*

John Ferguson. He came from Lunenburg, Mass. Tradition has it that he came to Peterborough before there were any inhabitants in town, and lived three months in a log cabin which he built a short distance west of Col. Norton Hunt's, and here sustained himself by fishing and hunting. If so, he was among the very earliest pioneers of the town. He purchased six hundred acres of land, comprising the Ferguson, Stuart, and Hadley farms. This he divided among his children. He probably came to town as soon as it was deemed safe after the close of the French war. He had six children, none of whom were born in town. *Vide Gen.*

*David Bogle** was at one time the owner of farm B, drawn by John Hill, one of the proprietors. He had two sons, Thomas and Joseph, who were bachelors, and one young daughter, named Martha, who was drowned in the Bogle brook, running through the same. This is all we know of the Bogle family. This farm contained five hundred acres, and extends nearly to the North Factory. A larger portion of it lies on the west side of the river. This farm was bought of the Bogles by Capt. William Alld, who came to town from Merrimack about 1778, and it descended from him to his son Samuel.

James McKean came from Londonderry about 1765, and

---

* S. S. Manuscript Notes, p. 139.

9

began the David Blanchard place. This lot lay east of the east line of the farm B, or Bogle farm, and was bounded on the north by Wiley, east by Miller, and south by Kelso Gray. The road began at the south-west corner and ran to the north-east corner, dividing it into about two equal portions. Jotham Blanchard took the north-west portion, and McKean held the eastern part. *Vide Gen.*

Jotham Blanchard. This is almost the only notice we have been able to make of this individual, aside from the town records. We know nothing of his family, or his antecedents, or the man, any farther than is recorded in the town records. He was a selectman in 1777, '78, '79; moderator in 1776, '77, '78, '80, '81. He was elected a representative to a convention held in 1783. With all these offices and honors of the town, not the least trace has been discovered in relation to him, as to where he came from, the time he first appeared, or whether he had a family, or what became of him after 1783, when he disappeared.

Maj. Samuel Gregg came from Londonderry and took up a tract of land in the north part of Peterborough, constituting a part of farm C, extending to the Contoocook River, about three miles north of the present village; the precise time is not known, but probably before 1760. It is the same farm afterwards owned by John S. White. His name does not appear on the town records till 1768. *Vide Gen.*

Lieut. John Gregg settled on the same lot C, on the east side of the Contoocook, and just south of Maj. Gregg, where his son James Gregg lived. It was deeded to him by his father, John Gregg, of Londonderry, Oct. 8, 1765. He came about 1759. It appears that the whole farm C was deeded to John Gregg by John Hill, of Boston, Dec. 6, 1743, as land granted to Samuel Hayward and others, " East Monadnicks." *Vide Gen.*

Hugh Wilson came to town for a permanent residence in 1752 or '53. He bought three lots a mile long that made six hundred acres, nearly a mile square, in the north part of the town. This land in the early settlement was supposed to be the most desirable in town, but was found by experience to be cold, wet, and unproductive. The Pratt farm, now abandoned, constituted one of the lots. It embraced parts of the Mussey, the Hagget, the Melvin, and the Green farms. This was among the first settlements in the north part of the town. *Vide Gen.*

William McCoy was an early settler, though we cannot determine just the time he came. He made one of the first settlements on the East Mountain, on the farm afterwards occupied by John Leathers. He probably removed here in 1752 or '53. All his children were born here; the oldest born July 2, 1753. *Vide Gen.*

George McClourge was an early settler, and settled somewhere near the hill now known as the McClourge Hill. Nothing more is known of him or his family, except the record of the births of six children from August 22, 1752, to January 10, 1760. *Vide Gen.*

Thomas McCloud settled in the east part of the town; had a family of eight children, all born in town, beginning with Sept. 2, 1769, and extending to July 29, 1783. Of this family we know nothing more. *Vide Gen.*

Capt. David Steele came to town from Londonderry, with family, in 1760, and purchased the farm where he always lived, — the same afterwards occupied by Gen. John Steele. *Vide Gen.*

Samuel Miller, of whom we know very little, only that he purchased certain lots of land in the north part of Peterborough, for his sons, from the thrift and earnings of his wife in the manufacture of linen. *Vide Gen.* Two deeds are found, one from Jeremiah Gridley to Samuel Miller, of lot No. 50, July 28, 1756, one hundred and fifty acres; the other from John Hill to Samuel Miller, No. 51, April 24, 1758, one hundred acres. More land than this was purchased, though we have not been able to find the deeds. He gave a lot of land to Matthew, his son, which embraced the widow Parker place and adjacent lands; then two lots to James and William; that on the east side of the road to William, that on the west to James. John was settled on what was afterwards the Dr.

Smiley place. They all came from Londonderry, but the precise time it is difficult to fix. It must have been near the time of the date of the deeds in 1756. Samuel Miller probably never resided here as a permanent location. *Vide Gen.*

Joseph Hammill. We know little of this man, or where he came from, only that somewhere not far from 1770, he began the farm at Bowers's Mill, so called, now Russell's; built a saw-mill in 1778, and a grist-mill in 1781, and was the owner of considerable land in the vicinity. *Vide Gen.*

Maj. Robert Wilson removed to Peterborough from West Cambridge, Mass., in 1761, or 1762, soon after his marriage, and bought the farm and succeeded to Alexander Scott in a tavern, a few rods south of the Capt. Wilson place, on the west side of the road. The buildings, long since, were all demolished, and the place has been abandoned.

Dr. John Young came to town in 1763, from Worcester, Mass., as a physician. He lived and owned land at Carter's Corner, it being a portion of the Mill lot, lying on the east side of the Contoocook. *Vide Gen.*

Samuel Brackett came to town from Braintree, Mass., soon after his marriage, Dec. 17, 1765, and settled on a farm situated on the north border of the Cuningham Pond. He reared a large family of thirteen children. *Vide Gen.*

Thomas Little came to town in 1763 or 1764, from Lunenburg, and settled on a lot of land east of the John Little farm, long since abandoned.

Abraham Holmes removed to town from Londonderry about 1765. He settled in the north part of the town, near the mills, now Russell's. He raised a family of eleven children. An exemplary and pious man. *Vide Gen.*

Abel Parker was an early settler; but it is not known where he came from. He began land on the East Mountain, near, or part of, the Samuel McCoy farm, probably before 1760.

Elijah Puffer came to town from Norton, Mass., in 1764. He first located himself north of the Gen. David Steele farm, which he exchanged with Gen. Steele for wild land in the north-west part of the town, where his descendants now live.

CHAPTER VI.

HOME LIFE.

THOUGH these homes might have been deficient in many of the amenities of modern life, yet there was a sincerity and truthfulness that made them beautiful. The state of the families and condition of society would be likely to give rise to a certain austerity in the heads of the same, and these might have seemed stern, allied somewhat to the old Scotch Covenanters; but it was not so. They were alive to all kinds of fun and humor, even sometimes of an undesirable kind to some individuals. No one's infirmity of temper or disposition was spared; no one's peculiarities respected; no one's mistakes or blunders palliated; all were made legitimate subjects of raillery and sport. They were especially addicted to bestowing on one another nicknames that followed them through life. And yet these homes were places where the sincere reading of the Bible and the daily worship of God were instituted; and where men were actuated by the truest and most substantial principle, always aiming to do right.

And here, too, at all times, from dire necessity, prevailed the greatest industry. All who were old enough were usefully employed. The children, from early childhood, were trained in the hard paths of toil and continued labor. The condition of the women was peculiarly hard. They were required to cook and to prepare the food from a very inadequate supply of the raw material; to make the best of their very scanty means, with an entire absence of any of the modern luxuries. In addition, it devolved on them to carry on the home manufactures, by which the clothing of the entire family was supplied. It was a life peculiarly trying and wearing, and yet borne with great patience, and with thankfulness for all the mercies that came by their means, to their families and possessions.

It has always been an enigma to us how these early settlers became so intelligent and well-informed. There were no books in these early homes, always excepting the Bible, and now and then a stray volume of theological and speculative discussion, such as the " Marrow of Modern Divinity," or the "Self-Justiciary Convicted and Condemned." The Bible was thoroughly read without note or comment, and made the rule of their lives, as hardly ever since; and the effects of its teaching was apparent in the lives of all our ancestors. It did more to make these men what they were than any other circumstance in their lives.

Without this influence upon them, isolated as they were in the midst of the dense forests, and without much association, they would have been little better than barbarians. Under these influences, with their active perceptive powers, and ardent desire for information, they were the ready recipients of a vast deal of oral instruction from the best-informed among themselves. Their common-sense was predominant above everything. They became intelligent, they hardly knew how. At the beginning of the Revolution they found themselves able to grapple with all the abstract principles of government, and to see their situation at a glance. It is said that New Hampshire presented less disloyal men, or tories, in the Revolution than any other State in the Union. An ignorant and stupid race would have said: " Let well enough alone; they were well off; the hard times had not reached them "; but these men looked farther on to the full demonstration of the principles avowed by their rulers, and gave up their wealth, their comfort, and their lives, even, to the support of their liberties.

The diet of the early settlers must have consisted principally of the products of the soil, together with the wild game of the forests and the fish of the streams. To the latter, always present when other things might fail, we are accustomed to attribute a great deal of their support. The woods were full of game, and fresh fish in any quantity could be obtained, with very little trouble, near their homes. The rest of their food must have been coarse. Indian meal, beans, salted beef and pork, milk, butter, and cheese, with such vegetables as they could raise, must have constituted their main living. We do not suppose, before the Revolution, that there was much indulgence in such luxuries as sugar, molasses, tea and coffee, spices, etc., and we are not informed that the sugar from the maple was much used. Flour, too, was not much indulged in. These articles named above, so indispensable now, could not then be easily obtained, if, indeed, they had any means for this purpose. Corn and rye bread made the great staple of general consumption for all classes.

But such food as they had was sufficient for all purposes of nourishment and strength in the elements of tissue-making; and their mode of living was one of their least deprivations in the new settlement. They had an abundance of such food as samp broth and bean porridge, coarse bread, milk, Indian puddings, and vegetables; so that only upon the women devolved the task of the preparation of an acceptable diet from so few materials.

The early settlers manufactured all their clothing at home. It consisted of fulled cloth for men's wear, and flannel striped with blue for frock and trousers. The women wore flannels dyed at home in such colors as they desired, with very little of the ornament found on the English or French goods of modern times. A calico dress, for a long time, was an expensive luxury that few indulged in. It has seemed to us, from all the facts we have been able to obtain on this subject, that the early settlers were not sufficiently warmly clad to

meet all the rigors of the climate that attended the first settlement in the primeval forests. We think of them as hardier
men, and having more stamina than ourselves, so that they
did not need all the warmth now required; as men who did
not suffer in winter from cold, even when clad in what would
hardly make summer clothing for us. Nevertheless, the
query comes up, whether there was as much longevity among
them as we have been accustomed to think, and whether these
hardy lives were not abridged from a scanty wardrobe, and a
bold disdain of the cold, as though they could vanquish the
elements by their will. To this we should add that their
dwellings lacked all the comforts and conveniences of modern
life. They were open, cold, and uncomfortable, and it required
much hardihood to endure the exposure to which all were
subjected in abodes so imperfectly, constructed. We can
hardly imagine how they could live in such houses, and carry
on so much work besides the regular household duties; but
they had made up their minds to receive everything in the
best spirit, in hopes of better and more prosperous times to
come, and thereby they made of their hovels, of their wretched
cabins, and half-built houses, homes consecrated to religion,
and to all the social and moral virtues. We suppose the
training of the children was in rather the patriarchial mode,—
the father's will being the rule and end of all domestic power.
The children were brought up to early and continued labor,
without much relaxation.

In the early settlement, all the people attended public
worship regularly. When they lived three or four miles from
the meeting-house, in bad weather or in the winter, the great
sacrifice it must have been to them in comfort and health,
cannot be easily estimated by those who are accustomed to
our comfortable and convenient houses, and warm winter
clothing. Most of them had to walk to church. There were
few horses, no carriages among them, and then with insufficient clothing for such an exposure as sitting in a cold meeting-house for two services, each from one and one-half to two
hours in length, they must have come home, not simply un-
refreshed, but chilled and fatigued by the hard service of the

day. It seems, for once, as if the common-sense of the people had forsaken them, in making their places of worship so repulsive, and so detrimental to health as well as comfort. It was little better than cruelty to inflict such duties upon these men; yet public opinion compelled all to comply with this custom ; and we suppose it might have been one of the duties of the tithingman to see to it if any one persisted in staying at home.

CHAPTER VII.

HOME MANUFACTURES.

FOR many years after the first settlement of the town, perhaps almost to the beginning of the present century, all the clothing of both sexes was manufactured by the women at home. The flax manufacture probably preceded the woollen, as the town was so exposed to wolves at that time that it was not safe nor profitable to keep sheep. It is related in the manuscript sketches of Samuel Smith that in 1783 they destroyed fifty sheep in one night, belonging to Capt. Thomas Morison and his son, Samuel Morison. Much wool no doubt was raised, notwithstanding these obstacles; they could not, at this time, have imported or paid for such a necessary article. This manufacture was then entirely accomplished by hand. The fleeces of wool were torn to pieces, and all the dirt carefully picked out. Then it was greased and prepared for the cards by placing boards on the wool, and on these heavy weights, and then pulling the wool from under the edges of the boards, in small parcels at a time. Wool-breaking was made a recreation. Invitations would be given to the women, for the distance of two or three miles to assemble with their cards, and assist in breaking the wool for carding.

It was a good task for fifteen or twenty young women to break as many fleeces in an afternoon; and it required a great deal of physical power to accomplish it. Such a recreation was succeeded by the assembling of the young men in the evening, and ended with the usual amusements and games of the day.

The wool manufacture was a very important item in the ancient household. It was all done by hand, there being at that time no labor-saving machines. The wool prepared as above represented was first carded and made into rolls, and then spun on the large wheel, to which a wheel-head, greatly increasing the speed of the spindle, was added about 1800.

It was then woven into the kind of cloth needed—for all the family were dressed in homespun,—thick cloth for men's wear, often not fulled; and flannel for women's garments, which when used for dresses was dyed at home, of such colors as they desired. In addition, large quantities of wool were used for making blankets, stockings, and leggings. The first clothier in town was William Powers, from Ireland, who commenced his business on the brook, near Mr. J. Milton Mears', in 1777. At first it is probable that he only colored and dressed cloth, but afterwards put in machinery for carding wool.

All the implements needed in these manufactures were made among settlers themselves,—the little foot-wheels for spinning linen; the large wheels, so called formerly, and the wheel-head subsequently invented; all necessary reels, quill-winders, spools, warping-bars, reeds, harnesses, and looms. They were almost independent of the rest of the world. Where their cards were procured, we do not know. Every home was furnished with a complete set of all these instruments and machines for manufacture. They were exceedingly cheap as well as rude, requiring little or no use of any iron appliances beyond the bare spindle. So great became the demand for these articles that a number of persons carried on the wheel-making business, so that the wheels were peddled through the country. The foot-wheels were usually sold at $2.00; the great wheel at $1.00, or with brass

boxes and iron axle, at $2.00. The patent head came into use
about 1800, and was first sold at $2.50; but the price was
afterwards reduced to 50 cents; the quill-wheel $1.00, and the
clock-reel sold for $1.00 each.

The flax culture was a great business with our fathers.
Every farmer had his plat of ground for flax, which was the
most profitable of all his crops. The seed would often pay
for the cultivation, which was generally sold in town, and
manufactured into linseed oil.

The flax, when grown to maturity, was often pulled by the
women; and, after the seed had been thrashed out, it was
spread out on the grass to rot; and when rotted sufficiently,
was bound up in bundles, and in this form was dressed; that
is, the flax and tow were swingled out from it. Scarcely any
crop, while growing, was so beautiful as the flax. From one-
half to two bushels of seed were sown on an acre, and the
crop amounted to about two hundred pounds. The flax was
usually manufactured by the families that raised it. Great
skill was required in the work, which we suppose they
brought with them from Ireland. Equally with the inhabitants of Londonderry, they produced manufactures which
always commanded the highest price in the market. And all
this was accomplished in the various households, and with
such machinery as they could cheaply supply themselves with
at home. It is confidently asserted that the sales of linen
thread, cloth, diaper, etc., amounted to more than all the
other products of the town, and was the most efficient cause
of its early prosperity. Hardly a family could be found that
did not, more or less, engage in this manufacture, enough certainly for its own consumption.* "It was by manufacturing
linen in its various forms, and butter (but principally the former), that the wife of Maj. Robert Wilson raised funds for
the education of her son, Hon. James Wilson, both at the
academy and college. She set herself (says her grandson,
Gen. James Wilson) to manufacturing linen and butter, and
everything else the farm would produce. These things she

---

* Letter Gen. James Wilson, Peterborough *Transcript*, Jan. 27, 1872.

would put upon a pack-horse, and taking another saddle-horse herself, she would start off leading the pack animal by the bridle, and thus she would make the journey to Boston and sell her marketing twice in the year, take the money to her son at Andover or Cambridge to pay his way,—for board, tuition, books, clothing, pocket-money, etc. Remember that Peterborough is over sixty miles from Boston; and that in 1783, and some years subsequent thereto, there were no open wrought roads for travellers to follow, only a line of marked trees, for much of the way, to guide the wayfaring man or woman."

Very much is due to the industry, skill, and economy of the women for the prosperity of this town, and for the education of so many of her sons abroad. The thirty-first chapter of the Book of Proverbs may be aptly applied to the mothers of Peterborough.

The linen manufacture was continued till the cotton mills were started in town, about 1810, when farmers began to raise less flax, and in a few years it entirely ceased. So the present generation, and almost its predecessors, never saw any flax growing in the fields.

All these things are entirely passed away. The great wheel with its wonderful new head, the wheel-pin, the little wheel and distaff, the quills and quill-wheel, the clock-reel, swifts and hatchel, coarse and fine cards for tow and cotton, spools and warping-bars, reeds and harness, looms and all their appendages,—all, all have long since gone to the attic or to destruction in all our households. The exhilarating buzz of the little spinning-wheels, the peculiar whirring of the large wheels, and the constant click of the loom are heard no more.

CHAPTER VIII.

AMUSEMENTS AND SOCIAL HABITS.

Difficulties of the Subject. — The Use of Spirit. — Its Dangers not known. — Its Excess an Abuse. — Wrestling an Amusement. — Quoits. — Social Gatherings. — Mode of Recreation. — Spirits used Freely. — Conversation Useful and Instructive. — Various kinds of Recreations. — Raisings, Huskings, Log-rollings, Quiltings, Apple-parings, and Parties to Destroy Wild Game. — Trainings and Musters. — Election Days. — Horse Racing and the Horse Jockeys. — Bowling Alleys.

THERE is much difficulty in fully ascertaining the facts in relation to the amusements of the early settlers. It is probable that in times of so much hardship, during the fierce French wars, and the constant fear of Indian depredations, there was very little of any kind of recreation among the people. Their first object was to live, and their bodily powers were already sufficiently taxed to forbid any kind of amusements that required much active exertion. The social element was always rife among them, — they were all brothers and sisters, and had one common interest in the general welfare of society. We often look with surprise, nurtured by this element more than any other, upon the habits of drinking rum, so common with all in those days. It seems never to have entered their minds that there was either crime, or folly, or uselessness in this habit. Liquor was found in all their houses, not for any domestic use externally, or simply for essences or camphor, but for a beverage. It was dispensed to all, both old and young, as the greatest token of hospitality that could be given. They never seemed aware that there was any danger from its use, — that it had any deleterious effects upon the body, or worked infinite mischief to mind and soul. It was the first thing in all the assemblages of men. At log-rollings, huskings, raisings, etc., it constituted an important appendage in all their visiting.

It was essential at all births, and, for a long time, at all funerals, so that our ingress into the world no less than our egress from it was accomplished by its aid. It was used equally by all classes; it was free in all the houses to its inmates and to strangers, and we can only wonder that they did not all of them become drunkards. No one then had come to see the evils of this habit; the drinking was thought all right, while they only condemned the abuse of it. Now and then a poor drunkard was made; he was pitied, but his case afforded no warning to the rest, and occasionally some of the best of society would be overcome by its influence, but it occasioned no alarm. They could not work without it, and they believed that they could not live without it. So it passed as one of the essentials of life. It seems strange to us that they were so slow to see the evils the habit brought upon them, for they often suffered from drunken broils, and were often spectators of quarrels and fighting produced by drink, — and yet they could not see the necessity of abandoning its use. Even when respectable and good men were carried away by their excesses, and lost their good character in the community, they yet failed to see the folly and mischief of such an extravagant use of spirits.

At all the public gatherings at an early period, the most prominent amusement was wrestling, and there was always a champion in these games in every community. It is said that when James Wilson entered Harvard College, 1785, that wrestling was then the most popular of college games; that he took the badge for this feat in his freshman year, and retained it during the whole period of his college life. There is good authority for this statement. Sixty years afterward, upon the introduction of his son (Gen. James Wilson) to the late Hon. John Q. Adams, he said, when ascertaining his parentage, "Your father was the best wrestler in college." It is to be inferred that Mr. Wilson was trained to these sports by the general resort to them in his native town. How long the custom prevailed we are unable to say. There has been but little of it since the present century came in. The sport, which so tested the strength and muscles of the contestants, was not altogether without danger, for it did occur occasionally that an individual became seriously injured for life.

The more innocent game of quoits was often engaged in. But men who had so much use for their muscles and activities at home, could not, we think, make these sports very frequent. In their social gatherings we do not know how the adults amused themselves; they had no cards or games, yet their meetings were pleasant and agreeable to them, — many think that there was much dancing among the older inhabitants at their social gatherings; the younger classes would resort to button, hunt the slipper, blind man's buff, and also to dancing.

It may be said, if it is any excuse for our fathers, that at these parties there was no serving of tea and coffee as now, so that ardent spirits were made the substitute. The people were eminently social, and many of them excellent talkers, so they could have an agreeable time without any artificial means. In this manner, probably, most of their social parties were conducted. In those times men's ears were open to hear the best informed talk, and these conversations were full of wit, sarcasm, and solid information. It was then almost the only mode of acquiring information of the passing events of the day. There were few newspapers or periodicals that came to their homes, and books were quite as scarce; it was only a few who could keep themselves posted up to the passing events. There must have been an interest in these conversations far beyond anything now existing, when every man is supposed to be capable of reading for himself with such increased facilities of information, and judging on all these matters which were then communicated orally.

There were other modes of recreation that were useful and remunerative. Huskings were often made, in which the people came together, and husked out all their neighbor's corn in one evening; and after free libations of liquor, a good supper, and a social chat, they returned home.

Raisings were another occasion of assemblage and enjoy-ment. Buildings were then made of such massive timber that it required a large force to erect a building, which was done solely by muscular power, all appliances of the modern invention of pulleys used now for this purpose being entirely ignored. On these occasions liquor was always free to all who came to work or to look on. These raisings were usu-ally important events in every neighborhood, and all the people near came to witness and enjoy them. Log-rolling was another mode of useful recreation. When a man had felled a considerable space of ground, covered as it was with its prim-itive growth of large timber, it was impossible for him, with-out aid, to get the logs together so as to burn them. He made a log-rolling, invited all his neighbors, who came, and with good will and strong muscles brought the logs together, and the work ended with a good supper and a social good time.

Quiltings were another mode that called the people to-gether, the women doing the quilting in the afternoon, and the men assembling in the evening for a social entertainment.

Apple-parings often called them together, when with a knife, for no apple-parers had yet appeared, the knurly and natural fruit of the orchard was pared for the apple-sauce of the winter. No grafted fruit was then known; and how very few native good apples then existed is only now known to the older inhabitants. The orchards were very productive, but the fruit was very poor. Another kind of recreation must be mentioned, but with very little approbation, for it was both cruel and destructive, — I mean that of parties pairing and pitting themselves against each other, to see which would destroy the most of the wild game of the forests, a scale of counting having beforehand been agreed upon. By this cruel and thoughtless destruction of wild animals for no useful pur-pose, our woods were often cleared of most of their game. This feat of useless and destructive policy against wild game has come down to our times. Within a few years a great

11

company was organized, and ranged through all the woods within twenty miles of Keene, to destroy all the wild animals that then existed, for mere sport!—to see which party could destroy the most!

We must not omit to mention the great place which the military trainings occupied in the public mind. These trainings were always attended by the people, and a deep interest manifested in keeping up this organization. Musters were afterwards very popular, and were frequented by large numbers and with much interest.

Also the election day, the first Wednesday in June, since the adoption of the present constitution of New Hampshire, has been kept as a holiday, and till within a few years very generally observed.

Late in the last century, and in the beginning of the present one, horse-racing was one of the sports of the time, and the general place of resort was the Evan's flat, on the road south of Albert Frost's. This, no doubt, originated with the horse-jockeys, a class of idle, gossipping, drinking fellows who, for a considerable time molested the community. They each owned one horse or more, and an old watch, and thus equipped they started out on their business. They would assemble at one of the stores in town, and here would banter, put their miserable steeds on trial occasionally, trade watches, — in the meanwhile, each in succession, unless other means were devised to obtain toddy, calling for the drink, till they were all pretty essentially intoxicated. We have a distinct recollection of John Taggart * (Pistol John, so-called), and his brother Abner, Theodore Broad, Jerry Carlton, and others not remembered. A more worthless set of vagabonds never infested society; nobody ever knew one thing that they were good for.

Still later the bowling-alley was much resorted to, and became such a source of dissipation, the games all being made for strong drink, that the Legislature of the State was obliged to interdict its use.

---

* At the Temple muster, in 1807, he was wounded in the neck by the wad of the pistol of some one near him, and his carotid artery injured. It so eroded in a few days that it burst while Dr. Twitchell was present. He took it up and tied it, and saved the man's life, though he had never heard that it had been done before.

CHAPTER IX.

ECCLESIASTICAL AFFAIRS.

First Meeting-houses. — Rev. John Morrison. — His Scandalous Ministry according to a Petition from Inhabitants of Town to be Released from his Support. — Dismission. — Settlement Rev. David Annan. — His Ministry. — Complaint of Elder Moore. — Dismission. — Calls to Rev. Abram Moore and to Rev. Zephaniah S. Moore, D.D. — Ordination of Rev. Elijah Dunbar. — His Ministry. — Causes of Dismission. — The Different Ministers in Congregational Unitarian Society. — Presbyterian Society. — Formation of New Society. — Methodist and Baptist Societies. — Catholic Church.

WE have no means of telling when the Presbyterian Church was formed in town. The records of the church were destroyed in the conflagration of Dea. Robert Morison's house, in 1791, and so through the ministry of Rev. John Morrison, and that of Rev. David Annan, we have no account of deaths or marriages. And then the affairs of the church were exceedingly complicated, being interwoven with the history of the town. The town managed all its financial matters, and all matters relating to the meeting-house. The ministerial support was levied by a public tax, and the procuring of preaching devolved on a special committee chosen for this purpose, or on the selectmen. A Presbyterian minister, by the name of Johnston, came early with the settlers, and remained about a year, after which they were subject to frequent changes, procuring supplies as they could. Rev. Mr. Harvey preached for a time, and in 1764 the Rev. Mr. Powers.

The first house for public worship was erected in the year 1752, under the proprietary management. It is first mentioned after incorporation, in 1761, when sixty-eight pounds were voted to repair the meeting-house, and purchase the land on which it stood. "To protect meeting-house from falling trees and fire, each surveyor, with all his gang, should work one day to clear about the meeting-house, and clear the graveyard and fence it." "Voted, To enlarge old meeting-house by an addition eighteen feet long on south side, and as wide as the old house is long, and join roof of addition to that of old house." In 1763, "voted to lay a floor and build plank seats, and glaze windows in meeting-house." "Voted, To demand of Alexander Scott the 'neals' given by the proprietors." The old house is not again mentioned except in the following vote of 1774; *viz.:—*

"Voted, To build a new meeting-house upon the ten acres of common land, where the old one stands and some distance west from said house." Chose William Smith, William Robbe, and Henry Ferguson a committee to carry the same into effect. "Voted also one hundred pounds toward the same, and that it should be framed, boarded, clapboarded, shingled, and glazed by the committee one year from the date, which will be in 1776." We know not the cause of the delay, but the house was not raised till 1777, and remained in an unfinished state a number of years.

In 1779 we learn that the town released Mr. Comings with regard to the obligation to build the meeting-house, and allowed him certain sums for his labor, and at the same time voted to finish the new meeting-house, and lay the under floor, and have windows for the lower story. The house remained unfinished till 1784, when a committee was chosen to let out the building of the pews and the finishing of the meeting-house, and in 1785 there was action of the town in relation to the galleries, and after this there was no more legislation, only votes to move the meeting-house to a more convenient place, in 1795; and if the town cannot agree, the subject to be submitted to a committee from out of town; in 1797, also to move meeting-house, if they can agree upon a place to set it; in 1798 it was "voted to set the meeting-house a little to the east of the house that Thomas H. Blood (Dr. Blood) now lives in (Carter's Corner) when built or moved." I find no other action in regard to the house, only that in 1812 it was voted to make a thorough repair of the meeting-house, and one hundred dollars voted for the same in 1813. In same year, April 6, "Voted that the town be at one-half of the expense of purchasing a stove, on condition that the other half of expense is done by subscription, said stove to be the property of the town, and to be kept in the meeting-house." In 1816 it was voted not to repair meeting-house, so no repairs were made on the house, nor, indeed, did a stove ever get within its walls.

An effort was made to fix upon a location for a new meeting-house in 1816, and a committee from out of town was selected; viz., Nahum Parker, of Fitzwilliam, Samuel Bachelder, of New Ipswich, and Benjamin Pierce, of Hillsboro. It was not till 1819 that this committee was called on to act. The town chose David Steele, Jonathan Faxon, Thomas Steele, Nathaniel Holmes, Jonathan Smith, James Cuningham, Robert Swan, Hugh Miller, David Carter, Adam Penniman to wait on committee of location and see that all necessary admeasurements be made, and all necessary information be furnished, and notify them to come as soon as convenient.

This committee was assembled in June. As preparatory to their decision, the distances were accurately measured from every dwelling in town to a central point, with the number of each household: those in the south-east to Hunt's Corner; those in the south-west to Carter's Corner; those in the west and north-west to Smith's Bridge; those in the north-east to John Little's Corner; the same being laid down on a plan, now in good preservation, by Caleb Searle, June 19, 1819.

This committee, after a careful examination, fixed the place of location for the new meeting-house, north of the house of James Wilson, on the west side of the street road, about midway between the house aforesaid and the old cemetery. The decision did not prove satisfactory to any body. At a town meeting, Sept. 13, 1819, Samuel Smith, moderator, "Voted not to accept the report of the locating committee." "Voted not to repair the meeting-house." The old house continued to be used for some years only during the summer season, the meetings being held in school-houses in the winter, till 1825, when it was finally abandoned. In 1829 we find the following vote, "Voted to sell the old meeting-house forthwith." Sold to William Scott for $75.25.

Rev. John Morrison, of a race entirely distinct from the Morisons of the town, was the first settled minister (see Genealogical Record for his history). Mr. Morrison was offered sixty pounds sterling and one hundred acres of land, or one hundred dollars in money, if he accepted the call. The land was given by the proprietors. His yearly salary was forty-five pounds in our currency, and an increase when the number shall increase to one hundred families. Then to be fifty pounds a year. It was voted that his settlement be assessed forthwith. Mr. Morrison complied with the offer, and was ordained Nov. 26, 1766, no account of the ordination having come down to us. It was an unfortunate ministry for the town, and great uneasiness and dissatisfaction were soon manifested by some of the best men of the church. It appears that a petition was made to the Provincial Legislature, dated Nov. 27, 1771, praying to be released from the support of Mr. Morrison, and was signed by the following persons; viz.:—

William McNee,	Hugh Wilson,
Samuel Miller,	Samuel Mitchell,
James Cuningham,	James Taggart,
William Cochran,	William McNee, Jr.,
John Wiley,	Alexander Robbe,
Matthew Miller,	David Steele,
James McKean,	John Smith,
William Miller,	Robert Morison,
James Miller,	Joseph Hammil,
Neal Hammil,	Samuel Cuningham,
Samuel Wilson,	Thomas Little,

James Wilson,	John Mitchell,
John Gregg, Jr.,	Elijah Puffer,
John Wilson,	John Puffer,
Daniel Mack,	Hugh Gregg,
Jasaniah Crosby,	Abraham Holmes.
William Moore,	

Journal C. & Assm., from May 22 to Dec. 31, 1771. The petition of Sundry of the Inhabitants of the town of Peterborough setting forth, that about 5 years ago the Rev'd John Morrison was ordained to the work of the Ministry there, since which, he has been repeatedly guilty of ye gravest immoralities, such as Profane Swearing, Drunkenness, Lewdness, &c., and therefore Praying the Interposition of the Legislature to release them from their obligation to support him, &c. Read and sent down to the assembly. Hearing ordered by the house. Provincial Papers, Vol. 7, pp. 291, 292.

The vote for a hearing in the Council was reconsidered, and Dec. 18, 1771, it was ordered that the petition be dismissed. And in the house of Representatives, Dec. 20, 1771, the above vote in the Council being considered, it was proposed that the petition should be dismissed; accordingly, the question being put, it passed in the affirmative. Provincial Records.

Mr. Morrison relinquished his connection with the society in March, 1772. During his ministry his conduct became so scandalous that at a Presbyterial meeting held at this time, he was for a time suspended from his office. He is represented as possessing more than ordinary talent. He was but twenty-three years of age when he commenced his ministry.

The town was without a minister till 1778, the pulpit being supplied by the town authorities with such men as could then be procured, preaching, nevertheless, being pretty constantly maintained. The early settlers had great faith in a regular maintenance of the preached gospel.

Rev. David Annan was called in 1778, having been ordained at Walkill, N. J., October, 1778, with Peterborough for his destination. He was brother of Rev. Robert Annan, a man of superior talents, who was for some time a pastor of the

Federal Street Church, in Boston. Mr. Annan came to America when young. He received his education at Rutgers College, New Brunswick, N. J., where the degree of A.M. was conferred on him in 1782. The pastoral connection of Mr. Annan with the society in Peterborough continued fourteen years, until it was dissolved at his request, in 1792, by the Presbytery of Londonderry. In a complaint against Mr. Annan by Elder Samuel Moore to the Presbytery of Londonderry, to be holden at Peterborough, Aug. 30, 1788, drawn up in the handwriting of Judge Jeremiah Smith, whether ever acted on we have no means of knowing, it charges, 1st, That the Rev. Mr. Annan, as appears from his private conversation, as well as his public performances, has neglected the study of useful knowledge, the reading of good books, and especially of the holy scriptures, — and hath not given himself to study, but has frequently, as he himself confesses, gone into the pulpit without any preparation, and thus hath served the Lord with that which cost him nothing, and hath not by his discourses edified or improved the flock committed to his care. That Mr. Annan's "conversation and behavior and manners have been of a kind different from those recommended by the apostle and essential to the character of a gospel minister, who is an example to the flock, — his conversation not seasoned with salt, but generally upon trifling subjects; his behavior not being sober, but light and vain; and his conduct and manners irreverent, sometimes indecent, and unbecoming the character of a gospel minister." "That he has attempted to extort from the town two fifty-acre lots of land which he knew were never designed for him, and were no part of the contract the town made with him; and to accomplish his purposes respecting this land, he has not scrupled, in several instances, to deviate from the truth." The complaint then charges him with being intoxicated on several specified occasions; viz., at an entertainment at the house of William Smith, Esq., about the 1st day of September, 1784, he became intoxicated with spirituous liquors; also the 1st day of February, 1785, at the marriage of Elizabeth Smith, he was intoxicated with liquor, and behaved very unbecomingly.

Several other instances are mentioned of his being intoxicated, and reference is made to the names of the witnesses to substantiate the charges. The complaint ends thus : —

Your complainant might have swelled the catalogue with Mr. Annan's faults as a minister, as a man, and a Christian to a greater bulk ; but if he should be able to justify the Presbytery that those which have been enumerated are true, he is persuaded that they will think it needless to adduce any more proofs to show that this people, as well as your complainant, have just cause to complain ; and that Mr. Annan's labors in Peterborough are without profit to the people, and that his conduct has been irregular, and unbecoming his station as a minister of the gospel and a member of your reverend Presbytery, and that you will proceed to inflict such censure on him as the nature of the offences merit, and as your wisdom shall direct.

We know nothing of the action of the Presbytery on this complaint. It is quoted here because it clearly expresses the grounds of dissatisfaction with Mr. Annan. It did not immediately prevail. It was not an easy thing to dispossess a minister in these early times ; and the people bore with all these flagrant vices for four years longer, when he voluntarily withdrew. No manuscript sermons of Mr. Annan's are within our knowledge, so that we have no means of knowing the precise character of his preaching. We suppose that he generally preached extempore, especially as the complaint says that "he went into the pulpit often without any preparation, and thus served the Lord with what cost him nothing." There was a prejudice against written sermons in the early settlement, as indicated by a vote in town-meeting, April 3, 1764: "Voted, That the Rev. Mr. Morrow, lately come from Ireland, and is shortly to return, should be our commissioner, and be invested with full power and authority to send us a faithful minister of the gospel, a Calvinist of the Presbyterian constitution, a *preacher* of the word, and not a *reader*." *! !*

Mr. Annan was a man of good attainments and of very respectable talents. *Vide Gen., under Annan.*

It appears that Watts' Hymns were introduced by a vote

12

of the town at a meeting, April 10, 1792. The following vote was passed: "Voted, That Dr. Watts' version of Psalms be used in the congregation of Peterborough for the future"; also, "Voted, To choose a committee to procure seats in the breast and front of the gallery, decent and comfortable, to accommodate a sufficient number of singers to carry on the singing in as good order as the circumstances of the congregation will admit of"; also, "Voted, That Robert Smith, John Moore, and Thomas Steele be said committee to buy or hire said seats or pews as they shall think best"; also, "Voted, That Jonathan Smith, John Gray, Oliver Felt, and Samuel Smith are to set the tune, and to invite such persons to assist them as they think proper."

The town continued without a pastorate until 1799, obtaining such supplies of preaching as offered, and giving a regular call to two different individuals. The first was to Rev. Abram Moore, a graduate of Dartmouth College, 1789. Sept. 25, 1795, a call was extended to him, and was signed by fifty-eight of the leading men in town, his salary voted, and Samuel Smith authorized to prepare a call, and present it to him or to the Presbytery to which he properly belongs. Nothing more is heard of this matter, whether he accepted or declined, or what broke off the expected engagement; and, with the exception of Mr. Elihu Thayer, no one in town ever heard that such a man existed. The following are the names of those who signed the call to Rev. Abram Moore, Sept. 21, 1795; viz., Moses Cuningham, Samuel Mitchell, David Steele, Samuel Gregg, John Morison, Joseph Hammil, William Alld, William Mulliken, Benjamin Mitchell, John Todd, Peter Thayer, John Gray, Robert Smith, James Miller, Nathaniel Holmes, Robert Swan, Jonathan Smith, Samuel Alld, Samuel Moore, James Richey, Abner Haggett, John White, Richard Finch, John Waugh, Samuel McNay, David Hovey, David Steele, Jr., Samuel Wiley, Samuel Miller, David White, Robert Morison, Ezekiel Morison, William Howden, John Gregg, Randall McAlister, Christopher Thayer, William Moore, Matthew Templeton, Henry Crane, Robert Richey, Samuel Gordon, John Barry, William Nay, Abraham Holmes,

Henry Ferguson, Heman. Evans, Samuel Smith, Nathaniel Moore, William Smith, John Steele, Bartholomew Thayer, Hugh Miller, Samuel Miller, Jr., William White, Richard Hovey, Elihu Penniman, Kelso Gray, Thomas Steele.

In 1797 Mr. Zephaniah Swift Moore appeared as a candidate, and it was voted at a meeting, June 27, 1797, that the town join the church in giving Mr. Zephaniah Swift Moore a call in the Congregational way. The call was postponed at this meeting; but at a later meeting, Oct. 30, 1797, it was voted to give Mr. Zephaniah Swift Moore a call, — eighty votes were given for the call and three against. Mr. Moore having declined to settle under the Presbyterian form, it was proposed to him to adopt the Congregational form, in a paper with the autograph signatures of some fifty or sixty members of the church and inhabitants of the town. This paper I have in my possession. We do not know just what the reasons were which induced Mr. Moore to decline the call unless he feared the discords which he may have found here, and that he would fail to harmonize the Congregational and Presbyterian forms to the acceptance of the people. He declines in a very fine letter, in which he expresses his high appreciation of the people, and the manner in which he had been treated, with his thanks and well wishes for their welfare. He was settled soon after at Leicester, Mass., and became an eminent man; he was the founder and the first president of Amherst College.

The next call was made to the Rev. Elijah Dunbar, Jr., June 5, 1799, to settle as a Congregationalist, when in a town meeting of the same date, sixty-one voted in favor of a call and twelve against it. His salary was fixed at four hundred dollars a year.

All the preliminaries to this event having been satisfactorily adjusted; viz., the invitation of a large council, from no less than seventeen churches, ten of them in Massachusetts, and a special invitation to Rev. Joseph Willard, D. D., LL. D., President of Harvard College, who being unable to attend, his place was supplied by Prof. Webber, afterwards also President of the university; the making all necessary preparations for the entertaining the multitude who might attend, for in those days, at the ordination of a pastor, all houses were open to the free and hearty entertainment of all who would come; also the propping up of the galleries of the meeting-house in expectation of a crowd, — the ordination took place Oct. 23, 1799.

The church in town had been Presbyterian probably from its organization (the records having been destroyed by fire), and had been early connected with the Londonderry Presbytery, until Mr. Annan's ordination, when, at his request, it was dismissed from the Londonderry and united with the New York Presbytery, which body becoming extinct, it again came under the jurisdiction of the Londonderry Presbytery. There being many in the congregation who were attached to the Presbyterian mode of worship, certain individuals petitioned the town to have services one day in the year in the Presbyterian form, when the following vote was passed by the town in 1804; *viz.*, "Voted, That the Petitioners have the privilege of the meeting-house one Lord's day in the year for the purpose of the administration of the Lord's Supper agreeable to the Presbyterian form of worship, which day the Petitioners may appoint, provided they notify Mr. Dunbar thereof one month previous to said day, and the members of Mr. Dunbar's church, in regular standing, may communicate with said Petitioners agreeable to the Presbyterian mode; and the expenses attending said performances to be defrayed by the town of Peterborough, provided the minister attending upon said ordinances lives within sixty miles of this place."

This arrangement, thus constituted, was continued until 1822, or until the separation of the Presbyterian from the old society and their formation into a new one. The Rev. William Morison, D. D., of Londonderry, was selected as the first preacher, and continued to officiate every year that the service was held, from 1805 to 1818, except the year 1817, when he was prevented from ill health. He died March 9, 1818, aged seventy. He was an excellent man, and his services here were always highly appreciated and fully attended.

The annual administration of the sacrament of the Supper in the Presbyterian form after 1804 to 1822 : —

Oct. 20, 1805, Rev. William Morison, D. D., Londonderry.
Aug. 30, 1806, Rev. William Morison, D. D.
1807, no record of any meeting this year.
Sept. 25, 1808, Rev. William Morison, D. D.
Sept. 4, 1809, Rev. William Morison, D. D.
Sept. 16, 1810, Rev. William Morison, D. D.
Sept. 22, 1811, Rev. William Morison, D. D.
Sept. 20, 1812, Rev. William Morison, D. D.
Sept. 12, 1813, Rev. William Morison, D. D.
Sept. 11, 1814, Rev. William Morison, D. D.
1815, no record this year.
Sept. 22, 1816, Rev. William Morison, D. D.
Nov. 2, 1817, Rev. Mr. Taggart, of Colerain, Mass.
Sept. 6, 1818, Rev. Mr. Taggart.
Sept. 12, 1819, Rev. Mr. Taggart.
Sept. 10, 1820, Rev. E. P. Bradford, of New Boston.
Sept. 16, 1821, Rev. E. P. Bradford.

At a meeting of the church in Peterborough, Nov. 28, 1799, the following persons were chosen rulling elders; *viz.*, William Smith, William McNay, Robert Morison, Jonathan Smith, Nathaniel Holmes; and it was voted that the Lord's Supper be administered on the first Sabbath in the months of May, July, September, and November.

Mr. Dunbar's ministry continued twenty-seven years, until he was dismissed June 27, 1827. He kept a most accurate church record during his ministry, which in all cases has been found to be authority in all it contains. All the funerals he attended, with the names and ages of the individuals, were strictly recorded, as also all the marriages he solemnized, three hundred and seventy-three of which are recorded upon the town books. This record has been of great aid in determining many dates not otherwise attainable.

Mr. Dunbar's ministry was attended with many difficulties, but was no doubt as successful as most of those in the vicinity. He had a large family, and his domestic cares became so great that he was obliged to forego all improvement, and merely meet his daily duties as he could. He did not keep up his theological studies, during a period of intense theological excitement in New England, neither possessing nor reading the new books or publications of his times. His preaching, though always above mediocrity, and always in pure Saxon English, was not so interesting as more culture would have infused into it. He was an excellent scholar to start with, and had great facility in composing, and also great powers of concentration, so that he wrote most of his discourses with all his family around him. It was not strange that in his sermons, and in his manner of delivery, he should fall behind the times, and that the people should desire a different kind of preaching, even before he had passed the maturity of his age.

So dangerous is it for a professional man, with any aspirations of true success in life, to intermit self-improvement and constant culture; he is surely sometime to feel the error of his course, and suffer in consequence. Mr. Dunbar's preaching, so fresh and new in the first part of his ministry, being so little enlivened by new recruits and aids in his reading, soon grew to be dull and monotonous.

The society, finding it impracticable to worship in the old meeting-house any longer on account of its uncomfortable location and dilapidated condition, determined to erect a new house, which was located in the village, and built during the year 1825, the same the society now occupies.

The church was dedicated Feb. 22, 1826. Rev. James Walker, D. D., preached the dedication sermon.

Mr. Dunbar preached in the new house till Feb. 25, 1827, when he preached from the Sixth and Tenth Commandments, to a very crowded audience, his last sermon as minister of Peterborough.

July 4, 1826, James Walker, John H. Steele, Timothy K. Ames, and others formed themselves into a society for the support of public worship, under the name of the "Congregational Society in Peterborough." The first meeting was called Jan. 27, 1827, at Samuel Smith's store, Gen. John Steele chosen moderator, James Walker clerk. May 19, 1827, letters of invitation were sent to Rev. Abiel Abbot,

D. D., to become their pastor. Mr. Abbot was installed June 27, 1827. He continued to supply the pulpit until 1839, when his health failed, and the Rev. Curtis Cutler was settled as a colleague, Jan. 29, 1840. He resigned April 30, 1848, and closed his ministry the last Sunday in May, in consequence of a bronchial affection, and soon after left the ministry for commercial pursuits. He died at Cambridge, Oct. 13, 1874, aged sixty-eight. Rev. Abiel Abbot resigned his pastoral relations with the society Sept. 9, 1848. He died at West Cambridge, Jan. 31, 1859, aged ninety-three. A call was extended to Liberty Billings, Sept. 10, 1848, and he, accepting the same, was ordained on the 27th of October, 1848. He resigned after a ministry of two years.

Rev. Charles Robinson was installed as pastor of said society Dec. 4, 1851, and closed his ministry July 1, 1859. He was born July 23, 1793, and died at Groton, Mass., April 9, 1862, aged sixty-eight years, eight months. Charles B. Ferry, a graduate of the Meadville Divinity School of 1859, having been invited to become pastor, was ordained June 13, 1860. After a very successful ministry Mr. Ferry resigned in August, 1869, his services ending Dec. 1, 1869. Isaac F. Porter, also a graduate of the Meadville School, was next invited to become pastor, by letter of Jan. 13, 1870, and was installed June 8, 1870. He resigned Aug. 1, 1872. Abraham W. Jackson, a graduate of the Divinity School at Cambridge, of the class of 1872, was ordained Jan. 2, 1873, and now continues in the pastoral relation.

An organ, built by E. & G. G. Hook was added to the church in 1867, at a cost of $2,600 for the organ, and $321 for fixtures for the same, — total, $2,921. The funds for the same were raised as follows: 1st, by a levee, Dec. 12, 1866, from which was realized $455; 2d, $1,040 received from former residents and members of the society, who had removed from town; 3d, $1,344.50 from a subscription of the members of the society and others in town favorable to the enterprise; 4th, from an organ concert in dedication of the organ, $60; and accrued interest on money received on deposit, $30, — total $2,929.50.

The semi-centennial of this church was observed Feb. 22, 1876. A sermon was preached on the occasion by Rev. M. J. Savage, of Boston, and an historical address read, prepared by Dr. Albert Smith, who was absent spending the winter in Newark, O. At an evening meeting addresses were made by Rev. C. B. Ferry and Rev. I. F. Porter, former pastors of the society, and by Rev. R. R. Shippen, secretary of the American Unitarian Association, and letters were read which had been received from former members of the society; *viz.*, Gov. P. C. Cheney, Abel Boynton, Henry F. Cogswell, Dr. E. M. Tubbs, N. H. Morison, William H. Smith, etc.

PRESBYTERIAN SOCIETY. — In 1822 a portion of the people, who had never been pleased with the Congregational form, and others who had never adopted the liberal views of Mr. Dunbar's society, withdrew, and formed a Presbyterian society. They maintained separate worship, at such places as could be procured, until 1825, when they built a house of worship of brick, at Gordon's Corner, which was completed and dedicated Oct. 4, 1825. The Rev. E. P. Bradford, of New Boston, preached the sermon. This house was used till 1839, when it was taken down, and its materials used towards a new house erected in the village, on Concord Street, in which the same society, under a different name, now worships. This house was dedicated Feb. 4, 1840. Soon after this house was dedicated, a call was extended to the Rev. Peter Holt, late of Epping, to become their pastor, and he was installed the succeeding March, 1826. He was a most excellent man and efficient preacher, but he had the misfortune that awaits us all who live to grow old; namely, less and less to interest the younger portion of the society, and his pastorate came to an end March, 1835. He continued to preach many years afterwards, in various places, and filled out a useful and beautiful life, with labor and effort to the last. He died at Greenfield. Rev. Nathaniel Pine was installed pastor June 8, 1836, and dismissed January, 1837, after a short pastorate.

The society was without a pastor from 1837 to 1840. Rev. Joshua Barrett was here until February, 1839. James

R. French was ordained March 18, 1840, and continued his ministry until 1847, when he was dismissed. Under his pastorate large additions were made to the church and society.

Rev. Henry J. Lamb was installed July 14, 1847, pastor of this society, and dismissed Dec. 31, 1852. During the year 1851, much dissatisfaction existing with the preaching of Mr. Lamb, a number of the members of the Presbyterian Church, by the decision of the Presbytery of Londonderry, were recommended to different churches in the vicinity. In 1853 the same persons, with others, were, by advice of council, organized into a Congregational Church, whose officers were Nathaniel H. Moore, Joel Fay, and Andrew A. Farnsworth. April 21, 1858, the Congregational and Presbyterian churches, by mutual consent, and advice of a reference committee for both parties, were organized into a church to be known by the name of the "Union Evangelical Church." The officers of this church, to the present time, have been Nathaniel H. Moore, George A. Jewett, Andrew A. Farnsworth, and James A. Collins.

Oct. 19, 1859, Rev. George Dustan, graduate of Dartmouth College, 1852, was ordained to the work of the gospel ministry, and installed as pastor of this church. The society and church have prospered under the wise and efficient labors of Mr. Dustan, who still continues their pastor. The church now numbers over two hundred members, with a large worshipping congregation. In the summer of 1866 the house was repaired and enlarged, at a cost of nearly $3,000. A donation of $350 was received from individuals in and out of town; the remainder was met by voluntary subscription, and a small tax on the pews. The first persons set apart to the office of elders were consecrated by the Rev. Robert Annan, of Boston, in 1778. They were William McNee, William Smith, Samuel Moore, and Samuel Mitchell. They adorned their profession, and died in the faith. Their successors, until 1826, were William McNee, Jr., Jonathan Smith, Peter Thayer, Robert Smith, Thomas Davison, Robert Morison, Christopher Thayer, Robert Thompson. Elders in 1826, Timothy Hunt, John Field, Jr. On the 21st of May the

13

following persons were elected elders; *viz.*, Peter Peavey, Stephen Holt, Timothy Fox, Solomon Holt; and May 22, 1830, Nathaniel Moore, John Todd, Jr.; and June 8, 1836, Henry Breed, Nathaniel H. Moore; and March 18, 1840, Samuel Maynard, Watson Washburn; and Feb. 17, 1850, John Vose, James B. Nichols, Joel Fay. The following persons were chosen deacons to the new society; *viz.*, Nathaniel H. Moore, A. A. Farnsworth, James H. Collins.

In the summer of 1873 this society erected a neat and commodious chapel, attached to the east of the church, at an expense of nearly $2,000. They were aided in the enterprise by the liberal gift of $275 from John Field, Esq., of Arlington, Mass., in addition to the numerous donations for various purposes heretofore made to said society.

METHODIST SOCIETY. — Introduction of Methodism into Peterborough, by Rev. Albert F. Baxter. Methodism was first introduced into Hillsborough County by Rev. Zenas Adams, who preached in Hancock for the first time in 1819. In the same year said Adams preached in Peterborough, and hence has the honor of first sowing the seed of Methodist doctrines here also.

In 1824 Brother Adams, in connection with Brother G. Campbell, visited this town, and formed a class consisting of six members; *viz.*, Adam and Phebe Penniman, John Shearer and Jean White, Elizabeth and Fanny Gregg. This class was the nucleus of the Methodist Episcopal Church in Peterborough, which may date its origin from October, 1824, and claim for its founders Zenas Adams and G. Campbell. Rev. Zenas Adams, who preached here in the fall of 1819, was the first Methodist preacher who entered Peterborough to represent the Methodist denomination.

A list of circuit preachers who occasionally preached in Peterborough : —

1826, Samuel Kelley, Matthew Newhall.
1827, James Smith, Joseph Allen.
1828, Joseph Allen, Calvin Walker, Goodyear Bassett.
1829, H. Cushman, S. P. Williams.

1830, H. Cushman, E. A. Rice.
1831, Nathaniel Ladd, E. Beede.
1832, S. Gleason, J. Scott, A. P. Brigham.
1833, S. Gleason, Henry Eliot.
1834, during this year Peterborough was made a station, and regular preaching was established.

The following are the preachers appointed here, and the time of their service: —

1834, '35, Joseph Allen.	1835, '37, Amos Kidder.
1837, '39, John Jones.	1839, '40, J. C. Cromack.
1840, '41, B. D. Brewster.	1841, '42, C. H. Chase.
1842, '44, James Adams.	1844, '45, Moses A. Howe.
1845, '46, Elijah Mason.	1846, '47, Franklin Furber.
1847, '49, Rufus Tilton.	1849, '51, John Hayes.
1851, '53, George S. Dearborn.	1853, '54, C. M. Dinsmore.
1854, '55, Kimball Hadley.	1855, '57, William H. Jones.
1857, '59, Linville J. Hall.	1859, '60, George S. Barnes.
1860, '62, R. E. Danforth.	1862, '64, S. L. Eastman.
1864, '65, Joseph Fawcett.	1865, '67, L. Draper.
1867, '68, Silas Quimby.	1868, '71, Frank P. Hamblet.
1871, '72, Samuel Beedle.	1872, '73, Samuel L. Beiler.
1873, Albert F. Baxter.	1876, I. H. Hillman.

The society had worshipped in school-houses and private dwellings, and for a few years occupied the town-house, up to 1839, and felt the need of a place of their own, where they could worship God according to the dictates of their own consciences. This being centenary year, they made an effort to build a house of worship. Some wishing to make a centenary gift, appropriated it to purchase a site on which to build a meeting-house, as a monument of their love to the cause of God and their attachment to Methodism. They obtained a very pleasant situation, which cost them eight hundred dollars. They agreed to build, and let out the work to Brother Caleb Beede. He was to put the house on the underpinning, and finish it all off for $1,300. The house was finished and dedicated to the worship of God the 16th day of September, 1840. Brother J. G. Dow, the presiding elder, preached the dedicatory sermon. The meeting-house and underpinning, fixtures, parsonage, and parsonage lot cost the society $2,429. During the year 1873 the church was repaired and refurnished, through the earnest efforts of Mr. B. F. Winn, and others.

BAPTIST SOCIETY. — The following history of the Baptist Church was furnished by Rev. W. O. Ayer, pastor of the same from 1871 to 1874 : —

It is not known that ever a Baptist minister preached in Peterborough before the fall of 1822. At that time it became known that there were persons in town inclined towards the Baptist faith; and Elder John Cummings, of Sullivan, was sent to spend a Sabbath and to inquire after them. The result of his visit was the baptism, that same Sabbath, of two young ladies, and the formation of the Baptist Church, Dec. 19, 1822, with a constituent membership of fifteen.

Immediately upon the organization of the church, quite a number were received, both by baptism and by letters, from other Baptist churches. Jonathan Faxon (died April 13, 1849, aged eighty-three years) was the first deacon, and Moses Dodge (died 1850, aged eighty-one years) was the first clerk. The church was without settled pastors for some years, but continued to be supplied with preaching every other Sabbath by Elder Cummings, under whose efforts the church was gathered. They held their meetings on the Sabbath in the brick school-house on High Street (now a private residence). Peterborough was not, in all respects, as civilized then as it is to-day; and more than once the little band of worshippers suffered a "lock-out," and were subjected to other petty persecutions from those who dissented from their religious opinions. But the church has lived to reap the benefits that result from the general acknowledgment and reception of the great principle for which Roger Williams and the Baptist fathers contended; namely, the right of man to worship God according to the dictates of his own conscience, without molestation.

The first meeting-house was erected in 1822, on High

Street. It still stands, being now used as a tenement house. In this house the church held their meetings for twenty years, and they were obliged to enlarge it about 1834. This build-- ing was destroyed by fire Nov. 29, 1875. The first regular pastor of the church was Rev. Asa Niles. His stay was short (1825, '26), but during his pastorate the church increased in membership materially.

From 1826 to 1837 the church was much of the time pastorless, and the ministers who settled with them remained but a short time. Progress, under such circumstances, was of course slow. In 1837 Elder John Peacock came to labor with them for a few months, and his work was signally successful. At the close of his labors the church registered ninety-seven members.

In the spring of 1840 they settled Rev. Zebulon Jones. His coming proved a great blessing to the church, and his pastorate was the longest that had been enjoyed by them. Under his lead the church decided to abandon their meetinghouse, and seek a more central location. The result was the purchase, Dec. 15, 1840, of a lot of land on Main Street, opposite the Unitarian meeting-house. On this site was erected the substantial brick edifice now occupied by the church. It was completed and dedicated in the summer of 1842. The same year twenty-three were added to the church by baptism.

After the departure of Rev. Z. Jones (1843) they were pastorless about one-half of the time until 1848, when Rev. J. M. Chick was settled, and remained more than four years.

From 1853 to 1866 the church passed through severe trials; was without pastoral oversight much of the time, and was very much reduced in membership.

During the pastorate of Rev. J. B. Breed (1866, '67) they were very much quickened, many joined their membership, and the meeting-house was very thoroughly and substantially repaired.

Two short terms of pastoral work and occasional supplies followed the departure of Rev. J. B. Breed until the church called and settled Rev. W. O. Ayer, September, 1871. He remained with them until October, 1874, since which time they were regularly supplied with preaching till November, 1875, when the society settled Rev. C. F. Myers as their pastor.

The fiftieth anniversary of the church was observed December, 1872. Two constituent members were present; *viz.*, Mrs. Hannah Davis and Mrs. Betsey P. Hadley. The church is now in a flourishing condition, united, and in good working order. They maintain a Sunday-school, under the efficient superintendence of Charles Wilder, which now numbers one hundred and twenty. The membership of the church in September, 1874, was sixty-six. During the winter and spring of 1876 thirty new members have been added.

CATHOLIC CHURCH. — The Catholic church in Peterborough is beautifully situated on high ground, a short distance north of the village, commanding a full view of the valley of the Contoocook, for a considerable distance up and down the river.

It was commenced in 1869, and has been in process of erection to the final completion, in February, 1876, when the pews were put in. There are forty-eight pews on the main floor and eight in the gallery, each capable of seating four persons.

The style of the building is gothic, and is thirty-one feet wide by seventy-three feet long, and surmounted by a gilt cross. The interior is tastefully arranged. The windows are variegated stained glass, the walls frescoed, and trimmings imitation of black walnut. The gallery, with the exception of either side, is devoted to the use of the choir and organ. The altar is a very pretty one, in front of which and across the church extends a very heavy black walnut balustrade. The cost of the church is about $5,000.

The Catholics of Peterborough had been attended by pastors from Nashua and Keene until June, 1874, when Rev. P. Holahan took up his residence in town, as their first resident pastor, and was succeeded in 1876 by Rev. Mr. Buckle.

This church was dedicated May 14, 1876, by the usual services of the order on such occasions, Right Rev. James A. Healy, bishop of the diocese, officiating. It received the name of St. Peter's Catholic Church.

CHAPTER X.

EDUCATION.

Schools before Incorporation. — No Money Raised from 1760 to 1772.
— The Sums Raised and Expended for this Purpose to 1790. — Five
New School-houses Built in 1790. — Agents Appointed for Schools.
— Long Struggle to Obtain a School-house in No. 1. — Description
of the New School-houses and Mode of Warming. — Districts De-
fined and Numbered. — The Old School-houses Replaced in 1824
by Seven Brick School-houses. — Peterborough Academy. — High
School.

WE have no means of ascertaining whether there were any
schools in town previous to the incorporation in 1760, but
suppose there were, either private, or supported at the public
expense, of which latter circumstance we have not been able
to find any account in the Proprietary Records.

At the very first meeting of the town, under the act of incorporation, £40 were voted for schooling; but the next year we
find no appropriation, but a vote that whatever of this sum
remained unexpended should be paid to Samuel Stinson
for work done on the meeting-house. There is not another
appropriation for schools till 1772. No doubt the general
instruction of the youth by private schools was kept up all
through this period, by the contributions of the inhabitants.
We suppose that more money has been expended privately
for education in town, through its whole history, than has
ever been appropriated by law for this purpose. We cannot
believe that the town had no schools in all this period, — that
the youth of that time just anterior to the Revolution were

entirely neglected, and had consequently grown up in ignorance. The events of the Revolution revealed a people sensible of their rights, and no less able to vindicate them by
argument than by physical force. But no record has come
down to us of any schools, and no individual is living who
knows anything of that period. In 1772 the town raised
£12 for schooling; in 1773, £15; 1774, £24; and the places
of the schools were ordered by a committee; viz., Capt. Alexander Robbe, William Moore, William McNee, Jr., Major
Robert Wilson, Dea. Samuel Moore, James Cuningham,
Capt. David Steele, Capt. William Alld, and Daniel Warren;
in 1775, £12, divided by a committee; in 1779, £100; in
1780, £100; in 1781, £18, or paper money equal thereto;
the selectmen were directed to divide the town into eight
parts, and the school to be kept equally in each part. In
1784, £15; in 1786, £30; in 1787, £40, "to pay a grammar-
school teacher, and Henry Ferguson being a committee to
hire the master and to expend the money." In April, 1788,
"Voted, To raise £25 in addition to the £40 that was
assessed last year to pay the grammar school that was kept
last winter, and furnish the town of Peterborough with a
grammar school the present year, as the law directs." In
1789, £30. March 17, 1789, "Voted, The diocese should not
send to any but their own, and that the said schools should
be under the direction of the selectmen." In 1790 "it was
voted to expend the school money of 1789, and that of this
year (probably the same amount, though we see no other
record of any sum being raised), in building school-houses."
At the same meeting it was voted, "To divide the town into
dioceses (as then called) to accommodate the town school";
also, "Voted that the selectmen be a committee to divide the
town into dioceses, and make a report."

At a meeting of the town, Sept. 20, 1790, "Voted, To have
but four dioceses." This vote was reconsidered at an adjourned meeting, and the number fixed at five. "Voted, That
the selectmen be a committee to vendue the building the
school-houses to the lowest bidder; also, that in case any
dispute should come in either diocese, where the school-house

should be set, the selectmen to decide the dispute, and establish the places for said houses to stand." "Voted, To choose men to notify the dioceses to meet and to pitch upon places in the several dioceses to set school-houses." Chose Charles Stuart, John White, Jr., Moses Cuningham, James Miller, Committee. "Voted, That the selectmen vendue the building of the school-houses upon the 18th of October next, at the adjournment of this meeting." These five school-houses were designated as the south-west (south factory), south-east (near the house of Charles F. Bruce), the middle-east (near Caleb Wilder's), the north-east (near Widow James Parker's place), the north-west (near the Faxon or Charles Stuart place). We find no record of any money being raised for school purposes in 1791, yet we think it was raised. After this time, the raising money for schooling follows regularly every year according to law, the constitution of the State, now in force, having been established. The sums raised varied for some years, but were constantly increasing. In 1792, £70; in 1793, £80; in 1794, £70; in 1795, £70; in 1796, $300; and ever after this in the Federal currency. In 1797, $300; in 1798, $300; in 1799, $333.33; in 1800, $300; in 1801, $200; in 1802, $300; in 1803, $300; in 1804, $300; in 1805, $400; in 1806, $400; in 1807, $400; in 1808, $400; and ever after that what the law required according to valuation. An increased attention to the schools was manifested in 1803 by the appointment of Rev. E. Dunbar, John Smith, and James Wilson a committee to examine school-masters.

It appears that the town appointed agents for each district, from 1798 to 1822, who were to receive their share of the money, and inspect the schools, and probably to perform all the duties that now devolve upon the prudential committees. After this the several districts were organized according to law, and did their own business. These persons, chosen by the town for the several districts, were variously called on the town books, superintendents, inspectors, and agents of the schools. There were only six districts to 1822.

We suppose that those living in the centre district, or near what is now the centre village, had to avail themselves of the

14

schools nearest to them, and that their taxes were not permanently attached to either of the districts.   This is implied
in the following vote, March 31, 1795: "Voted, That Mr.
Asa Evans' money be considered as part of the south-west
division in said Peterborough."

In regard to an article in the warrant for a town-meeting,
March 29, 1796: "To see if the town will vote (at their
expense) to build a school-house near to Asa Evans', and
disannex such as will be better accommodated at said school-
house, from the south-west, and with west and middle-east
school divisions, to be considered as members of said new
division."   The following vote was passed: "Voted, Not to
build a school-house."

Nearly the same article was in the warrant for the meeting, Nov. 7, 1796.   It was passed in the negative.   We find
another reference to this same subject in another article of
the warrant of March 28, 1797: "To see if the town will
build a school-house to accommodate a number of inhabitants
round Samuel Smith's and Asa Evans', and what sum of
money they will raise for the same."   At the meeting it was
passed in the negative.

Again this matter appears in an article of the warrant for
the meeting, Aug. 27, 1798, as follows: "To see if the town
will vote that Smith, Evans, and Osgood, and others shall
have their proportion of the school money for the present
year to pay a school they have had this summer, or any other-
school."   The matter seems now to have assumed some mag-
nitude, so that a large committee of twelve was chosen to
consider the subject; "and they were equally divided respecting the building of a school-house, and thus ended."

At a meeting, March 5, 1799, the following committee were
chosen to take into consideration the situation of the schools;
viz., James Wilson, Jonathan Smith, William White, Jr., Abner Haggett, and David Steele, Jr.   They recommended that
a sixth school-house be built; that John White, Jr., belong to
the same, also William Scott, Mrs. Morrison, the Bailey farm,
Kendall Osgood, Charles Davison, "and all who live within
the premises before mentioned."   Also, that the "school-house

be placed east of the great bridge, nigh the guide-post." The above report was accepted and recorded; and it was voted, "That the town give Samuel Smith and Asa Evans $150 to build said school-house,—$75 this year and $75 next."

At last the village or centre district were granted a school-house, with the pittance of $150 to build the same. But they were not satisfied with a common school-house merely, but must have in addition an academy. They erected a building two stories high, the upper room of which was intended as an academy, and the lower one for the district school. The academy room was pleasant and commodious, and the desks were arranged to seat two persons each; but the lower room was constructed in the usual style of the day. In that part of the room where the seats were built (and this description answers almost perfectly for all the six houses in town), the floor rose some three feet in an inclined plane; and both the seats and the desks were formed of one continuous plank, from one side of the room to the other, only leaving in the middle an alley some three feet wide. There was some kind of a fixture under the desk part for the books, slates, etc., but no backs to the seats. The very small scholars had a low seat in front, equally devoid of a back. All these houses were warmed by large, open fireplaces, the chimney being built on one side of the room, and taking a large space, leaving on one side of it an anteroom for entrance, and, in some cases, a small room on the opposite side, used as a dungeon for punishment. The school-rooms were open and cold, and it was fortunate if they had no broken glass in the windows for additional ventilators. There was generally no lack of fuel; but it was drawn to the school-houses from the woods green, and of sled length, requiring to be prepared for the fire by the older scholars. We should not be surprised that, from neglect to have the fire built early in severe weather, the business of the school should be retarded, the green logs requiring a long time to become sufficiently ignited to afford heat; and when the heat was attained, it was scorching on one side while the other was freezing. And so, under all those difficulties, these people gathered up their meagre share of education.

The new school-house, now the No. 1 in town, was built, no doubt, by a tax on the inhabitants in the diocese, with the exception of the town appropriation of $150, and the part appropriated for an academy by private contributions. We have no means of knowing anything more of the matter. The upper room was used as an academy for several years. We have heard of three teachers who were employed; *viz.*, Edmund Parker, graduate of Dartmouth College, 1803, Speaker of the House of Representatives, Judge of Probate, Hillsborough County; Reuben D. Musser, in 1804, graduate of Dartmouth College, 1803, who became a most distinguished man; and in 1805, '06, the school was kept by William F. Morison, son of Rev. William Morison, of Londonderry, graduate of Dartmouth College, 1806. After it ceased to be used for this purpose, it remained closed till the building was sold, and converted into a tenement house, and is the first building on Concord Street, on left-hand side from the bridge.

All these schools were in successful operation many years, and were of immense value to the town. Some of them were very large, numbering over ninety, and sometimes rising even to one hundred, scholars, especially the schools in the village and in the north-west districts.

In town-meeting, April 8, 1817, "Voted, That the selectmen number the school-houses." The lines defining the limits of the school-districts in town were presented for the first time by a committee, through their chairman, Samuel Smith, at the annual town-meeting, 1824, who also reported that the districts be numbered from one to nine; "that the school-houses be built hereafter by the districts, according to their taxes, and according to a just valuation of the same." By the report, the limits of District No. 7, North Factory, were defined.

The brick school-house in No. 1, now converted into a dwelling-house, was built near to Asa Evans' tavern-house, some years before the rest of the brick houses.

We have a distinct recollection of the old school-houses in 1824, all of them in a shabby, dilapidated condition, — shingles worn out, and roofs leaky; clapboards off, affording additional ventilation; of a dark wood-color, innocent of any paint, even the famous Spanish brown so common in those early times.

This year, 1824, seven new brick school-houses were built, all of which but four, *viz.*, Nos. 2, 3, 7, and 8, are now displaced by wooden structures. The following vote was passed, April 8, 1828: "Voted, That each school-district choose their prudential committees." It appears that for some years after this date a portion of the literary fund was appropriated to the smaller school-districts, and another portion to purchase books for the town library.

In 1833, the school in District No. 1 becoming very large, agreeable to the custom then, the only relief was division; so a new district, No. 11, was established, and another brick school-house built, just north of the Congregational (Unitarian) Church.

In 1840 a new school-district, now known as No. 4, was established in the south-west part of the town, on the petition of Samuel Adams, Samuel Robbe, and others. No record of the proceedings of the town-meeting held Nov. 2, 1840, in which this petition was acted on, were ever made by the then town clerk, A. C. Blodgett.

In 1844 it was voted in town-meeting that Districts Nos. 1 and 11 be united under the name of No. 1.

During this year the united districts purchased land in the centre of the village, and erected a large school-house containing three commodious rooms, with a seat for each scholar, and divided the scholars into three classes, for the several rooms; and have conducted their school matters in a similar manner to the present time.

In 1845 John Barber, Samuel Carey, John W. Barber, and Elijah Washburn were set off into a district called No. 10. A district has since been set off in the west part of the town, near Barker's Mill, and a school-house built called No. 11.

During the past years great changes have taken place in the school-districts in town. Those most distant from the village have dwindled in numbers, while those in the villages have greatly increased. The farms in many parts of the town, that were formerly very productive, and abounded in full houses, granaries, and barns, and generally large families, are now, by the deterioration of the soil, reduced to the lowest state of production, and begin to be abandoned for all purposes of tillage as fast as the buildings become untenantable. All the school-districts became more or less affected by these causes.

The policy of increasing the number of school-districts, and so further dividing the school money, has been erroneously pursued here as elsewhere, as the only remedy for those badly situated in regard to schools. The consequence has been a great expense to these individuals, of erecting new school-houses, and ultimately receiving but little instruction, and that of the most immature and inexperienced kind. Persons thus situated were obliged to send their children to neighboring districts when in session, or be at the additional expense of private schools, to derive the ordinary advantages of our common schools. There are now eleven districts in town. It will not be long before many of these must be abandoned for want of scholars, and the school money concentrated where it can be more usefully and economically expended. The experiment of small districts has been fully tried, and they have been found an insufficient remedy for the evils complained of.

PETERBOROUGH ACADEMY.—An act for the incorporation of an academy was obtained from the New Hampshire legislature, Dec 28, 1836, to be called the "Peterborough Academy." A sufficient subscription having been obtained for the purpose, a neat brick school-house, 47 by 30, was erected in the village, in the summer of 1837, on a beautiful and convenient site, presented by Gen. James Wilson for this purpose. The whole amount expended was $1,453.63. This sum included $100 appropriated to the purchase of philosophical apparatus, to which $80 more, raised by subscription, were added.

The opening services were held Aug. 21, 1837, and the academy commenced with a large number of pupils, under the instruction of Nathan Ballard, graduate of Dartmouth College, 1837, who remained but one year. The school was kept in operation many years with varied success, being more or less prosperous, according to the popularity or address of the teachers, until by a regular decadence it was reduced to two terms in á year, and still later to only one. In 1871, the house being needed for a high school, just then for the first time established in town, it was rented April 12, 1871, and is now occupied for this purpose. The property is yet in the hands of the corporation of the academy, a regular organization having been maintained through all the decline of the school.

HIGH SCHOOL. — The high school was established by the following vote of the town, at the annual March meeting, 1871 : On motion of Ezra Smith, "Voted, That we establish a high school in the town of Peterborough, and that all the school-districts in said town shall constitute said high-school district. The town shall annually choose a committee of three persons, who shall have the entire charge of said high-school district and school. There shall be a fall, winter, and spring term of school in said district each year. All persons offering themselves for admission to said school shall be examined by said committee, and if found to possess the qualifications required by the committee for admission, may be admitted to said school. The tuition shall be free to all those admitted, who are resident of said high-school district; and all others shall pay such a reasonable tuition as the committee shall require." $1,200 of the school money was appropriated for this purpose the first year. The school went into operation in August, 1871, under the instruction of Thomas P. Maryatt, graduate of Dartmouth College, 1871, with about fifty scholars. The same teacher continued with great success for four years. He was succeeded, 1875, by L. C. Cornish, A. B., graduate of Waterville College, Me. The school has thus far proved of great advantage to the young people of

Peterborough, and has been carefully improved by those who have been qualified to enter it.

The success of the high school has been greatly aided by a munificent donation of philosophical apparatus by Nathaniel H. Morison, LL. D., of Baltimore, Md. When he retired from his private school in Baltimore, over which he had presided more than a quarter of a century, to accept the position of Provost of the Peabody Institute, he presented all his philosophical apparatus, after having had the same put in perfect repair, which had cost him over $2,000, as a gift to the high school of his native town.

CHAPTER XI.

WE cannot learn of any library previous to the establishment of the "Peterborough Social Library" in 1811. This
consisted of one hundred volumes of exceedingly well-selected
books, every one of which could be read with profit. The
library was extensively used till 1830, when it was sold,
having been for some time much neglected, and considered as
old and out of date.

Another library was gotten up about this time by the Rev.
Abiel Abbot, D. D., which was very much used for many
years; but the conditions of membership requiring an annual
payment of fifty cents, which not being paid in a certain time
the share became forfeited, all the proprietors but two or
three suffered the shares to be forfeited, and these proprietors
made it over to the Ministerial Library, where it is now in
safe keeping.

The Union and Phœnix Cotton Factories had each a small,

15

well-selected library for their operatives, which was much read and very useful. The Phœnix Library, consisting of two hundred and one volumes, was presented to the Town Library in 1860.

The Peterborough Ministerial Library, connected with the Congregational Society (Unitarian), and principally for the use of their minister, was founded by the sole efforts of Rev. Abiel Abbot, who commenced it with a large donation of books from his own library, and labored assiduously in its behalf for several years. An act of incorporation was obtained for the same in 1838. It now numbers from twelve to fifteen hundred volumes.

TOWN LIBRARY. — The Peterborough Town Library was established in 1833, and was, without doubt, the first free public library in the United States. Thanks to such men as Abiel Abbot, John H. Steele, James Walker, Timothy K. Ames, James Howe, William Scott, Henry F. Cogswell, and many others, for this inestimable boon to this generation. It was a step in advance of the times, — they builded better than they knew. No town or place in all our country had conceived the plan of furnishing free reading to the community at their sole expense, till some time after our project was in full and successful operation.

The Peterborough Town Library claims, First, That it was founded by the town with the deliberate purpose of creating a free, general library, and has always been owned by it. Second, It has been managed by the town, and every year since its foundation the town has appropriated money for its support, has chosen a library committee to take care of the same, and has expended the yearly appropriation in books. Third, It is free to all citizens of the town, has books for all classes, and is, and always has been, in the widest sense, a free public town library.

Edwards, in his *Memoirs of Libraries*, an elaborate work, in two large volumes, octavo, page 214, says: "By town library, I mean a library which is the *property* of the town itself and enjoyable by all the townspeople. Such a library must be both freely, and of right, accessible and securely permanent. It must unite direct responsibility of management with assured means of support. No such library existed in the United States until that of Boston was founded in 1848. Nor did any such library exist in the United Kingdom until after the passing of the 'Libraries Act,' in 1850."

In a correspondence with the Commissioner of the Bureau of Education, at Washington, D. C., he says, in a letter of Aug. 7, 1875: "The first free public library supported or aided by taxation, of which this bureau has any account, was established at Wayland, Mass., and was opened to the public in August, 1850; the second at New Bedford, Mass., was opened in March, 1853. If the Peterborough Town Library was free to the inhabitants of the town prior to August, 1850, whether supported by municipal taxation or by the income of invested bonds, it furnishes the first example of a free library, and we shall be glad to give it the credit." In another letter of Aug. 12, 1875: "So far as any data are at present known to us, your library is the earliest of its kind. Should we obtain information of an earlier enterprise of the same kind, you will be duly informed."

The Department of Education, having obtained additional and important information on this subject, addressed us the following letter, of Jan. 11, 1876: "It appears that a youth's free library was established in Salisbury, Conn., in 1803, and that for many years it was supported, and additions of books made, by means of a tax; thus making it the first free library supported by taxation of which we have any account." In the beginning of 1803, Caleb Bingham, of Boston (of *Columbian Orator* memory, etc.), a native of Salisbury, presented to the town a juvenile library, and himself appointed a board of trustees to manage it, these trustees having power to fill vacancies. It was called the "Bingham Library for Youth." We are not informed whether it was received by a formal vote of the town or not. At all events, the town never assumed the ownership or care of the library, or by its contributions had anything to do with its being a free library. We know not how often, or how much, the town contributed to the library, — it was simply aided in its prosperous days, and in the end permitted to run down. Judge Samuel Church, in an address on the one hundredth anniversary of the first town-meeting, held in Salisbury, Oct. 20, 1841, in speaking of this library, says: "The books were sought after and read with avidity; the town, from time to time, by grants from its treasury, has contributed to its enlargement, and generous individuals, too, have made valuable additions." The town clerk of Salisbury, Daniel Pratt, Esq., informs me that this library has ceased to be used for the last thirty years or more; probably the books were worn out, or dilapidated so as to be unfit for use, and never renewed. In no sense can this be considered a town library. It was simply a free library, to which the town afforded an occasional aid in its prosperous days.

One other case is found, nearer to the point of becoming a free library under municipal authority. In the year 1700, Rev. John Sharp bequeathed his library to New York City for a municipal institution. Thirty years after, a second bequest came to it from an English clergyman, Dr. Wellington. But it fell into neglect, and it does not appear, so far as we can learn, that it received any support from the city. In 1754 a number of influential citizens added seven hundred volumes, and greatly improved its regulations. But the idea of a library owned and supported by the city, for the free use of its citizens, seems to have been entertained by almost no one save its founder. In 1772 it was avowedly converted into a proprietary library. In that year it was formally incorpo. rated as the Society Library of New York. It now prospers greatly as a proprietary library.

The school district libraries in New York, supported by taxation, and owned by the several districts, come the nearest to our town libraries of anything else known. But these were not established till 1835, and were only for the school district to which they belonged, — in no sense town libraries.

We were informed still later (June 10, 1876), by the Commissioner of Education, that the Castine, Me., free public library antedates ours. By a letter from P. J. Hooke, librarian of the same, we learn that this library went into effect March 5, 1855, by a vote of the town, twenty-two years after the beginning of the Peterborough library.

Thus giving all due credit for previous attempts to establish free public libraries, we think the claim of Peterborough to be the first to have succeeded in it is indisputable. Any library in this country, founded and owned by a town, supported by municipal taxation, maintained from its origin till now, and open to the free use of all its citizens, anterior to our own, is entirely unknown to us. We confidently claim the honor of being the pioneers in this enterprise, that our library is the first public free library supported at public expense in the United States.*

There has been more difficulty in ascertaining the history of the town library than we had anticipated. It being a matter of comparatively recent origin, it was thought that many persons living would remember about it, and be able to furnish all the requisite information; but it so happened that those most prominent in the matter were at, or past, the middle age of life, and are all now deceased, with the exception of Henry F. Cogswell, now residing in Buffalo, N. Y. The town records have been carefully examined, but they furnish poor and scanty materials for history; they faithfully record votes, and the results of various transactions, but of those who made the motions, or advocated the measures, they are entirely reticent.

The following are the first proceedings of the town in relation to the library, at a meeting held April 9, 1833 : —

"On motion, Voted, That out of the money to be raised the present year from the State Treasurer on account of the literary fund of the town, as to make the principal thereof amount to seven hundred and fifty dollars, to remain a permanent fund."

"Voted, that the remainder to be raised from the State Treasury, together with the interest of said fund, be appropriated the present year."

---

* In a letter of July 22, 1876, from John Eaton, LL.D., Commissioner of Education, Washington, D. C., he says: "So far, then, as the Bureau is at present advised, Peterborough may rightly claim the honor of having established the first free town library in the United States."

"On motion, Voted, That the portion of the literary fund and the interest thereof be appropriated this year; be divided among the small school-districts, and applied to the purchase of books for *a town library.*" *

We have reason to believe that this important town measure owed its origin in a great degree to the late Rev. Abiel Abbot, D. D., together with the earnest and hearty coöperation of Gov. John H. Steele, James Walker, Henry F. Cogswell, Wm. Scott, T. K. Ames, James Howe, and many others. The library has always been regarded with favor by the people, and has received more persistent support than almost any other voluntary institution in town.

In 1834 John H. Steele, Abiel Abbot, and Timothy Fox were chosen directors of the town library, which committee probably purchased the first books. The library started off this year with an appropriation, made in 1833, of $66.88; for the next two years, 1834, '35, $70, each, was appropriated. In 1836, $96.37 was appropriated, and in 1837, $75; 1838, $75; 1839, $89, and an addition, also, of $50; 1840, $70; 1841, $90; 1842, $50, and additional, also, $80; and then $45 for each year to 1865, except the year 1862, when no appropriation was made. In 1865, $60 was appropriated; 1866, $75; 1867, $95; 1868, $75; 1869, $75; 1870, $150; 1871, $75; 1872, $75; 1873, $75; 1874, $75: 1875, $75. In 1835 the first appropriation, of $42.09, was made to William T. Smith for taking care of the library, and subsequently a certain sum, from $30 to $50, was paid annually to different persons, till the removal of the library, in 1874, to the south basement of Town Hall, and its great enlargement, when the salary of the librarian was increased to one hundred dollars a year. The money above appropriated was derived from the literary

---

* The wording of these votes seems very obscure. The fact intended to be conveyed was, no doubt, this : —

1st, That of the money heretofore received by the town on account of the literary fund, with enough of this year's receipts to make $750, be formed into, and remain, a permanent fund, as it is at the present time.

2d, That what remains, after completing this fund, be appropriated, with the interest on said fund, the present year.

3d, Is a repetition of the last vote with the following, to be divided among the small school-districts, and applied to the purchase of books for a town library.

und, so-called, a state tax on banks, and distributed to the various towns, to be used for literary purposes.

The following are the various aids and donations in money, which have been extended to the town library, with the names of the individual donors. In 1868 one hundred dollars was subscribed, the following persons giving five dollars each, *viz.*, M. L. Morrison, Jonas Livingston, C. H. Brooks, H. A. Marsh, John Gates, A. J. Aldrich, Joseph Noone, C. B. Ferry, A. M. Pendleton, S. N. Porter, Marshall Nay, George T. Wheeler, S. I. Vose, John R. Miller, E. M. Tubbs, R. B. Hatch, O. Felt, A. P. Morrison; those giving two dollars each were Dr. Albert Smith, E. B. Dodge; and those giving one dollar each were William Lowe, E. R. Farnsworth, John Scott, John Wilder, Dr. J. F. Cutler, and P. McLaughlin. The above subscription was gotten up and collected by Rev. A. M. Pendleton.

In 1869 a levee was gotten up by Rev. A. M. Pendleton and Miss Catharine Smith for the purpose of procuring additional funds for the town library, and a committee, consisting of John R. Miller, Charles Scott, and Charles Wilder, were appointed to invite former residents and natives of the town to attend and partake of the festivities of the same. An agreeable response of $290.50 was generously made by the following persons, while $144.24 was realized from the levee, making a total of $434.74 : —

John Field, Arlington, Mass., $100; Wm. H. Smith, Alton, Ill., $50; Samuel May, Boston, $20; N. H. Morison, Baltimore, Md., $20; Mrs. S. W. Hogan, Woburn, Mass., $10; J. H. Morison, D. D., $10; Nathaniel Holmes, Cambridge, Mass., $10; K. C. Scott, Keene, $10; Geo. E. Forbush, Providence, R. I., $10; Perkins Bass, Chicago, Ill., $10; Mrs. Helen J. McCaine, St. Paul, Minn., $5; Albert B. Hannaford, Norwalk, O., $5; William M. Smith, Lowell, Mass., $5; Albert Field, So. Market, $5; George Howe, Lynn, Mass., $5; a Friend in Lynn, Mass., $5; ·Charles M. Townsend, Springfield, Vt., $3; Jona. Felt, Jr., Newton Lower Falls, Mass., $2; Mrs. Sarah E. Cheney, Chicago, Ill., $2; Laurence Daly, Perkinsville, Vt., $1.50; Elias Boynton, New

Lisbon, Wis., $1; Betsey J. Follansbee, Canaan, $1. The same year, the committee acknowledge the receipt of $11 from a ladies' calico ball. A few other donations were also made; in 1862, $20 by Mrs. Mortier L. Morrison, and $3.25 by a person unknown. In 1869, by a vote of the town, $108 was appropriated to the library, realized from the sale of the New Hampshire reports.

We have yet to mention the most remarkable aid to the library. Through the individual and unaided efforts of the Rev. A. M. Pendleton, a fund of $1000 was subscribed in 1873, '74, of which sum, $914.50, with $3, by Wallace Clark, of the same subscription, in 1875, was paid, and has been expended in books.

Towards this fund the following persons contributed $25 each: *viz.*, A. M. Pendleton, R. B. Hatch, Charles Scott, John R. Miller, I. F. Porter, A. S. Scott, S. I. Vose, James Scott, James S. Gray, David Barker, James Hannaford, T. S. Stewart, E. W. McIntosh, Jonas Livingston, Joshua Briggs, Joseph Noone's sons; $15 for the same, Charles H. Brooks; $10, Anna C. Payson, John Q. Adams, Levi Cross, John Gates, Sylvester Tenney, Samuel Adams, Jr., John Scott, M. L. Morrison, Joseph Farnum, George W. Farrar, James R. Miller, W. G. Livingston, Albert Smith, Albert Frost, Stephen Felt, B. S. Winn; $5 each, W. D. Chase, Sampson Washburn, W. G. Hale, George H. Longley, S. N. Porter, W. E. Davis, John Wilder, Abel Wilder, Asa Twitchell, D. W. Gould, Lorenzo Holt, J. M. Collins, W. F. Pratt, Smith Brothers, L. O. Forbush, W. S. Keyes, John Smith, Albert M. Smith, T. D. Winch, J. M. Macomber, C. W. Holt, Charles W. Barber, A. A. Sawyer, E. A. Fletcher, G. A. Hamilton, John Cragin, William F. White, Sargeant Bohonan, H. K. French, G. F. Day, George H. Scripture, Franklin Mears, William Moore, L. P. Wilson, Elbridge Howe, E. M. Felt, S. P. Longley, George Dustan, Charles H. Longley, Augustus Fuller; $3 each, N. C. Forbush, G. W. Towle, J. T. Regan, H. H. Templeton, M. M. Heath, A. A. Ames, J. H. Collins, Charles Jaquith, Jasper Elliot, C. P. Follansbee, C. L. Dodge, J. N. Dodge, W. H. Longley, Milton Carter, Franklin Field, G. W.

Wilson, G. B. **Priest**, S. A. Sawyer, N. H. Moore, C. P. Richardson, G. F. **Livingston**, J. M. Mears, Ebenezer Fairbanks, Harvey Hadley, **G. W.** Marden, E. B. Dodge; $2.50, C. Haywood; $2 each, **A. T.** Hovey, C. C. Clark, E. A. Towns, Ellen Forbush, A. C. **Frost**, W. E. Clark, F. J. Ames, S. H. Hardy, H. F. Preston, **J. N.** Thayer; $1 each, G. W. Conant, F. J. Shedd, Hiram **McCoy**, J. L. Carter, J. Stone, Sallie A. Crombie, David **Clark**, Samuel Weston, W. C. B. Spofford, E. N. Fish, C. L. **Richardson**.

In addition to these money donations, books have from time to time been presented. The first important addition made was that of the Phœnix Factory Library, in 1860, of two hundred and one volumes of well-selected and valuable books, presented to the town by the directors of the same; forty-two volumes from Hon. Mason W. Tappan, and five volumes public documents; in 1861, five volumes by individuals, names of donors not mentioned; in 1862, five volumes by Hon. E. H. Rollins; in 1863, six volumes by Hon. E. H. Rollins; in 1864, eight volumes presented by the librarian, John R. Miller, three volumes by Hon. E. H. Rollins, one volume each by Miss Anna C. Payson, and George Livermore, Esq., Cambridge, Mass.; in 1865, eighteen volumes by Hon. E. H. Rollins, four volumes by Hon. Daniel Clark, one volume by Nathaniel H. Morison, Esq.; in 1866, thirty-three volumes by the American Unitarian Association, twenty-one volumes by Messrs. Clark and Rollins, one volume by John H. Morison, D. D., one volume from the funds of the Young Men's Debating Club, and two volumes by an unknown friend; in 1867, one volume by Judge Nathaniel Holmes, — a copy of his work on the "Authorship of Shakespeare"; in 1868, thirty volumes by Miss Anna C. Payson, four volumes by Mrs. E. J. Hale; in 1869, thirty volumes of public documents by Hon. A. F. Stevens, three volumes by Senator Cragin, nine volumes of State Reports, seven volumes by the American Tract Society, one volume by J. A. Bullard, one volume by Asa Twitchell, one volume by Miss L. S. Fisk, five volumes by Miss Anna C. Payson; in 1871, three volumes by Mrs. Cochran, one volume by J. L. Emmons, ten

16

volumes by Horáce Morison, fifteen volumes by the American Unitarian Association; in 1872, three volumes by S. N. Haskell; in 1873, eight volumes by Hon. A. C. Cragin.

The greatest benefactor to the town library has been the Rev. A. M. Pendleton. He served gratuitously eight years on the library committee, and labored in season and out of season for its welfare. It is to him, more than any other person, that we are indebted for the judicious selection of the books, the largest portion of which was bought while he was a member of the board; for the careful supervision and management of the library; the securing a convenient place for the same; for the raising, by subscription, such large sums of money for its advancement, and a still-continued interest in its behalf. He merits the lasting gratitude of the town, and of all those who are enjoying the fruits of his labor, in the excellent books he did so much tó provide for them.

The library commenced with a very few books, and was gradually increased by the annual appropriations of the town, and the various donations in money and books which were made to it from time to time, the town in the meanwhile paying the expenses of furnishing a room and the taking care of it. The committees hitherto in charge of it have been very faithful in the discharge of their duties; and one is surprised to learn how few books have been lost during the forty years of its existence. In 1864 every volume was accounted for, and in 1865 only one volume was lost, and in other years but two or three volumes each year. Vastly more books were absolutely worn out than were lost. The committees often complain of the ill usage the books receive, and yet acknowledge, in almost every report, the very general use of the library by all classes. A considerable number of books are thrown aside every year as worn out, and unfit for further use; and those badly dilapidated have to be repaired, new covered, and new labelled, bringing a good deal of labor and care upon a committee whose services have hitherto been gratuitously rendered.

The library at the present date (by the report of the committee for 1876) contains three thousand seven hundred and thirty-two volumes. The books have all been very carefully selected, and are well suited to the wants of the people. The design has been to furnish useful and instructive reading, rather than that of a light or amusing character; and works of fiction, except those of the most acknowledged merit, have found little place among the books.

The library is rich in history, biography, travels, and ethics, furnishing to the public some of the best books in our language. Those who desire the lighter reading are obliged to seek it elsewhere. The library furnishes useful nutriment to all classes who read to become intelligent. It has become a great success, and is freely used by all, and has proved of inestimable value to the people.

The great desiderata for the future prosperity of the library are, First, that some public-spirited person, a descendant of the town or otherwise, should endow it with a fund that should yield it a larger annual income than it has ever yet had. Second, that some one should erect a building with all the accessories of a well-approved library, solely for its use. The annual income of the library has hitherto been small; and, in the action of the town, it has incurred the fate of other measures, that of always being fixed at the lowest minimum. But for the liberality of the inhabitants, and friends of the town abroad, the library, only increased and supported by the annual appropriation to this object, would now make a very insignificant appearance. Thanks to these donors, who have contributed so liberally to this purpose! they have accomplished a good that will long be remembered. It has now existed over forty years, and is more flourishing than ever. We trust that the town, on whom it must rely for its continuance and support, will ever keep up its interest in the library, and never suffer it to languish from want of support, or from the indifference of the people.

CHAPTER XII.

PROFESSIONAL HISTORY.

College Graduates. — Lawyers. — Those Educated as Lawyers, and Settled Elsewhere. — Clergymen. — Physicians. — Those who became Physicians, and Settled Elsewhere.

List of College Graduates from the Town of Peterborough.

JEREMIAH SMITH graduated at Rutgers College, N. J., in 1781, and received the honorary degree of LL. D. from Dartmouth College in 1804, and the same from Harvard University in 1807; Chief-Justice of Superior Court and Governor of New Hampshire in 1809; also Judge of United States Circuit Court, an eminent and distinguished lawyer. He died at Dover, Sept. 21, 1842, aged 82 years.

JAMES WILSON, son of Major Robert Wilson, graduated at Harvard College in 1789. Was educated a lawyer, and practised his profession in Peterborough till 1815, when he removed to Keene, where he died, Jan. 4, 1839, aged 73 years. He was a talented and successful lawyer. He was chosen Representative to Congress 1809–11.

WALTER LITTLE, son of Thomas Little (name changed to Fullerton), graduated at Dartmouth College in 1, 96. Was settled as minister in Antrim, before the Rev. Dr. Whiton. He remained but a few years, went to Maryland, and died in 1815.

JOHN WILSON, son of Major Robert Wilson, graduated at Harvard College in 1799; was a lawyer of some eminence; settled in Belfast, Me.; a Representative to Congress in 1813–15; died in 1848, aged 76 years.

STEPHEN MITCHELL, son of Benjamin Mitchell, graduated at Williams College in 1801; studied law, and practised his profession in Durham; died February, 1833, aged 53 years.

REUBEN D. MUSSEY, son of Dr. John Mussey, graduated at Dartmouth College in 1803; M. D. and LL. D.; professor at Dartmouth Medical College many years; also Professor of Surgery in the Ohio Medical College, Cincinnati, O.; author of various books; died in Boston, June 21, 1866, aged 86 years.

JOHN STUART, son of Charles Stuart, graduated at Williams College in 1804; a lawyer; died 1848, aged 65 years.

WILLIAM RITCHIE, son of James Ritchie, graduated at Dartmouth College in 1804; studied divinity, and was settled first at Canton, but removed to Needham, where he preached many years; died Feb. 22, 1842, aged 60 years.

STEPHEN P. STEELE, son of Gen. David Steele, graduated at Williams College in 1808. He studied law, and practised his profession in Peterborough; died July 22, 1857, aged 73 years.

CHARLES JESSE STUART, son of Charles Stuart, graduated at Dartmouth College in 1809; was a lawyer in Lancaster, where he died, May 17, 1836, aged 47 years, 7 months.

JAMES PORTER, Jr., son of James Porter, graduated at Williams College in 1810. He studied divinity, and was settled as minister in Pomfret, Conn., where he continued twenty-five years. He died June, 1856, aged 71 years.

DAVID STEELE, son of Gen. David Steele, a graduate of Williams College in 1810. He studied law, and practised his profession at Hillsborough Bridge; died Dec. 10, 1866, aged 79 years.

JONATHAN STEELE, son of Thomas Steele, graduated at Williams College in 1811. He studied law, and practised his profession at Epsom. He died September, 1858, aged 66 years.

ISAAC P. OSGOOD, son of Dr. Kendall Osgood, graduated at Harvard College in 1814; studied law, and settled in Boston; died in 1867, aged 74 years.

JESSE SMITH, son of Robert Smith, graduated at Dartmouth College in 1814. He studied the medical profession; lectured at Dartmouth Medical School, the sessions of 1820; and was appointed Professor of Anatomy and Surgery in the Ohio Medical College, Cincinnati, O., which office he held till his death. He died of cholera, in 1833, at Cincinnati, aged 40 years.

DAVID STEELE, son of Gen. John Steele, graduated at Dartmouth College in 1815. He was an attorney at law, with considerable distinction, at Goffstown, and died there, Oct. 1, 1875, aged 80 years.

JOSEPH BRACKETT, son of Samuel Brackett, graduated at Williams College in 1815. He was ordained at Rushville, N. Y., where he died, Sept. 24, 1832, aged 41 years.

CHARLES WHITE, son of John White, graduated at Dartmouth College in 1816. He went out to Mississippi to teach, and died at sea on his return passage, Aug. 10, 1817, aged 22 years.

AMASA EDES, son of Samuel Edes, graduated at Dartmouth College in 1817. An attorney at law at Newport.

JONATHAN SMITH, Jr., son of Jonathan Smith, graduated at Harvard College in 1819; studied law with the late Gov. Levi Lincoln, Worcester, Mass.; settled at Bath, where he died, Aug. 10, 1840, aged 42 years.

JAMES WILSON, Jr., son of James Wilson, a graduate of Middlebury College in 1820; an attorney at law at Keene, and for many years in San Francisco, Cal.; a member of Congress from New Hampshire, 1847–51.

ALBERT SMITH, son of Samuel Smith, graduated at Dartmouth College in 1825; received from the same the degree of M. D. in 1833 and LL. D. in 1870; Professor of Materia Medica and Therapeutics in the Dartmouth Medical School, from 1849 to 1870.

JOHN HOPKINS MORISON, son of Nathaniel Morison, graduated at Harvard College in 1831; studied divinity, and was first ordained at New Bedford, and afterwards at Milton, Mass., where he now resides; received the degree of D. D. from Harvard College in 1858.

JOSIAH BALLARD graduated at Yale College in 1833; studied divinity; ordained ——; died in 1863.

ARTEMAS LAWRENCE HOLMES, son of Nathaniel Holmes, Jr., graduated at Dartmouth College in 1835. He studied law, and for a time practised his profession in Peterborough; afterwards resided in New York, where he died in 1871, aged 57 years.

SOLOMON LAWS, son of Thomas Laws, graduated at Dartmouth College in 1836. He is a minister of the Universalist denomination; has removed to Ohio.

HORACE MORISON, son of Nathaniel Morison, graduated at Harvard College in 1837; spent most of his life in teaching in Baltimore; was, from 1840 to 1854, Professor of Mathematics in the University of Maryland; returned to Peterborough in ill health, a short time before his death; died Aug. 5, 1870, aged 60 years.

NATHANIEL HOLMES, son of Samuel Holmes, graduated at Harvard College in 1837; educated as a lawyer, and settled in St. Louis, where he became a Judge of the Superior Court of Missouri, afterwards Royal Professor of Law in Harvard Law School from 1868 to 1872. He now resides in St. Louis.

NATHANIEL H. MORISON, son of Nathaniel Morison, graduated at Harvard College in 1839. He prepared himself for the ministry, but devoted himself to teaching in Baltimore, Md.; appointed Provost of the Peabody Institute in that city in 1867; LL. D., St. John College, Annapolis, Md., 1870.

BARNARD BEMIS WHITTEMORE, son of Barnard Whittemore, graduated at Harvard College in 1839; was educated as a lawyer, but has devoted himself to journalism; editor of the New Hampshire *Gazette*.

DAVID YOUNGMAN, Jr., son of David Youngman, graduated at Dartmouth College in 1839; studied medicine, and practises in Boston.

OREN B. CHENEY, son of Moses Cheney, graduated at Dartmouth College in 1839. He was settled at Lebanon and Augusta, Me., six years at the former place, and five at the latter. He then devoted himself to the founding of a free Baptist school in 1854, at Lewiston, which eventuated in the establishment of Bates College, of which he has been president from the beginning. The honorary degree of D. D. was conferred on him by the Wesleyan University in 1863.

JOSEPH ADDISON WHITE, son of Robert White, graduated at Harvard College in 1840. He devoted himself to teaching, and died early, Jan. 20, 1843, aged 25 years, 7 months.

JAMES SMITH, son of William Smith, graduated at Yale College in 1840; an attorney at law in New Orleans, with flattering prospects, when he was cut off by consumption, and died at Peterborough, Jan. 1, 1847, aged 31 years.

GEORGE WALKER, son of James Walker, graduated at Dartmouth College in 1842; studied law, and was many years in Springfield, Mass., in the practice of his profession. He now resides in New York City, and devotes his time to various financial matters.

LUKE MILLER, son of Andrew Miller, graduated at Norwich University in 1841; studied medicine, and removed to Lanesborough, Minn., where he now practises his profession.

JAMES MORISON, son of Nathaniel Morison, graduated at Harvard College in 1844; was educated a physician; settled in San Francisco, Cal.; Professor of Theory and Practice in the Pacific University; now resides in Quincy, Mass.

JOHN G. PARKER, son of James Parker, graduated at Norwich University in 1847; M. D., Dartmouth, 1852. He studied medicine, practised at Dublin and Warner, and died at the latter place, Sept. 12, 1869, aged 51 years.

CHARLES GILMAN CHENEY, son of Moses Cheney, graduated at Dartmouth College in 1848; studied law; practised at Peterborough; cashier of the first bank established in town. He died at Hillsborough Bridge, Nov. 13, 1862, aged 36 years, 4 months.

SAMUEL ABBOT SMITH, son of Samuel G. Smith, graduated at Harvard College in 1849; studied divinity, and was ordained at West Cambridge (now Arlington), June 27, 1854, where he died, May 20, 1865, aged 36 years.

GEORGE WASHINGTON COGSWELL, son of Henry F. Cogswell, graduated at Harvard College in 1849. He died at LeRoy, N. Y., April 22, 1854, aged 23 years, 9 months.

FREDERICK AUGUSTUS SMITH, son of Albert Smith, graduated at Dartmouth College in 1852; also M. D. in 1855; commenced his practice ·in Leominster, where he died, Dec. 20, 1856, aged 26 years.

GEORGE ADDISON HUNT, son of Norton Hunt, graduated at Dartmouth College in 1852; an attorney at law, with considerable distinction, at Quincy, Ill., where he died, March 24, 1867, aged 39 years.

JOHN PERRY ALLISON, son of John Allison, graduated at Harvard College in 1854; studied law, and now resides in Sioux City, Ia.

ALFRED LAWS, son of Thomas Laws, Jr., graduated at Dartmouth College in 1858; is a teacher.

GEORGE MOORE, son of Nathaniel H. Moore, graduated at Dartmouth College in 1866; devoted himself to teaching; died at Cincinnati, May 5, 1867, aged 25 years.

AMOS KIDDER FISK, son of Francis Fisk, graduated at Harvard College in 1866; has become a journalist; engaged in the *Globe* newspaper office.

WILLIAM GARDNER HALE, son of William Hale, graduated at Harvard College in 1870; now a tutor in the same.

JONATHAN SMITH, son of John Smith, graduated at Dartmouth College in 1871; is now an attorney at law in Manchester.

FRANK LESLIE WASHBURN, son of George Washburn, graduated at Bates College, Lewiston, Me., in 1875.

Fifty graduates.

The following persons had only a partial course in college; there may have been more than these, but we have not been able to ascertain: —

SAMUEL A. HOLMES was in Dartmouth College two years, in the sophomore and junior classes, 1840, '41.

DAVID SMITH, son of Jenny Smith, was a member of Dartmouth College three years, in the class of 1823, but did not graduate.

ALBERT S. SCOTT was two years a member of the class of 1848.

CHARLES A. AMES, one year in Amherst College.

17

IRA ALLISON, one year in Dartmouth College, in the class of 1827.

THOMAS SPRING, two or three years in Williams College.

WILLIS A. FARNSWORTH in Amherst College a year and a half in the class of 1873.

List of the Lawyers of Peterborough.

Jeremiah Smith, James Wilson, Stephen P. Steele, James Walker, Artemas L. Holmes, David J. Clark, Edward S. Cutter, Charles G. Cheney, George A. Ramsdell, C. V. Dearborn, Albert S. Scott, Riley B. Hatch, Eugene Lewis, Ezra M. Smith, Frank G. Clark, Daniel M. White.

List of Natives and Inhabitants of Town who have Studied Law and Practised Elsewhere.

JONATHAN STEELE, son of Capt. David Steele, settled at Durham, and was a Judge in the Superior Court of New Hampshire, from Feb. 19, 1810 to 1812.

JOHN WILSON, son of Maj. Robert Wilson, practised his profession in Belfast, Me., and acquired much eminence. Was a Representative to Congress from Maine.

ZACCHEUS PORTER, son of James Porter, studied law, and was in partnership with John Wilson, at Belfast, Me., where he died at an early age.

DAVID STEELE, son of Gen. David Steele, at Hillsboro Bridge.

JONATHAN STEELE, son of Thomas Steele, at Epsom.

DAVID STEELE, son of Thomas Steele, at Dover.

DAVID STEELE, son of John Steele, at Goffstown; died Oct. 1, 1875, aged 80 years.

ISAAC P. OSGOOD, son of Dr. Kendall Osgood, at Boston

AMASA EDES, son of Samuel Edes, at Newport.

DAVID SCOTT, son of William Scott, at Columbus, O.

GUSTAVUS SWAN, son of John Swan, at Columbus; a judge in the courts in that state.

GEN. JAMES MILLER, in Greenfield.

THOMAS F. GOODHUE, in Greenfield.

STEPHEN MITCHELL, son of Benj. Mitchell, at Durham.

JOHN STUART, son of Charles Stuart, in Boston.

CHARLES JESSE STUART, son of Charles Stuart, at Lancaster.

JAMES WILSON, Jr., at Keene, and San Francisco, Cal.

JONATHAN SMITH, Jr., son of Jonathan Smith, at Bath.

GEORGE WALKER, son of James Walker, at Springfield.

NATHANIEL HOLMES, son of Samuel Holmes, at St. Louis; became a Judge of the Superior Court in Missouri, and Royal Professor of Law at Harvard College.

SAMUEL A. HOLMES, son of Samuel Holmes, St. Louis, Mo.

BERNARD B. WHITTEMORE, son of Bernard Whittemore, at Nashua.

JAMES SMITH, son of William Smith, at New Orleans.

GEORGE A. HUNT, son of Norton Hunt, at Quincy, Ill.

JOHN P. ALLISON, son of John Allison, at Sioux City, Ia.

SAMUEL JOHN TODD, son of Daniel Todd, at Beloit, Wis.

FREDERICK C. INGALLS, son of Cyrus Ingalls, at Chicago, Ill.

T. KNEELAND AMES, son of T. Parsons Ames, prepared for the law; went into the army and was killed, second Bull Run battle.

JONATHAN SMITH, son of John Smith, at Manchester.

Persons in Town who became Clergymen.

WILLIAM RITCHIE, son of James Ritchie. He was ordained at Canton first, and removed to Needham, Mass., where he died, Feb. 22, 1842, aged 60 years.

JAMES PORTER, Jr., son of James Porter, ordained at Pomfret, Conn., and remained pastor over one society twenty-five years; died at Pomfret, Ct., June, 1856, aged 71 years.

JOSEPH BRACKETT, son of Samuel Brackett; settled at Rushville, N. Y., where he died, Sept. 24, 1832, aged 41 years.

WALTER LITTLE, son of Thomas Little, changed his name to Fullerton; was settled at Antrim; died in Maryland in 1815.

NATHAN UPTON, a blacksmith, became a Methodist preacher; removed to Effingham, Ill.

Dr. DAVID SMILEY was a licensed Baptist preacher.

DAVID SMITH, son of Jenny Smith; went West.

JOSIAH BALLARD, son of William Ballard.

OREN B. CHENEY, D. D., son of Moses Cheney; President of Bates College, Me.

SOLOMON LAWS, son of Thomas Laws; Universalist clergyman.

JOHN H. MORISON, D. D., son of Nathaniel Morison; first settled at New Bedford, then at Milton, where he now resides.

S. HUDSON PARTRIDGE has had several pastorates; is now at Greenfield.

DANIEL MCCLENNING has had several pastorates.

SAMUEL F. CLARK; first settled at Athol; removed to Ware, where he died.

SAMUEL A. SMITH settled at Arlington, 1854, where he remained till his death, May 20, 1865, aged 36 years.

A List of the Physicians who have Practised Medicine in Town.

Dr. JOHN YOUNG was the first physician; he came to town in 1763 or '64; had an extensive practice. He died of a cancer on his face, Feb. 27, 1807, aged 68 years. *Vide Gen.*

DR. KENDALL OSGOOD came to town in 1788. He was a well educated physician, but did not do much business in town. He died Aug. 19, 1801, aged 45 years. *Vide Gen.*

Dr. JONATHAN WHITE, son of John White, Sen., was educated as a physician. He studied with Dr. Young, and received such training as he was able to give, but completed his studies in Boston, by attending the medical lectures just then instituted in New England for the first time. The blight of intemperance rested on this man early in his career, and closed his professional life almost as soon as begun. We find by the town records, in 1788, "that it was voted to engage Jonathan White to keep the grammar-school one year, if he could be engaged." We suppose he was engaged, by an anecdote told us only a short time since. A number of his scholars, almost men grown, had formed a plan to eject him from the school, and it was agreed that Daniel Robbe should take the initiatory steps in the affair. He exposed himself to discipline purposely, and was promptly called out by the teacher, who, seeing something wrong was afoot, by a rapid and violent seizure, thrust him headlong out of the house into the snow. The conspiracy was at an end at once.

They had mistaken their man. No school ever went on more successfully afterwards, and no teacher ever had better scholars than these same turbulent conspirators.

Dr. White seemed to be a man of rare accomplishments. His chirography was beautiful,—more like copperplate than anything else. It is supposed, by the writing, that he was employed by the then town clerk, Samuel Cuningham, to copy the proceedings of the town for the years 1785, '86, which come to the examiner of these records like an oasis in the desert. The spelling, punctuation, and use of capitals are all faultless, and show a man well versed in the English language. But he could do nothing as a physician; and after numerous attempts of his friends to reform him had utterly failed, he left town more than sixty years since, and died miserable and degraded, at Carlisle, Penn., having enlisted as a common soldier in the first part of the war of 1812.

Dr. DAVID SMILEY commenced practice in town as early as 1786, and continued it as long as his strength permitted. He died in extreme old age, Oct 3, 1855, aged 95 years, 5 months. *Vide Gen.*

Dr. THOMAS H. BLOOD. It is uncertain when he came to town. We know that when Samuel Smith removed to his mills, and occupied his new residence at the end of his large building, Dr. Blood occupied his house at the Corner, Jan. 1, 1795. In the proceedings of the town in 1798, the following vote was passed, *viz.*, " Voted to set the meeting-house a little to the east of the house that Thomas H. Blood lives in, when built or moved."

We learn from descendants of Dr. Blood something in relation to his after life. Between 1800 and 1801, he removed to Bolton, and subsequently to Sterling, giving up the profession, and engaging in the hatting business; he also devoted himself to public life, having been a Representative for Sterling, and also a State Senator to the Legislature. He also became a brigadier-general in the militia of Massachusetts. He acquired much property by his business, but lost it in 1829 by the great depression in business, and never regained it. He had eight children. One son, Oliver, graduated at

Harvard College in 1821; studied the medical profession and took his M. D. at same institution, in 1826. Afterwards he devoted himself to dentistry in Worcester, and died in 1858. Another son, Thomas S., took his medical degree of M. D. at Harvard College in 1838, and is now practising dentistry in Fitchburg, Mass. One of his daughters married Prof. Oliver Stearns, of the Divinity School at Cambridge. She died June, 1871. Dr. Blood died at Worcester, May 15, 1848, aged 73 years, 3 months.

Dr. John Mussey came to town in 1798. He never practised much in town, though a regularly educated man. He died Jan. 17, 1831, aged 85 years, 4 months. *Vide Gen.*

Dr. Thomas Peabody is remembered by some of the elderly inhabitants as an intemperate vagabond, who tramped about on foot, with a secret remedy, which he called his "arcanum." It was supposed to be some one of the preparations of antimony. With his secret remedy, he dispensed his skill equally to man and beast. He died at Greenfield, Nov. 6, 1822, aged 57 years.

Dr. Willis Johnson was born in Sturbridge, Mass., Dec. 21, 1786. He first commenced practice in Jaffrey, in 1807, and removed to Peterborough in January, 1808, where he remained till 1814, when he removed to Mason, where he remained the rest of his life. He died in 1859, aged 73 years.

Dr. John Starr came to town in 1808 or 1809. He was a graduate of Harvard College in 1804. He remained till 1814, when he removed to Northwood; married Sally Virgin, of Concord; died Sept. 8, 1851, aged 67 years.

Dr. David Carter removed from Marlboro to town in 1812, and remained till 1820. He spent a few years in practice in Dublin, where he died, January, 1828.

Dr. Jabez Priest commenced practice in town in 1816, and continued in the same till his death. He died of an epidemic dysentery, Aug. 17, 1826, aged 36 years. *Vide Gen.*

Dr. Samuel Richardson came to town in 1820, and was in active practice till he removed to Watertown, Mass., in 1838. *Vide Gen.*

WILLIAM FOLLANSBEE, M. D. He succeeded Dr. Priest in his practice. Received his degree of M. D. at Dartmouth College in 1825. He remained in successful practice till his death, May 30, 1867, aged 66 years. *Vide Gen.*

RICHARD STEELE, M. D., began practice in 1825 or '26, but did not succeed, and left town. A. M. and M. D., Dartmouth College. He died at Durham, 1870, aged 73 years.

DANIEL B. CUTTER, M. D., 1835, Yale College. A. M., Dartmouth College. Born in Jaffrey, May 10, 1808; removed from Ashby to Peterborough in September, 1837. Is yet in the practice of his profession in town. *Vide Gen.*

ALBERT SMITH, M. D., graduated at Dartmouth College, 1825. Received from the same the degree of M. D., 1833; of LL. D., 1870. After spending five years in practice in Leominster, Mass., he removed to Peterborough in 1837, where he now resides. *Vide Gen.*

JOHN H. CUTLER, M. D. Born in Rindge, Feb. 16, 1834. Received his M. D. at Burlington College, Vt., in 1861. Practised his profession in Mason Village; was in the army as assistant surgeon in 1864, and removed to Peterborough in the fall of 1865, and has remained here since. *Vide Gen.*

WILLARD B. CHASE, M. D. Born in Claremont. Received his M. D., Harvard College, 1866; practised for a while in Greenfield, and removed to Peterborough in 1869, where he now resides. *Vide Gen.*

Dr. GEORGE GREELEY came to town in ——, and remained a few years.

The following homœopathists have been here at various times, *viz.*, Drs. Seavey, Chase, Bradford, and Dodge.

Mary Ann Kimball, M. D., is the homœopathic physician in town at the present time.

Natives and Inhabitants of Peterborough who became Physicians and Settled Elsewhere.

REUBEN D. MUSSEY, M. D., LL. D. Professor at Dartmouth Medical College, and Ohio Medical College.

Dr. FREDERICK A. MITCHELL studied the profession and practised it at various places; died at Manchester, July 28, 1869, aged 80 years. *Vide Gen.*

Dr. DAVID MITCHELL located himself as a physician at Bradford, where he suddenly died of a heart affection, Jan. 21, 1821, aged 39 years. *Vide Gen.*

JESSE SMITH, M. D.   In Cincinnati, O.   Professor of Anatomy and Surgery in the Ohio Medical College.   Died of cholera, July, 1833, aged 40 years.   *Vide Gen.*

WILLIAM LITTLE, son of Thomas Little, settled in Hillsboro, and was drowned in the Contoocook.   *Vide Gen.*

ROBERT SMITH, son of John Smith.   He practised in various places; died at Addison, Vt.   *Vide Gen.*

WILLIAM H. PEABODY, M. D.   Dartmouth College, in 1826. Settled in Gorham, Me., and died there, March 2, 1843, aged 42 years.   *Vide Gen.*

ALBERT SMITH, M. D.   Five years at Leominster, Mass. *Vide Gen.*

HIRAM J. EDES, M. D.   Took his medical degree at the Hampden Sidney College, Va., and first practised in Kansas, and then removed to Cedar Rapids, Ia., where he now resides in the active practice of his profession.   *Vide Gen.*

DAVID YOUNGMAN, M. D., graduated at Dartmouth College in 1839, and also took his medical degree in 1846.   He practised ten years in Winchester, Mass., and is now in the practice of his profession in Boston, Mass.

GEORGE H. INGALLS, M. D., settled at Proctorsville, Vt., where he remained till the failure of his health, and died at Peterborough, May 26, 1849, aged 44 years.   *Vide Gen.*

LUKE MILLER, M. D., at Woodstock, Vt., 1843; A. B., Norwich University in 1841.   He is now practising his profession at Lanesboro, Minn.   *Vide Gen.*

JOHN G. PARKER, M. D. at Dartmouth College.   A. B. at Norwich University, Vt., in 1847.   He practised twelve years at Dublin, and then removed to Warner, where he died, Sept. 12, 1869, aged 51 years.   *Vide Gen.*

E. COOLIDGE RICHARDSON, M. D.; medical degree at Harvard College in 1842; now resides in Ware, Mass., in the practice of his profession.   *Vide Gen.*

JAMES MORISON, M. D.   Graduated Harvard College, 1844. Medical degree in Maryland University in 1846.   Resided many years at San Francisco, Cal.; was Professor of Theory and Practice in the Pacific University; now resides in Quincy, Mass., in the practice of his profession.

FREDERICK A. SMITH, M. D. Graduated Dartmouth College, 1852 ; M. D., 1855. Resided in Leominster, Mass.; died Dec. 20, 1856, aged 26 years.

18

CHAPTER XIII.

MUNICIPAL.

The Record of Town Meetings. — List of Moderators. — Town Clerks. — Selectmen. — Treasurers. — Representatives. — Committee of Safety.

THE town was incorporated Jan. 17, 1760, and the first meeting called by Hugh Wilson, authorized so to do by the charter, was held at the meeting-house, — the full proceedings of which are given in the fourth chapter.

The meetings of the town after this organization have been held continuously to the present time, of which there is a fair record preserved, with the exception of two meetings, one in 1770, under the clerkship of Deacon Samuel Mitchell, and the other, the presidential meeting in 1840, under the clerkship of A. C. Blodgett. The record is marred by only a few other omissions. In two or three instances, the warrant is not recorded, and a number of the clerks have neglected to certify to their record. The other errors are of minor importance; as bad spelling, a clumsy and obscure wording of the propositions before the meetings, a careless heading of the proceedings on the record, an omission of the date on the pages, and of marginal notices, rendering it often very difficult to consult it as a reference.

The names of all individuals who have held the principal offices in town, from 1760 to 1876, are here recorded, in the various lists which follow.

Those who have held offices the longest time are here presented :—

For Selectmen. — Hugh Miller held the office of selectman from 1805 to 1828, twenty-four years successively. Next to him is Thomas Steele, who held this office eighteen years. Asa Evans, Capt. William Wilson, twelve years each. Alexander Robbe, 2d, eleven years. Henry Ferguson and Charles Stuart, ten years each.

Town Clerks. — Rufus Forbush, to 1867, held this office twenty-one years. Thomas Steele, nineteen years. John Steele, fourteen years. Samuel Mitchell, thirteen years.

Moderators. — Samuel Smith, seventeen years. Timothy K Ames, fourteen years. Charles Scott, twelve years.

Treasurers. — James Walker, nine years. Hugh Miller, Henry Steele, Ervin H. Smith, seven years each.

Representatives. — John Smith, twelve years. James Wilson, Hugh Miller, and Jonathan Smith, nine years each.

List of Moderators of the Annual Meetings from the Incorporation of the Town to the Present Time, with the Years they Respectively Served, Arranged in the Order in which they first Appear upon the Record.

Hugh Wilson, 1760, 61, 62, 63, 64, 72, 73.

John Young, 1765, 66, 68, 69, 83, 84, 85.

Thomas Morison, 1767, 74.

Samuel Moore, 1771.

William Smith, 1775, 79.

Jotham Blanchard, 1776, 77, 78, 80, 81.

Samuel Mitchell, 1782.

David Steele, Sen., 1786, 87.

Jeremiah Smith, 1788, 90.

George Duncan, 1789.

Robert Smith, 1791.

Henry Ferguson, 1792.

John Smith, 1793, 97, 98, 99, 1801.

Samuel Smith, 1794, 1803, 12, 15, 16, 18, 19, 20, 21, 22, 23, 24, 25, 26, 27, 28, 29.

Kendall Osgood, 1795.

David Steele, Jr., 1796, 1802, 4, 6, 8, 11, 17.

James Wilson, 1800, 5, 9, 13, 14.

Thomas Steele, 1807, 10.

John H. Steele, 1830, 31, 32, 35, 36, 37.

Timothy K. Ames, 1833, 34, 38, 39, 40, 42, 43, 44, 45, 46, 47, 51, 55, 61.

David J. Clark, 1841.

Daniel B. Cutter, 1848, 49, 50.

Edward S. Cutter, 1852, 56, 57, 58.

Charles G. Cheney, 1853, 54.

Albert S. Scott, 1859, 62, 65.

Charles Scott, 1860, 66, 67, 68, 69, 70, 71, 72, 73, 74, 75, 76.

Samuel I. Vose, 1863, 64.

List of Town Clerks from the Incorporation of the Town to the Present Day, in the Order in which they Appear upon the Record.

John Ferguson, 1760, 61, 62, 63, 64, 65, 66.

Samuel Mitchell, 1767, 68, 69, 71, 72, 73, 74, 75, 76, 77, 78, 79, 80.

Matthew Wallace, 1781.

William Smith, 1782.

Samuel Cuningham, 1783, 84, 85, 86.

Thomas Steele, 1787, 88, 89, 90, 91, 92, 93, 94, 95, 96, 97, 98, 99, 1800, 1, 2, 3, 4, 13.

John Steele, 1805, 6, 7, 8, 9, 10, 11, 12, 14, 16, 17, 18, 19, 20.

Daniel Abbot, 1815.

Nathaniel Holmes, Jr., 1821, 22.

Stephen P. Steele, 1823, 24, 25, 26, 27, 28.

Cyrus Ingalls, 1829, 30, 31, 32.

Rufus Forbush, 1833, 34, 35, 36, 50, 51, 52, 53, 54, 55, 56, 57, 58, 59, 60, 61, 62, 63, 64, 65, 66.

Moody Davis, 1837, 38.

A. C. Blodgett, 1839, 40.

Samuel Gates, 1841, 42, 43, 44, 45, 46, 47, 48, 49.

Kendall C. Scott, 1867.

Daniel W. Gould, 1868.

Samuel N. Porter, 1869.

Charles A. Ames, 1870.

John H. Steele, 1871, 72, 73, 74, 75, 76.

A List of Selectmen from the Incorporation of the Town to the Present Day, with the Years they Served, Arranged in the Order in which they first Entered their Office.

Hugh Wilson, 1760, 64, 72.

Thomas Morison, 1760, 65, 66, 73, 79.

Jonathan Morison, 1760.

Joseph Caldwell, 1760, 67.

John Swan, Jr., 1760.

John Smith, 1761, 73.

William Mained, 1761.

William Smith, 1761, 67, 69, 71, 72, 73, 77, 78, 82.

John Taggart, Jr., 1761, 68.

James Robbe, 1761.

Samuel Mitchell, 1762, 66, 77, 78, 80.

William Ritchie, 1762.

John Morison, 1762.

William Robbe, Jr., 1762, 66, 74, 75, 77, 78, 85, 86.

John Gregg, 1762, 63, 67.

Samuel Moore, 1763, 72.

Hugh Gregg, 1763.

Alexander Robbe, 1763, 69, 71, 72, 83, 84, 85, 86.

Thomas Cuningham, 1763.

Samuel Todd, 1764.

John Cochran, 1764.

John White, 1764, 73.

John White, Jr., 1787.

Henry Ferguson, 1764, 71, 77, 78, 85, 88, 89, 90, 91, 92.

Robert Wilson, 1765, 71.

David Steele, Capt., 1765, 66, 69, 72, 73, 80.

Matthew Wallace, 1765, 80, 81, 82.

John Young, 1765, 66, 68, 74, 84.

William Miller, 1767.

John Wiley, 1767.

Samuel Gregg, 1768, 71, 80, 82.

Joseph Hammill, 1774.

Thomas Davison, 1774,

Robert Morison, 1774.
James Templeton, 1775, 76, 83, 84.
William McNee, Jr., 1775, 76, 79.
Samuel Cuningham, 1768, 76, 79, 81.
Thomas Turner, 1768.
William Moore, 1769.
James Miller, 1769.
James Cuningham, 1775.
Charles Stuart, 1775, 81, 84, 85, 93, 94, 95, 96, 97, 98.
Aaron Brown, 1776.
Kelso Gray, 1776.
Jotham Blanchard, 1777, 78, 79.
Jonathan Wheelock, 1779.
Robert Holmes, 1780.
Thomas Stuart, 1783, 84.
Robert Smith, 1785, 92.
Thomas Steele, 1786, 88, 89, 90, 91, 92, 93, 94, 95, 96, 97, 98, 99, 1800, 1, 2, 3, 4.
Nathaniel Evans, 1786.
Israel Taylor, 1786.
John Gray, 1787.
Nathan Dix, 1787.
George Duncan, 1788, 89.
George Duncan, Jr., 1805, 6, 7, 8, 9.
Jeremiah Smith, 1790, 91.
Asa Evans, 1793, 94, 95, 96, 97, 98, 99, 1800, 1, 2, 3, 4.
Jonathan Smith, 1799, 1800, 1, 2, 3, 4.
Hugh Miller, 1805, 6, 7, 8, 9, 10, 11, 12, 13, 14, 15, 16, 17, 18, 19, 20, 21, 22, 23, 24, 25, 26, 27, 28.
John Steele, 1805, 6, 7, 8, 9, 10, 11.
John Scott, 1810, 11, 12, 14, 15, 16, 17, 18.
Nathaniel Morison, 1812, 13.
Robert White, 1813.
William Wilson, 1814, 15, 16, 17, 18, 19, 20, 21, 22, 23, 27, 28.
Nathaniel Moore, 1819, 20, 21, 22, 23, 24, 25, 26.
Alexander Robbe, 1824, 25, 26, 30, 31, 32, 33, 34, 35, 43, 44.
Timothy Fox, 1827, 28, 29, 31, 32, 33.

Moses Dodge, 1829, 30, 31.
Samuel Holmes, 1829, 30.
George W. Senter, 1832, 33.
Timothy K. Ames, 1834, 35, 36, 37, 42, 46, 47, 49, 52.
Isaac Edes, 1835, 36, 37, 38.
William Scott, 1836, 37, 38, 42.
John Smith, 1838, 39, 40.
William M. White, 1839, 40.
John Todd, Jr., 1839, 40, 41.
Samuel Miller, 1841, 50, 51.
Samuel Adams, 1841, 59, 60.
Ezra Peavey, 1842.
Archelaus Cragin, 1843, 44, 45, 53, 54.
Abiel Peavey, 1843, 44, 45.
James G. White, 1845, 46.
John H. Steele, 1846.
James Scott, 1847, 48, 50, 56, 57, 65.
Isaac Hadley, 1847, 48, 49, 51, 52, 61, 62, 63.
Robert Fulton, 1848.
Josiah S. Morison, 1849, 50.
Edwin Steele, 1851.
William B. Kimball, 1852, 53.
Eri Spaulding, 1853, 54, 55.
Amzi Childs, 1854, 55.
Diocletian Melvin, 1855.
Thomas Little, 1856, 64, 65.
Samuel R. Miller, 1859, 60.
Asa Davis, 1856, 57, 58, 66, 67, 68.
Albert Frost, 1857, 58, 59.
William R. Heywood, 1858.
Charles H. Brooks, 1860, 61, 62, 63, 73, 75, 76.
Eli S. Hunt, 1861, 62, 63, 64.
Franklin Field, 1864, 65, 66.
John M. Collins, 1866, 67.
Samuel I. Vose, 1867, 68, 69.
Mortier L. Morrison, 1868, 69, 70.
Charles Barber, 1869, 70, 71.
John Q. Adams, 1870, 71, 72, 74, 75.
E. W. McIntosh, 1871, 72, 73.
John Cragin, 1872, 73, 74.
Augustus Fuller, 1874, 75, 76.
William Moore, 1876.

*List of the Town Treasurers from the Incorporation of the
Town to the Present Day, in the Order in which they
Appear upon the Record.*

William Smith, 1774, 75, 77.

Matthew Templeton, 1776.

William Alld, 1783, 84.

Robert Wilson, 1785, 86, 87, 88.

Thomas Steele, 1799.

Hugh Miller, 1821, 22, 23, 24, 25, 26, 27.

James Walker, 1828, 29, 30, 31, 43, 44, 45, 46, 47.

Cyrus Ingalls, 1832.

Riley Goodridge, 1833, 34, 35.

William Moore, 1837, 38, 39, 40, 41, 42.

Stephen P. Steele, 1848.

Henry Steele, 1849, 50, 51, 52, 53, 54, 56.

John Kinsley, 1855.

S. Hudson Caldwell, 1857, 58, 59, 60, 61, 66.

Kendall C. Scott, 1862, 63, 64.

Charles H. Brooks, 1865.

Ervin H. Smith, 1867, 68, 69, 70, 71, 72.

Ezra M. Smith, 1873.

Samuel N. Porter, 1874, 75, 76.

*List of Representatives from the Incorporation of the Town to
the Present Time, in the Order in which they Appear upon
the Record.*

Samuel Cuningham, April 25, 1775, to 3d Provincial Congress at Exeter.

William Smith, May 17, 1775, to 4th Provincial Congress at Exeter.

Samuel Moore, Dec. 21, 1775, to 5th Provincial Congress at Exeter.

Matthew Wallace, 1784.

Samuel Cuningham, 1786.

Nathan Dix, 1787.

Jeremiah Smith, 1788, 89, 90.

John Smith, 1791, 92, 93, 94, 95, 96, 97, 98, 99, 1800, 1, 2.

James Wilson, 1803, 4, 5, 6, 7, 8, 12, 13, 14.

Jonathan Smith, 1809, 21, 22, 23, 24, 25, 26, 27, 28.

John Steele, 1810, 11.

Hugh Miller, 1815, 16, 17, 18, 19, 20, 30, 31, 32.

John H. Steele, 1829.

James Walker, 1833, 34, 44.

Alexander Robbe, 1835, 36, 43, 44.

John Todd, 1837, 38, 39.

William Moore, 1838, 39, 40.

Timothy K. Ames, 1840, 41.

Stephen P. Steele, 1841, 42.

William Follansbee, 1842, 43.

Luke Miller, 1845, 46.

Josiah S. Morrison, 1845, 48.

Norton Hunt, 1847.

Samuel Adams, 1847.

A. P. Morrison, 1848, 62, 63.

Daniel McClenning, 1849, 50.

James Scott, 1849, 50.

Samuel Miller, 1851, 52.

Daniel B. Cutter, 1852.

Isaac Hadley, 1853.

Person C. Cheney, 1853, 54.

Asa Davis, 1854.

Albert Smith, 1855.

Albert S. Scott, 1855, 57, 66, 67.

Samuel Edes, 1857, 58.

Asa F. Gowing, 1858, 59.

John Smith, 1859, 60.

Andrew A. Farnsworth, 1860, 61.

Cornelius V. Dearborn, 1861, 62.

Granville P. Felt, 1863, 64.

Elijah M. Tubbs, 1864, 65.

Nathaniel H. Moore, 1865, 66.

John Wilder, 1867, 68.

Riley B. Hatch, 1868, 69.

Charles Wilder, 1869, 70.

George Dustan, 1870, 71.

Ezra M. Smith, 1871, 72.

Daniel W. Gould, 1872, 73.

Joseph Farnum, 1873, 74.

Levi Cross, 1874, 75.

Franklin Field, 1875, 76.

Charles Scott, 1876.

Committees of Safety for the Years 1775, 76, 77, 78, 79, *as they Appear upon the Record.*

1775.

Aaron Brown,

Henry Ferguson,

Kelso Gray,

Alexander Robbe,

William McNee.

1776.

William Robbe,

David Steele,

Jotham Blanchard,

Samuel Mitchell,

Robert Wilson.

1777.

John White,

Jonathan Wheelock,

Robert Gray.

1778.

David Steele,

Thomas Davison,

Matthew Wallace,

Matthew Templeton.

1779.

James Templeton,

Samuel Gregg,

James Cuningham,

Charles Stuart,

John White.

CHAPTER XIV.

No Records of the Military. — Efficient Military Training. — French and
Indian Wars. — American Revolution. — Association Test. — Men
who Served in the Revolution. — At Battle of Bunker Hill. — War of
1812. — The Late Rebellion. — Men in Service. — Soldiers' Monument.

It will be impossible to collect any information of the various military organizations that have existed in town; and any
attempts must result in only a fragmentary record, with little
that would be of interest to any one. From the frequency of
military titles in the town records — and our fathers were
particular in bestowing them, — we suppose the men thus
recognized by their titles were among the best citizens, and
were the leading men in the town. Military companies existed quite early — anterior to the Revolution, — and the men
who bore military titles were numerous. At one time the
street road divided the town as to the military, and all those
on the east side of it constituted the East Company, and those
on the west, the West Company. This arrangement was
sustained for many years. There was also a flourishing company of artillery, established about 1804, first commanded by
the late Hon. James Wilson, which was well sustained for
many years, till removed to Lyndeboro; and, still earlier, a
company of cavalry existed here, or in the immediate vicinity,
but when or how it flourished, and when it became extinct,
we do not know, — probably before the present century came
in.

Any attempts to investigate the early history of the various military companies that have existed in town, from time to time, would, in their results, be so unsatisfactory and meagre as to be of little or no value. The citizens of Peterborough participated largely in all the service of the field in times of war. They had a military training at home, and frequent experiences in the French and Indian wars, that made them ready and efficient soldiers at once. In the use of fire-arms they were always skilled; it was common to find a musket in every house, and those who could use them adroitly, either in securing wild game, or in protecting themselves against the incursions of the Indians, were numerous.

The French and Indian wars were a heavy drag upon all the infant and frontier settlements of New Hampshire. We shall see how readily and freely, at the call of the mother government, * they aided in the protection of their extensive frontier, by their services, their property, and their lives. We regret that there are so few data now existing by which we can do proper justice to these heroic men. We can only rely on the account given of them in a sketch of Peterborough, by Rev. Elijah Dunbar, in 1822, † and manuscript notes in 1833 or '34, by Hon. Samuel Smith, ‡ any other means of information being entirely unknown to us.

The following list of soldiers was furnished in the war of 1755: viz., James Turner, brother of Thomas Turner, Samuel Wallace, William Swan, son of old John Swan. Of these, James Turner died in camp at Crown Point, 1760. In 1756 Thomas Cuningham and Samuel Cuningham. The former, who was a lieutenant, died of small-pox.

In 1757, Charles McCoy, John Stuart, son of William Stuart, David Wallace, son of Maj. Wallace, Wm. Wilson, brother of Maj. Robert Wilson, Robert McNee, son of old Dea. McNee, John Dinsmore, John Kelley, brought up by

---

* Holmes' American Annals de French War, 1758, and a call for three hundred men from N. H. 2d vol., p. 225.

† Topographical and Historical Account of Peterborough, by Rev. Elijah Dunbar. Historical Collections.

‡ Manuscript Notes, by Hon. Samuel Smith, made in 1833 or '34.

Rev. Mr. Harvey.   All the above, being enlisted in Rodgers' Company of Rangers, were killed in one unfortunate moment, having fallen into an Indian ambuscade, March 13, 1758, near Lake George; while Samuel Cuningham and Alexander Robbe, being of this brave but unfortunate band, and in the same fight, escaped.

In 1758, Wm. Scott, Jeremiah Swan, Samuel Stinson, Alexander Scott. Of these, Jeremiah Swan died in camp.

In 1759, Robert Wilson, Daniel Allat, John Taggart, Wm. Scott, George McLeod.

In 1760, Samuel Gregg, John Taggart, Samuel Cuningham, William Cuningham, Moore Stinson, Henry Ferguson, John Swan, William Scott, Solomon Turner, John McCollom, John Turner, John Hogg, David Scott. Of these, John Turner and John McCollom died somewhere on the lake, and John Hogg and David Scott, son of Alexander Scott, both took the small-pox in returning, and died at home.

The whole number enlisted from Peterborough during the war was thirty-two, and fourteen were lost in this war, a great number from a settlement so small and weak. It must have been seriously felt, and been a heavy damper upon the progress of the town.

AMERICAN REVOLUTION. — The American Revolution came as the great event of the early settlers, although they had had various experiences in the French and Indian wars. We are surprised that they were not appalled by such imminent danger as they incurred by their bold and defiant course, and sometimes think that they did not realize what they were doing, or what mighty consequences might flow from their conduct. But they were intelligent men; they had weighed the whole matter in their minds; they were not rushing impulsively and rashly upon a great danger; they were ready, as their declaration in the Association Test avers, to meet the enemy with force of arms, and give their lives and their all, if need be, to the cause. They knew their prowess, too; they had had much experience in the French and Indian wars, and they were accustomed to the use of fire-arms, which they all possessed, and which were much used in the early settlements in securing wild game as a part of their support; so that they were already soldiers in skill in the use of fire-arms, in hardihood and courage, and in everything but the military drill. When the trial came, the town was truly patriotic and loyal to the principles of freedom. They never flinched or paled in the hour of peril, when the alternative seemed to be either ease and safety, by not engaging in the movement of the times, or, by action, the risk of all they had, their wealth, honor, and lives in an uncertain conflict.

When the Association Test, or virtual Declaration of Inde-pendence, was sent to the various towns in the State, by the General Committee of Safety, eighty-three persons in town, out of a population of only a little over five hundred, signed it. It probably embraced every efficient man in town, capa-ble of bearing arms. Not a single Tory was ever known. Our ancestors not only professed to be willing to risk everything for the cause, but they really did so; and during the war of the Revolution no town could be more patriotic in furnishing men and supplies to the army than Peterborough. So many went to the war, that it is a wonder to us how the out-door work at home was carried on. The noble women of that day kept all home-matters right and prosperous in their absence. They were hale and hearty, and could, if necessity required it, work as effectually out of doors as within. Their hearts were in the enterprise, as much as those of the men, and their hands and efforts were little less effectual in the ultimate success of the war.

It seems strange to us, and shows most conclusively the sagacity and foresight of our fathers, that they who had felt so little of the despotism of the mother country, who had enjoyed a continuous prosperity, and who were in comfortable circumstances, could, from apprehended danger to their liber-ties in the future, shown by the various arbitrary acts in relation to taxation without representation, and the transpor-tation of persons to England for trial, have engaged in such a perilous undertaking.

The following order was sent to the selectmen of Peter-borough.

IN COMMITTEE OF SAFETY, *April 12, 1776.*

In order to carry the underwritten resolve of the Honorable Continental Congress into execution, you are requested to desire all males above twenty-one years of age (lunatics, idiots, and negroes excepted) to sign the declaration on this paper; and, so done, to make return hereof, together with the name or names of all who shall refuse to sign the same, to the General Assembly or Committee of Safety of this colony.

M. WEARE, *Chairman.*

IN CONGRESS, *March 14, 1776.*

Resolved, That it be recommended to the several assemblies, conventions, and councils, or Committees of Safety of the United Colonies, immediately to cause all persons to be disarmed within their respective colonies who are notoriously disaffected to the cause of America, or who have not associated, and refuse to asso-ciate, to defend by arms the United Colonies against the hostile attempts of the British fleets and armies. — *Extract from the Minutes.*

CHARLES THOMPSON, *Secretary.*

In consequence of the above resolution of the Honorable Con-tinental Congress, and to show our determination in joining our American brethren in defending the lives, liberties, and properties of the inhabitants of the United Colonies:

We, the subscribers, do hereby solemnly engage and promise that we will, to the utmost of our powers, at the risque of our lives and fortunes, with arms, oppose the hostile proceedings of the British fleets and armies against the United American Colonies.

Neal Hammill,	Aaron Brown,
Thomas Morison,	Samuel Mitchell,
Thomas Cuningham,	Charles White,
James Templeton,	William Swan,
Thomas Davison,	Samuel Houston,
Samuel Miller, Sen.,	William White,

William McNee, Jr.,
James Cuningham,
Alexander Stewart,
Samuel Miller, Jr.,
James Ritchie,
William McNee,
John Scott,
William Smith,
William McCoy,
James Robbe,
Joseph Hammill,
Jonathan Wheelock,
John Gragg, Jr.,
Robert Smith,
John Smith,
Moses Cuningham,
William McKean,
John White, Jr.,
Samuel Moore,
William Robbe,
William Miller,
Samuel Mitchell,
John Young,
Abraham Holmes,
John Mitchell,
David Steele,
John McMurphy,
Robert Morison,
Thomas Turner,
John Smith,
John Morison,
Thomas Morison, Jr.,
Jotham Blanchard,
Samuel Cuningham,
Robert Wilson,
John Gragg,

John White,
William White,
David White,
Isaiah Taylor,
Charles Stuart,
Samuel Gragg,
William Spear,
Kelso Gray,
Matthew Templeton,
William Scott,
Thomas Steele,
James Taggart,
Elijah Puffer,
Daniel Mack,
Samuel Miller, ye 3d,
Alexander Robbe,
Samuel Hogg,
Samuel McAlister,
Robert Gray,
John Butler,
Isaac Mitchell,
Thomas Stewart,
John Blair,
John Taggart,
James Hockley,
William Moore,
Timothy Miner,
Hugh Willson,
Samuel Willson,
James Willson,
John Willson,
John White,
Benjamin Mitchell,
David Ames,
Adams Gragg.

PETERBOROUGH, *June 17, 1776.*

Pursuant to the within request, the inhabitants of the said town of Peterborough hath subscribed their names to the within resolve of the Continental Congress.

JAMES TEMPLETON, ⎞
SAMUEL CUNINGHAM, ⎬ *Selectmen.*
WILLIAM McNEE, ⎠

A true copy, examined and compared with the original.

N. BOUTON.

CONCORD, June 27, 1871.

The following persons served in the Revolution in time and place as designated after each name. This is exclusive of those who were mustered for the battle of Bunker Hill.

The account, as here presented, was found among some old papers in the ministerial library of the Congregational Society, in the handwriting of Judge Smith, drawn up, probably, with some view of presenting the services rendered by these individuals in a suitable form for adjustment. But we have no definite account that any or only slight remuneration was ever made to them by either the town or State. It shows how readily and promptly the various calls made upon this little community, for attaining and securing their liberties, were responded to.

D. Ames, served with Capt. Alexander Robbe, on alarm, from June 29 to July 3, 1777.

Thomas Alexander, mustered Dec. 17, 1777.

Benj. Alld, discharged Dec. 20, 1781.

Luther Adams, discharged Dec. 20, 1781.

John Alexander, mustered in April, 1777 ; Col. E. Hale's report.

Joseph Babb, alarm from June 29 to July 3, 1777. July, 1776, five months. Mustered in April, 1777. Report of Col. E. Hale. Served three years.

W. Blair, alarm June 29 to July 3, 1777. Army at Cambridge, 1775. For Bennington, July 19, 1777. Saratoga, Sept. 28 ; returned Oct. 25, 1777.

John Blair, raised July 19, 1777 ; discharged Sept. 26. Army at Cambridge, 1775. Served in Rhode Island, from Aug. 28, 1778. Mustered April, 1777, of twenty-two men for Peterborough. Report of Col. E. Hale.

Zaccheus Brooks, mustered June 15, 1779, by Enoch Hale; never joined.

John Barlow, by order of Committee of Safety, July 12, 1782.

John Burns, discharged Dec. 21, 1781.

Jacob Baldwin, discharged Dec. 21, 1781.

John Butler, served in the army at Cambridge, 1775.

Andrew Bailey, in army 1776, one year's man; army at Cambridge, 1775.

Ensign W. Cochran, in army at Cambridge, 1775.

James Cuningham, mustered Sept. 20, 1776, to serve two months. Served in Rhode Island, from Aug. 28, 1778.

Serj. Samuel Cuningham, alarm from June 29 to July 3, 1777. Raised July 19, 1777; discharged Sept. 26; for Bennington. Served in Rhode Island, from Aug. 28, 1778. Alarm at Lexington, April 19, 1775, one week.

Joseph Covel, from July 9 to Nov. 27, 1780.

W. De Cannon, among the claims; of Londonderry.

John Canada, of twenty-two men mustered April, 1777. Report of Col. E. Hale.

Samuel Caldwell, served in Rhode Island, from Aug. 28, 1778. Col. E. Hale's Regt.

Thomas Davison, three months, spring of 1777. Engaged July 7; discharged Oct. 21, 1780, three months, fifteen days.

Charles Davison, engaged July 9; discharged Dec. 26, 1779.

Solomon Dodge, engaged June 28, 1780; discharged in December.

Richard Emery, mustered Sept. 20, 1776, for two months. In army at Cambridge, 1775.

Lieut. Henry Ferguson, served forty-four days, at Cambridge, last of 1775.

Jeremiah Fairchild, in army at Cambridge, 1775.

Thomas Green, in army at Cambridge, 1775. Engaged June 28, 1780; discharged in December.

William Graham, in army at Cambridge, 1775; of twenty-two men furnished April, 1777. One year's men for 1776.

John Graham, in army at Cambridge, 1775. One year's men, 1776. Mustered by E. Hale, July, 1776, to serve five months.

James Gregg, served in army at Cambridge, 1775.

Samuel Gregg, alarm at Lexington, April 19, 1775, five days. Alarm at Walpole.

Adams Gregg, alarm at Lexington, April 19, 1775. Army at

Cambridge, last of 1775. On alarm from June 29 to July 3, 1777. Rhode Island, from Aug. 28, 1778, under Capt. Samuel Cuningham.

Hugh Gregg, alarm at Lexington, April 19, 1775. Alarm from June 29 to July 3, 1777.

John Gregg, alarm at Lexington, April 19, 1775.

Robert Gray, alarm at Lexington, April 19, 1775.

Richard Gilchrist, in army at Cambridge, 1775.

William Gilchrist, one year's men, 1776.

John Gray, in Rhode Island, Aug. 28, 1778, Co. of Capt. S. Cuningham. On alarm at Walpole.

James Gordon, engaged Sept. 19; dismissed Nov. 27, 1781.

James Hockley, in army at Cambridge, 1775. Of twenty-two men furnished April, 1777. One year's men, 1776.

Joseph Henderson, of twenty-two men furnished April, 1777. Raised July 19, 1777, for Bennington; discharged Jan. 1, 1778.

John Halfpenny, one year's men, 1776. In army at Cambridge, 1775.

Nathaniel Holmes, mustered Sept. 20, 1776, two months.

Simson Hogg, for Bennington, July 19, 1777; discharged Sept. 26.

Samuel Huston, alarm, June 29 to July 3, 1777, five days. Served in Rhode Island, Aug. 28, 1778.

Isaac Huston, alarm, June 29 to July 3, 1777, five days.

William Huston, alarm at Walpole, 1777.

John Kennedy, mustered July, 1776, five months. Town claims, — as paid by town.

Solomon Leonard, in army at Cambridge, 1775.

Samuel Lee, of twenty-two men furnished April, 1777. Alarm at Walpole.

Thomas Little, in army at Cambridge, 1775. For Bennington, July 19, 1777; discharged Sept. 26.

Robert Lakin, engaged July 7; discharged Oct. 21, 1780.

Timothy Locke, enlisted Capt. Scott's Co., Aug. 9, 1780. Engaged June 28, 1780; discharged December. Served six months.

Samuel Lewis, on alarm, in Capt. Alexander Robbe's Co., five days.

James Miller, alarm of Lexington, April 19, 1775.

William McNee, alarm of Lexington, April 19, 1775. Alarm at Walpole. To Saratoga, Sept. 28; returned Oct. 25, 1777.

John Mitchell, alarm of Lexington, April 19, 1775. In army at Cambridge, 1775. Alarm at Walpole.

Samuel Mitchell, alarm of Lexington, April 19, 1775. At alarm, in Capt. Alexander Robbe's Co., June 29 to July 3, 1777, five days. Of the twenty-two men mustered April, 1777. Town claim for three years. Alarm at Walpole. For Bennington, July 19, 1777. Discharged Sept. 26. Saratoga, Sept. 28 ; returned Oct. 25, 1777.

John Morison, alarm at Lexington, April 19, 1775. Served in Rhode Island, Aug. 28, 1778. On alarm, in Capt. Alexander Robbe's Co., from June 29 to July 3, 1777, five days. Bennington, July 19, 1777 ; discharged Sept. 26.

Benjamin Mitchell, alarm at Lexington, April 19, 1775. Mustered Sept. 20, 1776, to serve two months. For Bennington, July 19, 1777 ; discharged Sept. 26.

John Moore, alarm at Lexington, April 19, 1775.

Thomas Morison, in army at Cambridge, 1775. Mustered Sept. 20, 1776, for two months. Alarm at Walpole. Alarm, Capt. Alexander Robbe's Co., June 29 to July 3, 1777, five days. For Bennington, July 19, 1777 ; discharged Sept. 26. Saratoga, Sept. 28 to Oct. 25, 1777.

Ensign Munro, in army at Cambridge, 1775. Served in army, 1776, one year's men.

James Mitchell, in army at Cambridge, 1775. Alarm at Lexington, April 19, 1775. Bennington, July 19, 1777 ; discharged Sept. 26. On alarm, in Capt. Alexander Robbe's Co., from June 29 to July 3, 1777, five days.

Isaac Mitchell, in army at Cambridge, 1775. Alarm at Lexington, April 19, 1775. Of the twenty-two men furnished April, 1777. Alarm at Walpole. Returned from service April 2, 1781.

Samuel Moore, Jr., in army at Cambridge, 1775. Alarm at Lexington, April 19, 1775. Alarm, in Co. of Capt. Alexander Robbe, from June 29 to July 3, 1777, five days.

William Mitchell, in army at Cambridge, 1775. Served in army, 1776, one year's men.

Randall McAlister, in army at Cambridge, 1775. Alarm at Lexington, April 19, 1775. Three years. Town claims. Of the twenty-two men furnished April, 1777. Alarm, in Co. of Alexander Robbe, June 29 to July 3, 1777, five days.

John Mather, of the twenty-two men furnished April, 1777. Town claims. Suppose three years.

William McCoy, in army at Cambridge, 1775. Served in Rhode Island, Aug. 28, 1778. E. Hale's Regt.

George McCloud, mustered July, 1776, for five months.

Timothy Mixter, mustered July, 1776, for five months. Alarm,

20

in Co. of Capt. Alexander Robbe, from June 29 to July 3, 1777, five days. Town claims. Jackson's Regt., Mass. Of the twenty-two men mustered April, 1777.

Robert McCloud, mustered July, 1776, for five months.

John Murphy, mustered July, 1776, for five months.

William McKean, mustered Sept. 20, 1776, to serve two months.

Peter McAlister, from Dec. 5 to March 15, 1777.

Joseph Miller, on alarm, in Capt. Alexander Robbe's Co., from June 29 to July 3, 1777, five days. In Rhode Island, from Aug. 28, 1778. Col. E. Hale's Regt.

Samuel Miller, Bennington, July 19, 1777; discharged Sept. 26. Alarm at Walpole, 1777.

William Moore, Bennington, July 19, 1777; discharged Sept. 26.

Charles McCoy, in army in Rhode Island, from Aug. 28, 1778. Col. E. Hale's Regt. At Bennington, July 19, 1777; discharged Sept. 24.

John Miller, Saratoga, Sept. 28; returned Oct. 25, 1777. Alarm at Walpole.

Daniel Mack, alarm at Lexington, April 19, 1775.

Charles McClurg, engaged July 7; discharged Oct. 21, 1780, three months, fifteen days.

Robert Morison, alarm at Walpole.

Sergeant ―――― Page, mustered July, 1776, to serve five months. Bennington, July 19, 1777; discharged Sept. 26.

Abel Parker, engaged July 7; discharged Oct. 21, 1780.

Jeduthun Roberts, enlisted in camp. Entered by order of the Committee of Safety, July 12, 1782.

John Richey, in army at Cambridge, 1775; died there.

Samuel Robbe, Saratoga, Sept. 28, 1777; discharged Oct. 25. Engaged Sept. 19; discharged Nov. 27, 1781. On alarm, in Capt. Alexander Robbe's Co.

William Robbe, Bennington, July 19, 1777; discharged Sept. 26. Service from Dec. 5, 1776 to March 15, 1777.

James Richey, in army at Cambridge, 1775. On alarm, in Capt. Alexander Robbe's Co., five days.

R. Richardson, in army at Cambridge, 1775.

Capt. Alexander Robbe, on an alarm, June 29 to July 3, 1777, five days. Mustered July, 1776, for five months.

William Swan, alarm at Lexington, April 19, 1775. In army at Cambridge, 1775. On alarm, in Co. of Capt. Alexander Robbe, from June 29 to July 3, 1777, five days.

Alexander Stuart, alarm at Lexington, April 19, 1775.

Charles Stuart, alarm at Lexington, April 19, 1775. In army at Cambridge, 1775. Engaged from Dec. 5, 1776, to March 15, 1777, three months. In Rhode Island, Aug. 28, 1778. Alarm at Walpole, 1777, five days.

William Scott, alarm at Lexington, April 19, 1775. In army at Cambridge, 1775. Alarm, in Capt. Alexander Robbe's Co., from June 29 to July 3, 1777, five days. For Saratoga, Sept. 28, and discharged Oct. 25, 1777. Alarm at Walpole.

William Scott, Jr., alarm at Lexington, April 19, 1775. In army at Cambridge, 1775. Mustered July, 1776, for five months.

Capt. William Scott, in army at Cambridge, 1775. Served, 1776, one year's men.

Lieut. William Scott, in army at Cambridge, 1775. Served in 1776, one year's men.

James Stanford, alarm at Lexington, April 19, 1775. In army at Cambridge, 1775. Of the twenty-two men furnished April, 1777. On town claims ; a three year's man.

Ephraim Stevens, in army at Cambridge, 1775. Of the twenty-two men furnished April, 1777. Alarm at Walpole. Died in the service.

Thomas Scott, in army at Cambridge, 1775. Served in 1776, one year's men.

James Stinson, in army at Cambridge, 1775.

Thomas Sanders, of the twenty-two men furnished April, 1777.

David Scott, of the twenty-two men furnished April, 1777.

John Scott, of the twenty-two men furnished April, 1777.

John Smith, in army at Cambridge, 1775. Mustered to serve five months.

Robert Smith, mustered by E. Hale, to serve five months. Mustered Sept. 20, 1776, to serve two months.

James Smith, in alarm of Capt. Alexander Robbe's Co., from June 29 to July 3, 1777, five days.

Jeremiah Smith, raised for Bennington, July 19 ; discharged Sept. 26, 1777.

Thomas Smith, in Rhode Island, Aug. 28, 1778. Served from Dec. 5 to March 15, 1777, three months. Saratoga, Sept. 28. Returned Oct. 25, 1777.

R. Swan, mustered by Col. E. Hale, for five months. On alarm, in Capt. Alexander Robbe's Co., from June 29 to July 3, 1777, five days.

John Swan, Saratoga, Sept. 28 ; returned Oct. 25, 1777. March, on alarm of Capt. Alexander Robbe's Co., from June 29 to July 3, 1777, five days.

Thomas Steele, on alarm, in Capt. Alexander Robbe's Co., from June 29 to July 3, 1777, five days. Alarm at Walpole.

Capt. David Steele, alarm at Walpole.

Thomas Sanderson, alarm at Walpole, five days.

Amos Spofford, enlisted by Maj. Scott, Aug. 9, 1780.

Samuel Speer, three years ; town claims.

John Stroud ; town claims.

James Taggart, alarm at Lexington, April 19, 1775. In army at Cambridge, 1775. Served from Dec. 5, 1776, to March 15, 1777. On town claims ; three years. Of the twenty-two men furnished April, 1777.

S. Treadwell, in army at Cambridge, 1775. Served in army, 1776, one year's men.

Joseph Taylor, in army at Cambridge, 1775. Died in Cambridge, 1775.

Thomas Temple, in army at Cambridge, 1775 ; died in Cambridge, 1775.

Isaiah Taylor, served in Rhode Island, from Aug. 28, 1778.

John Taggart, alarm at Walpole, 1777. Of the twenty-two men furnished April, 1777. Served in Rhode Island ; he died, Mount Independence, 1777.

Capt. Robert Wilson, alarm at Lexington, April 19, 1775.

John White, Sen., alarm at Lexington, April 19, 1775. Alarm, in Capt. Alexander Robbe's Co., from June 29 to July 3, 1777, five days.

Corp. John White, at Saratoga, Sept. 28, 1777 ; returned Oct. 25. Rhode Island, 1779.

Charles White, alarm at Lexington, April 19, 1775. In army at Cambridge, 1775. Served in New York from Dec. 5, 1776, to March 15, 1777. Rhode Island from Aug. 28, 1778.

W. White, alarm at Lexington, April 19, 1775. In army at Cambridge, 1775. Served in New York, from Dec. 5, 1776, to March 15, 1777. Saratoga, Sept. 28 ; returned Oct. 25, 1777.

David White, alarm at Lexington, April 19, 1775. In army at Cambridge, 1775. Served in Rhode Island, Aug 28, 1778.

Titus Wilson, of the twenty-two men furnished April, 1777. Alarm at Walpole ; a negro ; died at Mount Independence, 1777.

Jonathan Wheelock, of the twenty-two men furnished April, 1777. Saratoga, Sept. 28 ; returned Oct. 25, 1777. Alarm, in Capt. Alexander Robbe's Co., from June 29 to July 3, 1777, five days. Served in Rhode Island, April 28, 1778.

M. Woodcock, in army at Cambridge, 1775. Mustered July, 1776, to serve five months. Served in Rhode Island, from Aug. 28, 1778.

James Wilson, mustered from July, 1776, to serve five months.

James White, Bennington, July 19, 1777, to Sept. 26. Served in Rhode Island, Aug. 28, 1778.

Lues Wheelock, engaged from July 7 ; discharged Oct. 21, 1780.

Thomas Williams, engaged from July 9 to Nov. 27, 1780.

John Wallace, enlisted by Committee of Safety, July 12, 1782.

A List of Those who Volunteered, on the 17th of June, 1775, to the Battle of Bunker Hill. Derived Principally from the History of Peterborough, by Rev. Elijah Dunbar, and the Manuscript Notes of Hon. S. Smith.

Capt. William Scott.. Short, by S. S.

Lieut. William Scott. Long, by S. S. Wounded.

George McLeod, wounded. His name does not appear again.

James Hockley.

John Graham, wounded.

David Scott, James Scott, Thomas Scott, David Robbe.

Randall McAlister, wounded.

John Taggart, died at Mount Independence, 1777.

Samuel Mitchell, Thomas Morison.

David Allat ; his name does not appear again.

Thomas Greene, wounded.

Joseph Henderson, Richard Gilchrist.

Ensign William Cochran, John Swan, and Jonathan Barnett; these three were on duty, but not in the battle.

Rev. John Morrison remained in camp, and excused himself from accompanying his friends, alleging that the lock of his gun was so injured as to be useless. Shortly after he passed over to Boston and joined the British.

McAlister and Greene were severely wounded. Greene, in a fainting and almost expiring state, was saved by his friend Gilchrist, who transported him on his back from Bunker Hill to Medford.

In addition to the above the manuscript notes of S. S. add the following names : —

William Scott, father to James Scott, Esq.

Joseph Greene.

Dudley Taggart (known as Judge Taggart). Samuel Morison thinks he was not in the battle.

William Gilchrist.

William Blair. Samuel Morison thinks he was not, — John Todd thinks he was.

William White. Samuel Morison thinks not.

Charles White, James McKean.

By the above account, one hundred and forty different men of Peterborough were called for longer or shorter periods, during the Revolutionary war, and, in addition to these, five more ; *viz.* : —

George McLeod, David Allat, Jonathan Barnett, Dudley Taggart, Joseph Greene, who were in the battle of Bunker Hill, whose names do not again appear, making in all one hundred and forty-five different persons from this infant settlement who rendered military service during the war.

THE WAR OF 1812. — We do not know of one single individual from this town who voluntarily enlisted as a soldier in the regular army of this war. A draft of soldiers from Peterborough for three months was ordered in 1814, for the defence of Portsmouth, and the following officers and men volunteered for the service, *viz.* : —

Col. John Steele, 2d Lieut. James B. Todd, Corp. Ahimaz Jewett, John Gray, John T. Hagget, David Miller, Robert Morison, Brown Shattuck, William Upton, Stephen Warner, John Ames, Nathaniel Smith, Daniel Edes, Russel Nay, David Wilson, David A. Hatch, Joseph Washburn, Nathan Wait, Nathan Upton, David Evans, Andrew Holmes, Samuel Pettes, Sergt. Isaac Hadley.

The British naval force did not attack Portsmouth, as was apprehended, and the soldiers were discharged without serving out their time.

The following vote was passed in town meeting, April 4, 1815 : —

"Voted, To give the soldiers that volunteered to go to Portsmouth last year five dollars per month in addition to what is allowed by the general and State government."

The town did not furnish much aid to this war, except in the unequalled services of Gen. James Miller, one of her sons, whose bravery and military exploits were more than equal to a regiment of men, and have afforded one of the brightest pages in the history of that war.

WAR OF THE REBELLION, 1861. — The war of the Rebellion, which came so unexpectedly to all, was met by our citizens, irrespective of party, with alacrity and zeal. In the first call for volunteers, after the fire on Fort Sumter, our citizens, from the promptings of patriotism and without any pecuniary inducements such as were subsequently held out for volunteers, came forward and eagerly enlisted, and were at once ready for service. In the first enlistment, May, 1861, into Capt. E. Weston's Company, 2d Regiment, Co. G, nineteen were enrolled, and at once marched forward and were engaged in the first Bull Run battle, that introduced the bloody scenes of the great civil contest. In the autumn of the same year, thirty-eight men enlisted into the 6th Regiment, and many others joined various regiments in the State till 1862, when twenty-eight enlisted in the 13th Regiment, commanded by Capt. Nathan Stoodley. All these enlistments were going on till the draft of 1864, in which the several towns offered large bounties, in addition to those of the State and general government, to make it an object pecuniarily for individuals to enlist. As the war terminated abruptly early in 1865, those who last enlisted were richly rewarded for their risk and adventure.

The whole number enlisted from town was two hundred and nine. We have, in the following list, the names, ages, terms of enlistment, the regiments joined, and the various incidents relating to the several persons, as to casualties, deaths, etc. : —

Officers, Soldiers, and Seamen of the Town of Peterborough, who have been in Service of the United States since the Commencement of the Rebellion.

ARMY.

April 22, 1861. George W. Rines, age 23, 1st Reg., Co. G. 3 mos.

May 20,   Elmer J. Starkey, age 21, 2d Reg., Co. G. 3 yrs.
                In second Bull Run battle severely wounded in
                the thigh, and left on the field of battle, where
                he was taken prisoner.

15,   John Reagan, age 23, 2d Reg., Co. G. 3 yrs.
                Wounded at first Bull Run battle, and subse-
                quently taken prisoner at Glendale, Va.

20,   Alpha E. Ames, age 20, 2d Reg., Co. G. 3 yrs.

24,   Joseph Bolio, age 28, 2d Reg., Co. G. 3 yrs.

15,   Daniel W. Gould, age 22, 2d Reg., Co. G. 3 yrs.
                Wounded in battle at Williamsburg, and had
                one arm amputated near the shoulder.

                Nicholas Duffey, age 21, 2d Reg., Co. G. 3 yrs.

                Charles O. Collister, age 23, 2d Reg., Co. G. 3
                yrs. In second Bull Run battle he was wound-
                ed in the bowels, left on the field, and reported
                afterwards as killed.

                Albert J. Farnsworth, age 19, 2d Reg., Co. G. 3 yrs.

24.   Abbot A. Forbush, age 21, 2d Reg., Co. G. 3 yrs.

15,   Gilman T. Gould, age 24, 2d Reg., Co. G. 3 yrs.
                Reënlisted Jan. 1, 1864. Promoted to 1st Lieu-
                tenant, Feb. 5, 1865.

                Alonzo M. Hannaford, age 20, 2d Reg., Co. G. 3
                yrs. Wounded at Gettysburg, July 2, 1863.

                Newman Hall, age 29, 2d Reg., Co. G. 3 yrs.
                Died at Washington, Dec. 11, 1862.

24,   Nelson Hurd, age 40, 2d Reg., Co. G. 3 yrs. Re-
                enlisted Veteran.

25,   John J. Moore, age 22, 2d Reg., Co. G. 3 yrs.

20,   James E. Saunders, age 30, 2d Reg., Co. G. 3
                yrs. Promoted to Sergeant Major, Sept. 1,
                1863. Reënlisted June 1, 1864, and promoted
                to Captain.

Aug. 6,   James M. Hannaford, age 28, 2d Reg., Co. G.
                3 yrs.

Sept. 10,   Frank E. Howe, age 19, 2d Reg., Co. G. 3 yrs. Killed at Fair Oaks, Va., June 23, 1862.

July 15,   Darius Hadley, age 19 ; George W. Hadley, age 22 ; William P. Coolidge, age 23 ; Elihu Wilder, age 21. 3 yrs. 2d N. H. Band. Mustered out, Aug. 8, 1862.

Aug. 1,   Richard B. Richardson, age 39, 3d Reg., Co. I. 3 yrs.

9,   Charles Jewett, age 34, 3d Reg., Co I. 3 yrs. Appointed Armorer, June, 1863. Reënlisted Feb. 15, 1865. 1 yr., 1st N. H. Cavalry.

30,   Frank Matthews, age 21, 4th Reg., Co. E. 3 yrs. Wounded at Drury's Bluffs.

Emery Wyman, age 18, 4th Reg., Co. E. 3 yrs. Wounded May 16, and Aug. 16, 1864.

Lyman Wyman, age 22, 4th Reg., Co. E. 3 yrs.

26,   Stedman W. Piper, age 18, 4th Reg., Co. I. 3 yrs. Discharged 1864 ; reënlisted, and afterwards deserted to the enemy at Cold Harbor, June 3, 1864.

George Welding, age 26, 4th Reg., Co. I. 3 yrs. Killed in battle, July 24, 1864.

27,   Henry S. Gould, age 35, 4th Reg., Co. I. 3 yrs. Discharged for disability. Reënlisted, substitute for Albert Stevens, Sept. 2, 1863, 8th Reg., Co. B.

28,   Luther G. Crosby, age 19, 4th Reg., Co. C. 3 yrs. Died in hospital, Beaufort, N. C., Aug. 26, 1863.

Sept. 10,   George Wyman, age 28, 4th Reg., Co. K. 3 yrs.

Aug. 26,   German N. Breed, age 26, 5th Reg., Co. K. 3 yrs. Died at Fairfax Court House, of typhus fever, March 27, 1862.

Oct. 12,   Ancil D. Holt, age 38, 5th Reg., Co. K. Discharged for disability, May 27, 1862.

Aug. 28,   George M. Spaulding, age 23, 5th Reg., Co. K. 3 yrs. Killed in battle at Cold Harbor, June 3, 1864.

Sept. 2,   James Nichols, age 28, 5th Reg., Co. K. 3 yrs. Wounded in arm at White Oak Swamp. Transferred to Invalid Corps, Jan. 1, 1863.

21

Nov. 28,   Charles Scott, age 32, 6th Reg.   Major, and pro-
                moted to Lieutenant Colonel.   Resigned, Oct.
                14, 1862.

                John A. Cummings, age 24, 6th Reg.   Lieutenant,
                and promoted to Captain.   Discharged for pro-
                motion, April 5, 1864.   Reënlisted, and appoint-
                ed a Major in the 1st N. H. Cavalry, Co. E,
                March 19, 1864.

Oct. 14,   John S. Smith, age 23, 6th Reg., Co. E.   3 yrs.
                Promoted from Sergeant to Adjutant, March 20,
                1863.   Wounded at Cemetéry Hill.   At expira-
                tion of his three years he was recommended as
                1st Lieutenant in U. S. Veteran Volunteers, and
                promoted to Captain in 1865 ; mustered out
                June, 1866, services no longer required.

       4,   Henry C. Lakeman, age 18, 6th Reg., Co. E.   3
                yrs. Transferred to Invalid Corps, May 13, 1865.

       9,   Osgood Hadley, age 24, 6th Reg., Co. E.   3 yrs.
                Discharged, and reënlisted as Veteran, Dec. 20,
                1863.

       7,   George W. Hadley, age 20, 6th Reg., Co. E.   3
                yrs.   Died March 3, 1863, at Newport News, Va.

Sept. 25,   John P. Webber, age 18, 6th Reg., Co. E.   3 yrs.
                Wounded May 12, 1864.   Reënlisted Feb. 15,
                1864.   Transferred to Veteran Reserve Corps.

       23,   Allison G. Howe, age 22, 6th Reg., Co. E.   Had
                a lung fever at Roanoke Island ; was transferred
                to hospital at Newport News ; subsequently dis-
                charged.

Oct. 11,   William H. Wallace, age 20, 6th Reg., Co. E.   3
                yrs.   Died at Memphis, Tenn., Sept. 15, 1863.

Sept. 30,   Lucius H. Farwell, age 24, 6th Reg., Co. E.   3 yrs.
                Died of measles, at Hatteras Inlet, N. C., Jan.
                29, 1862.

Oct.   1,   Henry E. Badger, age 18, 6th Reg., Co. E.   3 yrs.
                Reënlisted Dec. 30, 1863, as Veteran, and pro-
                moted to 2d Lieutenant, Jan. 1, 1865.   Wounded
                June 3, 1864, and July 30, 1864.

       15,   Martin White, age 21, 6th Reg., Co. E.   3 yrs.
                Wounded May 16, 1864, at Spottsylvania, Va.,
                through both thighs ; had gangrene in one leg,

which was lessened in size and weakened. Re-
enlisted as Veteran, Dec. 24, 1863. Had a 1st
Lieutenant commission sent him, but declined it.

Oct. 19, Christopher M. Wheeler, age 22, 6th Reg., Co. E.
3 yrs. Died of measles at Hatteras, N. C., Feb.
20, 1862. Interred in Peterborough.

5, David D. Page, age 20, 6th Reg., Co. E. 3 yrs.
Discharged for disability. Reënlisted Aug. 9,
1864, 1st N. H. Cavalry, Troop H.

3, Munro A. Smith, age 21, 6th Reg., Co. E. 3 yrs.
Chief Bugler.

Sept. 28, Cyrus Henry Farmer, age 21, 6th Reg., Co. E. 3
yrs. Died Aug. 17, 1863, at Covington, Ky.

Oct. 7, David A. Cram, age 18, 6th Reg., Co. E. 3 yrs.
.Killed at second Bull Run battle, Aug. 29, 1862.

Sept. 24, Allen T. Perry, age 20, 6th Reg., Co. E. 3 yrs.
Discharged for disability.

Oct. 15, Jackson Brackett, age 23, 6th Reg., Co. E. 3 yrs.
Wounded in right arm, Sept. 17, 1862. Discharged for disability, Nov. 6, 1862.

28, Alfred Perry, age 18, 6th Reg., Co. E. 3 yrs.
Wounded Dec. 13, 1862, and died after the am-
putation of his leg for injury to the knee, Jan.
27, 1863.

Nov. 1, Jonathan Smith, age 18, 6th Reg., Co. E. 3 yrs.
Discharged for disability. Reënlisted Aug. 16,
1864, in 1st N. H. Cavalry, Troop E.

28, Timothy K. Ames, 2d, age 24, 6th Reg. Sergeant
Major, promoted to 1st Lieutenant, Aug. 5, 1862.
Killed in second Bull Run battle, Aug. 29, 1862 ;
body never recovered.

26, Marshall K. Ames, age 20, 6th Reg., Co. E. 3
yrs. Wounded in right arm, by which he lost
the rotatory motion of the arm.

28, Charles L. Fuller, age 30, 6th Reg., 3 yrs. 2d
Lieutenant, promoted to 1st Lieutenant. Wounded in second Bull Run battle, Aug. 29, 1862, and
died in hospital, Sept. 11, 1862.

2, James K. Blake, age 40, 6th Reg., Co. K. 3 yrs.
Philemon W. Cross, age 37, 6th Reg., Co. K. 3
yrs. Died by collision of the steamers West

Point and the George Peabody, on the Potomac,
Aug. 13, 1862.

Nov. 23,   John M. Dodd, age 24, 6th Reg., Co. K. 3 yrs.
Sergeant Major, promoted to 2d Lieutenant.
Died May 14, 1864. Enlisted as Veteran.

7,   Charles H. Fay, age 20, 6th Reg., Co. K. 3 yrs.
Died Jan. 10, 1862, at Alexandria, Va., of pneu-
monia.

1,   Charles Nims, age 32, 6th Reg., Co. K. 3 yrs.
Discharged for disability, Aug. 12, 1863.

6,   Alvarado Robbe, age 30, 6th Reg., Co. K. 3 yrs.

2,   Charles C. Silver, age 22, 6th Reg., Co. K. 3 yrs.
Discharged for disability, Dec. 22, 1862.

15,   Washington Swett, age 24, 6th Reg., Co. K. 3
yrs. Wounded in second Bull Run battle, and
had his left leg amputated.

Oct. 28,   Henry C. Taggart, age 35, 6th Reg., Co. K. 3
yrs. Killed at second Bull Run battle, Aug. 29,
1862 ; body not recovered.

Nov. 8,   Thomas J. Vose, age 27, 6th Reg., Co. K. 3 yrs.
Sergeant. Died at New York, May 10, 1862.

Oct. 28,   Charles F. Winch, age 29, 6th Reg., Co. K. 3
yrs. Sergeant, and promoted to 1st Lieutenant.
Slightly wounded at Fredericksburg, Va.

26,   George W. Woods, age 25, 6th Reg., Co. K. 3
yrs. Discharged for disability ; returned home
and died of consumption.

Dec. 4,   Menville Bowers, age 34, 6th Reg., Co. K. 3 yrs.
Wounded Sept. 17, 1862, at Antietam, in side
and thigh. Discharged Jan. 30, 1863.

11,   Luther Starkey, age 24, 6th Reg., Co. K. 3 yrs.
George S. Clark, age 26, 6th Reg., Co. K. 3 yrs.
Discharged for disability, March 23, 1862.

14,   Wallace Scott, age 21, 6th Reg., Co. K. 3 yrs.
Drum Major, Jan. 1, 1864.

Oct. 1,   Josiah P. Smith, age 21, 8th Reg., Co. B. 3 yrs.
Killed in battle at Fort Hudson, La., June 14,
1863.

22,   Jonathan L. Powers, age 44, 8th Reg., Co. D.
Died in Camp Parapet, La., Oct. 20, 1862.

Aug. 15, 1862. Jeremiah Regan, age 25, 10th Reg., Co. F. 3 yrs. Wounded at Drury's Bluff, May 16, 1864; seriously, at Cold Harbor, June 3, 1864.

9, Nathan D. Stoodley, age 39, 13th Reg., Co. G. 3 yrs. Captain, promoted to Major, Oct. 28, 1864. Slightly wounded at the siege of Suffolk.

Gustavus A. Forbush, age 30, 13th Reg., Co. G. 3 yrs. 1st Lieutenant, promoted to Captain, May 5, 1863. Killed in storming Fort Harrison, Sept. 29, 1864.

Sept. 12, . Person C. Cheney, age 34, 13th Reg. 3 yrs. Quarter Master. Discharged on account of sickness, Aug. 6, 1863.

Aug. 30, Mortier L. Morrison, age 26, 13th Reg. 3 yrs. Quarter Master's Sergeant, promoted to Quarter Master, Aug. 12, 1863.

12, Henry B. Wheeler, age 28, 13th Reg., Co. G. 3 yrs. Sergeant, and promoted to 2d Lieutenant, May 30, 1864. Wounded at Fort Harrison, Sept. 29, 1864.

13, Oliver H. Brown, age 34, 13th Reg., Co. G. 3 yrs.

12, Ira A. Spafford, age 37, 13th Reg., Co. G. 3 yrs. Accidentally wounded at Cold Harbor, Va.

John Bolio, age 21, 13th Reg., Co. F. 3 yrs.

15, John Gafney, age 18, 10th Reg., Co. F. 3 yrs. Deserted at Washington, Sept. 28, 1862.

12, Edward Haskins, age 32, 10th Reg., Co. F. 3 yrs. Deserted at White House, Va., July 16, 1863.

13, John Kelly, age 21, 10th Reg., Co. F. 3 yrs. Wounded at Cold Harbor, June 3, 1864.

12, Thomas Mulhern, age 28, 10th Reg., Co. F. Wounded at Cold Harbor.

Nathan C. Forbush, age 24, 13th Reg., Co. G. 3 yrs. Promoted from Corporal to Sergeant.

13, Albert M. Smith, age 25, 13th Reg., Co. G. Promoted from Corporal to Sergeant.

20, Jeremiah D. Smith, age 20, 13th Reg., Co. G. 3 yrs. Discharged for disability, May 21, 1863.

18, Charles A. Ames, age 23, 13th Reg., Co. G. 3 yrs. Quarter Master's Sergeant; served as Clerk till promoted.

Aug. 18,   Charles W. Bailey, age 20, 13th Reg., Co. G.   3
            yrs. Ruptured at Fredericksburg, Va. Trans-
            ferred to Veteran Reserve Corps.

    12,   John A. Bullard, age 38, 13th Reg., Co. G.   3 yrs.
            Detailed as Hospital Nurse and Clerk most of
            his term of enlistment.

    13,   Rodney M. Brackett, age 25, 13th Regt., Co. G.
            3 yrs. Discharged for disability. Died at Peter-
            borough.

            Joseph A. Crosby, age 22, 13th Reg., Co. G.   3
            yrs. Killed in storming Fort Harrison, Sept.
            29, 1864.

    12,   Wallace Clark, age 18, 13th Reg., Co. G. Wound-
            ed slightly, Fort Harrison, Sept. 29, 1864.

            Jacob Chamberlain, age 36, 13th Reg., Co. G.   3
            yrs. Wounded at Fredericksburg, Va., and
            died Nov. 4, 1863, of consumption.

    18,   Harrison Evans, age 26, 13th Reg., Co. G.   3 yrs.
            Quarter Master's Clerk and Store Keeper.

    15,   Eugene G. Farwell, age 29, 13th Reg., Co. G.   3
            yrs. Died at Hampton, June 12, 1864.

    16,   Rufus R. Frair, age 18, 13th Reg., Co. G.   3 yrs.

    9,   Henry N. Frair, age 28, 13th Reg., Co. G.   3 yrs.
            Killed in battle near Petersburg, Va., June 15,
            1864.

    12,   Edmund S. Greenwood, age 42, 13th Reg., Co.
            G. 3 yrs. Transferred to Veteran Reserve
            Corps.

    13,   Charles W. Gould, age 20, 13th Reg., Co. G.   3
            yrs.

    12,   John J. B. F. Hardy, age 30, 13th Reg., Co. G.
            3 yrs.

    18,   Herbert Lee, age 26, 13th Reg., Co. G.   3 yrs.
            Died of diptheria, Aug. 31, 1863.

    13,   John Leathers, age 44, 13th Reg., Co. G.   3 yrs.
            Died of small-pox, at City Point, Va.

    12,   Henry K. McClenning, age 20, 13th Reg., Co. G.
            3 yrs.

    18,   Robert M. McGilvray, age 18, 13th Reg., Co. G.
            3 yrs. Wounded through both legs severely,
            June 1, 1864.

Aug. 18,	Daniel W. Osborne, age 22, 13th Reg., Co. G. 3 yrs.
13,	Cortes S. Osborne, age 18, 13th Reg., Co. G. 3 yrs. Died at Hampton, Va., Oct. 31, 1864.
7,	Andrew J. Robbins, age 26, 13th Reg., Co. G. 3 yrs.
13,	John B. Stevens, age 30, 13th Reg., Co. G. 3 yrs.
15,	Samuel M. Woods, age 31, 13th Reg., Co. G. 3 yrs. Transferred to U. S. Navy, April 28, 1864.
12,	Mark A. Wilder, age 19, 13th Reg., Co. G. 3 yrs. Discharged for disability, Jan. 16, 1863.
	William H. H. Wilder, age 22, 13th Reg., Co. G. 3 yrs. Served as Quarter Master's Clerk.
Oct. 23,	Francis S. Piper, age 16, 16th Reg., Co. I. Died.
Sept. 9,	Leroy P. Greenwood, age 24, 1st Co., Sharpshooters, Co. E. 3 yrs. Discharged Dec. 19, 1862. Drafted Sept. 2, 1863, 14th Reg., Co. G.
Jan. 1,	J. Clinton McDuffie, age 21, 3d Co., N. H. Cavalry. 3 yrs.
Aug. 25,	Joseph Tatro, age 38, 2d Reg., Co. G. 3 yrs. Deserted while at Concord, May 2, 1863.
	Edward Bolio, age 18, 2d Reg., Co. G. 3 yrs. Died June 16, 1864, of wounds in the thigh, at Cold Harbor, Va., June 3, 1864.
Jan. 6, 1863.	Alfonso E. Osborne, age 17, 3d Reg., Co. I. 3 yrs. Enlisted under the fictitious name of James Smith, being under age, so that his friends might not reclaim him.
	George A. Frost, age 17, 3d Reg., Co. I. 3 yrs. Enlisted under the fictitious name of George French, so his parents might not reclaim him from service.
Sept. 2,	David Burke, age 30, 7th Reg., Co. C. 3 yrs. Substitute for George E. Brackett.
	Patrick Glancey, age 21, 8th Reg., Co. H. 3 yrs. A substitute for Hiram McCoy. Deserted at New Orleans, La., July 11, 1864.
	Samuel Wiggins, age 20, 8th Reg., Co. I. 3 yrs. Substitute for D. M. McClenning. Transferred to Navy, June 16, 1864.
	James Smith, age 20, 8th Reg., Co. K. 3 yrs.

Sept. 2.   Substitute for Joshua Richardson. Transferred
              to Navy, Jan. 18, 1864.

Oskar Rosenthal, age 21, 8th Reg., Co. K. 3 yrs.
Substitute for Kendall C. Scott. Deserted at
Franklin, La., Dec. 19, 1863.

William Mitchell, age 21, 8th Reg., Co. I. 3 yrs.
Substitute for Francis Cragin.

Thomas Worth, age 31, 8th Reg., Co. D. Substitute for D. Lovejoy. Deserted at Franklin, La.,
Dec. 20, 1863.

Alexander Mc'Lenan, age 18, 8th Reg. Substitute for Henry M. Breed.

Patrick Carney, age 20, 8th Reg., Co. K. Substitute for Samuel W. Vose. Deserted at Natchez,
Miss., March 2, 1865.

Oct. 29,   James Fox, age 19, 4th Reg., Co. A. 3 yrs. Substitute for Rodney M. Wilder.

Aug. 23,   John P. Marsh, age 21. Heavy Artillery, Co. B.

Dec. 21,   Charles D. French, age 33, 13th Reg., Co. F. 3
yrs. Drafted Sept. 2, 1863.

     22,   Frank S. Ritter, age 16, 9th Reg., Co. G. 3 yrs.
Musician. A hired recruit.

     24,   Richard Carr, age 22, 9th Reg., Co. D. 3 yrs. A
prisoner of war; no discharge furnished. A
hired recruit.

John Smith, age 19, 13th Reg., Co. F. 3 yrs. A
hired recruit.

     26,   Frank Thurston, age 18, 9th Reg., Co. E. 3 yrs.
A hired recruit.

Thomas Rigley, age 22, 9th Reg., Co. C. 3 yrs.
Wounded Jan. 17, 1864. Deserted from hospital, Oct. 30, 1864. A hired recruit.

John Watters, age 22, 9th Reg., Co. E. 3 yrs.
Deserted at Annapolis, Md., Aug., 1864. A
hired recruit.

Daniel W. Kennedy, age 19, 9th Reg., Co. E. 3
yrs. Deserted, City Point, Va., August, 1864.
A hired recruit.

William Russell, age 32, 9th Reg., Co. F. 3 yrs.
A hired recruit. Absent from sickness. Transferred to 6th Reg., Co. F.

Dec. 28,   Peter Louis, age 18, 9th Reg., Co. G. 3 yrs. A hired recruit. Transferred to 6th Reg., Co. G.·

William A. Walker, age 18, 9th Reg., Co. E. 3 yrs. Wounded May 12, 1864. Transferred to 6th Reg., Co. E. A hired recruit.

Jacob Jackson, age 30, 9th Reg., Co. D. 3 yrs. Died Sept. 10, 1864. A hired recruit.

Abraham Heran, age 19, 9th Reg., Co. G. 3 yrs. Transferred to 6th Reg., Co. G. A hired recruit.

Peter Loran, age 19, 9th Reg., Co. G. 3 yrs. Transferred to 6th Reg., Co. G., June 1, 1865. A hired recruit.

Robert Warner, age 35, 9th Reg. Deserted *en route* to regiment; probably a hired recruit.

Samuel Woods, age 25, 9th Reg., Co. G. 3 yrs. Transferred to 6th Reg., Co. G. A hired recruit.

31,   James Dinwidder, age 33, 6th Reg., Co. I. 3 yrs. Deserted at Annapolis, Md., April 3, 1864; probably a recruit.

John Glover, age 25, 1st New England Cavalry, Troop I. Captured at Winchester, Va., Aug. 17, 1864; probably a hired recruit.

William Culberson, age 22, 6th Reg., Co. I. 3 yrs. A hired recruit.

Jan. 1, 1864.   George Wallace, age 28, 1st N. H. Cavalry, Troop D. Deserted *en route* to regiment; a hired recruit.

Aug. 5,   William Loftis, 14th Reg., N. H. Infantry, Co. E. 3 yrs. Substitute for Edwin A. Towne.

6,   John Higgins, 5th Reg., N. H. Infantry, Co. A. Substitute for George F. Livingston. Deserted at Alexandria, Va., June 5, 1865.

10,   Don Negretta, age 40, 1st N. H. Cavalry, Troop G. 3 yrs. Substitute for Charles J. Smith.

5,   James Conner, 14th Reg., Infantry, Co. C. 3 yrs. Substitute for Albert C. Frost.

6,   William Mahoney, 5th Reg., Infantry, Co. I. Substitute for Horace F. Whittemore.

12,   James Bennett, 5th Reg., Infantry, Co. B. Substitute for George Bruce. Deserted to the enemy, at Petersburg, Va., Oct. 11, 1864.

Aug. 15, George Hyatt, 5th Reg., Infantry. Substitute for William G. Livingston. Deserted *en route* to regiment.

Jacob Williams. Substitute for Richard H. Noone.

13, John Walker, 5th Reg., Infantry, Co. I. Substitute for J. Frank Noone. Deserted at Petersburg, March 29, 1865.

10, John Welch, 5th Reg., Infantry. Substitute for John D. Holmes. Deserted *en route* to regiment.

Sept. 15, Hans Nelson, 5th Reg., Infantry, Co. C. Substitute for Charles Barber.

9, Osburn Anderson, 5th Reg., Infantry, Co. B. Substitute for Jones C. Dodge. Deserted, apprehended, and mustered out without pay, July 5, 1865.

David Walker. Substitute for Person C. Cheney.

7, John Farrel, 5th Reg., Infantry, Co. B. Substitute for Sampson Washburn. Deserted to enemy, near Petersburg, Dec. 12, 1864.

Wm. McCoy. Substitute for Henry B. Kimball.

27, Frank Clark, 8th Reg., Infantry, Co. G. Representative recruit for Thomas Little.

Charles H. Robinson. Representative recruit for Charles H. Brooks.

28, Charles H. Littlefield, 8th Reg., Infantry, Co. E. 1 yr. Representative recruit for George T. Wheeler.

Patrick Mullin. Representative recruit for Andrew C. Cochran.

30, George Adams, 14th Reg., Infantry. 1 yr. Representative recruit for Eli S. Hunt.

William Simpson, 14th Reg., Infantry. 1 yr. Representative recruit for Abraham P. Morrison.

Benjamin A. Moodey. Representative recruit for Albert Smith.

Aug. 9, George W. Cummings, 1st N. H. Cavalry, Troop G. 3 yrs. Promoted to 2d Lieutenant.

Aug. 19, Charles E. Lakeman, 13th Reg., Go. G. 3 yrs.
Died March 10, 1865.

9, Daniel M. White, age 21, 1st N. H. Cavalry,
Troop E. 3 yrs. Promoted to 2d Lieutenant.

16, Willis L. Ames, 1st N. H. Cavalry, Troop F. 3
yrs.

John Scott, age 19, 1st N. H. Cavalry, Troop
G. Quarter Master's Sergeant. Accidentally
wounded by a gun-shot in foot, Nov. 2, 1864.

19, Albert Mason, age 22, 1st N. H. Heavy Artillery,
M. 3 yrs.

James B. Mooney, 1st N. H. Heavy Artillery.
3 yrs.

Sept. 2, Lewis F. Cheney, 1st N. H. Heavy Artillery, C.
1 yr.

Frank A. Robbe, 1st N. H. Heavy Artillery, C.
1 yr.

Aug. 30, Charles M. Moore, age 18, 1st N. H. Heavy Artillery, E. 1 yr.

Sept. 26, Samuel S. Hardy, age 42, 1st N. H. Heavy Artillery, L. 1 yr.

Mar. 31, Ervin H. Smith, age 24, 1st N. H. Cavalry, Troop
C. 3 yrs. Captured Nov. 12, 1864, at Cedar
Creek. Confined in Libby Prison, Richmond,
and Salisbury, N. C.; endured great sufferings
in the above prisons.

30, Stilman Dunn, age 27, 1st N. H. Cavalry, Troop
D. 3 yrs.

Allen R. Hood, age 22, 1st N. H. Cavalry, Troop
B. 3 yrs.

Benjamin F. Whitcomb, 1st N. H. Cavalry, Troop
B. 3 yrs.

Ambrose F. Upton, age 18, 1st N. H. Cavalry,
Troop B. 3 yrs. Captured June 29, 1864.
Died at Andersonville Prison, Ga., Oct. 7, 1864.

23, Wm. H. H. Pritchard, age 23, 1st N. H. Cavalry,
Troop A. 3 yrs. Wounded on picket, July
18, 1864.

Henry Field, age 40, 1st N. H. Cavalry, Troop A.
3 yrs.

Mar. 23,   John P. Farmer, age 22, 1st N. H. Cavalry, Troop
                  A. 3 yrs.

      31,   William A. Huntress, age 36, 1st N. H. Cavalry,
                  Troop E. 3 yrs. Wounded in leg. Trans-
                  ferred to Veteran Reserve Corps, April 17,
                  1865.

      19,   George E. Whitman, age 20, 1st N. H. Cavalry,
                  Troop B. 3 yrs. Captured, and died at An-
                  dersonville Prison, March 6, 1865.

      30,   William H. Drinker, age 19, 1st N. H. Cavalry,
                  Troop B. 3 yrs. Wounded severely in Laurie
                  Valley, Va., Sept. 22, 1864.

Feb. 15, 1865.   Charles Jewett, age 38, 1st N. H. Heavy Artillery,
                  K. 1 yr.

Mar. 10,   George D. May, 1st N. H. Heavy Artillery, Troop
                  K. 1 yr.

      23,   Charles S. Gray, age 40, 1st N. H. Cavalry, Troop
                  L. 1 yr.

                  George B. Tilden, age 42, 1st N. H. Cavalry,
                  Troop L. 1 yr.

                  George N. Bailey, 1st N. H. Cavalry, Troop K.
                  1 yr.

Feb. 25,   Wells E. York, 1st N. H. Heavy Artillery, M.
                  1 yr.

      14,   John C. Richardson, 8th N. H. Infantry, Co. A.
                  1 yr.

                  W. H. H. Greenwood, 1st N. H. Heavy Artillery,
                  M. 1 yr.

June 14, 1863.   John C. Swallow, Navy, 1st Class Boy. 1 yr.

SOLDIERS' MONUMENT. — The soldiers' monument erected
in Putnam Grove, Peterborough, consists of a bronze statue
of a soldier, six feet seven inches high, standing in full dress,
at rest upon his arms, upon a granite pedestal seven feet in
height. The statue was designed by Martin Milmore, Esq.,
of Boston, and cast by the Ames Manufacturing Company,
at Chicopee, Mass. The pedestal is of the Concord granite,
and was designed at Chicopee, and wrought by D. C. Hutchinson, of Manchester. The statue and pedestal are so well

proportioned that the artistic effect of the whole is very pleasant and admirable. Upon the face of the granite pedestal, in front, is inserted a bronze memorial tablet, bearing the following inscription : —

THE WAR OF THE REBELLION.

PETERBOROUGH SOLDIERS SACRIFICED.

Capt. Gustavus A.Forbush, 13th N. H. Regt.
Lieut. Timothy K. Ames, 6th N. H. Regt.
Lieut. Charles L. Fuller, 6th N. H. Regt.
Lieut. John M. Dodd, 6th N. H. Regt.

Charles O. Collister, 2d N. H. Regt.
Newman Hall, 2d N. H. Regt.
Edward Bolio, 2d N. H. Regt.
Frank E. Howe, 2d N. H. Regt.
George Wilding, 4th N. H. Regt.
Luther G. Crosby, 4th N. H. Regt.
German N. Breed, 5th N. H. Regt.
George N. Spaulding, 6th N. H. Regt.
George W. Hadley, 6th N. H. Regt.
William H. Wallace, 6th N. H. Regt.
Lucius H. Farwell, 6th N. H. Regt.
Cyrus Henry Farnum, 6th N. H. Regt.
Christopher M. Wheeler, 6th N. H. Regt.
David A. Cram, 6th N. H. Regt.
Alfred Perry, 6th N. H. Regt.
Philemon W. Cross, 6th N. H. Regt.
Charles H. Fay, 6th N. H. Regt.
Henry C. Taggart, 6th N. H. Regt.
Thomas J. Vose, 6th N. H. Regt.
George W. Wood, 6th N. H. Regt.

Josiah P. Smith, 8th N. H. Regt.
Jonathan L. Powers, 8th N. H. Regt.
Rodney M. Brackett, 13th N. H. Regt.
Joseph A. Crosby, 13th N. H. Regt.
Jacob Chamberlain, 13th N. H. Regt.
Charles E. Lakeman, 13th N. H. Regt.
Eugene G. Farwell, 13th N. H. Regt.
George J. Moore, 13th N. H. Regt.
Henry H. Frair, 13th N. H. Regt.
Herbert Lee, 13th N. H. Regt.
John Leathers, 13th N. H. Regt.
Cortes S. Osborne, 13th N. H. Regt.
Francis S. Piper, 16th N. H. Regt.
James L. Boyce, 16th N. H. Regt.
Ambrose F. Upton, 1st N. H. Cavalry.
Henry Moore, 11th Ill. Regt.
Joseph Clark, 2d Mass. Regt.
George M. Clark, 5th Conn. Regt.
John P. Cram, 15th Conn. Vol.

Drowned, by Sinking of Steamer on Potomac River :
Sophia, Wife of Lieut. Col. Charles Scott.
Katie, Wife of Capt. John A. Cummings.

The first steps taken to procure a soldiers' monument, in commemoration of those belonging to Peterborough who sacrificed their lives in the war of the Rebellion, were taken in the organization of a "Soldiers' and Sailors' Mutual Benefit Association." They elected a committee, April 4, 1866, to solicit funds for this purpose.

This committee held their first levee Dec. 25th, of the same year, and realized from its proceeds four hundred and eighty-one dollars and fifty-eight cents. Hon. P. C. Cheney, formerly of the 13th Regiment, generously added one hundred dollars to this auspicious beginning. The second levee was held Dec. 24, 1867, and three hundred and seventy dollars raised. A chowder-party, from West Peterborough, gave, as a surplus of a Fourth of July gathering, sixteen dollars and seventy-five cents. The town, at its annual March meeting in 1868, voted to raise the sum of one thousand dollars towards the monument, and chose a committee to act in connection with the soldiers' committee; *viz.*, Elijah M. Tubbs, Albert S. Scott, Charles H. Brooks, Albert Sawyer, Abraham P. Morrison, Charles Scott, Ervin H. Smith, James E. Saunders, John H. Cutler, Mortier L. Morrison. The third levee was held Feb. 26, 1869, and three hundred and eleven dollars and fifteen cents secured. The two "Ladies' Soldiers' Aid Societies," in dissolving their organizations, gave for the monument the unexpended money in their hands, amounting to thirty-five dollars. Miss Catharine Smith contributed ten dollars from an enterprise of hers. At the annual town meeting in March, 1870, the town voted six hundred and fifty-three dollars and forty-nine cents, to cancel the debt due for the monument. The several sums received were placed on interest, and the amount realized was one hundred and fifty-two dollars and ninety cents.

No part of the town appropriation was paid until the monument was completed.

The following is a financial report of the cost of the monument, with error of $60 in receipts, as per dedication pamphlet : —

Funds received.		*Expended.*	
Town of Peterborough,	$1,653 49	Foundation for Monu-	
Three Levees, ...	1,162 73	ment, ...	$14 25
Donation of P. C. Che-		Pedestal, ...	525 00
ney, ...	100 00	Statue and Tablet, . .	3,277 50
Ladies' Soldiers' Aid So-		Freight, ...	9 50
cieties, ...	35 00	Fence, removing stumps,	
Miss Catharine Smith, .	10 00	&c., in Grove, . . .	76 48
Chowder Party, . . .	16 75	Contracting, ...	28 45
A Friend, ...	800 00	Incidentals, ...	59 69
Interest, ...	152 90		
Error?	60 00		
	$3,990 87		$3,990 87

The monument was erected in Putnam Grove, on Grove Street, late in the fall of 1869, so late that the joint committee of soldiers and citizens decided not to dedicate it until the following spring or summer. The tablet was inserted in May, 1870. During the spring the grove, as yet entirely in a state of nature, underwent great improvements; it was neatly fenced and enclosed, suitable entrances were constructed, the trees trimmed, the grounds smoothed and partially terraced, and otherwise greatly improved. The 17th of June, 1870, was selected as the day of dedication. The following were the officers of the day: Albert S. Scott, President; Charles H. Brooks, Albert Sawyer, E. H. Smith, Committee of Arrangements; Daniel M. White, Toast-master; Col. Charles Scott, Chief-marshall; Aids, Lieut. M. L. Morrison, Capt. James E. Saunders, and Col. S. I. Vose.

Gen. Aaron F. Stevens, of Nashua, delivered the oration; Maj. N. D. Stoodley, of Wakefield, Mass., the poem, and Dr. E. M. Tubbs, of Manchester, the annals.

The following persons responded to toasts on the occasion: Rev. George Dustan, Dr. George B. Twitchell, of Keene, Maj. John A. Cummings, of Boston, Lieut. Daniel G. Gould, Col. Henry D. Pierce, of Hillsborough, and Rev. A. M. Pendleton, of East Wilton.

CHAPTER XV.

PAUPERISM.

Few Paupers Early. — Increased by the Revolution. — Jean Culberson. — Warning out of Town. — Lydia Peram. — Widow Mary Swan. — Margaret Caldwell and New Boston. — A Cow Lent to Jona. Barnett. — Dr. Young Aided. — William Powers. — Selling Paupers at Auction. — Poor Let Out on Contract. — Purchase of a Town Farm.

PREVIOUS to the Revolution there were very few paupers. If there were any from the earliest settlement to the incorporation of the town, we suppose that they were provided for by the proprietors, though no record of such aid has come down to us. Between the incorporation and Revolution the town authorities were seldom called upon to afford aid to any individual, but at the close of the war there was a great increase of those who came to want, caused by loss of wages in the war and impoverishment from long service, and in many instances from their vices and habits contracted in the army. It was a perplexing subject to deal with, as well as a heavy burden on the early settlers.

We find by the town records that in 1763 Jean Culberson was the first person warned out of town, and was probably the first pauper after incorporation. The following was the form generally used for warning persons out of town : —

Province of   }
New Hampshire. }

December ye 23d 1763

To James Templeton Constable of this town of Peterborough in His Majesty's name, we command you forthwith warn Jean Culberson now in this place forthwith to Depart out of this town, hereof fail not as you will answer the Contrary At y^r Perill. Thomas Cunningham Alex^r Robbe Hugh Gregg Selectmen &c.

December ye 24th 1763, according to the within request, I have Warned Jean Culberson forthwith to depart out of this town &c.

James Templeton Constable for the town of Peterborough &c.

This warning was to prevent individuals from gaining a residence; by which the town would be liable for their support if they should come to want. It was often carried to such an extent as, in many towns, to be practised indiscriminately upon all who came into town, so that often the best people of the settlement were warned out. It continued from 1760 to 1777, in which year occurs the last case on record.

It seems that the above process did not shake off Jean Culberson, as it was voted, in 1765, " That Jean Culberson should be maintained from house to house, as last year." After this, we hear nothing more of her. A Lydia Peram next appeared, who required a good deal of legislation in the town. An effort was made to induce Deacon Thomas Davison to support her, he having brought her into town, but I judge unsuccessfully, as the town in 1769 and 1772 voted money to her support and doctoring. She was probably sick, as the record speaks of her as being " under doctors," and probably soon after the last date deceased, as we hear nothing more of her. About this time [1773], it was " Voted that the selectmen should take care of Mrs. Braffy and her children." In 1782, widow Mary Swan turned up, and occasioned a good deal of trouble and expense, but was finally sold, as it is called in the warrant, to some relative, who obligated himself to support her during her natural life, for which the town was to pay thirty pounds.

The next case was that of Margaret Caldwell in 1785. It was voted in 1787 to move Margaret Caldwell, a town charge in Peterborough, to New Boston, " and that Jeremiah Smith should proceed in that way he thinks most regular, of moving said Margaret to New Boston, and likewise to recover the expense the said Margaret has been to the town of Peterborough." At a meeting Dec. 17, 1787, it was voted " To stop

23

process against the selectmen of New Boston respecting Margaret Caldwell, upon the condition that the selectmen of New Boston come with the present week and carry off the said Margaret Caldwell, and discharge the town of Peterborough forever hereafter for her maintenance." The selectmen of New Boston probably complied with the terms of this vote, as we hear no more of her.

In 1792, we find a vote "That the town pay the necessary expenses that arose upon the sickness, death, and funeral of Johnson, that lay sick and died at Richard Finch's in April, 1791." And in 1793, Richard Finch was allowed twenty shillings, in addition, for his trouble with Johnson in his last sickness. About this time, a vote was passed to lend a cow to Jonathan Barnett, till the town think proper to call for it. In 1796, the money for the poor was raised in the federal currency, and seventy dollars was raised for this year. The sum raised in the several succeeding years was constantly increasing till 1802, when it reached $170. We have already spoken of the kind and delicate manner in which Dr. Young was aided when dying with a cancer of the face, and have stated that in 1805 two cows were also voted for his use.

William Powers, who first introduced cloth-dressing and wool-carding into town, became poor, gave up his place to the town, and was many years, from 1801 to 1817, supported by the same. The town carried on his farm for a time, and the work was let out at public vendue, when, among many other things, the getting of ten cords of wood was taken by William Wilson, at ninety-three cents a cord.

The sums raised for the support of the poor varied from one to two hundred dollars up to the year 1815, when four hundred dollars was raised, and ever after the sums raised were rarely below this amount.

About this time, a new plan of selling the paupers at public auction for a year was instituted; and in 1816 we find that William Powers was bid off at one dollar and fifty-eight cents per week, and Benjamin Alld at ninety-six cents per week, and again in 1817 William Powers was struck off at one dollar and sixty-nine cents per week, which is the last we hear of him on the town records.

At these auctions, the peculiar qualities of each individual were described by the auctioneer, pretty much as he would speak of the qualities of any other live-stock offered for sale. We have a distinct recollection of the vendue of one of the paupers, who was subject to epilepsy, but well most of the time. Auctioneer, " Here is Mr. ——; he is a strong, hearty, sound man, who can eat anything, and a good deal of it; how much do you bid?"

This mode was continued till 1831, when the town authorized the selectmen to contract with some individual for the support of the poor for three years, or a shorter'time, as best to be obtained. Mr. Thomas Upton was the first contractor, and took them all to his farm, and continued to support them till 1836 or '7.

Before this experiment in supporting the poor was tried — when their year's residence was determined at a public vendue, — they were often treated very harshly, if not cruelly, for they fell into hands unable from disposition or circumstances to take proper care of them, but were induced to bid them off for the small sums of ready money paid for their support. The custom of selling the poor annually, both men and women, at public auction, like cattle or slaves, at length became abhorrent to the public sentiment, and a better and more humane method was sought. It was a practice that had obtained in all the neighboring towns as well as this; and in some of them this base thing was done in a still baser way.* Liquors, as at all other auctions, were furnished at the public expense in some places when the auction came off, but never, as we think, here, and under its influence, the poor creatures were bid off by those who had neither ability nor convenience to accommodate them, and at prices, too, not at all remunerative. The consequence was that the poor creature was made to suffer, and to wear out the weary year as he could, — a burden, a nuisance, and a great loss, too, to his supporter. It was bad enough to be poor, but to be punished for it, by being treated worse than we treat our dumb animals, was cruel and unjust

---

* History of Dublin, pp. 26, 27.

in the extreme. The poor who asked for aid were those, generally, past labor. They were old, broken-down in constitution by disease or their own vices, and were the most unfit inmates for any family; and we do not wonder that many who undertook to support them were disappointed, and could hardly extend to them any kind treatment, they were so repulsive and disagreeable in their habits and conduct. It is a class always difficult to please, and one that, with its poverty, seems to possess so large a share of the vices and corruptions of our nature as to be incapable of appreciating good and kind usage.

In 1836, a committee consisting of John H. Steele, Henry T. Cogswell, and Thomas Upton were chosen to inquire into the success of those towns which had begun to support their poor upon a town farm, and to report. The committee, satisfied with the experiment as witnessed in other towns, reported that it is expedient to purchase a farm. John H. Steele, Isaac Edes, and William Scott were chosen a committee to buy. Various farms in town were examined, *viz.:* Thomas Upton's, Jonathan Holmes' (the Deacon Holmes place), Adam Penniman's, Watson Washburn's, and John S. White's. The committee reported, 1837, in favor of Jonathan Holmes' farm, which was bought, and the town voted to adopt the system of keeping their poor on the farm purchased for this purpose.

The town "Voted, that the agents authorized to receive the surplus revenue appropriate so much of the money as to take up the note given to Jonathan Holmes."

And also to appropriate of their money the necessary expenses in relation to the poor farm, for stock, tools, and necessary expenses of the present year.

The poor have ever since been supported on the farm, it proving a very successful and economical measure for the town. The new poor laws, however, have so changed the terms of settlement, and thereby so reduced the number of paupers to be supported, that many towns have already abandoned or are abandoning the system, finding it too expensive to keep up such establishments for only two or three inmates. The great majority of the poor are now supported at the county poor farms.

CHAPTER XVI.

Legislation on Roads in Town Meeting. — Roads Poor before Incorporation. — A Road Cut and Cleared by Proprietors from Meeting. House to New Ipswich in 1738. — Object of Incorporation to Improve the Roads. — The Roads in Town.

On the subject of roads there was no doubt in all the New England towns a vast amount of legislation. The records are full of the petitions and votes to lay out and build new roads, the raising of money for the same, the various manœuvres for delay, for reconsideration, etc., and no little litigation has been incurred, occasionally, by individuals not satisfied with the awards of town authorities.

Before the incorporation of the town in 1760, we know very little about the roads, but suppose that they were little else than mere bridle-paths, the way only cleared of trees, with little or no attempt to smooth or work them. They were merely passable for horses, and perhaps an ox-cart could with much " geeing and hawing " get over them, laden with the families of the early settlers, and such necessary implements of household furniture as were indispensable.

The following vote was passed at an adjourned meeting of the proprietors held at Alexander Cochran's, at the " Three Horse Shoes," Boston, Dec. 4, 1738, *viz.:* " Voted, that the former committee (*viz.*, John Hill, Jeremiah Gridley, John Fowle, Jr., Jonathan Prescott, and Peter Prescott, or any three of them) be, and hereby are, empowered to agree with some suitable person, to cut and clear a good way or road from New

Ipswich to the meeting-house lot in said township, as soon as may be."

All the roads, such as they were, previous to the act of Incorporation, were either made by the proprietors, or by individual enterprise, for the petition for the act says "that we cannot hold any proprietors' meetings at all, to pass any vote or votes that will be sufficient to oblige any person to do any part towards supporting the Gospel, building a meeting-house and bridges, clearing and repairing roads, and all which would not only be beneficial to us settlers to have it in our power to do, but a great benefit to people travelling to Connecticut River and those towns settling beyond us." An *addendum* to the petition reads as follows: "Your Petitioners beg leave to add, as a matter of considerable importance, that the only road from Portsmouth through this province to 'number four' is through said township of Peterborough, and which makes it more necessary to repair said road within said township, and to make many bridges, which they cannot do, unless incorporated and enabled to raise taxes," etc.

We have, as briefly as we could and make them intelligible, traced out on the town records the transcript of all the roads of the town from the time of its incorporation, only omitting the many short pieces of road built especially for the accommodation of individuals. The roads will be described nearly in the order of dates.

Road from the middle of the town to Hugh Wilson, Esq.'s, Nov. yᵉ 11th, 1760, beginning about twenty rods north of William Robbe's, from the middle or great road. This is the old road leading from the Gordon corner, by the Dunbar place and past the house of Gen. David Steele, over the brook (Bogle) to widow James Parker's, and thence to the mills (Russell's) near which Hugh Wilson lived.

A road from the intersection of this road near David Blanchard's to where Robert Morison now lives, the Maj. Samuel Gregg place. Width of road, two and one-half rods.

A road leading from yᵉ meeting-house to the great bridge, to a road near great bridge, leading to south part of the town. This is the old road, long since discontinued, that went to meeting-house east of the Follansbee house on side of hill, Nov. yᵉ 11th, 1760.

Road from the street to the mountain. It passes about east of the house of James Robbe (supposed to be where Charles F. Bruce now lives) then east to the foot of the mountain, and then by marked trees to town line,— supposed to be the road over the mountain to Temple, Nov. yᵉ 18th, 1760.

A road from the grist-mill (site of the first Peterborough cotton factory) to John Smith's and Turner's, Nov. yᵉ 18th, 1760.

Begins at grist-mill, thence over the bridge by Samuel Mitchell's door, a little to the westward of south to the top of the hill (by A. Frost's house), thence along the road, now cleared and improved, by the south end of John Smith's house, thence to where it branches, the one part leading along by house of Moses Morison and east side of John Morison's house to the westerly end of Halbert Morison's house, the other branch leading along the road, now cleared and improved, to Thomas Davison's and Turner's, and thence to town line west of Turner's barn.

A road from the south line of town (Spalding's Corner) to grist-mill, Dec. yᵉ 17th, 1760.

Beginning at the south line of the town, on the east end of William McNee's lot, thence north along the east end of John Taggart's (the Shedd place), and across the land whereon William Richey now lives; then across land belonging to John and Moses Morison, and land belonging to Lieut. Thomas Morison, near to the place "where clay hath been dugg." Then it branches, the one part leading to his house (Thomas Morison's) and from thence to his saw-mill, "all on the place where it is now cleared and improved"; the other leading about north, and crossing land of Morison to old road and to a small brook (Cold Brook), and thence to a larger brook (Wallace Brook) on north line of said Morison's land, and thence to John White's house, thence till it comes to a small brook near Marshall Nay's, a little below the old ford, thence north to the old road formerly improved, thence along the old road over the great bridge, and thence to the grist-mill. Said road to be two and one-half rods wide.

A south road along the Main Street to the meeting-house. The Street Road, so called, Dec. y⁸ 17th, 1760.

Beginning at a bridge over the brook on the south line of this town (Town Line Brook), on land belonging to Jane McKay, and from thence on land of the same to Margaret Stewart's lot, and land of William Smith, John Scott, Robert Wilson, William Mitchell, and William Scott, on the old road as now cleared and improved. Said road to be as wide as originally allowed in the laying out of the same.

A road from meeting-house to Hugh Gregg's (Deacon Christopher Thayer's), and from thence over the river to John Ferguson's (supposed to be west of Col. Norton Hunt's house), Dec. y⁸ 17th, 1760.

A continuation of Main Street or Street Road. Beginning at the meeting-house, thence about north-east by land of William Robbe and west end of Samuel Stinson's land opposite his house, thence north on the east end of said Robbe's land, along the old road, as it is now cleared and improved, until it comes a little to the south of Hugh Gregg's house, and from thence keeping a straight line to a great rock that is in the line of John Ferguson's land, then leaving it to the discretion of the surveyors to lead down as near the Island Brook as the land will admit, to the bridge-place, or ford, by a great rock that stands in the river, and across the river by that rock, then turning up the river on the north side, and keeping as near the river as good land will admit of for making a road, until it comes into the Main Street again (the old road crossed the river about thirty-five rods above Col. Hunt's). Said road is to be five rods wide (the road which this superseded, from Samuel Stinson's, or the John Little place, was discontinued Aug. 27, 1798, and the land sold to Samuel Smith).

A road from School-house No. 2 (South Factory) to Alexander Robbe's or Samuel Adams'. Beginning at the crotch of the road that leads to John Smith's, and follows the old road, now occupied, to Alexander Robbe's. To be two

and one-half rods wide, Oct. yᵉ 1st, 1761. Transcript of said
road recorded Sept. yᵉ ——, 1772.

A road from Samuel Mitchell's to Samuel Moore's. From
near G. P. Felt's manufactories to Orrin Smith's in Windy
Row, Oct. yᵉ 1st, 1761. Beginning at the east end of Samuel
Mitchell's house, from thence to a stake and stones, it being
Mr. Gridley's south-east corner of his farm, from thence to
Samuel Moore's, as the road is now occupied, it being discre-
tionally left with the first surveyor to alter the same at any
particular " pleace," for the benefit of the road, not exceeding
two rods.   Said road to be two rods wide.

A road from Alexander Robbe's to Dublin line, Sept. yᵉ 26,
1763. This road is laid out in a westerly direction from
Alexander Robbe's house, by marked trees, to Dublin line.
To be two and one-half rods wide.

A road from Samuel Todd's to Peterborough north line,
June yᵉ 14th, 1764. To accommodate the settlers in " New
Limbrick." Beginning where the old road now leaves Samuel
Todd's east line of his lot, and thence leads northerly to the
town line, part on the aforesaid Samuel Todd's east line, and
part on the lots east thereof, and from thence to the aforesaid
Peterborough north line, to a rock-maple tree marked with
the letter H.   To be two and one-half rods wide.

A road from Capt. Thomas Morison's to "' Middleton" line,
laid out from Capt. Thomas Morison's over the new bridge
westward, as the road has been improved, by John Smith's
house, through his land to Thomas Davison's, and from thence
between said Davison's and Thomas Turner's land, as said road
has been improved, and so to the town line beyond said Turner's barn, Aug. yᵉ 13th, 1768.   The width of above road
fixed at two rods by selectmen, Oct. 22d, 1785.

A road from the great bridge (north factory) to the north-
west corner of Henry Ferguson's land, to the road that is already laid out from Charles Stuart's to the mills, July yᵉ 4th,
1768

A road from Matthew Templeton's (Caleb Wilder's) running
easterly, as the road is now cleared, to the east line, or common

24

land, towards Lyndeboro.   Said road to be two rods wide, Jan. yᵉ 6th, 1773.

A road from Peterborough to Temple, beginning on land between John Blair's and James Cuningham's, and running east, as the road is now laid out and cleared, thence by the north side of the pond until it strikes lot No. 13, and thence between lots No. 13 and 14, to the lot now improved by Moses Cuningham.   Width, two rods, Dec. 29, 1773.

A road from Charles Stuart's (or Faxon place) to Peterborough north line.   Beginning at Charles Stuart's house, running north by marked trees, as near to the ridge hill as the land will admit of, and by land of Robert Swan and others, and thence to the Peterborough north line.   Width, two and one-half rods, June yᵉ 16th, 1780.

A road from John Mitchell's causeway to Thomas Morison's bridge, over "pine hill."   Beginning at the west end of the great bridge west of Capt. Thomas Morison's house, and thence northerly, upon the line between said Morison's and John Smith's land, to the foot of the pine hill, so called, and from thence east of north through Capt. Thomas Morison's land to John White, Jr.'s, land, and to said White's house, and from thence northerly through said White's and John Mitchell's land, to the east end of the causeway upon the road leading from Alexander Robbe's house to John Mitchell's house. Width, two and one-half rods, Sept. 10, 1781.

A road from north bridge (north factory) to Thomas Steele's farm.   It begins at the north end of said bridge, and runs easterly to William Swan's, and thence by land of Samuel Jackson and said Swan till it strikes Thomas Steele's south line, to the westerly side of a beach stump.   Width, two rods, Aug. 10, 1786.

A road from William Miller's to the town line, Greenfield. It begins on a line between William Miller's and James Miller's, and runs one hundred rods on said line, thence through William Miller's land to his east line, thence through widow Miller's land, the same point of compass, to a bridge now built, then runs north of east on David Hovey's land, thence eastward south of said Hovey's house, then east and through Richard Hovey's land to lot No. 15, and then between lots No. 15 and 16 to the town line. Width, two rods, June 14, 1787.

A road from Thomas Morison's to Joseph Miller's in Sharon, or Sharon line. Beginning at the south-west corner of Jonathan Smith's pine field on the old road to Peterborough line by the Richey place, through land of James Richey and Daniel Gray to Samuel Morison's house, and thence on same course across said Morison's land and a corner of John Smith's (Stuart place), to John Gray's north line, and thence on said line to middle of said Gray's lot, thence southerly to Sharon line. Width, two and one-half rods, Oct. 28, 1793.

A road from William Moore's (Deacon N. H. Moore) to Jaffrey line. Beginning to the west of said Moore's barn, and running west on a line betwixt said Moore's and Robert Smith's land till it strikes Thomas Turner's land, and thence on said land to Jaffrey line. Width, three rods, Oct. 28, 1793.

A road from William Smith's to Samuel Morison's. Beginning at the said Smith's gate, past the south side of his house and barn, down through his field to his pasture, and near an old brick-yard into the old road. Width, two rods, Dec. 25, 1794. Discontinued in 1814.

A road from Oliver Carter's to old meeting-house. April 7, 1801, one hundred dollars awarded as damages to Oliver Carter or William Scott for the above road, and one hundred dollars to be awarded to the same next year, to be in full for land and fencing.

A road from Jonathan Faxon's to James Smith's, Windy Row, beginning at the east corner of Jonathan Faxon's field west of road that leads to Hancock, and running, on the road now occupied, south of Alexander Scott's house, to the west road that leads to Hancock. Width, two and one-half rods, Dec. 13, 1810. The road yet open, but not kept in repair.

A road from Capt. William Wilson's place due west to intersect the Dublin road near Warren Nichols'. This road was laid out by a court's committee in 1809, to be completed in eighteen months from Dec. 1, 1809. Extending from Warren Nichols' house to Contoocook River and across the river, by the house of the late Robert White's place, to the intersection of the roads near the Capt. Wilson house.

A road from Thomas Steele's to Hancock line, over the Ballard hill, beginning at said Steele's south line, at the road formerly laid out through Hunt's farm, thence north to William Stuart's land, and past the west end of his buildings, to James Gregg's south-west corner on his line near the river, thence across the brook, thence as near the river as the land will admit till the river turns to the right, thence to Antony Bullard's south-west corner, thence to William Bullard's house, then, as it is now travelled, past Abraham Moore's house, and through his land to Mr. Dennis' wall, within ten rods of Hancock line, then, bearing to the left, supposed to be Hancock line.   Width, three rods, Nov. 8, 1811.

A road from Bartholomew Thayer's (John Little place) to the great bridge.   No transcript can be found of this road but this vote of the town, March 5, 1799 : "Voted, that the selectmen lay out a road from Bartholomew Thayer's over the hill to the great bridge, and cause it to be made in the place where it has been proposed."   The road was built, and there was much legislation in town in regard to damages to Mrs. Morrison, supposed widow of Rev. John Morrison, who owned land.   Road discontinued.

A road from bridge near Reuel Richardson's, or Spring's bridge, so called, to Dublin, near to where the line between Peterborough and Dublin crosses said road, thence north, bounding on Dublin line, through land of Abijah Richardson till it intersects the road, as now travelled, from John Richardson's past Abijah Richardson's to Dublin meeting-house. Width, two and one-half rods.   To be opened one year from date, Oct. 1, 1816.

A road from Stephen Pierce's (the Jewett place) through West Peterborough, across the river, south to the old road from Peterborough to Dublin.   Width, three rods, Sept. 20, 1823.   The road to be opened for travel, June 1, 1824.—*Town Records, Vol. 2, p. 51.*

A road from great bridge to Presbyterian Meeting-house at Gordon's Corner. Beginning at the east end of the great bridge, near the house of Samuel Smith, Esq., thence north on said Smith's land twenty-four and a half degrees, ninety-eight rods, thence on land of said Smith till it strikes land of Capt. Moses Dodge and land of Rev. Elijah Dunbar, in front of the Presbyterian Meeting-house. The said road to be opened and made passable on or before the first day of November next, July 1, 1824.—*T. R., Vol.* 2, *p.* 81.

A road from north-east corner of Asa Carley's land, near Abel Weston's house, to the Street Road, near Deacon Samuel Maynard's house. Said road to be opened and made passable on or before Nov. 1, 1828. Width, two and one-half rods, March 1, 1827.—*T. R., Vol.* 2, *p.* 86.

A road from South Factory to Smith's Village. Beginning at the south-west corner of Capt. Henry F. Cogswell's land, thence running east forty-three degrees, north seventeen rods, on said Cogswell's land, to land owned by the second Peterborough cotton factory corporation, thence by the land of said corporation and Samuel Morison, and land of Robert White, to land of James Wilson, in various points of compass, till it reaches Goose Brook, to land of Samuel Smith and land of the Phœnix factory corporation to the road near the tavern house, now occupied by Charles Whitney (the site of the Town House). This road to be opened and made passable on or before Nov. 1, 1827. Width, three rods, July 1, 1826.—*T. R., Vol.* 2, *p.* 88.

A road to Greenfield by Holmes' mill. Beginning on the east side of the road between Asaph Evans' and David Wilson's, fifty rods west and twelve degrees south of Calvin Washburn's, thence on land of Calvin Washburn, John Steele, Mary Dickey, Samuel Straw, Jonathan Cudworth, to Greenfield line. Width, three rods, ——, 1828. — *T. R., Vol.* 2, *p.* 100.

A road from the paper-mill of Morrison, Hoit & Blodgett to the village. Beginning at the turn of the road west of the paper-mill, thence east three degrees, south twenty rods, to within half a rod from the north end of the paper-mill, thence on land of Isaac Hadley, William Scott, Jacob Flint, George W. Senter, and Samuel Holmes, in various points of compass, to the Priest house (the old Evans tavern house). Width, three rods, June 20, 1832. — *T. R., Vol.* 2, *p.* 134.

Widening and straightening the road in village, from Brown's store or the stone bridge to Bernard Whittemore's, east and opposite upper hotel. Beginning two rods north of the north bounds between Moses Chapman's and Phœnix corporation, thence east five degrees, south sixteen rods, across the bridge, thence from first-mentioned bound west nineteen degrees, north thirty rods, the point being forty-seven feet south of Riley Goodridge's store, the width of the point to be three and a half rods wide, thence west fifteen degrees, north fifteen rods, the width of which is three rods, thence west twenty degrees, north five rods, thence west thirty degrees, north seven rods, the width of which, to last points, to be two and a half rods wide, March 6th, 1834. — *T. R., Vol.* 2, *p.* 156.

Diamond road. Beginning at a stake in the bars on the south side of the road leading from the Street Road to the East Mountain Road, and about twelve rods easterly of the bridge, and running to a stake standing on the line, being the north line of said Diamond's land, and the south line of Asa Carley's land. Width, two rods, Sept. 11, 1835. — *T. R., Vol.* 2, *p.* 174.

Alteration of road round Capt. Alexander Robbe's hill, running south of his house, and laid out by the County Commissioners. At a town meeting, March 10, 1840, voted to raise four hundred dollars for the purpose of building the above road. — *T. R., Vol.* 2, *p.* 242.

Alteration of road over the mountain from the woods east of Samuel White's to the Richey house.

April 5, 1836, " Voted, That the selectmen be authorized and directed to lay out the road beginning at east side of the woods east of Samuel White's, from thence up the mountain until it intersects the old road near the Richey house, and cause the same to be built the present year." — *T. R., Vol.* 2, *p.* 183.

A road to North Factory from the village. Beginning at the centre of the small stone bridge north of the village cemetery, thence north sixteen degrees, east twenty-two rods, and, by various points of compass, on land of William Follansbee, Guy Hannaford, Ethan Hadley, Elihu Thayer, Timothy and Norton Hunt, Archelaus Cragin, and Robert Day, to old road between Timothy Ames' and Samuel C. Oliver's house, on the east side of the small bridge, Feb. 16, 1835. Width, three rods. — T. R., Vol. 2, p. 463.

The widening and straightening the road, laid out by a court's committee, round the Wilson hill, so called. Beginning at a stake easterly of Capt. William Wilson's, thence on his land till it strikes the old road near Locke's bars, so called. Width, four rods, June 24, 1839. — T. R., Vol. 2, p. 284.

A road from William Pratt's to School-house No. 10. Beginning at the corner of the wall near William Pratt's, thence north thirty-three degrees, west fourteen rods, and, by various points of compass, to the old road near the School-house No. 10. Width, three rods, May 25, 1843. — T. R., Vol. 2, p. 284.

A road from Eri Spalding's to Cyrus Blanchard's (called slab road). Beginning at a stump on highway at Bowers' mill, so called, and running to the old road near School-house No. 6. To avoid the "mill hill," so called, Aug. 26, 1843. — T. R., Vol. 2, p. 290.

A road from Eri Spalding's to brick-yard near North Factory. Laid out by the Road Commissioners for County of Hillsborough. Beginning at a point in the old road, at a stake on Eri Spalding's land, thence south forty-one degrees, west, and by various points of compass, through land of William M. White, Watson Washburn, the Swan farm, so called, Carter and White's land, Elihu Thayer's, to a point on the old road opposite to Carter's brick-yard, so called. Width, three rods, Aug. 27, 1844. — T. R., Vol. 2, p. 301.

A road from Nahor's to Hancock line, laid out by the County Commissioners, Apr. 8, 1817. In town meeting, "Chose a committee to view the land the road was laid out on, and report to the town the probable expense of making the road,

and the probability of getting rid of making said road, if con-
tested." No report of said committee is found, but three
hundred dollars is raised for the Hancock road, April 7, 1818.
April 6, 1819, the further sum of five hundred and eighty dollars was raised to pay damages on Hancock road and build it.
— *T. R., Vol. 2, p.* 13.

A road to School-house No. 1, in village. Beginning at a
stake on the east side of the road leading from the village to
the South Factory, near Brockway's store (now W. G. Livingston's), said stake being in the middle of the road ; thence south
sixty-six degrees, east and continued thirteen rods and twenty-
one links to a stake and stones in the wall near the south-east
corner of the Phœnix garden. Width, eighteen and a half
feet. By another transcript, March 31, 1846, the road is laid
out two rods wide, June 26, 1845. — *T. R., Vol. 2, p.* 317.

A road from Main Street to Joseph H. Ames'. Beginning
from a stake on the north side of the road leading through the
village, forty-four feet east from the south-east corner of the
yard in front of the Unitarian meeting-house, thence north
three degrees, east eight rods eleven links, and in a northerly
direction to a stake in the old pass-way of Joseph H. Ames'
house, passing through land of Job Hill and others, the same
to be three rods wide, May 22d, 1847; by a special vote of the
town, passed March 30, 1847. — *T. R., Vol. 2, p.* 350.

A road from Reuel Richardson's to West Petèrborough.
Laid out by the Road Commissioners, and damages awarded
as follows : Union Manufacturing Co., $107.50; Frederick Liv-
ingston, $75.00; Ivory Wilder, $128.60; Reuel Richardson,
$90.00; Charles R. Richardson, $145.00, Dec. 10, 1850. — *T.
R., Vol. 2, p.* 384.

A transcript is also found on the Town Records, p. 398,
of a road from Reuel Richardson's to land of Reuel Richardson, through land of C. D. Richardson, and damages
awarded to him of $185.00, a supposed amendment of the
road as laid out by the County Commissioners, Dec. 10, 1850,
being all merged in one, Sept. 10, 1851.

A road from Benjamin Hosmer's (the Robert Swan place) to

where it intersects the old road near where the School-house No. 5 stood. Width, three rods, Nov. 19, 1851. — *T. R., Vol.* 2, *p.* 403.

A road from Eri Spalding's to Greenfield line, laid out by the County Commissioners, March 13, 1855. In town meeting, "Voted, That the selectmen be authorized and instructed to borrow money to pay damages, and build the road laid out by the Commissioners from Eri Spalding's to the Greenfield line, if necessary." — *T. R., Vol.* 2, *p.* 443.

A road from Mitchell's Corner to near the house of Joseph H. Ames. Beginning at a stake in the highway at the foot of Mitchell's hill, so called, thence easterly and southerly trhough land of Norton Hunt and others, to the present highway, east of J. H. Ames' dwelling-house. The highway to be three rods wide for the first seventy-six rods, and for the next two hundred and eleven rods it is to be four rods wide, the remainder of the road to be three rods wide, April 8, 1855. — *T. R., Vol.* 2, *p.* 445.

A road from bridge near Barker's Mills to Sharon line. No transcript found; supposed laid out by a court's committee. The following article is found in a warrant for town-meeting, March 8, 1842 (T. R., Vol. 2, p. 268): "To hear the report of same committee, on the petition of Samuel Nay and others for a new road, commencing at the Jaffrey Road (so called), and extending to the Sharon line, and act thereon." "Voted [p. 272], that the petition of Samuel Nay and others be accepted; also voted at the same meeting to raise $450 for the Sharon Road."

A road from Spalding's Corner (so called) to the intersection of the road with that leading from Barker's Mills to Sharon line, not far from the bridge; said road laid out by the commissioners, after a public hearing, Aug. 10, 1859; probably built in 1860.

A road from Gulf Road, near Nathan Gould's, to where it intersects the old road leading from Timothy Hovey's to James Smiley's. Width, two and one-half rods; transcript, Oct. 3, 1859. — *T. R., Vol.* 3, *p.* 86.

25

A road from South Factory to Jaffrey line. It was vendued to various persons, Nov. 16, 1840, to the amount of $1,688.93.

Granite Street, beginning at the intersection of the road leading from bridge near Monadnock Railroad to N. H. Morison, Esq.'s; by first transcript, Nov. 30, 1868, to Amzi Mayo's house; by second transcript, Sept. 20, 1870, to Samuel Knight's house; by third transcript, Nov. 14, 1871, from Samuel Knight's house to Pine Street. The road built and made passable in 1872. Width, two and one-half rods.

A road to School-house No. 1, from Main Street, between Baptist Meeting-house and Asa Davis' store; transcript, Dec. 23, 1863. Width, three rods.

CHAPTER XVII.

MANUFACTURES.

Bell Factory. — Phœnix. — Eagle. — South. — North. — Union Manufacturing Co. — Paper Manufacture. — Woollen Manufacture. — Peg Mill. — Stone Grist-Mill. — Basket Shop. — Manufacture of Barometers and Thermometers. — Manufacture of Hand-Cards for Cotton and Wool. — Machine Shop and Foundry. — Marble and Granite Works. — Briggs' Manufactory of Portable and Patent Piano-Stools.

BELL FACTORY. — The first Peterborough cotton factory, known as the "Old" or "Bell" Factory, called the "old" from its being the first incorporated factory in town, and the "bell" from the circumstance of having introduced the first bell ever used in town, was erected in 1809, '10. It stands on the spot on which the first saw and grist mill was built in town, in 1751, on the north side of the Nubanusit River, at the head of a small fall of the same in the Centre Village. The privilege and lands connected with the same were purchased of Asaph Evans, Jan. 2, 1809. It was incorporated Dec. 20, 1808.

The first proprietors were as follows: Charles H. Atherton, Joseph Cushing, David Holmes, Frederick French, Samuel Bell, Edmund Parker, of Amherst; and John Smith, Samuel Smith, Jonathan Smith, John Steele, John Scott, Asaph Evans, Samuel Evans, John Field, George Duncan, Daniel Robbe, William Pettes, William Wilson, Edmund Snow, Nathan Scott, Hugh Miller, Nathaniel Morison, James Ferguson, Samuel Alld, Nathaniel Holmes, Matthew Templeton, of Peterborough. The stock was divided into one hundred shares, one-half of it owned in Peterborough, the other half in

Amherst.   The first assessment of $3,500 was made in 1809;
and in 1810 $10,000 was assessed, and four dwellings for
boarding-houses, thirty by twenty feet, were built on the
south side of the river opposite to the factory.

The first machinery of this mill was constructed at Peterborough under the charge of John Field, of Pawtucket, R. I.,
known here then, by the importance of his trust as Judge
Field.   He was one of the workmen employed by Samuel
Slater in the erection of the first cotton factory in the United
States.   Mr. Field was considered one of the best workmen
known; and the company gave him what was then called
extravagant wages, three dollars per day, and in addition kept
his horse, and furnished him with half a pint of rum a day!
Mr. Field built his machinery the exact pattern and type of
that in Pawtucket, for which he brought models and exact
measurements with him.   It was even better than its pattern,
and did good service for many years.   The Phœnix Factory,
built by Samuel Smith, was an exact imitation and reproduc-
tion of the first factory.

The machinery of the Bell Factory was put into operation
in 1810; the first cotton was purchased by John Smith,
Esq., at thirty-two and one-half cents per pound; in 1815 the
average cost of cotton was twenty-six and one-half cents per
pound; and the highest price paid was, in 1816, forty-one
cents per pound.   At first the yarn was divided among the
proprietors; and at one time, by a vote, the distribution was
made every week.   The cost of the cotton, and the expenses
of manufacturing, must have been met by assessments.   During 1812 the yarn was sold at the factory prices, which were
increased in 1814 seven cents on a pound of yarn up to No.
15, and five cents above that number.   After the close of the
war of 1812 there was a great depression in the value of yarn,
and it was sold at a discount of twenty-five, fifty, and even
seventy-five *per cent.* from factory prices.

In April, 1817, an addition of a brick building was made to
the factory, and looms added to the establishment under the
superintendence of John H. Steele, and the first cotton cloth
woven by water-power in New Hampshire was manufactured
in this mill in May, 1818.

Jonas Livingston

Mr. Steele had serious difficulties to encounter from a want of experience, with no aid from those who had already begun to weave by water-power. The irregular speed of the mill, no regulator as yet being invented, the newness and the breaking in of new machinery, were serious difficulties; and he says: "Never did I more sensibly feel the truth of the saying that patience and perseverance will accomplish all things, than I did in setting that loom in motion. My future prospects depended on my success; and accordingly all the patience and perseverance I could command were exerted. Three days, the longest and most toilsome I ever spent, were consumed before the purpose intended was accomplished." The difficulties of the undertaking are well expressed by the anecdote that Mr. Steele used often to tell, of the boy whose curiosity attracted him to the scene of action. Being unable to make out what was going on, he asked his sister, who was in attendance, what Mr. Steele was doing. "Why?" said she. "Because," said the boy, "it sometimes looks like cloth, and sometimes like the harness."

Mr. Steele remained in charge of this mill till 1824, when he resigned to take the superintendence of the building of the Union Mill in West Peterborough. It was then under the direction of various agents till purchased in part by Frederick Livingston in 18—, who superintended it till he sold out, in 1865, to Ammidown Lane & Co., of New York City, who are now the owners of the same. After they purchased the mill, it underwent an enlargement and thorough repair under their agent, A. J. Aldrich. It is now leased by E. B. Hill, for the manufacture of "curtain hollands," who employs between eighty and ninety hands, and has a monthly pay-roll of $2,000.

PHŒNIX FACTORY.—This factory stands on the site of the large building of two hundred feet in length and two stories high, erected by Samuel Smith, in 1793, '94, situated in the Centre Village, on the Nubanusit, some thirty rods above its junction with the Contoocook River. The water that drives this mill is used for various purposes of manufacture on its

passage to the Contoocook, at the west butment of the stone
bridge. In 1812 the north part of this building was converted
into a cotton factory by Samuel Smith, and put in operation in 1813 or '14, under the direction of his son, Frederick A. Smith; and was changed to weaving, under the direction of John and Robert Annan, in 1822; and sold to Samuel
May and others in 1823. The new company was organized
this year, held their first meeting in Boston, and divided their
stock into thirty-two shares, which were owned by D. D.
Rogers, Samuel Smith, Samuel Appleton, Pickering & Nichols,
Samuel May, Samuel Greele, Isaac Parker, Sewall Williams
& Co., and Jeremiah Smith. This company was incorporated
under the name of the "Phœnix Cotton and Paper Factory";
but by an additional act of the Legislature in 1832 this name
was changed to that of "Phœnix Factory," by which it is now
known. Under the new act the shares were divided into one
hundred instead of thirty-two shares. The paper-mill was
kept in operation for some years after the cotton factory
was built. It was not till 1823 that the paper-making was
given up, and the original building, south part, was taken
down, and a new brick building erected. This new building
was fitted up and put in operation by Samuel G. Smith, then
the agent of the company, during this same year. This same
building, with all its valuable machinery, was destroyed by
fire, Dec. 18, 1828. This was the largest and most destructive fire that had ever occurred in town. It took fire from a
small stove in the attic. The engine of the factory just west
of the building, after some delay caused by its not having
been used since the preceding October, and by the bursting
of the hose from the hurry and inexperience of the men, was
finally got into successful operation, which, together with the
engine from the Union Manufacturing Co., continued to throw
a large quantity of water for four hours, and greatly backened
the fury of the flames, and preserved the north half of the
building,—a wooden structure, only separated from the burning building by a brick wall. It was a terribly cold day;
water was easily congealed into ice, and many present who
came in contact with the water were covered with a coating

of ice from head to foot. The loss was estimated at $32,000. This mill was soon replaced and filled with machinery; and the north half of the establishment, which occupied the old wooden structure erected by Samuel Smith, was removed and a brick building erected in its place.

Samuel G. Smith resigned his agency in 1830, and removed to Baltimore. He was succeeded by John H. Steele, who superintended it many years, till he was succeeded by Frederick Livingston in 1834, Edward O. Abbot having held the office one year in the meantime. Jonas Livingston, having succeeded in purchasing a majority of the stock of the company, took possession and the superintendence of the factory in 1865, which he now manages. He has greatly enlarged and improved the establishment, so that it is now the most extensive manufactory in town.

EAGLE FACTORY. — This building was erected in 1795 by Daniel Abbot, and was for many years occupied by him as a cabinet-shop, chair-factory, and dwelling-house. It was converted into a cotton factory by him and others, under the name of Eagle Factory, in 1813, and the machinery for it was built by Harris & Dodge, of Peterborough. It was many years under the charge of Thomas Baker, and finally was purchased by Joseph and Abisha Tubbs. In 1833 it was sold by them to Moore & Colby, who, in the summer of that year, removed the old buildings and built their machine-shop, where the business of building machinery has been carried on ever since.

SOUTH FACTORY. — This factory was erected in 1809, on the west bank of the Contoocook River, in the South Village. It was put in operation in 1810, and was owned by Nathaniel Morison, Jonathan Smith, Jonas Loring, Nathaniel Holmes, Samuel Morison, William Smith, and Jacob Putnam. Benjamin Chamberlain was first employed, as master-workman, at two dollars per day, but, being found incompetent, Jacob Putnam was engaged to continue the work. It was finally completed by Nathaniel Holmes, Jr., and John H. Steele. It was in view of the high prices paid for labor at this mill that Samuel Morison, a sagacious observer of mankind, used to say that "Give a man fifty cents a day and he will work like a hero, give him one dollar a day and he will do tolerably well, but give him two dollars or more, and he will do nothing."

This property was purchased by Nathaniel Morison in 1814 or '15, and carried on by him for a few years, at such a loss as to prove his financial ruin. It was then sold to Barry, Senter & Brown, and subsequently by them to Stephen Felt, and was destroyed by fire, Nov. 29, 1849, and has never been rebuilt.

NORTH FACTORY. — This factory was built in 1813, and is situated on the Contoocook River, at the North Village, one and a half miles north of the Centre Village. It was started in 1814, and looms were introduced in 1823 under the direction of Stephen Felt. It continued in operation till 1860, when it was sold to Charles Wilder, and converted into a shop for the manufacture of barometers and thermometers.

UNION FACTORY. — The first mill was erected in 1824, also the same year a machine-shop, both under the care of John H. Steele. The first owners of this factory were Samuel May, Parker Blanchard & Co., Samuel Billings, and John H. Steele. The cost was $100,000. It has always manufactured very fine goods, — sheetings, of yarn as high as No. 40. In 1856 the original subscription was increased, and a new factory building, mill No. 2, erected and filled with the most modern machinery (for sheeting and shirting), under the care of Frederick Livingston. It was not put into operation till 1858.

This factory is situated in West Peterborough on the Nubanusit, each mill has a separate dam, so that the same water moves them both.

Gov. John H. Steele, who had the superintendence of this factory from its erection, sold out his interest in the same in 1845, when he resigned, and was succeeded by Frederick Livingston.

A. P. Morrison

He continued in charge till 1857, when he was succeeded by J. Wallace Little, who held the office till his death, Sept. 23, 1867. Levi Cross succeeded Mr. Little, and held it till his resignation in 1875. Joseph S. Moody is now the superintendent.

The usual number of operatives employed in both mills is about one hundred and ten. From the great depression in cotton manufactures at the present time (1876), these mills are suspended.

PAPER MANUFACTURE.—The first paper-mill in town was put in operation by Samuel Smith in his great building already alluded to, probably in 1795 or '96, and carried on extensively by him in the use of from two to four engines to grind the rags. The mill was furnished with the necessary vats, presses, etc., together with large lofts for drying the paper, the shutters of the same giving such a peculiar appearance to the paper-mills of the olden time. This mill was continued in operation till the erection of the brick cotton factory on its site in 1823. Up to this time all the paper was made by hand, none of the recent improvements in paper-manufacture having come into use or being even invented.

The next mill was erected by James Smith, now of St. Louis, and William S. Smith, in 1825, on the Nubanusit, near and east of the Union Mills. It was sold to Messrs. Morrison, Hoit & Blodgett, in May, 1835. Mr. Blodgett soon sold his interest in the same to Moses Cheney, of Holderness, who removed to town and remained here till 1846, when he returned to Holderness (now Ashland). The manufacture was then carried on by Mr. Morrison and his son till Mr. Morrison's death, in 1870, when the mill was sold to Samuel Adams, Jr., and J. Madison Nay, the present proprietors.

Another paper-mill was erected in the north-west part of the town, on an old site of Silas Spring's saw-mill, by Gov. P. C. Cheney. It was burned while he was carrying it on, and rebuilt; and on his removal to Manchester it was sold to John J. Barker, who has operated it since.

WOOLLEN MANUFACTURES.—William Powers, from Ireland, was the first clothier who settled in town, on the Wallace Brook, near I. Miller Mears', about 1777. Before this, cloth was carried out of town to be dressed. It is not probable that he commenced the wool-carding; for he became very poor, and the town took his farm and supported him many years. Samuel Smith built his clothier's mill about 1794 or '95, in the village, and continued it till near 1822 or '23. We are unable to fix the precise time or by whom wool-carding was first introduced, but most probably by Samuel Smith. Nathaniel Prentice was many years employed by Samuel Smith in his clothier's shop, and was probably his first clothier. Asahel Gowing carried on the business in 1813, and E. B. Kimball and Jefferson Fletcher in 1816 and '17, and Nathaniel Brown in 1820.

Calvin Chamberlin and James Perkins erected a building for carding wool and dressing cloth and the manufacture of wool, in 1813, at the South Village. In 1817 this mill was purchased by Henry F. Cogswell. It was greatly improved by him, by additions both to the buildings and the machinery. It was destroyed by fire in 1823, at a loss of $3,571.00, and rebuilt in a much improved form in 1824. Mr. Cogswell carried the business on very successfully for some years, and acquired considerable wealth, when he sold out to Joseph Noone in 1845. Mr. Noone continued the business till his death in 1870, and it has been continued since by his sons, R. H. and A. W. Noone. The mill was destroyed by fire in 1872, and has since been rebuilt in the most substantial manner, of brick, and greatly enlarged. The mill is now in successful operation, principally manufacturing a species of goods called roller-cloth for the cotton factories.

In 1828, Thomas Wilson purchased the house and the blacksmith-shop of George McCrillis, on the Contoocook River, north of Noone's woollen mill, and converted the shop into a mill for cloth-dressing and wool-carding, and carried on the business till his death in 1839. After his decease it was purchased by E. B. Kimball, who continued the business till the building was destroyed by fire in 1873. It has not yet been rebuilt.

PEG MILL. — A peg-mill was built by Mark Wilder in 1834, on the Nubanusit River, east of Morrison's mill, and on the Main Road. He commenced making pegs in 1835. He manufactured, the first year, one thousand bushels and averaged twenty-four hundred bushels for several years. The business was discontinued and the building converted into a saw-mill, and now constitutes the site of Briggs' great manufactory for piano-stools, etc.

STONE GRIST–MILL. — This is said to be the best grist and flouring mill in Hillsboro County. It was built in 1840 by Gen. James Wilson and Asa Davis, of split and squared stones from the quarries near. It is two stories high, with a large attic, and thirty-five by thirty-three feet in size.

It is now in successful operation as a grist-mill, a flouring-mill, and a grain-store, sustaining its former reputation, and commanding the confidence of the public. The upper part of this building constitutes the office of the Peterborough *Transcript*, and the printing-office of Farnum & Scott. It is now owned by J. F. Noone. There had been a grist-mill for some years on the spot on which the Stone Mill was erected, tended by Job Hill. It was originally an oil-mill, and is the first water-power below the junction of the Nubanusit and Contoocook Rivers.

BASKET SHOP. — This is the building erected by Moses Chapman, in 1830, for a wheelwright-shop, and was used for various purposes till purchased by Amzi Childs for a basket-shop, in 1854. It is situated near the Stone Mill, and receives its water from the Phœnix Factory into an artificial pond, made of sand carted, in 1825, from the bank to make a place for the Goodrich buildings, so called.

A considerable business is done in the basket line — being the first ever done in town, — the work being principally done by machinery. Amzi Childs is the proprietor of the same.

THE MANUFACTURE OF BAROMETERS AND THERMOME-

TERS. — This business was commenced in town by Charles Wilder, in 1860, in the buildings of North Cotton Factory, which he purchased for this purpose. It has been continued by him since, and is now extensively and successfully carried on, so that the sales vary from one to three or four thousand dollars per month. These instruments have attained such a reputation for accuracy and finish, that they are known and sought after in every part of our country.

The United States government, in some of the departments, after trying English, German, and French thermometers, give Mr. Wilder's instruments the decided preference. He has begun also to export his thermometers to South America, to the British American Provinces, and to Japan, and he is finding an increasing demand for them at home every year.

He employs seventeen persons in his works, and carries on all the processes needed in the operations of his factory, employing a glass-blower constantly for the tubes of his various instruments, and furnishing all the beautiful ornamental and useful mountings of the same.

This business has become a useful and important acquisition to the town.

.THE MANUFACTURE OF HAND-CARDS FOR COTTON AND WOOL. — This business was commenced here, in 1797, by Edmund * Snow, and continued by him till the erection of the cotton factories, when he removed to Amherst, in 1810 or '11.

The wire was prepared to be set into the leather by machinery, and the holes were pricked in the leather and the work of setting the same was done in families in this vicinity.

Isaac Parker, Esq., that late eminent merchant of Boston, in his answer to an invitation to attend the Peterborough Centennial in 1839, speaks of setting card-teeth by hand, for which he was paid fourpence per pair, and he says, "By close

---

* Drake's Dictionary of American Biography gives his name as Edward Snow; his name is Edmund.

yours with respect
William Moore

application in my leisure hours, I could set about one and a half or two pairs per week." Mr. Snow came from Liecester, Mass., where he first pursued this business in company with Pliny Earle, as early as 1785.* He was a great American inventor, and ultimately made such great improvements in the manufacture of cards that they could no longer be manufactured by hand, being entirely wrought by machinery.

Mr. Snow carried on this business in the basement story of the house which he is supposed to have built, directly opposite the factory brick house, east of the first Peterborough cotton factory.

MACHINE-SHOP AND FOUNDRY. — This is a large establishment in which all kinds of cotton, woollen, and wood-working machinery are manufactured. It stands on the site of the Eagle Factory, or original chair-factory, of Daniel Abbot. The business was first commenced here by Moore & Colby, in 1833, and subsequently carried on by William Moore. He sold out to Morrison & Felt, in 1848, who continued in business till 1851, when Granville P. Felt became sole proprietor, and greatly enlarged the same, and has carried it on extensively since. Mr. Felt added to the above, in 1865, a foundry, which escaped the conflagration of his works. In 1871, he commenced the manufacture of force and suction pumps, in which he has of late been largely engaged. He has employed from twenty-five to thirty hands, and his business has amounted to $30,000 a year.

This shop, with most of its valuable contents, was destroyed by fire, Nov. 16, 1875, at a loss of from $25,000 to $30,000.

PETERBOROUGH MARBLE AND GRANITE WORKS. — These were established in 1849 by Hubert Brennan. The marble business was commenced in town as early as 1848 by Hill & Gray, then by Gray, and subsequently by Goodyear Bassett, but with little success till the works were assumed by Hubert Brennan, of Lowell, in 1852.

---

* See New American Encyclopædia, article, Pliny Earle.

These works are at present located in the basement of Brennan's Block, on the west side of the granite bridge, on Main Street.

Mr. Brennan, by his workmanship, industry, and talent, has built up a large business, and acquired for his art a widespread reputation in the community.

Among the many elegant specimens of his art we may mention a monument to the late Charles G. Cheney, Esq., in the Holderness Cemetery; an elegant and extensive catacomb for John H. Elliot, in the Keene Cemetery; and a chaste and elegant monument, in the Village Cemetery, to the late Joseph Noone, Esq.; beside the beautiful soldiers' monuments erected in the towns of Sullivan, Dublin, and Temple. His business now takes in a large circuit, of twenty-five miles or more, and gives constant employment to eight hands. In point of skilful execution his work is not excelled in the State, if anywhere else.

BRIGGS' MANUFACTORY OF PORTABLE, PATENT PIANO-STOOLS. — This business was commenced in town, in a small way, by Joshua Briggs, in 1862. He made, at odd jobs, one dozen of piano-stools in 1863, occupying the basement of Robert Day's shop, near "Wilder's Manufactory," North Peterborough. In the spring of 1864 he rented the second story and attic of "Brennan's Building," in the village, and continued there until the whole building was too limited for his vastly increased business, when he purchased the saw-mill property of Sampson Washburn, the site of the old peg-mill of Mark Wilder, and erected for his manufactory, in the summer of 1873, his present large and commodious buildings. The progress of his business was gradual, from making a dozen piano-stools by himself, as in 1862, '63, and then with hiring one or two hands a part of the time, to his present condition. He now employs, when the business is good, from twenty-five to thirty hands in the shop, and at the same time hires all his iron-work, castings, screws, etc., done outside.

Mr. Briggs has secured five several patents on his piano-stools; *viz.*, two on the screw style, two on the ottoman style, one on the portable back.

"The Massachusetts Charitable Mechanics' Association," Boston, in September, 1869, awarded to him a diploma and honorable mention of his piano-stools. In September, 1871, at the New England Fair at Lowell, Mass., a silver medal was awarded him for his portable piano-stools.

CHAPTER XVIII.

TOPOGRAPHY.

PETERBOROUGH, County of Hillsboro, latitude forty-two degrees, fifty-two minutes, longitude seventy-two degrees, three minutes, is situated in the south-western part of the county, bordering on Cheshire County, and lies in an amphitheatrical form, with the Monadnock and the large elevated ridge of land north of it on the west, the Pack Monadnock and its range, extending through Sharon to New Ipswich, on the east. The village is situated on the Contoocook not far from the centre of the town, and is the place where these opposite sides converge. The village is thus conveniently situated, not less for business than beauty. It has been considered one of the most beautiful of our New England villages.

As originally laid out, by the first surveyor, the town had very little waste land, and would have been quite free from it, but that Col. Blanchard, the agent of the Masonian Proprietors, under their direction, cut off three-fourths of a mile from the west side of the town, and added as much to the east side, thus including most of the East Mountains within the limits of the town. As originally laid out, it was, without doubt, the best township in this vicinity.

In 1788 a small portion of the town situated on the southeast corner of the same, and on the east side of the mountain, was set off to Temple to accommodate those occupying the land, by the following vote of the town, July 8, 1788.

"Voted, that the following eight lots of land in the southeast corner of Peterborough be set off to Temple, to wit: No. 1, No. 2, No. 3, No. 4, No. 5, No. 6, No. 33, No. 34, upon the condition that any person or persons who now or at any time, when the said lots shall be annexed to Temple, shall reside or live on the same shall, in case they stand in need of relief, be considered as the proper charge of said Temple."

During the next Legislature, of 1789, an act was passed annexing the above named lots to Temple.

We find further, that when Greenfield was chartered, in 1791,* that the remainder of the range of lots which were annexed to Temple, of from one to six, was added to this town, the length of the line being one thousand four hundred and fifty rods.

The following is the article in the charter of the same: —

"Easterly on the north line of Peterborough about seven hundred and sixty-eight rods to the west line of the east range of lots in said Peterborough, then south on the west line of said east range of lots in said Peterborough, about fourteen hundred and fifty rods to the north-west corner of Temple."

It seems by this, that one entire range of lots on the east side of the town was cut off, and the east line of the town removed one lot or one-half mile further west. The action of Col. Blanchard in cutting off one and a half ranges from the west side of Peterborough and annexing the same amount

---

* Proceedings of the town. By Town Records, March 16, 1790, on the petition signed by a few inhabitants of Peterborough and a number of the inhabitants of Lyndeboro, Lyndeboro Gore and the Society to take the east range of lots of Peterborough to be annexed to the Society, Lyndeboro Gore and the westerly part of Lyndeboro to make a parish. It was voted not to grant the prayer of the petitioners. Another article was inserted in the warrant the same year, Aug. 12, 1790, to see what the town will do respecting the petition of sundry persons to be disannexed from Peterborough and incorporated into a town.

It was voted, Sept. 20, to grant to the persons petitioning the General Court for the east range of Peterborough, in case they obtain from Lyndeboro and other places what they have petitioned for, to be incorporated into a town.

to the east side, threw the East Mountains entire into Peterborough. After the east range had been disannexed and
added to Temple and Greenfield, the east line of Peterborough passed over the highest part of the first mountain,
and west of the other elevated land, so that only a part of the
highest mountain is now contained in Peterborough.

The town is very uneven in its surface, the hills rising both
on the eastern and western sides of the valley of the Contoocook to considerable height. On the eastern side of the village is an elevation rising rather abruptly to the height of
two hundred feet, where the old meeting-house stood, which
was used for public worship till 1825. Though so uneven in
its surface, the town has been considered to contain a large
amount of soil well fitted for cultivation, some parts being
better than others. The best portion of land in town was,
no doubt, the farm A, of five hundred acres, laid out for Jeremiah Gridley, one of the original proprietors, embracing part
of the farms of Cyrus Frost, Stephen D. Robbe, Charles
McCoy, and W. H. Longley, and extending across the Nubanusit and reaching near to the machine-shop of Granville P.
Felt; while the farms B, C, D, laid out for the other proprietors, situated on the Contoocook and extending to the Hancock line, were not nearly so good. Some of the hill land
was very good, especially that on the meeting-house hill,
where early settlements were made. The surface was mostly
covered with a heavy growth of wood. The principal of the
arboreal products were the pine, hemlock, beech, birch, and
maple. These dense forests extended as far as the eye could
reach. On the north it was one unbroken forest to Canada,
on the west Keene was the nearest point, and Townsend on
the south. Here was the pine in its pristine glory, the king of
the forests, so uniformly reserved, in all grants, for the masting of His Majesty's ships. Many of them were found one hundred feet in height, and six feet in diameter at the butt. All
these noble trees have been destroyed and burnt in the clearing of the land, till now hardly a vestige remains of the original forest. One of the sons of Peterborough, S. J. Todd,
Esq., of Beloit, Wis., writes me: "At my last visit to

Peterborough, in 1874, I found (after thirty-seven years' absence) that the heads of my old school-mates were turning gray, and that their faces were furrowed by time, and, sadder still, that which was the crowning glory of Peterborough (next to her sons and daughters) had nearly disappeared. Your noble forests were gone. Those hills which had been covered with grand trees had been stripped bare and naked. The beautiful groves, 'God's first temple,' had vanished." So it is ; the trees are nearly gone, leaving the hills bare and unproductive to cultivation, and mostly covered with white grass, and unsuited to furnish much pasturage to the cattle.

And the land, thus stripped of its trees, is in a worse condition. When the first settlers commenced, the land was in its virgin state, and was very productive without much fertilizing or labor; the same is now worn out and nearly worthless.

Many large, productive farms are now so run out that they have been abandoned, and others will be as soon as the present buildings grow tenantless.

We know not how these lands are to be recruited as long as the agricultural products of the West can be brought to us by a cheap transportation, so as to undersell our home productions raised on the hard soil and by the dear labor of New England.

It is doubtful if the wood now grows in town as fast as it is consumed, even with a considerable use of hard coal. Almost all wild game has disappeared, having no place of shelter now. The brooks, the home of the trout, have so dried up, with the clearing of the forests, as to afford hardly any retreat for them. We should be thankful that the birds will still remain with us, and accept our planted trees as a substitute for the primeval forests.

We are not aware that there has been any great change in the climate. There are with us the same great varieties of warm, mild, and intensely cold weather as with our ancestors. We have the same very cold winters as formerly, and the same deep snows, and when we begin to talk of an amelioration of the climatic influences, we often experience a variety of bad weather, intensely cold, or wet, or hot, never exceeded before.

We have summer enough generally to ripen our crops, though now and then some of them are cut off by the early frosts. Though rains are usually abundant enough, now and then an extreme drought comes on to destroy all vegetation, and cut off most of the crops of the season. But with common prudence and forethought the farmers usually secure their crops safely, the season being long enough to ripen such products as they raise.

If the winters are sometimes intensely cold and the summer intensely hot, it is very rare that these periods continue much length of time. The climate is considered salubrious, notwithstanding these great vicissitudes of weather, and tending to the longevity of the inhabitants. Many are of the opinion that the longevity of the early settlers far exceeded that of the present day. If a careful examination should be made from such data as we can command, it is pretty certain that the present generation would go far beyond their predecessors in longevity. Never were more persons above seventy living in Peterborough than at this very time. The number over seventy years of age, by an exact enumeration carefully made by George H. Longley, in June, 1876, has been found to be one hundred and fifty-one, with thirty in their seventieth year. The number over eighty is thirty-five, and three over ninety, *viz.:* Elihu Thayer, ninety-three, Mrs. Job Hill, ninety-three, and Nathan Gould ninety-one. The period of human life is prolonged by the progress of our age. There has been a great improvement in all that pertains to our living, a more judicious diet, a more comfortable and safe mode of clothing, better dwellings, and a more general observance of the laws of health. The early settler, by his dauntless spirit and daring courage in braving the perils of the forests, the dangers of war, the depredations of the Indians, and all with insufficient clothing, and often with a scanty and innutritious diet, often succumbed to these evils which assailed him, at an early age. We are surprised to see how many deaths have occurred in full manhood, but particularly how many are recorded at ages from sixty-five to seventy-two or three. It is evident that these men were not wise in regard

to themselves. The common precepts of prudence in regard
to life are never to be disregarded by any one with impunity.

There are only two important rivers in town, — the Contoocook and the Nubanusit. The Contoocook (meaning long
river), always called, on the plan, "the great river," takes its
rise from ponds in Rindge and a small branch from the foot
of the southern part of the Monadnock, which unite before
they reach East Jaffrey, where the stream is used largely for
manufacturing and mechanical purposes. Before it reaches
Peterborough it is enlarged by two brooks, the Mace Brook
and the Town Line Brook. It runs nearly north through the
town, and about a mile west of the centre. There are various
manufactories on it, — Barker's saw and grist-mill, near the
southern border of the town; Noone's woollen-mill, at South
Village; the grain-mill and other works in J. F. Noone's stone
buildings, in the village; a saw-mill and the barometer and
thermometer-shop of Charles Wilder, at North Village. On
it formerly stood, in the South Village, the second cotton factory built in town, which was burnt in 1849, and Kimball's
clothing mills, burnt in 1873. This stream is very readily
affected by large rains or by the effects of melting snow in
the spring, so that it was a common thing to have a bridge
carried off, as the south bridge, the new bridge, or the great
bridge at the village. The permanent stone bridge at the
village, built in 1842, has as yet stood all the freshets that
have occurred since.

The other river is the Nubanusit, situate in the north-
westerly part of the town, running in a south-easterly direction till it makes its junction with the Contoocook in the village. It has its rise from two sources. One branch (the
north) flows from Long Pond in Harrisville, which receives
as a tributary the stream used in all the manufactories of that
town. This pond is used as a reservoir for the large factories in Peterborough, and enables them in times of low water
or a drought to keep their mills in motion. Barker's paper-
mill is on this branch, a short distance above its junction with
the other branch of this river.

The other branch of the Nubanusit flows from Thorndike's

or Bullard's Pond, in the north-west part of Jaffrey, at the foot of the Monadnock, through the south part of Dublin, and unites with the Harrisville branch in the Spring Meadows above West Peterborough, as mentioned before. This river is now called Nubanusit (meaning little waters), from the Indian name of that portion of the "Town Line Brook" which flows through the meadows and flat lands east and south of the Dudley Chapman place, now occupied by Joseph McCoy, the lower part of the same stream being called "Hill's River." The name, long since disused, is now applied to this stream as a beautiful, euphonious Indian title that should by all means be retained in town. It is absolutely certain, from the old plan of the town, that the name of Goose Brook, which has prevailed about eighty years, was wholly unknown to the original settlers. It was probably adopted near the end of the last century, from the accident that the poultry-yard of Asa Evans stood on its banks, and his geese were constantly seen on its waters. This is a sure and never-failing stream, and is well adapted to the various purposes for which it is used. The principal manufactories in town are located on it, — the Union Manufacturing Co., Adams & Nay's paper-mill, and Briggs' manufactory, at West Peterborough; and in the Central Village, Felt's machine-shop, first Peterborough cotton factory, Phœnix Factory, and Farrar's shop. If the river has grown somewhat less from natural causes than formerly, it is yet of sufficient power for all needed purposes.

Turner's Brook rises in the south-east part of Dublin, runs through a corner of Jaffrey, then across the south-west part of Peterborough, and enters the Contoocook a little below Bacon's mills in Jaffrey.

The Mace Brook, called on the old map Gridley's River, rises in the south-east part of Sharon, and has been and is now improved for saw-mills in its course; and enters the Contoocook on the east side, about midway between the Turner and Town Line Brooks.

The Town Line Brook, called on the plans Hill's River, at its mouth rises near the notch of the mountain, on the south border of the town, and enters the Contoocook near Barker's Mill.

The Cold Brook, called, unaccountably, on the plan Isle Slow Brook, for it has no island, and is not slow in its flow, is a small stream rising in Cold Springs, east of the Samuel Morison house, and unites with the Wallace Brook in the White Meadow. Where it crosses the Mial Woods Road its waters are but a few inches deep; but they were deep enough to drown Lieut. Ephraim Smith (called Cady Smith), April 8, 1814, while intoxicated. His horse had stopped to drink; the rider, falling into the water with his face downwards, was unable to turn himself over, and was found with the back of his head actually above the water !

The Wallace Brook has its rise in the swamps east of the Capt. W. Wilson farm, with a small stream from the Cuningham Pond, and running down past J. Milton Mears', it enters the Contoocook in the White Meadow, west of the Bleak house.

On this stream are the cranberry meadows of Felt & Nay, near its origin; and it supplied the power for William Powers' clothing-mill and Moses Chapman's furniture-shop, situated near Mears' house. It is now used for some mechanical purpose by A. Z. Fuller, near where the stream crosses the Temple road; and a few years ago a saw-mill was erected west of this, where for a time much sawing was done.

The Bogle Brook has its source in a small pond on the East Mountain, and furnishes the water-power for John D. Diamond's mill, and was formerly used for a saw-mill by James Howe, and runs in a north-westerly direction, past the house of John Ramsey, to its junction with the Contoocook.

The Otter River, so called, is a brook that is used for the Holmes Mills near the Greenfield line, and Russell's saw-mill, and enters the Contoocook near the north line of the town.

A small stream passing through the Moore Meadows and entering the north branch of the Nubanusit is called Beaver River.

There are but two ponds in town, one of these being very small. There is a collection of water covering an area of eight or nine acres, high up on the East Mountain, some four or five hundred feet above the village, situated just north of the highest peak of these mountains, and some sixty rods or so from the east line between Peterborough and Temple. We are not aware that it has ever yet had any name. It is pure water, with sandy shores all round it, and said to abound with fish. Cuningham Pond is also situated in the east part of the town, consisting of about forty acres. It is said to have had no fish formerly; is pure, clear water, furnishing in abundance the best ice for summer use, and in a dry season it has no visible outlet.

Among the arboreal products are the ash, three kinds, white, red, and black; beech; birch, four kinds, black, white, yellow, and gray; basswood or linden; cherry-tree, black and red; elm, fir, hemlock, hornbeam, juniper, red oak, moose-wood, white pine, spruce, sycamore, poplar, rock or sugar maple, white maple, butternut, and witch elm. White oak, hickory, and pitch pine are not found here. The beautiful mountain ash is found on some of the hills.

WILD FRUITS. — The wild fruits are the upright blackberry, raspberry, blueberry, high and low, checkerberry, strawberry, and in some spots the black huckleberry and cranberry. The high and low blueberries are tolerably abundant in various places in town; and the high blackberries often yield a plentiful supply, are much used, and constitute a healthful fruit. Native strawberries are much less abundant than in former days, when the land was first cultivated. Raspberries are often found by the sides of the travelled roads and their fragrance is grateful.

WILD ANIMALS. — The moose, the largest wild animal in this part of the country, was killed in town as late as 1760.

Deer were often taken by the first settlers. Three were in town a part of the winter of 1809, and one passed through town in 1823.

Beavers were taken in town after the commencement of the settlement. Maj. Heald, of Temple, took several in Sharon. The last of the family left a leg in his trap, and
Mill

was taken by Mr. Taggart, of Dublin, more than twenty years after, about 1790.

Wolves were mischievous. In June, 1783, they destroyed about fifty sheep in one night, belonging to Capt. Thomas Morison and his son, Samuel Morison.

Bears were somewhat plenty. In 1801 one did damage in the cornfield of Samuel Smith, Esq. It passed through the village, and was not killed.

Wild-cats were here early, but how lately is not known.

The following wild animals are supposed to be in town at the present time: the yellow fox; raccoon; rabbit; skunk; woodchuck; squirrels, gray, red, striped; weazel; hedgehog or porcupine; otter, though exceedingly scarce (one was killed in 1826, and another taken by Mr. Barker near his mill in 1869); the muskrat; the mink.

River fish were very common and easily taken in the early settlement. They have now nearly disappeared. Salmon were plenty in town before the dams were built across the Contoocook. They were frequently taken, from 1793 to 1799.

INSECTS.—A new enemy to the success of our farmers has of late years appeared. Insects, though small in size, often become formidable by their numbers. Dr. Harris, some years since, published a treatise on some of the insects of New England which are injurious to vegetation. It should be in the hands of every farmer. Their destructive power is far greater than that of crows and foxes, for the heads of which the State has sometimes offered a bounty. It is said that* within the limits of Dublin more than two thousand different species of insects have been collected. Many more would be discovered by further investigation.

There has been here the usual variety of birds, as in other towns in the vicinity; but with the destruction of our forests, however, there has been a great diminution of them. The wild turkey was found early in the settlement. The partridge and

---

* History of Dublin, p. 120.

28

squirrel yet remain. The harmless, insect-destroying birds are much less numerous than formerly, and our vegetation has suffered much in consequence.

PUTNAM GROVE. — This grove is situated on the right bank of the Nubanusit and the west side of Grove Street, as you cross the stream to the south, by Farrar's shop. It consists of two and three-quarters acres of land, and is yet covered with its primitive trees. It is in the form of an amphitheatre from the river, which makes it exceedingly convenient for all great gatherings, especially where there is to be any out-door speaking. It has already proved a great comfort and convenience to the inhabitants of the town. It is set apart, for all time to come, for public gatherings, picnics, fourth of July meetings, etc. It is an evidence of the far-seeing sagacity, as well as munificence, of the donor; and her bounty will reach future generations, as the site is never to be appropriated to any other use than that of a public grove.

This grove was presented to the town at its annual meeting, March 11, 1862, by Miss Catharine Putnam, when the following vote was passed: "Voted, That a vote of thanks be presented to Miss Catharine Putnam for her very munificent gift of the grove to the town." After the presentation and acceptance of the grove, and before her decease, she expressed a wish that it might be called Putnam Grove. The following vote was passed at a town meeting held Aug. 12, 1862: On motion of George A. Ramsdell, Esq., by the request of the late Miss Catharine Putnam, "Voted, That the grove lot be hereafter known by the name of the 'Putnam Grove.'"

Miss Catharine Putnam, of Boston, the donor of the grove, was a lady of great wealth, and of unusual mental and moral endowments. In consequence of failing health in the city, she removed to town some years before her death; and, finding her health much improved, she made Peterborough her residence for the remainder of her life. She was constantly striving to do good to others, by her free and liberal gifts to persons of every class who were needy, by her personal attention to the sick, her sympathy to all in trouble, and by the

constant exercise of all the amenities of life. She was as
eminently good as she was cultivated and refined. No dim-
ness came over her path in her advanced age; old age was
hardly perceptible in her. She died suddenly of a heart
affection, without experiencing any sickness, and with hardly
any premonition of the event. She died at Peterborough,
March 27, 1862, aged eighty-four, and was buried at Mount
Auburn, Mass.

The town has surrounded the grove with a substantial
picket fence, and put up suitable gates and stiles for entrances, and smoothed and graded the ground for use.

The soldiers' monument is placed on the west side of the
grove.

CHAPTER XIX.

CEMETERIES AND BURIALS.

THREE cemeteries have been established in town since its settlement, *vis.:* the Old Cemetery, the Village Cemetery, and the Pine Hill Cemetery. The Old Cemetery has long since ceased to be used, and the second, the Village Cemetery, is now used only as families have lots in the same; the general place of burial being the Pine Hill Cemetery. In addition to the above, a few burials were made in a little graveyard on the meeting-house hill. This was probably laid out just after the first meeting-house was built, in 1752. It seemed the intention of the early settlers to have the graveyard just behind the church; and a few burials were made here. William Stuart, the first person who died in town, March 15, 1753, aged thirty-three years, was buried here, and then five other burials (which have stones) took place, and a few mounds and head-stones indicate a few graves beside. But the ground vas found so full of rocks, and so hard, that it was impossible to dig graves, and this site was abandoned and a new location sought. A spot was selected near, situated on the side of the hill, east of the meeting-house, of about one and a half acres, and walled in for this purpose, which is now known as the Old Cemetery. With our modern views of cemeteries, it had an exceedingly bad location; it was on ground, the most of it, wholly unsuitable for the purposes of burial; there was no order in the arrangement of the graves in the yard, only that the head was laid to the west. It was also too circumscribed, as though in this wide country, and where land was so cheap, a sufficient room could not be afforded for the final resting-place of our bodies without impinging on one another. The north side only of this yard was found suitable for graves, embracing but a little more than a half of the yard, while the remainder of it, in consequence of its rocks and ledges, was never occupied. So hardly an acre of ground constituted the burial-place of this town for more than eighty years, or through more than two generations. How such numbers were buried on such a small tract of land, and yet always room for more, is a mystery to us. Gravestones were not very common, in proportion to the number of deaths, and the graves soon became obliterated and gave space for new burials. In these times, very little attention was ever bestowed on cemeteries; they were sadly neglected, allowed to grow up with bushes and briars, to be overrun with cattle, and to become one of the most unsightly places in town. To narrow the precincts of man at death, when he requires so little space at the best, was a petty economy, a thoughtless act that should never have been tolerated.

The first burial in this yard was Samuel, son of Capt. Thomas and Mary Morison, died Dec. 22, 1754, aged one year; and then burials occurred in 1757, '58, '60, '62, '64, and '66, and so on till 1834, when most of the burials ceased, upon the establishment of a new yard. These are some of the earliest burials in the Old Cemetery: Elizabeth, daughter of Alexander and Elizabeth Robbe, died Nov. 29, 1757, aged ten months; Jenny, daughter of William and Mary Ritchie, died Oct. 1, 1758, aged two years; Mary, wife of Deacon William McNee, died October, 1759, aged forty-eight years; Hannah, wife of Samuel Todd, died November, 1760, aged thirty years; Samuel Todd, died March 30, 1765, aged thirty-nine years; Agnes, wife of James Brownlee, died March 17,

1762, aged seventy-nine years; Anna, daughter of Samuel Stinson, died Jan. 7, 1764, aged two years; Robert Smith, died Jan. 14, 1766, aged eighty-five years. As for ornamentation of the early cemeteries, it was never dreamed of; all agreed to let the graveyard be the most neglected of all places; but little effusions of fancy and sometimes grim humor would eke out on the gravestones, in the grotesque figures of death and death's head, sometimes an angel with a trumpet, and the memorable inscriptions of *"Moriendum est omnibus"* and the *" Memento mori"* so common in these times. Little scraps of indifferent poetry were often applied to individuals, as much out of place as could well be imagined; for instance, a rough, quarrelsome, and perhaps intemperate, person is lauded with all the choicest and mildest of the Christian graces, the quotation being as devoid of taste as of propriety of application.

The early inscription on the stones began with the real matter of fact, " Here lies the body of ——"; the next step was, " Sacred to the memory of ——"; and later to the plain "Memory of ——"; but subsequently with the plain " Mr. ——," with the date of death and the age, and perhaps with some scrap of poetry or a Scripture quotation on the bottom of the stone. The early gravestones very scrupulously notice all the titles of the individual, and if he had none he was sure to have the plain Mr. applied to his name on his gravestone.

In proportion to the large number of burials, very few gravestones were erected, and all of these were of slate. Many families were very culpable in this respect. No doubt it was attended with a great trouble and expense in these times, and then to be served with an ordinary article at the best. But some of these stones show the durability of slate, even compared with the modern marble. They stand yet — a good, fair record, — after more than a hundred years of exposure to the elements.

VILLAGE CEMETERY. — The subject of a new graveyard began to be agitated and the matter was brought before the town at a legal meeting, April 10, 1832, by an article in the warrant (the warrant of this year not recorded on town books), "and a committee, consisting of Deacon Jonathan Smith, Hugh Miller, Moses Dodge, James Walker, John Steele, were chosen to take the subject of a new graveyard into consideration, as to the propriety of establishing one or more new ones or enlarging the old one and report at the next meeting." At the same meeting it was "Voted, to enlarge the old burying-ground under the direction and superintendence of the selectmen."

At a meeting of the town, Nov. 5, 1832 (warrant not recorded), on the third article of the warrant, "Heard the report of the committee, chosen at the last town meeting, on the subject of a graveyard, which was against enlarging the old graveyard and in favor of purchasing land of Samuel G. Smith (in the village), for a new one."

"Voted to accept the report; and that the same committee be authorized to examine said ground, and if in their opinion it is suitable, to make a purchase of the same, and the selectmen be authorized and directed to fence it in a suitable manner."

"Voted, that the same committee be directed to lay out the said ground in suitable lots, with proper space between each lot, and that the same be staked out with stone posts and numbered."

At a town meeting, April 9, 1833, on motion, "Voted to accept the report of the committee on the subject of the graveyard." At a meeting, April 8, 1834, on motion, "Voted, that the town take one acre of land on the north end of the new graveyard, and that the selectmen fence what part of it they think proper."

So the town started off in 1834 with their new cemetery, instituted for all time, of two acres of land, with an addition of an acre on the north end, which the selectmen were authorized to fence, if they thought proper, it being a side hill so abrupt and steep as never to admit of burials or any other use, only as a link in the world's continuity.

With the use of this cemetery, new ideas began to prevail here as well as elsewhere in regard to places of burial. More elegant and costly kinds of gravestones began to be common, the slate was entirely discarded and the best specimens of marble substituted. Each family now had their own lot, upon which, often, much was expended in ornamentation, in grading the grounds, in iron fences or stone curbing. Very many expensive monuments of marble and granite were erected, which, together with trees, shrubbery, etc., make this cemetery altogether a beautiful and attractive place.

PINE HILL CEMETERY. — In 1866 and 1867 it was found that all the lots in the Village Cemetery had been taken up, and those, also, belonging to families who had left town with only one or two burials on a lot had been appropriated. It became a necessity then either to enlarge the yard or to select a new one. A committee was appointed at the annual meeting, 1867, to investigate the matter, consisting of Dr. Daniel B. Cutter, Riley B. Hatch, John N. Thayer, and Albert Frost, and report at a future meeting, not exceeding three months. This committee reported at a town meeting, held May 14, 1867. After examining the Village Cemetery, they reported against an enlargement. They say that " The land on the north and east was found hilly, some parts rocky, with deep ravines where water, at times, rushed with great power; it is difficult of access, and could be used only by grading and terracing at much expense." And then on the south side, six rods only in width could be added, that would furnish seventy-two burial-lots the size of those in the present yard, and this at a great expense and serious damage to the property adjacent. Two locations were then specially examined: one on land of Benjamin Buckminster and Watson Washburn, on the east side of the river and half a mile north of the Village Cemetery; the other on land on the Bailey Hills, so called, on the west side of the river, owned by Joseph H. Ames; the latter of which the committee recommended, with two members of the same dissenting — one of the said committee and one of the board of selectmen, — who were in favor of the lot owned by Buckminster and Washburn. The report was accepted, but it was voted, " That it is the sense of this meeting that the cemetery be enlarged."

This vote was reconsidered at a subsequent meeting, May 28, 1867, and at the same meeting the following action was had : "Voted, That the selectmen be authorized to purchase for the town, for a cemetery, land owned by Messrs. Buckminster and Washburn, or either of them; and that a committee of five be chosen to confer with the selectmen, and locate a cemetery as in their judgment they may think best; but that three-fourths of said committee and selectmen shall agree upon the location." "Albert S. Scott, John Smith, Joseph Noone, Charles Wilder, M. L. Morrison, were chosen said committee." The above committee, with the selectmen, it seems, agreed upon the location of a new cemetery on land of Messrs. Buckminster and Washburn. And a committee was chosen to make all due regulations in regard to the new yard, as to the laying it out in lots, the size of the lots, the price of the same, and give names to the avenues, paths, etc., as well as determine the name of the cemetery itself. They decided that it should be known by the name of the Pine Hill Cemetery.

The cemetery contains about forty acres, and is diversified with sufficient hill and dale. It has a large growth of pine, shrubs, and other kinds of trees to give great beauty and variety to the grounds.

After its adoption as a town cemetery, by the advice of the above committee, it was dedicated on Sunday P. M., July 4, 1869, in a hollow to the left as you enter the west gate. The attendance was very large and the services interesting. Rev. George Dustan delivered the dedicatory address.*

The yard has been enclosed with a neat picket fence by the town, and three gates of entrance have been erected at three different points, to accommodate the people and give easy access to the ground.

It is now, 1875, the general burial place for the town, except for those who have lots in the Village Cemetery, and friends buried there.

---

* The first burials in this yard were made in 1868, on Lot No. Three, and Rosa A. A., daughter of John C. and Ariannah A. Richardson, who died July 15, 1868, aged one year and six months, was the first person buried in the same.

HEARSES, BURIALS. — It appears that in the early settlement of the town it was the custom, at funerals, to place the body on a bier, and to have it borne on the shoulders of the bearers to the grave, from every part of the town, and sometimes even from neighboring towns. It became a serious grievance to the community, and gave rise to the following article in the town warrant for a meeting, March 30, 1802 : —

"Article 10. To see if the town will vote to take into consideration the burden our young men bear in carrying the dead to the grave, and the utility of purchasing, at the town's expense, a horse carriage, or carriages, to carry the corpses to the grave, and also a set of suitable tools to dig the graves."

"Voted, that the selectmen purchase a suitable carriage to carry the dead to their graves."

This was the first hearse bought in town, and was continued in use until 1868, when at a meeting held March 10, 1868, it was voted "That the selectmen be authorized to purchase a hearse at an expense not exceeding six hundred dollars, and that the said sum be raised and appropriated therefor." Agreeable to the above vote, a handsome and modern hearse was purchased, which is now in use.

A sexton is now appointed by the town, whose duty it is to dig all the graves, to attend all the funerals, to convey the bodies to the graves, and take care of the cemeteries at the expense of the town.

CHAPTER XX.

TOWN HALL. — The first town-house was built in 1830.
Previous to this time all the town meetings had been held in
the meeting-house, of which the town, in this as well as in the
adjacent towns, was always part owner. A vote was passed
at a meeting of the town, Aug. 31, 1829, in which the house
was located on the Mitchell Flat, so called; the selectmen
were authorized to purchase Lot No. 5, on which John N.
Thayer now lives, for this purpose; the house to be built of
brick, of one story, and to be completed by Oct. 1, 1830.
Many of the citizens of the town, being desirous of having a
room in the town-hall for public schools and other purposes,
petitioned the town to add another story to the building. At
a subsequent meeting, June 9, 1830, it was voted not to add
another story to the town-hall, and not to permit subscribers
to add one at their own expense! It was a very mean house,
seeming to be built in the narrow, jealous spirit which originated it, and continued to be used with universal discontent,
till the town outgrew its dimensions, and required larger
quarters.

At a meeting of the town, March 13, 1860, it was voted to
build a town-house; and, agreeable to this vote, a town-hall of
large dimensions was erected during the year 1860.

It is a large building, fifty-five feet by eighty-five feet. The hall is on the second story, and the entrance is by stone steps on the north end of the building.

This floor embraces a large hall, sixty-four and a half feet by fifty-five feet, and two anterooms, an entrance to hall and rooms, besides a passage-way to the attic, which is occupied by the Odd Fellows. The basement story is divided into four apartments, which are rented for various purposes, in the south of which the town library is placed.

It is a handsome and imposing edifice, but has never proved satisfactory for the purposes for which it was intended. The hall was constructed from an imperfect and incorrect plan, and which did not accord with any acoustic principles; so that both speaking and hearing are very difficult in the same. No remedy for this great defect has yet been devised, and it has to be endured with all its inconveniences.

MONADNOCK RAILROAD. — The necessity of railroad facilities had long been felt by the business community of Peterborough, and strenuous efforts had been made from time to time to secure a railroad connected with some trunk leading to Boston, but had all hitherto failed. The barrier of the East Mountains seemed to cut off the town from all connection with the Peterborough & Shirley Railroad at Greenville; and the continuation of the Wilton Railroad round the north side of the mountain not being accomplished, and also then deemed impracticable if not impossible, from the steep grade and unfavorable ground out of East Wilton, the people in 1867 began to agitate a south route to Winchendon, Mass., to connect with the Cheshire Railroad, the present Monadnock road. With much effort this road was pushed through in the year 1870, and opened for the general business of passengers and freight, June 6, 1871.

The town, at a legal meeting held March 12, 1867, voted five *per cent.* of its valuation for a railroad from Parker's Station to the Cheshire Railroad at the State line, so called, not to be paid till the road should be completed to the Centre Village. The Monadnock, having completed their road to the village from Winchendon, claimed the gratuity as before voted, when, at a town meeting held Oct. 6, 1870, it was voted to give the Monadnock Railroad $40,000, and the remainder of the five *per cent.* when the road should be completed to Hillsboro Bridge or Parker's Depot, Goffstown. Vote, 293 affirmative, 111 negative, there being twenty-three more than two-thirds.

The road has been in successful operation since it started, and has proved a great benefit by giving an impetus to individual enterprise and to all business affairs in town.

In the summer of 1874 the Boston, Barre, & Gardner Railroad leased the Monadnock road for ninety-nine years, and have successfully operated the same since.

The following are the officers of the road: President: Jonas Livingston; Clerk and Treasurer: William G. Livingston; Directors: Jonas Livingston, Willis Phelps, O. H. Bradley, J. H. Fairbanks, Peter Upton, H. A. Blood, H. K. French.

MASONRY. — The charter of Altemont Lodge, No. 26, which was established in Dublin, was granted by the Grand Lodge of New Hampshire, June 14, Anno Lucis 5815. It went into operation, and was formally consecrated, Sept. 18, 1816, on which occasion Rev. Thomas Beede, of Wilton, preached the sermon. The meetings· continued to be held in Dublin for some years, at one of which, May 7, 1816, the following vote was passed, *viz.:* "Voted to exclude the use of ardent spirits in this lodge, and substitute therefor crackers, cheese, and cider."

The subject of a removal of the lodge to Peterborough began to be agitated at a regular communication, May 15, 1825, when Amos Heald, Peter Tuttle, Levi Fisk, Henry Whitcomb, and Oliver Heald were appointed a committee to report whether, in their opinion, the interests of Masonry would be promoted by a removal of this lodge from Dublin to Peterborough. This committee reported: "that if the lodge can be removed from Dublin to Peterborough without disturbing the harmony of the same, it will be for the good of Masonry to have it removed." The report was accepted, and measures were · taken which resulted in the removal of the lodge to Bernard Whittemore's hall in Peterborough. Few, if any, of the Masons in Dublin followed it. One after another, as appears by the records, withdrew his membership; and some never met with the lodge again.

The lodge was kept in operation in town till 1834, when in consequence of the political excitement of the times in which Masonry had become involved, its meetings were suspended until 1849. The institution of Masonry at this time became very unpopular, and the lodges generally suspended operation through the country. The charter of the Altemont Lodge, in consequence, became forfeited in 1840, but was restored in 1849.

On the renewal of the lodge, in 1849, it became very popular, and now numbers about one hundred and twenty members, embracing some of our best citizens. It has recently taken possession of the beautiful and spacious hall over the Peterborough Savings Bank, which it now occupies. The Peterborough Royal Arch Chapter, No. 12, holds its meetings in the same hall.

INDEPENDENT ORDER OF ODD FELLOWS. — On the petition of Edwin Steele, John Parker, A. P. Morrison, Levi Cross, and J. H. Webber, a charter was granted by the Grand Lodge of New Hampshire, in February, 1846, to be located in Peterborough, and to be known as Peterborough Lodge, No. 15, of the Independent Order of Odd Fellows.

The members first initiated, when it was instituted into working order, the 18th of Feb., 1846, were Timothy K. Ames, Avery H. Hayward, James G. White, Nathan Whitney, Granville P. Felt, David F. Hall, Henry S. Carter, Samuel Jaquith, Hosea Pierce, and George Pritchard.

They held their meetings for nineteen years in the hall known as the Goodridge Hall, in the attic of the store formerly occupied by Samuel Smith, till 1864, when, jointly with the Masons, they leased the new hall fitted up in the Town Hall Building, where they still continue to hold their meetings, while the Masons have removed to the new hall in the Savings Bank Building.

Also with this order there exists a Rebekah Degree Lodge, No. 5, of Independent Order of Odd Fellows, confined to wives of Odd Fellows. "The degree of Rebekah" (says our informant, J. G. White, Esq.), "which has been in operation since January, 1852, has already won the approval and admiration of the fraternity. Thousands of ladies, the wives of Odd Fellows, have already availed themselves of its privileges, and thousands more are ready to receive them. It is chaste, beautiful, and admirably adapted to the object it designs to effect. Schuyler Colfax, the author of this new and popular degree, deserves and has received the sincere thanks of the fraternity for this ornament to the building which our fathers framed. The order is now in a flourishing condition."

In 1867, thirty of the younger members of Peterborough Lodge, No. 15, obligated themselves to revive and sustain the Encampment, No. 6, which had become extinct, provided seven patriarchs of the said order could be found who had been honorably discharged, who should petition for the restoration of the charter and property of said encampment. The following are the names of the petitioners, viz.: James G. White, John H. Webber, Granville P. Felt, Joseph Noone, Ira A. Spofford, Nathan Whitney, and D. F. Hall. The Most Worthy Grand Patriarch granted this request by dispensation. This encampment was instituted, Sept. 4, 1867, the officers were chosen and installed, and the lodge started off in good working order. To the present time, October, 1875, there have been admitted to the encampment sixty-four members. The present number is sixty. This encampment pays no benefits. It is at the present time in a prosperous condition.

Peterborough Lodge, No. 15, is in a flourishing state, and has admitted, during its thirty years of existence, by initiation, two hundred and forty-one members. The largest number of contributing members has been one hundred and fifty-three; the present number is one hundred and thirty-four.

A large number have withdrawn by card to join other lodges, a few have retired from disaffection, and quite a number have been suspended; four have been expelled, twelve have died, and seventy-seven have been rejected.

The lodge has paid, since it went into operation, for benefits, burying the dead, and for charitable purposes, $4,350; and
at the end of thirty years, the funds of the lodge amounted to
$5,000, with all its fixtures in good condition.

This institution is supported by the weekly dues of each
of its members, and confers upon them when sick a certain allowance per week during their illness. It exercises a
supervision over the conduct of all its members, especially
the younger part; it admits of no immorality or vicious conduct, or any crime amenable to the laws, but inculcates the
highest principles of morality and Christian benevolence.

It looks after the sick of the order, having a special committee for this purpose always appointed and in force, whose
duty it is to see if any one of the brethren is sick, and if needy
to help him, and provide watchers, or any other aid needed
by his family. It pays thirty dollars for burial expenses to
the family of every deceased brother, and fifteen dollars to
every brother losing his wife. It has a charitable and orphans'
fund, from which it dispenses to those of this class needing aid.

It has proved a useful and efficient aid to society in this
place, exercising a helpful hand to a large class of its members; in guarding the community from vice, by raising the
tone of public morals; in sustaining and taking care of the
sick; and in the prevention of suffering and destitution, by
its charities and services.

BANKS. — The Peterborough State Bank, with a capital of
$50,000, went into operation, Jan. 1, 1855; A. C. Cochran,
President, and Charles G. Cheney, Cashier. Mr. Cheney resigned, May 16, 1862, and William G. Livingston was elected
to fill the vacancy.

This bank closed its operations, May 27, 1865, when the
First National Bank of Peterborough was established, with a
capital of $100,000. The office of president becoming vacant
by the death of A. C. Cochran, Esq., June 27, 1865, Frederick Livingston was elected to fill the same, which office he
still holds. William G. Livingston resigned as cashier, Aug.
1, 1867, and Albert S. Scott was elected in his place. Mr.

Scott held the office till April 24, 1871, when he resigned, and was succeeded by the present cashier, Charles P. Richardson.

The bank was removed from the Granite Block, June, 1875, to the southern apartment, on the lower floor of the Peterborough Savings Bank, which has been rented for a series of years.

List of Directors for 1876: Frederick Livingston, Thomas Little, Amos Whittemore, Jonas Livingston, Henry K. French, David Hunt, William G. Livingston.

PETERBOROUGH SAVINGS BANK. — This bank was incorporated in 1847. It was organized in 1859, by the choice of John H. Steele, William Follansbee, Timothy K. Ames, Whitcomb French, James Scott, Albert Smith, Daniel B. Cutter, Samuel Nay, Abraham P. Morrison, Abial Sawyer, Norton Hunt, and Samuel Adams, as a board of trustees.

John H. Steele was chosen president and George A. Ramsdell secretary and treasurer. Jan. 12, 1863, John H. Steele resigned his position as president and trustee, and William Follansbee was chosen president of the board. George A. Ramsdell resigned as treasurer, April 30, 1864, and Riley B. Hatch was elected to fill the vacancy. The office of president becoming vacant by the death of Dr. William Follansbee, Dr. Albert Smith was elected to this office, July 6, 1867, which office he still holds.

The bank buildings of the Peterborough Savings Bank were erected during the season of 1870, and the first meeting for business was held in the new rooms, Feb. 20, 1871. R. B. Hatch resigned the office of treasurer, April 5, 1873, and Mortier L. Morrison was elected to fill the vacancy. He entered upon the duties of secretary and treasurer, April 17, 1873, and still holds the office.

Whole amount due depositors, Jan. 1, 1876, $611,676.76. Board of Trustees elected January, 1876: Albert Smith, James Scott, Whitcomb French, Norton Hunt, Daniel B. Cutter, Silas Sawyer, Thomas Little, Ebenezer Jones, Fred-

30

erick Livingston, Jonas Livingston, Andrew A. Farnsworth, Albert Sawyer, Albert S. Scott.

Standing Committee on Investments : James Scott, Daniel B. Cutter, Ebenezer Jones.

Auditors: Albert Smith, Thomas Little.

NEWSPAPERS. — The first newspaper in town was published by William P. and John S. Dunbar, and commenced in the last part of 1829, which was called the *Hillsboro Republican and New Hampshire Clarion.* It was edited by Rev. Elijah Dunbar. It was printed in the building near the bridge, on Main Street, afterwards known as Joel Brown's store. It had a short duration, for it closed, April 29, 1831, with the ninth number of its second volume.

The second paper, a little sheet in pamphlet form, called the Peterborough *Messenger,* was published by Samuel P. Brown, in the summer of 1847, and discontinued after about ten months.

The first number of the Contoocook *Transcript,* published by Miller and Scott (John R. Miller and Kendall C. Scott), was issued, June 2, 1849, with four hundred subscribers. It has been continued uninterruptedly to this time, the present proprietors having early changed the name to that of *The Peterboro' Transcript,* by which it is now known.

During the first two years of its publication, for a portion of the time, it was edited by Albert S. Scott, Esq., and they were also indebted, for many valuable contributions, to the students of Harvard College.

At the expiration of two years, the subscription list, in the meantime, having been doubled, the paper passed into the hands of K. C. Scott. Elias Cheney was the next proprietor, who sold out to Charles Scott, and by him it was again sold to K. C. Scott, and after some years passed into the hands of the present proprietors, Farnum & Scott.

TEMPERANCE. — This town has never been backward in this great enterprise. Though much good has been accomplished by the various efforts made in its behalf by the efficient organizations of the Sons of Temperance, the Good Templars, etc., yet the cause progresses slowly, and much remains to be done to inculcate the true principles of sobriety and temperance. Perhaps it may be said with truth, that there is now more total abstinence from intoxicating drinks among the young people than ever before; but the evil is yet great, and the remedy seems as yet unknown.

CASUALTIES. — Aug. 16, 1771, Anna, daughter of Maj. Robert and Mary Wilson, was killed by the falling of a log off a fence.

Dec. 31, 1795, Deacon Robert Smith, died in consequence of a slight wound of his knee, aged forty-three years.

June 25, 1793, Jabez, son of John Field, drowned in a tan-vat, aged four years.

May 19, 1801, Israel, son of John Leathers, and brother to John and Nathan Leathers, was killed by falling from a tree, aged twelve years.

June 29, 1801, Samuel McCoy, son of William McCoy, killed by the kick of a horse, aged thirty-four years.

Dec. 24, 1801, funeral of John Gray, who died instantly, just after sunset, by falling from the staging of Samuel Smith's new saw-mill, aged forty-six years. [Church Records.]

January, 1810, Nathan Sanders, drowned in the mill-pond near the great bridge, a son of Philip Sanders and wife, who were called the "King and Queen." Thomas Baker had taken the boy to bring up to the trade of paper-making, and when out this evening, with a party sliding on the pond, he slipped into an air-hole and was drowned, aged ten years.

June 15, 1810, Ebenezer Hadley, died in consequence of being thrown from his horse and one foot remaining in stirrup, by which he was dragged some distance on the ground, and so injured that he died the next day, aged fifty-nine years.

Jan. 13, 1812, Joseph, son of Capt. William Wilson, scalded to death by falling into hot water, aged two years.

March 27, 1812, Daniel Kimball, killed by being thrown from a horse, aged thirty-four years.

Jan. 13, 1813, a child of Eli Hunt's, scalded to death, aged two and a half years.

April 8, 1814, Lieut. Ephraim Smith, called "Cady Smith," was drowned in the Cold Brook just beyond Mr. Mears', the water but a few inches deep, aged seventy-five years.

June 17, 1816, Samuel Edes, Jr., fell from a barn, now owned by Charles McCoy, while raising, and instantly killed, aged forty-one years, three months.

Sept. 24, 1815, Nathan Smith, lately from Washington, committed suicide by cutting his throat.

Oct. 1, 1818, Thomas White, Jr., by kick of a horse, aged twenty-three years.

Aug. 7, 1821, John Smith, Esq., was instantly killed by falling from a load of hay in the meadow near the Samuel White place, aged sixty-seven years.

Oct. 16, 1822, Nathan Watts, blown up in a well in Dublin, aged thirty-five years.

May 28, 1824, Charles, son of William Smith, mortally wounded by a cart-wheel running over his head, aged seven years.

Sept. 25, 1824, Daniel Gibbs, the mail-carrier, mortally injured so that he died in a few hours, by being thrown out of his wagon and off the great bridge upon the rocks below, aged seventy-three years.

Dec. 25, 1824, David Scott, killed by a falling tree, aged eighteen years.

Dec. 20, 1825, Sarah, daughter of Jonathan Bowers, killed by accidentally falling down the cellar stairs, aged four years.

March 21, 1825, Noah Jackman, killed by the explosion of a rock, aged twenty-one years.

Dec. 28, 1826, Nancy, daughter of Deacon Samuel Maynard, scalded.

July 10, 1828, John Morison, son of John Morison, drowned in the Nubanusit River, in meadow above the Union Factories, aged thirty-one years.

Dec. 21, 1828, John Haywood, of Dublin, killed at the Daniel Robbe hill, by being thrown from his wagon and the wheels passing over his head, aged forty-three years.

April 17, 1829, Jonathan Mussey, son of Dr. John Mussey, accidentally shot himself, aged seventeen years.

April 8, 1832, B. Morse, suicide, aged twenty-seven years.

Jan. 31, 1833, R. W. Stebbins, drowned at the great bridge during a great freshet, body not recovered till the next June.

June 30, 1833, Luther, son of Jonathan Bowers, killed by the explosion of powder, aged fourteen years, seven months.

June 11, 1837, Rebecca Brackett, daughter of Samuel Brackett, committed suicide by hanging, aged fifty-four years.

Dec. 7, 1838, Jefferson Nay, suddenly, from a large infusion of alcohol, aged thirty-one years.

May 19, 1839, son of Paul Boyce, drank some strong ley and lived twenty-three hours, aged one year, nine months.

Sept. 30, 1839, son of —— Crawford, drowned at West Peterborough, aged five years.

March 14, 1841, Gilman Miller, shot himself.

June 21, 1841, Alfred and Albert, sons of Jonathan Bowers, drowned in the Nubanusit, aged six years, eleven months. .

July 12, 1844, Dexter Carley, drowned in North Factory pond, aged thirty-nine years.

April 27, 1845, Abby, daughter of Samuel Converse, drowned, aged two years.

Oct. 2, 1846, Charles Brackett, son of Josiah Brackett, killed at Waltham Factory, aged twenty-three years.

June 27, 1847, William, son of William D. Cogswell, drowned, aged eighteen years.

August, 1848, Joel B., son of D. B. Willoughby, drowned while bathing above the Bell Factory, aged eleven years.

June 2, 1838, Hannah Jane, daughter of John Chapman, killed by a window-sash falling upon her neck in her attempt to get into a school-house in Jaffrey, the blocking under her feet falling away and leaving her hung by the neck, aged twelve years, five months.

Dec. 4, 1851, Samuel Clark, hung himself, hereditary insanity.

Feb. 17, 1851, Charles F., son of Amasa Alexander, drowned by being swept over the dam at Granville P. Felt's shop, on a piece of ice on which he was standing, which broke off un-expectedly. His body was not recovered for six weeks, when it was found near the pine trees opposite to the Village Cemetery, aged fifteen years, seven months.

Aug. 13, 1862, Sophronia, wife of Col. Charles Scott, and Katie, wife of Maj. John Cummings, drowned by a collision of the steamboats "West Point" and "George Peabody," on the Potomac River.

Oct. 27, 1875, La Forrest Saunders, this day, was caught under the cars near the car-house, and both of his legs were broken and crushed as well as his left arm. He survived the accident four hours, aged fifteen years.

THE TOWN CLOCK. — The Town Clock was purchased and erected in 1856. The ladies of the town, determining that we should no longer be without this useful adjunct to our village, organized and carried through successfully "a clock festival," so called, at the upper hall in this village, Feb. 14, 1856, from which they realized four hundred dollars for this purpose. Another hundred was raised by subscription, the clock costing about five hundred dollars. They employed Mr. David Smiley, jeweller, as their agent to select, purchase, and erect as good a town clock as could be procured. In the discharge of his trust, he rendered a large amount of gratuitous services in the business, to the acceptance of all.

The clock was purchased of Howard & Davis, of Boston, in 1856, and erected in the tower of the Congregational Church the same year. It has proved an excellent time-keeper, and after a trial of nineteen years is now as good as ever. It has grown to be one of the indispensable things in our village. When the clock had been put in good running order, the ladies presented it to the town, and it was accepted by the following vote, March 10, 1857 : "Voted, That the town accept the clock presented by the ladies, and take charge of the same." Mr. Smiley has been employed to take charge of it since its erection.

FIRE-ENGINE. — Previous to 1856 there had been very inadequate means to extinguish fires in town. The only means were a large fire-engine belonging to and attached to the Phœnix Factory, being placed in a small building on the west side of the same, but from its weight incapable of being transported to any other place, and a smaller one belonging to the Union Manufacturing Co.; but these afforded very little security to the property of the town. Many individuals, feeling their great insecurity from fire, subscribed about $700 for a fire-engine, which induced the town to have the following action, May 3, 1856; "Voted, That the town purchase a fire-engine and the necessary apparatus for the extinguishment of fires."

"Voted, To raise eight hundred dollars for a fire-engine and apparatus."

"Voted, To accept the sums raised by subscription for the same." Chose John H. Steele, Thomas Little, and Granville P. Felt a committee to purchase the same.

In 1874, the town voted, for the security of their property, to lay down water-pipes from the Phœnix Factory to the Town-Hall, which pipes were to be connected with the force-pump of the factory. Individuals who owned property on Main Street raised by subscription between $1100 and $1200, to continue the same through the street, to the great bridge. The work was completed late in the fall of this year, tried, and found to be in perfect order.

In less than two weeks after the pipes were laid it was brought to a successful trial. A room in Henry K. French's building, just over the book-store, having been set on fire by an incendiary, at five different places, with kindlings, so as to insure a rapid fire, the water-works were brought into full play upon the same, in a very short time, and quickly extinguished the same, with but little loss to the building.

SURPLUS REVENUE. — During the administration of Andrew Jackson, President of the United States, a large amount of the revenues of the government was deposited with the several States, to be repaid when called for, and in the distribution to New Hampshire, Peterborough received her moiety of the State division.   An agent, Timothy K. Ames, was chosen by the town to receive their share, and the town was pledged, agreeable to an act of the Legislature, for the safe keeping and repayment of the same, if required to be returned.   The whole amount received in three several instalments, including interest, amounted to $5,695.38, all of which was appropriated to the payment of the Poor Farm and stocking the same for running order.

THE OSGOOD GRATUITY. — At a legal meeting of the town held March 10, 1868, "Voted, That the town accept the legacy bequeathed by the late Isaac P. Osgood, of Boston (son of the late Dr. Kendall Osgood), upon the conditions specified in his late will and testament, and that the selectmen be authorized to receive and receipt for the same."

The following is the article alluded to in the will: —

"I give to the selectmen, for the time being, of my native town of Peterborough, in the State of New Hampshire, one thousand dollars, to be by them invested in some safe security, bearing an annual interest of six *per cent.*, the annual income thereof to be by them distributed annually to such paupers of the town as they may judge to be worthy of such charity."

POST-OFFICE. - We suppose there were no postal facilities in town prior to the establishment of a post-office, and the appointment of John Smith, P. M., Oct. 1, 1795.   Whether there were any post-offices in any of the neighboring towns, by which letters were sent to the inhabitants of Peterborough, we have no means of knowing.   Postal facilities during the Revolution and the subsequent years, to the establishment of the Federal Constitution, 1789, must have been very meagre, if any really existed.   It is probable that all the correspondence of that day, which was very small, must have been done through private means.   The following are the names of all the postmasters who have held office in town: —

John Smith,　　1st Postmaster, appointed 1st of October, 1795
Samuel Smith,　　2d　　"　　"　　1st of July,　　1797

Jonathan Smith,	3d Postmaster appointed	15th of June,	1813
Samuel Smith,	4th " "	4th of January,	1817
Riley Goodridge,	5th " "	29th of October,	1833
Samuel Gates,	6th " "	10th of Febru'y,	1841
Henry Steele,	7th " "	15th of May,	1854
Miss S. M. Gates,	8th " "	1st of February,	1861
John R. Miller,	9th " "	17th of August,	1861

which office he now holds.

The mail was first carried from Brattleboro to Portsmouth once a week, by a Mr. Balch. This mail-route was among those first established in the State, under the Federal Constitution of 1789. We are uncertain as to the precise time that William Thayer succeeded Mr. Balch; but he continued to carry the mail till 1807, when he died suddenly, at Amherst, from an injury received in an innocent scuffle with one of his friends. Daniel Gibbs was the next mail-carrier, and continued to follow the business till his death in 1824, when he was accidentally thrown out of his wagon at the great bridge in the village, then under repair, and fatally injured. For many years he carried the mail on horseback, as his predecessors had done before him, till the one-horse wagons came into use. He at once adopted this vehicle, as more convenient for his mail-matter, and as enabling him occasionally to carry a passenger on his route. Asa Gibbs, his son, succeeded him, and for a few years carried the mail in a two-horse carriage, till the establishment of stages. The first mail-coach from Exeter to Brattleboro commenced running July 14, 1828, three times a week. It was first started and run by George W. Senter and I. N. Cuningham. These facilities were soon so increased as to have a daily mail from Boston, and a stage up and down each day through our village. This continued till the advent of railroad facilities in 1871.

POPULATION.—The first census of Peterborough was made in 1767, as follows:—

Unmarried men from 16 to 60,   .   .   33
Married men, ...   64
Boys 16 and under, ...   113
Men 66 and above, ...   13
Females unmarried, ...   149
Females married, ...   68
Male slaves, ...   01
Female slaves, ...   00
Widows, ...   02
                                                                ———
                                                                443

A census was taken again in 1775 as follows:—

Males under 16, ...   135
     "   from 16 to 50, ...   77
     "   above 50, ...   23
Persons gone to the army,   .   .   .   25
All females, ...   277
Negroes and slaves for life,   .   .   .   08
                                                                ———
                                                                545

We have no farther enumeration till the Constitution had been adopted, and the first census taken, in 1790.

In 1790 the population of Peterborough was,   861
  " 1800   "   "   1,333
  " 1810   "   "   1,537
  " 1820   "   "   1,500
  " 1830   "   "   1,983
  " 1840   "   "   2,163
  " 1850   "   "   2,222
  " 1860   "   "   2,265
  " 1870   "   "   2,228

It will be seen by the above, that the population of Peterborough has remained nearly stationary for the last forty years. The manufacturing interests have increased while the agricultural have greatly diminished. Many farms are so

run out, by the deterioration of the land and expense of cultivation, that they have already been abandoned, and many
more will be when the houses on the same become tenantless.
We know not how these lands are to be revived, as long as
the agricultural products of the West can be brought to us by
a cheap transportation, so as to undersell our products raised
on the hard soil and by the dear labor of New England.

The population on all the old farms in town is constantly
decreasing, while that of the villages scarcely increases in the
same proportion.

In the Centennial Address of 1839, the emigrants from
Peterborough, scattered through all the various parts of our
country, were estimated at four hundred and eighty. Mr.
W. S. Treadwell has, for a number of years, been carefully
engaged in ascertaining the number of emigrants since that
time, and has found it to be nine hundred and sixteen.

CHAPTER XXI.

. CONCLUSION.

Difficulties of the Work. — Changes in Town. — Number of Families
Left or Extinct. — Present Descendants. — Comparative Merits of
the Descendants with their Ancestors. — Character of the Adopted
Citizens. — Number and Character of the Professional Men.

This work is now completed, and no one more than myself
can feel how inadequately it has been done. I was too late
on the stage for the undertaking; and it should have been a
life work, rather than the eking out of the end of a hard professional life. The actors of these early times have passed
away, with no record left; their immediate descendants have
all disappeared, equally recordless, and the present generation
are far advanced in age, with little ability to aid the historian.
They were all too indifferent to dates, and too vague in their
relations, to be reliable without farther and accurate research.
It is true, nowadays, that very little importance is to be
attached to tradition, the facilities for writing and printing
having become so numerous and easy that no one thinks it
necessary to charge his memory with the details of events
that may be so well expressed and preserved in this manner.
Those men, with their great memories and with their full
store of facts, having all passed away before I began my
labors, I have had to grope my way as best I could, coming
far short of what I desired, or what should have justly been
expected in this work.

The changes in town have been very great. Many of the
families, large and influential a century ago, have now all left

town, and many of them have become extinct; while many others have become reduced to a very few individuals.

It is believed that, of the following families, there is not now in town a single descendant bearing the family name: Cuningham, Swan, Alld, Wallace, Stinson, Gordon, Mitchell, Todd, Stuart, Duncan, Ferguson, Milliken, Taylor, Powers, Evans, Young, Huston, Wiley, Ballard, McCloud, Hammill, Chubbuc, Finch, Crane, Loring, Holmes, Hale, Holt, Parker, Penniman, Allison, Haggett, Barker, Chapman, Mussey, Hugh Wilson, Whittemore.

The names of the descendants of the first settlers and of the early inhabitants of the town, which follow, in a few instances include a considerable race left, but many of them are reduced to a very small number:—

Robbe, Scott, Smith, Morison, Steele, Moore, Treadwell, McCoy, Hovey, Smiley, Diamond, Brackett, Ritchie, Upton, Laws, Leathers, White, Wilson, Field, Thayer, Hunt, Blair, Weston, Howe, Little, Hadley, Nay, Pierce, Carter, Barber, Puffer, Gowing, Miller, Felt, Davison, Turner, Spring, Gray, Porter, Grimes. The changes of residences, and of families from the old homesteads, have been very great; but very few places remain in the hands of the descendants of the early settlers.

The farms now owned by the descendants of the first settlers, or of those who took up their farms in a wild state, are as follows:—

The farms of Nathaniel H. Moore, Thomas Davison, John Field (occupied by his daughter's family), A. A. Farnsworth, James Wilson, Brackett heirs, Sally Spring, heirs of I. D. White, J. S. Diamond, Stephen D. Robbe, Silas Barber, Alvah Puffer, William Hadley, Frank Smiley, James Scott.

I think it may be within the truth to say that between one-fifth and one-sixth only of the inhabitants of to-day are the descendants of the early settlers and early residents of the town. In looking over the town, through the agricultural, mechanical, mercantile, and professional part of the community, they all seem new men. Where are the descendants? They have either died out, or gone to new homes; and we hope they have infused their good principles, learned and imbibed here, into other communities. The adopted citizens, who have been here longer or shorter periods, are good inhabitants, and do much to sustain the high character of the town for talent and probity. They are superior to the average of other communities for talent and business capacity, and will do their part faithfully in sustaining the character of this ancient town. They know its pioneers only through history; but they are proud of such an inheritance, — proud of the men who left, so unmistakably, the impress of their virtues upon the town.

We are so accustomed to laud our ancestors, that we are wont to attribute to them, besides their own good qualities, others which they did not possess. They were, undoubtedly, an extraordinary race of men; but, with all their excellences they had large failings.

They were unlearned men, with strong and vigorous intellects, with large common-sense, with a keen observation, and an inquisitive turn of mind, so they could learn orally what it is so hard for us to acquire by long discipline and teaching. They could listen well, if a man had anything to say worth hearing. Their judgment and sagacity easily detected all shams, so no one could gain a hearing who was not worthy. With books they had little to do except the Bible; and they drew from this, as from a great storehouse, in all the exigencies of life.

Many persons are in the habit of extolling the ancestors as vastly superior to their descendants. To this I can give no assent. In the course of my investigations, I have carefully looked through all the branches of the descendants down to the present time; and am more and more satisfied that they are in every way worthy of their parentage, and that there has been no deterioration, but rather an improvement, upon the whole.

In comparing the talents and virtues of the fathers with their children, we must take into the account the different spheres in which they were placed. The qualities and notions of these much-lauded men would be as much out of place at the present time as that of their children would have been in their day.

The times then required just such men, sagacious, honest, faithful, sincere, and upright, devoid alike of all the graces and refinements of modern society. They were clothed coarsely and lived upon a plain diet, free from all the modern luxuries. More independent men were never known; they felt themselves in their homespun the equals of any of God's creation. A few of them, as is always the case, towered above the rest, but there was, beside, much material that did little honor to the settlement. We do injustice to ourselves as well as to the truth, when we assume that all our ancestors were of this highest type of manhood. The same diversity existed then as now. There were then, as now, the good; bad, and indifferent.

It is often asked what we have to put against such men? I say a worthy list of descendants, such a list as we may well be proud of. In many families there has been a decided advance in their descendants. Many worthy men have done honor to the town, while their parents were little respected. They must have grown up under the influences that surrounded all our youth a century ago, and in this way they acquired correct principles and virtuous habits which were little known or inculcated at the paternal hearth.

This was true of these men, but how is it with the descendants of the best and most influential families? Have they sustained the characters of their fathers? I think they have. Not that they have exhibited the same kind of talent; that would be preposterous to expect, and such qualities now are not required.

The first settlers required peculiar qualifications for the work they had undertaken. They needed shrewdness, sagacity, and common-sense. They needed hardihood, boldness, and courage, for all the exigencies and trials of frontier life. High culture and refinement would have been entirely out of place, and would have been regarded as signs of effeminacy. The hardier virtues flourished, and admirably fitted the men for the peculiar duties of their times. At a later period, a new order of talent was required; men no longer became prominent by mere physical prowess, or by the robust and hardy endurance of such dangers and perils as was required in the early settlement.   In the new generation came up the enjoyment of greater advantages in education (the town had fifty college graduates to 1876), of more comfortable modes of living, of much improved dwellings, of many luxuries and indulgences not known before, of books, newspapers, and all the refining methods of a higher civilization. Did they deteriorate under these influences ? The age imposed upon them duties requiring a different order of talents, and in the discharge of their duties, they showed themselves as competent and able as their fathers had ever been.

We should not be considered as disparaging the talents and virtues of our ancestors by saying, that the great distance in time between them and us magnifies their good qualities, so that they appear to the best advantage, and that the memory of their virtues and their excellences has been preserved, while the foibles and deficiencies of their lives are little known.

I wish briefly to enumerate the professional men the town has sent forth. It has furnished some fifteen or sixteen clergymen, all of them respectable and useful men, one of them president of a college, and two of them honored with the title of D. D.

A large number of lawyers, about thirty, have gone forth. They proved men of ability and knowledge, and some of them became very eminent in their profession.   Two of them have held the highest judicial office in the State, and one held the same office in another State; some of them have been Representatives in Congress, and one has been Governor of the State. It has furnished about twenty physicians, many of them very efficient men, who have been eminent and useful in the sphere of their practice, three of this number having held the important offices of medical professors in the New Hampshire and Ohio Medical Colleges, and two of them honored with the highest literary title, of LL. D.

We have had, besides these professional men, two Governors from our town, and those who have held other responsible offices in the general and State government.

We have never lacked good material, at any time, for our town offices, the business of which has always been efficiently and correctly done.

Our present home talent is not to be disregarded, nor will it suffer in comparison with that of a century ago. "*Justitia fiat, cælum ruat.*"

We end our record in this Centennial year with many forebodings for the future, but we trust that with the new access of railroad facilities, our beloved and ancient town is not destined to sink into insignificance. May the future historian of Peterborough find clearer fields before him, and a better record of facts to resort to, and so make a more satisfactory history than this can be. We shall be content to have our book thrust aside, when it shall be superseded by a better one.

BUSINESS DIRECTORY OF PETERBOROUGH,

1876.

BANKS. — First National Bank of Peterborough, Savings Bank Building: Frederick Livingston, President; C. P. Richardson, Cashier. Peterborough Savings Bank: Albert Smith, President; M. L. Morrison, Treasurer.

DRY GOODS, GROCERIES, AND FURNITURE. — William G. Livingston, Grove Street; Sylvester Tenney, corner Main and Summer Streets; Asa Davis, Main Street; J. Fisher, West Peterborough; Smith Brothers, Tarbell's Block.

MILLINERY AND FANCY GOODS. — Mrs. F. A. Tracy, Grove Street; Mrs. T. D. Winch, Town Hall; New York Store, Brennan's Block; Miss Evleth & Co., French's Block.

BOOKS AND STATIONERY. — John H. Steele, French's Hotel Block; Miss M. J. Nichols, Town Hall.

ICE DEALER. — A. L. Shattuck, East Street.

MILKMEN. — D. Osborn, Concord Street; J. M. Collins, Union Street; Holt & Hunter, South Peterborough; G. F. Livingston, Grove Street.

LIVERY STABLES. — H. K. French, Main Street; John Rourke, Depot Street; M. A. Smith, Union Street.

TEAMING AND JOBBING. — Townsend & Lovejoy, Main Street; A. T. Hovey, Concord Street.

MEATS AND PROVISIONS. — C. F. & G. S. Peavey, Main Street; Eaton & Shedd, High Street; W. F. Pratt, Main Street.

FISH MARKET. — E. Goldthwait, Main Street; C. Silver, Union Street.

BAKERY. — George H. Longley, Proprietor, Main Street.

REFRESHMENT ROOMS. — E. H. Pierce, Brennan's Block.

WATCHES AND JEWELRY. — A. F. Grimes, Dell M. Nichols, Main Street; F. H. Coffin, Grove Street.

DRUGS AND MEDICINES. — John R. Miller, Main Street; George L. Forbush, Grove Street.

HARNESSES AND CARRIAGE UPHOLSTERY. — E. W. McEntosh, Main Street; G. W. Ames, North Peterborough; Frank Steele (Upholstery), Concord Street.

PAINTERS. — Lorenzo Holt (Carriage), Grove Street; L. P. Wilson (House), Grove Street.

CARRIAGE-MAKERS AND WHEELWRIGHTS. — Geo. W. Farrar, Grove Street; John D. Diamond, East Peterborough.

STONE MASONS. — Asa Davis, Pine Street; John N. Thayer, Concord Street; J. W. Macomber, South Peterborough; Dennis O'Keefe, Granite Street; Thomas Scott, High Street.

BRICK MASONS. — G. W. Marden, Concord Street; William Lawrence, North Peterborough; Amasa Alexander, Union Street; P. McLaughlin, West Peterborough.

TIN-WARE, &c. — Augustus Fuller, Main Street; Nichols Brothers, Main Street.

FLOUR AND GRAIN. — J. F. Noone, Stone Grist-mill, Main Street.

HATS, CAPS, AND CLOTHING STORE. — Marshall Nay, Grove Street; John Wilder & Co., corner Main and Grove Streets.

TAILORS. — H. H. Templeton, Grove Street; Osgood & Martin, Main Street.

SHOE STORES. — F. S. Bullard & Son, W. E. Baker, W. E. Dadman, Main Street.

MARBLE WORKS. — H. Brennan, Main Street; Spline & Wallace, Pine Street.

BLACKSMITHS. — G. W. Farrar, Grove Street; E. A. Robbins, Depot Street.

PAPER MANUFACTURING. — Nay & Adams, West Peterborough; J. J. Barker, West Peterborough.

CARPENTERS. — C. E. Jaquith, Grove Street; C. H. Longley, Union Street; George B. Priest, Concord Street; A. Abbot Forbush, Union Street; Ira Forbush, Union Street; Jeremiah Pritchard, Vine Street.

HOTELS. — H. K. French, French's Hotel, Main Street; M. A. Smith, St. James Hotel, Union Street.

LAWYERS. — Scott & Clark, Counsellors of Law and Insurance Agents, Grove Street; Ezra M. Smith, Counsellor of Law, Main and Grove Streets; D. W. White, Counsellor of Law, Main Street.

PHYSICIANS. — D. B. Cutter, M. D., Main Street; Albert Smith, M. D., Concord Street; John H. Cutler, M. D., Main Street; W. D. Chase, M. D., Concord Street.

CLERGYMEN. — Rev. George Dustan, Union Congregational; Rev. A. W. Jackson, Congregational; Rev. C. F. Myers, Baptist; Rev. J. H. Hilman, Methodist; Rev. Edmund Buckle, St. Peter's, Catholic.

MILITARY. — Cheney Guards, John D. Diamond, Captain, thirty-two men; Section B., N. H. Battery, thirty men, Lieut. A. A. Forbush; Co. A., 1st Reg. N. H. Cavalry, L. P. Wilson, Captain, sixty mounted men; D. M. White, Major 2d N. H. Reg.; W. H. Greenwood, Major 1st N. H. Reg.

PETERBOROUGH CORNET BAND. — C. E. White, Leader; W. E. Davis, Treasurer; E. A. Towne, Clerk.

COTTON FACTORIES. — Phœnix Corporation, Jonas Livingston, Superintendent; Union Manufacturing Co., J. S. Moody, Superintendent, West Peterborough; Peterborough Manufacturing Co., Main Street, E. B. Hill, Superintendent.

WOOLLEN MILL. — Joseph Noone's Sons, South Peterborough; R. H. Noone, Superintendent.

MISCELLANEOUS. — News and Telegraph Office, J. H. Steele, French's Hotel Block; United States and Canada Express, H. K. French, French's Hotel Block; Postmaster, John R. Miller, Town Hall; Postmaster, Justin Fisher, West Peterborough; Surgeon Dentists, S. N. Porter, Main Street; C. H. Haywood, Main Street; Peterborough *Transcript*, Farnum & Scott, Main Street; Undertaker, E. O. Willey, Grove Street; Hair-Dressing, &c., J. Gil. Fish, Main Street; Photographs, George H. Scripture, Main Street; Florist, F. F. Myrick, Grove Street; Organs and Pianos, J. M. Bruce, Grove Street; Auctioneers, Vose & Scott, Concord Street; Piano-Stool Manufactory, Joshua Briggs, Union Street; Barometers and Thermometers, Charles Wilder, North Peterborough; Machine-Shop and Foundry, and Manufactory of People's Pumps, Granville P. Felt, Elm Street; Truss Manufactory, Howe & Carter, Main Street; Basket Manufactory, Amzi Childs, Main Street.

STREETS AND AVENUES.

Concord Street, from Main Street, north.

Central	"	" Vale, south.
Depot	"	" Main, south, to School.
Elm	"	" Union, south-west.
Factory	"	" Winter, east.
Granite	"	" Pine, south.
Grove	"	" Main, south.
High	"	" Main, north-east.
Laurel	"	" Grove, west.
Main	"	" Concord, north-west, to Union.
Pine	"	" Main, south-east.
Phœnix Avenue,	"	Grove, west.
Prospect Street,	"	Union, north-west.
Summer	"	" Main, north.
School	"	" Grove, to Depot.
Union	"	" Main, north-west, to West Peterborough.
Vale	"	" Grove, to Winter.
Vine	"	" Main, east.
Winter	"	" Elm, south.

John H. Morison

AN ADDRESS

DELIVERED AT THE

CENTENNIAL CELEBRATION IN PETERBOROUGH, N. H.,

OCTOBER 24th, 1839.

By JOHN HOPKINS MORISON.

ONE hundred years ago this whole valley, from mountain to mountain, from the extreme north to the extreme southern limit, was one unbroken forest. The light soil upon the banks of the Contoocook was covered with huge and lofty pines, while the rocky hills and rich, loamy lands were shaded with maple, beech, and birch, interspersed with ash, elm, hemlock, fir, oak, cherry, bass, and other kinds of wood. Bogs and swamps were far more extensive then than now; and the woods in many parts, on account of the fallen timber and thick underbrush, were almost impassable. The deer and the moose roamed at large; the wolf and bear prowled about the hills; the turkey and partridge whirred with heavy flight from tree to tree, while the duck swam undisturbed upon the lonely, silent waters. The beaver and the freshet made the only dam that impeded the streams in their whole course from the highlands to the Merrimack; the trout, pickerel, and salmon moved through them unmolested, while the old Monadnock, looking down in every direction upon almost interminable forests, saw in the hazy distance the first feeble encroachments upon the dominion which he had retained over his wild subjects for more than a thousand years.

That an attempt was made to settle this town as early as 1739 there can be no doubt. The authority of the petition for incorporation as a town, of which, through the Secretary of State, we have been favored with a copy, is on this point decisive. The town was surveyed and laid out by Joseph Hale, Jr., in 1737. Of the party that came in 1739 no memorial remains. Probably they were driven away before any considerable clearing had been made. In 1742, five men,* each with an axe and a small supply of provisions upon his shoulders, came from Lunenburg, Mass., and cleared a few small patches of land near the old meeting-house. They abandoned the settlement at, or more probably considerably before, the alarm of war in 1744. Soon after this party, three men cut down the brush and girdled the large trees on the hill near the Ritchie place, at the south part of the town, but left before they had put in their seed. They probably returned the next year, with Thomas Morison and John Swan. It could not have been later than 1744, and must have been at a period when there were no other settlers here. For it is a story often told by the children of Thomas Morison, and which cannot well be doubted, that soon after they came several Indians called upon them just after breakfast, appeared friendly, and, after tarrying a short time, went away. When the cook, however, came from chopping to prepare a dinner for the party, he found not only the pot which he had left upon the fire robbed of its contents, but all their provisions carried off; and they were obliged to go to Townsend, twenty-five miles, for a dinner; which they would not have done had there been other inhabitants here at the time.

In 1744, the town was entirely abandoned, and the settlement was not resumed till the peace of 1749. Indeed, I have found little evidence that families † had established themselves here

---

* The traditions are by no means distinct, and it is possible that this party came as early as 1739. They may not have stayed more than a single season. Their names, according to Mr. Dunbar (see N. H. Historical Collections, Vol. I., p. 129), were William Robbe, Alexander Scott, Hugh Gregg, William Gregg, and Samuel Stinson. John Todd, Sen., a high authority in the antiquities of our town, says they were William Scott, William Robbe, William Wallace, William Mitchell and Samuel Stinson.

The second party were William M'Nee, John Taggart, William Ritchie.

† Catharine Gregg, mother of Gov. Miller, is said to have been baptized here in 1743.

previous to that period, and this presumption is confirmed by the fact that the first male child, John Ritchie, was not born till Feb. 22, 1751. All that was done, therefore, previous to the war of '44 was only to prepare the way for the future settlement, which was commenced in earnest in 1749. From that time the colony was rapidly increased by new accessions from abroad, till, in '59, there were forty-five or fifty families, from Lunenburg, Londonderry, and some immediately from Ireland. They all, however, belonged to the same stock. They came to this country from the north of Ireland, and were usually called Scotch-Irish.

Early in the reign of James I,* on the suppression of a rebellion by his Catholic subjects in the north of Ireland, two millions of acres of land, almost the whole of the six northern counties, including Londonderry, fell to the king; and his Scotch and English subjects were encouraged by liberal grants to leave their own country, and settle on these lands, in order to keep in awe the turbulent spirits who had so often defied the authority and arms of the British government. This accounts in some measure for the hatred which the English and Scotch population bore to the Catholics, who could not but hate the men who occupied the soil from which their countrymen had been forcibly expelled. The great Irish rebellion — for they were many — which happened thirty years after, in the reign of his son, doubtless had its origin in the attempt of the Irish Catholics to extort the redress of grievances and repel religious persecution; and we may well suppose that they had not yet forgotten the transfer of their property to foreigners of a religion different from their own. The plot of a general massacre of the Protestants was discovered in the southern part of the kingdom before the time fixed for its execution; but this was unknown in Ulster, and the most cruel destruction of lives and property ensued that has ever stained the bloody pages of history. Some of the first settlers of our Derry were probably alive at the time.

---

*Lingard, Vol. IX., p. 121. Hume, Vol. VI., pp. 433-6.

John Morison,* my great-great-grandfather, who died here in 1776, was born about thirty years after, but you may well suppose that vivid pictures of this dreadful time, when, according to some,† not less than one hundred and fifty thousand were victims, had been strongly impressed upon his mind.

In order better to understand these people from whom we are descended, we must remember that, in addition to those already mentioned, in the time of Cromwell, about 1656,‡ a large number of English and Scotch, mostly Scotch, were induced to settle in Ireland on lands forfeited for the Popish rebellion of 1641, or by the adherents of the king. All these circumstances must have greatly exasperated the original Catholic Irish against the foreigners who had thus been planted among them.

In 1689, James II. returned from France. His intention was to settle the affairs of Ireland. On the first alarm of an intended massacre the Protestants flew to arms, and shut themselves up in the strong places, particularly in Londonderry, where, under the command of Walker, an Episcopal clergyman, they defended themselves against the royal army. The ships sent to them with supplies were kept back by a boom across the entrance of the harbor, below the city. The French general who commanded the besiegers threatened to raze the city to its foundations and destroy every man, woman, and child, unless they would immediately submit to James. But these brave men, suffering at the time from hunger and every privation, treated the Popish general's threats with contempt. His next step was to drive the inhabitants, for thirty miles round, under the walls of the city. Among these miserable beings, exceeding four thousand in number, was the family of John Morison, then nine years old. The greater part, after being detained there three days without tasting food, were suffered to return to their habitations, plundered of everything, and many of them actually dying

---

* I have retained the spelling for this name which was used by his sons, Thomas and Jonathan in their signature to the petition for incorporation in 1759. It is the true Scotch orthography.

† Hume, Vol. VI., pp. 436, 7.   ‡ Hume, Vol. VII., p. 268.

upon the road of hunger and fatigue. His family were admitted into the famished city. The garrison, which consisted of about seven thousand, became greatly reduced* in numbers; but their courage and constancy remained unshaken. Just when their sufferings had reached the point beyond which human nature can suffer no more, Gen. Kirk, who had deserted his master and joined King William, sent two ships, laden with provisions and convoyed by a frigate, to sail up the river. One of them, after two unsuccessful attempts, and amidst a hot fire from both sides of the channel, at length reached the wharf, to the inexpressible joy of the inhabitants.

There are now alive† those who have frequently heard this youth, when near a hundred years old, relate the most striking incidents of the siege. Standing upon the walls of the city, where he could survey at once the besieging army surrounding them, and full of a more savage cruelty than any other army had ever possessed, ready to execute their threats of indiscriminate rage and slaughter against the miserable sufferers within, the frigate and transports just heaving in sight, the foremost in full sail, with a strong wind, prepared to cut the boom. Amid a severe fire from the enemy, on both sides of the channel, she strikes against it, and bounds heavily back, to the consternation of the inhabitants. Again she advances; new hopes are kindled; she strikes, and again bounds heavily back, in full sight of the pale and starving multitude. A third attempt is made; the chain creaks and breaks. The old man could resume the boy, and describe most graphically the universal joy when the ships reached the city.

I have dwelt long on this part of the subject. For John Morison, the oldest man that was ever buried in our place, had, among our early settlers, three sons, four sons-in-law, and the numerous family of Steeles ‡ were descended from his

---

* Burnet says that near two-thirds of them perished by hunger. Burnet's Own Time, Vol. III., p. 20.

† This whole account I have received from his grandson, Hon. Jeremiah Smith, who remembers distinctly the tall, erect form, the engaging countenance, urbane manners, and " peculiar native eloquence," which, together with the remarkable scenes through which he had passed, made a strong impression upon the young.

‡ Capt. Thomas Steele came in 1763 from Londonderry, N. H.

sister; so that he has been connected far more extensively than any other man with our inhabitants, and may in some measure be looked back upon as the patriarch of the town.* But in addition to this, it is necessary to bear in mind the circumstances that have been mentioned, in order to understand the character of the emigrants from the north of Ireland. They have been often confounded with the Irish, and yet at the time of their emigration there were perhaps no two classes in the United Kingdom more unlike, or more hostile. Every circumstance in their history, for more than a hundred years, had served only to inflame them against each other. The original strong traits which separate the Scotch and Irish had been gathering strength through more than a century of turbulence and bloodshed, in which they had been constantly exasperated against each other by their interests, by secret plots and open rebellions, by cruel massacres, by civil wars carried on through the most black and malignant of all passions, religious hatred.

It is not, therefore, wonderful that even after the establishment of the Protestant cause by the accession of William, Anne and the house of Hanover to the throne of Great Britain, they should still have found their position in Ireland uncomfortable. They considered themselves a branch of the Scotch Presbyterian Church, and, though permitted to maintain their own forms of worship unmolested, a tenth part of all their increase was rigorously exacted for the support of the established Episcopal Church. They also held their lands and tenements by lease, and not as the proprietors of the soil.† They were a religious people, with an inextinguishable thirst for liberty, and could not therefore bear to be trammelled in their civil and religious rights.

For these reasons, and influenced particularly by the representations of a young man named Holmes, the son of a clergy-

---

* By marriage, or direct descent, he has been connected with the families of Steele, Wilson, Smith, Wallace, Moore, Mitchell, Todd, Jewett, Gregg, Ames, Holmes, Gray, Field, Stuart, Little, Swan, and probably some others, without including the last generation.

† See Century Sermon, by Rev. Edward L. Parker, of Londonderry, p. 7. See also Farmer's Belknap, p. 191.

man, who had been here, four Presbyterian ministers,* with a large portion of their congregations, determined to remove to this country. They belonged not to the lowest class in the country from which they came, but perhaps to the lower portion of the middling class. They had the cool heads which their fathers had brought from Scotland, and doubtless counted well the cost of the step they were about to take. It required no small strength of character to leave a country where they *could* live quietly and in tolerable comfort for an untried region, with an ocean between, and a full prospect before them of the labors and sufferings incident to planting a new country with slender means. In the summer of 1718, they embarked in five ships for America.† About one hundred families arrived in Boston ‡ Aug. 4th; and twenty families more, in one of the vessels, landed at Casco Bay, now Portland. Among these were three of the families, Gregg, Morison, and Steele, who afterwards settled in Peterborough. The vessel had intended to put in at Newburyport, but arrived at Casco Bay so late in the season, that she was frozen in, and they, unable to provide more comfortable quarters, were obliged to spend the whole winter on board, suffering severely from the want of suitable accommodations and food. It is said that on first landing upon that cold and cheerless coast, the wintry ocean behind them and naked forests before, after the solemn act of prayer, they united in singing that most touching of all songs : " By the rivers of Babylon, there we sat down ; yea, we wept, when we remembered Zion "; and with peculiar feelings, as they surveyed the waste around them, and remembered the pleasant homes which they had

---

* Holmes, James M'Gregore, William Cornwell, and William Boyd. The Federal Street Church in Boston was founded by this same class of emigrants.

† From a manuscript left by Rev. James M'Gregore, and seen by Mr. Parker, it would appear that he preached to them on leaving Ireland, stating distinctly that they were coming to America in order " to avoid oppression and cruel bondage; to shun persecution and designed ruin; to withdraw from the communion of idolaters, and to have an opportunity of worshipping God according to the dictates of conscience and the rules of his inspired Word."

‡ They brought with them, according to Dr. Belknap, the first little wheels turned by the foot that were used in the country, and the first potatoes planted in New England; which from them have ever since been called *Irish* potatoes.

left, might they add : " How shall we sing the Lord's song in
a strange land ? "

They left Casco Bay early in the spring, and began their
settlement in Londonderry, April 11, O. S., 1719. The
people of the neighboring towns, supposing them to be Irish,
harbored strong prejudices against them, and wished to have
them driven out from the country. Soon after they began
their settlement in Londonderry, a party from Haverhill,
headed by one Herriman, came, in order forcibly to expel
them. It was on Friday afternoon, and the settlers, with
their wives and children, had come together under an old oak,
to attend, according to the good old Presbyterian fashion, the
lecture preparatory to the communion, which was to be administered the following Sabbath. Herriman stopped his
party and listened till the services were over, when, deeply
affected by what he had seen and heard, he said to his follow-
ers, " Let us return ; it is vain to attempt to disturb this
people ; for surely the Lord is with them."*

In September, 1736 or '37, another party came over from
Ireland. Among them were the Smiths, the Wilsons, and Lit-
tles. Mrs. Sarah M'Nee, or, as she was called, old Aunt Nay,
who died within my memory, aged ninety-seven, or, as some
supposed, one hundred years, was one of this party, and used
to relate, with much satisfaction, that as the vessel approached
the wharf in Boston, a gentleman there, after inspecting
them closely, said, " Truly, these are no poor folk; and,"
she always added, " he was an awfu' great gentleman ; for he
had ruffles on his fingers." It † was noised about that a pack
of Irishmen had landed, and they were much annoyed by the
observations that were made upon them. " Why," said one,
with evident surprise, " these people are white." " So they
are," said another, with not less astonishment ; " as white as
you or I." " It made my blood boil," said the elder William

---

* This account I have taken partly from Mr. Parker's sermon, and partly from the lips of John
Todd, Sen.

† For this I am indebted to my great-aunt, Sally Morison, who, though always feeble, and for
many years an invalid, retains now, in her eighty-fifth year, a very perfect recollection of what she
heard more than seventy years ago.

Smith, who was then about eighteen years old, "to hear our-selves called a parcel of Irish." The prejudice subjected them to a more serious inconvenience, and rendered it difficult to procure lodgings. They, however, succeeded in getting a Mr. Winship, in the east part of Lexington, to take them for the winter. His neighbors, especially during the intermission on Sundays, would crowd around him and remonstrate loudly against his harboring these Irishmen. At last he would listen no longer, but told them that if his house reached to Charles-town, and he could find such Irish as these, he would have it filled up with Irish, and none but Irish.

The spring or summer following (1737), they came to Lun-enburg, Mass., from which place, and from Londonderry, small parties, as we have seen, came out between '39 and '49 to make a settlement in Peterborough. The township had been granted by the General Court of Massachusetts, on the supposition that it was within their limits, to Samuel Hay-wood * and others, but soon after was transferred to the famous Jeremiah Gridley, of Boston, John Hill, John Fowle, and William Vassal, who were become the sole proprietors of the soil. Under purchases made from them the first settle-ments were made, and the town is said to have taken its name from Peter Prescott, of Concord, Mass.

Till 1749, almost nothing was done. It is impossible to say how many came then; but from that time the growth was rapid. The hardships of the first settlers cannot be under-stood from anything that is now experienced by the pioneers in our Western territories. Being recently from a foreign country, they were unaccustomed to the axe, and by no means acquainted with the best method of clearing away the timber; and yet, here they were in the midst of an unbroken forest, to which alone they must look for support. The gloom and loneliness of the place, the hollow echoing of the hills and woods as the first tall pine fell groaning by their side, the sound of strange birds and insects, the dismal creaking and

---

* The petition for incorporation (Oct. 31, 1739) says, . . . "in consequence of a tract of land had and obtained from the Great and General Court or Assembly of the Province of the Massachu-setts Bay, by Samuel Haywood and others, his associates," etc.

howling among the trees upon a stormy night, connected with
what they had heard of destructive beasts and snakes, and the
frightful acts of Indian cruelty which were going on all around
them, must have made an impression upon them which we can
hardly conceive. Add to these the superstitious fears, the
religious awe, that overcame them as they stood here, apart
from the civilized abode of man, and it will not seem strange
if again and again they abandoned what they had begun, even
from imaginary fears, and withdrew that they might, for a
season, be within the sympathy and security of an older settlement.   A single incident will show the constant apprehension
under which they lived. About twelve o'clock, on one of
those autumnal nights when the moon, rising late, hangs with
a sort of supernatural gloom over the horizon, the family of
William Smith were suddenly startled from their sleep by
shrieks of murder in the house of their nearest neighbor.
Immediately, without waiting to put on a single garment, the
father and mother, each with a child, left their log-hut, and forc-
ing their way, no one could ever tell how, more than two miles
through the woods, arrived at the log-house of her brother,
near where the South Factory now is, and spread the alarm
that they had barely escaped with their lives from the Indians.
Capt. Thomas Morison, who was a man of greater martial
coolness than his brother-in-law, after supplying them with
clothes, joined them, with his own wife and children, one an
infant, and after hiding them in the woods south of his house,
set out for the fort, about a mile further south, saying, as he
left them, that if he should meet the enemy before reaching
the fort they would know it, because he should certainly have
time to fire, and kill at least one man before he should himself
be killed or taken.   Meanwhile, the Swans, another family at
the south, had taken the alarm and fled for the fort. Soon
after, a younger Swan, returning home at that late hour, from
what to young men is a very pleasant as well as important
business, and finding his father's boots and clothes by the
bedside, and the house deserted, ran out almost frantic, and
spread the report that his whole family had been murdered
and carried away by the Indians. The consternation was

general and intense; and it was not discovered till morning that the whole panic was occasioned by some thoughtless young men at Mr. Cunningham's, who had screamed and shrieked simply to frighten their neighbors, the Smiths.

This incident, trifling as it is, shows the constant apprehension in which our fathers every night retired to their beds; and yet they were brave men. About the same time with this alarm, perhaps the following summer, a report was spread here that the Indians had fallen upon the settlements at Keene. Immediately Capt. Morison with his company set out, and in the heat of summer marched more than twenty miles through the woods to rescue their brethren from an enemy of unknown strength, who seldom spared a foe. Upon arriving at Keene, the men there were found mowing peaceably in the field, and so much were they affected by this act of kindness, that they could not refrain from weeping.*

Such was the continual fear of midnight fire and murder from the Indians for twenty years from the commencement of the settlement, being several times, as their petition says, driven off by the enemy, and "many of them almost ruined." "Yet," to use their own affecting language, "what little we had in the world lay there; we, having no whither else to go, returned to our settlement as soon as prudence would admit, where we have continued since, and cultivated a rough part of the wilderness to a fruitful field."

But aside from the apprehension of danger, they surely had difficulties and hardships enough. Till 1751, they had no grist-mill, and were obliged to bring all their provisions upon their shoulders five-and-twenty miles. For many years there was not a glass window in the place. Their dwellings were miserable huts, not a board upon or within them till 1751, when three frame-houses were erected. Most of the frame-houses first made, were poorly built. In one,† considerably later than this, when the family had gathered round the table, the floor suddenly gave way, just as the good man was asking

---

*This was told me by his daughter, Elizabeth Morison.

† The house was William Moore's, and William Smith, Esq., the man who was asking the blessing as they sunk.

a blessing, and the whole party, dinner and all, found themselves in the cellar. The first meeting-house,* which must have been erected as early as 1752 or '53, for several years was furnished with no other seats than rough boards laid loosely upon square blocks of wood. For a long period there were no oxen, and still later no horses. The first mill-stone used was drawn, in 1751, more than a mile and a half by seventeen men and boys. Their food was meagre in kind, and not often abundant in quantity. Bean porridge, potatoes, and samp (corn) broth were, for the first twenty years, the principal articles of diet. The women vied with the men, and sometimes excelled them, in the labors of the field. There was no bridge till 1755, and the roads were fit only for foot-passengers. But notwithstanding their privations and hardships, with insufficient clothing and almost without shoes, except in the severest weather, the first settlers lived to an unusually advanced period, and the three oldest people that have ever died in the place were natives of Ireland, and among our earliest inhabitants.†

Such was the condition of the town for the first twenty years after its settlement. About that period many new comforts began to be introduced. Oxen became more common. The richer part of the inhabitants might be seen going to meeting on horseback, the good man before, his wife on the pillion behind, while at noon the children would gather round, with almost envious eyes, to admire this curious and sumptuous mode of conveyance. All marketing was done with a horse. Butter was carried by tying two casks together, and placing them across the horse's back like panniers. In this way the wife of Major Wilson often carried her spare articles to Boston, while her son James was in Harvard College, between the years 1785 and '89. The first chaise was introduced in 1793, and the first one-horse wagon in 1810.

---

* It was thirty feet square, and stood a little to the east of what we call the "old meeting-house," which was raised in 1777. During the raising, a deep gloom was thrown over the whole assembly by the arrival of a courier, who announced that our troops had left Ticonderoga, and that a new levy was called for. In 1760, the first meeting-house was enlarged by an addition in front, considerably broader than the main body.

† John Morison and Sarah M'Nee, who died in their ninety-eighth, and Mrs. Cunningham in her ninety-ninth year.

Few things could have given our ancestors more annoyance than their extreme awkwardness in the mechanical arts.* For this reason their houses must have been loose, cold, and deficient in almost every article of domestic convenience. Jonathan Morison † was the first, and for a considerable time the only, mechanic in town. He was a mill-wright, a blacksmith, a carpenter, a house-joiner, a stone-cutter, a gun-maker, and had the reputation of being really a workman at all these trades. He was the son of John Morison, and was considered the most gifted of the family, being a man of quick parts, great ingenuity, and generous in the extreme, but unfortunately possessed, what is too often the curse of superior endowments, a violent temper, and a want of self-control, which led sometimes to intemperance. To crown his misfortunes he had a wife who, in all but his bad qualities, was the opposite to himself. A separation took place when he removed to Vermont, where he lived for some time. He finally returned to Peterborough, and was killed by a fall from his horse in 1787. The second and third mechanics were William Cochran and James Houston, both blacksmiths. From these small beginnings we have gone on till now there is hardly a product of the mechanic arts, belonging either to the comforts or elegances of life, which may not here be furnished.

The first use made of our water-privileges ‡ was for a saw and grist-mill, on the spot where the Peterborough Factory now stands. It was built by Jonathan Morison, in 1751. This was an important event to the neighboring towns, which for several years brought all their grain to this mill. It was built for William Gordan, of Dunstable, Mass., and passed through several owners into the hands of Samuel Mitchell,

---

*This was well taken off by Uncle Mosey (as every one called him) in his account of Deacon Duncan's hewing, and Deacon Moore's ladder. "As I was ganging," said he, "thro' the woods, I heard a desprite crackling, and there I found a stick of timber that Deacon Duncan had hewn, sae crooked that it could na lie still, but was thrashing about amang the trees. I tauld him that he must go and chain it doun, or it wad girdle the hail forest."

"Deacon Moore," he said. "made a ladder, and it was sae twisting, that before he got half way to the top he was on the under side, *looking up*."

† The first male child born in Londonderry.

‡ For a very full and exact account of this part of the subject, see, in the Appendix, the reports prepared by John H. Steele.

34

in 1759. The grist-mill was usually tended by his wife, and it was thought could hardly be a source of much profit; for she would take no toll from the poor, and when her customers were there at meal-time, she would constrain them to partake of her fare, and often to remain through the night. The second saw-mill, where a saw and grist-mill now stands, near the South Factory, was built by Thomas Morison in 1758; and the grist-mill added in 1770. The race-way to these mills is through a ledge of a sort of trap-rock, on which it is extremely difficult to make any impression by blasting with gunpowder. Besides, the use of gun-powder for blasting seems to have been unknown here at that time. Large fires were therefore built upon the ledge, and when it was heated, water was thrown on. This scaled or cracked the rocks; all that was loosened was removed, and the same process repeated till a sufficient depth was gained.*

At this period (1770), log-huts were little used; substantial frame-houses, many of them two stories high, had been erected,† and, though hard labor and a homely fare were their portion, our people perhaps enjoyed as much then of the real comforts of life as at any subsequent period. Robust health, and confirmed habits of industry and exposure, enabled them to enjoy what would now be esteemed intolerable hardships. Four bridges had been built across our two principal streams;‡ the roads had greatly improved; there were no longer apprehensions of danger from the Indians or wild animals. I cannot well picture to myself happier domestic scenes than might then be found in one of those spacious kitchens which some of us have seen, though not in their glory. The kitchen stretched nearly across the house; at one end was the ample *dresser*, filled up with pewter platters and basins of every size, all shining bright, and telling many a

---

* There are now in town six grist-mills and seven saw-mills.

† Hugh Wilson moved into the first two-story house, in 1753. The first brick house was built by Nathan Richardson, in 1811 or '12; the second by Jonas Loring, in 1815. The whole number now in town is twenty-three.

‡ The first near the great bridge in 1755; the second across Goose Brook previous to 1760; one at the North, and one at the South, Factory in 1765, by labor from the town.

story to the beholder, of savory broths,* and Indian puddings, and possibly of pumpkin pies, even. The fire-place, which seemed to reach through half the length of the room, and was four or five feet high, not only contained, between its capacious jambs, logs two or three feet in diameter, and almost sled length, heaped one above the other, with the proper accompaniments of fore sticks and small wood; but back in one corner was an oven big enough to receive the largest pots and pans in which beans and brown bread ever were baked; and in both corners, under the chimney, was room for benches, where the children might sit on a winter's evening, parching corn, while the huge, green back-log and back-stick were simmering and singing, and three or four little wheels, with various tones, were joining in the concert; and the large cat upon the wide, stone hearth, interrupted occasionally by a gruff look from the dog, was industriously purring out her part of the accompaniment. There by the blazing fire, for it would have been extravagance to burn any other light, the children sit, with attention divided between the stories and the corn, and the young people, stealing now and then a sly glance or joke at the expense of their elders, burst out often into a chorus of laughter, as their fathers, with grotesque humor, narrate the hardships and strange adventures of their early settlement, or dwell upon their favorite theme, the wonders of the old country, and especially " the preëminence of Ireland," against which all their anger is now forgotten. At length the time for retiring has come; apples† and cider, after taking their station for a time upon the hearth, are served up. And now (for the guests, though neighbors, are expected to remain till morning) a candle is lighted, the big Bible is brought out; the oldest man receives it with reverence, and after singing a portion of the Psalms, from their

---

* Broth (barley or corn) was the favorite food. It is said that one of our eminent men, when a boy, wished that he could only be a king, for then he might have broth every day, and as much as he wished.

† The first apple-tree in the town was set out by John Swan, and is still alive. Apples must have been seldom used in the way I have mentioned, so early as 1770. The first cider was made by Mrs. John Smith. The apples were pounded in a barley-mortar, and pressed in a cheesepress.

Presbyterian or Scottish version, to such tunes as " Dundee," " Martyrs," " Coleshill," or " Elgin," and reading a chapter with a voice of peculiar and unaffected solemnity, all join in prayer, and the elder people withdraw. Now is the time for the young. No longer with suppressed laughter, but with loud and boisterous merriment, the evening is prolonged. The call from the sleepers, whose slumbers they have broken, produces only a momentary check. How long they sit up nobody knows; but before light the young men are gone, for they must spend the day in the woods. The common mode of neighborly visiting among the women was to go in the morning, carrying with them, not unfrequently a mile or more, their little wheels, and returning before dark; thus en-joying all the advantages of good-fellowship, without loss of time.

This period of quiet, however, was of short duration. The difficulties with England soon began. Our fathers were too zealous in their love of liberty to remain indifferent spectators at a time like that. They entered warmly into the dispute. Private feelings were merged in their anxiety for the public good. News of the Lexington. battle fell upon them like a sudden trump from heaven, summoning them to the conflict. " We all set out," said one who was then upon the stage, " with such weapons as we could get, going like a flock of wild geese, we hardly knew why or whither." The word came to Capt. Thomas Morison at daylight, that the regulars were upon the road. In two hours, with his son and hired man, he was on his way to meet them, they on foot, he on horseback, with a large *baking* of bread, which had just been taken from the oven, in one end of the bag, and pork in the other. This is but a sample of the general spirit which spread through the town, among men and women. " I was willing," said an old lady, whom I was questioning about those times, her pale cheeks kindling as she spoke, "that my father and brothers should run their chance with the rest." " I will not taste your tea," said another woman, this same day; "I would as soon drink a man's blood."

At the battle of Bunker Hill, though there could not have

been more than seventy or eighty families in the town, twenty-two of our citizens were present, and seventeen actively engaged in the fight. The night after the battle information was brought to Major Wilson,* who then commanded the company, that the British were advancing upon the American lines, and at break of day every able-bodied man in town, with such weapons as he could procure, was on the march. At Townsend, those who went on foot heard the result of the battle and returned;† and then the old men, who had sons in the battle, set out to learn whether their children were yet living, and had acquitted themselves like men.

Seventeen days before the Declaration of Independence, the following resolution was signed by eighty-three of our citizens, which included all the strong men, except those who were in the army, and possibly one or two besides:—

" In consequence of the Resolution of the Continental Congress, and to show our determination in joining our American brethren in arms, in defending the lives, liberties, and proper-ties of the United Colonies,

" We, the subscribers, do hereby solemnly engage and promise, that we will, to the utmost of our power, at the risque of our lives and fortunes, with ARMS oppose the hostile proceedings of the British fleets and armies against the United Colonies."

It has always been a matter of wonder to the world how our American Congress, which had no legal authority, whose strongest enactment was nothing more than a recommendation, should dare to make the Declaration of Independence, and, still more, be able to carry out their measures through a long and discouraging war. The secret of their success is contained in the resolution which I have just read. It was the spirit which pervaded the people in their individual capacity, that nerved their arm and gave them strength. It was the solemn engagement and promise of the people, " at

---

*This anecdote is told me by his grandson, Gen. James Wilson, of Keene, who had it from his father, James Wilson, Esq., who was born in this town, 1766, and died in Keene, January, 1839.

† The greater part, however, were on horseback, and proceeded as far as West Cambridge, where they broke into a large, vacant house, and passed the night.

the risque of their lives and fortunes, with ARMS, to oppose the hostile proceedings of the British fleets and armies," that enabled Congress to take and carry through those strong measures which have been the admiration of every student of history. And in privations and hardships, that school of stern and manly virtues, in which not only here, but throughout the United Colonies, men were brought up, may we not see the hand of God stretched out to provide them with courage to declare, and strength to maintain, their rights? that while He was elsewhere raising up men to direct the councils and lead the armies of the nation, He was here, and in places like this, making ready the strong nerves, the hard muscles, the unflinching souls, to fight the battles that should set them free. " He found them in a desert land, and in the waste, howling wilderness; he led them about, he instructed them," and when the great day had come, through the discipline which he had imposed, they were found equal to their work.

It is impossible now to paint the anxieties which prevailed through this little town during the war. Their remoteness from the scene of action, while it lessened their dangers, by no means diminished their fears. Rumors of terrible defeats and slaughters, of victories that had never been gained, and battles that were not fought, swayed them back and forth with doubts more cruel than the worst certainty. They were constantly in the dreadful expectation and suspense that precedes the conflict, and tries the soul more sharply than the hottest fight. No stranger made his appearance but the town was full of surmises, suspicions, and strange reports. He must be stopped, examined, and, when fairly gone, suspicions were again afloat. The sufferings of those left behind were greater than of those in the war. It is sufficient, however, to say that our citizens nobly redeemed the pledge they had given at the commencement of hostilities. During the war there were no mobs against the Tories, for there was not a man here who favored the British cause.

Of our political history I shall say little. The terms on which the original settlement was made, were such that no provincial* meeting could be held, or vote passed, "obliging any person to do any part towards supporting the gospel, building a meeting-house and bridges, clearing and repairing roads." The act of incorporation was passed, Jan. 17, 1760. These corporate townships are a peculiar feature in our government; and, so far as I know, have received only from a single author† anything of the attention which is due to so important a subject. Townships, with their peculiar rights, sprang, as I suppose, from the form of church discipline which was originally introduced into New England. Being composed entirely of the people, they contain in themselves all the elements of a pure democracy, and exercise all the functions of a more extended government. They are the schools in which young men are educated for higher offices, and in which all may be taught their duty as citizens. But the great purpose which they answer is, that they serve as a barrier against the encroachments of the State and federal governments.

A great danger in every government is, the centralization of power. For this reason only that which relates to the whole nation in its federal capacity should be placed in the hands of the general government; and only that which relates to the whole State should be placed in the hands of the State government. All that remains should be left with the towns, and, as a matter of fact, nine-tenths of the real, effective legislation in New England is performed by the towns. They raise the taxes, support the schools, roads, bridges. The parts of our general government which tend most to the centralization of power, and from which we have most to apprehend, as they, more than all others, tend to corruption, are the revenue and post-office departments. Now, were it not for our townships, the same influence which pervades those departments would take to itself, as it does in Prussia, the control of our roads, our schools, of all the taxes that are raised; and there would be at the heart of the republic an accumulation of power with which no government on earth can be safely

---

* See petition for incorporation.   † De Tocqueville.

trusted. To prevent this dangerous result, we have in the first place our State governments, and then, what is of far greater importance, our town governments, which hold in their own hands more than nine-tenths of the real power which, so far as they are concerned, belongs to government.

Our town government, from the commencement, has been efficient and liberal. The town-meetings in old times were often stormy, and ended in small results.* At all times of great party warfare in national politics, the contest here has been warm; and it has been well for the town, that while the same party, the conservative, has prevailed in every severe trial, it has, at all times, been confronted by a large and respectable minority. The severity of the contest kept alive the interest; it obliged men to examine and to think; and though, when parties are nearly equal, the temptation to gain a momentary triumph by dishonest artifice is sometimes too great to be resisted, the consciousness on each side that they are closely watched, and cannot escape detection and exposure, will, where higher considerations fail, make them peculiarly circumspect in their movements. While the strong character of our citizens has done much to make political contentions severe since the first formation of parties under the federal government, the nearly equal division of parties has done much to sharpen the intellects, and restrain, if it did nor correct, purposes grossly unjust.†

The ministerial history of the town is the darkest page in our calendar; but those whose feelings might be injured are now gone, and it is time that the subject should be placed in its true light. A Presbyterian minister, by the name of Johnston, came with the first settlers, and tarried with them about a year. Another by the name of Harvey, whose wife was the first person laid in the old graveyard, was here for a time.

---

* An old man returning, many years since, from town meeting was asked what had been doing. "Oh," said he, "there was George Duncan, he got up and spakit awhile, and Matthew Wallace, he got up and talkit awhile, and Matthew Gray, he got up and blathered awhile; and then they dismissed the meeting." A fair account of many town meetings.

† Party spirit in politics has, perhaps, in no town been more violent than here, but it has never been permitted to disturb the cordiality of social intercourse.

A Mr. Powers supplied the desk in 1764. This is all that we know of them. John Morrison, of a family entirely distinct from our first settlers, was born at Pathfoot, in Scotland, May 22, 1743; was graduated at Edinburgh, Feb. 17, 1765; arrived at Boston the May following, and was ordained at Peterborough, Nov. 26, 1766. From all that I can learn he was a man of decided talents; but it must be borne in mind, that the same ability will appear always more conspicuous in a bad than in a good man, just as a horse or a building of perfect symmetry will always appear smaller than another of the same dimensions whose parts are out of proportion. But after making all due allowance, we must, I believe, conclude that Mr. Morrison possessed more than common powers, for good or for evil. But soon he proved himself an intemperate, licentious man, dangerous alike as the companion of either sex. A charitable construction was put upon the first symptoms of intemperance. At a party he was found unable to walk, and 'it was necessary to take him through the room where the young people were collected, in order to place him upon a bed. This was managed with so much adroitness, that no suspicion was raised, except with three or four church-members who were disposed to view it as an accident, at a time when similar casualties were not uncommon. But soon, while his bad habits in this line became notorious, his evil passions in another direction flared out, to the general scandal of the town. 'A presbytery was held; he was suspended from his office for two or three months, a thing probably to his taste, as his salary was *not* suspended. At length; however, the people could no longer tolerate him; he relinquished his connection with the society in March, 1772; visited South Carolina, returned and joined the American army at Cambridge in '75. He was present at Bunker Hill, but excused himself from entering the battle, on the ground that his gunlock was not in order. The next day he joined the British, and continued in some capacity with them till his death, which took place at Charleston, S. C., May 26, 1782. He became a professed atheist. It is said that he spent his last days, when he was daily sinking to the grave, among profli-

35

gate, abandoned associates, taking his part in every species of dissipation which his decaying strength would permit; and just before his death gave a sum of money to his companions, requesting them to drink it out upon his coffin. His wife, Sarah Ferguson, in every respect a true, exemplary woman, never, to the time of her death, November, 1824, aged eighty-four, lost either the interest or the confidence with which she had first joined her fortunes to his. It is refreshing to add, that their son, John Morrison, who died more than forty years ago, was, by the uniform consent of all who knew him, one of the most pure-hearted and clear-headed men that our town has produced. I have never heard him mentioned by one who had known him except with strong affection and respect. He received his education at Exeter, where for a time he was also a teacher. When, many years after, I went to Exeter, and was there in a very humble employment, a friendless, ignorant boy, the fact that my name was the same with his had, I have no doubt, a very considerable influence in bespeaking for me unusual kindness on the part of my employer,* who had been his early friend.

From 1772 to '78 our people had no settled ministry. The meeting-house was built in '77, and traditions are handed down respecting a Mr. Clarke, who was preaching here at the time. Many who heard him testify that the following is nearly an exact account of the exordium to one of his discourses. "This is a stately house; and who meet here? The folk, they meet here, and the de'il, he meet here too; and he is amang the foremost and the fattest† o' ye. An' he's peeking at ye, like a wee mouse in the wa'; ye dinna see him, but he kens ye. An' now where is the gun to shoot him wi'? Here it is," said he, lifting up the Bible and taking aim, "here, is the gun. _Too! too!_ he's deed, he's deed." The preaching of that period was usually without notes, the sermons very ordinary, very long, and made up very much of repetitions, especially of a continual play upon the words of the text.

---

* Joseph Smith Gilman.

† This, it was thought, might apply to Deacon Mitchell and his wife, as he was usually foremost, and she the fattest in the assembly.

The second settled minister of the place, David Annan,* was born at Cupar of Fife, in Scotland, April 4, 1754, came early to America, was educated at New Brunswick College, N. J., was ordained for Peterborough, at the call of the people here, by the Presbytery which met at Wallkill, N. Y., October, 1778, and was dismissed from this society at his own request, by the Presbytery of Londonderry, at their June session here, in 1792. He was deposed from the ministry by the Presbytery of Londonderry in 1800, and died in Ireland in 1802. The people received him with high expectations, and were slow to believe anything against him. Though in talents inferior to his predecessor, he was a man of more than common endowments, but was intemperate and morose, uniting in his character the extremes, which sometimes meet in smaller tyrants than Nero, of levity and cruelty. With the elders of the church he was stern, inflexible, and austere. With young men his conversation was loose, licentious, corrupt. He was easily flattered, but being opposed, haughty and overbearing. When *treated to toddy* at a public house by a man of no good repute, he expressed himself delighted with his companion, and wished he had a whole church like him; and when one of the most upright of his society† attempted in private and with great kindness to remonstrate with him on his conduct, his only reply was, "It is a wise people that can instruct their minister"; "and a foolish minister," it might have been rejoined, "who cannot be instructed by his people." Rev. Mr. Miles, of Temple, used to relate, that once on coming to his house to exchange with him, he found him sitting at a table with a fiddle, made by his own hands, a bottle of rum and a Bible before him. In his own house he was the severest of tyrants. His wife, an amiable, discreet, patient, uncomplaining woman, often retired at night amid actions and

---

* His brother, Robert Annan, was first at Wallkill, N. Y., then pastor of the Federal Street Church in Boston, then of a society in Philadelphia, where he died. He was a man of uncommon power and of great austerity.

† Henry Ferguson, a thoroughly excellent man. Not one of the name is now among us. Three of the sons removed to South Carolina, where the last of them, having accumulated a large property, died within a few years.

threats which left to her scarcely a hope that her life would be spared till morning, and sometimes she passed the whole night with her children in the woods. After the birth of their last child his conduct towards her and her children was so brutal that it could no longer be borne. She fled from his house with her child, and a petition for a bill of divorce, on the ground of extreme cruelty, was granted at once by the court, with a feeling almost of horror at the disclosures then made.

The only organized mob, of which I find any evidence in our history, was against Mr. Annan. Just at the time of his wife's flight with her child, when stories were spread through the town, and every one was burning with indignation, the young men who were collected at a ball, talking over the circumstances till they had wrought themselves into a perfect rage, determined to take the matter into their own hands. Blacking their faces with soot, disguising themselves in every uncouth dress, and provided with a rough spruce pole, at the dead of night, in the autumn of 1799, they knocked at the door of Mr. Annan's house, and when he, suspecting no harm, came to them as if from his bed, three* of the strongest among them seized him, placed him upon the pole, and the whole party, with shouting and howling, the tinkling of cow-bells, the blowing of horns and pumpkin-vines, carried him a full half mile, and threw him into a muddy pond. An attempt was made by Mr. Annan, who always after went armed with pistols, to bring the rioters to justice. Writs were issued against them, and had he possessed a single friend, he might have succeeded. But nothing could be proved; the feelings of those who had been most severe against him began to relent, and they looked with pity on the solitary, friendless, dejected old man.

The provocation in this case undoubtedly was great. But never, we may safely say, in a well organized society, can an emergency arise where individuals may be justified in taking

---

* "What do you want o' me?" he inquired, sternly. "Only a little of your good company," was the reply from a young man, whose name has since been known through the United States (Gov. James Miller, from whom I received the account).

upon themselves that which belongs to the natural retribu-
tions of Providence and the authorized laws of the land to
inflict. It may pain and vex us to see the oppressor go untouched; but sooner or later punishment will overtake him,
and we know not how severely he may suffer at the very moment when he seems most happy.

Mr. Morrison and Mr. Annan were the only settled ministers in the place for fifty years. Two questions naturally
come up : How could such men be tolerated so long; and how
could religion be kept alive under such instructions ?

They were tolerated, in the first place, because of the great
veneration which was then attached to the profession. "Ministers," said one, at the commencement of the difficulties with
Mr. Morrison, "are edged tools, and we maun aye be carefu'
how we handle them." "Keep yoursel' to yoursel'," said an
elder of the church, with great solemnity, to his son, who was
beginning to intimate that Mr. Annan was not what he should
be. Another reason which made many, and those among the
most rigid disciplinarians, more tolerant than they would
otherwise have been was that the ministers, though wrong in
practice, were yet sound in faith; and error in belief was
esteemed far more dangerous than in heart or life. This doctrine of antinomianism was then carried to a degree of extravagance which finds no sympathy now. An illustration
may be given. A Mr. Taggart, one of the straightest in faith,
but who was intemperate in his habits, had a remarkable gift
in prayer, and this gift was rather increased than diminished
by the exhilaration of ardent spirits. At funerals, where
there was no minister, he was usually called upon to pray;
and sometimes when unable to stand would kneel by his
chair, and edify the assembly by the readiness and fervor of
his devotions. Henry Ferguson once met him lying in the
road, and after helping him up told him that this conduct was
inconsistent with his place in the church. "Ah," said he,
"but we are not our own keepers." Some time after, Mr.
Ferguson was nominated an elder, and Mr. Taggart, on the
strength of this conversation, publicly opposed him as a man
who trusted entirely to works. These two reasons, in their

influence upon some of our own people, and still more upon the presbyteries with which they were connected, together with the personal influence of Robert Annan, who was a strong man in the church, will sufficiently account for the long infliction upon the patience and moral feelings of the community.

The next question, How could religion be kept alive under such circumstances, is readily answered. Our people were always readers, and the Bible was almost their only book. Here they went for counsel and support. It was, to them, prophet and priest. With all their reverence for the public ministrations of religion, their reverence for the written word was far greater. In the next place, the practice of family prayer was faithfully observed. Morning and evening the Scriptures were read; and if the flame of devotion burnt dim in the house of public worship, it was not permitted to go out upon the family altar. Besides, they had preachers more powerful than man. They were strangers in a strange land, in the midst of perpetual alarms and dangers; sickness, death, and all the vicissitudes of life entered their dwellings in the wilderness, and through its loneliness spoke to them as they never can speak in a more cultivated place. They had, before coming here, been well imbued with the principles of religion; and, besides, the human soul is so constituted that it cannot live and be at peace without a religious faith. Rites and ordinances are an important means of advancing the cause of religion. But they are not all. God has never left himself without witness among men. The success of his word does not rest upon a mortal priesthood. Religion is an essential want of the soul, deeply fixed in its nature. Men may stifle its cravings, may, for a time, suppress them, and unhallowed servants at the altar may help to keep them down. But they cannot be destroyed until the soul itself is crushed. Religion, dishonored by its ministers, degraded by the false ideas that have gathered round it, can never be banished, so long as these human hearts, beating with hopes, anxieties, and fears, look round upon a world of change and weakness, and find nowhere here the object that fills up their wants.

The church thus far had been Presbyterian. After Mr. Annan left, the late Rev. Zephaniah Swift Moore was invited to remain, but declined, not wishing to settle as a Presbyterian. After he left, a paper was handed round and signed by all, or nearly all, the church, expressing a willingness to settle Mr. Moore in the Congregational form; but he, in the meantime, had found another place, and the town continued without a settled minister till Oct. 23, 1799, when Rev. Elijah Dunbar was ordained. Originally the church had belonged to the Londonderry Presbytery. At the settlement of Mr. Annan, by his request, it received a dismission from this and joined the New York Presbytery. When Mr. Dunbar was settled, that Presbytery had become extinct, and the church here was left an independent body. It then adopted the Congregational form, and though there were still some who preferred the Presbyterian mode, all attended upon his ministry, with the understanding, however, that once a year the communion should be administered by a Presbyterian, and in the Presbyterian manner. For many years the Rev. Dr. Wm. Morison, of Londonderry, administered the ordinance every autumn. It was always a day of uncommon interest; the house was crowded; and though but a child when he last came, I well remember the solemnity and awe with which I was impressed by the countenance, accent, and manner of that aged and faithful minister of Christ. Mr. Dunbar, with unsullied character, remained the minister of the town till June 19, 1822, when a portion of his people who had never liked the Congregational form, and others who had never been quite at ease under an Armenian preacher, withdrew and formed the Presbyterian society. Mr. Dunbar continued pastor of the Congregational society till February, 1827. He was succeeded, in June of the same year, by Rev. Abiel Abbot, D. D., who had preached in town a short time, thirty years before, and who is still the pastor.

The Presbyterian Church was built in 1825, about half a mile north of the old meeting-house, and during the present year has been removed to the village. Rev. Peter Holt was installed pastor, March, 1827, and resigned, March, 1835.

Rev. Mr. Pine was installed, June, 1836, and dismissed, January, 1837. Rev. Joshua Barret was pastor from February, 1837, till February, 1839.

The Baptist Church was constituted, November, 1822, containing forty members. Rev. Charles Cummings was the first pastor; Rev. Mr. Goodnow, from June, 1831; Rev. George Daland, from March, 1834, till 1836; Rev. John Peacock, one year, from September, 1837, have been the ministers. Rev. J. M. Willmorth, the present pastor, was settled September, 1838.

There has been for some years a Methodist society; ;and the Universalists have sometimes had preaching in the Congregational meeting-house.

Of our public schools, important and vitally connected as they are with all the better prospects of our country, my limits will allow me to say but little. From 1760 till 1797, the annual appropriations were small, never more than one hundred dollars, seldom fifty dollars, and often nothing. I do not find that any school-houses were erected by the town before 1790, when the town was divided into five districts, and provision made for the erection of five buildings.* From 1797 to 1805, three hundred dollars were annually raised for schools, except in 1801, when the appropriation was but two hundred dollars. From 1805 to 1808, four hundred dollars were raised annually; and since then the town has uniformly raised what the law required, and, I believe, no more, except that, for a few years past, one-half the literary fund, about seventy-five dollars per annum, has been given to aid the feeble districts. The school-tax now, and it has not materially varied for several years, is eight hundred and eighty-one dollars and thirty-six cents.

The condition of the schools, public and private, during the last, and the first twenty years of the present, century, was

---

* There were school-houses long before this, which had been erected by neighborhoods. In the same way schools also were supported. The public appropriations give a wrong idea of what has actually been paid for this purpose. The sum now paid for private schools is at least equal to what is paid by the town. There are now in town eleven districts, each with a brick school-house.

decidedly bad. Some improvement has been made since then; and great credit is due to the spirited exertions of a few individuals in different parts of the town. Still, for I should pervert the purposes of this day, if I stood here only to flatter or to praise, *the subject has not received the attention which its importance demands, and our public schools do not take the place that we should expect, from the general intelligence of our citizens.* They are peculiarly the property and province of the whole people, by whom they live and prosper, and without whose hearty assistance and' coöperation committees and teachers can accomplish nothing. All who take an interest in the welfare of their children or of society will not be slow to do what can be done for these, the true nurseries of a nation's mind. They will not grudge to the teacher his hard-earned pay, nor forget to do at home that which alone can render his labors easy and effective.

Our libraries demand a moment's attention. There had been, previously, a library of a similar character; but as early as 1811, the Peterborough Social Library was gotten up, containing not far from one hundred volumes. So judicious a selection I have never seen. There was hardly a book which did not deserve its place. I well remember the astonishment with which, at the age of eleven, I first looked on what seemed to me such an immense collection of books; nor can I soon forget the uniform kindness with which my early reading was encouraged, and in some measure directed, by the librarian, Daniel Abbot. In an intellectual point of view, I look back on no period of my life with so much satisfaction, as on the two years when, at the age of fourteen and fifteen, I lived with Samuel Templeton, as honest a man as this or any town has ever produced. During the hour which he always gave me at noon, and in the evening by fire-light, I read the standard histories in our language, and made myself acquainted with the important events of the ancient world. When a volume was finished, I would set out at dark, after a hard day's work, walk three miles to the village, and, enriched with a new treasure, would return almost unmindful of the woods and their near vicinity to the graveyard and old meeting-house, which, especially on a wintry, autumnal night, standing there naked, black, and lonely, was, as I know full well, a fearful object enough to a child. The Peterborough Social Library became gradually neglected, and was sold about 1830, when a new library on the same plan was gotten up, and contains now about three hundred volumes. The Union and Phœnix Factories have each a library of about one hundred and fifty volumes. The Ministerial Library (an excellent institution) contains five hundred, and the public town-library about nine hundred volumes; so that, besides private collections, there are now in town, for the use of readers, two thousand volumes.

One word let me here say to the young. These schools and libraries are for you. All that is most valuable in education is within your reach. Many have been the bitter but unavailing regrets of those who, despising these precious advantages in youth, have found themselves, as men and women, ignorant and incompetent to the great duties that were before them. The busiest day has intervals of rest, and he who is in earnest for knowledge will receive it. Let your leisure moments be sacredly devoted to the improvement of your minds. You might not covet the honors of a professional life, if you knew its painful watchings, anxieties, and toils; but as you value the esteem of others, or your own happiness, as you would do your part to carry on the progress of the world, as you would be useful and respected in manhood, and escape a leafless, neglected, old age, do not fail now, while the time is, to use every means that is held out for your intellectual advancement.

Another subject of much interest in our history I can but just sketch out. Early in our history, the hand-card, the little wheel, and the loom with the hand-shuttle, were almost the only instruments of manufacture in the place. The grandmother of Gov. Miller paid for four hundred acres of land in fine linen, made entirely, except getting out the flax, by her own hands. With the exception of hats and the wedding gown, which was usually of satin, and handed down as a sort of heir-loom to children and grandchildren, even three generations not unfrequently being married in the same dress, all the articles of clothing were manufactured at home. There the wool was carded, spun, woven, colored, and made up into garments. The hides were indeed sent away to be tanned; but the same hides were brought home as leather, and the shoemaker came always to the house, with his bench, lasts, and awls. To use foreign goods was considered, as indeed it was, great extravagance. After the first store was opened here, in 1771, one hundred pounds of butter was the price usually paid for a calico gown. Almost every article of food and clothing was then prepared at home. The first clothier's shop, for taking in wool to card and cloth to dress, was built by William Powers, in 1780, and this was the only factory in town till 1793; when, on the spot now occupied by the Phœnix Factory, "a* wooden building two hundred feet long, and two stories high, was erected by Samuel Smith, and was the wonder of the whole country. Mr. Smith had in this building a paper-mill, a saw-mill, an oil-mill, a clothier's shop, a trip-hammer shop, a wool-carding machine, and a dwelling-house." This bold step gave the first decided impulse to the manufacturing enterprise of the place. It brought into notice the great water-privileges that were here possessed. The first cotton factory for the manufacture of yarn was started in 1810. And from that time to this, one after another place has been taken up, until the capital vested in and upon the different water-privileges — not forgetting the peg-mill, in which twenty-five hundred bushels of shoe-pegs are made annually — is now estimated at three hundred thousand dollars; the cotton factories alone producing, annually, one million seven hundred and twenty-five thousand yards of cloth; and the amount of property annually imported and sold in our stores, it is estimated, cannot be less than seventy-five thousand dollars. With this change there has been a great influx of

---

* I have received from John H. Steele, Esq., a very full and exact account of all our manufacturing establishments from the beginning, which, in a condensed form, may be found in the Notes.

people from abroad; the habits and pursuits of the town have undergone an important revolution.*

But with all this show of enterprise and prosperity there is danger. Our young women, the future mothers, who are to form the character of the next generation, are not educated as their mothers were, at home, in comparative solitude, where the mind had leisure to mature, and the affections to expand, but are taken from their homes, work together in large companies, and board in crowded houses. It is surely a solemn responsibility that rests upon the owners and agents of these establishments. Thus far, their conduct has been marked by generosity and high principle. But it is well for all to be awake; for the operatives to remember that they have rights and duties for themselves beyond the mere comforts and luxuries of an animal life. They have minds, they have hearts, which require to be clothed and fed, and unless now, in season, they provide for their intellectual, moral, and spiritual wants, for the support of a refined intelligence, a modest but true moral independence, we shall repent the day that has clothed our bodies with improved garments, but left us with inferior minds, — with souls robbed of their pure affections, lofty freedom, and immortal hopes.

The notice of our early history would be incomplete without some scattered facts of a different character. Our ancestors, with all the rest of the world, believed in the bodily manifestation of the devil, in the existence of witches, and the appearance of ghosts. It is not my purpose to do anything more than relate what they believed. A small, lean, aged woman, by the name of Stinson, was uniformly regarded as a witch. A cat somewhere in town was observed to act strangely, hot water was thrown upon her, and straightway Mrs. Stinson's back was dreadfully afflicted with the St. Anthony's fire. On another occasion, a good man near

---

* A post-office was established in town about 1795; John Smith was the first postmaster. A Mr. Balch first carried the mail. William Thayer was carrier from 1803 to 1807. He was succeeded by Daniel Gibbs, who for many years rode on horseback from Portsmouth to Brattleboro once a week. At last he rode in a little wagon, and carried a few passengers. He was killed in 1824, by falling from a bridge. He was succeeded by his son. Stages began to run in 1826 or '27, and now a daily stage each way is crowded with passengers.

Sharon shot at a crow many times, but the bird only flew round and laughed at him. He at last took off a silver sleeve-button, and with it broke the crow's wing; whereupon Mrs. Stinson was found with a lame arm. At her funeral, which was about fifty years ago, though she was hardly more than a skeleton, the strong men who bore her to the grave were almost crushed to the earth by the weight of sin, and their shoulders remained for weeks black and blue.

There was also one Hannah Scott, who supposed herself bewitched by an old woman named Aspy, of Hancock. The girl lay more than a month without the power of opening her eyes, any more than she could open a part of her cheek. While in this state, she could tell exactly who were passing, how they looked, what they had with them, and what was going on in different houses, and in different parts of the town.. She always said that if old Aspy would come and bless her she should recover. The witch came, and passing her hands over the girl's forehead, with the words, " Your God bless you and my God bless you," ended the charm. This, it will be seen at once, is but the counterpart of what has recently taken place under the name of Animal Magnetism.

All this was religiously believed. And we in our day have known one* who, to his dying hour, firmly believed that he had twice been honored by a personal interview with the devil. Old Baker — what child in Peterborough within the last sixty years has not danced to his fiddle, with an ecstasy which no other music ever gave? Who does not remember the benevolent, complacent smile with which his honest, black face and white teeth and eyes shone, as raising his instrument to his chin, and producing the first sweet notes, he looked about on the delighted children that were listening or romping round him? But when we knew him, " the

---

* Baker Moore, a colored man, born in Boston, 1755, bought as a slave and brought to this town by Deacon Moore, in 1763. At the age of twenty-two, he purchased his freedom for two hundred dollars, which he never felt obliged to pay, nor was it exacted. He died January, 1839. There have been in this town eight slaves; two, Baker and Rose, belonging to Deacon Moore; two to David Steele; two to Samuel Alld; one to Isaac Mitchell; one to Capt. Robbe. There may possibly have been others.

minstrel was infirm and old," and now he is gone, — light
may the turf rest upon his bosom.   Such men are like
fossil remains and petrifactions, which preserve the exact
lineaments of plants and animals centuries perhaps after
the living species has become extinct.   Their minds receive in youth the impressions then current, and there
remain fixed through life; so that Baker, in these matters,
may be considered a fair sample of the belief which prevailed sixty or seventy years ago.   It was seldom that he
could be induced to speak upon the subject, and then with
symptoms of terror which it would be difficult to describe.
I remember, however, to have heard him once,-after casting
round a fearful look to be sure that the doors were shut, and
the evil spirit not actually in the room.   As he was driving
the cows to pasture, he said, one evening he met a man who
very kindly accosted him, and in the course of the conversation told his fortune, mentioning things that no mortal could
have known.   He gave him a book, with the request that he
would read it.   Baker took the book; but it hung like lead
upon his spirits.   He carried it constantly with him, for he
was afraid to leave it behind, and at last, having met "the
man" again on horseback, in the north-west part of the town,
he returned the book; whereupon the man's eyes glistened
like fire, his cloven foot appeared, and he was terribly angry.
Baker looked up a moment after and he was gone.   All this
our good friend as much believed as he believed in his own
existence, and it is but a fair sample of what our fathers also
believed.   One man, William M'Nee, had horse-shoe nails
driven into the horns of all his cattle, to save them from the
witches, and it was generally believed that horse-shoes, witch-
hazel rods, and silver, were effectual securities against their
influence.

Another singular fact may be here added, to illustrate this
part of their character.   William Robbe — his mother was
always supposed to have saved the life of the elder William
Smith, by sucking the wound made by a poisonous snake in
Lunenburg, and both he and his parents were modest, excellent people, — William Robbe was a seventh son; and it was

generally thought that certain diseases could be cured by him. He was not a quack; receiving pay destroyed the charm. He gave a small silver coin to those who came. The visits became so numerous that he left the town, in consequence, and went to Stoddard; but, being unfortunate there, was obliged to return, and bear the onerous duties which the accident of being the seventh son imposed upon him. The belief in his power was general, and borne out by reputed facts, which we cannot here stop to examine or even specify.

I would now speak of the characteristics of our inhabitants.

In the first place, they have been always distinguished for their mental activity, and love of knowledge. The original emigrants from Ireland were by no means an ignorant people. They were brought up in the common school education of the day, and most of them were imbued with the religious education then more common in Scotland and the north of Ireland than in the sister kingdom of England. What was wanting in outward instruction was, in some measure, supplied by their own intellectual energy and zeal. The respect which has always been paid to learning may in part be understood from the number and character of our educated men. Thirty-two[*] have graduated at our different colleges. James Wilson, for a time Representative in Congress, and Jonathan Steele, a Judge of the Supreme Court, were widely known. Nor must we omit the name of Jesse Smith, who, having graduated at Dartmouth College in 1814, studied medicine with Dr. George C. Shattuck, of Boston, and afterwards established himself in Cincinnati, where, as a professor in the Medical College and a practitioner, he stood decidedly at the head of his profession. He died of the cholera in 1833, universally lamented, having fallen a victim to his humane and fearless

---

[*] Jeremiah Smith, 1781; James Wilson, 1789; Walter Little (name changed to Fullerton), 1796; John Wilson, 1799; Stephen Mitchell, 1801; Reuben D. Mussey, 1802; John Stuart, 1804; William Ritchie, 1804; Stephen P. Steele, 1808; Charles J. Stuart, 1809; James Porter, 1810; David Steele (son of Gen. David), 1810; Jonathan Steele, 1811; Isaac P. Osgood, 1814; Jesse Smith, 1814; David Steele (son of Gen. John), 1815; Joseph Brackett, 1815; Charles White, 1816; Amasa Edes, 1817; Jonathan Smith, 1819; James Wilson, 1820; Albert Smith, 1825; John H. Morison, 1831; Josiah Ballard, 1833; Artemas L. Holmes, 1835; Solomon Laws, 1836; Horace Morison, 1837; Nathaniel Holmes, 1837; Oren B. Cheney, 1839; Nathaniel H. Morison, 1839; Bernard B. Whittemore, 1839; David Youngman, 1839.

exertions for the suffering, during the ravages of that frightful pestilence.

Among the educated sons of Peterborough is another, yet
happily numbered with the living, who was your first choice
for the task which I am now laboring to perform. I cannot
but regret that it was out of his power to accept your call;
for there is no man alive so intimately acquainted with our
history, or so well able to do justice to the character of our
people. He was born Nov. 29, 1759; his father, William
Smith, perhaps the best-educated of our early settlers, and
who was a delegate to the Provincial Congress in 1774, was a
man of singular discretion, modesty, and goodness; and his
mother, the daughter of John Morison, was a driving, energetic woman. He was one of seven sons,* all, except one
who died before his strength was brought out, uncommon
men. Until recently, for the last sixty years, they have had
here an influence possessed by no other family, and have done
more than any others to form the character and advance the
prosperity of the town. Seventy years ago, if we may trust to
one who then knew them well, a more rude, uncouth, impudent set of boys was not to be found in Peterborough. Very
early, however, Jeremiah's enthusiastic love of knowledge began to act. But the facilities for learning within his reach
were greatly inferior to what may now be enjoyed by the
poorest and most neglected child among us. There were no
books to be had; and the schools were wretched. I have
heard him speak of going, when a small boy, three or four
miles to procure the loan of some ordinary volume, and the
tears of disappointment with which he often came away from
his teacher's blundering explanation of subjects which he was
longing to understand. But never yet did the youth, urged
on by an unquenchable desire to know, stop short through
outward obstructions. They only quicken his zeal, and give
new energy to his powers. So was it with our townsman.
At the age of twelve he began to study Latin at the public
school, which was then kept in the old meeting-house, by Mas-

---

* Robert, John, William, James, Jeremiah, Jonathan, and Samuel.

WILLIAM ALBERT

ter Rudolphus Greene. After this, he studied for a short time with a Mr. Donovan at New Boston, and then with Rev. Mr. Emerson, of Hollis, where he began Greek, and finished his preparation for college. He entered Harvard College in 1777. Just at this time, he enlisted for two months in the service, was present at the battle of Bennington, where a portion of his gun was shot off in his hands, and a musket-ball grazing his throat left its mark there for many years. He left Cambridge in 1779, and was graduated at Rutgers College, N. J., in 1781. He now began the study of the law in Barnstable, Mass., 1782, '83, spending, after this, a year at Andover and two years in Salem, filling at each place the office of teacher, in connection with his studies.

He began to practise here as a lawyer in 1787, was a member of our Legislature three years, during which time he revised the laws of the State. Previous to this time, Peterborough had been notorious for its lawsuits, and furnished no small portion of the whole litigation of the county. These foolish disputes he always discountenanced, sometimes cooling down his angry client by pleasantry, and sometimes dissuading him by more serious considerations. It was the opinion of our most intelligent people at the time, that the town might afford to pay Jerry Smith five hundred dollars a year, simply for his influence in preventing lawsuits.

But a wider field was opening. In 1791, he was chosen a Representative to Congress. To this office he was appointed at four successive elections, and, continuing in it through nearly the whole of Washington's Administration, he resigned during the Presidency of the elder Adams, after the May session of 1797. Here it was his privilege to become acquainted with the great men of the time ; with Washington, with John Adams, with Jefferson and Madison, with John Jay, John Marshall, Samuel Dexter, and Fisher Ames, during the interesting period when the French Revolution was breaking out with the suddenness of a new volcano. Upon leaving Congress, he was appointed United States Attorney for the District of New Hampshire, and soon after, while holding this office, was made Judge of Probate for the County of Rocking-

37

ham, having in the meantime removed to Exeter. In 1801, he was appointed Judge of the Circuit Court of the United States, and during a part of the year 1802 was at the same time Judge of Probate, Judge of the United States District Court, and Chief-Justice of the Supreme Court of New Hampshire. He continued Chief-Justice till 1809, when he was chosen Governor of the State. He returned to the bar in 1810; in 1813 was again made Chief-Justice, and continued in this office till 1816, when he withdrew from public life. In 1820, he gave up his practice at the bar. It is not my purpose, nor am I 'competent, to speak of the ability, learning, uprightness, and independence with which the duties of these high, various, and responsible offices were discharged. His acts, are they not written in the chronicles, and themselves an important part of the public history, of our State? The assaults of party violence are over; and they who were once the most earnest to assail are now among the foremost to acknowledge his intellectual vigor, great learning, and, above all, the spotless purity of his character as a public man. It is not for such as I to praise or censure him. The verdict has been made up by his peers; and if they are to be trusted, his name will be handed down as one of the two most able and accomplished public men that New Hampshire, during the first two centuries of her political existence, has produced.

In this our great family meeting, may we not indulge in the expression of personal feeling? Especially, may not a younger brother speak of what he owes to one full of honors as of years, whose heart is with us, though he be not here? From my childhood up, I have been the creature of kindness, and should I die with the consciousness of having done no other good than to have called out the kind acts which have been extended to myself, I shall go down to the grave feeling that I have not lived in vain. There are others towards whom the fulness of my gratitude can be known only by the Searcher of all hearts. But for them, I should not now be among the living. What I should have been without him I almost tremble to think. Just standing upon the verge of life, with principles unformed, with a yearning, indeed, for knowledge, which had followed me like some mystic spell from my earliest recollections, hoping and yet despairing, with no claim but inexperience and helplessness, I received from him all the kindness that a father could give. Dull, indeed, must I have been, if I have not profited from the richness of his mind and the advantages which his aid has placed within my reach.

I have dwelt on this example, not for the purpose of gratifying private feelings, but because it is the brightest illustration that our town has furnished to the young, of a really great intellect strengthened and adorned by a finished education. When I see such a man, and feel his strength of mind, the richness and variety of his intellectual stores, his vivacity and wit, and, more than all, his utter scorn for everything mean or dishonest, I forget the offices through which he has passed. They have borrowed much, but added little to the dignity of the man. And the elements which have made him what he is belong peculiarly to the Peterborough mind, and may be seen, less clearly developed indeed, in many of our citizens.

But while the intellect of our people is shown in the number and character of educated men that have gone from among them, it is shown still more in their general character. I might select many among those whom I have personally known, who, if not polished so as to bring out all the shades and rich veins of intellect, have yet been sufficiently cultivated to show minds capable of grasping strong thoughts, and acting upon the most important interests of public and private life. Many excel them in every species of intellectual refinement, in the taste for poetry, the fine arts, and the niceties of literature. But in sterling good sense, in close and severe reasoning, in solid information, especially in acquaintance with the standard works of history, theology, and some branches of philosophy, the people of few towns are superior, if indeed, as a whole, they are equal, to those who have lived here for the last twenty or thirty years. Like every place, it has those who recognize no such thing as purely intellectual tastes and wants. But thanks be to heaven they are few, and their influence in the town has been only to make men shun their example. Our young men, kindling with nobler hopes, look to other quarters for instruction.

The next remarkable feature of our town during the past century has been courage. It was shown by our fathers in Ireland, and has not deserted their sons. As a people, they have never shrunk from peril. At the first sound of danger, their custom has been to fly to the scene of action. So was it in the Indian and French wars, in which, when there were not in town more than forty families, six of our citizens were slain in a single day.* So was it after the news of the battle of Lexington. Of the seventeen engaged at Bunker Hill, one man, John Graham, remarkable for his skill in throwing stones, after exhausting his ammunition, unwilling to retire, seized upon stones and hurled them, not without effect, against the enemy; another, John Taggart, after fighting as long as it was possible to fight, in the retreat stopped his companions while yet in the midst of danger, and, when they had refreshed themselves from their canteens, exclaimed, " Neu let us trust in God and tak the tother run." Randall McAlister was severely shot through the neck; Thomas Green, in a fainting and almost expiring state, was saved by his friend Gilchrist, who carried him on his back from Bunker Hill to Medford. Lieutenant (afterwards Captain) William Scott, early in the action, had one of the bones of his leg broken just below the knee. He continued coolly paring musket-balls and handing them to his soldiers. He was among the very hindmost in the retreat, when he received in his thigh and the lower part of his body four additional balls, and, bleeding at nine orifices, fainted upon the field. When he came to himself, a British soldier was standing over him, with his bayonet, and asked with an oath if he did not deserve to be killed. " I am in your power," was the reply, "and you can do with me as you please." He was rescued by a British officer, and permitted to remain unmolested upon the field through that night. The next morning he

---

* In a ranging company commanded by Robert Rodgers, in 1757. See Farmer's Belknap.

was taken to Boston, and thence to Halifax, where he was imprisoned. With a gimblet, a bayonet, and an old knife, furnished by a friend without,* he, and six of his companions broke the prison, and by the help of that same friend got on board a vessel, and reached home the following August. He set out immediately for the American army, which he joined on Long Island, was taken with two thousand others at the capture of Fort Washington;† but the night after, tying his sword to the back of his neck, and his watch to his hat-band, he swam a mile and a half to Fort Lee, upon the Jersey shore, eluding the vigilance of the British frigate that had been stationed there to guard the prisoners. He continued in the army till after the retreat of Lafayette before Cornwallis, and from that time was engaged upon the ocean.

The same intrepidity which he had shown in war continued in peace. The following is from the Boston *Independent Chronicle*, of July 12, 1792, under the head of news from Philadelphia, July 2d. After stating in general terms a terrific tempest that occurred the day before, and some of the accidents caused by it, they add: "Since writing the above account, we further learn that a boat from this city to the Jersey shore was overset within fifty rods of Samuel Cowper's wharf. There were in the boat Captain Scott, Mr. Blake, his wife, and four small children, a young woman, and Mr. Betis—in all nine persons,—none of whom could swim but Captain Scott. The captain, by the most astonishing and praiseworthy exertions, was able, providentially, to save them all. He swam ashore with one child hanging to his neck and one to each arm, and he returned to the boat amidst the boisterous waves raging in a furious and frightful manner, and brought the others, who had, with much difficulty held by the boat, safe to land."

The editor of the Boston paper adds: "For the honor of Capt. Scott, an old and valiant soldier, a son of Massachu-

---

* John Morison, Esq., the brother of Thomas and Jonathan. He lived in Nova Scotia, was a Whig, and like others of the family, not being able to keep his opinions to himself, became suspected, fled from the British Provinces, and lived for a time in Peterborough.

† November 16, 1776. See Holmes's Annals of America, Vol. II., p. 251.

setts, this circumstance should be handed down to posterity. Those who revere the virtues of the benevolent Howard must ever remember with veneration the successful exertions of Capt. Scott."

He fell at last a sacrifice to a higher spirit than can ever be shown by mere courage in the field. "In 1793, he went in the suite of Gen. Lincoln, to settle a treaty with the Six Nations of Indians at or near Sandusky, where his health was impaired. In 1796, he was connected with a party in surveying lands on the Black River, near Lake Erie, and in the vicinity of the smaller lakes. They were attacked by the lake fever, and he returned with a division of the sick to Port Stanwix. Finding it difficult to procure any to go back after the sick persons left behind in the wilderness, he determined to go himself, though strongly dissuaded by the physician, who affirmed that he could not return alive. 'I think I shall,' was his reply, 'but if not, my life is no better than theirs.' He succeeded in his benevolent attempt, but died on the tenth day after his return, at Litchfield, N. Y., Sept. 19, 1796, in his fifty-fourth year."*

This instance, which by no means stands alone in our history, may serve to illustrate the courage which has been always a prominent feature in the character of our citizens. And it has run through their whole character, distinguishing alike their habits of thought, of social intercourse, of public and private enterprise. In whatever they have undertaken, they have gone forward with the same fearless spirit. If at any time a man has had hard thoughts of his neighbor, he did not whisper it about in private scandal, but the offender was the first to hear it. There has been no secret, underhand dealing, but their voices were always loud,† their gait erect, their conduct open. While ready to maintain their own and their neighbors' rights, they have also, it must be

---

* See N. H. Historical Collections, Vol. I., p. 135.

† Loud talking has always prevailed here; and at least in one case served an important purpose. At Bennington, the company belonging to New Ipswich and Peterborough were surprised by an ambuscade of Tories, when Lieut. Cuningham, of Peterborough, cried out with the voice of a lion, "Bring up those four hundred men," which put the Tories to flight, and left an open passage to the main army.

acknowledged, never been backward in proclaiming their own merits. Yet they have not been a conceited, boasting race, but men who knew their strength, who judged correctly of their merits, and would not suffer others to destroy or impair their just appreciation.

Closely allied to this was another prominent trait in their character. They were always a high-minded, generous people. Though poor, they were never mean in spirit. Sometimes, indeed, a foolish pride has been among them. It is related of the wife of the oldest John Morison, that when her husband was building his first habitation in Londonderry, she came to him, and in a manner unusually affectionate, as is sometimes the custom of wives when they have a great favor to ask, said, " Aweel, aweel, dear Joan, an it maun be a log-house, do make it a log heegher nor the lave " (than the rest). A portion of this spirit may have come down to some of her descendants, and perhaps to a few who are not her descendants. But if they have had a little sprinkling of this, they have also been marked by a true loftiness and generosity of soul, which in all their trials has not forsaken them. It mingled with their courage in war. We have seen how prominent it was in the character of Scott. And in the last war, when our townsman made himself conspicuous in the eyes of the nation, by his coolness and gallantry, in the most perilous enterprise ever ready to " try," and to succeed where he tried, he gained the confidence of his soldiers and townsmen, by his humane, and generous attention, even more than by his unquestioned military ability and courage.* The same spirit of liberality guided their intelligence in politics. When it was proposed in our Legislature to give some assistance to Dr. Belknap, who was then preparing his invaluable history of the State,

---

* James Miller, son of James and Catharine Miller, born in 1776, began to practise law in 1807, and was appointed Major in the U. S. service in 1808. The family from which he sprang lived in the north-east corner of the town, which seemed cut off from the rest. James Miller, Senior, and a twin brother inherited a farm together, which they lived upon fifteen or sixteen years, enjoying the produce in common, with no exact division of labor or the fruits of their labor. The whole family were remarkable for simple-hearted truth and kindness, and at the same time great manliness and courage. Gen. Miller's history after entering the U. S. service is too well known to be given here.

the Representative of a neighboring town objected, saying
that he would as soon support an appropriation for the purchase of Tom Thumb. The next morning your representative,* in the presence of the House, gave to him a copy of
Tom Thumb, adding that it afforded him much pleasure to be
able to make the gentleman a present so appropriate in size and
character to the liberality which he had shown the day before.
In their influence, great or small, in high or in low stations,
upon the councils of the State or nation, our people, as a body,
have always been on the side of a liberal, generous policy,
whatever might be its effect upon their private interests.
The same may be said of their conduct as a town. The
whole amount of their property at the present hour would
not probably exceed five hundred thousand dollars; yet the
amount of taxes this year (and for several years past they
have varied little) is four thousand seven hundred and sixty-
eight dollars and twenty-two cents. If to this we add nine
hundred dollars paid for the support of private schools, one
thousand five hundred for the support of public worship, and
remember that of three hundred and eighty taxable polls
only two hundred and six, and many of them by no means
the most competent, contribute anything towards the maintenance of religion, we certainly must conclude that our citizens now are by no means backward in their contributions
for public objects. In addition to the usual taxes, in 1825
fourteen thousand dollars were raised, without great effort, for
the erection of churches and school-houses, and in roads the
town has been liberal almost to excess.

The same spirit has been even more conspicuous in private
donations. Losses by fire have sometimes been more than
made up to the sufferers by voluntary subscription, and generally he whose house has been burnt has hardly borne a
greater share of the loss than many others, in proportion to
their means. Nor has this liberality been confined to cases

---

* John Smith, Esq., whose sudden death in 1821 threw a gloom over the whole town. He perhaps united in himself all the characteristics of our town in a more remarkable degree than any
other man, joining to the gushing emotions of a child, strong powers of thought, integrity, courage, and an infinite fund of wit.

of want; but it has often happened that when, by the sudden providence of God, a portion of a man's goods has in this way been destroyed, many whose property was less than what remained to him have cheerfully contributed to make up his loss. There have been, we all know, and still are, mean men among us, but I do not believe that in the history of the town a single instance can be found in which a mean act, public or private, has been for a single day countenanced by the general feeling of the community. It has been my privilege, beyond the lot of most men, to reside among high-minded, generous people, but I have never lived in a place where, in thought, speech, and conduct, there has been so general a detestation of what is paltry and little as in my native town.

The same spirit has been carried into their quarrels and enmities. Who has ever heard in Peterborough of a sullen, Indian-like hatred, cherished for years or even weeks, watching stealthily for the opportunity of revenge; or of a fawning dislike, veiling itself under the semblance of friendship till the secret stab might be given? They have been impetuous in their feelings, and have given way too readily to the impulse of anger; but the cloud passed quickly off. The storm was too violent to last. They who have quarrelled to-day are to-morrow the more earnest to do each other a kind act; and acts of neighborly kindness in the common intercourse of life have been a leading feature, from the earliest settlement of the town. It has made an important part of the good-fellowship of the place; and if the kind office had not its intended effect, instead of going sulkily away and determining to do so no more, they enjoyed it as a good joke, and were quite as ready to repeat the act when a new occasion might require it. A man who had not been long in town was poor, lazy, and shiftless; the neighbors came together and mowed his grass, leaving it for him to do the rest. "It is very light," said the old man, after they went away, "very light; worth mowing indeed, but not worth mowing and raking too," and so he permitted it to lie upon the ground. They were not angry, but simply laughed at his awkward excuse, and for aught that I have heard to the contrary may have mowed and raked his hay, too, the year following.

This brings me to what has, perhaps, from the beginning been their *one* trait, standing out from all the rest; I mean their love of fun. The sun would go down before I could tell half the stories we still have which might illustrate this point.* No occasion, no subject, was kept sacred from their wit. The thoughtless and the grave, the old and the young, alike enjoyed it. When Capt. Scott had been pierced by five bullets, and his life almost lost, he said the minister had prayed in the morning that their heads might be covered in the hour of battle. "His head," he added, "was safe enough, but the prayer should have extended to the rest of his body."† Relatives and friends were never spared, when they offered a good subject for laughter, but were rather dealt with the more freely. From the cradle to the grave there was no circumstance which at one time or another did not administer to their mirth. Even their superstitions had in them a mixture of drollery that took much from their terror. The bird that was bewitched "only laughed" at the man who shot at it. They who believed most fully in the reality of the account, and who never doubted that Satan was actually present at the scene, could yet, with shouts of laughter, tell how, at a certain place, when Mr. Morrison and Mr. M'Lellan, another minister, were there, the evil spirit came, and the bed on which a young woman lay actually rose from the floor, and the ministers, terribly frightened, called upon each other to pray, and Mr. Morrison would not pray, but at the prayer of Mr. M'Lellan the spirit was driven off. Our fathers were serious, thoughtful men; but they lost no occasion which might promise sport.

---

* Moses Morison, the prince of story-tellers, usually manufactured his stories for the occasion. The wit consisted in a wild and comical exaggeration of real facts, and was the offspring of a prolific fancy. It had, however, an unfavorable influence; for though these stories were told and heard merely as romances, the habit of exaggeration thus produced was likely to extend itself to more serious matters, so that strict verbal accuracy has been too little regarded.

† A story has been told, which, though perhaps without foundation as a matter of fact, may yet show the extent to which they often indulged their wit in serious matters. The story is, that when they were first forming a church, almost every one propounded was set aside on account of some objection (particularly intemperance), till it became doubtful whether a church could be established, when one of their number rose, and gravely said, "If God chooses to have a church in this place, he must take such as there be."

Weddings, huskings, log-rollings, and raisings, — what a host of queer stories is connected with them!

At weddings* seventy years ago, the groom usually proceeded from his dwelling with his select friends, male and female. About half-way on their progress to the house of the bride, they were met by her select male friends. There each party made choice of a champion to run for the bottle to the bride's house. The victor returned to the party with the bottle, gave a toast, drank to the groom's health, passed round the bottle, and the whole party proceeded, being saluted by the firing of muskets from the houses they passed, and answering the salutes with pistols. When they arrived at the bride's house the groom was stationed upon the floor, the father led his daughter, dressed usually in white satin, and delivered her up to the groom, and the rest of the ceremony was performed nearly as at the present time. The evening was filled up with all imaginable sports, and closed with a ceremony which it will hardly do now to mention. This is the way in which our grandparents were married.

The other merry-meetings then common, I cannot stop to describe. Huskings, log-rollings, apple-parings, and raisings,† most of those now in middle-life have seen; and as they think of the new cider, the smoking Indian puddings, and huge loaves of brown bread, such as our grandmothers made, with perhaps a whole quarter of mutton, and pork and beans, smoking also from the same oven, and followed by

---

* The first notice given in town publicly of intended marriage was in 1749. William Ritchie agreed with Alexander Robbe, for half a pint of rum, to give notice of his intentions, which he did by nailing the publishment to a beech-tree near the old meeting-house. The first oral notice (which mode prevailed for a long time) was given thus by Alexander Robbe: "Marriage is intended between Joan Robbe and Betty Creighton. If ony man or man's man has ony objections, let him speak neu, or forever after haud his clash."

The above, with other curious particulars relating to our early history, was furnished me by John Todd, Jr.

† At the raising of the third two-story house (in 1764), all the men, women, and children of the town were gathered together. After the sills were levelled, prayers were offered, and a psalm sung. Seventeen gallons of rum had been provided, and none of it remained the next morning, except half a pint, which had been stealthily put aside. At a training, much later than this, a barrel of rum was placed upon the field, and the head knocked out, so that each, without loss of time, could dip from it what he wanted. Before night an express was sent for more. One man, on returning home, said they had had an excellent training, and he believed they were to have more of it the next day, "for he saw many of the soldiers lying upon their arms."

pumpkin, apple, and mince pies, such as they also made, not thin, depressed, or all outside, but thick and plump, and remember the jokes, the plays, the peals of merriment, and the sound night's rest that followed, their childhood and the dawning hopes of life rise again; the father and the mother, the brother and the sister that are gone, come before them, and what would they not give to renew but for once those ancient times? But they cannot be renewed, and we must soon follow them into the pale and shadowy past, and be known here among our native hills only as a memory more and more dim, till it shall vanish clean out.

But I may not dwell on subjects like these. Our ancestors dearly loved fun. There was a grotesque humor, and yet a seriousness, pathos, and strangeness about them which, in its way, has perhaps never been excelled. It was the sternness of the Scotch Covenanter softened by a century's residence abroad amid persecution and trial, wedded there to the comic humor and pathos of the Irish, and then grown wild in the woods among these our New England mountains. I see in them and their genuine descendants the product of the heaths and highlands of Scotland with their border wars, of the rich, low fields of Ireland with their mirth and clubs, modified afresh by the hardships of a new settlement and the growing influence of a free country.*

In nothing here was the Irish character more visible than in the use of ardent spirits.† When the entrance of death‡ into the little colony had suspended the sound of the axe, and a strong arm was laid low, all the people gathered together at the house of mourning, and through the long, dark, dismal night watched by the body of their friend. The eldest and

---

* See Notes, No. 1.

† I had thought our ancestors an intemperate people, but it was not so. Some never drank; but there were loose men who would always, when an opportunity offered, get intoxicated, and be quarrelsome. The great body of the people were not in the constant habit of using inebriating drink; but on great occasions there were few of whom it might not be said, as of Tam O'Shanter, that if they "were na fou," they "just had plenty," — enough to put them in the best possible trim for telling their "queerest stories."

‡ The first death in town (March 15, 1753) was that of William Stuart, aged 53, who was buried in the Old Cemetery.

most sacred of their number, with the holy volume before him, and with an iron sternness of manner, from time to time administered the words of divine consolation and hope. This was the offspring of Scotland, and betokened at once the sublime and severe character of the highlands. But ever and anon another comforter came in, of Irish parentage; the long countenance became short, the broad Irish humor began to rise, and before the dawn, jokes and laughter had broken in upon the slumbers of the dead. Again at the funeral the same mixed custom prevailed. After the prayer had been offered, and the last look taken, and the coffin closed, spirit was handed round, first to the minister and mourners, then to the bearers, and finally to the whole congregation. All followed to the grave. The comforting draught was again administered at their return, and a sumptuous supper prepared. So did they bury their dead in the days of our fathers.

And yet they were a devout, religious people. With their Presbyterian predilections confirmed by the inhuman massacres, extortions, and wars through which they had passed, their first object in settling here was that they might be free in their religious faith. And nowhere upon the shores of New England, every part of which was sought for a religious end, have prayers been offered more fervent and sincere, or the Scriptures read with more constancy and reverence, than in the first rude dwellings of our fathers. The fact that with such religious teachers they should still have preserved a religious character shows how deeply those principles had been implanted in their minds. What had clung to them in Ireland, the disposition to humor, rioting, and laughter, was only upon the surface, playing there and varying the outlines of the countenance, while the strong, granite features of Scotland were fixed deep in the soul. The unbending purpose, the lofty principle, the almost haughty adherence to what they believed true, and high, and sacred, resting on a religious basis, was the real substance of their character. They had foibles, they had weaknesses and errors. But well may it be for us if the refinements of a more advanced society and a more liberal culture should serve to give grace, beauty, and light to the same strong powers of thought, the same courage, though in a different sphere, the same generous elevation of soul, the same vivacity, and, above all, the same deep, thoughtful, religious principle that belonged to them. .

I have now before me a list* of four hundred and eighty emigrants, who, scattered through sixteen different States, and, if not greatly distinguished, yet holding a respectable place, retain these same strong features. Here, though at times we have felt as if strangers who came among us could only spy out the nakedness of the land after the fruitful gatherings of the harvest, there is still, enriched as the town has been by new accessions, enough to perpetuate the character which we have received from our fathers. Their faults were usually virtues carried too far. The strong mind sometimes became dogmatical, impatient, overbearing; their courage became rashness, their generosity extravagance, their wit levity; their piety was sometimes proud, formal, severe; and all these incongruous excesses were not seldom mingled in the same mind. Such were our fathers, the substantial elements of their characters well deserving attention, especially in these days of timid virtue; their faults, partly belonging to the times, but more the effect of strong feelings without the advantages of early discipline. At the same time, they had in them the rudiments of a real refinement — warm, kind, and gentle feelings, — and specimens of politeness were found among them worthy of the patriarchal age.

A century has gone by since the solitude of our forests was first broken by the sound of their axe; and within that century what events have successively risen upon the world! The old French war; our own Revolution, one of the few great events in the history of man; Washington and his associates, — they have come and gone, and the noise of their actions is like the distant murmurings of the sea, heard inland when the storm is over, and the waves are sinking to their repose. Then there was the French Revolution, filling the world at once with hope and terror, the rise and fall of

---

* Prepared with much care by Capt. Isaac Edes.

that wonderful man, who, beginning and ending his life in a narrow island, dethroned monarchs, shook empires, ploughed through kingdoms in his bloody course. During all this while, our mountain retreat remained, answering only with a faint echo to the tumults that were agitating all the great interests of the world. The common incidents of time passed over it. Our fathers sowed, and, with the patience of hope, waited the result of their labors; they laughed and mourned, performed or neglected the great work that was before them, and went off one by one to their reward. All of the first, and almost all of the second, generation are now gone. The few that linger with us will soon be gathered to their fathers, and no link will be left connecting us with the first settlers of our town. They are going, they are gone; a strongly-marked race, — bold as the craggy summits of our mountains, generous as our richest fields, impetuous as the torrents that came tumbling down our hills, kind and gentle as the same streams winding through the valleys, and watering the green meadows.

They, and all that they loved, hoped, or feared, their intelligence and strength, their warm sympathies and strong hearts, their loud jests and solemn prayers, are gone from their old homes. Their bones repose on yonder bleak hill-side, near the spot where they were wont to assemble, as a single family, to worship the God of their fathers. Blessings rest upon the spot. The old meeting-house, as if it could not longer, in its loneliness, look down day and night upon the graves of those who had once filled its walls with prayer and song, has gone like them, and the ploughshare has removed every mark of the place where it stood. The graveyard alone remains. It is overgrown with wild bushes, briers, and thistles. There let them in summer spread their shade over the ashes of the dead, and in winter let the winds whistle and howl through them, a fitting emblem of the desolation which must sooner or later strip off every earthly hope. May the blessings of heaven rest still on that spot. Fresher tears may be shed, and more sumptuous ornaments prepared for the new ground, but many are the hearts, of children and brothers and parents, which still cling to the old graveyard, bleak, and wild, and lonely as it is. And some there are who, when the paleness of death is creeping under their thin gray locks, shall leave the parting charge of the patriarch: " Bury me with my fathers on the old hill-side. There they buried Abraham and Sarah his wife; there they buried Isaac and Rebecca his wife; there I buried Leah, and there let my bones be laid."

A hundred years have gone by. What unlooked-for events in the great wheel of human life shall rise before another century has closed, it were vain for us to inquire. But when a remote generation shall come next to celebrate this day, not one of us, not one of our children, except as a gray and wrinkled relic from the past, shall be found among the living. The Monadnock then, as now, will catch the first glimmerings of morning, and the last rays of evening will linger upon his bald and rugged brow; the Contoocook will journey onward to the sea; but of all that our hands have wrought, and our hearts have loved, not a vestige will remain as we now behold it. What future good or ill, what storms of civil violence or public war, may pass over the land, we know not. But so may we live that the inheritance which we have received, of freedom, truth, intelligence, virtue, and faith, may be handed down unspotted to those who shall succeed; and the blessing of Almighty God will go with it, and go also with us.

NOTE. — My object throughout has been to state facts, and not to give opinions. In noticing at the beginning of the discourse, for instance, the long and bitter contests between the native Irish and the Scotch who had settled on their lands, I wished to say nothing of the blame attached to either party. My sole object was to state the facts as viewed at the time by the Scotch emigrants, in order to show the influence upon the character of their descendants. The Irish may have been guilty of cruelty and madness, but it was the cruelty and madness into which a sensitive, generous, enthusiastic people were goaded by oppression.

I cannot let this opportunity pass without expressing my obligations to several members of the Committee of Arrangements at Peterborough, without whose assistance in the collection of facts, this Address, imperfect as it is, could not have been prepared.

NOTES.

No. I.

THE union of opposite qualities, which has sometimes prevented our character from being rightly estimated by strangers, is, with great justice, expressed in the following account of Dr. Jesse Smith, which I have been permitted to extract from a manuscript sermon preached after his death (Sept. 22, 1833), by my friend, Rev. Ephraim Peabody, who had been his pastor.

"There were united in him qualities which, in so eminent a degree, are rarely seen combined. His mind was thoroughly possessed by that foundation of every virtue — a sense of his own personal responsibility — which governed his life with the omnipotence of habit. Hence that firmness and independence of purpose which kept its calm and even way, equally incapable of being seduced by the solicitations, or overawed by the fear, of man. His iron firmness of resolve seemed almost to partake of obstinacy, till a more intimate acquaintance showed that it was the result of a character where the mental and moral powers were peculiarly active, but peculiarly well-proportioned, — where habits of independent, clear thought left no wavering of mind, and the moral energy fully sustained the intellectual decision. And interfused through these more rugged features was a true tenderness of nature, which softened down everything like austerity, and preserved for manhood the simple feelings of the child. It struck men almost strangely, who had seen him only in the struggle of life, to witness how quickly and deeply he was touched by everything that interested others, until it was remembered how much better the firm character preserves the original susceptibilities of the heart, than the feeble. . . . But that which shed beauty over his character, and commanded the love and respect of his friends so deeply, was the light and strength it received from religious faith."

In conversation, my friend speaks also of his fearless intrepidity of spirit, which, united with the Peterborough humor, that spared no one, and with a frame of mind so vigorous, gave to those who knew him little the idea of coarseness and levity, hiding at once the nice susceptibilities, deep feelings, and lofty principle which were really, with him, the controlling powers.

No. II.

PROVINCE OF NEW HAMPSHIRE.

To his Excellency, Benning Wentworth, Esq., Commander-in-chief and over his Majesty's Province of New Hampshire; the honorable his Majesty's Council of said Province.

The Humble Petition of us, the subscribers, being Inhabitants of a tract of Land (lying in said Province on the West side of Merrimac River, of the contents of about six miles square, commonly called and known by the name of Peterborough) in behalf of ourselves and others, the inhabitants of said tract of land, most humbly shews — That about the year of our lord 1739, a number of Persons in consequence of a Grant of a tract of land, had and obtained from the Great and General Court or Assembly of the Province of the Massachusetts Bay, by Samuel Haywood and others his associates, granting to them the said tract of land on certain conditions of settlement. And in pursuance whereof a number of People immediately went on to said tract of land and began a settlement, (tho then very fur from any other inhabitants) which we have continued increasing ever

39

since the year 1739, except some times when we left said Township for fear of being destroyed by the Enemy, who several times drove us from our settlement soon after we began and almost ruined many of us. Yet what little we had in the World lay there, we having no whither else to go returned to our settlement as soon as prudense wood addmitt where we have continued since and have cultivated a rough part of the Wilderness to a fruitful field — the Inhabitants of said tract of land are increased to the number of forty-five or fifty familys, and our situation with respect to terms we at first settled on are such that we cannot hold any Provincial meetings at all, to pass any vote or votes that will be sufficient to oblige any person to do any part towards supporting the Gospel building a Meeting-house and Bridges, Clereing and repairing Roads and all which would not only be beneficial to us settlers to have it in our power to do but a great benefit to people travelling to Connecticut river and there towns settling beyond us —

Therefore we humbly request of your Excellency and Hon' to take the premises under consideration and Incorporate us, that we may be invested with town privileges and immunities as other towns are in this province and your petitioners as in duty bound shall ever pray, &c. Oct. 31, 1759.

THOMAS MORISON,
JONATHAN MORISON,
THOMAS CUNINGHAM.

Your petitioners beg leave to add, as a matter of considerable importance that the only road from Portsmouth thro this Province to number four is through said township of Peterborough, and which makes it more necessary to repair said Road within said Township, and to make many bridges which they cannot do unless incorporated and enabled to raise taxes, &c.

No. III.

MORTALITY. — The average annual mortality, according to an estimate made from tables furnished by Dr. Follansbee, was, from 1801 to 1806, one in ninety-three; from 1806 to 1816, one in eighty-one; from 1816 to 1826, one in seventy-eight; from 1828 to 1838, one in sixty-eight; which shows a very considerable increase, notwithstanding all the comforts which have been brought in.

EPIDEMICS. — In 1777, the dysentery prevailed severely; in 1800, it prevailed in the north part of the town, particularly among children. Number of deaths, twenty-three. In 1826, it prevailed under a more malignant form among adults as well as children. Number of deaths, fifty-eight.

CASUALTIES. — There have been, since 1751, fifty-eight cases of death by accident; but no person or building has ever been destroyed by lightning.

PAUPERISM. — The first pauper in town was Jean Culberson, 1764; the largest number (seventeen) in 1821. In 1826, the expense was four hundred and ninety-nine dollars and fifty-four cents, and the average annual expense, from 1815 to 1836, was about four hundred dollars. Since then the poor have been on a farm purchased by the town, and maintained without cost.

POPULATION in 1775, five hundred and forty-six; in 1790, eight hundred and sixty; in 1800, one thousand three hundred and thirty-three; in 1810, one thousand five hundred and thirty-seven; in 1820, one thousand five hundred; in 1830, one thousand nine hundred and eighty-four; in 1839, two thousand three hundred.

No. IV.

WATER PRIVILEGES. — The following is condensed from Mr. Steele's report. I regret that an abstract of his full and exact account of the subject is all that our limits will admit.

On the spot where the Peterborough Factory now stands, a saw and grist-mill was erected about 1761. The grist-mill ceased operation in 1817. The mills were burnt in 1772, and rebuilt. The South Factory Mills were built in 1758, burnt 1768, rebuilt 1770. Bowers' Mills, — saw mill built 1778, grist-mill added 1781. The Moore Saw-Mill built 1780, burnt 1790. Hunt's Mills, — saw-mill 1799, grist-mill 1803. Both have ceased. The present saw and grist-mill began 1826. The Spring Saw-Mill built 1810; James Howe's Saw-Mill, 1814; City Grist-Mill, 1820; Union Saw-Mill, 1823; Grist-Mill, 1828; Holmes' Mills, 1827; Upton's Saw-Mill, 1837.

COTTON FACTORIES. — The Peterborough Factory, or the Old Factory, or the Bell Factory, incorporated December, 1808, started 1810; the brick part with looms added 1817. The first cloth woven 1818, under direction of John H. Steele. It now contains one thousand two hundred and eighty spindles, and forty-two looms, making three-fourth drillings and shirtings of No. 16 yarn, four hundred thousand yards per annum.

The South or Second Factory erected 1809, machinery started 1810; now employed in making satinet warps and yarn for the market.

The North Factory, started 1814, contains now eight hundred and forty-eight spindles and twenty looms, making drillings and shirtings of yarn No. 16, four hundred thousand yards per year.

The Phœnix Factory began, in 1813 or 1814, to make yarn; looms added in 1822; the southern half burned in 1828; rebuilt 1829; the northern half rebuilt 1831. It contains now three thousand eight hundred and eighty spindles, and seventy-eight looms, and makes shirtings and sheetings, part No. 16, part No. 30, five hundred and seventy-five thousand yards per year.

The Union Factory, erected 1823, cost one hundred thousand dollars, contains two thousand five hundred and sixty spindles, and seventy-four looms, and makes seven-eighth and four-fourth shirtings, of No. 40, three hundred and fifty thousand yards per year.

The first clothier's shop was built in 1780; the second, 1794; the third, 1801; the fourth (now Henry F. Coggswell's), 1811; the fifth, now run by Thomas Wilson, 1826.

The other factories which have been or now are in town, carried by water, are the Eagle Factory, Moore & Bement's Machine-Shop, the Batting-Shop, seven trip-hammer shops, an oil-mill, an iron furnace and stone shop, a shoe-peg factory, two paper-mills, two bark-mills, six shops for turning cabinet and wheelwright work.

The whole manufacturing power is estimated at three hundred thousand dollars.

PROCEEDINGS

CENTENNIAL CELEBRATION.

AT

PETERBOROUGH, N. H.

At a legal town-meeting of the inhabitants of Peterborough, holden at the town-house in said town, Oct. 5, 1839, the following votes were passed and proceedings had, *viz.:* —

Balloted for and chose John H. Steele, Moderator, who was sworn to the faithful discharge of the duties of his office, by William M. White, First Selectman of Peterborough.

On motion, *Voted* unanimously to celebrate, on Thursday, the 24th instant, the *First Centennial Anniversary* of the settlement of the town.

Voted, To choose a Committee of Arrangements, whose duty it shall be to invite such guests as they may see fit, and do and provide all things necessary for the celebration.

Chose Jonathan Smith, David Smiley, John Scott, John Steele, Nathaniel Moore, Hugh Miller, William Wilson, Stephen P. Steele, John H. Steele, Timothy K. Ames, John Todd, Jr., Albert Smith, A. C. Blodgett, George W. Senter, William Follansbee, William Scott, Robert White, Henry F. Coggswell, Alexander Robbe, William M. White, Isaac Edes, William Field, Frederick Livingston, James Scott, Jonathan Faxon, Reuben Washburn, William E. Treadwell, John Smith.

Voted, To publish in a pamphlet form the Address, together with such other facts and proceedings as the Committee of Arrangements may see fit, and that a copy of the same be distributed to each family in town.

Voted, To appropriate two hundred dollars out of any money in the treasury, for the purpose of defraying any expenses incident to the celebration; and that the Selectmen's order on the Treasurer shall be his voucher for the amount so drawn, not exceeding the above-named sum.

A true copy from the records.

Attest, A. C. BLODGETT, *Town Clerk.*

Saturday, Oct. 5, 1839. Meeting of the Committee of Arrangements. Chose John H. Steele, Chairman, and Albert Smith, Secretary.

Voted, That all the sons of Peterborough who have distinguished themselves abroad be invited to attend the celebration.

Committee to Invite Guests : John H. Steele, Albert Smith, Stephen P. Steele.

Voted, That John Steele, William Scott, A. C. Blodgett, Isaac Edes, John Smith, be added to the former committee, to prepare sentiments for the celebration.

Voted, That the Secretary be authorized to insert a notice of the celebration in five neighboring newspapers, *viz. :* the two Keene papers, the two Nashua papers, and the *Farmer's Cabinet* at Amherst.

The following notice was accordingly sent to the above papers : —

" The Centennial Celebration of Peterborough will take place on Thursday, the 24th instant. An address will be delivered by the Rev. John H. Morison, of New Bedford, Mass. The exercises will commence at 11 o'clock, A.M. All the absent natives and those who have resided in Peterborough are respectfully invited to attend on this occasion. Peterborough, Oct. 13, 1839."

Voted, That a cold collation be prepared for dinner.

Chose Gen. John Steele, Marshal, with authority to appoint such assistants as he may think proper.

Voted, That a Committee of Three be appointed to confer with the Presbyterian Society, in relation to the obtaining of their unfinished church for the dinner.

John Todd, Jr., William Field, Isaac Edes, *Committee.*

Voted, That a Committee be chosen to prepare seats and make the necessary preparations for the dinner.

James Scott, William Scott, William M. White, *Committee.*

Voted, That a Committee be chosen to contract for and procure the dinner.

Timothy K. Ames, Samuel Swan, William Scott, *Committee.*

Voted, That A. C. Blodgett and James Scott be a committee to see to the ornamenting of the meeting-house, and that they invite the ladies to assist, and that they be controlled by their taste.

Voted, That a Committee of Three be chosen to invite the independent companies, and all the singers and the instrumental music of the town to take a part in the celebration.

Albert Smith, William Scott, William Follansbee, *Committee.*

Voted, that a President of the Day be chosen.

Chose Jonathan Smith, *President ;* David Smiley, John Scott, *Vice-Presidents ;* Albert Smith, *Toast-Master.*

Voted, That this meeting be adjourned to Monday, Oct. 14th, at 4 o'clock, P.M.

ALBERT SMITH, *Secretary.*

Monday, Oct. 14, 1839. Met agreeably to adjournment.

Voted, That the procession form at the town-house on the day of the celebration.

Voted, That the Committee of Invitation be requested to invite all the regular clergymen of the neighboring towns, together with Rev. A. A. Livermore and Rev. Z. S. Barstow, of Keene, and Rev. Mr. Whitman, of Wilton.

Voted, That a Committee of Three be chosen to designate the clergy-. men who shall take part in the religious services of the day.

Rev. Dr. Abbott, Rev. John H. Morison, Rev. J. M. Wilmarth, *Committee.*

Adjourned to Monday, Oct. 21st.

ALBERT SMITH, *Secretary.*

Monday, Oct. 21, 1839. Met agreeably to adjournment.

Voted, That a Committee be chosen to procure extra seats for the meeting-house on the day of the celebration.

Chose Frederick Livingston, Jonas Livingston, Riley Goodridge.

Order of the Procession: the Military; Orator; President and two Vice-Presidents; Clergy; Invited Guests; Committee of Arrangements : the elderly Citizens of the Town; Citizens.

Voted, That the above be the order of the procession.

Voted, That all the lower pews of the Unitarian Church be appropriated to the ladies, except those on the broad aisle.

Meeting adjourned.

ALBERT SMITH, *Secretary.*

Thursday, 11 *o'clock, Oct.* 24, 1839.

Sung an *Anthem.*

Invocation, by Rev. Solomon Laws.

Reading the Scriptures, by Rev. J. M. Wilmarth.

Hymn, composed for the occasion by Henry Dunbar, a blind boy.

> To thee, O God, we joyful raise
> Our songs of gratitude and praise;
> Thy mercies like thy dews descend;
> O'er all thy care and love extend.
>
> We thank thee, Lord, that thou didst bless
> Our fathers in a wilderness;
> That where the forest darkly frowned
> The smiling cottage now is found.
>
> We thank thee that to us is given
> Freedom, the richest boon of heaven;
> And may our country ever be
> The land of true equality.

The poor man, in his humble cot,
Is not, O Lord, by thee forgot;
And they whose mansions higher rise
Receive their blessings from the skies.

Then, Father, grant that we may stand
Protected ever by thy hand;
And while thy power our life sustains,
We'll sing thy praise in joyful strains.

Prayer, by Rev. William Ritchie.

Anthem.

Address, by Rev. John H. Morison.

Ode, written for the occasion by Nathaniel H. Morison.

TUNE — "*New England Fathers.*"

Through devious ways and paths unknown,
    Through forests dark and drear,
Our fathers sought these mountain streams,
    To plant their offspring here.

They came not forth from princely halls,
    To wasting pleasures sold;
They came not as the Spaniard came,
    To seek for mines of gold.

But, strong in purpose, high in soul,
    In virtue armed secure,
They came from homes affection blessed;
    They sought for homes as pure.

Through years of toil, through years of want,
    They bravely struggled on,
And lo! the forest melts away;
    The prowling wolf is gone.

Their flocks increase, and fields of corn
    In summer breezes wave;
And plenty crowns the smiling board,
    When winter tempests rave.

And soon, while busy life flows on,
    And hardship slowly flies,
They see on fair Contoocook's banks,
    Their pleasant hamlets rise.

Their names are left for us to bear;
    Their spirits — they are fled;
And yon lone hill has gathered in
    The harvest of their dead.

Their homes, their graves, may be forgot;
    And yet they will be blessed,
So long as we, their sons, shall own
    The spirit they possessed.

Anthem.

Benediction.

Blessing at the dinner table by Rev. Elijah Dunbar; thanks returned by Rev. Peter Holt.

AFTERNOON.

Toast 1st — The memory of the early settlers of Peterborough; let us not forget the perils and hardships which they endured, while we are enjoying, in peace and plenty, the fruits of their labors.

Deacon Jonathan Smith, President of the Day, rose and said:—

FELLOW-CITIZENS,—The sentiment just read relates to the sufferings and hardships of our fathers in their first settlement in this place. The orator of the day has related many incidents of the perils they endured, yet the half has not been told. I well recollect many of the meetings of the first settlers, at my father's house and elsewhere, when they used to relate the privations, hardships, and dangers of their first settlement; and it seemed as though they were enough to break down their spirits, and cast a gloom over every countenance. Was it so? No. Notwithstanding all they suffered and all they feared, there was a joyful countenance, —there was more mirth, pleasantry, wit, and humor, at that time, than at the present. There was another good thing attending those meetings: there was more friendship towards one another; more acts of kindness in relieving each other in their distress. The singing of the old Scotch songs generally closed these meetings.

In truth, their lives were soldiers' lives, though they were not so well fed or clothed. These scenes and trials admirably fitted them for brave and hardy soldiers, to fight our battles and gain our independence. If the times and condition of the country raised up men eminently qualified to lead our armies, no less did they raise up soldiers, making them patient of suffering, persevering and confident of success. Had it not been for this, we have no reason to believe that we should have gained our independence. Now shall their sons, well clothed and fed and at their ease, lose what their fathers so hardly earned? I hope not; but that the same Divine Hand that so abundantly cherished and sustained their fathers in attaining will also qualify them to keep and improve the blessings of liberty they now enjoy; and that another century from this will find a people *here* improved in all knowledge, virtue, and every moral principle, so that our independence will be preserved to the latest ages.

MUSIC — "*Oft in the Stilly Night.*" Sung by the Choir.

2d — The memory of the patriotic eighty-three of this town, who signed a virtual Declaration of Independence, June 17, 1776.

[A copy of the document alluded to was read by Thomas Steele, Esq., one of the signers, now in his eighty-sixth year, who gave a short account of every signer, where they lived, and where they died. No more than three of the eighty-three remained, namely, Thomas Steele, Esq., Capt. William Robbe and Benjamin Mitchell, all of them present.]

Music — " *Ode on Science.*" Sung by the Choir.

3d — The Clergy; may their united labors, as heretofore, prove a strong citadel of our free institutions and sacred rights.

Rev. William Ritchie rose and said : —

Mr. President, — It is probably expected that I, the eldest of the clerical sons of Peterborough, should respond to this compliment to the clergy. In the faithful discharge of the duties of their office, the clergy are necessarily important aids to civil government. Whilst they advance the spiritual interests of men, and prepare them for a higher and more perfect state of being, they make them better in all the relations, social and civil, they sustain on earth. Their ministrations strike at the root of those disorganizing principles and vices which endanger the rights, disturb the peace, destroy the liberty and happiness of society. The good done by many other classes of the community is palpable ; but frequently the happiest influences of our ministry can never be known until the secrets of all hearts are revealed. Then it will be seen how often, by the faithful ministrations of the clergy, slumbering conscience has been aroused, incipient crime checked, languishing virtue revived, and the intellectual and moral nature awakened into vigorous exercise, and man no longer permitted to live, a libel on his form and on his Maker.

In the eloquent and interesting Address of this morning, its author, as by enchantment, caused our ancestors, in all their privations and sufferings, excellences and defects, to pass before us. The first and second clergymen of this town, we were told, and some of us recollect, were neither an honor to their profession ·nor a blessing to the community. Such examples are, however, rare ; and their successors still live and fully redeem this order of men from the reproach cast upon it by their predecessors in this place. Not only the faithful ministrations of the clergy, but their example, is well calculated to guard our free institutions and sacred rights. We are sometimes, indeed, told the clergy have no concern with politics, and should never leave their proper sphere for one so uncongenial to their sacred office. Party politics, the arts of office-seekers, are sufficiently disgraceful not only to exclude the clergy, but all honest men, from them. The man, however, who devotes himself to the ministry does not by that act surrender his social and civil rights. He has, and should feel, all the interest in the political prosperity of his country which every good man does ; and having no selfish purpose to serve, no office to look for, one would suppose this, added to intellectual acquirements, would render his opinion at least as important and valuable as that of other members of the community. So long as the minister of religion discharges faithfully and independently his duty, expresses fearlessly and courteously all his opinions, without a wish to dictate or control the opinions of others any farther than light and conviction should control them, his influence must be highly beneficial to the religious, social, and civil institutions of his country.

I have no wish that former days should return, when respect was paid solely to the office, however unworthy the occupant. Intelligence and character in the clergy should alone command respect and confidence. The clergy have also manifested a deep interest in the cause of education ; and been efficient in elevating the common schools. This is the very corner-stone on which all our valuable free institutions rest. Valuable as are our high schools and academies, the town schools are the

40

fountains from which knowledge flows to the people. An overwhelming majority of the community and of the electors receive all their education at the town schools. No greater service can be done for the community than to elevate the standard of education in the public schools. In this important work the clergy have taken an active and leading part. May every class of the community coöperate, until our common schools are what the wants of the community demand, affording to every portion of the republic the means of a good education. It is always pleasant to look back to the place where we first acquired a taste for learning. Indeed, everything which reminds us of the place of our birth, and of those dear parents and friends whose affection cared for us, when we could not care for ourselves, is deeply interesting. Yes, I have often hailed as a friend the dark Monadnock, at a great distance, raising his head above the hills and looking far off on the land and on the sea; and around its barren top have clustered the most delightful associations and reminiscences of by-gone days, of parents and ancestors whose remains now sleep on the side of yonder hill, on which they uniformly worshipped, and to which they early directed my feet.

I have already occupied more time than I intended. The rapid advancement of my native town in mechanic arts, the increase of wealth, the improvement in public buildings and private dwellings, has given a new aspect to this place. May the cause of education equally advance, giving a permanent glory to the prosperity of a place we all delight to honor. I conclude with this sentiment: Intellectual and moral culture; the only conservative principles of the republic; may they ever have an increasing interest in our hearts.

MUSIC—"*Old Hundred*." Sung by the Choir.

4th — Hon. Samuel Smith, whose activity, energy, and enterprise put the first wheels in motion that have rolled this village on to its present flourishing condition.

Dr. Albert Smith rose and said:—

It is with great reluctance and embarrassment that I feel myself obliged to respond to the sentiment just read. I regret to consume any time in which you might be entertained by others, who are now ready to speak. You have seen fit, kindly, to notice my father on this occasion,—one of the greatest and most important in the history of our town. But the fast-creeping infirmities of age have rendered him unable to express, in a manner agreeable to his feelings, the sincere gratification which this kind and flattering notice has given him. You will permit me to speak for him who, you all know, has heretofore so well and ably spoken for himself.

What he has been and all that he has done belong to this town alone; here he was born and here he has always lived. The sentiment alludes to his efforts as the founder of this village. He did here only what he would have done elsewhere,—with such energy of character, such ardor and enthusiasm in his projects; for he had all the Morison failing of being a great projector, and was withal somewhat visionary. Such men often do great good. It is well that, now and then, an individual can disregard all the minor considerations of prudence and economy, and go on fearlessly in his course. Thus great plans are carried out, villages arise, business is increased, and what is ordinarily the work of years is accomplished at once.

It was thus with my father. Almost any man, with his limited means when he came to this village, instead of building all kinds of mills, dams, walls, stores, houses, etc., would, in Scripture language, have counted the cost; and then the progress of this village would have been slow, and what was accomplished at one effort would have been the work of years.

It is now forty-seven years since he first commenced in this part of the village. There was then but one house standing, and one family only, near the spot where we are now assembled. All else was in the rude state of nature, untouched and unsubdued. From yonder hill, what a contrast would a view of this place now present! Then all was dreary and desolate. A thick, tangled forest, abounding with lofty pines and hemlocks in all the grandeur of mature age, was flourishing, where now resound the efforts of active and constant industry. There was nothing in the prospect to give pleasure; for should you look with attention, a high and extensive sand-bank, that had withstood the elements for ages, would meet your view; then you would observe abrupt hills, and the two rivers almost choked with the inroads of the forest. Only now and then might be seen a human being along its narrow and crooked road. The out-settlers of the town could not use too opprobrious terms to express their dislike of the place. But now how changed! from the same spot there would meet your view, or I am deceived, one of the most beautiful villages of our country. You would see this beautiful river at your feet winding its course through highly-cultivated fields; at a little distance the green, but, at this time, deeply variegated, woods; then the *hills*, the grand hills, some of them rising abruptly, others in a gradual slope from its banks. When your eye rests on the village, you would see the happy homes of hundreds, and of all these only two (my parents) remain who were here in the infancy of the place. Again, you would see churches, houses, factories, stores, mechanic shops, and all the busy hum of men, — the stir and bustle of business from morn to eve. You would see the evidence of enterprise on every hand, the well-marked and not-to-be-mistaken signs of a prosperous and flourishing community. Well might it excite astonishment that one individual, alone and unaided, and with limited means, should have pitched upon this spot, as forbidding as it then was; should have reared up such a building of Babel dimensions as justly to be considered the wonder of the day; should have filled the same with all kinds of mills and machinery then in use and needed by the community, and persevere till he had made a village of his own. But the greater the difficulties, the more ardent and persevering was he in overcoming them. His life has been a lesson of perseverance, whatever other lesson it may have exhibited to mankind. The pecuniary embarrassments which he sustained for years would have prostrated almost any other mind; but he preserved an equanimity through them that few men possess; and nothing but the ruthless hand of age and infirmity could depress or break him down. I trust I shall be pardoned for speaking thus. No one *now* can feel any other than sentiments of respect towards him, unless it be of commiseration. For here is a noble mind in ruins. He has now passed the active scenes of life, he has long since ceased to be an object of jealousy or envy to any living being, and soon, in all human probability, must his earthly career be closed. What he has done in life, it is not for me to say. His labors are ended, and whether they be for weal or woe, those who come after him and us will judge.

I offer the following sentiment in behalf and at the request of my father: May the present enterprising spirit and increased prosperity of Peterborough — which is so highly honorable and praiseworthy — ever continue.

Music — "*Who is this.*" Sung by the Choir.

5th — Gen. James Miller; a brave man, never to be forgotten by his country or native town.

Gen. Miller rose and said : —

MR. PRESIDENT and Fellow-Citizens of my Native Town, — I return to you my sincere thanks for your flattering notice of me on this memorable occasion, — an occasion which once more gives me the pleasure of meeting and taking by the hand so many of my old and valuable friends and acquaintances, and of again witnessing the marked improvements of my native place. That her march may still be onward in every useful improvement is the sincere wish of my heart.

Mr. President, I offer as a sentiment: May we encourage literature, revere religion, and love one another.

Music — "*Gen. Miller's March.*" By the Band.

6th — First Light Infantry and Peterborough Guards; a citizen-soldiery the best in the world.

Capt. Samuel C. Olliver rose and said : —

MR. PRESIDENT, — My situation is such as to render it inconvenient for me to come forward to speak. But after hearing the sentiment just offered I feel obliged to respond. Although an adopted son of Peterborough, I am proud on all occasions to acknowledge myself one of her sons, — even one of her citizen-soldiery. Yes, Light Infantry and Peterborough Guards, we have in the sentiment just read the honorable title of a citizen-soldiery given us. We are so indeed, — members of that institution which gained for us the blessings of liberty and freedom which we now enjoy, and descendants of those noble patriots who won them, with whose praise we are all familiar. We cannot, we will not, prove ourselves unworthy of the sires who, reared in those valleys, went forth at the first call of their country, met the British lion on the plains of Bennington and Saratoga, and bravely took him. History responds to their heroic deeds ; and the echoes of those hills answer nobly to the tune of "Yankee Doodle," and fill the air with victory. We are all familiar, too, with the condition of the American people. Every child knows and adopts the popular sentiment, that ours is the happiest nation on the globe, — and is it not so? We are able to enjoy ourselves independently of others. Although other nations may trouble and even threaten us with destruction, yet we know the strong arm of the militia will defend our families and homes.

It is our own prerogative, and the distinction of the true Yankee, to be prepared to defend, but not to invade. Mark the improvement. One hundred years ago, those limpid waters that flow along our river witnessed in their course only the yell of the savage and the howl of wild beasts. Now a civilized and industrious people rise up in clouds before them, — a people, too, whose homes and firesides have become academies of useful learning. One hundred years ago, the inhabitants of this fertile soil knew naught but the enslaving maxims that enchain the mind. Now every man is a student. Then none sought to improve by the past, but were content with the pleasures of the moment; in a word, they were savages. Now all look forward to a nobler and higher state of improvement. Having been sufficiently educated to become instructors of themselves, they reach forward with slow but sure march to jewels that are laid up in store for them. Moreover, we here breathe the pure air of freedom, where all are born equal, where there are no kings, no princes, no nobility, no titles; in a country that is destined to grow on, to fill the Valley of the Mississippi, to spread itself along the Red River, the Arkansas, the Missouri, climb the Rocky Mountains, descend upon the Columbia, and overspread the shores of the Pacific Ocean with a hundred millions of human beings as free and independent as ourselves. We have something to do in this matter. Mr. President, upon us rests the responsibility for the safe keeping of those institutions, and transmitting them untarnished to millions yet unborn.

Fellow-citizens, citizen-soldiers, when our country, with all her noble institutions, shall cry, Defend, are we ready? Aye, ready.

Mr. President, permit me to offer the following sentiment: The fair; it is but fair that the fair partake of our fare on the present occasion.

MUSIC—"*Gen. Washington's March.*" By the Band.

7th—Our Absent Sons; we gladden at your prosperity, we mourn if you attempt to do evil; though we grow old we do not forget you.

EXETER, Oct. 22, 1839.

Gentlemen,—I regret that it is not in my power to accept your invitation to attend your Centennial Celebration on Thursday. Nothing, I assure you, could give me more pleasure. I am sure none of the sons of old Peterborough would enter more into the joyous feelings of the day. I have known her nearly as long as any of her children still alive, and yield to none in attachment. I have experienced nothing but kindness and confidence from her ever since I was capable of knowing good from evil; and I pray heaven to reward her for all her goodness to me. Allow me to offer this sentiment: Peterborough; may she be as distinguished in the next century for moral worth, as she has been for intellectual superiority and business enterprise in this.

I am, gentlemen, with much regard, your obedient servant,

JEREMIAH SMITH.

NEW YORK, Oct. 17, 1839.

Gentlemen,—I assure you, with the most perfect truth and sincerity, that I received the invitation with heart-felt satisfaction, considering the place whence this gratifying testimony proceeds. It being the place of my early and late associations, it demands the expression of my profound and grateful acknowledgments. It occasions me painful regret not to be able to accept the invitation, and I cannot conclude without tendering to you, and those whom you represent, my respectful thanks for the honor done me on this occasion. Permit me, gentlemen, to propose the following sentiment: Peterborough; what was she a century ago, what was she half a century ago, and what is she now? May her industry, enterprise, improvements, prosperity, and happiness continue to advance onward for centuries yet to come.

Your obedient servant,

DANIEL ABBOT.

———

BOSTON, Oct. 17, 1839.

Dear Sirs, — Accept my hearty thanks for your invitation to the Centennial Celebration at Peterborough. I should most certainly attend, were I not denied that pleasure by ill-health. But, gentlemen, I shall not be unmindful of so interesting an event; for I intend to celebrate the day at my own residence in Boston. I shall be *with you* then, though not actually in my native town.

Your kind letter brought to my mind many pleasing reminiscences of days gone by — of the scenes, the times, the associates, and friends of my youth. The Wilsons, Steeles, Mitchells, and Smiths; the Morisons, Stuarts, and Moores; the Millers, Whites, and many other worthy citizens, whose names are familiar to you, appeared before me. They had a rugged path to walk; but they were industrious and persevering. They were open-hearted, public-spirited, and independent men; and it is gratifying for me, a native, though non-resident of Peterborough, to know that the present inhabitants are the true representatives of such predecessors.

On the 24th inst., and while you are publicly rejoicing, I shall fill my glass with wine in honor of the day, in remembrance of the first settlers and my old comrades and friends, and to the health of their descendants and the present inhabitants of the town, giving this sentiment: The pioneers of Peterborough; let us cherish their memories, and teach our children to emulate the labors and virtues of the first settlers of the town.

Renewing to you, gentlemen of the committee, and through you to the citizens, my regret that "though with you, I shall not be *there*" on the occasion in question, I remain an ardent friend of my native town, and

Most respectfully your obedient servant,

SAMUEL GREGG.

———

BELFAST, Oct. 15, 1839.

Gentlemen, — A short absence prevented the receipt of your letter a day or two. But the first occasion is embraced to say that the pleasure of attending your Centennial Celebration would overcome all objections as to distance, if it were not that the Court of Common Pleas sits in this county on the first Thursday of next month, and that will prevent attendance.

With leave, the following sentiment is offered: The town of Peterborough; may her prosperity be as rapid and lasting as her streams.

Yours, with sentiments of high respect,

JOHN WILSON.

CINCINNATI, Oct. 18, 1839.

Gentlemen, — I am much obliged by your kind invitation to be present at the Centennial Celebration at Peterborough. It would give me a peculiar pleasure to be there on an occasion so interesting, and especially as I should find myself among many old friends; but it will be wholly impracticable. If there were time — I received the letter yesterday, — I could not come. Our lecture-term is at hand and I must be on the ground.

Be pleased to present my affectionate regards to the Rev. Mr. Morison, if he be the same gentleman who was once my patient; and my sincere respects to my old friends, the recollection of whose kindness, years and years agone, I fondly cherish.

Very respectfully, your friend,

R. D. Mussey.

BOSTON, Oct. 16, 1839.

Gentlemen, — Your kind letter of the 7th instant, inviting me to join the citizens of Peterborough in the celebration of the approaching Centennial Anniversary of the town, on Thursday, the 24th inst., was received in due course of mail. I feel highly gratified with being remembered on this occasion by the inhabitants of my *native* town; the town where I spent the pleasant hours of my early childhood; where the remains of my beloved parents, now long since mingled with the dust, were deposited. But I should feel a much higher gratification, if my daily engagements would permit me to meet with my brethren, the sons of the town, and interchange with them the feelings which belong to such a relation, and respond, in such manner as I might be able, at the moment, to sentiments suitable to such an occasion. Since this gratification is denied me, I take pleasure in saying that I feel proud in numbering myself, here in Boston, among those who hail from the "Granite State," the birthplace of a statesman who has acquired for himself the exalted appellation of "The Defender of the Constitution"; and more especially among the sons of the town of Peterborough, the nativity of many industrious, frugal, enterprising agriculturalists, the "*bone and sinews* of our country," and other men who have eminently excelled in the manufacturing art, at the bar, and upon the bench, in the senate and on the field. That the town of Peterborough may flourish in the coming century, as she has during the past, and continue to send forth her sons with the spirit of their fathers, to excel in all the useful occupations of life, is the sincere sentiment of one of her sons, and, gentlemen, your brother,

I. P. Osgood.

FRANKLIN, Oct. 21, 1839.

Gentlemen, — When I received your kind invitation to attend the celebration, I was determined to do so; but circumstances have occurred since which render it impossible for me to attend.

Although I cannot be present on the occasion, my heart and soul will be with you. I claim to be a native son of Peterborough, and feel proud of my maternal home. The occasion brings to my mind many pleasing recollections of by-gone days, the days of my childhood, when seated with others of my father's family around the winter evening fire, listening to the traditionary tales of the first settlement of the town.

I will conclude this communication by proposing the following sentiment: The adopted sons of Peterborough; however distinguished or exalted may have been many of her native sons, may her adopted sons be equally distinguished.

Yours, in the bonds of affectionate brotherhood,

JOHN ANNAN.

NEWPORT, Oct. 22, 1839.

Gentlemen, — It would have given me great satisfaction to meet my early associates, and join with them in the festivities of that occasion.

Peterborough is dear to me, and I feel proud of being recorded among her sons, of whom so many have distinguished themselves in the different professions and departments of active life. She has within my own short recollection sent forth four or five respectable clergymen, and fifteen or sixteen lawyers, four members of Congress, and four or five respectable physicians. She can point to the Hon. Jeremiah Smith, for a long time Chief-Justice of the Superior Court of Judicature, truly a sage of the law, and a former Governor of this State, as one of her sons; and to Dr. Mussey, now of Cincinnati, as not less distinguished in the medical department; and to Gen. James Miller, not less distinguished in our military annals.

Suffer me, in conclusion, to offer the following sentiment: The citizens of Peterborough; may they continue to cherish literature and the arts and sciences; may they be distinguished for their morals and those virtues which elevate and ennoble man; and may she send forth men who shall protect and defend the rights of our country, and perpetuate our free and liberal institutions.

With sentiments of respect and high consideration,

Yours truly,

AMASA EDES.

BATH, Oct. 19, 1839.

Gentlemen, — I received your invitation a few days since to attend the Centennial Celebration of the settlement of the town of Peterborough, on the 24th inst.

My attachments to my native place are strong, and though I have spent a large portion of my life elsewhere, those attachments have not diminished, nor has a link of the chain that bound me there ever been severed.

It would give me great pleasure to be present with you and participate in the celebration, but it is otherwise ordered; and though I may never again see the place of my birth, or again mingle with my fellow-citizens there, for whom I have such strong sympathies and attachments, I may be present with you *in spirit* on this occasion.

I was early taught to entertain high respect for that hardy and enterprising band who, in 1739 and the ten following years, established the settlement of our native town. They possessed certain traits of character of high excellence doubtless mingled with faults of as strong a character, yet those of excellence so far predominated as to give a marked and distinctive character of excellence to the people of the town.

I trust some one of her many talented sons will be found ready, on this occasion, to do justice to their memory and character. Permit me, gentlemen, to offer you the following sentiment: May the generation that now is exhibit all the excellencies of character, without any of the faults, of the generation that is past, for the instruction of those who are to come; that the town may continue to have a name and a praise, for the worth of her citizens, when those present are gone from the stage and rest with their fathers.

I am, gentlemen, very truly yours,

JONATHAN SMITH.

NEW YORK, Oct. 19, 1839.

Gentlemen, — Your kind invitation of the 8th instant came duly to hand. I have delayed replying, hoping to do it in person; but I very much regret that my engagements are such as I cannot remove, and will consequently prevent my attendance.

That you will have a gratifying celebration I have no doubt, and that you may is the sincere wish of

Yours very truly,

JEREMIAH SMITH.

BOSTON, Oct. 22, 1839.

Gentlemen, — I have delayed giving you an answer, in hopes of being able to be present on the interesting occasion, and now I am truly sorry to find myself unable to leave my business affairs at this time; otherwise it would afford me the greatest pleasure to be present.

It is pleasant to visit the home of our childhood at any and all times, but especially on such an occasion as the present.

Your obedient servant,

DAVID CARTER.

BALTIMORE, Oct. 15, 1839.

Gentlemen, — Nothing could give me greater pleasure than to be present at your celebration, but circumstances will necessarily prevent. Allow me, therefore, to express myself, though now adopted elsewhere, still a son of my native town, good and true to the core in feeling and every wish for her prosperity, and to propose the following sentiment, as my *representative* among you: Our native town: her *intelligence*, the *boast;* her *success*, the *joy;* her *hills*, memory's dearest *shrine;* her *all*, the *pride* of her absent sons.

With great respect, I am yours, etc.,

HORACE MORISON.

41

BALTIMORE, Oct. 15, 1839.

Gentlemen, — Your letter of the 9th instant was received, inviting me to attend a Centennial Celebration in Peterborough on Thursday, the 24th of October. Nothing could give me more pleasure than meeting on that occasion my townsmen, the inhabitants of Peterborough, and her many distinguished sons from abroad; but circumstances beyond my control render it impossible. I trust, however, I shall be there in spirit, and, like a true-hearted son, enjoy in imagination the festivities in which I can take no part. I hope my native town will accept, in my absence, the following lyric, * from one of the humblest of her bards, as a fit offering on such an occasion.

Accept for yourselves personally my warmest regards, and believe me truly your fellow-townsman,

NATHANIEL H. MORISON.

MUSIC — "*The Winding Way.*"   Sung by Messrs. Carter and Dunbar.

8th — Non-Resident Owners in our Manufacturing Establishments; for their liberality in aiding the public and private institutions of Peterborough, we return them our sincere thanks.

BOSTON, Oct. 22, 1839.

Gentlemen, — I have received your letter of the 16th instant, with a polite invitation to attend the celebration of the First Centennial Anniversary of the town of Peterborough, on the 24th instant. I much regret that it will not be in my power to attend said celebration, as it would afford me much pleasure to meet my friends and acquaintances at that place.

I have known Peterborough for about sixty years, and observed with pleasure its rapid growth in population, agriculture, manufactures, arts, sciences, literature, etc., etc.

My first visit to Peterborough I will relate, merely to show some of the changes that have taken place since my recollection. Fifty-nine years ago last April, a man with a drove of cattle passed my father's house in New Ipswich, on his way to a pasture for his cattle in the town of Hancock. Being in want of assistance to drive his cattle, and seeing a flaxen-haired boy at the door, he bargained with my father that I should assist him on his way as far as the mills in Peterborough, distance ten miles; for this service to be performed by me, my father received *nine-pence, lawful money;* we arrived at the mills — a rickety saw and grist-mill, standing on the site where the Peterborough Factory now stands — about four o'clock. The man of cattle then offered me half as much as he had paid my father, and a night's lodging, if I would go on with him through the woods three miles to Taylor's Tavern. I readily consented, and pocketed the cash. At that time there was only one house (Dr. Young's) between the mills and the tavern. All the rest of the way was a dreary wilderness. But enough of my first visit to Peterborough. I propose, with your permission, gentlemen, the following toast: The first settlers of the town of Peterborough; the Smiths, the Wilsons, the Steeles, the Morisons, and many others; celebrated for their industry,

---

* Inserted on page 311.

perseverance, prudence, and honesty. Also their sons and grandsons, whether at home or abroad; they have done honor to themselves, to their native town, and to their country. Their virtues and talents have shed a lustre on every profession, political, judicial, ecclesiastical, medical, military, and scientific. *

I have the honor to be, most respectfully, gentlemen, your obedient, humble servant,

SAMUEL APPLETON.

P.S. — Gentlemen, if you have not on hand more toasts than time, I beg leave to propose the following: The first matrons of Peterborough, who, like the matrons of King Solomon's time, laid their hands to the spindle and distaff, made fine linen and sold it to the merchants, † and looked well to the ways of their household. Also, their fair daughters of the third and fourth generation, who, without handling the distaff, by the almost magical use of the spinning-jenny and the shuttle, can clothe themselves in silks and fare sumptuously every day.

BOSTON, Oct. 19, 1839.

Gentlemen, — Your favor of the 16th inst. came duly to my hands, and I accept and thank you for the invitation to attend the Centennial Anniversary of your town on Thursday next.

I fear that it may be impracticable for me to be absent from Boston at that time, and shall much regret if such shall prove to be the fact. In any event, my sympathies and feelings will be with you; for I have witnessed with lively interest the growth and improvement of Peterborough, and find it my pride and pleasure to associate with her sons.

Very respectfully yours,

SAMUEL MAY.

Should I be prevented being with you on the interesting occasion, allow me to offer through you as a sentiment: The town of Peterborough; forward in the ranks of agriculture and manufactures; high in the scale of education, morals, and religion; she has sent forth her full quota of eminent and excellent laborers in Church and State. May she go on "prospering and to prosper."

BOSTON, Oct. 23, 1839.

Gentlemen, — This will be handed you by my son. I regret very much that I cannot be with you to-morrow, but having only within a few minutes returned from a journey of some fifteen or sixteen days, it is impossible that I can have that pleasure. I have many pleasant reminiscences connected with Peterborough. Born, as it were, upon the borders of the town, her brooks and rivers were familiar to me, for I was in the habit of fishing from them the wily trout, before factories were hardly thought of, other than the then common ones for manufacturing meal and boards. I

---

* Among my acquaintances may be reckoned Judge Smith, General Wilson, Doctor Smith, o f Cincinnati, Rev. Mr. Morison, General Miller, etc., etc.

† Fifty years ago the writer of this kept a small store at New Ipswich, and exchanged tea, sugar, coffee, pins, needles, etc., for home-spun fine linen, made by the matrons and fair daughters of Peterborough.

should there find myself surrounded by many old friends and acquaintances, and might, perhaps, point out in the assembly the man who used
to purchase of me the skins of the muskrat,* which I entrapped to supply
myself with change for election and training days; and I trust I should
then meet my much respected and ever valued friend† — Peterborough's
most enterprising son, — who, when I came of age, and was about to
leave New England to seek my fortune and business in Western wilds,
unsolicited, took me by the hand and established me in business with
himself in Keene; a change which no doubt has much promoted my
prosperity and happiness, and for which I trust I shall ever feel grateful.

With manufacturing in Peterborough I can claim an early connection,
as well as one of more recent date. More than forty years ago I was an
operative, and used to set card-teeth by hand for one of her citizens, for
which I was paid fourpence a pair, not in cash, but "store pay." By close
application in my leisure hours, I could set about one and a half or two
pairs in a week. I was an owner in the Peterborough Factory, and was
present at the commencement of its operations in 1810, and that, I believe, was the second cotton factory in the State; since then I have been
interested in *most* of the factories established there, and have done business to a considerable extent for them *all*.

In many towns where manufactories have been established within the
last twenty years, the inhabitants have looked upon them, and especially
upon the proprietors who were non-residents, with jealousy and distrust;
but it has not been so with the citizens of Peterborough. They have
been governed by more enlightened and liberal views, and with few, very
few, exceptions, they have fostered and aided the corporations by all the
means in their power; and from them the proprietors abroad have ever
received the most kind and courteous consideration and support, for
which they are entitled and through you I would most respectfully
present to them, my sincere acknowledgments. To you, gentlemen,
personally, for your kind invitation to be present on this interesting occasion of the Centennial Celebration, I tender my thanks, and offer the annexed sentiment to be used as you may deem proper.

Very respectfully, your obedient servant,

ISAAC PARKER.

Peterborough: prosperity to her people, to her manufactories, her fur
trade and her fisheries.

MUSIC — "*Hill of Zion.*" Sung by the Choir.

9th — *Our Adopted Citizens;* may we never in action or in word say to any one
of them, Thou art the son of a stranger.

John H. Steele, Esq., rose and said: —

MR. PRESIDENT, — Had I the ability to do justice to my own feelings,
or to the feelings of many others who like myself are adopted citizens of
Peterborough, the present occasion would have been eagerly sought. No
minor considerations could have prevented me from embracing this op-

---

* Jonas Loring; for a long time the only hatter in town.
† Samuel Smith, Esq.

portunity to return thanks, in the warmest language of the heart, for the many proofs we have received, not only of your kindness and open-handed hospitality, but for the free, warm-hearted welcome invariably extended to every stranger whose fortune it is to make his residence among you.

No diversity of opinions has at any time prevented that cordial interchange of sentiment or free discussion which is the parent of every improvement. All here meet as men should meet. No fancied distinctions or differences of opinions are suffered to destroy that sociability which is at once the pride and boast of Peterborough.

The stranger, as well as native, share alike the honors and pleasures of society. No wonder, then, that your sons, where'er they roam, in whatsoever situation they may be placed, whether on the tented field, in the senate, on the bench, in the pulpit, at the bar, following the plough, or hammering on the anvil, — all cheerfully own their native home, all proudly hail from Peterborough.

Mr. President, if the sentiment which has brought me forward is to be considered as a call *now* made on the native citizens of this town, never, in action or in word, to say to any one of their adopted citizens, "Thou art the son of a stranger," it will not convey a reproach either now or in times gone by. No, sir; nearly thirty years' residence among you enables me to say that for the past you can have no reflections to cast; the stranger is here sure to find a resting-place, a *home*.

To those who have never wandered far from their paternal firesides, I would say: You know not the feelings of the immigrant, the longing desires of the homeless stranger. No one who has wandered far from the home of his youth but must have felt a loneliness, a depression of spirits, a yearning after his native land, an almost irresistible impulse to return to the place that gave him birth; it is of little consequence where that place may be, whether on the borders of the burning desert, amid the chilling blasts of the frozen North, or the yet more fatal stagnant swamps of the South. Let him be a forced or willing exile; let him have received the kindest or the most cruel treatment that the ingenuity of man can inflict; all, all, cannot, will not, and, let me add, should not, wean him from his native land. He that can forget the land that gave him birth must be unworthy to be called an adopted citizen of any other. Such a man deserves not the sympathy of others. On such a being the kind and generous greetings of his adopted home are lost. He careth not whether you say to him, Thou art welcome, stranger, or that "Thou art the son of a stranger." Far different are the feelings of him who never hears the name of his native land without emotion. Although alive to the interests of the home of his childhood, he will not neglect or forget the interests of his adopted home. By such a man a cheerful, hearty welcome will be duly appreciated; it will cheer him on, and bring forth whatever there may be of the man in him; while a different reception, if it did not destroy, would paralyze his future efforts, and perhaps extinguish forever all the energy of his character. His usefulness would be impaired, his previous acquirements lost, and all his future prospects blasted; the home of his adoption would only be able to number one more human being among them, who would probably live a life of wretchedness instead of one of usefulness, and die a neglected, forgotten stranger.

Yes, fellow-citizens, on you in a great measure depends the usefulness of every stranger who may permanently settle among you. It is true you cannot give youth to the aged, neither can you make the stupid active, nor yet entirely wean the sluggard from his slothful ways; but

you have, time and again, by your open-heartedness, not only encouraged all who were disposed to help themselves, but have effectually
rebuked, both by precept and example, the vicious and evil-inclined.
Many a youth, who from previous associations had acquired a thoughtless, if not a ruinous, habit of extravagance, has been by the example of
your industry reclaimed, and made to bless the day that led him to choose
this as his abiding-place.

Mr. President, the allusions of the orator of the day to the old meeting-house on yonder hill brought forward in bold relief the remembrance
of one of Peterborough's brightest, noblest sons; one whose influence
has contributed much towards giving a distinct character to the town.
A friend whose departed spirit, if permitted to leave the realms of bliss
where it long since has taken its abode, is now within these walls. The
noble, manly, generous spirit that animated him while here must now
look down on this crowded assembly, while, with a tear on his manly
cheek, ready to drop and wash away all that his purer soul finds to con-
demn, his cheerful eye eagerly scans this animated collection of human
beings, and returns thanks to the Author of all good for the prosperity
of his native town.

Mr. President, I hardly need add that I allude to your departed
brother, John Smith, Esq. If Peterborough can boast of a better, more
useful, brighter, purer-hearted son than was John Smith, I know him not.
That she can point to many whose exterior, both in dress and address,
comes much nearer to what is generally termed a finished gentleman, no
one will doubt. But where now is the man who never lets a human being
pass him unheeded; whose ever active mind and ready talent can draw
forth alike the budding powers of childhood, or those of ripened age; who
is ever ready to aid, council, or direct, with wisdom, purse, or hand, his
fellow-man? Such a man was John Smith. With an address which to a
stranger appeared as rough and rugged as the mountains which surround
his native town, he possessed a heart as tender and pure as ever animated the breast of man. To him I owe more than I can express. He
was not only a friend, but a father. He taught me to believe that there
is nothing impossible; nothing that a willing mind and active hand cannot
accomplish. I yet seem to hear his voice reproving me for saying, *I
cannot do it!* He would say, "Steele, Steele, you booby, why don't you
try, and not stand there looking as if you were in a trance?" Shade of
my departed friend, permit me to say that your reproofs, councils, and
aid have not, I hope, been entirely lost.

But, Mr. President, I detain you, and keep back others who are much
abler, from giving to you and this assembled multitude matter more pleasing and better suited to the present occasion. Yet I must beg your
patience for a few minutes longer. I cannot sit down, sir, without saying
one word to the ladies. In attempting so to do I am not compelled, but
willingly throw myself on their well-known generous kindness. It has so
often been said that it is believed, at least by every gay Lothario, that the
way to win the good-will of the ladies is to flatter them. Is this so,
ladies? If it is, I had better stop where I am. Should I at this time of
life attempt to turn flatterer, it would, it must, prove a failure. No, I
shall not attempt it. My fate has been cast in a sterner mould; nor do I
believe one word of this slander. Such a libel on your good, sound sense
and well-known discriminating powers must have been penned or uttered
by one of those nondescript beings frequently seen hovering around the
fair daughters of the land, like a gay, gaudy butterfly around the beautiful
half-blown rose, and like that transient insect chased away by the approach of the first active, useful, busy bee. Would you know them, mark

well their confident air, their tight-bound waist and gay clothing, the closely cramped toes, the never-forgotten silk or embroidered kid gloves, the rattan or other useless switch. Useless, did I say? Not so; its repeated raps on their well-polished boots or full-cushioned legs will at least give you warning that a flatterer is approaching; and if age has furnished him with a beard, you will be almost sure to see the face half covered with a carefully curled pair of whiskers. Although they are called, as I suppose by way of derision, "ladies' men," avoid them as you would a viper. They are mere peacocks. Their hats may be of the latest fashion, but there is nothing in their heads. With the lighter, vainer portion of young and thoughtless females, who, like themselves, think gay clothing must make their charms irresistible, they may pass for men. To such, if any such there are among the many bright faces around us, I have nothing to say. They must be left to smoother tongues than mine.

It is to the more staid and useful I would say, Go on as you have done; encourage your husbands, sons, and brothers in everything that is manly and generous.

To you are or will be committed the destinies of our town. The results of the past are before us; the changes and improvements are great. Will the coming century produce as great? No one here can answer. No one here will in all probability live to see. One hundred years hence, when your descendants assemble, as we this day assemble, to commemorate the second centennial anniversary of their native or adopted town, will they be able, as I believe you *now* are, to say that all the good our mothers taught us we have kept and practised. To your mothers, as well as to yourselves, do we mainly, if not entirely, owe that public spirit, that love of order, that open, generous, manly bearing, which always did, and still does, distinguish your husbands, sons, and brothers.

To your influence are we, the adopted citizens of Peterborough, indebted for our privileges. Your influence enables us to say that this is truly the home of the stranger.

Guard well the rising generation. To you, to your guidance, it must be committed. *Must?* No! I take back that word, and say, To none other should so important a trust be committed. Without your fostering care, without the anxious care and instruction of a mother, what would man be? Deprive man of his natural and best companion, woman, he would then be, or soon become, a fit companion for the tiger. Degrade and debase woman from her proper sphere, and man at once sinks to the level of a savage. Give her full and free scope, and man rises to a higher destiny as fast or faster than generations pass away.

Mr. President, permit me to offer as a sentiment: Peterborough; may she ever continue to be, as she has heretofore been, the stranger's home.

———

Rev. Elijah Dunbar rose and said: —

MR. PRESIDENT, — An adopted son of Peterborough, following the example of our respected friend who has just spoken, would also briefly respond to the kind notice which has been offered. My adoption, which was confirmed forty years ago yesterday, *you* well remember. The venerable council of the ordaining clergy, with a very few exceptions, are gathered to their fathers; and it is with a great, though a mournful, satisfaction that we welcome the last survivor in this immediate vicinity, the Rev. Mr. Ainsworth, to our celebration. It reminds us of his venerable colleagues whom we shall see no more till we meet on the shores of eternity.

My long residence here; my long-continued and intimate connection with generations past and present; the continued kindness and support I have experienced; and the identity of national descent, from Scotch origin, almost persuade me.that I am a native.

The enterprise, the benevolence, and the liberality of the natives of Peterborough form a distinguished and highly honorable characteristic.

Among the evidences this day exibited,.permit me to notice the handsome military display. It may remind us of those who fell and those who triumphed in the war of 1755; of the enterprise, perseverance, and intrepidity of our Revolutionary heroes; and of the more recent glory of the battle-field of Bridgewater.

I would offer this sentiment: The citizen-soldiery of Peterborough; may they continue to cultivate the martial spirit; may they be ever prompt at their country's call; and he that hath no sword, let him sell his coat and buy one.

———

Mr. Thomas Payson rose and said : —

MR. PRESIDENT, — The toast to which my valued friend, an adopted son of Peterborough, has so justly and happily, although, considering the time is so far spent, rather too lengthily, responded, I had intended to notice in a more extended manner than, from the lateness of day, is now in my power. That friend has handsomely anticipated something which I contemplated to say on this occasion, as one of the fortunate, though lately adopted, citizens of this memorable town.

I will, however, with your good leave, state, in a few plain words, what my impressions of the inhabitants were before I knew them.

In early life it was my chance to make acquaintance with one of the natives of Peterborough, and to have no very favorable report of some others. He possessed not a few of the reputed characteristics of his fellow-townsmen, which the distinguished orator of the day has so justly and impartially portrayed.

This personal knowledge of one and historical reputation of others predisposed me to entertain no very favorable opinion of the place and people. Nor was this opinion lessened by the story of the outrageous application of Lynch law to an unhappy clerical subject, who had by that same people for many years been retained in the sacred office, to his own and his people's disgrace.

With these things fresh in my recollection, it so happened that a few years since I was called on to consider the proposal of making this same Peterborough my place of rustication.

Can any one of this respectable auditory who hears me indulge in wonder that, under such circumstances, I should feel a strong repugnance at making my future residence and closing my life among a people so famous? I assure you, sir, that repugnance was great, and that this was among the last places in New England, of which I had any knowledge, that I should voluntarily have made my home.

Circumstances, however, overruled my volition and repugnance. Twelve years since I removed to this town. How great was my suprise and disappointment, after a short residence here, in the appearance of the place and in the character of the people, I hardly need now repeat. I had looked at them through a foggy medium. I had judged of the *whole* by a *part* only. Instead of being stared at as a stranger, and treated as the son of a stranger, I found myself among a friendly set of men, was taken cordially by the hand, kindly and even respectfully received, and treated as a native son or brother. The people with as few exceptions as can be found in any other place, were open-hearted, hospitable, independent, intelligent, and more than usually well read, with good feelings and good manners. Modern degeneracy had not yet reached them. Had I come earlier in life among them, and possessed a reasonable talent for improvement, I might have profited more by their society and example. As it is, I owe them much. May the legitimate fruits of such social qualities constantly crown their future honest enterprise and labor.

In conclusion, allow me to offer the following toast: The pioneers of Peterborough in the eighteenth century, their posterity of the present day, and the generation yet to come; may their progressive advancement in knowledge, morals, the arts of life, and religion, prove commensurate with their years and their privileges.

MUSIC — "*Home, Sweet Home.*" By the Band.

10th — *The Agriculturists, Mechanics and Merchants of Peterborough*, the three great founts of our industry and prosperity; may they ever encourage and support each other.

William Scott, Esq., rose and said: —

MR. PRESIDENT, — I will make a few remarks in answer to that part of the sentiment just given, touching the class of citizens to which I am proud to belong, and to which belonged those bold pioneers, the first settlers and fathers of the town. The cultivation of the earth is the primitive and the most honorable employment in which men can engage. Every individual should feel an interest in agriculture. Considered as an art it is the foundation of all others. The wealth and unparalleled prosperity of this country may be attributed to the industry of the tiller of the soil. From this source all real wealth is derived. The employment is healthful and invigorating to body and mind, and operates powerfully and beneficially upon the morals and constitutions of those engaged in it, giving a right and permanent tone to our national character. I believe that open-hearted generosity and hospitality are more generally found to animate the rough, home-spun farmer than the more polite citizens of cities and villages; and if they take temperance and virtue for their guide, the tillers of the soil enjoy more of ease, more of the real luxuries of life, and undisturbed sleep than the debilitated inmates of counting-houses and city work-shops. They may justly be said to be the happiest class of people on earth. The torch of liberty has ever burned with a purer light on the hills and mountains, among the farmers, than in cities and villages. This was the case in Switzerland in the days of William Tell, and thus it was in this country in the struggle for independence. The agriculturists compose, in a great measure, the present defence of the Union. Standing upon the soil which they own and cultivate, they are every ready to catch their muskets and march to defend the liberties of the country. They can be relied upon with more certainty, in case of sudden invasion, than those engaged in commerce and trade, not being so likely to suffer loss by sudden fluctuations; for from these sources the farmer derives only a part of his luxuries, the necessaries of life being produced by the labor of his own hands. Notwithstanding these high claims in favor of the persuit of agriculture, it has been considered in years gone by as a low, unpopular, if not vulgar, employment. This undoubtedly arose from the sudden accession of wealth amassed by merchants and commercial men, and the high price paid for labor in and about our manufacturing establishments. These causes led many of our young men to forsake the occupation of their fathers in hopes of finding a more speedy road to wealth, preferring the meanest drudgery in the shop or counting-house to the hoe and rake. To such an extent has this unbounded desire of wealth been carried, that our counting-houses in particular have become full to overflowing. The slightest revulsion in trade turns loose upon society numbers of no profession, no occupation. Being so long habituated to a city or village life, to return to the occupation of their fathers, they become dead weights upon the community, — mere idle loafers, a name unknown in the days of our fathers.

But, Mr. President, I believe the days in which agricultural pursuits have been considered degrading are numbered. Many of our most respectable mechanics, as well as professional men, have, within a few years, turned their attention to the tilling of the soil, occupying the hours they can spare from the calls of their customers or books in the healthful as well as profitable pursuit of agriculture. This has caused a rise of lands, particularly in the vicinity of this village, almost beyond belief. This course, continued throughout the country, will create a taste for agriculture, and will prove instrumental in causing more of our youth to embark in this laudable pursuit. The time is not far distant, I hope, when our schools and colleges will be more anxious to instruct our youth in agriculture than in the dead and almost useless languages.

A few words to my brother farmers, and I will close. While we are pursuing that best and most independent of all arts, agriculture, let us not forget the duties which we owe to our fellow-citizens. Let us aid with a liberal hand and cheerful heart the various useful institutions of our country, encourage and support our mechanics and merchants. As to the lawyers and doctors, may we be so fortunate as to need but little of their assistance.

I conclude by offering as a sentiment: The laboring portion of our citizens; may their numbers be increased by accessions from the ranks of those of no profession, until all become usefully employed.

Mr. A. C. Blodgett rose and said:—

MR. PRESIDENT,—after so distinguished a display of talent and eloquence as that which has preceded me, I must acknowledge I feel somewhat diffident in attempting to make any response to the sentiment which has just been offered. But, sir, we have some thoughts which we won't conceal, some feelings which we can't disguise. Perhaps, sir, no one feels more than I do how much we owe to each other, not only in regard to our welfare and prosperity in business, but in the kindnesses and courtesies of civil and social life. It is but a few years since, when I was as it were but a youth and just entering the drama of the world, that I left my native home and came a stranger among you; "but a welcome smile and a friendly face" seemed to whisper in fancy's ear that, though a stranger, I should not long be among strangers. You have been pleased to take me by the hand and adopt me as a citizen, and now I feel that I am one among my townsmen who have come together within this temple, this day, to commemorate that epoch in our history which lies buried beneath the dust and darkness of a by-gone century. One hundred years have now rolled away since our forefathers first broke the gloom of that wilderness, which for thousands of years before had hung brooding over the land upon which we now live, move, breathe, and tread; and, standing as we now do on the line which divides one century from another, looking backward through the vista of years, let us for a moment contemplate Peterborough as she then was, a howling and hostile wilderness. The same old Contoocook, whose waters now whirl by us, passing on through flowery vales and banks of green, moving and aiding in her course almost every mechanical invention and enterprise, was then overshadowed by sylvan bowers, and her shores trod by the feet of savages. In the midst of this wild and romantic scene the echo of the white man's axe is heard by day, and his lowly hut receives his wearied frame by night; but he receives not there the feast to which as a reward for his daily labor he is entitled. "His needy couch and frugal fare" are all the luxuries of his home and fireside. Day after day the echo answers back again, until here and there is to be seen a little cleared spot, a log-house, and a field of grain springing up in the wilderness. They have now, to be sure, a home in the forest; but they have not the comforts nor conveniences of civilized life. Afar off in the world lay those blessings in store. For more than thirty years did they seek abroad, in other towns, all their merchandise.

Their numbers at length invited hither the merchant; and how willing and ready the farmers and mechanics were to sustain him, you, Mr. President and fellow-citizens, can judge for yourselves by the specimen of calico which the orator has exhibited to you this day, and for which one hundred pounds of butter was paid. And for the same compensation at this day I would cheerfully part with twenty such dress-patterns of the same quality. But, sir, I do not wish to be understood by this that farmers and mechanics are not as ready and willing to sustain the merchants as they were at that day. I say it to you, sir, and to all this assembled multitude, in the language of sincerity and truth, that I have ever found them ready to pay a fair and honorable consideration for all necessary articles of merchandise. It is not they, nor the want of encouragement and support from them, which retards the prosperity of the merchant; but it is the spirit of jealousy, envy, rivalry, and competition which exists among the merchants themselves that is so detrimental to their prosperity. If the merchants here do not prosper as well, and heap up golden treasures as fast as they wish, let them blame and censure each other, and not the farmers and mechanics who have patronized them with a generous hand and liberal heart. But while I as a merchant feel grateful for the liberal patronage so generously bestowed upon me, I cannot think the reciprocity is all, or should be all, on one side. If I buy one hundred pounds of butter or cheese, or bushels of corn or grain, of the farmer, and pay him a fair market price, and he buys a corresponding amount of goods of me, and pays a fair price, I am at a loss to know whose business it is, or should be, to say, "Thank ye." I owe to him, and feel under the same obligations, which man should ever feel due and bound to perform towards his fellow-man,— that of philanthropy and good-will. The great object of us all is to be free, independent, and happy; but there is a mutual dependence which we have upon each other, and a mutual advantage arising from it, which has a tendency to refine and perfect those blessings, not only as relative to business, but in all the relations of life. Trade in this place has had its ups and downs, its lights and shades. Its whole history is checkered o'er with the smiles and frowns of fortune; for here fortunes have been lost and won. Stores have multiplied from one to seven; the amount of goods has increased from two thousand to thirty thousand dollars. Circumstances have invited merchants from abroad, and fortune wafted them away to crowded cities and climes that echo farther West. Here people have commenced trade in early life, and continued until it was in the "sear and yellow leaf," and their children have risen up and become merchants abroad in the world, and ere another century shall roll away, who can dream of the changes which time may bring about? All of us, who are now on the stage, will have passed through the dark wilds of life. Our stores, with all of our existence that is mortal, will alike have crumbled into dust beneath the ravages of time. As the old Persian monarch, when he sat upon the brow of the mountain "which looks o'er sea-born Salamis," and surveyed the vast multitude of human beings which composed his army, wept that, ere a hundred years should pass away, not one among them all would be numbered among the living, even so might we at this time and on this occasion weep that, of all who are here assembled, not one will come forth a living monument at the next Centennial Jubilee to rehearse to posterity the scenes of this day. It will be for their children and their children's children, who may rise up in generations to come, to read from history and tell from tradition.

My worthy friend who has preceded (Esquire Scott) has portrayed to you in glowing colors, "in thoughts that breathe and words that burn," the merits of his own profession, and how much the community and country are indebted to them for their strength and prosperity. They give a complexion to the age; they are the stamina of the land, the palladium of civil liberty, and the bulwark of public safety. Now, Mr. President, I acknowledge the truth and force of the gentleman's remarks. Every year that rolls round furnishes us with satisfactory proofs, as we behold the fruits of their industry and enterprise springing forth in flowers of beauty; and like that virtue which lives when beauty dies, ripening into the fruits of promise, while their sons and daughters are rising up to call the nation blest. But may I not, sir, with equal justice and pride, claim the same honors and merits not only for my own profession, but also for the mechanics, who, though silent and voiceless on this occasion, are by the works of their hands daily showing forth to the world in characters of living light, too bold and indelible to escape observation and admiration, how much this town and the whole country are indebted to them for their present flourishing and prosperous conditions? Under their auspices and emulation, as a community and nation, we are constantly rising in the scales of laudable improvements, and marching on from strength to strength in the fulness of prosperity. "All are but parts of one stupendous whole," a mutual coöperation and combination of men. Business and professions have their benign and salutary influence in heightening the charms of society, imparting a zest to life, and a weal to the land. Fortune, and the fate of things, has allotted to us different parts to perform on this transitory stage of action; and all are alike honorable in themselves, and essential props and pillars to each other. The professors alone elevate or depress the professions. Every noble feeling should then animate us to "act well our parts"; so that in all the various callings of genius and fortune we may look back upon the past without remorse, and forward to the future without fear, setting an example to the generations who may succeed us, which they shall be emulous to imitate, by making some laudable pursuit the object of each passing moment, with constant endeavors to grow wiser and better to the end of time. I will trespass no longer, Mr. President, upon the patience of the audience. I will only, in conclusion, offer as a sentiment: Mental endowment; may its bright and chastening influence be breathed into all ranks of society, and equalize all business and professions.

MUSIC — "*Mehul*." Sung by the Choir.

11*th* — *The Music, Vocal and Instrumental;* may their combined and animating influence never be exerted for any but a useful purpose.

MUSIC — "*Multitude of Angels*." Sung by the Choir, led by Mr. Milton Carter.

12*th* — *Woman*, the last and best gift of God. May her amiable qualities teach men to love virtue.

Gen. John Steele, Marshal of the Day, rose and said: —

MR. PRESIDENT, — We look back to the wives, sisters and daughters of the early settlers of this town. No hardship could discourage, no allurements divert them from industry. Although all their industry could not procure them costly attire, it gave them and their families comfortable clothing, and assisted their husbands and brothers to convert the wilderness into a field for the growth of rye, potatoes, and flax, and aided in the raising of sheep and cows to help in the support of the family. The mother taught her children that strength, honesty, and virtue were the rubies that were highly to be valued; that virtue and industry were the smoothest path to journey through life. They took much pride in keeping their children trim and neat, and regularly sent them to meeting. If they had shoes it was well; if not they must go that part of the season which was comfortable without. No excuse about dress, even if the feet were bare, would satisfy. If the youngster said no, the little bunch of rods was pointed to, and the youth thought it best not to have them taken down. After meeting, inquiry was made of the children about the text and sermon, and they were seated to say the catechism. Let us look back to the time when the eighty-three husbands and sons signed the virtual Declaration of Independence which was read this day by one of the signers. Cut off from all connection with the parent country, they were deprived of every article not only of luxury but of clothing. They had to depend entirely on the large or foot-wheel, with their skill in turning them. Not one word of complaint was heard. When a neighbor or friend came in, the buzzing wheel was set aside, and a cheerful conversation introduced. Soon came the song, — very often the "Battle of Boyne," and many others, as each one had a store of them. They passed the evening in cheerfulness. If a stranger was among them they made great exertions to treat him with the best they had. They sometimes talked on religion; were not very superstitious, although some few thought that a good sound Presbyterian stood the best chance in a future state. One of the elderly mothers,* on hearing that the reverend found fault with young men and women for dancing together, said, "The minister had better take his dram out of his own bottle, play his own fiddle, and let the young people's innocent amusements alone."

When the old ladies saw their children's children walking in the path they so highly recommended, it brought a smile of approbation on their wrinkled countenances.

Ladies of the present day! will you go back and view those old-fash-

---

* Mrs. Gordon.

ioned women, though poorly dressed? I trust you can find something to
venerate, something to admire in their characters. When you consider
the vast importance of your precepts and example to your families and
society at large, will you not think, with those good old dames, that honesty, wisdom, and virtue are the most precious ornaments to grace the
youth of the present day?

MUSIC — " *The Mellow Horn.*" Sung by Two Young Ladies.

13*th* — *Emigrants;* well may we be proud of them. They exhibit in manhood characters that began their infancy on these our sterile hills. May they
never forget the land that gave them birth.

Gen. James Wilson rose and said : —

MR. PRESIDENT, — I regret that I am called on to respond to the sentiment which has just been announced, and received with so much approbation by this great assembly. On looking over the list of sentiments
yesterday, I was informed that the one just read was designed to call
out that highly-respected, time-honored gentleman, Hon. Jeremiah Smith,
of Exeter; a man who feels proud of the place of his nativity, and who
on all proper occasions has a good word to say of and for old Peterborough. We should have been delighted to have seen that venerable
and venerated man here, and to have heard from him, in his usual eloquent and forcible manner, his reminiscences of by-gone times.

He has indeed grown old, but not old enough yet to forget any good
thing. His mind is richly-stored with varied learning, and his knowledge
of the early history of the town, the peculiarities of its early inhabitants,
his great fund of wit and anecdote connected with the first settlers, very
far exceeds that of any living man ; and there is now no one of the emigrants who could so well give an apt response to your highly-compli-
mentary sentiment as that worthy octogenarian. I was heart-pained to
learn, last evening, that his attendance is prevented by physical infirmity.
In his absence I could have wished that another highly respected son of
Peterborough, of the Smith family, had been here to have spoken in our
behalf. I allude to one more nearly allied to you, Mr. President, — your
eldest son, my most esteemed friend. We are of nearly the same age.
Our friendship dates back to the days of our childhood. Our intimacy
commenced in that little, square, hipped-roof school-house that formerly
stood between your homestead and the homestead of my honored father.
It was an intimacy in the outset characterized by the ardor of youth, and
grew with our increasing years into the strong and unwavering friendship
of mature manhood. There has never been a moment's estrangement.
For thirty years no frost has chilled it, nor can it grow cold until the
clods shall rumble upon our coffins. Glad, indeed, should I have been
to have met once more my friend here, to have grasped him by the hand,
to have looked upon his slender form and his pale features, to have listened to the tones of his clear voice, to have caught and treasured up
the sentiments of a mind as clear as the atmosphere upon the summits of
our native hills, and a heart as pure as the fountains that gush from their
base. From the sad tidings that I hear of his declining health, I fear
that I shall never meet him on this side the grave. May a merciful God
bless him.

Well may Peterborough express her joy at the success of her absent
sons, and pride herself upon them when she numbers such men as these
among them.

Your sentiment, sir, breathes the prayer that we, the emigrants, may not forget the place of our nativity. I can hardly realize that I am an emigrant. True, sir, a wave of Providence has taken me up, wafted me onward, and cast me upon land not far distant. Although my domicile is in another place, it is here that I seem most at home. It is here that I enjoy all those pleasures derived from early recollections and early associations. It is here that every natural object that meets my eye has some story to relate of high interest to my mind; here every house and tree, stump and stone, hill and brook, presents to me the image of some old, familiar, well-loved friend. It is here that I meet my earliest friends, and their greeting seems warmer and more cordial here than elsewhere. It was here that I first enjoyed that substantial Peterborough hospitality so well understood and so highly appreciated by every one at all acquainted with the people of the town some thirty years ago. Let me not be understood, Mr. President, as drawing a comparison unfavorable to the good people with whom I am in more immediate intercourse at the present time. No, sir; I reside among an excellent and a worthy community, to whom I am bound in a large debt of gratitude. They have manifested towards me a kindness and a confidence vastly beyond my merits; and I am sure they will not esteem me the less for finding me susceptible of emotion at the recollections and fond associations of my childhood.

Forget Peterborough! How can I forget her? Why, sir, I was born just over *there*. The bones of my ancestors, both paternal and maternal, are deposited just over *there*. And among them *there* repose the remains of *my mother*. Oh! sir, it would be cold and heartless ingratitude to forget the place where one's earliest and best friend slumbers in death: —

> "Ingratitude! Thou marble-hearted fiend,
> More hideous, when thou show'st thee in a child,
> Than the sea-monster!"

Spare me, oh! spare me such a reproach. My prayer to heaven is, that when this eye shall grow dim, this tongue become dumb, when these lungs shall cease to heave, and this heart to throw off a pulsation, then this head and these limbs may be laid to crumble down to dust by the side of thine, *my mother!*

Sir, when I learned some few weeks ago that it was proposed to celebrate this Centennial Anniversary of the settlement of my native town, I resolved to be present; and in the expectation that I might be called on for a word, I began to search the by-places and corners of my mind to ascertain whether anything connected with Peterborough history had been stored away there that might be brought out to contribute to the interest of the occasion. When I heard who was appointed to address us, I had my fears that all the choicest and gayest flowers would be forestalled. My worst fears have been more than realized; but I have learned one thing with sufficient certainty, — that it is hopeless to attempt to keep any good thought out of the reach of the Morisons. They have a wonderful tact at seizing every grand, intellectual conception, and surprising facility in appropriating it exclusively to their own use. If, in my effort to brush up my recollection, I have had the good fortune to find anything worthy of remark, I find myself anticipated by my learned friend, the orator, to whose eloquent and excellent Address we have listened with so much interest. I ought, perhaps, to rejoice, that the evening is so far advanced that I have time only for a very few words, since all that I could have said has been so much better said by that worthy gentleman.

We have heard of the patriotism of our ancestors, of their unanimity in sustaining, and devotion to, the American cause in her early efforts for free government. They sought for a government of equal and impartial laws. Permit me to relate to you an anecdote illustrating their profound respect for sound laws.

My grandfather, as you know, Mr. President, kept a tavern in a small house, the shape of which sets all description at defiance; but its rickety remains are still to be seen upon the farm of your townsman, Capt. Wm. Wilson. A number of persons being assembled at his public house, an occurrence happened not unusual in the town at that time; to wit, a fight. There was a blow, and blood drawn. The defeated party threatened an immediate prosecution, but the spectators interposed their friendly advice, and a reference of the matter was agreed to by the parties. Five good men and true were designated as referees, who undertook to arbitrate upon the momentous matter. A solemn hearing was gone into. Every person present was inquired of as to the fact. After a deliberate hearing of the parties, their several proofs and allegations, the referees awarded that the aggressor should pay the cost of reference by a full treat for all the company, and give as damages to the injured man for the blood lost an equal quantity of cherry rum, which they appraised at half a pint. Ill-blood is sometimes created between the parties to a lawsuit that continues to circulate in the veins of succeeding generations. No such result followed the Peterborough lawsuit above reported. The wisdom of the referees was universally commended as manifested in their liberal award of damages, and their sagacity highly extolled for the discovery of an adequate and proper remedy for healing the wound inflicted upon "the peace and dignity of the State." The referees, the parties, and their witnesses all separated perfect friends.

We have heard that one of the prominent traits of the early inhabitants was a fondness for fun. It was on all occasions sought after, and it mattered little at whose expense it was procured. The name of one has already been mentioned, famous for his singular cast of mind and his witty sarcasms, — "Old Mosey Morison." I at this moment have in mind an anecdote which, by leave, I will relate, and if I omit the name of the individual upon whom the wit was perpetrated, I suppose the Chief Marshal of the day will take no exception to the relation of the story. Mosey Morison was here universally called, in common parlance, "Uncle Mosey." A young gentleman of no small pretensions to learning and high standing in this town, some forty years ago, went to the town of Nelson, then called Packersfield, to instruct a winter school. In the course of the winter "Uncle Mosey" happened to call at the store of a Mr. Melville, where a large number of the people of Packersfield were assembled, and there met the young Peterborough school-master. The school-master accosted him in the familiar salutation of "How do you do, Uncle Mosey?" The old gentleman, looking away, and manifesting no sign of recognition, replied in a cold, disdainful tone, "Uncle Mosey! uncle! to be sure! I'm na uncle of yours; I claim na relationship with you, young man." On his return to Peterborough, Mr. Morison related the incident to his blood relations, the Smiths, who asked him why he denied the relationship of the school-master. "Why," replied the old man, "I did na wish the people of Packersfield to understand that a' the relations of the Morisons were consummate fools."

I fear, Mr. President, that I am taking too much time in the relation of Peterborough stories. I will detain you with only one more. At one of the stores in town, upon a cold winter's night, quite a number of the people being present, the toddy circulated freely, and the company became somewhat boisterous, and, as usual, some of them talked a good deal of nonsense. An old Mr. Morison,* who plumed himself—and not without much reason—upon his talking talent, had made several unsuccessful attempts to get the floor (in parliamentary phrase) and the ear of the house. The toddy had done its work too effectually for him, and he gave it up as desperate, and taking a seat in a retired part of the room he exclaimed, in utter despair, "A' weel, a' weel; here ye are, gab, gab, gab, gab, and common-sense maun set ahind the door."

I have watched with intense interest the wonderful improvements that have been carried forward in my native town within the last thirty years. When I was a boy, a weekly mail, carried upon horseback by a very honest old man by the name of Gibbs, afforded all the mail facilities which the business of the town required. Now, sir, we see a stage-coach pass and repass through this beautiful village every day, loaded with passengers and transporting a heavy mail. Your highways and bridges have been astonishingly improved, showing a praiseworthy liberality on the part of the town to that important subject. Your progress in agriculture, manufactures, and the mechanic arts exhibits striking evidence of the progress of improvement. Look abroad now upon the finely cultivated fields, the substantial fences, the comfortable, yea, elegant dwellings, the superb manufacturing buildings, the splendid churches and seminaries of learning, and in view of all these let the mind for a moment contrast it with the prospect which presented itself to the eye of the first settler as he attained the summit of the East Mountain, one hundred years ago. Then not a human habitation for the eye to repose on over the whole extent of this basin-like township, — one unbroken forest throughout the eye's most extensive range. No sound of music or hum of cheerful industry saluted his ear. It was only the howl of the savage beast, or the yell of the still more savage man, that broke the appalling stillness of the forest. What a wonderful change hath a hundred years wrought here, and what unshrinking energy of character was requisite to induce the commencement of the undertaking!

Some of the old objects of interest to me in my younger days are gone; their places, indeed, have been supplied by more expensive and elegant structures. Still, I must say, I regret their loss. And let me ask, Mr. President, are you quite sure that the loss may not manifest itself in some future time? I allude, sir, to the loss of the old church on the hill there, and the old beech-tree that stood hard by. I look, even at this period of life, upon that spot with a kind of superstitious reverence. Many are the noble resolutions that young minds have formed under the shade of the old beech-tree. Intellectual indolence is the prevailing fault of our times. Under the old beech, in my young days, the great and the talented men of this town used to assemble, and there discuss with distinguished power and ability the most important topics. Religion, politics, literature, agriculture, and various other important subjects were there discussed. Well, distinctly well, do I remember those debates carried on by the Smiths, the Morisons, the Steeles, the Holmeses, the Robbes, the Scotts, the Todds, the Millers, and perhaps I may be excused here for adding, the Wilsons and others. No absurd proposition or ridiculous idea escaped exposure for a single moment. A debater there had to draw himself up close, be nice in his logic, and correct in his language to command respectful attention. Abler discussion was never listened to anywhere: Strong thought and brilliant conceptions broke forth in clear and select language. They were reading men, think-

---

* Jonathan, the first mechanic in town, and the first male child born in Londonderry.

43

ing men, forcibly talking men, and sensible men. Bright intellectual sparks were constantly emanating from those great native minds, and, falling upon younger minds, kindled their slumbering energies to subsequent noble exertion. The immediate effect of those discussions could be easily traced in the beaming eye and the agitated muscles of the excited listeners. It was obvious to an acute observer that there was a powerful effort going on in many a young mind among the hearers, to seize, retain, and examine some of the grand ideas that had been started by the talkers. This rousing of the young mind to manly exertion, and aiding it in arriving at a consciousness of its own mighty powers, was of great advantage where the seeds of true genius had been planted by the hand of nature. If any of the Peterborough boys, within the last thirty years, have attained to anything like intellectual greatness, my life on it, they date the commencement of their progress from the scenes under the old beech-tree. A thousand times have I thought, Mr. President, if I had the world's wealth at my command I would cheerfully have bartered it all for the ability to talk as well as those men talked. Antiquity may boast of her schools of philosophy; the present may point to her debating clubs and lyceums, and talk loud as it will of modern improvement; give me the sound good-sense that rolled unrestrained from eloquent lips under the old beech, and it is of more worth than them all. I shall always respect the spot where it grew, and even now it grieves me to see the greensward that sheltered its roots torn too roughly by the ploughshare.

I had purposed, Mr. President, to have asked the attention of the audience to some few remarks upon the all-important subject of education. Old Peterborough has hitherto given her full share of educated men to the public, and I cannot but hope that she will not now permit her neighbors to go ahead of her in this particular. The shades of evening, however, admonish me that I must not trespass further. I must tender my thanks to the audience for the very kind and polite attention they have given me during the remarks I have felt constrained to make at this late hour in the afternoon. Allow me to say in conclusion : The sons and daughters of Peterborough, native and adopted; in all good deeds may they prove themselves worthy of the noble stock that has gone before them.

At the close of Gen. Wilson's speech, when it was so dark that the audience could hardly distinguish each others' faces, a general invitation was given to attend a ball in the evening at Col. French's. On motion of Albert Smith, the meeting was adjourned for a hundred years. And with shouting and the clapping of hands — joy mingling with many pensive thoughts,— the assembly of fourteen or fifteen hundred persons separated to lie down in their graves long before the next meeting shall be held.

MONDAY, Nov. 4, 1839.

Met agreeably to notice.

Voted, That the proceedings of the celebration, the sentiments, and the responses be published with the Address.

Voted, That the Committee of Invitation, *viz. :* John H. Steele, Albert Smith, and Stephen P. Steele, be requested to write to those absent who responded to sentiments, and also obtain and prepare for publication all the remarks made by others.

Voted, That a copy of the Address be deposited in each of the following places for safe keeping, *viz. :* In the Library of Dartmouth College; in the Library of Harvard College; in the Collections of the Historical Society of New Hampshire; and with the Antiquarian Society at Worcester, Mass.

Voted, That this meeting be dissolved.

ALBERT SMITH, *Secretary.*

The Committee return their thanks to the citizens of Peterborough for the confidence reposed in them, and hope that the services rendered will prove acceptable.

To the fault-finders, if any such there be, we would say (in the language of one of the boys who assisted in clearing away the decorations of the church), "You are welcome to this, but at your next Centennial Celebration you may do it yourselves."

APPENDIX.

A COPY OF THE RECORDS OF THE PROPRIETORS OF PETERBOROUGH, N. H., FROM JULY 25, 1738, TO MARCH 25, 1769, AND OTHER PAPERS.

JEREMIAH SMITH.

Province of the Massachusetts Bay :—

To his Excellency, Jonathan Belcher, Esq., Captain-General and Governor-in-Chief, to the honorable his Majesty's Council and House of Representatives in Great and General Court assembled this fifth of December, 1737. Humbly shew:—

Samuel Heywood and others, the subscribers, that in the year 1721 they humbly preferred their petition to the Great and General Court then sitting, praying, for the reason there mentioned, they might be granted a tract of land upon the Souhegan River for a township, being without land for their posterity, and desirous they should not remove from out of the Province, but settle together under the laws and liberties of this government where they were born, and that the honorable House of Representatives then passed a vote in favor of them, but the Indian war then breaking out, they dropt their petition, and that ever since they have held together, and have petitioned this Honorable Court for a tract of unappropriated land for a township, and often had the encouragement and grant of the Honorable Board and House, as by their vote appears, but by the carelessness and indiscretion of those who appeared for the petitioners the petition never passed this Honorable Court till the year 1735, when the Honorable House of Representatives at first voted them a town six miles square, but presently, afterwards, the whole court voted they should be grantees of one of the townships which were then to be laid out, commonly called the line of towns, whereupon a committee of the petitioners repaired to the lands when laid out, to observe the circumstances and situation of the several townships, and among themselves made choice of one, hoping that the Honorable Committee of the General Court, appointed for that purpose, would admit the petitioners grantees of that township, but upon debate of that matter, the Honorable Committee assigned that township to the Hopkinton petitioners, which, although they do not doubt the justice of it, so far broke our committee's measures and discouraged them that they left their trust and companions, and most of them were admitted grantees in other townships; but, however, the far greater number of the petitioners kept to their first intention, of settling together, though this accident made them quite irresolute for a season, and was the occasion that hitherto they have unhappily failed of it. Whereupon the petitioners would humbly represent to your Excellency and Honors, that their design of settling together was, as they conceive, laudable in itself, and conducing to the public good in cultivating the waste lands of the Province; that they have a long while persevered in this design, from the year 1721 to this time, wherein they have had many meetings, of all which they have kept particular accounts, whereby it appears, upon computation, that this matter has already stood them upward of five hundred pounds, as they are ready to show; that they have frequently been encouraged in their designs by this Honorable Court, and at last they thought they were crowned with success, but unfortunately to them it has happened otherwise.

Wherefore they would humbly supplicate your Excellency and Honors, that they may have a grant of the unappropriated lands of the Province, to them and their associates, of six miles square for a township, to be settled under such conditions and regulations as your Excellency and Honors, in your consummate wisdom, shall think fit. And your petitioners shall ever pray, etc.

Samuel Heywood.
Joseph Barrett.
Timothy Minott.
Ebenezer Hubbard.
Joseph Hubbard.
Jonathan Willey.
Samuel Wooley.
Benjamin Barrett.
Joseph Flagg.
Israel Putnam.
John Brown.
Joseph Stratton.
Amos Brown.
John Miles.
Uriah Wheeler.
Eleazer Stearnes.
Josiah Jones.
Peter Holden.
John Lamon.
William Wheeler.
Richard Wheeler.
Elnathan Jones.
John Whiting.
Thomas Cutler.
Jonathan Whitney.
Joseph Wheeler.

Hezekiah Wheeler.
Jonathan X Harris.
Nathaniel Paige.
Thomas Fox.
Joseph Fitch.
James Horsemore.
Nathaniel Horsemore.
Mehitable X Horsemore.
Thomas Jones.
John Dodd.
Peter Bulkley.
Joseph Brandon.
Benj. Barrow.
Isaac Whitney.
James McFarland.
Andrew Dunn.
Jonathan Prescott.
Edward Bulkley.
Asa Douglas.
Solomon Taylor.
Andrew McFarland.
Ebenezer Heath.
Thomas Wheeler.

In the House of Representatives, Dec. 6, 1737.

Read, and ordered that the prayer of the petition be granted; and John Chandler, Josiah Willard, Nahum Ward, Esq., are a committee to consider of some suitable place of the contents of six miles square, of the unappropriated.lands of the Province, for the petitioners and their associates to bring forward the settlement of said township upon such conditions and regulations as may be proper. The committee to report hereon as soon as may be.

In the House of Representatives, Dec. 8, 1737.

Read, and ordered that the petition be granted, and the petitioners and their associates be, and hereby are, empowered, by surveyor and a chainman on oath, to survey and lay out a township, of the contents of six miles square, in some of the unappropriated lands of the Province, suitable for a township, and that they return a plat thereof to this court within twelve months, for confirmation.

And for the more effectual bringing forward the settlement of said new town, ordered that there be sixty-three house-lots laid out in a suitable and defencable manner, one of which to be for the first settled minister, one for the second settled minister, and one for the school, each of said three lots to draw equal divisions with the other grantees of the said sixty lots. That the grantees do within three years from the confirmation of the plan have settled on each home lot a good family.

And in order thereto, that they build thereon a dwelling-house of eighteen feet square and seven feet studs, at the least, and finish the same, and have well-fenced and brought to English grass, or ploughed, six acres on each of the home lots; that they settle an Orthodox minister, and build a decent, convenient meeting-house for the public worship of God; and that Col. Josiah Willard and Capt. John Hobson, with such as shall be appointed by the Honorable Board, be a committee for admitting the grantees or settlers; and that they take effectual care that no persons are admitted as such who have had any grant for the space of three years; and that each grantee give bond to the Province treasurer or his successor, in the sum of forty pounds, for his faithful fulfilling or complying with the terms or conditions of the grant; and if any of the said settlers fail of performing the said conditions, then his or their rights or share to revert to, and be at the disposition of, the Province.

Sent up for concurrence.

J. QUINCY, *Speaker.*

In Council, Dec. 14, 1737, read and concurred, and William Dudley, Esq., is joined in the affair.

J. WILLARD, *Secretary.*

January 16, consented to.

J. BELCHER.

Copy examined.

SIMON FROST, *Dept. Sec.*

WOBURN, March 17, 1737-8.

At a meeting of the committee appointed by the Great and General Court for admitting grantees or settlers into a township granted to the petitioners and their associates, whose names are entered in a petition of Sam'l Heywood and others, *viz.:* Wm. Dudley, Josiah Willard, and John Hobson, Esqs., the following persons were admitted, they not having had any grant of land within three years last past, to wit:—

Joseph Barrett, Petitioner, Timothy Minott, Jonathan Wooley, Sam'l Wooley, Benj. Barrett, Joseph Flagg, Israel Putnam, John Brown, Joseph Stratton, Amos Brown, John Miles, Uriah Wheeler, Eleazer Stearns, Peter Holden, John Lamon, Wm. Wheeler, Richard Wheeler, Elnathan Jones, Jonathan Whitney, Joseph Wheeler, Hezekiah Wheeler, Jonathan Harris, Nathaniel Page, Thomas Fox, Joseph Fitch, James Hosmore, Nath'l Hosmore, Mehitable Hosmore, John Dodd, Peter Bulkley, Joseph Brandon, Benj. Barrow, Isaac Whitney, Andrew Dunn, Edward Bulkley, Solomon Tailor, James McFarland, Ebenezer Heath, Thomas Wheeler;

Henry Wylee, associate in the room of Sam'l Heywood; Alex. Cockburn, associate in the room of Ebenezer Hubbard; John Prescott, associate in the room of Joseph Hubbard; Richard Gridley, associate in the room of Josiah Jones; Dudson Kiluep, associate in the room of John Whiting; Ezekiel Lewis, Jr., associate in the room of Thomas Cutler; James Smart, associate in the room of Thomas Jones; John Wilson, associate in the room of Andrew McFarland; Jonathan Prescott, Jr., associate in the room of Jonathan Prescott; Nathan Brooks, associate in the room of Asa Douglas; Jonathan Hubbard, associate in the room of Joseph Fitch; Isaac Gridley, Charles Prescott, John Wheeler, Sam'l Cox, William Clark, Peter Bliss, Hugh Sunderland, Amos Wood, Roland Cotton, John Healy, Edward Fennell.

Dated as above.

> WM. DUDLEY, ⎫
> JOSIAH WILLARD, ⎬ *Committee.*
> JOHN HOBSON, ⎭

[For a report of the Surveyor, Joseph Wilder, Jr., with a plat of the town, May 21, 1738, with the Act of the House of Representatives, confirming the land to the grantees, see pages 24, 25, of the history.]

In the House of Representatives, June 28, 1738.

Ordered, that Mr. Jonathan Prescott, one of the grantees of the new township granted to Sam'l Heywood and others be and hereby is fully authorized and empowered to notify and warn the said Proprietors or Grantees to assemble and convene as soon as may be in some convenient place, to choose a Proprietors' Clerk, and pass such votes and orders for the effectual bringing forward the settlement of said township agreeable to the conditions of the grant, and also to choose such other officers as they may think proper, and agree upon a method of calling future meetings agreeable to the rules of the law.

Sent up for concurrence. J. QUINCY, *Speaker*

In Council, June 28, 1738, read and concurred.

J. WILLARD, *Secretary.*

Consented to.

J. BELCHER.

Copy examined.

July 25, 1738. Pursuant to the foregoing order I have notified the Proprietors of the aforesaid township to meet this day at the house of Mr. Luke Verdy, in Boston, for the purpose there mentioned.

JONATHAN PRESCOTT.

July 25, 1738, at a meeting of the Proprietors of the township granted to Samuel Heywood and others, by the Great and General Court of the Province of Massachusetts Bay, on the 16th Jan., A.D. 1737, at the house of Mr. Luke Verdy, in Boston:

1. *Voted,* That John Hill, Esq., be moderator of this meeting, *nem. con.*

2. *Voted,* That Peter Prescott be clerk of the Proprietors, *nem. con.,* and he was sworn to the faithful discharge of his said office before me, Jacob Royall, Justice of the Peace.

3. *Voted,* That this meeting be adjourned to Monday next, at five of the clock, post meridian, at said Luke Verdy's.

Attest: PETER PRESCOTT, *Pro. Clerk.*

July 31, 1738, at a meeting of the Proprietors of the above township, held by adjournment at the house of Mr. Luke Verdy at five of the clock, post meridian, the following votes were passed, *viz. :* —

1. *Voted,* That there be a committee of five persons chosen to view said township, and to agree upon some suitable place for to lay out the home lots and to manage the prudentials of the said township, and the majority of the committee to govern in all affairs, *nem. con.*

2. *Voted,* That John Hill, Esq., Jeremiah Gridley, John Fowle, Jr., Jonathan Prescott, and Peter Prescott be the committee for the purposes above mentioned, or any three of them (they each were chosen separately), *nem. con.*

3. *Voted,* That it be left to the discretion of the committee to lay out what number of acres they shall think proper for the home or house-lots.

4. *Voted,* There be a treasurer chosen to receive and collect all taxes that shall be raised on each lot.

5. *Voted,* That John Hill, Esq., be treasurer and collector for the purpose.

6. *Voted,* That a tax of ten pounds on each right be raised to defray former charges, as also to enable the committee to lay out the home lots and pay other necessary charges.

7. *Voted,* That the said committee, or any three of them, be and hereby are empowered to agree with a surveyor and chainmen to lay out said lots, and that they accordingly proceed to view said township and some convenient place therein, to lay said lots out as soon as may be.

8. *Voted,* That the committee, or any three of them, be and hereby are empowered to agree with some person to build a saw-mill, either to pay cash for the same and so to be for the use of the Propriety, or to give such a quantity of land as they shall think proper for the building the same, together with the use and benefit of the stream whereon the said mill shall stand, as also to agree with any such person or persons who shall undertake said mill, for the price of sawing boards and such other lumber as may be wanted by the Propriety.

9. *Voted,* This meeting be adjourned to the house of Mr. Luke Verdy, at nine of the clock, A. M., on the 12th of August, *nem. con.*

Aug. 12, 1738, at a meeting of said Proprietors held by adjournment at said Verdy's, at nine of the clock on said day :

1. *Voted,* That the Proprietors' clerk, at the request of three, at least, of the Proprietors, be and hereby be empowered to call meetings, for the future, by posting up notifications at Concord, in the County of Middlesex, where great numbers of the Proprietors dwell, or at Mr. Luke Verdy's, at Boston, in the County of Suffolk, and some other public house in said Boston, said notification to be posted up fourteen days before the meeting begins.

And then the moderator dismissed the meeting.

Attest: PETER PRESCOTT, *Pro. Clerk.*

Nov. 29, 1738, at a meeting of the Proprietors aforesaid, duly notified to meet and convene at the house of Mr. Luke Verdy, in Boston, in the County of Suffolk, at ten of the clock before noon on said day :

1. *Voted,* That John Hill, Esq., be moderator of said meeting.

2. *Voted,* That the meeting be adjourned to the house of Mr. Alexander Cochran, at the Three Horse Shoes in said Boston, there to meet at three of the clock in the afternoon.

At the adjournment of said meeting, as aforesaid, the following votes were passed, *viz.* : —

1. *Voted,* That the farm marked with the letter A upon each corner be Jeremiah Gridley's and his heirs', said farm containing five hundred acres of land in the township aforesaid.

2. *Voted,* That the farm marked with the letter B upon each corner be John Hill's and his heirs', said farm containing five hundred acres of land in said township.

3. *Voted,* That the farm marked with the letter C upon each corner be Peter Prescott's and his heirs', containing five hundred acres of land in said township.

4. *Voted,* That the farm marked with the letter D upon each corner be John Fowle, Jr.'s, and his heirs', said farm containing five hundred acres of land in said township, and that he have liberty to add thereto two hundred and fifty acres of land at either end of said farm, and equal in breadth with said farm as an equivalent.

5. *Voted,* That the said John Hill should have liberty to pitch for the following lots in said township, to be his and his heirs', to wit: lots No. 6 and 69, and lots No. 36 and 98, which lots he did pitch and were accordingly confirmed to him.

6. *Voted,* That said Peter Prescott should have liberty to pitch for the following lots, to be his and his heirs', in said township, *viz.:* lots No. 7 and 70, and lots 50 and 112, which lots were pitched and accordingly confirmed to him.

7. *Voted,* That said John Fowle, Jr., should have liberty to pitch for the following lots in said township, to be his and his heirs', *viz.:* lots No. 4 and 67, and lots No. 5 and 68, which lots he pitched and accordingly they were confirmed to him.

8. *Voted,* That the said Jeremiah Gridley should have liberty to pitch for the following lots in said township, to be his and his heirs', *viz.:* lots No. 9 and 72, and lots No. 51 and 113, which lots he accordingly pitched and they were confirmed to him.

9. *Voted,* That the lot No. 71 in said township be the first settled minister's and his heirs'; " and that there be first reserved out of said lot ten acres for a meeting-house lot, burying-ground and training-field."

10. *Voted,* That the lot No. 76 be the second settled minister's and his heirs'.

11. *Voted,* That the lot No. 13 be for the use of the school forever.

12. *Voted,* That the remainder of the lots be drawn for according to the usual manner, both the first and second divisions.

John Hill, Esq., drew the following lots, as assignee to fourteen of the original grantees and their associates, to be his and his heirs', *viz.* : —

No. 1 Lots.		No. 2 Lots.	No. 1 Lots.		No. 2 Lots.
30	and	93	12	and	75
32	"	95	17	"	80
40	"	102	18	"	81
42	"	104	19	"	82
43	"	105	26	"	89
48	"	110	27	"	90
Pitched 6	"	69	29	"	92
Lots, 36	"	98		Fourteen Lots.	
	Sixteen Lots.				

44

Mr. Jeremiah Gridley drew the following lots as assignee as aforesaid, to be his and his heirs', *viz. :* —

No. 1 Lots.		No. 2 Lots.		No. 1 Lots.		No. 2 Lots.
Pitched Lots, 9	and	72		14	and	77
51	"	113		22	"	85
47	"	109		24	"	87
53	"	115		33	"	96
55	"	117		37	"	99
56	"	118		39	"	101
57	"	119		41	"	103
	Fourteen Lots.				Fourteen Lots.	

Mr. John Fowle, Jr., drew the following lots as assignee as aforesaid, to be his and his heirs' forever, *viz. :* —

No. 1 Lots.		No. 2 Lots.		No. 1 Lots.		No. 2 Lots.
Pitched } 4	and	67		34	and	97
Lots, } 5	"	68		38	"	100
11	"	74		44	"	106
16	"	79		49	"	111
21	"	84		54	"	116
25	"	88		58	"	120
28	"	91		59	"	121

Peter Prescott drew as assignee as aforesaid the following lots, to him and his heirs', *viz. :*—

No. 1 Lots.		No. 2 Lots.		No. 1 Lots.		No. 2 Lots.
Pitched } 7	and	70		1	and	64
Lots, } 46	"	108		2	"	65
50	"	112		3	"	66
52	"	114		10	"	8
60	"	122		15	"	73
61	"	123		20	"	83
				31	"	94
				45	"	107

Jonathan Prescott drew the following lots, to him and his heirs, *viz.* : Number of his lot in first division was sixty-two, and the number of his second-division lot was one hundred and twenty-four.

Jonathan Hubbard drew the following lots, to him and his heirs, *viz. :* Number of his first-division lot was sixty-three, and the number of his second-division lot thirty-five.

13. *Voted,* That this meeting be adjourned to Monday next at ten of the clock before noon, to this place.

December 4. At meeting of said Proprietors held by adjournment as aforesaid :

1. *Voted,* That the general plan of said township whereon the farms and lots are delineated be fixed in the Proprietors' book, and that the plan of each particular farm and lot be recorded in said book and attested by the clerk.

2. *Voted,* That the former committee be and hereby are empowered to agree with some suitable person to cut and clear a good way or road from New Ipswich to the meeting-house lot in said township as soon as may be.

3. *Voted,* That this meeting be adjourned to Monday, the first day of January next, to this place at four of the clock, P. M.

Attest: PETER PRESCOTT, *Pro. Clerk.*

Then follows the record of the plan, dated March 26, 1739, and description of the various lots divided among the different Proprietors.

Aug. 20, 1739, at a meeting of the Proprietors aforesaid, duly notified and warned to meet at the house of Mr. Luke Verdy, in Boston, in the County of Suffolk, on the 20th of August, instant, at ten of the clock in the forenoon: Voted that John Hill, Esq., be moderator of said meeting.

1. *Voted,* That the meeting be adjourned to three of the clock, P. M., at which time the meeting was adjourned from time to time, without passing any further votes till the 21st of December, 1744, and then at said meeting John Hill, Esq., was appointed Proprietors' Clerk, in the room of Peter Prescott, the then Clerk, who resigned said trust and delivered said Hill the Proprietors' book and writings to said Proprietors belonging.

At the above said meeting of said Proprietors they passed the following vote, *viz.:* that there be granted to Peter Prescott, his heirs and assigns forever, four hundred acres of land, to be laid out as the said Proprietors should hereafter agree.

Attest: JOHN HILL, *Pro. Clerk.*

Oct. 16, 1749, at a meeting of the Proprietors aforesaid, duly notified and warned to meet at the house of Robert Stone, the Royal Exchange Tavern, in Boston, on Monday, the 16th day of October, 1749.

1. *Voted,* That John Hill, Esq., be moderator, and then the meeting was adjourned until Monday next, ten of the clock in the forenoon, to the same place, the 23d of October, 1749.

Met accordingly, and voted that the whole or greatest part of said township be laid out in lots not exceeding two hundred acres, and not less than one hundred acres, as the land will best allow of; and that the grant made to Peter Prescott (at their meeting A.D. 1744), of four hundred acres of land, be drawn with said Proprietors after the land is laid out as above said.

Attest: JOHN HILL, *Pro. Clerk.*

BOSTON, Dec. 11, 1730. Know all men by these presents, that I, Peter Prescott, within named grantee, for and in consideration of the sum of thirty-five pounds lawful money to me in hand paid, before signing and delivering hereof by Benjamin Pollard, Esq., of Boston, in the County of Suffolk, do hereby give, grant, sell, and make over to him and his heirs forever all that tract and parcel of land within mentioned and granted to me and my heirs, to him, the said Benjamin Pollard and his heirs, with all the benefits and privileges whatsoever that would accrue to me and my heirs by virtue of said grant. In witness whereof I have hereunto set my hand and seal, day and year, first above written.

PETER PRESCOTT, and seal.

.Signed, sealed, and delivered before us.

NATHANIEL HATCH,
EZEKIEL PIERCE.

SUFFOLK SS.   BOSTON, Dec. 11, 1750.

The above said Peter Prescott acknowledged the above instrument to be his free act and deed before me.

EDWARD WINSLOW, *Jus. Peace.*

The above instrument was received and recorded the 20th of August, A. D. 1751, by me.

JOHN HILL, *Pro. Clerk.*

1750. At a meeting of the Proprietors of said Peterborough, being legally warned and notified, at the house of Robert Stone, Royal Exchange Tavern, in Boston, the 14th day of December, A.D. 1750:

Voted, That Jeremiah Gridley, Esq., be moderator.

Voted, That every grantee of said Proprietors shall within three months from the date hereof pay his proportion toward the maintenance of preaching in said town, and the assessment made by the inhabitants for the roads, to such persons as shall be appointed by the inhabitants for that purpose ; and upon the expiration of three months aforesaid settle his lot or lots, and continue and diligently perform his duty upon them. And in case any grantee shall not pay his proportion or settle as aforesaid, the inhabitants of said town are hereby empowered to dispose his lots to such other persons as will go and settle immediately in said town, and perform the delinquent's duty.

Voted, That the ten pounds of powder and twenty pounds of lead delivered to Mr. Scott by John Hill be for the use of the settlers, and said Hill to charge it to said Proprietors.

Attest: JOHN HILL, *Pro. Clerk.*

1753. At a meeting of the said Proprietors of Peterborough, being legally warned and notified, at the said Robert Stone's house, the 5th day of July, 1753:

Voted, Jerry Gridley, Esq., be moderator.

Voted, That if any of the settlers neglect to pay any sum or sums of money due for public uses, which was voted by the settlers or the major part of them, until the 15th day of September next, we will then dispose of their lots to the highest bidder.

Attest: JOHN HILL, *Pro. Clerk.*

SUFFOLK SS.   DECEMBER 21, 1744.

Col. John Hill made oath that in the office of Clerk of the Proprietors of Peterborough (a new plan taken so called) he would diligently and faithfully attend and discharge the duty of that office, and duly observe the directions of the law in all things whereto said office hath relation, and thereby committed to his care and trust.

Before me :   S. DANFORTH, *Jus. Peace.*

Sept. 26, 1753, at a meeting of the Proprietors of said Peterborough, being legally warned and notified, at the house of Alexander Scott in said Peterborough, Sept. 26, 1753:

Voted, That Jerry Gridley be moderator.

Voted, That there be granted to John Taget, his heirs and assigns, lot No. 39. containing one hundred acres, lying west of his settling lot, No.

48; in consideration thereof he relinquisheth his right to said Proprietors to lots Nos. 13 and 24, containing together one hundred acres ; they lie on the settlers' second division; the lot No. 13 is bounded south on lot No. 12, north on lot No. 14, east on lot No. 21, and south on lot No. 5. The said lot No. 24 is bounded south on lot No. 23, west on No. 16, north on No. 27, and east on No. 26.

Voted, That there be granted to William Richey, his heirs and assigns, lot No. 32, third division, containing fifty acres; it lieth north of lots No. 46 and 49; in consideration thereof the said William Richey relinquisheth his right to said Proprietors to lot No. 8 in the second division, containing fifty acres, lying west and north of the pond.

Voted, That there be granted to William McNay, his heirs and assigns, the fifty-acre lot lying west of his settling lot, No. 110, south on the town line, and north on lot No. 39, granted to John Taget ; in consideration thereof the said McNay relinquisheth to said Proprietors his right in lot No. 19, containing fifty acres, in the second division ; it bounds south on No. 18, and west on No. 11, and north on No. 20, and east on No. 25; necessary roads to be allowed out of each of the foregoing lots.

Attest: JOHN HILL, *Pro. Clerk.*

At the same meeting, on said 26th day of September, 1753, voted that there be granted to Samuel Miller, his heirs and assigns, lot No. 123, adjoining to his settling lot, No. 61 ; in consideration thereof the said Samuel Miller relinquisheth his right to said Proprietors to his second division lot No. 8, containing fifty acres ; it bounds south on No. 7, west on No. 60, north on No. 31, east on No. 16; necessary roads to be allowed out of each lot.

JOHN HILL, *Pro. Clerk.*

At the same meeting, on said 26th day of September, 1753, John Hill granted to Gustavus Swan lot No. 89, adjoining to his settling lot, No. 36, to his heirs and assigns ; in consideration thereof the said Swan relinquisheth to said Hill his right in lot No. 20, second division, containing fifty acres; it bounds south on No. 19, west on No. 12, north on No. 21, and east on No. 25; the above granted lot, No. 98, contains fifty acres, and necessary roads to be allowed out of each lot.

Attest: JOHN HILL, *Pro. Clerk.*

On the same 26th day of September, 1753, John Hill granted to Thomas Turner No. 92, containing fifty acres, adjoining to his settling lot, No. 29; in consideration thereof the said Turner relinquisheth his right to said Hill to No. 7, in second division, containing fifty acres ; it bounds south on No. 6, west on No. 121, north on No. 8, east on No. 15; necessary roads to be allowed out of said lot.

Attest: JOHN HILL, *Pro. Clerk.*

On the same 26th day of September, 1753, John Hill granted to Thomas Davison No. 93, containing fifty acres, adjoining to his settling lot, No. 30; in consideration thereof the said Davison relinquisheth to the said Hill his right to one hundred acres in the second division, granted to him for settlement on the same 26th day of September, 1753, *viz. :* Nos. 6 and 8.

John Hill granted to William McNay, his heirs and assigns, No. 110, containing fifty acres, adjoining to his settling lot, No. 48; in consideration thereof the said William McNay relinquisheth his right to the said Hill to his second division lot No. 10, bounded south on No. 9, west on No. 2, north on No. 11, and east on No. 18; necessary roads allowed out of each lot.

Attest: JOHN HILL, *Pro. Clerk.*

On the same 26th day of September, 1753, John Fowle granted to James Archibald his right in No. 88, adjoining to settling lot, No. 25; in consideration thereof the said Archibald relinquisheth to said Fowle fifty acres in his second division.

Attest: JOHN HILL, *Pro. Clerk.*

Then the meeting of the said Proprietors was adjourned to the next day, being the 27th day of September, 1753, to the said house of Alexander Scott, in Peterborough, to nine of the clock in the forenoon. Then met and passed the following vote: —

Voted, That there be granted unto John Richey,* son of William Richey, lot No. 19, containing fifty acres, to him, his heirs and assigns forever; said lot bounds south on lot No. 18, north on No. 20, east on No. 25, and West on No. 11, necessary roads to be allowed out of said lot.

Attest: JOHN HILL, *Pro. Clerk.*

1754. At a meeting of the Proprietors of Peterborough, being legally warned and notified, at the dwelling-house of Jeremiah Gridley, Esq., in Boston, on Tuesday, the 4th day of June, 1754, and passed the following vote: —

1. *Voted,* That John Hill be desired, at the charge of said Propriety, to purchase *half a barrel of gunpowder, one hundred weight of lead, and two hundred flints,* and send them by Mr. Alexander Scott to said town, there to be for a town stock for the use of the settlers in case of a war.

2. *Voted,* That the settlers of said town or their Committee chosen by them for that purpose be empowered, where any of the settlers have removed off their lots and don't return in three weeks from public notice being given by said Committee in said town and the town they shall be removed to, if it be known by said Committee, by posting up the same in some public place in each of the towns aforesaid; and also that any of the settlers that shall remove out of said town within six months from this date, the said Committee be empowered to dispose of such settlers' lots to such persons as will immediately enter into possession and improve said lots, and continue inhabitants in said town.

3. *Voted,* That John Hill, Esq., be desired, at the charge of the said Proprietors, to purchase a gun and send it to Peterborough by Alexander Scott, and the said Scott be desired to deliver said gun to the *Rev. Mr. Harvey, minister there,* for his use so long as he continues to be an inhabitant of said town.

Attest: JOHN HILL, *Pro. Clerk.*

At a meeting of the Proprietors of Peterborough, being legally warned and notified, at the house of John Fowle, Esq., in Woburn, on the 4th day of June, A. D. 1756 — present, Jeremiah Gridley, John Hill, and John Fowle, Esqs.:

---

* First child born in Peterborough. J. S.

Voted, That Jeremiah Gridley, Esq., be moderator.

Voted, That the Proprietors proceed to draw the lots in the list presented; and John Hill, Esq., drew the lots in the list No. 1 as is here set forth, to be to him, his heirs and assigns forever.

Location.	No. of each Lot.		Number of Acres.
First Range,	1 and 2	Mason P.,	200
Second "	31 and 32	"	200
First "	7 and 8	"	200
Second "	25 and 26	"	200
First "	13 and 14	"	200
Second "	105 and 106		200
First "	19 and 20		200
Third "	111		193
" "	48		150
Third East Range,	43		150
West from Farm B and C,	94 and 95		203
Fourth Range from West Line,	84 and 85		206
Fourth " " " "	91		75
Third "	74 and 75		203
" "	80		102
Second "	71 and 72		200
First "	63 and 62		200
Second "	64		100
First "	54		100
Third East Range,	52 (sold Hammill)		193
Fourth "	41		120

The above said lots are marked with the letter H on each lot in the plan annexed to this book, on pages 6, 7.

Recorded and attested: JOHN HILL, *Pro. Clerk.*

And John Fowle, Esq., drew the lots set forth in the list No. 2, as is here set forth, to be to him, his heirs and assigns forever.

Location.	No. of Lots.		No. of Acres.
Second East Range,	34 and 33	Mason P.,	200
First "	5 and 6	"	200
Second "	27 and 28	"	200
First "	11 and 12	"	200
Second "	21 and 22	"	200
First "	17 and 18	"	200
Second "	101 and 102		200
Third "	110		193
" "	47		150
Near Farm B,	93 and 92		200
West from Farm C,	96		137
Fourth Range from West Line,	86 and 98		200
" "	90		75
Third "	76 and 77		204
" "	81		102
Second and Third Ranges, West Line,	73 and 83		203
First Range from West Line,	60 and 61		75
Second Range from West Line,	65		100
Third Lot from South Line,	38		100
Third East Range (sold Riddle),	49		193
On West Line of the town,	53		102

The above said lots are marked with the letter F, in each lot, in the plan annexed to this book, pages 6, 7.

Recorded and attested: JOHN HILL, *Pro. Clerk.*

And Jeremiah Gridley, Esq., drew the lots set forth in the list No. 3, as is here set forth, to be to him, his heirs and assigns forever.

Location.	No. of Lots.			No. of Acres.
First East Range,	3 and	4	Mason P.,	200
Second "	29 and	30	"	200
First "	9 and	10	"	200
Second "	23 and	24	"	200
First "	15 and	16	"	200
Second "	103 and	104		200
First and Second East Ranges,	99 and	100		200
Fourth East Range,	112 and	113		192
West from Farm C.,	97			100
Fourth Range from West Line,	87 and	88		200
Fourth West Line,	89			103
Third Range from West Line,	78 and	79		204
" " " "	82			103
Second " " " "	69 and	70		200
First " " " "	58 and	59		200
Second Range from South Line,	39			106
Third Range from West Line,	50 (sold Miller)			151

The foregoing lots are marked with the letter G in each lot, in the plan annexed to this book, on pages 6, 7.

Recorded and attested :   JOHN HILL, *Pro. Clerk.*

Location.	No. of Lots.		No. of Acres.
Fourth East Range,	114 and	115	192
Third " "	46		150
" " "	45		150

The above four lots were drawn by Jeremiah Gridley, Esq., at the same time, and with the others recorded to him, and were contained in the list No. 3, but omitted in the recording, and are now recorded to him and his heirs and assigns forever.

By   JOHN HILL, *Pro. Clerk.*

At the same meeting the Assignees of Peter Prescott drew the following lots, *viz.:* —

Location.	No. of Lots.	No. of Acres.
Third East Range,	42	150
" " "	44	150
First West "	55	100

Conformable to a grant of said Proprietors at their meeting, the 21st day of December, 1744, as recorded in this book, page 56.

Recorded by   •   JOHN HILL, *Pro. Clerk.*

At a meeting of the Proprietors of Peterborough, being first legally warned and notified, at the house of John Fowle, Esq., in Woburn, on Wednesday, the 21st day of June, 1758, they passed the following votes :

Voted, That Jeremiah Gridley, Esq., be moderator.

Voted, That whereas two hundred and fifty acres of land at either end of the farm, and of an equal breadth therewith, was granted to John Fowle, Jun., and his heirs, at a meeting of the said Proprietors held the 29th day of November, 1738, recorded on page 11 of this book, as an equivalent to either of the other farms marked with the letters A, B, and

C; and whereas James Gordon, the assignee of John Fowle, has made his election of said two hundred and fifty acres on the east side of said farm, and laid said equivalent land out there, which takes in the lots Nos. 115, 114, and part of lot No. 113, which in the last division made by said Proprietors were drawn by Jeremiah Gridley, Esq. :

Voted, Therefore, that in lieu thereof there be, and hereby is, granted to said Jeremiah Gridley, his heirs and assigns forever, two hundred and fifty acres, adjoining to said farm D on the west side thereof, as an equivalent for the said lots, Nos. 115, 114, and part of No. 113, taken by said Gordon as aforesaid.

Voted, That whereas there was granted unto John Taget lot No. 39, containing one hundred acres lying on the west side of his settling lot, No. 48, at their meeting of said Proprietors, Sept. 26, 1753, recorded page 58 of this book, in lieu of said lot No. 39, he, the said John Taget, relinquished his right to said Proprietors in lots Nos. 13 and 24, in second division, laid out for said settlers ; and whereas Jeremiah Gridley, at the last division made by said Proprietors, drew the said lot No. 39, therefore, in lieu thereof, the said lots, Nos. 13 and 24, are granted to the said Jeremiah Gridley, Esq., and his heirs.

Voted, That the clerk be desired to make the following memorandum in the Proprietors' book, *viz.* : —

" That the heirs of John Vanall, etc., have not, by themselves nor any other person, appeared in any of the Proprietors' meetings, nor contributed anything towards the settlement of said town of Peterborough, and their guardian, the Hon. Spencer Phips, Esq., refused to pay anything towards the expenses the Proprietors were at in bringing forward said settlement, although application was often made to said guardian by John Fowle and John Hill, Esqs., as they have declared in this meeting of said Proprietors."

Voted, That there be and hereby is granted unto Richard Gridley, Esq., and to his heirs and assigns forever, for his good services to said Proprietors, a fifty-acre lot in said township of Peterborough, bearing No. 8 ; it bounds south on lot No. 70, north on lot No. 71 ; it buts east on lot No. 31 or the highway, west on the Mill farm. It is more particularly planned, described, butted, and bounded on page 15 of this book, and recorded by Peter Prescott, the then Proprietor's Clerk, Dec. 18, 1738.

Recorded and attested by   JOHN HILL, *Pro. Clerk.*

On pages 59, 60, of this book there is recorded as follows, *viz :* Sept. 26, 1753, John Hill granted to Thomas Davison No. 93, containing fifty acres, adjoining to his settling lot, No. 30 ; in consideration thereof the said Davison relinquisheth to said Hill his right to one hundred acres of land in the second division, granted to him for settlement on the same 26th day of September, 1753, and the said Hill has drawn for his the said second division, *viz.,* No. 6, containing fifty acres, bounding west on No. 61, east on No. 14, south on No. 5, north on Nos. 7 and 8 ; and the lot No. 8, containing fifty acres, is bounded south on lot No. 7, north on lot 31, east on No. 16, west on Nos. 60 and 122.

Recorded by   JOHN HILL, *Pro. Clerk.*

On pages 61, 62, there is recorded to John Hill, Esq., his draft of lots, and the following lots that are marked Mason P. are set off to the Pro-

45

prietors of Mason's claim, as their reservation in their grant to the Proprietors of Peterborough, for said Hill's part of said reservation.

In First East Range as on Plan in this Book.

No. 1,	containing	100 acres.
" 2,	"	100 "
" 7,	"	100 "
" 8,	"	100 "
" 13,	"	100 "
" 14,	"	100 "
" 19,	"	100 "
" 20,	"	100 "

In Second East Range, &c.

No. 25,	containing	100 acres.
" 26,	"	100 "
" 31,	"	100 "
" 32,	"	100 "

On page 62 there is recorded to John Fowle his draft of lots, and the following lots that are marked Mason P. are set off to the Proprietors of Mason's claim, as their reservation in their grant to the Proprietors of Peterborough, for said Fowle's part of said reservation.

In First East Range.

No. 5,	containing	100 acres.
" 6,	"	100 "
" 11,	"	100 "
" 12,	"	100 "
" 17,	"	100 "
" 18,	"	100 "

In Second East Range, &c.

No. 21,	containing	100 acres.
" 22,	"	100 "
" 27,	"	100 "
" 28,	"	100 "
" 33,	"	100 "
" 34,	"	100 "

On page 63 there is recorded to Jeremiah Gridley, Esq., his draft of lots, and the following lots that are marked P. Mason are set off to the Proprietors of Mason's claim, as their reservation in their grant to the Proprietors of Peterborough, for said Gridley's part of said reservation.

In the First East Range.

. No. 3,	containing	100 acres.
" 4,	"	100 "
" 9,	"	100 "
" 10,	"	100 "
" 15,	"	100 "
" 16,	"	100 "

In Second East Range, &c.

No. 23,	containing	100 acres.
" 24,	"	100 "
" 29,	"	100 "
" 30,	"	100 "

Nota bene, said Gridley has one hundred and thirty-three and one-third less taken out of his part or share of the lands to satisfy Mason's grant than Hill and Fowle have, so that Hill and Fowle must have each of them sixty-six and two-thirds acres allowed them, to make up so much for their part taken out and recorded to said Mason Proprietors.

On page 60 in this book is recorded, Sept. 26, 1753: John Fowle granted to James Archibald his high No. 88, adjoining to his settling lot, No. 25; in consideration thereof the said Archibald relinquisheth to said Fowle fifty acres in his second division, and the said Fowle has drawn lot No. 24, for his second division; it buts south on lot No. 23, north on lot No. 27, east on lot No. 26, west on lot No. 16.

Recorded: JOHN HILL, *Pro. Clerk.*

At a meeting of the Proprietors of Peterborough, duly notified and warned, at the chamber of Jeremiah Gridley, Esq., in Mr. Bagnall's dwelling-house, in Boston, on the 25th day of March, in the year 1767:

Voted, That there be and hereby is granted (at the request of the inhabitants of said Peterborough) unto the Rev. Mr. John Morrisôn, he being the first settled minister, the lots. Nos. 15 and 78, in the first division of lots as they are now laid out (they contain together one hundred acres), to him, the said Morrison, his heirs and assigns forever, on the following condition, *viz.:* lot No. 78, that he continue minister in said town of Peterborough for the space of seven years from his ordination, or to his death, if that should first happen; and in case the said Morrison should not remain minister of said Peterborough for the space of seven years, and so long live, then the said lot No. 78 is hereby granted unto the said town of Peterborough for their next settled minister.

Recorded by   JOHN HILL, *Pro. Clerk.*

[The end of page 67 of the Proprietors' Record.]

Pages 68 and 69 of the Proprietors' book contain an exact copy of the grant of the Masonian Proprietors to the Proprietors of Peterborough, etc., which is recorded on pages 1, 2, 3, and 4 of this book.

Transcribed Oct. 21, 1787. Finis.

For an attested copy, by Jeremiah Smith, of the above quitclaim of the Masonian Proprietors to the Proprietors of Peterborough, see pages 47, 48, and 49 of this History.

A COPY OF THE ACT ANNEXING A CERTAIN PART OF PETERBOROUGH TO TEMPLE.

State of New Hampshire.   •

In the year of our Lord one thousand seven hundred and eighty-nine.

[L. S.]

An act for annexing a certain part of the town of Peterborough in the County of Hillsborough to the town of Temple in said county:

WHEREAS, The following lots of land, lying in the south-east corner of said Peterborough, to wit, lots numbered one, two, three, four, five, and six in the first East Range, and the lots numbered thirty-three and thirty-four in the second East Range, are separated by a very high mountain from the other parts of said Peterborough, and are commodiously situated for said town at Temple, and the said towns of Peterborough and Temple have agreed that the said lots of land be disjoined from said town of Peterborough and be annexed to said town of Temple, therefore:

Be it enacted by the Senate and House of Representatives in General Court convened, that the said lots be and they hereby are disjoined from said town of Peterborough and annexed to said town of Temple; and the said lots of land with the inhabitants thereon shall forever hereafter be considered as a part, and belonging to, said town of Temple, as though the same had been originally incorporated therewith; and the person or persons who, on the 1st day of September last, or at any time since, lived, or are now living, on said lots of land, and who by living thereon may have gained a residence in said town of Peterborough, shall, in case they shall ever stand in need of relief, be considered as the proper charge of the said town of Temple, in the same manner as though the same lots at the time of such person or persons coming to reside thereon, and ever since, had been a part of said Temple, any law, usage, or custom to the contrary notwithstanding:

Provided, nevertheless, that nothing in this act shall be considered to affect the right of said Town of Peterborough to assess levy and collect any taxes now due from said lots, but the same shall be assessed, levied, and collected in the same manner as though this act had not been made, anything therein to the contrary notwithstanding.

In the House of Representatives, Jan. 28, 1789. The foregoing bill having been read a third time, Voted, That it pass to be enacted. Sent up for concurrence.

THOMAS BARTLETT, *Speaker*.

In Senate, Jan. 29, 1789. This bill having been read a third time, Voted, That the same be enacted.

JOHN PICKERING, *President*.

True copy examined by Joseph Pearson, Secretary.
True copy examined by Jeremiah Smith.

EXPLANATION,

By N. H. MORISON,

OF LAND-MAP TRANSCRIBED BY JUDGE SMITH IN 1787, FROM THE
PROPRIETORS' RECORDS.

In laying out a town six miles square, there can be little doubt that the surveyor *intended* to make the junction of the Contoocook and Nubanusit Rivers its centre, and to run its boundaries due east, west, north, and south.

FIRST SURVEY.

The first survey of lots was made by Joseph Wilder in the spring of 1738. The four great farms of 500 acres each (320 by 250 rods) for the proprietors were first laid off, farm A (Gridley's) being thrown perpendicularly across the Nubanusit River. To farm D (Fowle's), on account of the swamps in which much of it lay, was granted an addition of 250 acres, which, in 1758, were selected by James Gordon, the assignee of Fowle, on the east side of the farm, including lots 115, 114, and part of 113 of the second survey, these numbers being transferred to other lots west of the farm.

Beside the great farms the survey laid off the 63 lots required by the grant, 60 for the settlers, 1 for the first minister, 1 for the second minister, and 1 for the school. The settlers' lots were scattered over the various parts of the town and around the large farms in such a way as to give the greatest value to the lands retained by the proprietors. Each "home" or "settler's" lot contained 50 acres; but, at a later period (1753), the settler who had complied with the conditions of the settlement received another 50 acre lot. To each settler's lot of 50 acres was joined a proprietor's lot of the same size and dimensions, making each full lot contain 100 acres (160 by 100 rods) divided equally between settler and proprietor. Each lot of this first survey, therefore, contains two numbers, those from 1 to 63 designating the settlers' halves of the full lots, and the numbers from 64 to 125 marking the parts belonging to the proprietors. These double numbers are the characteristic feature of the first survey, and render it easy to trace the lots then laid out, over the different parts of the town. This first survey ran thus: —

1. South line, 1st range west of Street Road, running north 12 lots, 1, 64 — 12, 75.

2. 2nd range west of farm B, running south 5 lots, 13, 76—17, 80.

3. 1st range east of farm B, running north 3 lots, 18, 81 —20, 83.

4. Two ranges (14 lots) were then surveyed outside the present limits of the town, beginning west of 54, second survey (Alexander Robbe's).

West line, 1st range, running south 6 lots and 2 half-lots, 22; 21, 85; 23, 86; 24, 87; 25, 88; 26, 89; 27, 90; 28; 2d range, running north 6 lots and 2 half-lots, 91; 29, 92; 30, 93; 31, 94; 32, 95; 33, 96; 34, 97; 35.

These numbers were all transferred to other parts of the town after the western boundary was altered by Blanchard. Lot 21 is the companion lot of 84. Lot 35, granted to J. Hubbard, an early small proprietor, had no settler's lot attached, so that up to 34, 97 the difference between the two numbers in the lots is always 63, but after 35 this difference is 62.

5. South of farm B, 1st range east of Street Road, running south 5 lots, 36, 98 —40, 102.

6. South of farm B, 2d range east of Street Road, running north 4 lots, 41, 103 —44, 106.

7. South line, 2d range west of Street Road, running north 3 lots, 45, 107—47, 109.

8. South line, 3d range west of Street Road, running north 2 lots, 48, 110—49, 111.

9. East, north, and west of farm A, 7 lots, 50, 112—56, 118.

10. 1st range, east of Street Road, running south, 7 lots, 57, 119—63, 125, ending on the town line near the place of beginning, and completing the survey.

Three numbers of the Jaffrey lots (28, 91—30, 93) were retained in the half range left by Blanchard on the west side of the town. The other numbers were transferred to the 2nd and 3d ranges east of the Street Road, 28, 91 being found in both places.

SECOND SURVEY.

The second survey was made some time, but not long, after Oct. 16, 1749, when it was ordered. The name of the surveyor is not known. In the south-east part of the town, beginning on south line, 2nd range east of Street Road, 31 lots of 50 acres each were laid off. In 1753, these lands were divided by lot among such settlers as had complied with the conditions of settlement, and were styled 2nd division lots, the original settler's lot being his 1st division lot. Lots numbered 32, 3d division, south of 31, 2d division, and 32, 3d division, in the south-west part of the town, marked Richey, were also 50 acre lots, probably given to later settlers, and so called 3d division lots.

Lots 32, 33, 34, 35, 36, 37, in the south-west part of the town, were settled before the second survey was begun, and the bounds of these lots were probably arranged to suit the settlers actually in possession of them. This only will account for the great size and irregularity of these farms, for the fact that they were never divided among the proprietors, and that no mention of them whatever appears in their records. The survey proceeded as follows:—

1. N. E. part of town, 31 lots, 1–31, called 2d division lots.

2. S. W. "   "   6 " 32–37, settled before they were surveyed.

3. S. W. "   "   3 " 38–40.

4. East line, 4th range, 1 lot, 41.

5.   "   "   3d "   11 "   42–52.

6.	West	"	1st	"	11	"	53–63.
7.	"	"	2d	"	10	"	64–73.
8.	"	"	3d	"	10	"	74–83.
9.	"	"	4th	"	8	"	84–91.
10.	"	"	5th	"	6	"	92–97.
11.	"	"	4th	"	1	"	98.
12.	East	"	1st	"	1	"	99.
13.	"	"	2d	"	7	"	100–106.
14.	"	"	3d	"	5	"	107–111.
15.	"	"	4th	"	1	"	112.
16.	West	"	5th	"	3	"	118–115.
17.	South-east of farm A		1	"	116.

On the east line, 1st and 2d ranges, thirty-four lots were also laid out for the Mason proprietors, and numbered in a separate series from 1 to 34.

The lots above described constitute the entire town with the exception of two lots, not numbered, but marked Hill, in the extreme south-west corner of the town, the companion lot of 63 of the 1st survey (should be 125); the lot south of farm A, marked 81 (a number already appropriated elsewhere), and the "Mill Farm," granted to the builder of the first mill. The records contain no account of the survey or the assignment of these five lots.

Three divisions of lands were made. The first division took place in 1738, among the proprietors, of all the lands of the first survey. The second division was made in 1753, among the settlers, of thirty-one fifty-acre lots. The third division was made in 1756, among the proprietors, of all lands not previously disposed of. Gridley's lots are all marked on the map with G; Hill's with H; Fowle's with F; Prescott's with P, or P P (Peter Prescott, to distinguish him from Jonathan Prescott); and Hubbard's two lots with Hub.

At the third division, lots 55, 1st west range, 42, 44, 3d east range, were allotted to Benjamin Pollard, as assignee of Peter Prescott, and so do not bear a proprietor's name. Lots 56, 66, 67, 68, marked Todd in the 1st and 2d west ranges, lots 107, 108, 109, marked Willson, and lot 51, marked Wm. Miller, all in 3d east range, were never divided among the proprietors, and must have been sold to the persons whose names they bear after the survey of 1749-50, and before the division of lots in 1756. The same is true of lots 32, 33, 34, 35, 36, 37, in the south-west, which have no proprietors' names. The second division lots were never divided among the proprietors, and their names are only found in such of them as were obtained from the settlers by exchange for lots in other parts of the town. In 1767 the proprietors granted lots 76 and 15, in the 4th west range, to Rev. John Morrison, the first settled minister of the town.

Eight lots in the south-east corner of the town, six on the 1st and two on the 2d east range, were annexed to Temple in 1789; and the remainder of the 1st east range, from lot 7 northward to the town line, was annexed to Greenfield in 1791.

The line crossing the south-east corner of the town diagonally from lot 63 of the 1st survey on the south line, to lot 11 in the Mason series on the east line, shows the limit of the Mason Grant as finally fixed by the survey of Joseph Blanchard, son of Col. Blanchard, and Charles Clapham. In 1787 these surveyors, under the authority of the State, ran a line ninety-three and one-half miles long, from a point one and one-

fourth miles east of the south-west corner of Rindge to a point on the
east line of Eaton, both of which points they fixed by their survey.
This line passed through Peterborough as above described, and fixed, by
an authority from which there was no appeal, exact limits to the Mason
Grant. A dispute was thus settled which had raged, at times with great
violence, for more than one hundred and fifty years.

All the streams on this map are more or less out of their true positions, and the bounds of many lots are very inaccurately drawn, rendering it of little use to the surveyor; and yet the map is of great historic
value as showing the relative position of the farms, and the exact location
of all the earliest, and many of the subsequent, settlers of the town.

GENEALOGY AND HISTORY

OF THE

PETERBOROUGH FAMILIES.

I have combined under this head both the genealogy and history of the various families and individuals in town. It is more full and complete than any town register I have ever seen. It comprises all I have to say of the different families. It is in fact a history of the families, — their births, deaths, marriages, residences, etc. All due care has been taken to make it as accurate as possible. But when we are dealing with births and deaths of over a century, with imperfect records, it is all more or less uncertain. I have solicited information and data publicly and privately, and often by long-continued persistence to those who were slow or indifferent. Many of the genealogies have come in an imperfect state, which I had to correct from other sources of information. Many were not reliable, — often prepared in such a confused manner that it was like deciphering hieroglyphics to read them. And then sometimes they were in pencil, as if it was a matter that did not require much attention; often with the omission of the initials of the names, and the Christian names given carelessly, so that it would be doubtful whether Hattie was to be an abbreviation for Harriet, or Freddie for Frederick. Of course I was often at a loss what to do.

Sometimes my efforts grew importunate to get the true record, when I knew it was attainable. I did not let the care-

1

lessness and indifference of friends prevent my getting all the facts that existed. The labor of such a course may well be imagined. And if, after all, many families find a poor record, they must take the blame to themselves. I could not invent records, and if they were not furnished or were destroyed, I could only make such a record as the data afforded.

Much trouble and inconvenience have been experienced from ignorance of ancestors shown by their descendants. The excellent motto of my book cannot too often be inculcated, — " *Memor esto majorum.*"   In many cases they could go no farther back than their grandfathers, and often had but slight reminiscences of them.   This put a heavy labor on me. The facts, if they existed, were to be attained in some way, and every effort was made through more distant relatives to obtain the desired information.   If many mistakes occur in data thus obtained of these far-off persons, I must be pardoned when I say that I have done all I could to insure correctness.

There is, at the present time, great carelessness in keeping family records.   The old style of making the record in the family Bible, seems now, in a great degree, to have gone out of fashion.   Are there no family Bibles now?   In very many instances I found families who had never made any record at all, trusting entirely to their memories.   My record will be the first and only one they ever had.

I could not, of course, embrace all the families in town in my genealogy.   It would have involved a herculean labor. All the families down to between forty and fifty years past have been included, and if omissions or imperfections occur in regard to the record of some of the old families, I can only say, it is because I could get no data in relation to them.   The historical relations have been prepared with a good deal of labor and care.   They were written by myself, where credit is not otherwise given.   I regret that such meagre and contracted relations should have been made of many of these men; it was all that could be done now.   It will convey some idea of what the descendants of the early settlers have been and are now.

In the arrangement of the genealogy and history I have

adopted the plan used in the "History of Lexington," by Charles Hudson.

In these tables the name of the parent is given in small capitals as No. 1, and then follows the place of residence, any history in relation to him, offices held, marriages, deaths, etc. A short line is then drawn thus:

———

And then his children's Christian names are given in *italics*. The first name numbers 2, with one at the left hand to indicate the parent thus: 1-2. Then follows the family, 3, 4, 5, 6, 7, etc.; to each of them is added the birth, marriage, removal from town, etc. If any of the sons remain in town and have families, the names are marked with an obelisk † thus, showing that the family is next to be recorded; otherwise the names are dropped from the genealogy. A line is then drawn across the page transversely. Then comes the name of the first son with an obelisk, say 1-2. The history of the individual is given as above, and then the short line and his family follows, counting 8, 9, 10, 11, as may be. And if any one or more of his family settles in town, with a family, an obelisk is put to his name, and the record carried on in the *same manner*.

The following explanation will enable the reader to understand the genealogical tables : —

ABBREVIATIONS. — b. stands for born; æ. for age or aged; m. married; unm. unmarried; d. died; dau. daughter, or daughters; h. husband; w. wife; wid. widow; r. resides, or resided; re. removed; ad. admitted; ch. children; c. childless; q. v. for see register for his or her family; J. P. Justice of Peace; Rep. Representative; un. names unknown.

GENEALOGICAL, HISTORICAL, AND STATISTICAL REGISTER.

THE ABBOT FAMILY.

1   ABIEL ABBOT, H. U. 1787, D. D. 1838, was the son of Dea. Abiel and Dorcas Abbot, of Wilton. The parents were most excellent persons, and attained the utmost success by their industry and perseverance in the new settlement, so as to be enabled to give a collegiate education to three of their sons. Abiel was the oldest of a large family, and was born in Wilton, Dec. 14, 1765.* He graduated at Harvard University 1787, and received the degree of D. D. in 1838. He sustained a good standing in his class at college, and a character unstained. After teaching in Phillips Academy at Andover about two years, pursuing a course of theological studies, and being tutor in H. U. one year, he was ordained, in October, 1795, minister of the first church in Coventry, Ct. · Owing to differences of opinion between himself and the church, he left Coventry in June, 1811, and the September following was appointed Principal of Dummer Academy. In 1819 he resigned the charge of the academy, and moved to Andover, where, and at Chelmsford, in various pursuits, he remained till 1827 when in June he was installed minister of the Congregational Church in Peterborough. He continued to supply the pulpit until 1839, when his health failed, and the Rev. Curtis· Cutler was installed as his colleague. He resigned his pastorate Sept. 9, 1848.

Few men have ever lived that have sustained a better character than Dr. Abbot. His life was adorned with all the attainments, virtues, and excellences that belong to the Christian or man, and it would be difficult to say

---

* Genealogical Register of Abbot Family.

Abiel Abbot

what his faults or errors in life were, he was so pure and upright in everything. He was always planning and doing good to some one, or to society in general. The Ministerial Library of the Congregational Society was established by his own individual exertions and private contributions from his own library, and now numbers about twelve hundred volumes. He also was the prime mover, and one of the earliest supporters, of the Town Library. He was always untiring in his efforts for the common schools, and long after the period most men retire, on account of their age, from active pursuits, his zeal and interest remained unabated. As a preacher he was always plain, clear, and interesting, and as a pastor always kind and sympathizing. He was always greatly beloved by the people. He was scholarly in his habits, and kept alive a knowledge of the Greek and Latin classics, as well as an intimate knowledge of the progress of his times, all through his life. No language can be an exaggeration in speaking of the character and virtues of such a man. He removed to West Cambridge in 1854, to reside with his grandson, Rev. S. A. Smith, where he d. Jan. 31, 1859, æ. 93. He was buried in Peterborough. He m. Elizabeth Abbot, dau. Capt. John A. Abbot, Andover, 1796, and she d. in Peterborough, April 6, 1853, æ. 87.

"He published, in 1811, a statement of the proceedings which resulted in a dissolution of his ministry in Coventry; and in 1829 published a history of the town of Andover, Mass." *

2   *Elizabeth*, b. May 22, 17r8; m. 1822, Rev. John A. Douglas, Waterford, Me. She d. Oct. 12, 1823, æ. 25 yrs., 4 mos.

3   *Abigail*, b. Oct. 17, 1799.

4   *Sarah Dorcas*, b. June 22, 1801; m. 1828, Samuel G. Smith, of Peterborough. She d. June 11, 1831, æ. 30.

1   DANIEL ABBOT, born in Lyndeboro, July 31, 1769, was a descendant of one of the six early progenitors of the Abbot family, but which one is not known. He came to Peterborough, when twelve or fifteen years old, to learn the carpenter's trade. When quite young he worked on the old meeting-house, and afterward built the Bleak house, now owned by Nathaniel H. Morison, Esq. Early in the century he engaged in the business of chair-making, and manufactured such a thorough article, that many specimens of them are now in use in town. He removed to Newburyport, Mass., and spent four or five years, when he returned again to Peterborough, and was en-

* Genealogical Register of Abbot Family.

gaged in the mercantile business a number of years be-
fore he left town, in 1834. He m. July 5, 1798, Sally
Allison, of Londonderry, b. Dec. 17, 1769, and d. in New
York, Nov. 22, 1837, æ. 67 yrs., 11 mos. He d. at West-
ford, Mass., Jan. 27, 1854, æ. 84 yrs., 5 mos. He was
Town Clerk in 1815.

---

2 *Jane*, b. Sept. 30, 1800; m. John Scott; re. to Detroit,
   Mich.

3 *Sarah*, b. Nov. 3, 1806; m. May 6, 1830, Jefferson
   Fletcher. Ch., (1) Mary L., b. Oct. 15, 1835; m.
   Robert B. Hallock, New York City; (2) Sarah A.,
   b. July 26, 1841; (3) Edmund, b. Oct. 15, 1849.

4 *Daniel*, b. Apr. 11, 1808; m. 1838, Dorothy E. Cutter, b.
   Sept. 20, 1809. Ch., (1) Laura Jane, b. Nov. 7, 1842;
   m. 1862, Albert Stevens; one ch., Ida M. He d. in
   New York, Sept. 2, 1854, æ. 46 yrs., 4 mos.

5 *John*, b. Jan. 24, 1810; m. Jan. 2, 1834, Pamelia Beach,
   Monroe, Mich.; d. in Michigan, Nov. 30, 1834, æ. 24
   yrs., 5 mos.

THE ADAMS FAMILY.

1 SAMUEL ADAMS, son of Moses and Hannah Wilson,
   was b. in Dublin, May 3, 1794, where he lived until 1837,
   when he purchased the farm of the late Daniel Robbe,
   and removed to Peterborough. He has since resided
   here. He has held various offices in town. Selectman
   1841 and 1859, 1860; he also represented the town in
   the Legislature in 1847. He m., 1st w., Almira Kendall,
   who d. June 25, 1823; 2d w., Dec. 3, 1824, Martha
   Broad, who d. June 20, 1825; 3d w., Azuba Broad, Jan.
   23, 1827. She d. May 30, 1854, æ. 60; b. March 17,
   1794.

---

2 †*John Quincy*, b. Oct. 27, 1827; m. Sept. 29, 1853, Abbie W. Fisk, b. June 9, 1831, of Weston, Mass.

3 *Sarah B.*, b. July 18, 1829; d. Aug. 10, 1869, æ. 40.

4 †*Samuel*, b. Sept. 14, 1831; m. Matilda Nay.

5 *Hannah A.*, b. July 8, 1833; d. Nov. 1, 1857, æ. 24.

1–2 JOHN QUINCY ADAMS, m. Abbie W. Fisk, dau. of Sew-
     all and Martha S. Fisk, of Weston, Mass. He succeeded
     his father on the homestead. Has been selectman 1870,
     '71, '72, '74.

---

6 *Wallace P.*, b. Dec. 23, 1854; d. Nov. 30, 1864, æ. 9 yrs.,
   11 mos.

Henry F., b. May 30, 1857.

7	*Herbert G.*, b. May 14, 1860; d. Aug. 21, 1865, æ. 5 yrs.,
8	3 mos.
9	*Helen F.*, b. June 25, 1864.
10	*Mary M.*, b. Aug. 6, 1873.

1— 4   SAMUEL ADAMS, m. Matilda Nay, Apr. 21, 1853. He is a paper manufacturer at the mill formerly owned by A. P. Morrison.

11	*Loren W.*, b. Nov. 14, 1857.
12	*Clarabel F.*, b. Oct. 1, 1861.
13	*Kate A.*, b. Sept. 2, 1864.

THE ALEXANDER FAMILY.

1   AMASA ALEXANDER was b. in Marlboro, Feb. 18, 1798, and came to Peterborough about 1812, and lived with Dr. David Carter. He has resided in town ever since. He is a brick-mason by trade. He m. Eliza Woods, May 11, 1826, of Hillsboro, b. June 29, 1803.

2   *Harriet M.*, b. Nov. 25, 1829; d. Mar. 3, 1832, æ. 2 yrs., 3 mos.

3   *Lucien A.*, b. in Amoskeag, Aug. 13, 1832; m. Jan. 19, 1856, Bethiah A. Greenfield. He d. Aug. 16, 1873, æ. 41. One ch., Lizzie M., b. July 28, 1860.

4   *Charles F.*, b. July 3, 1835. Drowned Feb. 17, 1851, being swept over the dam at Granville P. Felt's shop, on a piece of ice which broke off unexpectedly, on which he was standing. His body was not found for six weeks, after every effort to recover it had proved unavailing. It was finally found in the river, near the pine trees opposite the village cemetery.

5   *Wilbur G.*, b. June 19, 1839; d. Oct. 5, 1840, æ. 1 yr., 3 mos.

6   *Louisa A.*, b. Dec. 10, 1849; d. Nov. 5, 1859, æ. 9 yrs., 10 mos.

THE ALLD FAMILY.

1   WILLIAM ALLD (Capt.) was b. in Ireland, 1723, and was among the early settlers of the town. He came here from Merrimack, in 1778, and purchased the farm on which the Bogle family lived, in the north part of town, which descended to his son, Samuel Alld. He held many offices in town: Town Treasurer, 1783, '84; Tithing-man, 1785, and Surveyor a number of years; and on Committee for the Amendment of the Constitution, in 1782, with Samuel Cunningham, Joseph Hammill, Jere-

miah Smith, and James Cunningham. **He m. Lettuce
——, who was b. 1725, and d. March 5, 1807, æ. 82. He
d. Aug. 25, 1805, æ. 82.**

---

2 *John*, b. 1756; d. July 14, 1790, æ. 34.
3 *Benjamin*, b. 1759, m. Nancy White. He d. Nov. 4,
   1823, æ. 64. He served three years in the Revolutionary War.
4 *Jenny*, b. ——, 1762; m. Capt. Robert Swan, q. v.
5 †*Samuel*, b. ——, 1766; m. Martha Swan and Lydia
   Perry, q. v.

1– 5 SAMUEL ALLD succeeded his father, and occupied the
Bogle farm so-called, where he resided nearly all his life.
He m., 1st w., Martha Swan, who d. Oct. 23, 1821, æ. 51 ;
He m., 2d w., Lydia Perry, of Rindge, Dec. 30, 1823.
Two ch. by 1st w., one by 2d w. He d. Dec. 24, 1841,
æ. 75.

---

6 *Hannah*, b. ——, 1795 ; m. John Metcalf, Nov. 18, 1816.
   Three ch. now living ; *viz.*, Samuel and John in San
   Jose, Cal. Mary Jane, m. Edwin P. Worcester, of
   Weymouth, Mass., a broker in Boston. Mrs. Metcalf
   d. May 13, 1832, æ. 37.
7 *Lettuce*, b. ——, 1797 ; m. 1st h. Loren Way, of Lempster, Feb. 25, 1816. Ch. (1) Samuel S., b. Dec. 17,
   1816 ; d. Jan. 4, 1872, æ. 55. He had been eminently
   successful in life, and d. with a property of about three
   millions ; (2) William S., b. ——, 1818, d. in California in 1854 ; (3) Jasper F., b. ——, 1820, r. in Boston ; (4) Martha Jane, b. ——, 1822, r. West Ran-
   dolph, Vt ; (5) Sarah Jane, b. 1824, d. 1840, æ. 16 ;
   (6) Addison L., b. 1826, in Rochester, Vt., r. Warren,
   Vt ; (7) John M., b. May 29, 1829, m. ——; a lawyer
   in Boston. Mrs. Way was divorced from Loren Way
   in 1829, and in 1830 m. John Whitten, of Rochester,
   Vt., by whom she had two ch., Charles F., and George
   S. Mr. Whitten d. 1846.
8 *James Miller*, by 2d w., b. Feb. 4, 1829 ; d. April 2,
   1829, æ. 1 mo., 28 days.

THE ALLISON FAMILY.

1 JOHN ALLISON came to Peterborough, Sept. 25, 1801,
and on the same day he said he walked into town through
the Street Road to John Little's, and then took the old
road—the Bart. Thayer road—west of the meeting-
house hill to the village, where he remained the rest of
his life. He was employed in the factories many years,

—a wood-workman and turner by trade. He was an honest and worthy man. He was born in Dunbarton, March 23, 1776, and d. in Peterborough, Aug. 13, 1864, æ. 88 yrs., 4 mos. He m., 1st w., Rachel Ladd, of Dunbarton, in 1805; b. June 9, 1780; d. Sept. 3, 1824, æ. 44. He m., 2d w., Abigail Perry, of Rindge, b. May 15, 1791, and d. at Sioux City, Iowa, Feb. 13, 1873, æ. 81 yrs., 8 mos.

2 *Ira*, b. June 11, 1806; m. Catharine Gillis, b. Nov. 12, 1812; r. New York State.
3 *Fanny Ladd*, b. March 4, 1811; d. Feb. 24, 1847, æ. 35 yrs., 11 mos.
4 *Mary B.*, b. Jan. 31, 1813; m. Rev. Zebulon Jones, Apr. 18, 1843; ch. living, Maria Frances, Ella Carrie, Willie Allison, Frank Irving.
5 *Caroline P.*, b. Sept. 9, 1817; m. Moses Wilkins, Sept. 5, 1866; d. July 29, 1867, æ. 49 yrs., 10 mos.
6 *Abigail Maria*, b. Sept. 22, 1827; d. Dec. 23, 1835, æ. 8 yrs., 3 mos.
7 *Elizabeth Sarah*, b. July 5, 1829; d. Dec. 21, 1864, æ. 35 yrs., 5 mos.
8 †*John Perry*, b. July 28, 1831; m. Lizzie Ann Thing, Exeter.
9 *Henry J.*, b. Feb. 5, 1837; d. Aug. 19, 1839, æ. 2 yrs., 6 mos.

1–8 JOHN PERRY ALLISON was fitted for college at Exeter Academy, and graduated at H. U. 1854. He studied law and commenced his practice at Sioux City, Iowa, where he now resides. He m. May 20, 1858, Lizzie Ann Thing, of Exeter, b. May 8, 1833.

10 *Fannie*, b. July 31, 1859.
11 *Mary Olive*, b. July 2, 1861; d. Sept. 21, 1862, æ. 1 yr., 2 mos.
12 *Hattie*, b. May 6, 1863.
13 *Mabel*, b. Aug. 11, 1867.

THE AMES FAMILY.

1 TIMOTHY AMES was b. in Andover, Mass., Sept. 26, 1765; m. Sarah Kneeland, March 22, 1787. Removed to Peterborough in 1793, first living in the north part of the town, and subsequently in various places, till late in life, when he built a house near the North Village, where he lived till his death. He d. suddenly, May 14, 1835, æ. 69. His w. survived him many years, and d. Nov. 13, 1861, æ. 92.

2

He was a cheerful, industrious and honest man. He was not successful in life, and had a hard struggle to rear up his large family, which, nevertheless, he did faithfully. Mr. Ames played the violin excellently well for those days, and for many years he supplied all the music demanded for the dancing parties for a large extent of territory around Peterborough. He derived a good deal of income from this source, which he followed through life, though his pay was small. During the season of dancing he was employed a good deal of the time, and often played night after night, with little rest, and with great acceptance to the young people. He entered with great glee into the enjoyment of the young, and was never weary, nor ever relaxed his efforts, as long as it was a pleasure to them.

2 | *Sally*, b. in Andover, Feb. 21, 1788; m. Aug. 16, 1812, George Henry. She d. May 12, 1825, æ. 37. Had two sons: George, who d. at Peterborough, Feb. 18, 1871, æ. 57; and John, who r. in Stoneham, Mass.

3 • | †*Timothy Kneeland*, b. Aug. 16, 1789; m. Dorothy Evans, dau. Asa and Dorothy Buss Evans.

4 | *Samuel*, b. Oct. 6, 1791; m. Sally Scott; five ch. He r. in Constantia, N. Y.; d. in Peterborough, Jan. 31, 1872, æ. 81.

5 | *John*, b. Aug. 3, 1793; unm.; d. July 16, 1816, æ. 23.

6 | *Benjamin*, b. July 30, 1795; d. July 6, 1797, æ. 2.

7 | *Benjamin*, b. June 25, 1797; d. March 24, 1812, æ. 14 yrs., 9 mos.

8 | *Mary K.*, b. June 1, 1799; m. May 23, 1818, Stephen Felt.

9 | *Ruthy S.*, b. March 12, 1802; m. May 1, 1821, John Hadley.

10 | *Hepsibeth C.*, b. Dec. 25, 1803; m. March 10, 1831, Jacob Longley.

11 | †*Alvah*, b. April 5, 1806; m. May 21, 1828, Betsey Little; 2d w., Rachel A. Watts.

12 | †*Joseph H.*, b. April 9, 1808; m. Aug. 28, 1832, Mary Melvin.

1– 3 | TIMOTHY KNEELAND AMES, m. Jan. 16, 1813, Dorothy Evans, dau. of Asa and Dorothy Buss Evans. She d. March 28, 1873, æ. 82 yrs., 11 mos. He died Aug. 25, 1874, æ. 85.

Mr. Ames was born in Andover, Mass., and was four years of age when his father removed to Peterborough, in 1793. His youth was spent in town. He was in the employ of Judge Theophilus Parsons, of Boston, as his personal attendant and coachman for a number of years

Tisdale K. Ames

previous to 1812, a circumstance that modified all his after life. Being of a quick and observing turn of mind, he acquired much information by such an intercourse, and an address and manner that was of great service to him through his life. He faithfully improved all these advantages.

He returned to Peterborough in 1812, and soon commenced the business of auctioneer, in which he was very popular and successful, not only in town, but in all the adjoining towns for a circuit of twenty-five miles. His first sale was the property of James Ferguson. He sold a large amount of property for Hon. Samuel Smith, and a larger number of acres for Gen. James Wilson. In the autumn of 1821 he sold at auction for sixty-five days before the first of January. In 1861, finding his labor too severe, and his business increasing rapidly, he associated with him in this business Col. S. I. Vose, under the firm of "Ames & Vose," which partnership continued to his death. The last sale to which he gave his personal attention, was in January, 1871, at East Jaffrey.

In 1819 he received his first appointment as deputy sheriff, from Gen. Benjamin Pierce, and held this office until his death, under all the successive administrations of the various high sheriffs of either political party. He was commissioned as justice of the peace in 1820, of the quorum in 1857, of the State in 1862. He was moderator for fourteen annual meetings of the town ; viz., 1833, '34, '38, '39, 1840, '42, '43, '44, '45, '46, '47, 1851, '55, 1861. He was selectman nine years, and represented the town in the Legislature in 1840, '41.

He was always interested in the affairs of the town, earnestly aiding and supporting all good measures for its peace and welfare. He was always public spirited, always liberal in donations to all charitable purposes. It was easy to know where he would be found when any new enterprise needed aid. He was always ready and foremost in any good work in town or in his own religious society. Of this he was one of the main pillars. He was deeply interested in a railroad to Peterborough, and sustained serious losses by his zeal and enterprise. He enlisted with much interest in the Monadnock Railroad, and was delighted to sit at his window and hear the shrill whistle of the locomotive, and see the train of cars come into the village.

3– 13 † *Theophilus Parsons*, b. Aug. 22, 1813 ; m. Almira P. Farnum ; 2d w., Julia Ann Peaslee.

14 *Alpha E.*, b. Oct. 9, 1815 ; d. Oct. 4, 1826, æ. 11.

15 *Sarah*, b. April 8, 1816 ; d. Aug. 11, 1822, æ. 6 yrs., 4 mos.

16 | *Charlotte*, b. April 8, 1818 ; m. Nathaniel Whittemore, Jr., Rome, N. Y.

17 | *Mary E.*, b. Feb. 8, 1820; m. Wm. Wallace, of New Boston ; q. v.

18 | *Eliza G.*, b. Aug. 5, 1821 ; d. Oct. 8, 1822, æ. 1 yr.

19 | *John A.*,
20 | *Benjamin F.*, } b. March 18, 1823 ; d. in infancy.

21 | †*George W.*, b. April 25, 1824 ; m., 1st w., Julia J. Greene ; and 2d w., Eliza Brown.

22 | *Louisa E.*, b. Nov. 6, 1825 ; m. Feb. 5, 1863, John E. Needham, who d. Aug. 29, 1870, æ. 49 yrs., 10 mos. ; ch., Walter B., b. Nov. 12, 1863 ; d. Sept. 28, 1870, æ. 6 yrs., 10 mos ; Clara Ednah Ames, b. July 3, 1850 ; m. Charles B. Davis, of Jaffrey, June 11, 1871 ; ch., Willie Burt, b. June 7, 1872. Mrs. Needham m., 2d h., William Burt.

23 | *Joseph Kneeland.*, b. Jan. 3, 1828; d. Oct. 24, 1844, æ. 16 yrs., 9 mos.

24 | *Abbie E.*, b. June 5, 1829 ; m. March 22, 1854, Henry M. Breed ; ch., (1) Harry A., b. May 18, 1856 ; (2) Arthur G., b. Oct. 16, 1864 ; (3) Marshall E., b. July 28, 1866 ; d. Aug. 26, 1866.

1– 11 | ALVAH AMES, m. Betsey Little, May 21, 1828 ; she d. March 27, 1872, æ. 68 ; 2d w., Nov. 26, 1872, Rachel A. Watts. He has always lived in the village, and for many years carried on the beef and provision business.

---

25 | *Elizabeth L.*, b. May 2, 1829.

26 | *Sarah Maria*, b. April 15, 1831 ; d. Feb. 25, 1833, æ. 1 yr., 10 mos.

27 | *Alvah A.*, b. April 15, 1834 ; d. Sept. 4, 1835.

28 | *Sarah M.*, b. Sept. 27, 1835 ; m. June 7, 1854, Charles A. Miller ; ch., (1) Lizzie M., b. June 2, 1856 ; (2) Fred M., b. Oct. 8, 1860 ; (3) Frank E., b. West Meriden, Ct., May 5, 1866 ; d. Sept. 6, 1866, æ. 4 mos.

29 | *Albert A.*, b. Feb. 24, 1845 ; m. Alice L. Kimball, 1871, of Chicopee Falls, Mass.

1– 12 | JOSEPH H. AMES, m. Aug. 21, 1832, Mary Melvin. He erected the buildings where he now lives, on what is called the "Bailey place," directly north of the Congregational Church. He was a cabinet-maker by trade. He was many years undertaker for the town. A deacon in the Congregational Unitarian Church.

---

30 | *J. Melvin*, b. Sept. 8, 1835 ; d. April 19, 1850, æ. 15.

31 | *Augusta F.*, b. Dec. 2, 1836 ; m. Oct. 9, 1865, William A. Smith. He d. Feb. 24, 1870, æ. 34. Ch., (1) Mar-

garet E., b. Oct. 3, 1866 ; (2) Frederick W., b., Feb. 23, 1869.

32   *Charles A.*, b. Jan. 1, 1839; m. Oct. 13, 1865, Annie Marden ; ch., (1) Willis M., b. Dec. 29, 1867 ; (2) Arthur M., b. July 13, 1871 ; d. July 12, 1872, æ. 1 yr. ; (3) Leslie W., b. March 29, 1873 ; r. in Bay City, Mich.

33   *Marshall*, b. July 14, 1841 ; m. 1869, Jennet Butman, of Bay City, Mich. Ch., (1) Henry M., b. July, 1870 ; (2) Howard B., b. Peterborough, Aug. 2, 1874.; r. Bloomington, Ill.

34   *Agnes*, b. Sept. 23 1843 ; m. Chester C. Wheeler ; r. Leavenworth, Kan. One ch., b. Peterborough, Oct. 15, 1875.

35   *Willis L.*, b. Sept. 29, 1845 ; m. 1868, Ella Butman. She d. Dec. 13, 1872 ; ch., (1) Charles B., b. April 27, 1869.

3– 13   THEOPHILUS PARSONS AMES, m. Nov. 17, 1835, Almira P. Farnum. She d. Dec. 18, 1835, æ. 27 ; 2d w., Julia Ann Peaslee, Nov. 27, 1836.

---

36   *Timothy K.*, b. Sept. 25, 1837 ; m. April 1, 1858, Louisa W., dau. Thomas and Lucretia Munson Little. Ch., Freddie, b. June 20, 1860 ; d. Aug. 29, 1860. He was educated to the law, but at the breaking out of the Rebellion he promptly enlisted, and was appointed a Lieutenant, and was killed in the 2d Bull Run battle, Aug. 29, 1862. He was an educated and promising young man.

37   *Almira*, b. Aug. 11, 1839; m. Frank Wheeler ; r. in Boston.

38   *Alpha E.*, b. April 21, 1841 ; r. New York City.

3– 21   GEORGE W. AMES, m. March 27, 1845, Julia J. Greene. She d. Feb. 4, 1859, æ. 33, two ch. ; m., 2d w., Eliza Brown, Jan. 4, 1860, six ch.

---

39   *Frederick J.*, b. Dec 25, 1851.
40   *Charles G.*, b. Sept. 22, 1853 ; d. April 19, 1854, æ. 6 mos.
41   *Julia A.*, b. April 13, 1861.
42   *Timothy K.*, b. Sept 21, 1862.
43   *Dora L.*, b. Dec. 21, 1865.
44   *George W.*, b. July 11, 1866.
45   *Emma B.*, b. July 2, 1867.
46   *Mary E.*, b. Aug. 6, 1871 ; d. Jan. 14, 1872, æ. 5 mos.

THE ANNAN FAMILY.

1   DAVID ANNAN (Rev.) was the third son of his father, John Annan, of Ceres, near Cupar of Fifeshire, Scotland. He was the next younger brother of Robert Annan, who was for some time pastor of the Federal Street Church in Boston. He was b. April 4, 1754, and came to America when quite young. He received his education at Rutgers College, New Brunswick, N. J.

His name does not appear among the graduates of the college, but in 1782 he received the honorary degree of A. M., it being the first name on the list of honorary degrees conferred by the college. He was ordained by the Presbytery which met at Walkill, N. J., October, 1778, with Peterborough as his destination. He remained the pastor of the Presbyterian Church in Peterborough till 1792, when his pastoral connection was dissolved at his request by the Presbytery of Londonderry. He was by the same Presbytery deposed from the ministry in 1800. After his withdrawal from the ministry he seems to have lost all restraint, and became so openly vicious and intemperate as not any longer to be endured. His conduct towards his family became so brutal, that his wife was often compelled to pass a whole night with her children in the woods, from fear of violence. To rebuke such conduct as this, a party of young men of the town, in 1800, every one of whom is now deceased, thoroughly blackened and disguised, came to his house in the night to give him a ride upon a wooden horse. Having roused him at the door, he came out to drive away the intruders, when two of the party deputed for this service, seized him in his nude state, and placed him on the pole. The party now proceeded down the road as far as where Cyrus Frost now lives, and threw him into a morass just east of his house, and fled. Though Mr. Annan knew many of the perpetrators of this act, yet he was so unpopular that he could not bring them to justice. Though this mode of procedure was contrary to the wishes and feelings of the people, yet they very quietly acquiesced in the matter, thinking that little more than justice had been done. In 1801 he went to Scotland, and d. in Ireland in 1802, on his return home. He m. Sarah Smith, dau. John Smith. She lived with him till 1800, when on account of his cruel treatment she sought and obtained a divorce. She m., 2d h., John Todd, Dec. 31, 1816, and d. April 6, 1846, æ. 85.

---

2   *Sarah,* b. Nov. 21, 1783 ; m. Benjamin Chamberlain.

3   *David S.,* b. July 10, 1784 ; d. ——.

4 | *John*, b. Oct. 30, 1787 ; d. Lowell, æ. 64.
5 | *Mary*, b. Sept. 5, 1789 ; m. Samuel Holmes.
6 | *Robert*, b. March 15, 1792 ; d. Manchester.
7 | *James*, b. Sept. 28, 1794 ; unm. ; now living as supposed.
8 | *Jane*, b. May 10, 1797 ; d. Dec. 30, 1819, æ. 23.
9 | *Amelia*, b. Aug. 30, 1799 ; m. —— Clements ; d. Concord.

THE BAILEY FAMILY.

1 | JOSHUA BAILEY came to town in 1822 or '23 ; m. Mary Spring, dau. of Silas Spring, and r. in the east part of the town, near to the farm of his father-in-law. He was b. May 7, 1798, and d. Feb. 18, 1873, æ. 74 yrs., 9 mos. She d. April 4, 1862, æ. 62.

2 | *Stephen*, b. Dec. 23, 1824 ; m. Cornelia W. Horton, Boston, April 4, 1867. One ch., Maud Abbot, killed by falling out of a window, June, 1873, æ. 3 ; r. Charlestown, Mass.

3 | *Mary E.*, b. Sept. 26, 1826 ; m. Jonathan E. Drake, of Easton, Mass., May 16, 1853 ; ch. (1) Lewis E., (2) Albert B., (3) Flora P., (4) Charlie E. ; r. New Bedford, Mass.

4 | *Harriet*, b. June 27, 1829 ; unm.

THE BAKER FAMILY.

1 | THOMAS BAKER, b. in Dorchester, Mass., Feb. 23, 1779, and d. in Perington, N. Y., Feb. 23, 1851, æ. 72. He learnt his trade in Waltham, Mass. (paper-making), and in 1802 he came to Peterborough to work for Samuel Smith, who had just then commenced the manufacture of paper in town. Mr. Smith associated him and Samuel Russell in partnership with himself in 1806, which was dissolved Sept. 18, 1811. In the subsequent year, 1812, in connection with Samuel Russell, John White (son John White, Jr.), Mr. Baker went to Hoosac, N. Y., and there erected the first cotton factory built in that State. He soon returned to Peterborough, and was engaged in manufacturing cotton yarn in the Eagle Factory until April, 1822, when he removed to Franklin, and in company with John Cavender and John Smith, Jr., built a cotton factory. He remained here till 1832, when he removed to Fairport, in Perington, N. Y., and remained there till his death. The following is an extract from a short obituary in the Peterborough *Transcript* at the time : "He was intimately known to all the older inhabitants of the town as an honest, upright, and intelligent man, but blunt and outspoken, even to a fault. Yet no man

ever cherished kindlier feelings than he towards his friends, or was more ready with kind offices. It was his abhorrence of hypocrisy and deceit that often made him seem rough. Never was the oft-repeated and quoted line of Pope better illustrated than in this instance:—

"'An honest man is the noblest work of God.'"

He m. June 12, 1812, Hannah Bright, b. in Watertown, Mass., June 24, 1781. She d. in Perington, N. Y., Jan. 11, 1860, æ. 78 yrs., 6 mos.

2 *Jeremiah Smith*, b. in Hoosac, N. Y., May 3, 1813. He r. in Perington, N. Y.; m., 1st w., Oct. 8, 1839, Adaline Sturtevant; 2d w., Nov. 4, 1869, Almira T. Pepper. Three ch., (1) Emma B., (2) Frances A., (3) Mary E.

3 *Catherine Frances*, b. in Peterborough, Jan. 16, 1815; unm.; r. Fairport, N. Y.

THE BARBER FAMILY.

1 SILAS BARBER was b. in Worcester, Mass., April 7, 1754; m. Prudence Rice, of Barre, Mass., who was b. Dec. 7, 1752. He removed to Peterborough about 1780, from Worcester, and first located on the Dunbar place, afterwards removed to what was called the Mitchell place, just south of the Faxon farm, and then to the place where the family now live. This place was probably occupied about 1783. He d. April 19, 1850, æ. 96. She d. May 19, 1849, æ. 97.

2 *Mercy*, b. Oct. 18, 1782; m. Frederick Poor. She d. Feb. 13, 1875, æ. 93 yrs., 3 mos.
3 †*John*, b. March 31, 1783; m. Betsey Washburn.
4 *Jonas*, b. Aug. 12, 1787; m. Hannah Gates; d. Feb. 23, 1831, æ. 45, c.
5 *Martha*, b. June 25, 1789; m. Thomas Hadley.
6 *Lucy*, b. Dec. 18, 1791; m. William Allen; re. to New York.
7 †*Silas*, b. Feb. 12, 1794; m. Lydia Washburn.

1–3 JOHN BARBER settled in the northwest corner of the town, until a few years before his death, when he removed to the village. He m. Betsey Washburn, of Hancock, b. March 27, 1792. He d. Dec. 22, 1848, æ. 65. She d. in Le Roy, Barton Co., Mo., Aug. 12, 1872, æ. 80 yrs., 4 mos.

8 †*John W.*, b. Nov. 1, 1810; m., 1st w., Elmina D. Davis; 2d w., Eliza Carley; 3d w., Mrs. Penelope Holden.

9   *Silas*, b. Nov. 27, 1811 ; d. Aug. 22, 1813, æ. 1 yr., 8 mos.

10   *Elizabeth*, b. April 21, 1816 ; m. George Haywood Hancock. Two ch.

11   *Prudence*, b. May 17, 1818 ; m. Rev. John Jones ; r. Le Roy, Barton Co., Mo. One ch.

1–7   SILAS BARBER settled on the homestead, and now lives there. He m. Lydia Washburn.

---

12   *Lydia Ann*, b. Dec. 18, 1820 ; m. A. C. Blodgett. She d. Nov. 6, 1843, æ. 22. One ch. John H. Blodgett, b. Nov. 6, 1842. M. D. University, Vt., 1866, now a physician in Concord, N. H. A. C. Blodgett d. Sept. 23, 1858, æ. 48.

13   *William*, b. March 27, 1824 ; d. ——, 1825, æ. 1.

14   †*Charles*, b. Sept. 22, 1826 ; m. Abby A. Parker.

15   *Louisa*, b. Dec. 19, 1830 ; m., 1849, Jones Dodge ; ch. Ella L., b. March, 1851 ; Albert J., b. Aug. —, 1857.

3– 8   JOHN W. BARBER, m., 1st w., Elmina D. Davis, of Hancock, who d. July 30, 1846, æ. 34 yrs., 3 mos. ; 2d w., Eliza Carley, dau. Jabez Carley, who d. at Grasshopper Falls, Jefferson Co., Kansas, March 10, 1862, æ. 34 ; 3d w., Mrs. Penelope Holden, of Grasshopper Falls. Mr. Barber removed from Peterborough to Grasshopper Falls in March, 1855, where he now resides, engaged in farming. Five ch. by 1st w., and three by 2d w.

---

16   *Frances Elmina*, b. Nov. 7, 1838 ; d. Dec. 29, 1844, æ. 6.

17   *Marietta L.*, b. Dec. 22, 1840 ; m. Sidney J. Squiers ; r. Grasshopper Falls.

18   *Albert D.*, b. Oct. 6, 1842 ; d. in Kansas, March 10, 1862, æ. 19 yrs., 5 mos.

19   *Ellen Maria*, b. Sept. 26, 1844 ; m., Nov. 26, 1863, Riley B. Hatch, a native of Williamstown, Vt. He was educated at Middlebury College, in class of 1857, and came to town in 1859 to take charge of the academy. He afterwards studied law and commenced the practice in town. He was appointed Treasurer of the Peterborough Savings Bank in 1864, which office he held until 1873. He represented the town in the Legislature in 1868–9. He first started the business of Fire and Life Insurance in town in March, 1863, and built up a large and successful agency here for numerous insurance companies. He still resides in town. Ch., Charles A., b. July 25, 1865 ; Ida Frances, b. Nov. 1, 1866 ; Ellen Maria, b. April 20, 1868 ; George Ernest, b. Jan. 22, 1870 ; d. Nov. 22, 1870, æ. 10 mos.

20	*James D.*, b. July 21, 1846 ; d. Aug. 25, 1846, æ. 1 mo., 4 days.
21	*Francis W.*, b. May 13, 1851 ; d. Aug. 23, 1852, æ. 1 yr., 3 mos.
22	*Frances E.*, b. Nov. 17, 1852, m. Henry James ; r. Barton Co., Mo.
23	*Alfred C.*, b. July 3, 1861 ; d. July 22, 1862, æ. 1 yr.

7→14   CHARLES BARBER settled on the homestead, as his father did before him.   He m. Abby A. Parker.   Selectman 1869, '70, '71.

24	*Gilbert A.*, b. May 2, 1856.
25	*Charles P.*, b. Oct. 28, 1858 ; d. March 21, 1866, æ. 7 yrs.
26	*Nellie,* ⎫ b. Feb. 1, 1860 ; ⎰ d. 1860.
27	*Ednah M.,* ⎭
28	*Clifford P.*, b. March 5, 1870 ; d. April, 1871, æ. 13 mos.
29	*Ida Mabel*, b. Oct. 17, 1872.

THE BLAIR FAMILY.

1   JOHN BLAIR.   It cannot be determined when he came to town.   He was an early settler.   It seems he had two wives, the first, Nancy Brown, of Groton, Mass. ; 2d w., Mary Freeman.   He d. March 9, 1780, æ. 63.

2	*Mary*, b. March 4, 1749 ; m. Randall McAllister. One ch., Mary, m. Wm. Field.
3	† *William*, b. May 20, 1750 ; m. Elizabeth Little.
4	*John*, b. —— ; re. to New York.
5	*Nancy*, b. —— ; m. —— Willard, Westminster, Vt.
6	*Margaret*, b. —— ; m. —— Mixer, Brattleboro, Vt.
7	*Samuel*, b. ——. (8) *George*, b. ——.
9	*Anna*, b. —— ; d. when about 20 yrs. of age.

There was said to be an Esther, who was very small in size, and unm.   She left town with George.   She was by the 1st w.

1–3   WILLIAM BLAIR.   He served in the Revolutionary war, and was present at the battle of Bunker Hill.   He lived in the east part of the town, near to the Cuningham Pond, on the farm now occupied by Franklin Field.   The house has been demolished.   He m. Elizabeth Little, dau. Thomas Little, Sen., Dec. 2, 1787.   He d. Oct. 13, 1825, æ. 76.   She d. Jan. 12, 1842, æ. 86.

10	*Agnes Nancy*, b. Sept. 22, 1788 ; m. James W. Swan.
11	† *William*, b. Oct. 13, 1794 ; m. Abigail Palmer.
12	*John*, b. July 1, 1796 ; d. Albany, N. Y.

3– 11 | WILLIAM BLAIR. He succeeded his father on the homestead. He m. Abigail Palmer, b. Feb. 12, 1800. He d. Aug. 2, 1852, æ. 58. She d. March 2, 1859, æ. 59.

13 | *John,* b. July 24, 1818 ; m. Eliza Thurston, Jan. 1, 1846 ; r. Fayville, Mass. Two ch.

14 | *William,* b. Dec. 24, 1819 ; d. June 22, 1826, æ. 6 yrs., 5 mos.

15 | *Elizabeth,* b. Oct. 4, 1821 ; m. Silas Bullard, Aug. 10, 1841 ; r. Mason.

16 | *Joseph L.,* b. July 28, 1823 ; d. May 13, 1824, æ. 9 mos.

17 | *Lucinda,* b. Feb. 6, 1825 ; d. Sept. 24, 1826, æ. 1 yr., 7 mos.

18 | *William,* b. Sept. 13, 1827 ; m. Elizabeth A. Pease, Dec. 21, 1852 ; r. Brighton, Mass.

19 | *Abbie Jane,* b. Jan. 11, 1830 ; m. George H. Gleason ; d. May 16, 1861, æ. 31 yrs., 4 mos. ; r. Marlboro, Mass.

20 | *Charlotte A.,* b. May 26, 1832 ; m. Henry W. Nieman ; d. Sept. 21, 1865, æ. 33 yrs., 3 mos.

21 | *Agnes Maria,* b. July 23, 1834 ; m. Christopher Decker, Aug. 10, 1854 ; d. April 25, 1869, æ. 34 yrs., 9 mos.

22 | *Mary Catharine,* b. Nov. 12, 1836 ; d. Aug. 28, 1848, æ. 11 yrs., 8 mos.

23 | †*George W.,* b. Dec. 16, 1839 ; m. Susan F. Goodhue.

24 | *James P.,* b. March 19, 1842 ; m. Elvira D. Clark, May 26, 1864.

25 | *Mary L.,* b. Aug. 24, 1844 ; m. George W. Towle, Nov. 16, 1869.

11–23 | GEORGE W. BLAIR, m. Susan F. Goodhue, June 17, 1864 ; b. in Hancock, Oct. 29, 1842.

26 | *Anna J.,* b. Nov. 23, 1866.

27 | *Lucy G.,* b. July 30, 1868 ; d. Nov. 25, 1872, æ. 4 yrs., 3 mos.

28 | *Ned G.,* b. Nov. 3, 1873.

THE BLANCHARD FAMILY.

1 | JOTHAM BLANCHARD (Capt.). His farm lay east of the east line of the farm B, or Bogle farm. It was bounded on the north by Wiley, and east by Miller ; south by Kelso Gray's farm. The road began at the south-west corner, and run to the north-east corner, dividing it into two equal parts or proportions. Jotham Blanchard took the north-western portion, and lived on the Alld place probably in 1776, '77, '78, '79, '80, '81 ; and James McKean occupied the south-eastern part.

Blanchard attached his portion to the Alld farm. Capt. Blanchard appears by the records of the town to have been an important character in its proceedings. We find that he was first made moderator at a town-meeting, April 5, 1774, and this is his first appearance; and then also moderator 1776, '77, '78, '80, '81, and selectman 1777, '78, '79, '80, '81, and on committee of safety 1776. After this his name does not occur again. There is no record of his family, or tradition how he disappeared from town without leaving some traces behind.

---

1   CYRUS BLANCHARD is entirely distinct from the family of the above. He was born in Milford, Oct. 9, 1781, and was the son of Stephen Blanchard. He m., 1807, Mary, dau. of Samuel and Mary Blanchard, of Billerica, Mass. He purchased the farm where he lived (the McKean place), and moved to town in 1807. He d. March 31, 1851, æ. 70 yrs., 5 mos. She d. Aug. 4, 1872, æ. 91 yrs., 7 mos.

---

2   † *Cyrus*, b. Sept. 15, 1809; m., 1st w., Maranda Persons; 2d w., Abigail Davis.

3   *David*, b. Oct. 10, 1813; m. Maria J. Moar, of Milford, Feb. 10, 1844; c.

4   *William*, b. Aug. 7, 1816; m. Elizabeth Edes, dau. Isaac Edes, August, 1859. He d. April 23, 1861, æ. 44 yrs. She d. Oct. 22, 1867, æ. 41 yrs.

1- 2   CYRUS BLANCHARD, Jun., m., 1st w., Feb. 22, 1834, Maranda Persons. She d. July 11, 1836; 2d w., Sept. 10, 1840, Abigail Davis. He lives on the Andrew Miller place.

---

5   *Mary E.*, b. April 5, 1843; m. B. Wyman Crosby, d. July 7, 1872, æ. 29 yrs., 3 mos. One ch., Wm. Wyman, b. Aug. 11, 1865.

6   *Fanny M.*, b. Nov. 26, 1844; m. Joseph Crosby, killed in battle in war of the Rebellion. Ch., (1) Gentianella, b. Sept. 6, 1860; (2) Etta M., b. October, 1862; m., 2d h., Charles Austin. Two ch., Freddie and Eddie.

7   *Abigail A.*, b. Sept. 16, 1846; m. R. M. McGilvray. Two ch., Frankie R. and Nellie.

8   *Harriet J.*, b. Feb. 27, 1848; m. George May; r. Wilton. Four ch.

9   *Sarah J.*, b. Feb. 27, 1854; d. August, 1856, æ. 2 yrs., 6 mos.

10   *Carrie M.*, b. May 21, 1858.

11   *Willie*, b. April 29, 1861.

12   *Emma*, b. Oct. 18, 1864.

THE BOWERS FAMILY.

1   JONATHAN S. BOWERS came to Peterborough from Dublin probably about 1821, being first taxed this year. He was a shoemaker by trade; m. Elizabeth Nay, dau. George and Sally Nay. He was b. Sept 19, 1786; d. Jan. 23, 1871, æ. 87 yrs. She d. March 16, 1873, æ. 78 yrs.

---

2   *Orinda*, b. March 17, 1817; m. Frank Twitchell. Four ch; r. Nashua.

3   *Luther*, b. Nov. 22, 1818; d. June 30, 1833, by explosion of powder, æ. 14 yrs., 7 mos.

4   *Sarah*, b. March 26, 1821; d. Dec. 20, 1825, æ. 4 yrs., by accidentally falling downstairs.

5   *George*, b. April 6, 1823; m. Nancy Lawrence. One ch.

6   *Alonzo*, b. June 22, 1825; m. Mary Ann Scott; r. Waltham, Mass.

7   *Melville*, b. Oct. 3, 1827; unm.; served in army of Rebellion; was wounded.

8   *Levi*, b. July 14, 1830; m. Julia A. Bemis; r. Waltham. Three ch.

9   *Alfred*, ⎱ b. June 29, 1834; both drowned June 21, 1841,
10 *Albert*, ⎰   æ. 6 yrs., 11 mos.

---

1   FRANCIS BOWERS (Capt.); a distinct race from the above. He came to town in 1800, and lived many years on the David Holt place. He purchased about 1820, and carried on until his death, the "Holmes' Mills," so called, at Spaulding's Corner. He was b. in Chelmsford, Mass., May 20, 1775. He d. Oct. 15, 1835, æ. 60 yrs. He m. Chloe Holt, dau. of Joshua and Phebe Farnum Holt, of Andover, Mass.; b. May 27, 1775. She d. Nov. 6, 1849, æ. 74 yrs., 5 mos.

---

2   *Chloe*, b. Jan. 15, 1799; m. John Dane; d. Oct. 8, 1844, æ. 45 yrs., 8 mos. Two ch., John B. and Fannie B.

3   *Ruth D.*, b. Jan. 20, 1803; m., 1831, Dea. Samuel Miller.

4   *Benjamin*, b. March 16, 1807; d. March 16, 1811, æ. 4 yrs.

5   *Phebe F.*, b. April 18, 1809; d. Feb. 28, 1811, æ. 1 yr., 10 mos.

6   *Francis H.*, b. Feb. 24, 1812; m. Martha A. Sherburn, of Lowell; d. Feb. 5, 1864, æ. 51 yrs., 11 mos.; r. Billerca, Mass.

7   *Hannah*, b. June 11, 1812; m., 1st h., Ezra Dane; 2d h., Dr. Luke Miller, Lanesborough, Minn.

8   *Betsey H.*, b. Nov. 28, 1820; d. Oct. 15, 1861, æ. 40 yrs., 10 mos.

9   *Phebe F.*, b. Oct. 12, 1823; unm.

THE BOYNTON FAMILY.

1   ABEL BOYNTON was the sixth son of Elias and Betsey Blood Boynton, b. in Temple, Feb. 22, 1793. When seventeen years of age he was apprenticed to Josiah Wheeler, of Lyndeboro, for the term of four years, to learn the carpenter's trade. He was m. to Serena Lawrence, of Lexington, Mass., May 17, 1817. He removed to Peterborough in March, 1819, purchasing a farm near Samuel Morison's place, where he lived till June 9, 1836, when he bought of William Smith the "old John Smith Farm," to which he removed, and continued to reside there until March 29, 1856, when he removed to New Lisbon, Juneau Co., Wis., where he and his wife live in a ripe old age.

While in Peterborough he worked at his trade at intervals from his farm. All his leisure was filled up with reading; few men read as many volumes as he did. His reading was general, embracing all subjects he could understand, but was not digested enough to render the various subjects about which he read very available for use. He read too much and thought too little.

---

2   *Mary Ann*, b. July 22, 1822 ; d. Jan. 15, 1855, æ. 32 yrs., 6 mos.

3   *Abel S.*, b. Dec. 25, 1824 ; a woolen manufacturer ; m. Sarah B. Tyler, of Lyndeboro. Now r. in New Lisbon, Wis.

4   *Samuel*, b. Feb. 24, 1828 ; machinist and sailor ; m. Margaret Townsend, 1874 ; r. Siegal, Wood Co., Wis. He has been all over the world, — is intelligent and philosophical in his habits of thought and in action.

5   *George*, b. May 3, 1830. Attended Phillips Academy, at Exeter, where by undue application to his studies he broke down, and had epileptic fits, which resulted in insanity. He d. Feb. 5, 1854, æ. 24 yrs.

6   *Elias*, b. Nov. 30, 1832 ; r. New Lisbon, Wis. A teacher and supervisor of schools in New Lisbon ; also assessor, justice of the peace, and town clerk, etc.

7   *Syrena*, b. May 23, 1834 ; m. John H. Crandall, of Lake George, N. Y., Oct. 13, 1864 ; r. New Lisbon. Ch., (1) James Cramer, (2) Jessie Alice.

8   *Edmund*, b. May 18, 1836 ; d. of typhoid fever at Marlow, where he had located himself in the tin and sheet-iron business, Oct. 1, 1856, æ. 20 yrs.

9   *Frederick E.*, b. March 19, 1839 ; m. Anna E. Temple, Point Bluff, Wis. Was in 6th Regiment Wisconsin Volunteers in the war of the Rebellion ; was in the battles of South Mountain and 2d Bull Run ; r. New

Lisbon. Ch., (1) Frank Leslie, (2) Nellie M., (3) Winnifred.

10   *Elnathan*, b. July 28, 1842. Enlisted in 4th Wisconsin Volunteers, infantry, afterwards changed to cavalry. Was in Gen. Butler's expedition to New Orleans, and saw much military service; m. Annie E. Marshall (b. in Virginia) in Baton Rouge, Feb. 5, 1864; r. New Lisbon; a carpenter by trade. Ch., (1) Sarah Lorena, (2) Halber Elnathan, (3) Roberta Lee, (4) Arthur Stilwell.

THE BRACKETT FAMILY.

1   SAMUEL BRACKETT was b. in Braintree, Mass., in 1742, and m. Rebecca Hayward, Dec. 17, 1765. They came to Peterborough about this time. He lived on the north side of the Cuningham Pond, where his descendants now live. He d. March 16, 1826, æ. 84 yrs. She d. July 7, 1832, æ. 86 yrs.

2   *Sarah*, b. Oct. 21, 1766; unm.; d. April 25, 1790, æ. 24 yrs.
3   *Samuel*, b. Nov. 26, 1768; d. unm. An imbecile.
4   *Betsey*, b. Nov. 7, 1770; m. John Collins; d. ——.
5   *Dorothy*, b. Oct. 7, 1772; m. John Bertram, name changed from Woodcock.
6   † *John*, b. June 24, 1775; m., 1st w., Elizabeth Stuart; 2d w., Elizabeth Lewis.
7   *James*, b. May 10, 1777; m., 1803, Hannah Carr; re. to Antrim.
8   † *Josiah*, b. Jan. 28, 1779; m. Mary Stuart, April 9, 1801.
9   *Isaac*, b. July 1, 1781; m. Nancy Field, of Quincy; r. Charlestown, Mass.
10   *Rebecca*, b. Aug. 15, 1783; unm.; d. 1837, æ. 54 yrs.
11   *William*, b. May 11, 1786; m. Sarah Ward; r. Colebrook; d. April 19, 1835, æ. 48 yrs., 11 mos.
12   *Ebenezer*, b. Nov. 27, 1788; m. Clarissa Hildreth, Oct. 1, 1817. He d. March 19, 1830, æ. 41 yrs. Six ch.
13   † *Joseph*, b. March 31, 1791; m. Sarah Bliss.
14   † *Benjamin*, b. Aug. 21, 1795; m., 1st w., Lavinia Cuningham; 2d w., Sally Wilcox, of Nashua.

1– 6   JOHN BRACKETT; m., Dec. 7, 1801, Elizabeth Stuart, dau. Thomas Stuart; she d. in Peterborough, Oct. 12, 1813, æ. 37 yrs.; m., 2d w., Elizabeth Lewis, who had two ch. He d. Dec. 8, 1852, æ. 77 yrs., 5 mos.

15   *Henrietta*, b. ——, 1822; m. Charles Caverly, Boston. Five ch.
16   *Mary*, b. ——, 1829; m. James A. Dale; c.

1– 8 | JOSIAH BRACKETT, m., April 9, 1800, Mary Stuart, dau. Thomas Stuart. He d. Jan. 31, 1855, æ. 76 yrs. He wandered into the woods, and was frozen to death. She d. March 6, 1871, æ. 90.

17 | *Rebecca*, b. July 6, 1801 ; m. Joel Tufts ; he d. May 7, 1852 ; 2d h., Col. Norton Hunt, March 14, 1860.

18 | *Jane S.*, b. Dec. 18, 1802 ; m. Nathan Bailey.

19 | *Mary*, b. Dec. 31, 1804 ; m. Samuel G. Pierce ; r. Belfast, Me. ; returned to Peterborough, 1874.

20 | †*Josiah, Jr.*, b. Feb. 11, 1807 ; m., March 19, 1835, Mary Piper.

21 | *Thomas*, b. Dec. 11, 1808 ; m. Rebecca Tuft ; r. Harvard, Mass. She d. July 17, 1853, æ. — ; ch., Ann R., and Sarah E.

22 | *Elizabeth S.*, b. Feb. 16, 1811 ; m., March 31, 1846, Nathan B. Buss.

23 | *Joseph*, b. May 26, 1815 ; m., Oct. 1, 1846, Lucretia L. Hunt ; r. South Acworth. He d. Jan. 18, 1871, æ. 56 yrs. Ch., (1) Albert, b. Jan. 2, 1850 ; (2) Laura L., b. April 15, 1854.

24 | *Sarah*, b. June 8, 1820 ; m. Albert P. Brown ; r. Amherst.

25 | *Charles*, b. June 24, 1823 ; d. Oct. 2, 1846, æ. 23 yrs.

1–13 | JOSEPH BRACKETT (Rev.) was educated for the ministry. He graduated at Williams College, Williamstown, Mass., 1819. He m. Sarah Bliss, dau. George Bliss, of Springfield, Mass. ; she d. 1826. He m., 2 w., ——. He d. in Rushville, N. Y., where he was settled as a minister, Sept. 24, 1832, æ. 41 yrs. He was a man of excellent character, and a worthy son of Peterborough.

26 | *George Ellis*, b. —— ; educated for the ministry ; r. New Orleans.

27 | *Henry Martin*, b. —— ; a real estate agent, Washington Territory.

1–14 | BENJAMIN BRACKETT occupied the old homestead. He m., 1st w., March 22, 1825, Lavinia Cuningham, b. Dec. 4, 1802 ; she d. Aug. 7, 1863, æ. 61 yrs., by whom he had all his children. He m., 2d w., Mrs. Sally Wilcox, of Nashua. He d. Feb. 2, 1876, æ. 80 yrs., 5 mos.

28 | *Samuel*, b. Dec. 27, 1825 ; m. Sarah Palmer, Waltham ; one ch., Mary Cora, b. March 7, 1858. He is a constable in the Municipal Court, Boston.

29 | *Henry*, b. Sept. 11, 1827 ; d. Oct. 11, 1849, æ. 22 yrs.

30 | *Joseph*, b. Nov. 24, 1829 ; unm. ; in Boston Police force.

31 | *George G.*, b. Sept. 13, 1833 ; unm.

32 | *Sarah A.*, b. Nov. 26, 1836. Principal in Licensed Minor's School, Boston.

33 | *Rodney M.*, b. Aug. 9, 1838 ; d. at home April, 1864, having lost his health in the military service of his country in the war of the Rebellion.

34 | *William G.*, b. June 25, 1839.

8–20 | JOSIAH BRACKETT, Jr., m., March 19, 1835, Mary Piper, b. Feb. 2, 1808, and lived many years in Sharon, where his ch. were b. She d. in Peterborough, Nov. —, 1871, æ. 63 yrs. He d. July 17, 1875, æ. 68 yrs., 5 mos.

35 | *Annie E.*, b. Nov. 17, 1836.
36 | *George*, b. Dec. 18, 1837.
37 | *Jackson*, b. April 5, 1839.
38 | *Maria Louisa*, b. Feb. 1, 1841.
39 | *John Piper*, b. June 3, 1842 ; d. Aug. 26, 1851, æ. 9 yrs.
40 | *Rosanna*, b. April 11, 1844.
41 | *Joel Tufts*, b. Dec. 30, 1845.
42 | *Charles*, b. May 22, 1848 ; d. Aug. 24, 1851, æ. 3 yrs.
43 | *Albert L.*, b. June 13, 1850 ; d. Aug. 25, 1851, æ. 1 yr.
44 | *Mary Rebecca*, b. Jan. 24, 1857.

Three of the above, *viz.*, John P., Charles, and Albert L., d. of dysentery, Aug. 24, 25, 26, 1851, and were buried the same day, and in the same grave, in the new cemetery in Sharon.

THE BRENNAN FAMILY.

1 | HUBERT BRENNAN was b. in Savagh, Co. Roscommon, Ireland, March 20, 1823. He came to America in 1845, and for a time worked at his trade of marble working in Lowell, where he remained till the 5th of September, 1851, when he removed to Peterborough, in response to a call for a competent marble-worker. He has continued to reside here since, and has built up the "marble works" alluded to elsewhere. He has proved an enterprising and useful citizen, and done much toward the prosperity and advancement of our village. He m., July 29, 1850, Mary Mahoney, b. in Callau, Co. Kilkenny, March 13, 1824, and emigrated to America. 1849, '50. Mr. and Mrs. Brennan visited the places of their birth in 1875, and were fortunate enough to be present at the grand demonstration of the O'Connell Centenary at Dublin, Aug. 5. They travelled extensively through all Ireland ; and Mr. Brennan, in describing the present condition of the country, says: "Where thirty years ago were thriving little villages and hamlets, now in many instances not a vestige of them is to be

4

found; and the country generally shows a fearful example of depopulation, and a lack of the brains and muscle that have helped very largely to make America what she is."

———

2   *Mary A.*, b. Lowell, June 13, 1851; m. Nov. 6, 1871, John F. Snow; r. St. Louis, Mo.

3   *James F.*, b. Peterborough, March 31, 1853; marble-worker.

4   *Hubert*, b. March 19, 1855; d. Sept. 4, 1855, æ. 5 mos.

5   *Alice*, b. Aug. 10, 1856.

6   *Catherine*, b. July 15, 1858; d. April 20, 1859, æ. 9 mos.

7   *Sarah J.*, b. Feb. 8, 1860.

8   *Ella T.*, b. Sept. 15, 1861.

9   *John M.,* } b. June 12, 1865; d. Nov. 12, 1865, æ. 5 mos.
10   *Hubert H.,* }   d. Nov. 10, 1867, æ. 2 yrs., 5 mos.

———

THE BRUCE FAMILY.

1   KENDALL BRUCE (Dr.) came to Peterborough in the winter of 1812, from Washington, where he had practiced his profession some years previous. He lived on the old road from South Village to Centre Village, — house now demolished. He was a native of Marlboro, Mass. He followed the lumbering business in Canada, after he gave up his profession. He removed from Peterborough to Calais, Vt., where he d. Jan. 12, 1832, æ. 64 yrs. He m. Rebecca Barnard. She d. at Peterborough, Sept. 10, 1852, æ. 84 yrs.

———

2   *Luther*, b. ——; unm.; d. ——.

3   †*Peter*, b. Jan. 30, 1790; m. Eliza French.

4   *Jerusha*, b. ——; m. Hollis Bruce.

5   *Kendall*, b. ——; m. Nancy Carr; r. Plainfield, Vt.; d. 1866.

6   *William*, b. ——; m. Lydia Carr; r. Worcester, Vt.

7   *Louis*, b. ——; unm.; d. Oct. 4, 1861, æ. 63 yrs.

8   *Solomon*, b. ——; unm.; nothing known of him.

9   *Bernard*, b. ——; unm.; probably lost at sea.

———

1–3   PETER BRUCE, a soldier in war of 1812, always resided in town after his father removed here in 1812. He m. Eliza French, Dec. 27, 1815. He was b. Jan. 30, 1790; d. March 1, 1850, æ. 60 yrs. She d. 1873.

———

10   *Kendall*, b. May 24, 1816; unm.; d. Feb. 5, 1850, æ. 33.

11   *John F.*, b. Aug. 31, 1818; m., Jan. 1, 1846, Martha Burt; 2d w., June 11, 1854, Salena Burt. Three ch.

12 | *Harriet M.*, b. March 20, 1821 ; m., May 7, 1843, George
W. Taggart ; d. Feb. 19, 1845, æ. 24 yrs.
13 | †*George*, b. June 29, 1823 ; m., 1st w., Nov. 18, 1851,
Abby Kimball ; 2d w., Arvilla Holbrook.
14 | †*Charles F.*, b. Oct. 16, 1826 ; m. Mary E. Crombie.
15 | *Eliza*, b. June 22, 1829.
16 | *Sarah M.*, b. Sept. 25, 1831 ; m. John F. Bruce, Lemp-
ster. Four ch.
17 | *Alfred A.*, b. June 21, 1833 ; m., April 23, 1852, Julia
Burt ; r. Morrison, Ill.
18 | *Harry*, b. Aug. 22, 1835 ; d. April 11, 1838, æ. 2 yrs.,
9 mos.
19 | *French*, b. Aug. 14, 1837 ; m., Jan. 9, 1863, Frances Bas-
sett. He d. July 3, 1871, æ. 34 yrs. One ch.

3–13 | GEORGE BRUCE, r. at the South Factory Village ;
m., 1st w., Nov. 18, 1851, Abby Kimball, who d. Aug.
15, 1856, æ. 27 ; 2d w., Arvilla Holbrook ; she d. Nov.
29, 1872, æ. 41 ; c.

20 | *George K.*, b. April 20, 1856.

3–14 | CHARLES F. BRUCE. He is a machinist by trade. He
now occupies the farm of the late Jonathan Felt. He
was in the naval service in the late war. He m., May
26, 1848, Mary E. Crombie, b. Dec. 26, 1828.

21 | *Harriet E.*, b. Dec. 27, 1849 ; d. Aug. 7, 1852, æ. 2 yrs.
22 | *Anna E.*, b. Dec. 12, 1851 ; m., Dec. 8, 1872, Bernard
Morloch. She d. in childbirth, Oct. 9, 1873, æ. 21 yrs.
23 | *Charles C.*, b. Feb. 5, 1854 ; m.
24 | *Frank C.*, b. April 1, 1860.
25 | *Mary A. W.*, b. June 14, 1870.

THE BULLARD FAMILY.

1 | JOHN A. BULLARD came to town in 1856. He was a
carpenter by trade, and lived in and owned the house built
by Dr. S. Richardson. He owned a number of other
houses which he built to rent. He m., Harriet N. Porter, April 27, 1856. He served in the war of the Rebellion. He d. Dec. 19, 1874, æ. 51 yrs.

2 | *Eddie P.*, b. April 16, 1857 ; d. Oct. 27, 1864, æ. 7 yrs.

THE BUSS FAMILY.

1 | RICHARD T. BUSS was b. in Wilton, Sept. 7, 1772 ; m.,
May 13, 1794, Betsey Ballard, b. Aug. 19, 1771 ; re. to

Peterborough in 1813, and lived there till his death. He
d. Oct. 20, 1861, æ. 90 yrs. She d. Nov. 5, 1856, æ. 85 yrs.

---

2 *Betsey*, b. June 26, 1795 ; m. Charles Crane, September,
    1817. He d. at Milton, Mass., May 18, 1824, æ. 32 yrs.
3 *Achsah*, b. Sept. 5, 1797 ; m. Elijah B. Kimball.
4 *Richard Taylor*, b. July 27, 1799 ; m., 1st w., Abigail
    Hunt. She d. Oct. 12, 1838, æ. 40 yrs., 6 mos.; 2d
    w., Persis Holmes, February, 1844 ; r. Bridgeport, Ct.
5 *Abel F.*, b. July 9, 1802 ; m. Mary W. Danforth. She d.
    at Taunton, Mass., Oct. 18, 1836. He d. at Ports-
    mouth, O., September, 1838, æ. 36 yrs.
6 †*Nathan Ballard*, b. July 24, 1804 ; m., 1st w., Arvilla
    Nay, of Sharon, b. Nov. 28, 1804 ; d. Nov. 11, 1844,
    æ. 40 yrs.; 2d w., Elizabeth Brackett, March 31,
    1846 ; c.
7 *Mary Ann*, b. Oct. 2, 1807 ; d. Sept. 12, 1826, æ. 19 yrs.
8 *Eunice*, b. Oct. 2, 1809 ; m. Amos Gutterson, of Milford,
    Nov. 23, 1837.
9 *Julia*, b. Oct. 7, 1811 ; d. Dec. 2, 1861, æ. 50 yrs.

1– 6 NATHAN BALLARD BUSS m., 1st w., Arvilla Nay ; 2d
w., Elizabeth Brackett ; c. His ch. were b. in Dublin.
He now lives in the village.

    George W., b. May 21, 1827 ; m. Syrena Jaquith, Jan. 3,
10 1850 ; r. in Auburndale, Mass.
    Mary Ann, b. April 14, 1829 ; m. Harrison Church,
11 March 23, 1854 ; re. to South Hadley, Mass.
    Lydia, b. Sept. 4, 1831 ; m. Amos A. Sawyer, May 26,
12 1852.
    Elizabeth, b. June 13, 1833 ; m. William E. Baker, March
13 8, 1855.
    Eunice, b. June 11, 1835 ; m. S. Hudson Caldwell, Dec.
14 24, 1861 ; d. April 16, 1866, æ. 30 yrs., 10 mos.
    Cynthia, b. Sept. 6, 1837 ; m. Benjamin F. Sawyer, June
15 7, 1860 ; r. Springfield, Mass.
    Myraette Vail, b. June 7, 1840 ; m. Marcellus L. Morse,
16 May 1, 1865 ; r. Keene.

THE CALDWELL FAMILY.

1 ENSIGN JOSEPH CALDWELL (so called) came to town
early, not far from 1751 or '52, and purchased the farm
afterwards known as the Dea. William McNee farm, of
John Taggart. He erected the first building on the
farm. How long he remained in town is not known.
He appears to have been a man of education, and spent
his winters in teaching. It is inferred that he came from

Londonderry, as it is reported that his first children were born there. We know nothing more of his wife or children than is related here. He was chosen as one of the first selectmen at the first meeting after the incorporation of the town, 1760, and again selectman in 1767.; also moderator in the same year at three of the meetings. After this we do not meet with his name in the records. It is not exactly known when he left town, probably about 1770. It is supposed he removed to Colerain, Mass., as many of his children settled there. His wife's Christian name was Ann; surname not known.

2   *William*, b. Sept. 27, 1750, Londonderry.
3   *Annie*, b. July 29, 1751, Londonderry.
4   *Joseph*, b. Jan. 23, 1752, Peterborough; m. Rachel McGee, Colerain, Mass.
5   *Mary*, b. Jan. 26, 1754, Peterborough; m. Jonas McGee, Colerain.
6   *John*, b. Dec. 20, 1759.

1   THOMAS CALDWELL, a race entirely distinct from above, was the son of William and Agnes Caldwell, and b. at Bedford, Mass., Nov. 20, 1773. He came to Peterborough when quite a boy, and lived with his uncle, Capt. William Alld, in north part of town on Farm B, to his manhood. He m. Eliza Cuningham, dau. Capt. Samuel Cuningham, Feb. 12, 1808. He d. March 18, 1856, æ. 82 yrs. She d. Feb. 19, 1851, æ. 67 yrs.

2   *Susan C.*, b. May 20, 1809; m. Jonathan Felt.
3   *Catherine M.*, b. Oct. 3, 1810; unm.
4   *Jane*, b. Jan. 5, 1813; d. Jan. 26, 1817, æ. 4 yrs.
5   *Nancy*, b. April 26, 1815; m., June 4, 1839, Silas G. Williams, Newton, Mass. Eight ch.; *viz.*, Ellen A., Maria F., Eliza E., Caroline W., Eva R., Janette W., Nancy C., Silas W.
6   *Eliza*, b. Oct. 3, 1817; m., Feb. 1, 1849, Augustus Fuller.
7   *William*, b. Dec. 24, 1819; unm.; d. Sept. 14, 1854, æ. 34 yrs., 8 mos.
8   †*Samuel Hudson*, b. Jan. 15, 1822; m. Eunice A. Buss.
9   *Mary E.*, b. April 20, 1824; d. Aug. 26, 1826, æ. 2 yrs., 4 mos.
10   *Thomas*, b. Nov. 26, 1826; unm.; d. March 23, 1871, æ. 44 yrs., 3 mos.
11   *Joseph*, b. Nov. 16, 1828; m., November, 1867, Lizzie Shaw, Rockford, Ill. One ch., Edith Eliza, b. ——.

1–8   SAMUEL HUDSON CALDWELL carried on the tin-plate and sheet-iron business in this village many years, till his health failed and compelled him to retire. He was a worthy and useful citizen, and his early death was much lamented.   He m., Dec. 24, 1862, Eunice A. Buss, dau. N. B. Buss.   She d. at birth of child, April 16, 1866, æ. 30 yrs., 10 mos.   He d. Nov. 13, 1867, æ. 45 yrs.

12   *William Hudson*, b. April 16, 1866.

THE CAREY FAMILY.

1   SAMUEL CAREY, son of Samuel and Mary Smith Carey, was b. in Jaffrey, June 1, 1799.   He came to town in 1814, when his mother, who was then a widow, moved here, and he has resided here since.   He is a farmer, and by his industry and economy has acquired a large estate.   He first purchased the Samuel Moore place, and carried it on for many years, when he removed to the village, and now owns and occupies the south dwelling of the "Brick Block."   He m. Harriet Olcott, 1822.

2   *Jane*, b. Oct. 20, 1822 ; m. Munro Johnson, of Hancock ; d. Sept. 30, 1852, aged 29 yrs., 11 mos.

3   †*Willard O.*, b. June 10, 1824 ; m., 1st w., Julia Ann Robbe ; 2d w., Emma T. Perry.

4   *Eliza Ann*, b. Sept. 22, 1826 ; m. George Everett ; r. New Jersey.

5   *Warren*, b. June 11, 1828 ; d., being scalded with hot water, June 1, 1831, æ. 3 yrs.

6   *Mary Ann*, b. Sept. 6, 1830 ; m. —— Elliot.

7   *Samuel W.*, b. June 20, 1832 ; r. Iowa.

8   *Harriet R.*, b. April 26, 1835.

9   *Almena*, b. April 6, 1838.

10   *John*, b. Dec. 8, 1839 ; m. —— Annette ; r. Nebraska.

11   *Charles A.*, b. July 6, 1842 ; d. September, 1852, æ. 10 yrs.

1– 3   WILLARD O. CAREY, a machinist by trade, has succeeded his father on the homestead ; m., 1st w., Julia Ann Robbe, b. April 23, 1827 ; d. June 19, 1850, æ. 23 yrs. ; m., 2d w., Nov. 6, 1853, Emma T. Perry, dau. of Dea. Ebenezer Perry, b. Oct. 9, 1826.   One ch. 1st w. ; five ch. 2d w.

12   *Rosa Julia*, b. Nov. 14, 1849 ; m. Willis H. Winn.

13   *Willis H.*, b. Sept. 1, 1854 ; d. May 11, 1857, æ. 2 yrs., 8 months.

14   *Alice Emma*, b. Jan. 25, 1857.

15   *Herbert Willard*, b. July 14, 1858.

16   *Hiram A.*, b. in Brooklyn, Sept. 17, 1860.

17   *Mabel Jane*, b. in Milford, Nov. 5, 1863.

THE CARLEY FAMILY.

1   Asa Carley was the son of David Carley, of Hancock. He came to Peterborough in 1812, and was foreman on Samuel Smith's farm many years, till he bought a farm in the east part of the town, where he lived till his death. He m. Kate Barry, June 19, 1803. He d. March 25, 1846, æ. 68 yrs. She d. Feb. 16, 1867, æ. 82 yrs., 9 mos.

2   †*Dexter D.*, b. July 1, 1805 ; m. Nellie White.
3   *Mary*, b. Aug. 13, 1807 ; m. David Sprague, 1835.
4   *Eliza A.*, b. Aug. 4, 1809.
5   †*Peter*, b. Oct. 27, 1811 ; m. Louisa J. Clark, 1849.
6   †*Asa, Jr.*, b. Dec. 21, 1813 ; m., 1st w., Sarah B. Pillsbury, 1840 ; 2d w., Mrs. Hobart.
7   *John*, b. March 15, 1816 ; m. Almira Crockett ; ch., George A., b. 1849.
8   *James M.*, b. Feb. 7, 1818 ; m. Malvina Crockett ; 2d w., Lizzie E. Burleigh, 1866 ; ch., Earnest, b. 1867 ; Bennie, b. 1869 ; Alice, b. 1872.
9   *Sarah*, b. April 8, 1820 ; m. James B. Campbell, May 9, 1847 ; r. Manchester ; ch., Lizzie, b. Dec. 24, 1849 ; d. Jan. 16, 1866 ; Charles Sumner, b. Dec. 24, 1855.
10   *Jane*, b. Aug. 14, 1825 ; d. Aug. 31, 1827, æ. 2 yrs.
11   *Jane C.*, b. Sept. 17, 1828 ; m. Parker Butterfield, Manchester, June 24, 1850 ; ch., Albert P., b. July 10, 1851 ; d. Aug. 16, 1853, æ. 2 yrs. ; George P., b. Oct. 30, 1854 ; Charles F. W., b. July 12, 1858.

1– 2   Dexter D. Carley m. Nellie White, dau. William White, June 2, 1831. She d. at Hanover, Ill., January, 1874, æ. 72 yrs. He was drowned in the North Factory Pond, July 12, 1844, æ. 39 yrs.

12   *William*, b. May 29, 1835 ; m. Mary J. James, June 17, 1856, Hanover, Ill.
13   *Mary Jane*, b. June 22, 1839 ; m. John L. Phillips, May 3, 1860 ; five ch. ; r. Hanover, Ill.

1– 5   Peter Carley has always resided in town ; m. Louisa J. Clark, 1849. He has for many years worked in the paper-mill in West Peterborough.

14   *Sarah J.*, b. Jan. 1, 1850.
15   *Estella*, b. ——, 1852 ; m. William Delmage, 1870.
16   *James M.*, b. ——, 1854.

1– 6   Asa Carley, Jr., settled on the homestead, but subsequently sold it and moved to Bedford, where he now

lives. He m., 1st w., Sarah B. Pillsbury, April 1, 1840;
2d w., widow —— Hobart, of Bedford, 1863.

17 | *Sarah C.*, b. May 20, 1841; m. —— Putnam, Lyndeboro.
18 | *Charles B.*, b. Nov. 9, 1843; supposed lost in the Chicago fire, 1871.
19 | *George A.*, b. Nov. 10, 1847; d. Mch. 14, 1866, æ. 18 yrs., 4 mos.
20 | *Albert B.*, } b. Feb. 5, 1851; { d. Mch. 18, 1866, æ. 15 yrs.
21 | *Mary M.*, } { d. Mch. 11, 1852, æ. 1 yr.
22 | *Etta J.*, b. April 24, 1855.

2 | JABEZ CARLEY, son of David Carley, of Hancock, and
brother to Asa Carley. After a successful term of lumbering in the British Dominions, he returned to Peterborough, and bought the "Taylor place," so called, of
James Smith, and erected an entire new set of buildings,
where he lived till his death. He m., 1st w., April 10,
1821, Mary Washburn, of Hancock, and sister of Reuben Washburn, of this town. She d. in childbirth Aug.
25, 1838, æ. 48 yrs. He m., 2d wife, Emma Pratt, Oct.
24, 1839; c. He d. Jan. 27, 1848, æ. 64 yrs. She d.
April 23, 1876, æ. 81 yrs.

23 | *David*, b. ——, 1819; d. Aug. 18, 1820, æ. 1 yr.
24 | *Henry*, b. ——, 1822; d. Aug. 11, 1826, æ. 4 yrs.
25 | *Eliza*, b. June 22, 1827; m. John W. Barber; r. in Kansas.
26 | *Mary Jane*, b. June 17, 1832; m. David M. Cavender; re. to Illinois.
27 | *Sarah*, b. March 7, 1835; m. Edmund S. Hoyt, of Warren, N. H., Aug. 8, 1861. She d. at Portland, Me.,
May 9, 1869, æ. 34 yrs. Ch. (1) Mary Brigham, b.
Jan. 27, 1866; (2) Sarah Carley, b. Aug. 8, 1868.

THE CARTER FAMILY.

1 | OLIVER CARTER, Jr., son of Oliver Carter, of Leominster, Mass., came to town in 1795, and succeeded Samuel Smith as a trader at the "Corner," and afterwards
bought the property, and continued business until his
death. He m. Jenny Stuart, dau. Charles Stuart. He
d. April 5, 1812, æ. 49 yrs. His widow afterwards m.
Capt. Thomas Sherwin. Capt. T. Sherwin d. Nov. 15,
1827, æ. 67 yrs. She d. March 8, 1857, æ. 82 yrs.

2 | *Franklin*, b. Nov. 19, 1795; m. Kate Whitbeck; re. to Lima, N. Y.; c.

3 | †*Milton*, b. Dec. 2, 1797; m. Fanny Dean; b. May 15, 1812.

4 | *Eliza*, b. Dec. 21, 1799; d. May 25, 1818, æ. 19 yrs.

5 | *Charles*, b. Jan. 25, 1802; m. Almira Ingalls, May 8, 1827; r. Leominster.

6 | †*Henry S.*, b. Dec. 17, 1804; m. Eunice H. Searle, June 8, 1828.

7 | *Oliver*, b. March 15, 1807; m. Kate Gardner. She d. 1865; he d. 1863.

8 | *David*, b. Oct. 14, 1810. He spent a few years in the store of Samuel Smith previous to 1829, and then for a time resided in Boston, and afterwards went to California. Samuel A. Morison, formerly of this town, now residing in San Francisco, Cal., says that David Carter was the first man who carried gold from the California mines, 2000 ounces, to the Philadelphia mint. At the time of his death he was in the wholesale leather business in Boston. He d. in Boston, April 5, 1849, of an aneurism of the arch of the aorta, æ. 39 yrs.

1– 3 | MILTON CARTER. He always resided in town. He was a teacher of vocal music in town and the vicinity for many years. He m. Fanny Dean, Nov. 27, 1838. He d. Oct. 30, 1864, æ. 67 yrs.

9 | *Ann Eliza*, b. Nov. 29, 1840; d. May 27, 1844, æ. 3 yrs., 5 mos.

10 | *Fanny*, b. Dec. 3, 1844; d. Sept. 4, 1848, æ. 3 yrs., 10 mos.

11 | *Milton*, b. Dec. 2, 1850.

1– 6 | HENRY STUART CARTER. He devoted much time in learning to play the violin, and became so skilled that his services were in great demand for many years for dancing-parties and schools in all this vicinity. He m. Eunice H. Searle, June 8, 1828. She was b. March 10, 1804. He d. April 12, 1873, æ. 69 yrs.

12 | *Anstiss M.*, b. Oct. 29, 1830; ch., Joseph C. Parsons [son of Anstiss M.], b. April 8, 1849; m. Eben G. Goldthwait, Jan. 3, 1852.

13 | *Eliza J.*, b. July 25, 1834; m. Benjamin F. Clark, June 16, 1860; ch., Charles, b. June 6, 1862. She d. July 2, 1862, æ. 27 yrs., 11 mos.

14 | *Emma G.*, b. Nov. 23, 1840; m. Sylvester Sweatt; r. Claremont; c.

15 | *Henry D.*, b. Sept. 5, 1847; d. Aug. 14, 1849, æ. 1 yr., 11 mos.

5

THE CHAPMAN FAMILY.

1   DUDLEY CHAPMAN came from Londonderry to Peterborough in 1788, and lived on the west side of the street
road, near to the town-line brook. His wife's name
was Eliza; surname unknown. He d. Oct. 18, 1832, æ.
67 yrs. She d. Nov. 28, 1826, æ. 66 yrs. He is remembered as one of the early bass singers in the church.

---

2   *Mary L.*, b. ——; m. Isaiah Emerson, Dec. 15, 1808 ; r.
Haverhill, Mass.

3   *Betsey*, b. ——, Londonderry; m. Samuel Hazletine,
March 22, 1810 ; r. Haverhill, Mass.

4   †*John*, b. ——, 1792, Peterborough ; m. Hannah Noyes.

5   †*Daniel*, b. ——, 1794, Peterborough ; m. Peggy Gowing, March 11, 1824.

6   †*Moses*, b. March 16, 1796 ; m. Polly Pierce, of Hillsboro.

7   *Gates*, b. Feb. 8, 1798 ; m. April 24, 1824, Mary Burnham, of Meredith. Was a machinist by trade, at
which he worked till failing health obliged him to relinquish it. He d. March 25, 1873, æ. 75 yrs. ; r. New
Ipswich.

1- 4   JOHN CHAPMAN lived and died on the homestead in
town. He m. Hannah Noyes, 1815, dau. Eliphalet and
Hannah Noyes, of Haverhill, Mass. He d. June, 1832,
æ. 40 yrs. She was b. March 18, 1795; d. Jan. 14,
1873, æ. 77 yrs., 9 mos.

---

8   *Hannah*, b. March 24, 1816; d. April 8, 1816, æ. 15 dys.

9   *Laura*, b. Oct. 15, 1817 ; m. George Goodnow ; r. Man-
kato, Minn.

10   *Charles*, b. July 5, 1819 ; d. June 25, 1824, æ. 4 yrs., 11
mos.

11   *John D.*, b. July 29, 1821 ; m. Eliza Cutter Jaffrey ; r.
Keene.

12   *Mary Ann*, b. Dec. 12, 1823 ; m. Henry Steele, Aug. 6,
1846.

13   *Hannah Jane*, b. Dec. 15, 1825 ; killed by a window-
sash falling upon her neck, in attempting to get into a
school-house in Jaffrey, the blocking under her feet
falling away, and leaving her hung by the neck, June
2, 1838, æ. 12 yrs., 5 mos.

14   *George W.*, b. April 18, 1828 ; m. Sarah J. Parker ; r.
Boston.

15   *Margaret L.*, b. June 2, 1830 ; m. Charles Morrison ; r.
San Francisco, Cal.

1– 5 | DANIEL CHAPMAN m. Peggy Gowing, dau. William Gowing, March 11, 1824; he d. Nov. 11, 1832, æ. 38 yrs.; she d. May 22, 1867, æ. 70 yrs.

16 | *Louisa*, b. ——, 1825; d. April 19, 1828, æ. 3 yrs.
17. | *William Wallace*, b. April 19, 1827; m. Lydia Hannaford; r. Ashburnham, Mass.; ch., (1) Charlie H., (2) Fred W., (3) Kate M., (4) Nettie M., (5) Jessie D., (6) Hattie P.

1– 6 | MOSES CHAPMAN was a cabinet-maker by trade, and carried on this business many years in a shop on Wallace's brook near the Powers, now Mears place, and then removed to the village where he built a house and buildings for carriage-making, in which he then engaged. He m. Polly Pierce, Dec. 25, 1823; he d. March 3, 1859, æ. 62 yrs., 9 mos.; she d. July 11, 1867, æ. 72 yrs., 9 mos.; b. Sept. 30, 1794.

18 | *Andrew J.*, b. Oct. 18, 1824; m. June 19, 1845, Ann Black, Haverhill, Mass.; r. Haverhill, Mass.
19 | *Albert P.*, b. March 29, 1826; d. Feb. 18, 1858, in Palmer, Mass., æ. 31 yrs., 10 mos.; m. Oct. 25, 1847, Mary Blanchard, of Palmer. A man of much promise.
20 | *Julia A.*, b. Jan. 22, 1828; m. George Handy, Dublin, Dec. 24, 1849; d. Jan. 5, 1872, æ. 43 yrs., 11 mos.; one ch., Emma M.; 2d hus. —— Sutherland; one ch.
21 | *Adaline P.*, b. Aug. 11, 1830; d. Sept. 14, 1848, æ. 18 yrs.
22 | *Jerome B.*, b. June 25, 1832; d. Oct. 25, 1863, æ. 31 yrs., 4 mos.
23 | *Martin*, b. Oct. 3, 1834; d. Sept. 29, 1865, æ. 30 yrs., 11 mos.
24 | *Walter D.*, b. Dec. 13, 1836; d. May 20, 1858, æ. 21 yrs., 9 mos.
25 | *Harriet M.*, b. April 11, 1839; d. June 17, 1864, æ. 25 yrs., 2 mos.

1 | JERRY CHAPMAN came to town, and lived in the south part of the town on the place afterwards occupied by Samuel Clark on the town-line brook. He was a shoemaker by trade. The name of his wife unknown, as also the deaths of both.

2 | *John*, b. ——; (3) *Zadoc*, b. ——.
4 | † *Joshua*, b. ——; m. Mary Robbe; b. Sept. 27, 1790; r. Elmira, N. Y.
5 | *Patty*, b. ——; m. —— Banks.
6 | *Betsey*, b. ——; m. David Robbe; re. Pennsylvania.

1– 4 | JOSHUA CHAPMAN m. Mary Robbe, Sept. 5, 1811, dau. Capt. William Robbe ; r. Elmira, N. Y.

7 | *William*, b. Feb. 25, 1812.
8 | *Maria Louisa*, b. Aug. 26, 1813.
9 | *John*, b. Nov. 17, 1814.
10 | *James Robbe*, b. Oct. 16, 1816.
11 | *Mary*, b. Sept. 20, 1818.
12 | *Jeremiah*, b. July 14, 1820.
All born in Peterborough.

THE CHASE FAMILY.

1 | WILLARD DUNLAP CHASE, M.D., son of Willard W. and Maria Dunlap Chase, b. in Claremont, Dec. 4, 1836. He received his education at the district school and academy in the town. At the age of twenty he entered the apothecary shop of Edwin Ainsworth, of Claremont, and at about the age of twenty-four commenced the study of medicine, under the instruction of Drs. S. G. Jarvis and C. A. Volk. He attended his medical lectures at Dartmouth Medical College and at Harvard Medical University, and in March, 1866, received the degree of M.D. from the latter institution. He settled at Greenfield immediately on graduation, and after remaining there two years he removed to Peterborough in the spring of 1868, where he now resides as a practising physician. He is now one of the superintending School Committee of Peterborough ; m. Dec. 30, 1869, Josephine L., dau. of Moses Clark, Esq., of Wilton.

2 | *Blanche M.*, b. Feb. 16, 1871.

THE CHENEY FAMILY.

1 | MOSES CHENEY was b. in Thornton, Jan. 31, 1793, and was the son of Elias Cheney, b. in Newbury, Mass., April 18, 1768, and Sarah Burbank, his w., born in Newbury, Mass., Nov. 22, 1766. He m. Abigail Morison, b. March 25, 1796. He was a paper manufacturer at Holderness, from which place he removed to Peterborough in 1835 to engage in the same business with his brother in-law, A. P. Morrison, of this place. He remained in town ten years, when he returned to Holderness, or Ashland, severed from that town, and spent the rest of his life there. He was a good and highly respected man, and held many important offices in the town in which he lived. He died while on a visit at Lebanon, July 17, 1875, æ. 82 yrs., 5 mos.

2 | †*Oren B.*, b. Dec. 10, 1816 ; m., 1st w., Caroline Adelia Rundlett ; 2d w., Nancy St. Clair Perkins.

3 | *Esther M.*, b. Sept. 27, 1819 ; m. John M. Merrill, Holderness ; d. ——.

4 | *Sarah B.*, b. March 30, 1821 ; m. S. G. Abbot ; r. Needham, Mass.

5 | *Moses, Jr.*, b. June 28, 1822 ; m. —— ; r. Henniker.

6 | *Abigail M.*, b. Dec. 21, 1823 ; m. George Washburn ; r. Ashland.

7 | †*Charles G.*, b. July 8, 1826 ; m. Sarah E. Smith, of Holderness.

8 | †*Person Colby*, b. Feb. 25, 1828 ; m., 1st w., Anna Moore ; 2d w., Sarah W. Keith.

9 | *Ruth E.*, b. May 28, 1830 ; m. Joseph W. Lord ; r. Wollaston, Mass.

10 | †*Elias H.*, b. Jan. 28, 1832 ; m. Susan W. Youngman.

11 | *Marcia A.*, b. Sept. 26, 1834 ; m. I. P. F. Smith ; r. Meredith.

12 | *Harriet O.*, b. in Peterborough, Feb. 27, 1838 ; m. Dr. C. F. Bonney ; r. Manchester.

All the above born in Holderness, now Ashland, but the last.

1– 2 | OREN B. CHENEY, D.D., was b. Dec. 10, 1816, in Holderness, now Ashland. He was prepared for college at New Hampton, and entered Brown University in 1835, but took up his connections and entered Dartmouth College in the spring of 1836, and graduated in 1839. During his college course he kept schools every winter, and in one of them he had an experience that may have been serviceable to him in all his after life. A certain important man in the district did not approve of prayers in school, and was determined that he should not offer them, and he, being disinclined to acquiesce in such a demand to discontinue the exercise, the district were summoned to decide the matter ; but they could not be made subservient to this man's view, and he went on, nothing awed or intimidated, to the close of his school as he had begun. He learned a lesson of perseverance, self-reliance, and self-control from this circumstance that has, no doubt, had much to do in making him the great educator and efficient man he is at the present time.

After graduation he was engaged in teaching in academies some two or three years in various places, and commenced preaching in 1842. He had two pastorates ; he was six years at Lebanon, Me., and five at Augusta. He started a movement for a Free Baptist School in 1854. It was located at Lewiston, Me., and existed until 1863 as a seminary. In 1863 it became "Bates College," now in a flourishing condition, with 125 students. Mr. Cheney has been president of the institution from the beginning. The college has a campus of 50 acres, — three large buildings and president's house ; total value of college property about $300,000, and also a fund of $100,000, and an effort is now making to add $200,000, of which $150,000 has been already subscribed. Connected with the college is a theological department, and there is also near by a preparatory school. The college is named after Benjamin E. Bates, of Boston, who has subscribed $200,000.

Mr. Cheney received the degree of D.D. from the Wesleyan University in 1863.

He m., 1st w., in 1840, Caroline Adelia Rundlett, dau. of James and Betsey Rundlett, of Stratham. She died in June, 1846. He m., 2d w., August, 1847, Nancy St. Clair Perkins, dau. of Rev. Thomas and Rebecca Perkins, of New Hampton ; 1st w., one ch. ; 2d w., two ch.

13　*Horace Rundlett*, b. Oct. 29, 1844. Graduated Bowdoin College, Me., 1863. Studied law at Harvard Law School ; is now settled in the practice of law in Boston, and for the past three years has been Assistant District Attorney of Suffolk Co.

14　*Caroline A.*, b. July 30, 1848 ; m. Charles H. Swan, of Providence, R. I.

15　*Emeline R.*, b. Jan. 23, 1850 ; m. J. Frank Boothby, of Lewiston, Me.

1- 7　CHARLES GILMAN CHENEY came to Peterborough with his parents while young, — was fitted for college, and graduated at Dartmouth College in 1848. He studied law in the office of Nesmith & Pike, of Franklin, and commenced the practice of his profession in town in 1851, but on account of ill health was obliged to relinquish it, and accepted the office of the first cashier of the Peterborough Bank, in 1854. He held this office till the spring of 1862, when, his health failing entirely, he was obliged to resign. By a severe rheumatic affection he lost the use of his lower limbs for some three or four years before his death, and was in constant suffering for the last years of his life. His life opened with the promise of great usefulness and honor, which was blighted by ill health from his first beginning to the end. He was a man of sterling integrity, of manly and honorable attainments, and of kindly affections, and his loss was deeply deplored by the community. He m., Oct. 25, 1851, Sarah E. Smith, dau. of Obadiah Smith, of Hol-

Eng. by A. H. Ritchie.

P. C. Cheney

derness. He d. at Hillsborough Bridge, Nov. 13, 1862, æ. 36 yrs., 4 mos.

_____

16   *Albert P.*, b. Feb. 2, 1853 ; d. March 8, 1862, æ. 9 yrs.

_____

1- 8   PERSON COLBY CHENEY (Gov.) was seven years of age when his father removed to Peterborough, to engage in the paper-making business, in company with his brother-in-law, A. P. Morrison. He was here trained to paper-making in all its modern forms, devoting all his early life to it, aside from the time spent in his education. He commenced business in the west part of the town, erected the paper-mill now owned by John J. Barker, and carried on the paper manufacture successfully until he removed to Manchester in 1866, to engage in the paper and stock business, where he now resides. He enlisted in the war of the Rebellion, and was appointed quartermaster of the 13th Reg. of N. H. Vols., August, 1862, and was honorably discharged August, 1863, on account of a severe sickness, which assumed a chronic and dangerous form that threatened life ; but after a long and tedious illness, he finally and fully recovered his health. He represented Peterborough in the legislature in 1853, '54 ; was elected Railroad Commissioner in 1864 for three years ; elected Mayor of Manchester for 1872, which office he held but one year, being obliged, on account of the urgency of his business, peremptorily to decline a reëlection, which was earnestly proffered to him. Mr. Cheney's removal from Peterborough was a source of sincere regret to his many friends, and a great loss to the community. He at once became popular at Manchester by his honest and upright business relations, by his kind and unselfish manner, and his sincerity and integrity of character.

Though denied, by the circumstances of his early life, the highest mental culture, yet it is supplemented to him with a far-seeing sagacity, and a common-sense application of his powers that render him an exceedingly useful man in society, and particularly to his political party, over which he exercises such an extensive control. He possesses, in all the relations of life, the very soul of honor. He can never do too much for his friends ; he cherishes no resentments against any one, — no vindictive feeling against his enemies, if he has any, or his political opponents.

His judgments of men and things are almost always singularly correct and just, and he is considered a safe adviser in any exigency of business or of party. Though unhackneyed in political life, and unwilling to yield his time and services to public office, to the great injury of his private business, yet his uncommon qualifications pointed him as perhaps the only man who could be successful against the great odds in the election of March, 1875. An uncommon unanimity in the party induced him to yield to the public call to be considered a candidate for Governor of the State. The result of the election was a surprise to every one, — a triumphant and confident party was defeated, and he was almost elected by the popular vote. His election was consummated by the legislature in June, 1875. Gov. Cheney was a candidate again for Governor in the March election of 1876, and was triumphantly elected by over 3,000 majority, and is the Governor of New Hampshire during this Centennial year. He m., 1st w., May 22, 1850, S. Anna Moore, dau. of S. Morison Moore. She d. Jan. 7, 1858, æ. 27 yrs.; m., 2d w., Mrs. Sarah W. Keith, dau. of Jonathan White, Esq., of Hanover, Ill., June 29, 1859.

17   *Agnes Annie*, b. Manchester, Oct. 22, 1869.

1– 10   ELIAS H. CHENEY m. Susan W. Youngman, of Peterborough, b. April 11, 1831. He was fitted for college at New Hampton and Exeter Academy. Having become a printer by trade, he purchased the Peterborough *Transcript* in 1853, and published it two years. In 1855, he removed to Concord, and took charge of the New Hampshire *Phœnix*, and subsequently purchased, in 1861, the *Granite State Free Press*, published at Lebanon, and has published that paper since. He represented the town of Lebanon in the legislature in 1867, '68.

18   *Fred. W.*, b. Peterborough, May 19, 1853.
19   *Harry M.*, b. Newport, March 8, 1860.
20   *Susie Y.*, b. Lebanon, Dec. 23, 1863; d. Jan. 28, 1864, æ. 1 mo., 5 dys.
21   *Helen Gray*, b. Lebanon, Nov. 5, 1865.

THE CHILDS FAMILY.

1   AMZI CHILDS, son of Henry and Matilda Billings Childs, of Deerfield, Mass., was b. Nov. 1, 1817. His father was the descendant of persons of that name that first came to Deerfield one hundred and sixty years ago. He lived and died there. Amzi Childs received his education at the common schools and at the academy in Deerfield. His early life was spent on the farm. He removed to Peterborough in 1841, and carried on, for thirteen years, the manufacture of lead pipe, the first

manufactory of the kind in this region. He then commenced the manufacture of baskets in 1854, having
purchased the large building erected by Moses Chapman for a wheelwright shop — which he rebuilt and
remodelled for this purpose, — and has continued the
same business on an extensive scale to the present time.
His wares are sold and known all through the New
England States. He lives on Pine Street, in a house
built by himself in 1849, situated a few rods south,
and on the same side of the road, of the house of M.
L. Morison and James Scott. Selectman, 1854, '55; m.
Jan. 28, 1846, Sarah D. Manahan, of Francestown. She
d. March 24, 1856, æ. 36 yrs.; m., 2d w., July 7, 1859,
Margaret A. Brenan of Francestown. One ch., 1st w.

2 | *Henry*, b. Sept. 21, 1849.

THE CLARK FAMILY.

1 | SAMUEL CLARK, son of Samuel and Rebecca Miller
Clark, dau. of Samuel Miller of Peterborough, residents
of Sharon, was b. Dec. 13, 1793; m. Lucy McCoy,
May 14, 1829, dau. of William and Lucy Ryan McCoy,
born in Sharon, Sept. 25, 1798. They removed to Peterborough March 4, 1834, and occupied the Jerry Chapman place in south part of town, his farm lying on the
town-line brook. He d. Dec. 4, 1851, æ. 57 yrs., 11
mos. She d. Oct. 26, 1861, æ. 63 yrs.

2 | *Lucia A.*, b. in Sharon, May 6, 1830; m., 1851, Kendall
C. Scott.
3 | *Sarah E.*, b. in Sharon, July 4, 1832; m., April 12, 1860,
Sampson Washburn.
4 | *Albert S.*, b. Sept. 1, 1834; m., April 4, 1867, Ellen E.
Taggart, dau. of Phineas Taggart, of Sharon.
5 | *Abbie F.*, b. Aug. 4, 1839; d. Oct. 7, 1861, æ. 22 yrs.

THE COGSWELL FAMILY.

1 | HENRY FRANCIS COGSWELL, son of William and Abi-
gail Dowes Cogswell, was b. in Marlborough, Mass.,
May 3, 1796; m. Rebecca P. Hosmer, dau. of Cyrus
and Polly Hosmer, of Concord, Mass., Sept. 14, 1818, b.
in Concord, Nov. 28, 1797. He is a woollen manufacturer, having served his apprenticeship of four years at
the business in Concord, Mass. During this time he
had a short service in the war of 1812. He says: "I
spent three months in the war in 1814, at South Boston,
in the company of light infantry, which consisted of

fifty men ; and I am the *only* man living out of the fifty, — rather extraordinary, as I always had a feeble body!'" He purchased the woollen-mill and clothier's-shop of Calvin Chamberlain, in 1817, built and operated by Perkins and Chamberlain for wool-carding and cloth-dressing, and removed to Peterborough and commenced business the same year. He manufactured satinets, cassimeres, and roller-cloth. While owned by him, the mill was destroyed by fire, with a loss of $3,571 in 1823, and promptly rebuilt in. 1824. In 1831 this mill was remodelled with new machinery and the power looms. He remained in the woollen business till 1845, when he sold his factory and other property to Joseph Noone, and that same year removed to Buffalo, N. Y., where he now resides. He was very successful in business, and before he retired had acquired a large estate.

2 *Martha R.,* b. May 26, 1820 ; d. June 23, 1836, æ. 16 yrs.
3 *Caroline H.,* b. May 26, 1823 ; m. Ethan H. Howard ; r. Buffalo, N. Y.
4 *William Henry,* b. June 10, 1826 ; d. Hudson, Mich., · March 28, 1858, æ. 31 yrs., 9 mos.
5 *Albert Smith,* b. Nov. 23, 1827 ; d. at Buffalo, Sept. 13, 1848, æ. 20 yrs., 9 mos.
6 *George W.,* b. July 1, 1830 ; d. Le Roy, N. Y., April 22, 1854, æ. 23 yrs., 9 mos. Graduated H. C. 1849.
7 *Eliza,* b. Feb. 17, 1832 ; d. Buffalo, Jan. 3, 1855, æ. 22 yrs., 10 mos.
8 *Sarah,* b. Feb. 10, 1834 ; m. Joshua O. Whitcomb, June 2, 1852 ; r. New York.

THE CONVERSE FAMILY.

1 SAMUEL CONVERSE came to town from Cambridge, Mass., about 1833. A blacksmith by trade. He still resides in town, having given up his trade. He m. Elizabeth, dau. of Samuel and Betsey Stuart Turner, Sept. 1, 1835.

2 *Emma,* b. April 14, 1837 ; m. Timothy M. Longley.
3 *Sarah Jane,* b. Oct. 26, 1840 ; m. S. P. Longley.
4 *Abby,* b. May 27, 1841 ; drowned April 27, 1843, æ. 2 yrs.

THE CRAGIN FAMILY.

FRANCIS and ARCHELAUS CRAGIN were the sons of Capt. Francis and Sarah Cummings Cragin, of Temple, both of which parents were b. in Temple, and d. there ; he d. Jan. 18, 1852, æ. 79 yrs.; she d. March, 1867, æ. 93 yrs.

1 | FRANCIS CRAGIN, Jr., was b. in Temple, Aug. 15, 1796; died in Peterborough, Nov. 23, 1866, æ. 70 yrs. He m., 1st w., Alice McKean, June, 16, 1824; b. in Windham, Aug. 28, 1796; d. Sept. 17, 1825, æ. 29 yrs. He m., 2d w., Hannah Boynton, b. in Temple, June 17, 1804; d. March 11, 1872, æ. 68 yrs. He came to Peterborough in 1832, and worked in the north cotton factory many years in the repair shop. He was a carpenter.

2 | *William M.,* b. Aug. 21, 1825; m. Emily L. Wilson, of Gilsum, March 29, 1860; she was b. Sept. 26, 1839; d. July 30, 1860, æ. 21 yrs., c.; 2d w., Emeline L. Wilson, May 26, 1862.

3 | *Francis, Jr.,* b. Jan. 24, 1831; m. Eliza R. Baldwin, Oct. 24, 1854, of Greenfield, b. Oct. 6, 1831; d. July, 1872, æ. 41 yrs.; ch., Emma Florence.

4 | *Alice Jane,* b. Aug. 17, 1834,; m. John H. Vose, Jan. 1, 1857.

5 | *Hannah M.,* b. Oct. 28, 1836; m. Samuel W. Vose, May 6, 1869.

6 | *Samuel O.,* b. March 30, 1840; m. Jan. 1, 1870, Mary H. Ricker, of Great Falls; b. Dec. 9, 1843; r. Lawrence, Mass.; one ch., Charles S., b. Aug. 25, 1871.

2 | ARCHELAUS CRAGIN, b. in Temple, April 28, 1798; m., 1st w., Martha Horsely, b. in Temple, Nov. 14, 1800; d. March 31, 1852, æ. 52 yrs. He m., 2d w., Barbara Maxwell, Oct. 27, 1853; b. in Pictou, N. S., June 1, 1822; d. ——, 1874, æ. 52 yrs. A carpenter by trade. Lived in south-west part of town, on Eli Upton, or old Robert Smith, place. 1st w., five ch.; 2d w., four ch.

7 | *Eveline,* b. Jan. 31, 1824; m. Joshua Dean, Sept. 11, 1857; he was b. in Easton, Mass., March 25, 1820; r. Bridgewater, Mass.; ch., (1) Martha F., b. June 25, 1852; d. Sept. 14, 1853, æ. 1 yr.; (2) Clarrie, b. Aug. 26, 1855; d. July 29, 1863, æ. 8 yrs.; (3) Jennie E., b. July 14, 1861; (4) Carrie E., b. Feb. 11, 1865.

8 | †*George,* b. Dec. 2, 1825; m. Sarah Miles.

9 | *Martha A.,* b. Sept. 20, 1829; d. Jan. 7, 1845, æ. 15 yrs.

10 | †*John,* b. Nov. 2, 1831; m. Maria S. Ober.

11 | *Sarah,* b. Dec. 19, 1833; m. Nelson Washburn, Nov. 20, 1855; c.; d. 1875.

12 | *Charles T.,* b. Aug. 13, 1854.

13 | *Edward,* b. March 8, 1857; d. Jan. 2, 1862, æ. 4 yrs., 9 mos.

14 | *William N.,* b. Nov. 22, 1858.

15 | *Julia M.,* b. April 5, 1866; d. Aug. 13, 1869, æ. 3 yrs., 4 mos.

2– 8 | GEORGE CRAGIN m. Sarah Miles, Nov. 7, 1851 ; b. in Salem, Mass., June 6, 1832.

16 | *Sarah Ella*, b. Nov. 13, 1862.

2– 10 | JOHN CRAGIN occupies the Thomas Upton farm. He m. Maria S. Ober, dau. of Hezekiah and Prudence Poor Ober, Dec. 16, 1858. Selectman in 1873, '4.

17 | *Lizzie Maria*, b. Jan. 21, 1863.

THE CRAM FAMILY.

1 | NATHAN CRAM, son of Nathan Cram, of Lyndeboro, m. Elizabeth White, dau. of John White, of Peterborough. He removed to Belfast, Me. He was drowned in 1815, and his wife returned to Peterborough, and subsequently married Michael McCrillis, and d. Feb. 9, 1858, æ. 77 yrs. He was b. 1780, and d. Oct. 23, 1815, æ. 35 yrs.

2 | *Almira*, b. Belfast, Me., June 2, 1806 ; m. Rufus Forbush ; r. Peterborough.

3 | *Hannah M.*, b. Belfast, Me., July 4, 1808 ; m. Bowdoin McCrillis ; r. Clarendon, N. Y.

4 | *Sarah E.*, b. Belfast, Me., Oct. 20, 1810 ; m. William Stanley ; r. Winchendon, Mass.

5 | *Elisabeth R.*, b. Belfast, Me., Feb. 28, 1812 ; d. Oct. 9, 1835, æ. 23 yrs.

2 | JOSEPH CRAM was a brother of the above, b. March 26, 1791 ; m. Sally White, dau. John White, July 4, 1817. He first settled in Belfast, Me. Returned first to Hancock, and then to Peterborough. She d. Aug. 19, 1864, æ 73 yrs., 10 mos. He d. at Brattleboro, Vt., Nov. 30, 1874, æ. 83 yrs., 8 mos.

6 | *Elizabeth*, b. Belfast, March 15, 1822 ; unm. ; r. Brattleboro, Vt.

7 | *Hannah Jane*, b. Waldo, Me., April 20, 1825 ; m. Oct. 27, 1847, B. N. Chamberlain, Brattleboro, Vt. ; one ch. living, Herbert B., b. Newport, Aug. 15, 1849.

8 | *John W.*, b. Waldo, Me., July 5, 1830 ; d. March 12, 1840, æ. 9 yrs.

9 | *Harriet H.*, b. Antrim, Feb. 25, 1833 ; m. John P. Liscom ; r. Brattleboro.

THE CRANE FAMILY.

1 | HENRY CRANE was b. Milton, Mass., Feb. 22, 1758, and moved from Newton to Peterborough in 1795. He was a

paper-maker, and probably came to town to work in Samuel Smith's new mill, just then put in operation. He m., 1785, Elizabeth Thompson, dau. Dea. Robert Thompson, who d. July 10, 1808, æ. 84 yrs. They removed to Franklin late in life, and died there. He d. Aug. 3, 1829, æ. 71 yrs., 5 mos ; she d. Aug. 2, 1835, æ. ——.

2   *Edith S.*, b. Oct. 2, 1786 ; m. William Bent ; d. June 12, 1866 ; r. Enfield, Conn.

3   *Betsey T.*, b. Jan. 1, 1788 ; m. Moses Hayden ; r. Ohio.

4   *Patience*, b. March 20, 1789 ; m., 1st hus., Wm. Bailey ; 2d hus., Jonathan Marsh. She d. Aug. 13, 1850, æ. 61 yrs., 4 mos.

5   *Henry*, b. March 2, 1791 ; m. Catharine Richards ; d. April 30, 1852, æ. 61 yrs. ; r. Dorchester, Mass.

6   *Charles*, b. Newton, November, 1792 ; m. Betsey Buss, September, 1817 ; ch., (1) Ariana B., b. Milton, July 25, 1819 ; d. Peterborough, July 8, 1836, æ. 16 yrs., 11 mos. ; (2) Augusta B., b. Dec. 14, 1821 ; m. Prof. Ephraim Knight, A.M., of New London, April 20, 1847 ; ch., Sherbert, b. Jan. 1, and d. Jan. 27, 1850, æ. 27 dys. ; Carl Ephraim, b. May 6, 1851 ; William M., b. May 20, 1855 ; Mabel Adele, b. April 17, 1859 ; d. July 25, 1871, æ. 12 yrs., 2 mos. ; (3) Charles T., b. March 28, 1823 ; m. Oct. 10, 1850, Jerusha Johnson ; ch., Flora M., Julia Buss, George F., Allen O. Charles d. at Milton, May 18, 1824, æ. 31 yrs.

7   *Robert T.*, b. in Newton, ——, 1794 ; m. Miriam Sanborn, of Franklin ; had nine children. He d. March 20, 1845, æ. 51 yrs.

8   *Isaac*, b. in Peterborough, May 20, 1796 ; m. Louis Greenleaf, of Salisbury ; five ch. He d. Nov. 7, 1857, æ. 61 yrs., 5 mos.

9   *Jeremiah S.*, b. June 4, 1798 ; a blacksmith ; went South and has never been heard of.

10   *Sally Jane*, b. June 17, 1800 ; unm. ; d. in Dorchester, Feb. 4, 1862, æ. 61 yrs., 7 mos.·
Children born before the family removed to Peterborough, and who never lived in town :—

THE CUNINGHAM FAMILY.

The history of this important family among the early settlers of Peterborough, must necessarily be very imperfect, as but few materials for this purpose are to be found in any quarter. We suppose they emigrated from the north of Ireland, and were of Scotch-Irish descent.

1   THOMAS CUNINGHAM, the name always spelt by the early settlers with one n, as here spelt, came to Peter-

borough about —— from Townsend, Mass. He was b. in 1706, and had two wives. Elizabeth, the 1st w., was b. 1706, and d. in Townsend, May 17, 1748, æ. 42 yrs. The 2d w., Elizabeth Creighton, came to Peterborough, and d. April 22, 1805, æ. 99 yrs. We are uncertain when he first came to town. He lived near the Dea. John Field place, just north, on the same side of the street road. He d. Sept. 23, 1790, æ. 84 yrs.

2	*Dohn*, b. ——; re. to Maine.
3	*William*, ——; re. to Maine.
4	† *James*, b. 1744; m. Mary Nay.
5	†*Samuel*, b. July, 1739; m. Susan M. Carter, of Hollis.
6	*Elizabeth*, b. ——; m. Alexander Robbe.
7	*Mary*, b. ——; m., 1st hus., James McKean; 2d hus., Samuel Treadwell.
8	*Moses*, b. 1751; m. Elizabeth Miller; he d. Oct. 25, 1822, æ. 71 yrs.
9	*Thomas*, b. ——; re. to Maine.

1– 4   JAMES CUNINGHAM lived in the east part of the town, directly west of the Cuningham Pond, on the place afterwards occupied by his son James. We do not know the precise time when he first occupied this farm, probably not far from 1770, though he had lived in town some years previous. He m. Mary Nay, dau. of Dea. William and Mary Ecles Brownlee McNee. He d. Oct. 29, 1826, æ. 82 yrs. She d. Jan. 31, 1811, æ. 66 yrs.

Not a single inhabitant of this name and race now remains in town, and only a few descendants. The name was formerly spelled Kinacum, and, thus pronounced, was in common use in our early days. It is a name that occurs often in the early records of the town. Thomas Cuningham, the father, was selectman in 1763, and tithingman in 1764; but his son James was much more employed in the town affairs. He was selectman in 1775, tithingman 1774, '80, '83, and one of the Committee of Safety 1779.

10	*Sarah*, b. Dec. 11, 1771; m. Paul Hale.
11	*Thomas*, b. Oct. 26, 1773; m. Susan Cuningham, dau. Samuel Cuningham.
12	*William*, b. May 18, 1775; m. Susan Carter, Northport, Me.
13	† *James*, b. April 27, 1777; m., 1st w., Hannah Porter; 2d w., Sarah M. Cuningham.
14	*Samuel*, b. June 22, 1779; m. Dorothy Bachelder; r. Maine.
15	*Elizabeth*, b. May 2, 1783; m. Thomas F. Goodhue, June

2, 1808; ch., (1) Elizabeth; (2) Thomas; (3) Jane; (4) Charles.

16 *Robert*, b. Nov. 2, 1785; m.; re. to Canada.

17 *John*, b. ——.

1– 5 SAMUEL CUNINGHAM (Capt.) was the most distinguished of this family. It is related, in a note in[*] Mr. Dunbar's sketch of Peterborough, that Thomas Cuningham (son of Old Mose, so called) and Samuel Cuningham were out in the French war in 1756, when he was only seventeen years old, and that in Rodgers' fight, March 13, 1758, he and Alexander Robbe only escaped, while seven men from Peterborough were slain. He was a stern patriot in the times of the Revolution, and served his country faithfully; but just how long or much we are unable to say. We have no means of accurately tracing his military career. He was among those who volunteered on the alarm of the Lexington battle, April 19, 1775. He was a captain in the Revolutionary service, and was with the army in Rhode Island in 1778. He was a lieutenant in a company raised in Peterborough and New Ipswich to resist the progress of Burgoyne, and joined the army at Bennington, Vt. When the company in their course had fallen into an ambuscade of the tories, Cuningham's coolness saved it.[†] "With the voice of a lion he called out to one of the officers to bring up a body of five hundred men to flank the enemy; at which the tories fled, leaving behind them all their baggage and plunder, and an open and unmolested road to the main army. In this encounter, Hon. Jeremiah Smith, then a private, and several others were wounded." He held many offices in town; was selectman in 1768, '76, '79, '81; town clerk 1783, '84, '85,' '86; and representative to the legislature in 1786. He m. Susan Carter, of Hollis, in 1774. He lived on the place afterwards occupied by Capt. Robert Swan, in the east part of the town. Late in life he re. to Belfast, Me., and d. there. He d. February, 1828, æ. 89 yrs. She d. October, 1842, æ. 86 yrs., b. June 27, 1756.

---

18 *Susanna*, b. April 1, 1778; m. Thomas Cuningham; d. Belfast, Me.; seven ch.

19 *Thomas*, b. Feb. 10, 1780; m. Charlotte Elwell; d. Belfast, Me.; five ch.

20 *Mary*, b. Feb. 6, 1782; m. Samuel Jackson; d. Belfast, Me.; four ch.

[*] Sketch of Peterborough, Rev. E. Dunbar, Historical Coll., note, page 138, vol. 3.
[†] Sketch of Peterborough, Rev. E. Dunbar, Historical Coll., note, page 138, vol. 3.

21 | *Elizabeth*, b. March 15, 1784 ; m. Thomas Caldwell.
22 | *Sarah M.*, b. May 4, 1786 ; m. James Cuningham, Jr.
23 | *Rachel*, b. May 10, 1788 ; m. Zacheus Porter ; r. Belfast, Me.
24 | *Jane*, b. June 10, 1790 ; m. Hudson Bishop ; r. Belfast, Me.; d. Jan. 21, 1874, æ. 84 yrs., 7 mos.
25 | *Samuel*, b. Nov. 5, 1792 ; m. Eliza Dummer ; r. Bucksport, Me.; d. November, 1870, æ. 78 yrs.
26 | *William*, b. June 17, 1795 ; m. Charlotte Nesmith ; r. Montville, Me. ; d. Sept. 9, 1871, æ. 76 yrs.
27 | *James*, b. Jan. 5, 1800 ; unm.; d. Belfast, Me.

4- 13 | JAMES CUNINGHAM, Jr., settled on the homestead, and took care of his parents in their last days. He m., 1st w., May 6, 1802, Hannah Porter. She d. July 10, 1804, æ. 25 yrs.; c. He m., 2d w., Sarah M. Cuningham, dau. of Samuel Cuningham, March 20, 1806. He re. to Rockford, Ill., in 1835, and d. there. She d. at Rockford.

---

28 | *Isaac Newton*, b. July 14, 1806 ; m. Nancy White, dau. Robert White.
29 | *James P.*, b. July 9, 1808 ; d. June 6, 1836, æ. 28 yrs.
30 | *Samuel*, b. ———, 1810 ; d. Aug. 5, 1813, æ. 3 yrs.
31 | *Thomas*, b. March 7, 1813 ; m.
32 | *Samuel*, b. Aug. 15, 1815 ; m. Emily Cutter, of Jaffrey ; r. Rockford, Ill.
33 | *William*, b. Nov. 5, 1817 ; went to California.
34 | *Benjamin F.*, b. Feb. 3, 1820.
35 | *Sarah H.*, b. Sept. 14, 1822 ; d. Sept. 10, 1835, æ. 13 yrs.
36 | *Rachel*, b. ———, 1824 ; d. Sept. 8, 1826, æ. 2 yrs.
37 | *George J.*, b. July 1, 1827 ; d. Aug. 8, 1831, æ. 5 yrs.

THE CUTLER FAMILY.

1 | JOHN H. CUTLER, M. D., son of Charles Cutler, of Rindge, and Melinda Wright, of Ashby, was b. Feb. 16, 1834. He received his education at the common and high schools of his native town, the Merrimack Normal Institute at Reed's Ferry, and at the Westminster Seminary, Vt. He pursued his medical studies in the office of Dr. O. H. Bradley, of East Jaffrey ; attended medical lectures at Pittsfield and Burlington, at which latter place he took his medical degree of M.D., June 9, 1861. After practising his profession in New Ipswich and Mason Village, he entered the army as assistant surgeon in the spring of 1864, and remained till the close of the war. After leaving the United States service, and looking at several fields for practice, he located himself in Peter-

Daniel B. Cutter

borough, in the fall of 1865, and has resided here since ;
m., June 6, 1865, Martha Louise Ryan, b. in Sharon,
Nov. 30, 1845.

2 | *Samuel Ryan*, b. April 29, 1866.
3 | *Charles Henry*, b. Sept 9, 1867.
4 | *Castella Melinda*, b. Nov. 21, 1869.
5 | *Martha Evangeline*, b. Oct. 20, 1875.

THE CUTTER FAMILY.

1 | DANIEL B. CUTTER, (Dr.) son of Daniel and Sally Jones
Cutter, of Jaffrey, b. May 10, 1808, came to town as a practising physician in 1837. He graduated at Dartmouth
College in 1833, and took his medical degree at Yale
College, New Haven, in 1835. He spent two years in
the practice of medicine at Ashby, Mass., before he removed to Peterborough. He has held important offices
in town ; moderator for 1848, '49, '50 ; representative
to General Court, 1852. He m., 1st w., Clementine Parker, dau. of Hon. Asa Parker, Jaffrey, Dec. 8, 1835 ;
she d. Aug. 28, 1870 ; 2d w., Mrs. Tryphena T. Richardson, Dec. 5, 1872.

2 | *Lucia Antoinette*, b. Sept. 7, 1836 ; d. July 25, 1854, æ.
18 yrs.
3 | *Isabella P.*, b. July 6, 1847 ; m. Albert Noone ; d. March
16, 1871, æ. 23 yrs.

2 | EDWARD S. CUTTER, a graduate of Dartmouth Col-
lege, 1844, son of Daniel and Sally Jones Cutter, of
Jaffrey, was b. March 27, 1822. He studied law, and
practised his profession in town until he was appointed
Clerk of the Court of Hillsboro Co., when he removed
to Amherst. He was moderator in town, 1852, '56, '57,
'58. He m., 1st w., Janet Swan, May 21, 1850. She d.
1873, æ. 42 yrs.; m., 2d w., Dec. 21, 1874, Sarah A. Lord,
of Boston.

4 | *Edward J.*, b. July 5, 1855.
5 | *Henry A.*, b. Oct. 27, 1857.
6 | *Anna L.*, b. June 13, 1863.
7 | *Leonard T.*, b. Nov. 3, 1871.

THE DAVIS FAMILY.

1 | ASA DAVIS, son of Asa and Lydia Laughton Davis, of
Hancock, was b. Oct. 7, 1806, received his education at
the common schools, which were then very limited, and

7

spent his early life on the farm with his parents to his majority. The first three years after were spent in stone work and road building; the first year in stone work, and in the subsequent two years he contracted and built ten miles of the Forest Road, so called, between Marlow and Hancock. He then purchased the Bradford Mills in 1833, and carried them on six years. In 1839 he re. to Peterborough, having purchased of Gen. James Wilson a half of the old grist-mill formerly owned by Job Hill, and in partnership with him built the granite-mill as it now stands. After its erection it was fitted up in the best possible manner for grinding all kinds of grain, and especially for a flouring-mill. It was soon, under his care, one of the best establishments of the kind in the State. The adjoining dwelling-house was built in 1841. He carried on this mill for nine years with great success and reputation, so that it was resorted to from all this region which imposed upon him such a degree of labor that his health failed, and he was compelled to withdraw from the business. He sold out in 1848 to Thayer & Buckminster. He commenced trading in "Powers Building" in 1848, having purchased the same in 1846, which business he still continues at the same place. He also carries on a large business in quarrying stone on Granite Street. He lives on Pine Street, in the house south of Albert S. Scott's, on same side of the road, and opposite to the house of F. A. Tarbell; Representative 1854; Selectman 1856, '57, '58, '66, '67, '68; Overseer of the Poor eight or nine years; Road Agent nine years, and also many minor offices in town. m., Dec. 15, 1831, Permelia Washburn, dau. John Washburn, of Hancock; b. Lempster, June 28, 1810.

2   *Adelia A.*, b. in Hancock, Oct. 19, 1832.
3   *Anna M.*, b. in Hancock, Dec. 14, 1833.
4   *Wilbur E.*, b. in Hancock, March 7, 1838; m. Aug. 19, 1864, Ann E. Carson, of Chicopee, Mass., one ch., Marion, b. Aug. 26, 1875.
5   *Charlie Freddie*, b. April 10, 1850; d. Sept. 13, 1853, æ. 3 yrs., 5 mos.

THE DAVISON FAMILY.

1   THOMAS DAVISON (Deacon) came to this country from Ireland, and settled in Londonderry when he was quite a young man. His brother, John Davison, and his father-in-law, Matthew Wright, came with him when he emigrated to Peterborough, and settled in Jaffrey. Matthew Wright's oldest daughter is said to be the first

child born in Jaffrey. Deacon Davison had a large family of ten children. He was b. in 1727; m. Anna Wright, 1757. He d. April 11, 1813, æ. 86 yrs. She d. Jan. 4, 1823, æ. 88 yrs. He began the place in the south-western part of the town where he lived and died. There is some uncertainty as to the precise time he came to town. It must have been after his marriage, which occurred not far from 1757, as the first child, Thomas, was b. Dec. 20, 1758. It was probably in 1757 that he took up his permanent residence here.

Mr. Davison was a deacon in the Presbyterian Church, and his name is among the remonstrants to Mr. Dunbar's settlement in 1799; but he subsequently joined his church in 1802, and retained his connection till his death. As to his religious character we know nothing. It is supposed that he met all the requirements of his office. Mr. Dunbar, April 12, 1813, makes this record in the Church Book: Attended the funeral of the aged and venerable Deacon Thomas Davison; preached at the house of the deceased from Luke 2d ch., 29, 30 vs. Deacon Davison's name appears on the Town Records in 1764 as Deer-keeper (what was his function?), and in 1778 as one of the Committee of Safety, an office which none could hold but tried patriots.

He was a man of much energy of character, and by his industry and perseverance succeeded well in life. He first purchased one hundred acres of land, and after making some improvements upon it, he bought land in Jaffrey, near the south-west corner of Peterborough, and built a saw-mill on the Contoocook River, probably on the spot of the Chamberlain Mills, so called. This mill he carried on for many years, going from home in the morning and returning in the evening, a distance of more than two miles. He gave his sons farms, and to most of his daughters he gave land. To his son William he gave the home farm, and all the land west of Deacon Robert Smith's farm to the Jaffrey line, and the land south to the Sharon line. He was considered a temperate man in his day, and it is not supposed that he transmitted tastes and appetites to his descendants that have resulted in the ruin of so many of his sons and grandsons. It has been supposed that the tendency to this vice in Deacon Davison's family came from the maternal side, and was owing to the injurious influence of Matthew Wright upon the young men. Mr. Wright was a man of superior talents and attractive powers, but very intemperate. He professed to be an infidel, and wished everybody he met to be like himself. His opinions were very abhorrent to the people of his day. It

was said that, on the day of his death, he called his son
Francis to his bedside and said : "When I am dead, I
want you to *tak* the big jug and gang down to New
Ipswich and get it filled with rum, and when I am buried
give the poor divils all the rum they want." We are indebted to George W. Moore, of Medina, Mich., for most
of the above.

---

2 | *Thomas,* b. Dec. 20, 1758 ; m. Betsey Pierce, of Dublin ;
two ch., Asa and Jonas.

3 | *Charles,* b. Sept. 10, 1760 ; m. Abigail Evans, June,
1785 ; c. He d. Dec. 31, 1831, æ. 71 yrs. She d.
April 4, 1842, æ. 74 yrs. ; b. Sept. 15, 1768.

4 | *Mary,* b. May 2, 1762 ; m. Maj. Jotham Hoar.

5 | *Sarah,* b. Feb. 15, 1766 ; m. Samuel Patrick, of Jaffrey ;
six ch.

6 | † *William,* b. Feb. 6, 1768 ; m., 1st w., Abigail Hunt ; 2d
w., Jane Wright.

7 | *Betsey,* b. —— ; m. Dr. —— Frisby ; r. Phelpstown, N.
Y. ; three ch.

8 | *John,* b. —— ; was in U. S. service, war of 1812 ; d. at
Lewiston, N.Y.

9 | *Robert,* b. —— ; m. Dolly Phelps ; re. to Canada ; nine
ch.

10 | *Anna,* b. —— ; m. Capt. Alpheus Dodge ; r. Derby, Vt. ;
eight ch.

11 | *Hannah,* b. —— ; m. Dr. Ezra Clark ; re. West ; two ch.

1— 6 | WILLIAM DAVISON. He settled on the homestead and
lived there during his life. He m. Abigail Hunt, sister
to Deacon Timothy Hunt, July 9, 1795. She d. Feb.
29, 1796, æ. 24 yrs. He m., 2d w., Nov. 15, 1798, Jane
Wright, his cousin, b. Nov. 18, 1777 ; d. April 1, 1860,
æ. 82 yrs. She was the mother of all his children. He
died of a cancer Jan. 29, 1838, æ. 70 yrs. The farm is
yet in possession of the family.

---

12 | *Matthew W.,* b. Feb. 27, 1799 ; unm. ; d. Sept. 25, 1835,
æ. 36 yrs.

13 | *Abigail,* b. Jan. 27, 1802 ; m. Moses Cutter Jaffrey ;
three ch.

14 | *Thomas,* b. Aug. 28, 1806 ; unm.

15 | *Francis,* b. Sept. 6, 1808 ; unm. ; d. Oct. 31, 1832, æ.
25 yrs.

16 | *William,* b. Sept. 9, 1810 ; unm. ; in poorhouse, Branch
County, Mich., by intemperance.

17 | *John,* b. Dec. 3, 1812 ; m. —— ; r. Holyoke, Mass.

18 | *Charles,* b. Feb. 19, 1816 ; d.

19 | Calvin, b. Nov. 16, 1818 ; unm. ; d. May 7, 1850, æ. 31
yrs.
20 | Jane, b. Jan. 25, 1821 ; m. —— Nichols ; d. about 1848.

THE DAY FAMILY.

1 | JOSEPH DAY was the son of Robert Day, who lived in the south part of Greenfield. He was b. in Andover, Mass., Sept 19, 1777 ; m. Esther Tuel. After marriage he moved to Vermont. She was the mother of his six children. Mr. Day moved to Peterborough in 1823, and bought and occupied the place on which John H. Holt now lives, till 1843, when he re. to Bennington, where he d. June, 1850, æ. 72 yrs., 8 mos. ; 1st w. d. at Antrim, 1829 ; m., 2d w., Widow Peavey.

2 | Joseph, b. Sept. 19, 1801 ; d. in Georgia, 1841.
3 | Esther S., b. Dec. 21, 1803 ; m. —— ; d. 1871, æ. 68 yrs.
4 | Mary, b. March 1, 1805 ; d. July, 1829, æ. 24 yrs., 4 mos.
5 | Robert, b. Washington, Nov, 23, 1807 ; m. Lydia N. Carr.
6 | Henry Payson, b. Rindge, April 8, 1812 ; d. 1815.
7 | George J., b. Feb. 16, 1816 ; d. young.

1- 5 | ROBERT DAY came to town with his father's family in 1823 ; was trained to the cabinet-making trade. Commenced business in 1832, having bought the shop of Moses Dodge, situated near to the North Factory ; m. Lydia N. Carr, Dec. 4, 1832. He sold his property in town, and re. to the North Branch, Antrim, April, 1874, where he now resides.

8 | German, b. April 17, 1834 ; m. Hannah Forbush, Oct. 10, 1861 ; one ch., Katie H.
9 | Edwin, b. July 5, 1836 ; now lives in Exeter ; of firm of Hobbs & Day, photographic artists.
10 | Mary, b. Sept. 8, 1838 ; m. Samuel S. Sawyer, of Antrim, May 15, 1861.
11 | Louisa, b. Feb. 9, 1841 ; m. Horace Gowing, July 13, 1869 ; r. Wakefield, Mass.
12 | Harry, b. Jan. 21, 1845 ; d. of consumption Aug. 17, 1867, æ. 22 yrs., 6 mos.

THE DIAMOND FAMILY.

1 | WILLIAM DIAMOND was b. in Boston, July 21, 1755, where he served his time in apprenticeship to the wheelwright trade. He re. to Lexington in 1775, where he continued to reside till he came to Peterborough in 1795.

He first occupied the place where Asa Carley lived for five years, and then bought and begun the farm where John D. Diamond now lives. He d. on this place, suddenly, July 29, 1828, æ. 73 yrs. He m. Rebecca Symonds, of Lexington, b. Sept. 1, 1762. She d. April 8, 1855, æ. 92 yrs., 7 mos.

Mr. Diamond was a drummer in the military service of his country, and said that he learned this art of a British soldier who was stationed at Boston. Mr. Diamond was the drummer of the sixty or seventy militia or minute men who stood on Lexington Common on the morning of April 19, 1775. He said he knew the name of every man who was on parade that morning. Whether there was anything menacing in the attitude or appearance of these men, history does not tell us. It is certain they evinced no fear, and probably cast a look of defiance upon their invaders. • They did not mean to be the aggressors, but waited till they were attacked, slaughtered, murdered, before they fired. The British, on their refusal to surrender, thought to make summary work with such a handful of men, and at once poured into their ranks a deadly volley of shots. At the first fire five were killed, and as many at the second, and a considerable number wounded. It was a dastardly act, — so many well-armed and disciplined soldiers firing a deadly volley into a handful of undisciplined, unarmed militia. It gloriously opened the ball of the Revolution. After the first fire, Capt. Parker told every man to take care of himself. Mr. Diamond said he had to step over the body of one of his comrades when he started to run, and that he took the Bedford road from the Common, and wishing to disencumber himself of his drum, he found he could not detach it, so he slipped it over his head, and by so doing he threw off his hat. He then threw his drum over the wall, and stooping to pick up his hat he saw the British bayonets so near him that he had to run for life and leave it. Nothing daunted, and having obtained a musket and ammunition of a man who had neither the courage nor the disposition to use it himself, he rushed on to Concord, and reaching the town before the British troops, he took part in the fight there, and with his brave comrades hung on the rear of the invaders all the way from Concord through Lincoln and Lexington, till the British were reinforced by twelve hundred men below Lexington. Mr. Diamond recognized among the troops the soldier who had taught him to drum, who endeavored to make a sign to him of the hostile and deadly intent of the invaders, but he was not then understood.

Mr. Diamond at once entered the service of the Colonies, and was subsequently at the Battle of Bunker Hill. He thought that Gen. Warren threw his life away by needlessly exposing himself during the battle. He served all through the war of the Revolution as a drummer. He received a pension in his last days, which at his death was continued to his wife during her long life.

---

2   *Rebecca*, b. Lexington, Sept. 20, 1783; m. Joseph Mace.

3   † *William*, b. Lexington, Nov. 20, 1785; m. Lucinda Haggett, Nov. 18, 1824.

4   *Mary*, b. Lexington, April 5, 1788; m. Joseph Johnson, Greenfield; d. 1857, æ. 71 yrs.

5   † *John S.*, b. Lexington, Aug. 9, 1790; m. Octavia Davis, of Concord, Mass.

6   *Elizabeth*, b. Lexington, March 4, 1792; m. James Barker; re. Wisconsin.

7   *Lydia*, b. Peterborough, May 6, 1797; m. Aaron Avery; re. Wisconsin.

1– 3   WILLIAM DIAMOND. He lived in the east part of the town on a farm directly west of his father's. He m. Lucinda Haggett, dau. of Abner Haggett, Nov. 18, 1824. He d. Jan. 25, 1872, æ. 86 yrs. A few years before his death he sold his farm, and bought the William White place, where he died.

---

8   *Mary Louisa*, b. ——; m. Frank Condy; one ch., Ida.

9   *Caroline*, b. ——; m. Joseph Fifield, Roxbury, Mass.

10 *Elizabeth*, b. ——; m. Gorham Hall, Manchester; d. ——.

1– 5   JOHN S. DIAMOND m. Octavia Davis, of Concord, Mass., Dec. 28, 1819; b. Oct. 12, 1800. They have always lived in town. He is a wheelwright by trade. He is now living on the old homestead.

---

11 † *John Davis*, b. Aug. 6, 1821; m. Laura Ann Farwell.

12 *Octavia Lavina*, b. Aug. 18, 1825; m. Daniel Edes, Jr., March 29, 1853.

5– 11   JOHN DAVIS DIAMOND. He lives on the old homestead, and is a wheelwright by trade. He m. Laura Ann Farwell, b. June 23, 1834.

---

13 *Laura Ada*, b. July 21, 1854.

14 *George F.*, b. July 26, 1856.

15 *John C.*, b. Oct. 23, 1863.

16 *Nettie Helen*, b. July 12, 1870.

THE DODGE FAMILY.

1 MOSES DODGE, son of Nathaniel and Sally Bailey Dodge, was b. in New Boston, March 17, 1779, where he spent his youth. He learned the carpenter's trade in Vermont. Came to Peterborough in 1814 to build the machinery of the North Cotton Factory in company with Andrew Harris. He remained here through his life. He at one time carried on the cabinet-making business. He d. 1850, æ. 71 yrs. He m. Sally Richardson, of Holliston, Mass. He was Selectman 1829, '30, '31. He was much respected as a worthy and honest man.

THE DUNBAR FAMILY.

1 ELIJAH DUNBAR, Jr., (Rev.) was the son of Elijah and Sarah Dunbar, of Canton, Mass., and grandson of Rev. Samuel Dunbar of that part of Stoughton now Canton. He was b. July 7, 1773. A sermon preached by Rev. Jason Haven in Dedham, Mass., on Sunday, June 18, 1783, at the funeral of the Rev. Samuel Dunbar, pastor of the first church and society in that town gives the following facts : He was in the seventy-ninth year of his age and the fifty-sixth of his ministry. Mr. Dunbar was a decided friend of the liberties of his country. In 1775 he was Chaplain to Col. Brown's regiment in the expedition against Crown Point. His zeal and firmness in the Revolution contributed not a little to support the hopes and sustain the sinking spirits of the people when cloud and darkness shrouded our prospects. This man was reported to have left seven thousand manuscript sermons. They were written in characters peculiar to himself, so that no one now can decipher them, and, perhaps, with no great loss to the world either.

Rev. E. Dunbar was fitted for college by his grandfather, the above, and entered Harvard College in 1790, and graduated in due course in 1794. We may form some idea of his scholarship in college from the fact that immediately on graduating he was selected as a tutor in Mathematics in Williams College, Williamstown, Mass., just then organized and commencing operation. He remained here two years and then studied divinity. It seems that he came and preached at Stoddard before he was engaged in this town. He was ordained over the church and society Oct. 23, 1799, and remained pastor of same twenty-seven years, till Feb. 25, 1827, when he preached his last sermon as minister of this society, and was formally dismissed June 27, 1827. He never en-

gaged in another pastorate. He preached occasionally
for some years, retaining his faculties in full to the last.
For the last five years of his life he resided at Milford
with his wife's sister, Clarissa Peabody, where he died
Sept. 3, 1850, æ. 77 yrs. His funeral was held at the
Unitarian church in Peterborough on the 7th of September, and the services were conducted by Rev. Levi W.
Leonard, D.D., and the Rev. Liberty Billings, then pastor of the Congregational Society. Mr. Leonard
preached a sermon on the occasion; and then his remains were consigned to that last resting-place on the
Meeting-house Hill, where he had so long ministered in
all seasons and weathers, and to the old cemetery hal-
lowed by so many associations of the old and venerated
inhabitants of Peterborough. He always lived on the
same place in town after his marriage,—the farm north
of the John Little place, which he held in his possession
till his death.

Mr. Dunbar published very little during his life. All
that has been found is a catechism called the "Peterborough Catechism," prepared to aid him in catechising the
children in 1815. It is very rare, and mankind will sustain but little loss if it becomes entirely extinct. He
also published a sermon preached at the funeral of Rev.
Edward Sprague, Dec. 18, 1817; and a sketch of Peterborough in Moore and Farmer's Historical Collections
in 1822, which has been the basis of all the gazetteer notices of Peterborough hitherto.

It is not the antiquary alone that has to lament that
during the late war of the Rebellion the price of old paper became so high that almost every family, all through
the country, cleared out their attics of all accumulated
papers, pamphlets, and useless books, to the serious det-
riment of literature and of all town historians. It is to
this cause no doubt that these publications have become
so scarce.

Mr. Dunbar had few of the graces of oratory, or even
of good elocution, but his enunciation was always good,
his voice sufficiently loud and clear to be heard in all
parts of the house. He was free from any disagreeable
intonation, or any peculiar or sanctified tone, and was
always natural in his manner of speaking. This is more
than could be said of the clergy generally seventy-five
or even fifty years ago. There was almost always a
peculiar manner assumed in the services of public worship, such as a drawl, or a peculiarly holy tone, or a
wrong emphasis or accent on certain words, or a vitiated
pronunciation of words which were of most frequent occurrence, and indeed such a manner of speaking as was

8

met with nowhere else but in the pulpit. We could not say that Mr. Dunbar's manner of speaking was pleasing, but it was respectable and free from great faults. He stood up without a single gesture and read his sermon, holding it up with one hand before him, which was written on paper folded in a duodecimo form (6x3½ inches size), — the usual form of the sermons of that day.

The sermons, as I remember them, would vary from three-fourths to an hour in length, and the whole service was rarely less than an hour and a half long ; and will it be believed in this generation that all this must take place in cold weather, in a cold house, to which no fire ever approached, so that it got to be the general belief that public worship and artificial heat were incompatibles ? How often Mr. Dunbar has preached in the old meeting-house on the hill in dead of winter one sermon, for his hearers could endure no more, for fear of freezing to death, and yet all these same worshippers would have deemed a fire in the church an effeminacy and impropriety of the grossest kind. In all his ministry he never knew the luxury of a fire in the meeting-house till his last year, when he preached in the new church.

Many persons not acquainted with Mr. Dunbar have thought that he was a man of inferior talents, because he knew so little of men and things, and withal was so credulous and unsuspecting. This was a great mistake. He possessed an intellect of a high order ; he was a brilliant scholar, and if he could only have been able to keep pace with the progress in his profession, could have had leisure and the books and literature of his time, he would have left a name among the very first.

He had never kept up with the times, a thing impossible for him, situated as he was, and perhaps it might have been this circumstance more than any other that led to his dismission, while he was yet in his full prime. He was called old-fashioned ; his preaching was dull, his manner uninteresting ; he used the old phraseology without the old dogma ; was entirely unacquainted with what was going on in the theological world at the very time when Unitarianism was just emerging to the light in Massachusetts, in the controversies of Channing, Wood, and Stuart. Mr. Dunbar was always genial and pleasant, and in his manner polite and courteous. In his conversation he always used the best language, never in his life uttering a low or slang phrase. He was an agreeable talker, always clearly and directly expressing what he wished to say, though it could not perhaps be said that he was very highly gifted in this respect.

Mr. Dunbar never spoke *extempore*. On all occasions he committed to writing all he had to say. This was peculiarly the case at funerals, where the addresses to friends were carefully prepared beforehand. He never cultivated his powers of *extempore* speaking, in which I have no doubt he might have been eminently successful, from his ready command of language and the choice of the best words in his common conversation. This seems the more strange as he was cast into the midst of a generation distinguished above all things else for their wonderful faculty in public speaking. It was rare in the history of any town that so many ready, fluent, and forcible speakers should appear at one time, as were exhibited some fifty or seventy-five years ago,—such men as John Smith, James Wilson, Thomas Steele, John Steele, Jona. Smith, John Scott, Daniel Robbe, Samuel Smith, and many others. It may be that Mr. Dunbar was fearful to try his powers of *extempore* speaking in the presence of such men, and, like Addison, being conscious that he could draw for a large amount if he had but a small amount in his pocket, he went on through life without any effort to improve this faculty.

He was always very happy in his funeral exercises. His pleasant countenance and sympathizing words afforded great comfort to mourners. In these services he always felt warmly and sincerely for the bereaved, and his utterances of sympathy and condolence were always natural, and the result of a kind heart and disposition. It may be that by his kind feelings he was prompted to laud the deceased more than circumstances would warrant ; nevertheless, it was all heartfelt and sincere. He strictly adhered to the old Latin motto, " *Nil de mortuis nisi bonum,*" to say nothing of the dead but good. His manner of addressing mourners sometimes seemed inflated and somewhat theatrical ; yet it was all so sincere and solemn no one ever felt that there was any impropriety. He was always exceedingly respectful in the adoption of terms, though those terms would remind one of the high-wrought and princely expressions of Shakespeare rather than the beautiful simplicity of the Bible.

He was a man of large stature, with a pleasant, genial face, and agreeable manners, and one of the very pleasant reminiscences of him is that of his passing into church (the old meeting-house), bowing gracefully to the various persons in the pews on each side of the broad aisle, and doing the same at the conclusion of the services. As long as he preached it was the custom for the congregation to remain standing in the pews until the minister had passed out, and this custom was only changed in 1827 or 1828 by a direct vote of the Congre-

gational Society. He enjoyed uniform good health all
his life down to his last sickness. He never failed in
his services on the Sabbath, unless such inclemencies of
the weather occurred that no one could venture out, or
dared to endure the hardship of hearing a long sermon in a cold and open meeting-house, situated more
than half a mile from any human habitation or fire.
Although he was allowed three Sundays in a year, yet
he never once thought of appropriating them except for
necessary absence to visit friends. He knew nothing of
the modern idea of a minister's vacation ; his only idea
was to work on, to work on to the end. He m. Anna
Peabody, dau. of Wm. Peabody, Esq., of Milford, Dec.
15, 1803. She d. July 25, 1828, æ. 44 yrs.

2 | *William P.*, b. Sept. 20, 1804 ; unm. ; r. Hancock.
3 | *Abigail W.*, b. Jan. 15, 1806 ; unm.; r. Hancock.
4 | *Horatio N.*, b. March 5, 1807 ; m. Sarah J. Robinson ; r.
     Milford.
5 | *Stephen*, b. June 22, 1808 ; m. Jane Bruce, Mount Ver-
     non.
6 | *Sarah A.*, b. Oct. 12, 1809 ; m. Nahum Warren ; d. in
     Dublin.
7 | *John S.*, b. Aug. 2, 1811 ; unm. ; d.
8 | *James M.*, b. Dec. 4, 1817 ; m., 1st w., Harriet D. Gould ;
     2d w., Irena Holden.
9 | *Henry W.*, b. June 28, 1822 ; m. Maria A. Holt ; di-
     vorced 1874.
10 | *J. Quincy A.*, b. July 20, 1824.

THE DUNCAN FAMILY.

1 | GEORGE DUNCAN was the son of John and Rachel
Todd Duncan, and grandson to George Duncan, who
emigrated to America, and lived and d. in Londonderry.
We are unable to fix the time he came to town, but it
was quite early. Most of his children were born in
Londonderry. He lived on the farm afterwards occu-
pied by Capt. Isaac Hadley. He m. Mary Bell, dau. of
John and Elizabeth Bell. She d. at Peterborough, Jan.
23, 1812, æ. 84 yrs. He d. May 29, 1810, æ. 86 yrs.
He was selectman in 1788, '89.

2 | *Betsey*, b. —— ; m. Rev. Samuel Taggart, of Colerain,
     Mass.
3 | *Rachel*, b. 1759 ; m. John Todd.
4 | *Esther*, b. —— ; m. Moses Black ; r. Boston.
5 | *Rosanna*, b. 1765 ; m. Ebenezer Moore.

6 | † *George, Jr.*, b. June 10, 1767 ; m., 1st w., Jane Ferguson ; 2d w., Betsey Taylor.
7 | *Sarah*, b. —— ; m. Robert McClellan, Colerain.
8 | *Mary*, b. —— ; m. Rev. Hugh Wallace ; r. Pompey, N. Y. ; d. 1802.

1– 6 | GEORGE DUNCAN, Jr., settled near his father's farm, long occupied afterward by William Gray, and now owned and occupied by the widow of Charles S. Gray. He was a man of talents, and was held in high estimation by his townsmen when he removed to the West. He held various offices in town ; was selectman 1805, '6, '7, '8, '9 ; surveyor of highways many years, from 1798 to 1807. He m., 1st w., Jane Ferguson, dau. of Henry Ferguson, March, 1798. She d. Jan. 16, 1802, æ. 29 yrs. She left one ch., Mary, who m. Judge Daniel Wells in 1824, of Greenfield, Mass. He m., 2d w., Betsey Taylor, widow of Charles Taylor, Dec. 2, 1805. She was the mother of the rest of his children. She d. at Preble, N. Y., Jan. 1, 1829, æ. 52 yrs. He m., 3d w., Annis Orr. She d. Feb. 9, 1868, æ. 78 yrs. He re. to Preble, N. Y., in 1813, and d. there Sept. 13, 1851, æ. 84 yrs.

9 | *Mary*, b. Dec. 28, 1798 ; m. 1824, Judge Daniel Wells ; r. Greenfield, Mass. ; he d. June 22, 1854.
10 | *Jane F.*, b. —— ; m. Silas Cummings, Preble, N. Y.
11 | *Henry*, b. —— ; d. in Byron, N. Y.
12 | *George*, b. —— ; d. in California.
13 | *Daniel*, b. —— ; d. Weedsport, N. Y.
14 | *Elizabeth*, b. —— ; m. Andrew Godcheus, Homer, N. Y.

THE DUSTAN FAMILY.

1 | GEORGE DUSTAN (Rev.), son of Jonathan and Sarah Morrison Center Dustan, was b. in Lebanon, Nov. 26, 1828. He graduated at Dartmouth College in 1852, and subsequently taught the academy at McIndoes Falls, Vt., for several years. He graduated at the Andover Seminary in 1859, and was ordained pastor over the Union Evangelical Church in Peterborough, Oct. 19, 1859, which position he now holds. He represented the town in the New Hampshire Legislature 1870, '71 ; was appointed by Gov. Stearns a Trustee of the State Normal School in 1870 ; has been a member of the School Board in Peterborough several years, and one of the Superintendents of the High School since its organization. He m., 1st w., Lucy A. Marsh, only dau. of Rev. Joseph and Lucy Dana Marsh, of Thetford, Vt., Feb. 14, 1855.

She d. Sept. 14, 1862, æ. 31 yrs. He m., 2d w., Sarah
L., only dau. of Deacon James B. and Adelaide Field
Nichols, May 4, 1864. Two ch., 1st w.; two ch., 2d w.

2 | *Dana M.*, b. Tunbridge, Vt., June 14, 1859.
3 | *George P.*, b. Peterborough, July 4, 1860.
4 | *Gertrude L.*, b. Aug. 19, 1868.
5 | *Grace Nichols*, b. Feb. 27, 1875.

THE EDES FAMILY.

This family traces its descent from the Eastern counties of England, as far back as 1517. The genealogy
has been carefully traced, with great labor and research,
by Richard S. Edes, of Bolton, Mass., and Henry Edes,
of Cambridge, Mass. It was a family of a good deal of
standing in society.

1 | SAMUEL EDES came to Peterborough in 1799, after all
his children were born. He was b. in Needham, Mass.,
Oct. 15, 1753, and d. in Peterborough, July 10, 1845, æ.
92 yrs. His 1st w., Elizabeth Baker, d. before he came
to Peterborough, and was the mother of all his children.
His 2d w., Sarah Hutchinson, d. in Peterborough, Oct.
20, 1816, æ. 64 yrs. His 3d w. was Widow Mary Eaton.
She d. June 4, 1864, æ. 89 yrs.

Mr. Edes was in the Battle of Lexington. He reported himself and seventeen others as being separated in
this battle from his companions, and being exposed to
great danger thereby. The night before the Battle of
Bunker Hill he was employed all night in driving oxen,
and was not allowed to speak above a whisper. He always lived on the same place in town, the same occupied
by his son, Isaac Edes.

2 | †*Samuel*, b. March 15, 1775; m. Mary Waite.
3 | *Catharine*, b. Feb. 16, 1777; m. Robert Carr; r. Hills-
boro. She d. ——.
4 | *Elizabeth*, b. July 15, 1779; m. —— Walker; re. Maine.
5 | *Sarah*, b. Sept. 6, 1781; m. John Howe; r. Temple, Me.
6 | *Joseph*, b. Sept. 10, 1783; re. Temple, Me.; was killed
by a neighbor 1863.
7 | *Jeremiah*, b. Aug. 24, 1785; re. New Jersey. Two ch.
8 | *Rebecca*, } b. Sept. 17, 1787. { m. —— Smith, Dedham.
9 | *Patience*, }
10 | †*Daniel*, b. Jan. 2, 1790; m. Jane Craige, Feb. 12, 1817.
11 | †*Amasa*, b. March 21, 1792; m. Sarah Hart, Keene.
12 | †*Isaac*, b. March 31, 1795; m. Elizabeth Mitchell.
13 | *Polly*, b. Dec. 6, 1797; m. Andrew Templeton; re. New
York.

1– 2 | SAMUEL EDES, Jr., m. Mary Waite, of Londonderry, May 9, 1794. He resided in Rome, N. Y., many years, where his first five ch. were b. The rest were b. in Peterborough. He was killed by the falling of the barn now owned by Charles McCoy, 2d, in the raising of the same June 15, 1816, æ. 41 yrs., 3 mos. She m., 2d hus., Dec. 4, 1820, Robert Carr, of Hillsboro ; d.

---

14 | *Mary*, b. April 27, 1796 ; d. Hillsboro.

15 | *Elizabeth*, b. Aug. 25, 1799 ; m. William Carter, Jaffrey ; d. Aug. 11, 1822, æ. 23 yrs. He d. Nov. 17, 1821.

16 | *Deidamia*, b. May 10, 1802 ; m. Hooper Runnels, Greenfield. He d. Aug. 30, 1862, æ. 64 yrs. She d.

17 | *Sarah*, b. Oct. 6, 1804 ; m. Gilman Bailey, Washington ; d. Washington.

18 | †*Samuel*, b. July 17, 1807 ; m., 1st w., Maria Corbin ; 2d w., Mrs. Miranda Corbin ; 3d w., Jennie Wilson.

19 | *Clarissa*, b. Greenfield, Feb. 27, 1810 ; m. —— Severance ; r. Washington.

20 | *Catharine*, b. Aug. 13, 1812 ; m. Joseph Tabor ; re. Minnesota.

21 | *Hiram Jason*, b. July 17, 1815 ; m. Ann Kelley in 1840. She d. in Missouri ; 2d w., Agnes P. Wood, 1856. She d. 1871, leaving one son, William Jason, b. April, 1858.

Hiram Jason Edes was early deprived of his father, and like his brother was thrown upon his own resources at an early age. He entered the Andover Academy, where he remained three years, during the time keeping a winter school each year. His health having failed he went to Virginia, and here attempted to complete his education at the Richmond College. But his health proving inadequate, he commenced the study of medicine, and attended his first course of Medical Lectures in the Medical Department of Yale College, Ct., and his second at Hampden, Sydney College, Prince Edwards County, Va., where he took his medical degree in 1844. He commenced practice in the city of Weston, Platt Co., Missouri, where he remained until the atrocious Kansas troubles arose, when he was proscribed and driven off on account of his political principles, and removed to Cedar Rapids, Ia., where he now resides in the practice of his profession. Since he was twelve years of age he has made his own way under all difficulties, getting a respectable education, and establishing himself in business, and suffering the great drawback the Kansas difficulties interposed, and finally building up a good character as a physician and a man. He says very modestly of himself that he is indebted for all his success in life to a good, Christian mother, to whom he promised in childhood never "to drink, play cards, or go to the theatre," and he has never disobeyed her.

I— 10   DANIEL EDES resided in various places in town, and at one time he owned and occupied the old farm of John Morison, in north-west part of the town, now abandoned. He m. Jane Craige, Feb. 12, 1817. She was b. Oct. 13, 1788; d. May 17, 1856, æ. 68 yrs. He d. June 22, 1860, æ. 70 yrs.

---

22   †*Daniel Edes, Jr.*, b. Nov. 3, 1817; m. O. Lavinia Diamond.
23   *Elizabeth Jane*, b. Oct. 22, 1819; unm.
24   *Isaac*, b. Jan. 17, 1826; d. March 6, 1829, æ. 3 yrs., 1 mos.

I— 11   AMASA EDES. He graduated at Dartmouth College in 1817. He studied law at Belfast, Me., with Wilson & Porter one year, and finished his studies at Keene with Hon. James Wilson, Sen. He was admitted to the bar in Cheshire County, October, 1822, and commenced the practice of his profession at Newport in 1823, where he now resides. He is now the oldest lawyer in the practice of law in the State; has, for many years, been president of the bar in Sullivan County. After his graduation in college, and until he was admitted to the bar in 1822, he was a very successful teacher, having for three years been the Principal of New Ipswich Academy, having taught an academical school in Hancock for six months, and also for three months in Newport in 1823. He represented the town of Newport in the Legislature of the State in 1834. He m. Sarah Hart, of Keene; b. in Chesterfield, July 5, 1795; d. Oct. 8, 1869, æ. 74 yrs., 3 mos.

---

25   *Joseph W.*, b. May 30, 1823; d. June 8, 1828, æ. 5 yrs.
26   *Samuel Hart*, b. March 31, 1825; graduated Dartmouth College 1844; m., Dec. 30, 1848, Julia A. Nourse, of Acworth. He is a lawyer by profession; has been Solicitor for the County of Sullivan; and also represented the town in the State Legislature in 1860.; ch., (1) George C., b. April 25, 1849; m. Lizzie M. Lyons, Nov. 10, 1873; (2) William A., b. Dec. 5, 1854; d. Sept. 22, 1872, æ. 17 yrs., 9 mos.; (3) Samuel W., b. Sept. 4, 1857; d. Sept. 23, 1858, æ. 1 yr.; (4) Maria J., b. Sept. 5, 1859.

1– 12 Isaac Edes succeeded his father on the old homestead. He m. Elizabeth Mitchell, April 24, 1823. She
d. Sept. 8, 1873, æ. 80 yrs., 4 mos. He was killed by
falling from a tree while picking apples. A limb broke,
and precipitated him with such force to the ground as to
destroy life immediately. He d. Oct. 26, 1859, æ. 64
yrs. He was much engaged in teaching in early life,
and was a deservedly popular instructor. He was selectman in 1835, '36, '37, '38. He was a respectable
and worthy man.

---

27 *Isaac*, b. Feb. 22, 1824; d. Feb. 25, 1824, æ. 3 dys.
28 *Elizabeth*, b. April 17, 1826; m. Aug. 23, 1859, William
Blanchard. She d. Oct. 22, 1867, æ. 41 yrs.
29 *Henry B.*, b. Jan. 24, 1829; d. Nov. 7, 1850, æ. 21 yrs.
30 *Martha M.*, b. Nov. 17, 1832; m. Robert B. Chalmers,
March 21, 1866; ch., (1) Annie Lizzie, b. July 26,
1867; (2) Henry Edes, b. Sept. 30, 1869; (3) Grace,
b. June 21, 1872; d. Aug. 9, 1872, æ. 1 mo., 18 dys.

2– 18 Samuel Edes, 3d. Being deprived of his father when
quite young, and his mother being left in a dependent
situation with a large family, he was early thrown upon
his own resources. When seventeen years of age he
went to New Ipswich and worked one year and a half in
the machine shop of Bachelder & Brown, and several
years as an overseer in their Cotton Factory. He returned to town in 1834 or 5, and carried on extensively
the Tin and Stove Manufacturing for some years, and
acquired, by his industry and attention to business, a
considerable wealth. He represented the town in the
State Legislature in 1857, '58. He m., 1st w., Feb. 2,
1830, Maria Corbin. She d. July 4, 1850, æ. 40 yrs.
He m., 2d w., Mrs. Miranda Corbin, March, 1853.
Failing to find harmony in his domestic relations, he
sought and obtained a decree of divorce from the Court
in September, 1868. He m., 3d w., Jennie Wilson, Oct.
1, 1868. He removed from Peterborough to Lake City,
Minn., 1860, where he now resides.

---

31 *Maria Eliza*, b. Nov. 4, 1831; m. Rev. Samuel Abbot
Smith, June 27, 1854.
32 *Samuel M.*, b. Aug. 12, 1833; d. Oct. 9, 1856, æ. 23 yrs.,
1 mos.
33 *Sarah A.*, b. October, 1837; d. 1838, æ. 9 mos.
34 *Sarah A.*, b. ——, 1839; m. Elbridge Sanderson, of
Boston, August, 1862; one son; d. when 3 years old.
She d. Nov. 1, 1866, æ. 28 yrs.

9

10– 22 | DANIEL EDES, Jr., m. March 29, 1854, O. Lavinia Diamond. He lives on the mountain, on a farm formerly occupied by Thomas Laws.

35 | *Helen Amanda*, b. May 6, 1855.

THE EVANS FAMILY.

1 | ASA EVANS was b. in Leominster, Mass., Oct 4, 1760. He came to town in 1784 or 5. We find him elected as one of the selectmen as early as 1793, and chosen to the same office for the twelve succeeding years. There was associated with him Thomas Steele, who was chosen every year from 1793 to 1805, and with them, Charles Stuart, six years to 1799.

Mr. Evans appears to have been one of the most enterprising and influential men of the town. He built and kept a public house, or in the language of the day "a tavern," in the same building now occupied for the same purpose, in the upper part of the village beyond the Peterborough Cotton Factory. He was also many years engaged in the mercantile business, and at the same time carried on a large farm. He had a large family of twelve children, the two eldest being born in Leominster, *viz.*, John and Asaph, and the rest in Peterborough. He m., 1st w., Oct. 25, 1781, Dorothy Buss, b. May 8, 1761. She d. Peterborough, Dec. 24, 1807, æ. 47 yrs. She was the mother of all his children. He m., 2d w., Margaret Moore, widow of late John Moore, and dau. of Charles Stuart, July 13, 1809. He d., after a short illness of five and a half days, Oct. 16, 1813, æ. 57 yrs. Mrs. Evans m. Richard Gilchrist, Sept. 15, 1816. She d. Aug. 7, 1818, æ. 50 yrs., 8 mos.

2 | *John*, b. Leominster, March 9, 1782 ; m. Martha Stuart, April 22, 1805 ; d. Boston, 1854, æ. 72 yrs.

3 | *Asaph*, b. Leominster, July 13, 1784 ; m., 1st w., Betsey Ferguson ; 2d w., Mary Green, of Concord ; 3d w., Widow Almira Davis. He d. New York City, February, 1842, æ. 58 yrs.

4 | *Samuel*, b. May 2, 1786 ; m., 1st w., Margaret Allison ; 2d w., Sarah Chase. He d. Hopkinton, Jan. 25, 1868, æ. 82 yrs.

5 | *Prudence*, b. Aug. 25, 1788 ; m. Dr. Wm. P. Cutter, of Jaffrey, March 26, 1807 ; m., 2d hus., Frederick Read. She d. Nov. 16, 1828, æ. 40 yrs.

6 | *Dorothy*, b. April 24, 1790 ; m. Timothy C. Ames, Jan. 14, 1813.

7 | *Artemas*, b. Jan. 29, 1792 ; m. Widow —— Wiggins, Concord. He d. May 25, 1818, æ. 26 yrs.

8 | *Luke,* b. Sept. 13, 1793. Nothing known of him.

9 | *Nathaniel*, b. Dec. 22, 1795 ; m. Harriet Wiggin, of Concord. She d. 1835, æ. 35 yrs. ; 2d w., Mary Ann Stanley, Hopkinton ; r. Hopkinton. He d. May 23,

10 | 1876.

Alpha, b. July 3, 1797 ; m. Hannah Emery ; d. Roxbury,

11 | Dec. 2, 1828, æ. 32 yrs.

Stephen, b. Nov. 3, 1799 ; d. Little Rock, Ark., 1825, æ.

12 | 26 yrs.

Mary, b. Sept. 27, 1801 ; m. Capt. Charles Chase, Hopkinton ; 2d hus., Samuel R. Adams, Hopkinton. She

13 | d. July 30, 1874, æ. 72 yrs., 11 mos.

Louisa, b. Aug. 10, 1803 ; d. Oct. 2, 1826, æ. 23 yrs.

THE FAIRBANKS FAMILY.

1 | EBENEZER FAIRBANKS is the son of the late Asa Fairbanks, of Dublin, and was b. May 28, 1794, and is uncle to Moses A. Fairbanks, hereafter mentioned. He m., 1st w., Betsey Wilder, b. Nov. 6, 1794, in Peterborough, and re. to Mount Tabor, Vt., where they lived five years, and then returned to Peterborough in 1822. He has lived in the village since his return, and is now one of the oldest inhabitants of the place. He is a carpenter by trade. His 1st w. d. Sept. 23, 1828 ; m., 2d w., Eleanor C. Farnsworth, dau. Timothy Farnsworth, Dublin, b. Jan. 28, 1801. Six ch., 1st w. ; seven ch., 2d w.

2 | †*Amaziah*, b. Dublin, Sept. 7, 1814 ; m., 1st w., Lucinda Pierce ; 2d w., Mary Ann Holt ; 3d w., Phila Ann Pierce.

3 | *Betsey*, b. Mount Tabor, March 6, 1817 ; m. William Grimes.

4 | *Nancy H.*, b. Mount Tabor, June 15, 1820 ; d. Peterborough, Jan. 30, 1827, æ. 6 yrs.

5 | *James W.*, b. Mount Tabor, Dec. 14, 1822 ; m. Lydia Searles. He d. June 28, 1865, æ. 42 yrs., 6 mos.

6 | *Lorenzo*, b. Peterborough, April 21, 1825 ; d. Feb. 22, 1827, æ. 1 yr., 10 mos.

7 | *Nancy A.*, b. May 29, 1828 ; m. Daniel Carter ; ten ch.

8 | *Eleanor H.*, b. Jan. 29, 1830 ; m. Levi Fairbanks, May 19, 1847.

9 | *Lorenzo A.*, b. Nov. 9, 1831 ; d. Aug. 15, 1833, æ. 1 yr.

10 | *Elvira F.*, b. Oct. 28, 1833.

11 | *George W.*, b. Oct. 14, 1835 ; m., 1st w., Sarah H. Rodman ; 2d w., Dora Abbot.

12 | *Merrick G.*, b. Jan. 9, 1838 ; m. Mary A. Larkin. He d. Nov. 2, 1866, æ. 28 yrs., 9 mos.

13 | *Amna C.*, b. Nov. 23, 1839 ; m. Charles Upton ; b. Jan.
6, 1837.

14 | *Josephine C.*, b. June 13, 1845 ; m., 1869, Charles H.
Townsend ; b. March 1, 1842 ; ch., (1) Willis M., b.
Jan. 30, 1870 ; (2) Frederick C., b. Dec. 11, 1873.

1 — 2 | AMAZIAH FAIRBANKS. He m. Lucinda Pierce. She
d. Aug. 17, 1841 ; 2d w., Mary Ann Holt ; d. Sept. 19,
1860 ; 3d w., Phila Ann Pierce, July 3, 1868 ; d. June 21,
1873.

15 | *Mary L.*, b. March 28, 1844 ; m. George A. Towns, Jan.
1, 1861 ; two ch.

16 | *Alfred*, b. 1858 ; d. young.

17 | *Lizzie Eldora*, b. April 20, 1860.

1 | MOSES A. FAIRBANKS, son of Moses and Jane Harper
Fairbanks, of Dublin, b. Sept. 29, 1822 ; m. Aug. 9,
1844, Abigail Hadley, dau. Thomas Hadley. He d.
April 10, 1862, æ. 40 yrs., 7 mos.

18 | *Mary S.*, b. Feb. 15, 1845 ; m. Ezra M. Smith, Esq.,
lawyer in Peterborough.

19 | *Albert H.*, b. Nov. 17, 1846 ; re. to Missouri.

20 | *Ellen L.*, b. Sept. 3, 1848.

21 | *Abbie E.*, } b. May 23, 1851. { d. 1874.
22 | *Etta J.*, }   { d. March 16, 1861, æ. 9
yrs., 9 mos.

THE FARNSWORTH FAMILY.

1 | ANDREW A. FARNSWORTH (Deacon), the son of the
late Andrew Farnsworth, of Bakersfield, Vt., was b.
there Oct. 30, 1817 ; came to Peterborough, Nov. 10,
1832.   He m. Sarah T. Field, dau. of Deacon John and
Beulah Reed Field, Sept. 6, 1841.   A tanner by trade,
he has carried on the business of tanning at the old shop
of Deacon Field, father and son for twenty-four years.
He is a deacon in the Union Evangelical Church in
town ; has held various offices in town ; Representative
to the State Legislature in 1860, '61.

2 | *Henry A.*, b. Nov. 23, 1843 ; m. June 1, 1870, Laura J.
Neville, b. in New Boston, July 4, 1847.

3 | *John Hermon*, b. June 17, 1846.

4 | *Willis Andrew*, b. Aug. 2, 1849.

THE FARNUM FAMILY.

1 | JOHN FARNUM was the son of Joseph and Arathusa
G. Farnum, of Wilton.   He came to Peterborough about
1820 ; worked for Samuel Smith for a time, afterwards

drove his heavy horse-teams to and from Boston ; and
still later he bought the teams, and performed all the
teaming for the stores and factories to Boston for this
town, and some of the adjoining towns, for many years,
until the railroad was completed from Boston to Nashua.
He also kept a hotel in the "Loring Block" at Carter's
Corner (so-called) for several years. He m. Mary N.
Withington, March 17, 1829. He d. Feb. 25, 1850, æ.
49 yrs. Mary N. d. Sept. 19, 1856, æ. 46 yrs.

2   *Justina M.*, b. Feb. 21, 1830 ; m. George Ditton, Iowa.
3   *Aurelia*, b. Oct. 12, 1831 ; m. George A. Damon ; r.
      Boston.
4   † *Joseph*, b. June 29, 1833 ; m. Mary A. Emerson.
5   *Mary E.*, b. Dec. 16, 1834 ; m. —— Garritt, Rockford,
      Iowa.
6   *John W.*, b. Sept. 13, 1836 ; d. Nov. 10, 1860, æ. 24 yrs.
7   *Almira*, b. May 22, 1838 ; m. T. E. B. Whitmore ; r.
      Chickasaw, Iowa.
8   *C. Henry*, b. Jan. 29, 1840 ; d. in military service in
      Covington, Ky., Aug. 17, 1863, æ. 23 yrs., 6 mos.
9   *Charles*, b. April 12, 1842 ; d. July 3, 1844, æ. 2 yrs., 2
      mos.
10   *George F.*, b. Sept. 14, 1845 ; r. Cochituate, Mass.
11   *Ellen M.*, b. Nov. 20, 1847 ; d. Feb. 20, 1849, æ. 1 yr., 3
      mos.

1- 4   JOSEPH FARNUM lives on Concord Street, first house
south of the Union Congregational Church, on the same
side of the road. He commenced to learn the printing
business in the *Transcript* office in June, 1850. Removed to Chickasaw, Iowa, in June, 1855, having purchased government land. Was engaged in farming and
teaching for a time, when he resumed his trade of
printing at Charles City, Iowa. Returned to Peterborough in Sept., 1857, and again entered the *Transcript*
office as a journeyman, which place he held, with the
exception of a few months, until March, 1866, when he
became editor and senior proprietor of the Peterborough
Transcript, which position he now holds. He was Representative to the legislature 1873, '74 ; m. May 9, 1852,
Mary A. Emerson, dau. of David and Lorinda Gray
Emerson.

12   *Charles F.*, b. Jan. 16, 1855.
13   *William D.*, b. Charles City, Iowa, Jan. 8, 1857.
14   *Harry E.*, b. Nov. 6, 1858.
15   *Nellie M.*, b. Aug. 22, 1862.
16   *John H.*, b. March 9, 1865 ; d. Aug. 21, 1865 ; æ. 5 mos.
17   *Mary Alice*, b. Oct. 8, 1872.

THE FAXON FAMILY.

1   JONATHAN FAXON (Deacon), was b. in Braintree, Mass., July 23, 1765, and m., in 1793, Abigail Ellis, of Sandwich, Mass., and re. to Peterborough about the year 1797. He d. April 13, 1849, æ. 83 yrs. She d. April 11, 1843, æ. 74 yrs. His father and mother both came to Peterborough and d. here. He·was a deacon in the Baptist Church, and one of its earliest supporters, and highly esteemed for his integrity, honesty, and Christian spirit. He was the salt of the earth. He purchased the Charles Stuart farm, and lived there some years, where both he and his w. d.

———

2   *Jonathan*, b. Sept. —, 1796; unm.; d. Oct. 15, 1862, æ. 66 yrs.

3   *Eliza*, b. April 30, 1800; m. Ethan Hadley; d. July 25, 1825, æ. 25 yrs.

THE FELT FAMILY.

1   OLIVER FELT was the seventh ch. of Jonathan and Lovell Felt, of Dedham, Mass. Jonathan Felt was b. June 3, 1719, and d. from an injury occasioned by falling from his cow-yard bars at Peterborough, May 16, 1786, æ. 67 yrs. Oliver Felt was b. in Dedham, Dec. 3, 1758, and d. Dec. 19, 1829, æ. 71 yrs. He m. Mary Dunlap, Aug. 14, 1788, in Peterborough, who d. Sept. 9, 1830, æ. 64 yrs., 8 mos., b. Dec. 22, 1765. His father, Jonathan Felt, came to Peterborough with his family, in 1780, and settled on land purchased of John White, on Street road, north of the John Smith place. Oliver succeeded him in the same place as a blacksmith, and followed the occupation until late in life.

———

2   *Tryphena*, b. Sept. 26, 1790; m. James Buckley, Feb. 17, 1820; r. Cape Vincent, N. Y.

3   *Mary*, b. Oct. 30, 1792; m. Samuel May, April 13, 1815; r. Sharon.

4   *Irene*, b. Oct. 9, 1796; m. Jeremiah S. Steele, April 29, 1823,

5   †*Ira*, b. April 28, 1799; m. Elizabeth Jewett, April 28, 1825.

6   † *Jonathan*, b. April 25, 1802; m. Susan Caldwell, May 18, 1829.

7   *Oliver*, b. June 18, 1804; d. Montebello, Ill., Aug. 29, 1834, æ. 30 yrs.

8   †*Cyrus*, b. July 27, 1807; m. Abby R. Brown; 2 w., Martha S. Marsh; 3 w., Caroline Lyman.

1- 5   IRA FELT m. Elizabeth Jewett, dau. John and Margaret Moore Jewett, April 28, 1825. He settled on the homestead, where he d. Oct. 11, 1826, æ. 27 yrs., 5 mos.

9   *Elizabeth*, b. ——, 1826; d. Sept. 2, 1830, æ. 4 yrs.

1- 6   JONATHAN FELT. He always r. in town. He m. Susan Caldwell, dau. Thomas and Eliza C. Caldwell, May 18, 1829. He d. March 30, 1870, æ. 68 yrs.

10   *Jonathan*, b. Feb. 19, 1830.
11   *George*, b. April 23, 1832; d. Oct. 20, 1852, æ. 20 yrs., 6 mos.
12   *Oliver*, b. July 14, 1834; m. Rosa Como, Feb. 22, 1872; r. Newton.
13   *Eliza Jane*, b. Sept. 14, 1838; d. Nov. 7, 1857, æ. 19 yrs.

1- 8   CYRUS FELT. He re. to Montebello, Ill., about 1832. He m. Abby R. Brown, Jan. 5, 1834. She d. Sept. 3, 1834; m., 2d w., Martha S. Marsh, Sept. 29, 1836; she d. Jan. 29, 1852, æ. 34 yrs., 9 mos.; 3d w., Caroline Lyman, March 21, 1856, of Rose, N. Y.; d.; ch. One son was killed in the late war, and only one dau. survives, who m. —— Brown. He d. suddenly at Montebello, Ill., Jan. 16, 1872, æ. 65 yrs.

2   STEPHEN FELT is of a family distinct from the preceding. He was b. in Temple, Sept. 15, 1793. He came to Peterborough as a machinist in 1816, and was engaged principally in the cotton manufacture till he left the business in 1845. He has since r. at the South Village; m., 1st w., Mary K. Ames, dau. of Timothy and Sarah Kneeland Ames, May 23, 1818. She d. Oct. 21, 1844, æ. 45 yrs. She was the mother of five ch.; 2d w., Eliza H. Morison, Sept. 18, 1845. She d. Aug. 14, 1867, æ. 62 yrs. She had one son.

14   *Sarah M.*, b. Aug. 29, 1820; d. April 23, 1822, æ. 2 yrs.
15   †*Granville P.*, b. Aug. 22, 1822; m. Jane B. Kimball, Dec. 3, 1846.
16   *Mary K.*, b. Nov. 11, 1824; m. Charles Spaulding; r. Milford.
17   †*George A.*, b. July 22, 1834; m. July 29, 1855, Eliza Hadley.
18   †*John Ames*, b. May 8, 1837; m. Aug. 1, 1860, Emma Ann Willers.
19   †*Edward M.*, b. Nov. 27, 1847; m. Jan. 9, 1873, Josephine Rolf, of Jaffrey.

2- 15   GRANVILLE PARKER FELT. He received his education in the common schools. He learned the machinist's trade of Gay, Silver & Co., North Chelmsford, Mass., and first engaged in business in Peterborough in company with Josiah S. Morrison, they having bought out William Moore's machine-shop. They manufactured cotton and woolen machinery, and wood-working machines. Mr. Felt bought out his partner in 1851, and has since conducted the business alone. He built a foundry just west of his shop, in 1865, in which he has done much business. In 1871, he commenced the manufacture of force and suction pumps, in which business he is now largely engaged. He has constantly employed from twenty-five to thirty hands, and his yearly business has amounted to $30,000 a year.

On Tuesday, Nov. 16, 1875, his shop took fire about 11, P. M., and was entirely consumed, with a large amount of stock, and almost all his valuable tools. The loss cannot be less than twenty-five to thirty thousand dollars, with only a small insurance. Being a man of indomitable perseverance, he again immediately resumed his business in the shop opposite to his works, which had fortunately been preserved in the conflagration, and will no doubt again recover what he has lost. He represented the town in the Legislature in 1863, '64. He is a director of the Peterborough Railroad. He has been too busy a man in his own affairs to find much time for public offices. He m. Jane B. Kimball, dau. Elijah B. Kimball, Dec. 3, 1846.

20 | *Granville*, b. Dec. 2, 1848; d. June 10, 1850, æ. 1 yr., 6 mos.
21 | *Annie J.*, b. Nov. 22, 1852; m. David A. Rogers, Dec. 16, 1872; 1 ch., Arthur Granville, b. Aug. 23, 1873; d. Sept. 13, 1873, æ. 20 dys.
22 | *Abby K.*, b. June 20, 1859.

2– 17 | GEORGE A. FELT. Is a machinist; m. July 29, 1855, Eliza Hadley, dau. Joel Hadley.

23 | *Albert*, b. March 29, 1857.
24 | *John Ames*, b. June 24, 1859.

2– 18 | JOHN AMES FELT re. to Ohio; m., 1st w., Aug. 1, 1860, Emma Ann Willers, b. July 24, 1842; 2 ch. by 1st w. She d. ——; m. 2d w.

25 | *Emma C.*, b. Sept. 26, 1861.
26 | *Elmer J.*, b. May 4, 1865.

2– 19 | EDWARD MORISON FELT; r. at South Village. He m. Jan. 9, 1873, Josephine Rolf, of Jaffrey.

27 | *Elmer Morison*, b. Aug. 4, 1873; d. Sept. 9, 1873, æ. 35 dys.

THE FERGUSON FAMILY.

1 | JOHN FERGUSON was b. 1704. It is supposed that he was born in Ireland, and probably came to this country in the company of the Smiths, Wilsons, and Littles, who made their first settlement at Lunenburg, Mass., about 1736 or '37. He no doubt accompanied these emigrants to Lunenburg, and with them took up his residence in the north part of the town. This residence at Lunenburg seems to have been but a temporary abode; a waiting till some new location, in the numerous towns about this time granted by the Massachusetts Legislature, should open to them. The early history of this man is somewhat obscure. He is supposed to have been one of the earliest settlers of the town. It is reported that he came to town the first time, which was between 1738 and '40, with one of the original proprietors, about the time the town was surveyed. It must have been some years before he removed his family. He soon afterwards purchased six hundred acres of land, which land, many years ago, was known as the Henry Ferguson farm, the Hadley farm, with a part of the Barber farm, and a part of the Norton Hunt place. After the purchase of this land, and before his final settlement, he visited Peterborough a number of times, and, at one time, he stayed there alone for three months, clearing a small piece of land, but spending most of his time in hunting and fishing. He carried the furs which he had taken to Lunenburg on his back. The town was then an unbroken wilderness, no roads, no mills, no bridges, or houses. The roof and floor of the first log-cabin, built by Mr. Ferguson, was made of split pine lumber. His first and second cabins were situated on the north bank of the Contoocook River, directly west from the present dwelling-house of Col. N. Hunt. The exact time of his settlement is uncertain, though most probably not far from 1750, at which time many families from Lunenburg came to town. He gave his son, Henry, two hundred acres of his purchase, or the Ferguson farm so called; to his daughter Esther, who married Charles Stuart, two hundred acres, where they lived, now known by the name of the Faxon farm; and to his daughter, Sarah Morrison, land in Windy Row, known as the Spring farm.

We can learn but little of his standing in society as a man, or his ability in point of talents. We know that when the town first organized, under the Act of Incor-

10

poration in 1760, he was chosen the first Town Clerk;
at which time he uniformly spelled his name on the records as Farguson. We have no means of telling when
the *a* was changed to *e* in the name; probably soon. He
continued in the office seven years, and until only two
years before his death. His record is a very good one;
the writing plain, but crowded so as to occupy as little
space as possible. Stationery, in those times, was scarce
and dear. His record of the proceedings was in plain,
clear language, and with the fewest words.

He appears to have been a well-educated man, and,
feeling a deep interest in the education of his own children, he set apart some hours each day for their instruction. It was soon known that John Ferguson was teaching his children at home, and his school rapidly increased to ten or twelve. Some of the scholars, coming
from a distant part of the town, brought with them the
material for their bean porridge, and an axe which they
used morning and evening, to pay their tuition. Great
pains were taken in this school with the branch of handwriting. The ink used was made from the bark of the
white maple; and their pens from the quills of the wild
turkey; and for paper they used the inner bark of the
white birch. White birch bark was used in all the
schools by the juveniles in writing until after the Revolution. Deacon Nathaniel Moore and wife both learned
to write on white birch bark. He m. Sarah McDaniel,
in Lunenburg, who was b. in 1710; d. Dec. 20, 1791, æ.
81 yrs. He d. May 13, 1769, æ. 65 yrs.

---

2 | *Mary*, b. Dec. 22, 1734; m.
3 | †*Henry*, b. Sept. 18, 1736; m. Martha Wilson.
4 | *Sarah*, b. Aug. 4, 1740; m. Rev. John Morrison.
5 | *Catrin*, b. June 8, 1742.
6 | *John*, b. Nov. 13, 1744; d. young.
7 | *Esther*, b. March 30, 1746; m. Charles Stuart.

1- 3 | HENRY FERGUSON was son of John Ferguson, but
where born I am yet unable to ascertain. He came
to Peterborough with his father, when he was about
thirteen or fourteen years old, about 1748 or 9 — a year
when many of the early settlers came to town from
Lunenburg and Townsend. We know very little of his
early life, of his childhood nothing; only that a life that
proved such a blessing to society must have had early
Christian culture. His father, being an intelligent and
educated man, gave his children better opportunities for
an education than most of the children of that period
enjoyed.

Yet without books or any of the modern means of instruction, we can hardly see how the work of teaching (mostly oral) could have resulted so well. Mr. Ferguson, with such instruction and training as his father could give, was considered one of the best-educated and intelligent men of his day. I find from the town records that he held the office of moderator in 1792, and was selectman for nine years, *viz.*, 1771, '7, '8, 1785, '8, '9, 1790, '1, '2 ; tithing-man for two years, *viz.*, 1783, '6. These were all the town offices he ever held, though he occasionally served on committees, and no doubt always kept his interest in the municipal affairs of the town. From my earliest days I have heard only the praise of this sainted man, and if he had faults, the sharp eyes of his contemporaries failed to discern them ; and he has come down to us as the salt of the earth.

There was a long and intimate friendship between Henry Ferguson and William Smith (the father of the great Smith family), which continued through their lives. There was no doubt great congeniality of feeling between them. They were both mild, social, and discreet men, and loved the quiet of their homes more than the hurry and excitement of frontier life ; they shunned rather than courted popular favor, and only took office for the benefit of others, and not for their own gratification. In a letter from George W. Moore, Esq., of Medina, Mich., he says: "My grandfather, Henry Ferguson, died before I was born, but all that I have heard of him has led me to form a very excellent opinion of him as a man of candor, justice, sobriety, and all those virtues that should adorn a true man and a real Christian. In matters of religion he put little stress in the creeds or ceremonies of this or that particular church, or in loud professions of religion that did not bring forth the fruits of righteousness. Religion with him was a simple covenant with his God, which he strove daily to keep. The most prominent trait of his character was his kindness to the poor, to the sick and unfortunate. His hands were always open to relieve their sufferings. They always found a shelter under his roof, and a seat at his table. If there was any poor family in town, he knew it. I have heard my mother [Sarah Ferguson, w. of Dea. Nathaniel Moore] say that he often went to mill with two or three bags of corn, and returned with but one of meal, having given away a large part of it. He was also a man of strict honesty in all his dealings, always scrupulous to represent an article just as it was, and always careful to give good measure, choosing rather to suffer wrong than to do wrong. About 1786 he bought a lot of land of a Mr. A., of Stoddard, upon which the last payment was to be one hundred bushels of rye. The rye was ready for delivery, and my grandfather sent his son James and his hired man with two ox-teams to deliver the same. The roads were bad, and they did not reach Stoddard until late at night. In the morning James, being anxious to get an early start for home, told Mr. A. that his father had carefully measured the rye, and that all he would have to do was to empty the bags. Mr. A. told James that he had a half-bushel measure that was correct, and that the rye must be measured with it. After measuring a few bags, it was evident the rye would overrun measure, and Mr. A. told James that he would take it at his father's measure, since the roads were so bad, and he was so far from home. But James told him, as his half-bushel was a correct measure, and he had questioned his father's honesty, that the rye should be measured again if he did not get home till the next morning. When the task was completed, they found one hundred and two bushels, and he brought the two extra bushels back to Peterborough.

"My grandfather would not tamely submit to a wrong, or allow his friends so to do, if he could prevent it. His sister, Mrs. Morrison, was engaged in a lawsuit in regard to some land. She had the right of the case, but had no money to carry on the suit. He borrowed money for this purpose of Dr. K. Osgood, to the amount of $500, and with this aid she gained her case; but he neither expected nor would receive any remuneration for the services rendered." Thus far Mr. Moore. It has been reported that Mr. Ferguson did not come in readily to the measures of the Revolution — not that he was a Tory by any means,—but he might have thought the action of the Colonies premature, and that there was no hope in contending, in our weak state, with so powerful a nation as Great Britain. There can be no doubt that he ultimately came in heartily with his friends to the support of the cause, if indeed he was ever lukewarm and backward, for we find his name, as Lieut. Henry Ferguson, among eleven others from town, who served in the army at Cambridge for forty-four days in the latter part of 1775. Mr. Moore, in another letter, has furnished me the following, as a reason why his grandfather, Henry Ferguson, did not and could not, under the circumstances, sign the Association Test or Declaration of Independence with the eighty-three others of his townsmen and neighbors. The Rev. John Morrison joined the British army at Boston soon after the Battle of Bunker Hill, June 17, 1775, and he deserted his wife, who was a sister of Henry Ferguson, with four small children, and with little means of support. After a few months the small stock of provisions became exhausted, and Henry Ferguson took his sister and her children to his own home. During this period letters passed between Mr. and Mrs. Morrison, and her situation was known to him. He says: "Mr. Morrison wrote to my grandfather that he had money which he would send to his wife if any one would come and get it. He also designated where he would meet the person sent, which was near New York City. My grandfather concluded to go himself, and after consulting with Deacon Samuel Moore, it was thought best that the journey should be kept secret. He therefore left Peterborough in the night on horseback, and was gone some days before his neighbors knew that he was away from home. Capt. David Steele, being one of the Committee of Safety for that year, with Wm. Robbe, Jotham Blanchard, Samuel Mitchell, and Robert Wilson (who had been severely censured by my grandfather at a public gathering in town not long before, for conduct he did not approve), taking advantage of his absence, started a report that he had given up the American cause, and had gone to join the British army in Canada. About the first of July my grandfather returned, and brought with him a certain quantity of gold, estimated at one pound of gold, or some three or four hundred dollars.

"The next day, Capt. Steele, with six of his neighbors, came to his house, and meeting him at the door said to him, 'Henry Ferguson, we understand that you have been to Canada, and we want to know your business, and examine your papers.' He asked them to go into the house, and handed the key of his desk to Capt. Steele, saying: 'I have not been to Canada. I have been about my own legitimate business, and the business of my family. I have conducted myself with propriety in my absence as I have always done.' Mrs. Morrison, fearing that the house would be searched and the gold found, went and hid it in the barn. But the frankness of Mr. Ferguson convinced the party of his honesty, and here the matter ended."

From the above it would be evident that Henry Ferguson was absent when this declaration was signed by his friends. It was presented the 17th of June, 1776, and immediately signed, as there could be no delay in that crisis of the country. So no imputation of disloyalty can rest upon him, for all the circumstances of his life indicate his earnest patriotism and zeal in the cause of liberty. He m. Martha Wilson, who d. Oct. 30, 1815, æ.

76 yrs. This excellent man became a victim of an epidemic fever which prevailed in town, April 1, 1812, æ. 75 yrs., and well may it be said of such a man, as quoted by Rev. E. Dunbar, in his notice of his death on the church records : —

> "Incorrupta fides, undique veritas, quando ullum ·
> Invenient parem, multis ille flebilis occidet."

8 | *John*, b. 1768. He went South in early life, and became a successful merchant in Coosawhatchie, Beaufort Co., S. C. In 1807 he gave up his business, and retired to his plantation, Coosawhatchie Swamp, where he d. March 28, 1828, of a cancer in the eye. He was never married, though he left children out of the pale of wedlock, to whom he willed his large property of money, lands, and negroes.

9 | † *James*, b. Feb. 13, 1770; m. Mary Howard, July 18, 1811.

10 | *Jane*, b. 1773 ; m. George Duncan, Jr.

11 | *Sarah*, b. Aug. 4, 1775 ; m. Deacon Nathaniel Moore.

12 | *Henry*, b. 1777 ; unm.; d. in the autumn 1818, at Coosawhatchie, S. C.

13 | *Thomas*, b. 1779 ; unm. ; d. at Ashapoo, Colleton Co., S. C., April 14, 1834, æ. 54 yrs., 7 mos.

14 | *Martha*, b. 1781 ; m. Gen. James Miller ; d. Greenfield, May 12, 1805, æ. 23 yrs.

15 | *Betsey*, b. Nov. 28, 1783 ; m. Asaph Evans, Aug. 30, 1808 ; d. Aug. 18, 1816, æ. 33 yrs.

3- 9 | JAMES FERGUSON. He m. Mary Howard, July 18, 1811. He settled on the homestead, and d. April 30, 1814, æ. 44 yrs. She m., 2d hus., Elias Boynton, of Temple.

16 | *Jane*, b.——— ; m. ——— Whiting, Wilton, 1834 ; c.

17 | *Martha*, b.———.

18 | *James*, b. Sept. 10, 1814 ; m. Sylva Stevens, 1836 ; d. Brooklyn, N. Y., Feb. 10, 1869, æ. 54 yrs., 5 mos.

THE FERRY FAMILY.

1 | CHARLES BRACE FERRY (Rev.), son of Benjamin and Hannah Street Ferry, was b. in Moscow, Livingston Co., N. Y., April 11, 1832. His parents originated in Connecticut. He had the ordinary advantages of the schools of Livingston Co., and for some years after he was seventeen years of age he taught winter schools, and worked on the farm during the summer. In 1852 he commenced learning the printer's trade, at Elmira,

N. Y., and subsequently spent four years at this business in Cincinnati, O. In 1856 he entered Meadville School, and remained there till 1859. In April of 1860 he received a call to settle over the Congregational Society (Unitarian) in Peterborough, and was ordained June 13, 1860. He remained pastor of this society till Sept., 1869, when he resigned and was installed at Manchester, Dec. 9, of the same year. He left Manchester early in 1874, and is now settled at Northampton, Mass. He m. Ellen Matilda Haywood, dau. of E. W. and Susan B. Haywood, of Uxbridge, Mass., June 11, 1860. She was. b. Aug. 11, 1834.

2 | *Catharine P.*, b. Aug. 8, 1862; d. Jan. 15, 1863, æ. 5. mos., 7 dys.
3 | *Ebenezer H.*, b. June 14, 1864.
4 | *Charles*, b. Feb. 10, 1868.
5 | *Henry B.*, b. Feb. 5, 1872, at Manchester.

THE FIELD FAMILY.

1 | JOHN FIELD came to Peterborough, in company with Dea. Christopher Thayer, May 8, 1786, from Braintree, now Quincy, where he was b. April 16, 1752. He was a tanner by trade, and settled just north of the farm of William Smith, Esq., where some vats had been made and some tanning done by Robert Smith, father to William Smith. These vats are now in a perfect state of preservation, having been made not far from 1760. He m. Ruth Thayer, in Braintree, Nov. 11, 1775, who was b. July 2, 1752. She d. in Peterborough, Aug. 7, 1846, æ. 94 yrs., having been blind some thirty years before her death. He d. Jan. 8, 1826, æ. 74 yrs.

2 | † *John*, b. Braintree, Oct. 27, 1777; m., 1st w., Beulah Reed; 2d. w., Tabitha Colburn.
3 | † *William*, b. Nov. 18, 1782; m. Mary McAlister.
4 | *Elisha*, b. Aug. 2, 1784; d. Aug. 19, 1861, æ. 77 yrs.
5 | *Jabez*, b. Jan. 4, 1789; drowned in tan vats, June 25, 1793, æ. 4 yrs.
6 | *Sally*, b. March 7, 1791; m. Noah Youngman, Lempster; d. March 24, 1854, æ. 63 yrs.
7 | *Otis*, b. Jan. 12, 1794; m. Lydia Dodge; six ch.; d. 1863, æ. 69 yrs.
8 | *Ruth*, b. April 3, 1796; m. David Youngman; 1 ch., Dr. David Youngman, of Boston. She d. Sept. 5, 1817, æ. 22 yrs.
9 | *Mary*, b. March 10, 1798; m. Timothy Bruce, Lempster; seven ch. She had five sons who went to the war, and all returned safe but one, who d. in the service.

1– 2 | JOHN FIELD (Dea.). He was nine years of age when his father moved to town. He followed the occupation of his father, and carried on extensively the business of tanning, for many years, at the same place his father began. He m., 1st w., Beulah Reed, of Lempster, June 20, 1802, who was the mother of all his ch. She d. July 30, 1835, æ. 57 yrs. He m., 2d w., Tabitha Colburn, April 5, 1838; d. Oct. 7, 1848, æ. 52 yrs. He d. Nov. 18, 1856, æ. 79 yrs.

---

10 | *Adelaide*, b. April 29, 1803 ; m. James B. Nichols, Feb. 4, 1830. He d. Aug. 3, 1852, æ. 46 yrs. She d. May 4, 1872, æ. 69 yrs. ; ch., (1) John F., b. Jan. 7, 1831 ; r. Chicago, Ill. ; (2) James, b. April 1, 1833 ; r. Alabama ; (3) Sarah, b. Aug. 29, 1835 ; m. Rev. George Dustan, May 4, 1864.

11 | *Isaac*, b. July 11, 1804; m. Mary Greene, Charlestown, Mass., May 20, 1830 ; c. He r. in Boston twelve years, was engaged in the hide and leather business, and then re. to Denmark, Ia., and has lived there since.

12 | *Louisa*, b. March 20, 1806 ; m. Benjamin Norton, Abington, Mass., May 13, 1841. She d. 1843, æ. 37 yrs.

13 | *Sylvina*, b. Dec. 21, 1807 ; m. John W. Shepherd, Oct. 17, 1839 ; r. Woburn, Mass. ; ch., (1) Horatio N. ; (2) Louisa C. ; (3) Sarah J. ; (4) Henry M. ; (5) Emma.

14 | *Ruth*, b. June 22, 1809 ; m. John E. Leiper, of Bethel, Ill., Jan. 4, 1842 ; ch., (1) Mary Louisa ; (2) John F. ; (3) Curtis M. ; (4) Edward F. ; d. Peterborough, April 22, 1850, æ. 14 mos. ; r. Denmark, Ia.

15 | †*John, Jr.*, b. Nov. 22, 1810 ; m. Sarah E. Worcester ; 2d w., Sarah A. Baldwin, Brighton, Mass.

16 | *Horatio N.*, b. March 25, 1813 ; m. Charity Taylor, Oct. 29, 1839 ; ch., (1) Emily ; (2) Charles ; (3) Ellen ; (4) Walter ; r. Chicago, Ill.

17 | *William*, b. April 27, 1814 ; m. Sophia Cone, Illinois. Two ch.

18 | *Mary Ann*, b. Nov. 22, 1815 ; d. April 4, 1816, æ. 4 mos.

19 | *Mary*, b. Jan. 13, 1817 ; m. Luther Noyes, of Abington ; d. Sept. 25, 1840, æ. 23 yrs. ; one ch., Mary Jane, b. May 10, 1840; d. young.

20 | *Marcy C.*, b. Dec. 23, 1817 ; m. Moses Thompson, Feb. 20, 1840 ; two ch.; (1) Mary Noyes ; (2) William E. She d. February, 1860, æ. 43 yrs.

21 | *Sarah T.*, b. Aug. 3, 1819 ; m. Andrew A. Farnsworth.

22 | *Louis Jane*, b. June 14, 1821 ; m. Luther Noyes, Abington, May 13, 1841. She d. Jan. 11, 1850, æ. 29 yrs. One ch., James B., b. June 14, 1844 ; d. young.

Yours truly
John Field

1– 3 | WILLIAM FIELD. He lived in the east part of the town, adjoining the old Blair place, where he raised his large family. He was a farmer. He m. Mary McAlister, dau. of Randall McAlister, April 17, 1808. She d. May 21, 1853, æ. 67 yrs. He d. April 23, 1863, æ. 80 yrs.

23 | *William J.*, b. Jan. 4, 1809 ; d. Aug. 4, 1828, æ. 19 yrs.
24 | *Alexander H.*, b. Dec. 22, 1809 ; m. Jane Brackett ; r. Lawrence, Kan. ; ch., (1) Ella ; (2) George ; (3) Edward ; (4) Mary ; (5) Jane.
25 | *Mary A.*, b. March 26, 1811 ; m. George Brackett ; d. Jul7 27, 1846, æ. 35 yrs.
26 | *John G.*, b. April 14, 1812 ; m. Rachel Marcy, Denmark, Ia. ; d. April 12, 1852, æ. 40 yrs. ; ch., (1) Albert ; (2) Henry A. ; (3) Charlotte ; (4) William G..
27 | *Katharine*, b. April 20, 1813 ; m. Horace Huse ; re. to Missouri ; eight ch.
28 | *Charles*, b. Sept. 18, 1814 ; m. Electa Brockway, Denmark, Ia. ; ch., (1) Charlotte A. ; (2) Henry S. ; (3) Charles F.
29 | *Harriet*, b. May 7, 1816 ; m. Abiel Niles, Lowell, Mass. ; ch., (1) Alonzo ; (2) Albertus ; (3) Frederick ; (4) Harriet E. ; (5) John.
30 | *Jeremiah S.*, b. July 10, 1817 ; m., June 7, 1842, Mary Harvey ; 2d w., Sarah M. Moore, Aug. 12, 1852 ; ch., (1) Fanny ; (2) Frederick ; (3) Herbert W. ; (4) Katharine C. ; r. Lawrence, Mass.
31 | †*Franklin*, b. May 1, 1819 ; m. Luvia Miner, of Lowell.
32 | *Ruth*, b. Oct. 9, 1820 ; unm. ; r. Boston.
33 | *Charlotte*, b. March 11, 1822 ; d. Jan. 2, 1844, æ. 21 yrs.
34 | †*Henry*, b. Oct. 30, 1823 ; m. Lucy Farmer.
35. | *Albert*, b. July 14, 1825 ; m. Mehitable Perkins, Jan. 14, 1851 ; 1 ch., Lizzie P. ; r. New Market.
36 | *Lois*, b. Oct. 23, 1826 ; m. Samuel Cannon, Oct. 16, 1852. He d. April 6, 1860, æ. 32 yrs., 9 mos. ; m., 2d hus., George M. Pierce, Jan. 23, 1866 ; r. Worcester, Mass.
37 | *Eunice*, b. Aug. 9, 1829 ; unm. ; r. Cambridge, Mass.

2– 15 | JOHN FIELD, Jr. He went to Boston in 1831, and succeeded his brother Isaac in the hide and leather business, under the firm name of Field & Converse. By his assiduity and industry he became eminently successful in business, and acquired wealth sufficient to be able to retire partially from active pursuits, 1863. In all his business relations he was an honorable and upright man, never yielding principle, in any instance, to expediency. He was a good citizen, a sincere Christian, and a true

11

man, and his life abounded with active benevolence and kind works and good deeds. He was deeply interested in many of the benevolent enterprises of the day, to which he freely gave his attention and labor, and also rendered largely of his means. He was a Director in the State National Bank, Boston ; also a Director of the American Peace Society, a corporate member of the American Board of Foreign Missions, and for many years has held a prominent office in the Orthodox Congregational Church, at Arlington. He m., 1st w., May 2, 1836, Sarah E. Worcester, granddau. of Noah Worcester, D. D. She d. June 20, 1839. She was the mother of the first two ch. He m., 2d w., Sarah A. Baldwin, of Brighton, Mass., Oct. 13, 1840; he d. July 31, 1876, æ. 66.

38   *Henry M.*, b. Oct. 3, 1837 ; m. Lydia M. Peck, Arlington. Appointed Professor of Materia Medica and Therapeutics in the Dartmouth Medical College, Hanover, 1871, and now holds the office. Graduated Harvard University 1859. Medical degree at the College of Physicians and Surgeons, New York City, and is now in the practice of his profession, Newton, Mass.

39   *John Worcester*, b. June 11, 1839 ; m. Amelia C. Reed, of So. Weymouth, Mass. ; r. Boston.

40   *Sarah Ann B.*, b. May 9, 1846 ; m. Arthur C. Lawrence ; r. Newton.

41   *William Evarts*, b. May 29, 1848 ; m. Louisa T. Swan ; r. Arlington.

42   *Arthur D.*, b. Dec. 21, 1849.

43   *George A.*, b. Nov. 10, 1854.

44   *Lilla Frances*, b. June 25, 1857.

3- 31   FRANKLIN FIELD. He lives on a part of the old homestead. He has held important offices in town. Selectman 1864, '65, '66 ; surveyor, &c. Representative in 1875, '76. He m. Luvia Miner, of Lowell, Jan. 19, 1847, b. in Coventry, Vt., July 30, 1827.

45   *Clara J.*, b. Lowell, Feb. 15, 1850; d. at Peterborough, April 17, 1865, æ. 15 yrs.

46   *William F.*, b. Peterborough, Feb. 16, 1852.

47   *Martin E.*, b. Dec. 30, 1854.

48   *Forrest G.*, b. Feb. 20, 1856.

49   *Charles G.*, b. Jan. 27, 1859 ; d. March 22, 1865, æ. 6 yrs.

50   *Walter E.*, b. Dec. 14, 1861.

3- 34   HENRY FIELD m. Lucy Farmer, b. Francestown, May 3, 1834. Is a carpenter by trade. He lives on the place begun by Moses Chapman, near the Mears place.

51 *Mary E.*, b. Oct. 18, 1855.
52 *Charles A.*, b. Dec. 23, 1857.
53 *Emma J.*, b. Nov. 27, 1859.
54 *Alice H.*, b. May 28, 1867.

THE FINCH FAMILY.

1   RICHARD FINCH was a British soldier. He came over
early in the Revolutionary War, probably in 1775 or '76,
and deserted from the British ranks while in Boston,
and went to Reading and worked for a Mr. Melendy, a
shoemaker. He was a boot-maker by trade, and here
first became acquainted with his wife, Hepzibeth Melendy. He married, and after a short residence in Amherst he removed to Peterborough, and bought land in
this village, on site and north of the Unitarian Church,
where he built a house on the very ground on which the
church now stands, and lived here till his death in 1797.
No person now living remembers him, though many
recollect the widow, who survived him many years. She
d. at Waltham, Mass., Feb. 11, 1837, æ. 83 yrs., 8 mos. ;
b. May 27, 1753. Richard Finch's name appears last
on the tax-list of 1797.

2   *William*, b. 1783 ; d. at Woodstock, Vt., while away
from home, about 1813 or '14, æ. 27 or 28 yrs.
Taxed 1807, '8, '9.

3   *Fanny*, b. 1786 ; m. Charles Martin, a paper-maker, Feb.
1, 1803 ; two ch., William and Mary. Mary was b. in
1805 ; d. May 19, 1812, æ. 7 yrs. The mother d.
Aug. 29, 1810 ; in the church records no age, but it
says of her, "a victim of intemperance" ; æ. about
24 yrs.

4   *Sarah*, b. Nov. 2, 1788 ; m. Francis Field, Oct. 12, 1812 ;
d. Dec. 9, 1858, æ. 70 yrs. Three ch. ; (1) Francis ;
(2) Joseph Badger ; (3) Mary Gridley ; r. Waltham.

5   *Harriet*, b. Feb. 12, 1793 ; m. Zaccheus Farwell, March
4, 1810. He d. April 15, 1861 ; ch., (1) Zaccheus, b.
Oct. 20, 1810 ; d. July 10, 1840 ; (2) Harriet, b. in
Peterborough, Nov. 26, 1812 ; m. Jesse E. Farnsworth ; r. Waltham, Mass. ; (3) Mary, b. in Peterborough, May 3, 1815 ; m. Daniel Smith Baxter ; r.
Brighton ; (4) Sarah, b. July 13, 1817, at Mount Tabor, Vt. ; m. Almon H. Hemenway ; r. Waltham ; (5)
Lucy, b. March 29, 1820, at Mount Tabor, Vt. ; m.
Nahum Chapin ; r. Boston ; (6) Frances, b. July 15,
1828 ; d. Oct. 29, 1832 ; (7) Elizabeth, b. June 26,
1833 ; m. Noah W. Sanborn ; r. Brighton.

6   *Mary*, b. —— ; m. Richard Moules ; re. to North Carolina, and d. there.

THE FOLLANSBEE FAMILY.

1   WILLIAM FOLLANSBEE, M.D., came to Peterborough from Francestown in 1826, and on the death of Dr. Jabez B. Priest, he succeeded him in the practice of medicine, and continued in the same until his death. He took his medical degree at the Dartmouth Medical College in 1825. He was a good practitioner of medicine, and a worthy and respectable man. He represented the town in the State Legislature in 1842, '3. He was b. Dec. 12, 1800; d. of an affection of the heart May 30, 1867, æ. 66 yrs. He m., 1st w., Hannah J. Follansbee; b. May 24, 1805, who was the mother of all the children. She d. Aug. 27, 1849, æ. 43 yrs. He m., 2d w., Rachel P. Moore, widow of Deacon William Moore, and dau. of Capt. Alexander Robbe.

2   † *George Fred.*, b. July 26, 1825; m. Mary C. Pierce, East Jaffrey, Aug. 29, 1846.

3   † *Charles P.*, b. Aug. 28, 1828; m. Charlotte E. Whitcomb.

4   *Henry A.*, b. Aug. 16, 1833; m., July, 1857, Lucy Ann Law; r. Manchester.

5   *Orrin C.*, b. Sept. 24, 1846; d. Oct. 26, 1846, æ. 1 mo.

1–2   GEORGE F. FOLLANSBEE m. Mary C. Pierce, Aug. 29, 1846; re. to Pierpont, O., and d. there, Sept. 27, 1858, æ. 33 yrs. After his death his family returned to East Jaffrey, where they now reside. He was a harness-maker by trade.

6   *Ella M.*, b. East Jaffrey, July 3, 1847; m. Addison Pierce, Jr., March 29, 1869.

7   *Annie S.*, b. Peterborough, Jan. 29, 1850; m. John H. Steele, Nov. 6, 1867.

8   *George W.*, b. Cleveland, O., March 19, 1853.

9   *Fred. A.*, b. Cleveland, O., July 20, 1855.

10   *Ida M.*, b. Pierpont, O., Nov. 10, 1857.

1–3   CHARLES P. FOLLANSBEE, after residing in various places, returned to Peterborough in 1867, and has resided here since. He m. Charlotte E. Whitcomb in 1855; b. Sept. 15, 1828.

11   *Frances E.*, b. Peterborough, Jan. 29, 1856; d. Dec. 6, 1870, æ. 14 yrs., 10 mos.

12   *Hattie A.*, b. Peterborough, Jan. 12, 1859.

13   *William Fred.*, b. Enfield, April 12, 1861.

14   *Lizzie E.*, b. Enfield, June 11, 1865.

15   *Lottie W.*, b. Peterborough, Oct. 25, 1868.

THE FORBUSH FAMILY.

1   SIMEON FORBUSH was b. in Acton, Mass., Feb. 22, 1770; d. at Peterborough, April 13, 1860, æ. 90 yrs. He m. Catharine Hosmer; b. in Acton, June 3, 1774; d. Sept. 13, 1841, æ. 67 yrs. They came to Peterborough in 1804, and lived on the Capt. Thomas Morison place, in the same house with Betty and Sally Morison.

2   †*Luke*, b. Jan. 31, 1799; m. Nancy Carey.
3   †*Rufus*, b. Sept. 9, 1800; m. Almira Cram.
4   †*Stephen*, b. Feb. 2, 1803; m., 1st w., Esther P. Hill; 2d w., Esther S. Smith; 3d w., Eleanor Machett.
5   †*Ira*, b. March 17, 1805; m. Hannah Brown.
6   *Sally*, b. March 15, 1807; m. Leonard Hill; re. to Utah, and d. there.

1— 2   LUKE FORBUSH. A carpenter by trade. He m. Nancy Ann Carey; b. March 16, 1802; d. March 1, 1869, æ. 66 yrs., 11 mos. He d. May 11, 1836, æ. 37 yrs.

7   †*Luke O.*, b. Nov. 8, 1823; m., March 2, 1846, Hannah M. Stearns; b. Aug. 27, 1824.
8   *Alpha A.*, b. Aug. 23, 1825; d. June 15, 1865, æ. 40 yrs.; m., 1st w., Eliza Ryder; 2d w., Emily B. Dexter; one daughter by last wife.
9   *Simeon*, b. Jan. 28, 1827; d. Aug. 15, 1828, æ. 1 yr., 6 mos.
10   *George E.*, b. Jan. 15, 1830; unm.
11   *Henry C.*, b. Sept. 20, 1831; m. Lydia A. Shores. Four ch.
12   *Chancellor S.*, b. March 15, 1834; m. Nancy J. Ethridge, July 17, 1853.

2— 7   LUKE O. FORBUSH. A machinist. Has erected buildings directly south of the Senter place, — near old Baptist meeting-house. He m., March 2, 1846, Hannah M. Stearns, b. Aug. 27, 1824.

13   *Lucinda C.*, b. June 26, 1847; m., May 1, 1866, John Scott.
14   *Abbie G.*, b. Aug, 30, 1849; m. Willard Lee; r. Claremont.
15   *George L.*, b. Oct. 4, 1851; m., 1875, Clara W. Keith. Druggist in town.

1— 3   RUFUS FORBUSH. He had the misfortune to lose his right arm at West Cambridge, Mass., in May, 1822, while tending a machine for preparing hair for stuffing furniture. Under this great loss he has been able comfortably to support and educate his family by his industry and perseverance. He soon qualified himself for teaching and surveying, and has been much employed in these pursuits. Having acquired facility in writing with his left hand, his fellow-citizens elected him town clerk, at first out of sympathy on account of his misfortune, and subsequently because no one could discharge the duties of the office better. He held this office twenty-one years, longer than any other person since the incorporation of the town. Thomas Steele, Esq., came next to him, having been town clerk nineteen years. The records during this long period that Mr. Forbush held this office are plain, clear, and legible, and will compare favorably with any records of the town before or since. He m. Almira W. Cram, dau. of Nathan and Elizabeth Cram, of Belfast, Me., Nov. 16, 1828.

16 | *Elizabeth E.*, b. April 3, 1829 ; m. Frederick W. Nichols.
17 | *Augusta A.*, b. March 17, 1831 ; m. Capt. Louis E. Crone, from Leipsic, Germany, now residing at East Lexington.
18 | *Annie J.*, b. March 19, 1834 ; m. Abel G. Alexander, Woburn, Mass.
19 | †*Nathan C.*, b. June 15, 1838 ; m. Clara J. Blodgett, of Chesterfield.
20 | *Sallie W.*, b. June 20, 1840 ; d. Nov. 1, 1856, æ. 16 yrs., 4 mos.

3- 19 | NATHAN C. Forbush. He was a soldier in Company G., 13th Regiment N. H. Vols., in the war of the Rebellion, and returned slightly wounded, for which he receives a small pension. He m. Clara J. Blodgett.

21 | *Lizzie Maria*, b. Feb. 27, 1862.

1- 4 | STEPHEN FORBUSH. A carpenter by trade. By his labor and industry he raised a large family. The few last years of his life he lived on the Deacon Samuel Maynard place, which he bought, and occupied at the time of his death. He m., 1st w., Esther P. Hill, Oct. 28, 1824 ; b. Oct. 25, 1802 ; d. June 29, 1835, æ. 33 yrs. ; 2d w., Esther S. Smith, Aug. 16, 1835 ; b. June 10, 1802 ; d. May 22, 1862, æ. 60 yrs. ; 3d w., Eleanor Machett, b. Nov. 24, 1802 ; m. Aug. 27, 1863. He d. July 30, 1873, æ. 70 yrs., 5 mos.

22 | *Leonard A.*, b. April 3, 1825 ; d. Sept. 10, 1826, æ. 1 yr., 5 mos.

23 | *John R.*, b. Feb. 28, 1827 ; m. Lucinda F. Foster, Oct. 11, 1846 ; d. Jan. 30, 1857, æ. 30 yrs.

24 | *Catharine H.*, b. Sept. 8, 1828 ; m. Amos B. Drown, Nov. 29, 1848 ; one ch., Isabel A., b. Jan. 22, 1850.

25 | *Stephen*, b. March 12, 1831 ; m. Abby C. Smith, June 10, 1853 ; d. Jan. 18, 1855, æ. 23 yrs., 10 mos. ; r. Maine.

26 | *Lucy E.*, b. June 7, 1833 ; m. Wilson Cobb, Sept. 18, 1853.

27 | *Charles S.*, b. June 2, 1838 ; m. Mary Davis, Nashua, Sept. 6, 1871 ; r. Nashua.

28 | *Mary Ann*, b. Feb. 19, 1841.

29 | *Sarah A.*, b. Dec. 22, 1842 ; d. 1875.

30 | *Martha E.*, b. April 22, 1844 ; d. Aug. 25, 1845, æ. 1 yr., 4 mos.

31 | *Martha E.*, b. Feb. 17, 1846 ; d. April 20, 1873, æ. 27 yrs.

1– 5 | IRA FORBUSH. A carpenter by trade. He m. Hannah Brown, of Andover ; has always lived in the village.

---

32 | *Elvira J.*, b. July 21, 1825 ; m. Charles J. Smith ; d. Aug. 20, 1857, æ. 32 yrs.

33 | *Amos B.*, b. Sept. 3, 1827 ; m., 1st w., Lydia Haggett ; 2d w., Louisa —— ; r. Buffalo, N.Y.

34 | *Maria L.*, b. Sept. 14, 1829 ; m. A. H. Stebbins ; d. Feb. 11, 1857, æ. 27 yrs.

35 | † *Gustavus A.*, b. Dec. 31, 1831 ; m. M. Frances Colman, Oyster Bay, Long Island.

36 | *Hannah C.*, b. June 4, 1834 ; m. German F. Day ; one ch., Katie H.

37 | *Ariana W.*, b. Dec. 21, 1836 ; m. A. H. Stebbins.

38 | *Abial A.*, b. Nov. 13, 1839 ; m. Lizzie Putnam, of Mason.

39 | *Ellen*, b. Feb. 11, 1844 ; m., April 22, 1874, E. Harris Jewett ; one ch., H. Paul, b. Feb. 11, 1876.

40 | *Orrin*, b. Nov. 5, 1846 ; m. Margaret Burns, of Clinton, Mass. She d. March, 1873, æ. 23 yrs. ; one ch., Harry O., b. March 2, 1873.

5– 35 | GUSTAVUS A. FORBUSH. A carpenter by trade. He enlisted in the United States service in the war of the Rebellion, Aug. 9, 1862, as First Lieutenant in the 13th Regiment, Company G., New Hampshire Volunteers. He was promoted to a captaincy May 5, 1863, and transferred to Company F. He was in the battles of Fredericksburg and Cold Harbor, sieges of Suffolk and of Petersburg, and at Fort Harrison, in storming of which, Sept. 29, 1864, he was killed, while leading his men to the attack, just as he had attained the parapet, and had secured the taking of the fort. His commanding officer, Gen. A. F. Stevens, who received a very serious wound in the same battle, from the effects of which he has never yet fully recovered, says of Capt. Forbush, in a letter of April 29, 1875 : "Captain Forbush was a man moderate in thought and action, yet quite methodical and thorough. Hence in time he made himself a fair proficient in company and regimental drill, in which he always evinced a sincere interest, and in which he assiduously sought to improve his command. Towards his men he was considerate and kind, though not wanting in the average discipline of the volunteer service. His moral character was exemplary, his habits correct, his patriotism firm and strong, and his desire and determination to remain in the service so long as his efforts were needed overcame all obstacles, and closed only with the heroic termination of his life. He was, in a military view, a good lieutenant and captain, and would in the course of events have deserved and attained promotion in the service. I can only add to these few words the assurance of my personal esteem for Capt. Forbush as a man, and my satisfaction and pride, as his regimental commander, in his military service and record." He m. M. Frances Coleman, of Oyster Bay, L. I. She d. Jan. 11, 1866.

41   *Willis Herbert*, b. Oct. 7, 1861 ; d. Dec. 24, 1862, æ. 1 yr., 2 mos.

42   *Addie Frances*, b. July 16, 1864 ; d. Sept. 29, 1864, æ. 2 mos.

✎ THE FRENCH FAMILY.

1   WHITCOMB FRENCH was the son of the late Whitcomb and Sally Patrick French, b. in Dublin, July 9, 1794. He m., Nov. 27, 1817, Mary Kendall, dau. of Joel Kendall, of Dublin, b. May 25, 1797. He had r. in various places, as in Nelson, Jaffrey, Keene, &c. Engaged in staging and in the livery-stable business till he moved to Peterborough, 1833. He had charge of the hotel in town to December, 1849, nearly seventeen years. He was a very acceptable landlord, and kept a very respectable house, with a good reputation far and wide. When he left the hotel he bought the Ferguson farm, and occupied it for some years. Unable to carry on a large farm, on account of his declining years, he sold the same, and purchased a residence in the village, where he now r.

Their golden wedding was celebrated Nov. 27, 1867, by a gathering of all the children, grandchildren, and other friends, on this occasion. Of their eight ch., all

Whitcomb French

were alive, the youngest being twenty-six years old, and five of them were present; and of the thirteen grand-children and four great-grandchildren, seven grand-children were also present.

2 | *Eliza G.*, b. in Nelson, Sept. 2, 1818 ; m., Sept. 28, 1840, Jesse C. Little ; r. Salt Lake City, Utah. Had eleven ch., five of whom are now living in Utah Territory.

3 | *Granville*, b. Dublin, July 2, 1820; m., April 26, 1843, Relief Walker, b. in Dummerston, Vt., Sept. 15, 1817. 1 ch., Frederick W., b. July 19, 1847 ; r. Epworth, Ia.

4 | *Mary S.*, b. Jaffrey, Dec. 4, 1823 ; unm.

5 | †*Henry K.*, b. Jaffrey, Jan. 21, 1826; m., 1st w., Harriet N. Gray ; 2d w., Amanda Adams.

6 | *Marshall W.*, b. Jaffrey, Sept. 4, 1827 ; m., Jan. 10, 1855, Lizzie T. Wales, b. Sept. 26, 1830 ; r. Palmer, Mass.

7 | †*Charles D.*, b. Keene, March 29, 1830 ; m., Jan. 23, 1851, Nancy L. Holbrook.

8 | *Sarah F.*, b. Keene, Feb. 22, 1832 ; unm.

9 | *William P.*, b. in Peterborough, June 4, 1841 ; m., June 29, 1868, Helen A. Shearer, of Palmer, Mass., b. Nov. 2, 1841 ; 2 ch., Willie S., and John W. ; r. Palmer.

1– 5 | HENRY K. FRENCH. He succeeded his father in the same house, and has shown himself eminently possessed of all the qualities necessary "to run a hotel." He thoroughly repaired and enlarged the house at a great expense, and has ever since kept a first-class hotel. He m., 1st w., July 9, 1850, Harriet N. Gray, of Wilton, b. Aug. 21, 1829 ; d. Oct. 13, 1852, æ. 23 yrs. ; 2d w., Nov. 20, 1855, S. Amanda Adams, b. Mason, July 10, 1834 ; 1st w., one ch. ; 2d w., three ch.

10 | *Frank G.*, b. June 10, 1852.

11 | *Charlie H.*, b. Dec. 22, 1856.

12 | *Hattie A.*, b. Aug. 27, 1858.

13 | *George A.*, b. Sept. 22, 1860.

1– 7 | CHARLES D. FRENCH. He re. to Chickasaw and Deerfield, Ia., and after a short residence returned to Peterborough in 1858, where he now resides. He served in the war of the Rebellion. He m., Jan. 23, 1851, Nancy L. Holbrook ; b. Swanzey, Aug. 1, 1827.

14 | *Charles W.*, b. Nov. 20, 1854 ; d. Feb. 26, 1856, æ. 1 yr., 3 mos.

15 | *H. Edward*, b. March 15, 1857.

16 | *Minnie M.*, b. June 17, 1861.

17 | *Katie H.*, b. Nov. 11, 1871.

THE FROST FAMILY.

1   CYRUS FROST, son of Benjamin and Annis Pierce
Frost, was b. in Dublin, May 12, 1807. He lived on the
old homestead in Dublin till March 13, 1852, when he
re. to Peterborough, and occupied the Charles Davison
farm, being a part of the Gridley farm, or farm A, so
called, of five hundred acres. He m., 1st w., November,
1829, Cyntha Nay, of Sharon. She d. Jan. 20, 1837;
2d w., Betsey McCoy, of Sharon, Nov. 9, 1837; b. Sept.
24, 1807. She d. Sept. 3, 1858, æ. 50 yrs., 11 mos.;
1st w., one ch.; 2d w., three ch.

2   *Lydia Ann*, b. July 30, 1831.
3   *Charles Albert*, b. Sept. 9, 1838; m., June 16, 1868,
Sarah A. Garfield, b. May 22, 1841, dau. of Wm. and
Annis Walker Garfield, of Claremont.
4   *Sarah E.*, b. Dec. 15, 1839; m. Miflin Bailey, Tremont,
Ill.
5   *Cyntha A.*, b. Aug. 6, 1843; m., 1876, Henry F. Mears;
r. Nashua.

2   ALBERT FROST, a brother of Cyrus Frost, was b. in
Dublin, March 20, 1817. He m., Feb. 21, 1843, Mary
Boutelle, of Antrim. He came to Peterborough in 1848,
and bought the Daniel Abbot place, where Dr. Young
formerly lived, and has resided there since. He has
been sexton for the town for a number of years. He is
a carpenter by trade.

6   *George A.*, b. March 23, 1844. He m. Oriseville S.
Fisher, b. Jan. 21, 1848; ch., Albert Orvis, b. Dec. 10,
1869.
7   *Mary E.*, b. April 30, 1847.
8   *Eugene L.*, b. Aug. 30, 1849; d. Aug. 21, 1852, æ. 2 yrs.,
11 mos.
9   *Emma J.*, b. July 17, 1851; d. Aug. 10, 1852, æ. 1 yr.

THE GATES FAMILY.

1   SAMUEL GATES was the son of Samuel and Susanna
Laughton Gates, of Hancock, b. Feb. 15, 1791. His
parents came from Rutland, Mass. His father d. in
Hancock, Aug. 28, 1838, æ. 86 yrs., 9 mos.; his mother
d. May 15, 1857, æ. 99 yrs. Samuel Gates was a blacksmith by trade, came to Peterborough in 1814, and carried on his business half a mile west of the village, on
High Street, near where Isaac F. Preston now lives, and
continued his work till his health failed in 1841, when he

was appointed postmaster, which office he held till his death, 1854. He was also made town clerk, which office he held nine years, from 1841 to 1850. During the last years of his life he suffered from a severe paralysis, which hopelessly impaired the use of his limbs ; and the duties of the post-office were very acceptably performed for some years by his dau. Susan, afterwards Mrs. M. L. Morrison. He m., 1st w., Sarah S. Ferguson, Sept. 3, 1816. She d. June 25, 1822, æ. 27 yrs.; 2d w., Oct. 26, 1824, Charlotte Mitchell. She d. Oct. 16, 1851, æ. 53 yrs. He d. May 7, 1854, æ. 63 yrs.; 1st w., three ch.; 2d w., five ch.

2   *George S.*, b. July 23, 1817 ; m. Christine Fletcher ; r. Groton, Mass. ; c.

3   *Sybil E.*, b. April 14, 1819 ; m. John Holmes, June 15, 1858 ; r. Springfield, Vt. ; d. April 24, 1863, æ. 43 yrs., 9 mos. ; ch., George G., b. July 15, 1859 ; d. Sept. 15, 1860, æ. 1 yr., 2 mos.

4   *Sarah S.*, b. June 8, 1822 ; d. July 27, 1822, æ. 1 mo., 19 dys.

5   *Henry*, b. May 3, 1825 ; d. July 5, 1826, æ. 1 yr., 2 mos.

6   *John*, b. Feb. 27, 1827 ; m., Sept. 21, 1856, Octavia Sampson, of Hartford, Me.

7   *Charlotte M.*, b. Feb. 14, 1830 ; m., Dec. 23, 1860, Chas. M. Townsend ; r. Springfield, Vt. ; ch., John G., b. Dec. 19, 1865.

8   *Henry*, b. March 24, 1832 ; r. at the South ; d. Savannah, Ga., 1875, æ. 43 yrs.

9   *Susan M.*, b. March 13, 1835 ; m. Mortier L. Morrison, Aug. 4, 1861.

THE GIBBS FAMILY.

1   DANIEL GIBBS, as near as can be ascertained, came to Peterborough about 1793 from Ashburnham, Mass. He moved to the place he occupied during his life, in the east part of the town, one-half a mile directly north of the Cuningham Pond. He began to carry the mail on horseback in 1804, and continued to do so for about ten years, from Brattleboro, Vt., to Portsmouth, once a week. All Boston mail-matter came by way of Keene every Saturday afternoon — a mail once a week from Boston ! After this Mr. Gibbs carried the mail in a little one-horse wagon. He was as regular on his course as the sun. He pursued this course about twenty years, and just before the mail was to be carried on a stage, then about to be established, he was killed in passing the great bridge in the village, then under repair, by one

wheel of his vehicle running off the bridge, and he being precipitated with the seat of the wagon down upon the rocks below, and so injured that he lived but two hours. The first words that he uttered to those who came to his assistance were: "Take care of the mail," and then "that he was fatally injured." He was an honest and worthy man. He m. Lydia Woods, of Ashburnham, Mass., who d. April 14, 1836, æ. 75 yrs. He d. Sept. 25, 1824, æ. 74 yrs.

---

2 *Polly*, b. April 1, 1780; d. April 17, 1795, æ. 14 yrs.
3 †*Asa*, b. Aug. 29, 1783; m., 1st w., Polly Gregg; 2d w., Sally Porter.
4 †*Abel*, b. July 18, 1787; m. Nancy Porter.
5 *Lydia W.*, b. Aug. 29, 1798; m. John Gardner; 2d hus., Rev. Wm. Hogan, January, 1828, in Savannah, Ga. He d. January, 1848, æ. 52 yrs. She d. at Peterborough, Sept. 20, 1875, æ. 77 yrs.
6 *Sally J.*, b. 1800; d. May 29, 1820, æ. 20 yrs.

1- 3 ASA GIBBS. He m., 1st w., Mary Gregg, dau. Major Samuel Gregg, March 16, 1809. She d. Feb. 24, 1813, æ. 31 yrs. He m., 2d w., Sally Porter, dau. James Porter, July 4, 1815. She d. Oct. 24, 1859, æ. 77 yrs. He d. May 27, 1849, æ. 65 yrs. After the death of his father, Mr. Gibbs carried the mail in a two-horse carriage until stages were established in 1826 or '7; 1st w., two ch.; 2d w., two ch.

---

7 *Mary*, b. Dec. 10, 1808; m. Philip Alexander; d. at Woburn, Sept. 14, 1872, æ. 64 yrs.
8 *Sarah S.*, b. May 7, 1812; m. James G. White.
9 *Nancy Curtis*, b. May 1, 1820; d. Dec. 18, 1866, æ. 46 yrs.
10 *Elizabeth*, b. Jan. 28, 1823; d. Dec. 2, 1861, æ. 39 yrs.

1- 4 ABEL. GIBBS m. Nancy C. Porter, dau. James Porter, March 13, 1816. He d. in Savannah, Ga., in 1819, æ. 32 yrs. They had one ch.

---

11 *James Porter*, b. Sept. 11, 1816; d. at Woburn, Mass., Oct. 9, 1842, æ. 26 yrs. Mrs. Gibbs afterwards m. Deacon Samuel Maynard.

THE GOODRIDGE FAMILY.

1 RILEY GOODRIDGE was b. in Westminster, Vt., June 18, 1795. He came to Peterborough to work at machinery. He was postmaster a number of years, and

having gone West on some business he d. at Council Bluffs City, Ia., Sept. 8, 1851, æ. 56 yrs., 2 mos. He m. Polly D. Powers, dau. Whitcomb and Merriam B. Powers, Nov. 8, 1830. She d. at Peterborough, June 12, 1870, æ. 77 yrs.

2 *Mary Antoinette*, b. Aug. 24, 1831; m. Charles Gold-thwaite, Sept. 13, 1859. One ch., Mary Louisa, b. May 8, 1862.

3 *Louisa T.*, b. June 25, 1833; m. Josephus Emery, Nov. 23, 1854. She d. April 27, 1860, æ 26 yrs., 10 mos.; r. Lowell.

THE GORDON FAMILY.

1 SAMUEL GORDON came from Ireland when he was seventeen years of age, and was the son of Nathaniel Gordon, who was b. in the county of Tyrone, Ireland, 1700; m. Sarah Martin; had four ch., *viz.*, John, James (who d. young), Samuel, and Hannah. About the year 1749 Nathaniel Gordon and family arrived in Boston. John, his son, b. in 1729, was a brewer by trade, and went into business in Boston, with the great Samuel Adams, between 1750 and '60. Nathaniel, the father, and Samuel, went to Dunstable, Mass., in the employ of William Gordon, an English merchant of that place, and remained five years, then bought a farm in Shirley, when the father and two sons, John and Samuel, re. to it, The next move was to Peterborough. Samuel and family re. in 1780; their parents, Nathaniel and Sarah Martin Gordon, came with them. Mrs. Gordon d. in Peterborough in 1781, and Nathaniel Gordon d. in 1788. There are no gravestones for them in the old cemetery.

Eleanor Mitchell, w. of Samuel Gordon, re. from Ireland to Cape Breton, when the French and English were at war, where her father was killed, and all the rest of the family but her mother, brother, and herself, were carried off by the small-pox. Her mother, after they came to Boston, m. a Mr. Holden, and had several ch.

Samuel Gordon was b. in Ireland, May 17, 1732, and d. in Peterborough, Dec. 2, 1818, æ. 86 yrs. His w. d. Nov. 2, 1820, æ. 74 yrs. He always lived on the same place that he first occupied in town, known as the Gordon farm. He and his wife were strict Presbyterians, good and pious persons. Mr. Gordon was the first to sign a remonstrance, with twenty others, against the ordination of Rev. Elijah Dunbar to the Christian ministry in Peterborough. We suppose that he was a man of moderate talents. Among the town offices held by him we find that he was pound-keeper eight years, and tithing-man three years before 1804.

---

2 †*Samuel*, b. in Shirley, May 27, 1765 ; m. Lydia Ames.

3 *Sally*, b. in Shirley, Feb. 10, 1767 ; r. Charlestown, with her uncle Holden.

4 *Betsey*, b. in Shirley, Jan. 23, 1769 ; m. Joseph Barnes, Sharon, Sept. 17, 1801 ; d.

5 *Hannah*, b. 1772 ; m. Stephen Pierce.

6 *Nathaniel*, b. —— ; re. to New York ; d. 1827 ; frozen to death.

7 *Eleanor*, b. —— ; m. Capt. Andrew Cochran, U. S. A., March 11, 1816.

8 *Jane*, b. —— ; unm. ; r. Milford.

9 *Polly*, b. —— ; m. Adam Dickey, Milford, Nov. 7, 1808.

10 *Nehemiah*, b. —— ; unm. ; went to sea ; d. at Martha's Vineyard.

11 †*John*, b. Dec. 20, 1790 ; m. Betsey Smith.

12 *Nancy*, b. —— ; m. Thomas M. Dickey, Jan. 26, 1815 ; r. Amherst.

1– 2 . SAMUEL GORDON was a man of superior talents. He first located himself at Hancock as a trader, and soon became the leading man in that town. He removed from Hancock to Charlestown, Mass., and kept a hotel. At one time public suspicion rested on him as being concerned in the robbery and murder of David Starrett, on Charlestown bridge, who was a guest at his hotel, and who all at once mysteriously disappeared, his rifled trunk being found on the bridge, but who, after some ten or twelve years, his estate in the meanwhile being settled in probate in New Hampshire, was found to be living in one of the Western States. Mr. Gordon removed to Hallowell, Me., and d. there, June 23, 1853, æ. 88 yrs. He m. Lydia Ames, dau. David Ames, of Hancock, May 20, 1790. She d. at same place, July 5, 1853, æ. 79 yrs. ; b. Feb. 19, 1774.

---

13 *Samuel*, b. Aug. 7, 1791, in Hancock ; d. in infancy.

14 *Yorick S.*, b. Jan. 9, 1793, in Hancock ; d. Pineville, S. C., 1820, æ. 27 yrs.

15 *Oliver H.*, b. June 27, 1794 ; d. Woodside, N. J., 1869, æ. 75 yrs.

16 *Lydia*, b. Dec. 25, 1795 ; m. —— Kimball ; he d.

17 *Isabella*, b. June 14, 1798 ; m. —— White ; he d.

18 *Eleanor*, b. Jan. 30, 1800 ; d. Sept. 8, 1808, in Hancock, æ. 8 yrs., 7 mos.

19 *Elizabeth*, b. Oct. 13, 1805 ; m. Thomas B. Brooks ; d. Brooklyn, N.Y., 1871, æ. 66 yrs.

20 | *Rebecca C.*, b. Feb. 29, 1808 ; d. June 27, 1808, in Hancock, æ. 4 mos.

21 | *Samuel A.*, b. Oct. 3, 1810 ; d. Hallowell, Me., Feb. 26, 1845, æ. 35 yrs.

22 | *Sarah M.*, b. March 6, 1813 ; m. Dr. Justus Hurd ; r. St. Louis, Mo.

23 | *John Clark*, b. Oct. 12, 1818 ; d. Oct. 19, 1818, æ. 7 dys. The first nine were b. in Hancock, the remainder in Charlestown, Mass.

1– 11 | JOHN GORDON succeeded his father on the homestead, and remained there till after the death of his parents. He re. to Montebello, Ill., in 1831, where he d. April 3, 1839, æ. 48 yrs. He m. Betsey Smith, dau. Deacon Jona. Smith, Dec. 31, 1819, who d. Aug. 12, 1845, æ. 50 yrs.

24 | *Jona. S.*, b. Oct. 20, 1822 ; d. Montebello, Ill., March 27, 1839, æ. 17 yrs.

25 | *Samuel*, b. May 3, 1825 ; m. Permelia A. Alvord, April 3, 1851 ; ch., (1) Ella E., b. Oct. 1, 1852 ; (2) John A., b. Aug. 21, 1855 ; (3) Alice A., b. Jan. 14, 1858 ; (4) Agnes C., b. Dec. 17, 1860 ; (5) Robert Smith, b. Dec. 10, 1866 ; (6) Mabel B., b. Dec. 30, 1870. Samuel Gordon r. in Hamilton, Ill.

THE GOWING FAMILY.

1 | WILLIAM GOWING was the son of James and Lydia Wellman Gowing, of Dublin, — one of twelve children. He re. to Peterborough in 1794 ; m. Abigail Miller, dau. Samuel Miller, Sen., Jan. 6, 1795. She d. Feb. 23, 1830, æ. 72 yrs. He m., 2d w., Lucy Adams, of Sharon, Nov. 25, 1830. She d. in Sharon, Nov. 27, 1862. He was b. in Lynnfield, Mass., March 1, 1766 ; d. at Peterborough, Oct. 25, 1854, æ. 87 yrs. He lived on the Miller place, directly east of the Smith farm.

2 | *Margaret*, b. in Dublin, Jan. 1, 1796 ; m. Daniel Chapman.

3 | *William H.*, b. Oct. 21, 1798 ; m., May 6, 1830, Laura Hale ; r. East Wilton. He d. July 8, 1859, æ. 60 yrs., 8 mos. ; ch., (1) Ariana ; m. Warren Jones, East Wilton ; (2) Sarah ; m. Joseph Langdell, East Wilton. Mrs. Gowing d. 1875.

4 | †*Moses*, b. Sept. 11, 1800 ; m. Mary Jewett.

1– 4 | MOSES GOWING. He succeeded his father on the homestead, and r. there till 18—, when he sold his farm and removed to the village where he now lives.

He m. Mary Jewett, dau. of John and Margaret Jewett, Sept. 8, 1825. They celebrated their golden wedding Sept. 8, 1875, by a large assemblage of their friends, and were made the recipients of many useful and substantial presents.

5 *Sophia M.*, b. Dec. 28, 1826 ; m. Albert Sawyer.
6 *Mary E.*, b. Nov. 30, 1828 ; m. Albert Taggart.
7 *Henry M.*, b. Sept. 11, 1832 ; m., Oct. 15, 1866, Tillie E. Irving ; r. New York City.

8 ASA F. GOWING was the son of Joseph and Hepzibeth Fairbanks Gowing ; b. Dec. 8, 1808, in Dublin. He came to Peterborough to reside in 1840 ; m., Dec. 2, 1845, Agnes Robbe, dau. Samuel and Betsey Scott Robbe. She d. May 20, 1852, æ. 37 yrs. ; 2d w., May 31, 1853, Catharine Robbe, sister of above ; c. He d. June 30, 1872, æ. 63 yrs., 6 mos.

9   *Lizzie R.*, b. Dec. 15, 1847.
10 *Frederick*, b. Aug. 15, 1851 ; d. Dec. 4, 1851, æ. 3 mos.

THE GRAY FAMILY.

1 KELSO GRAY came from Pelham to Peterborough probably about 1766 or '67. The record of the family must be very imperfect from the scanty materials furnished. He m. Phebe Gray, who d. March 27, 1814, æ. 74 yrs. He d. Oct. 28, 1824, æ. 86 yrs. He began the Gray farm, south of David Blanchard's.

2   *Hugh*, b. —— ; m. Jenny Moore, of Sharon ; re. to Montpelier, Vt.
3   *Reuben*, b. —— ; r. Montpelier, Vt.
4   *Esther*, b. 1770 ; d. March 5, 1795, æ. 25 yrs.
5   *Kelso*, b. —— ; m. Anna Wilson ; r. Montpelier, Vt.
6   †*Matthew*, b. Dec. 9, 1772 ; m. Polly Conner, of Poplin.
7   *Jean*, b. 1776 ; m. John Shearer White.
8   † *William*, b. Dec. 3, 1781 ; m. Harriet Scott.
9   *Phebe*, b. —— ; m. Adam Penniman.
10 *David*, b. —— ; m. Drusilla La Baines ; r. Montpelier, Vt.

1- 6 MATTHEW GRAY succeeded his father on the old place. He m. Mary Conner, of Poplin. She d. Jan. 8, 1846, æ. 75 yrs. He d. Dec. 25, 1841, æ. 69 yrs.

11 *Matthew, Jr.*, b. May 3, 1797 ; m., 1st w., Nancy Clark ; 2d w., Mrs. Rhoda Hutchinson Bartlett ; r. Milford. Only one dau. survives of all his ch. ; she by 2d w.

12 | *Mary*, b. Aug. 3, 1799; m. Wm. Miller; 2d hus., Wm. S. Smith.

13 | *Azuba*, b. Nov. 27, 1801; m. Hiram Chapman.

14 | † *William Conner*, b. June 8, 1804; m. Lucinda Parker.

15 | *Lorinda*, b. Nov. 14, 1806; m. David Emerson; 2d hus., Warren Woods Hancock. She d. Hancock.

1– 8 | WILLIAM GRAY settled and lived on the George Duncan, Jr., place until within a few years before his death, when he re. to the village, where he died. He m. Harriet Scott, dau. John Scott, Esq., April 4, 1811. He d. March 31, 1855, æ. 74 yrs.

16 | *Bethiah*, b. Jan. 7, 1812; m. Moses Greenfield, Jan. 19, 1835. He d. Nov. 28, 1844; ch., (1) Bethiah, b. Oct. 25, 1835; m. Lucien Alexander; 1. ch., Lizzie, b. 1861; (2) Maria, b. June 10, 1845; d. 1846.

17 | † *John S.*, b. June 11, 1813; m., Dec. 21, 1842, Elizabeth H. Flint.

18 | *Jane*, b. July 8, 1815; m., March 25, 1832, Lyman Knowlton. He d. in Nelson.

19 | *Harriet*, b. Jan. 30, 1818; m., Jan. 1, 1839, Horatio Nelson.

20 | *William S.*, b. Oct. 13, 1819; m. Louisa Whitcomb; r. ——.

21 | *Adam P.*, b. June 10, 1823; d. Aug. 15, 1842, æ 19 yrs.

22 | † *Charles S.*, b. Nov. 25, 1824; m. Lydia Ann Stevens.

23 | *James S.*, b. March 9, 1829; m., 1st w., Mary Ann ——, in New York City. She d. Aug. 8, 1852, æ. 20 yrs., 11 mos.; 2d w., Ada Lewis; c.; r. Peterborough.

24 | *Samuel*, b. April 29, 1832; d. 1832.

25 | *Sarah E.*, } b. Feb. 22, 1835; { m. Reuben Baldwin; d.
26 | *Mary Eliza*, } { d. in 1836.

6– 14 | WILLIAM CONNER GRAY. He r. in various places in town, and devoted himself principally to farming. He m. Lucinda Parker, Jan 23, 1834. He d. May 25, 1865, æ. 61 yrs. She d. Nov. 17, 1870, æ. 62 yrs.; b. Nov. 2, 1808.

27 | *Helen J.*, b. June 18, 1836; m. William McCain; r. St. Paul, Minn.

28 | *Clara L.*, b. Nov. 25, 1842; m. Ervin H. Smith; r. Springfield, Mass.

8– 17 | JOHN SCOTT GRAY. He was engaged in the mercantile business in the village, when he was attacked with a prevailing typhoid fever, and d. Oct. 13, 1843, æ. 30 yrs. He m. Elizabeth H. Flint, dau. of Jacob Flint, Dec. 21, 1842. Mrs. Elizabeth H. Gray, widow of John S. Gray,

13

m., 2d hus., Samuel Nay, Esq., of Sharon, April 3, 1863 ; r. in town.

29　 *John Flint*, b. —— ; d. Oct. 17, 1848, æ. 5 yrs.

8– 22　 CHARLES SCOTT GRAY. He fell from his buildings while repairing the same, and fractured the fourth vertebra of his spine, of which he d., after a painful sickness, Oct. 26, 1868, æ. 43 yrs., 11 mos. He m. Lydia Ann Stevens, dau. of Joshua Stevens, Nov. 4, 1847. He lived on the homestead.

30　 *Charles S.*, b. Sept. 1, 1848 ; d. Aug. 29, 1849, æ. 1 yr.
31　 *Lissie Ann*, b. Aug. 12, 1850 ; d. Dec. 24, 1850, æ. 4 mos.
32　 *Fred A.*, b. June 13, 1852.
33　 *John S.*, b. Dec. 27, 1854.
34　 *Arthur H.*, b. Oct. 4, 1857.
35　 *Annie C.*, b. Aug. 17, 1859.
36　 *Franse S.*, b. Dec. 17, 1861 ; d. Sept. 12, 1870, æ. 8 yrs., 8 mos.
37　 *Addie L.*, b. Feb. 3, 1863.
38　 *James S.*, b. Sept. 16, 1864.
39　 *Charles S.*, b. Oct. 15, 1865.
40　 *Perley B.*, b. July 22, 1867 ; d. Feb. 6, 1871, æ. 3 yrs., 6 mos.

THE GREGG FAMILY.

1　 MAJOR SAMUEL GREGG was the son of John Gregg, and grandson of Capt. James Gregg, who was one of the first sixteen who settled in Londonderry, and who was b. in Ayrshire, Scotland, and emigrated with his parents to Ireland about the year 1690.* He was a linen draper, and acquired considerable property before he emigrated to America. He embarked for America in 1718, and spent the winter at Cape Elizabeth, Me., amid many trials and much suffering. He had four sons and one daughter ; of these John was the father of Major Samuel Gregg above. He moved on to a tract of land in the north part of Peterborough, situated on the Contoocook River, about three miles north of the village, as a squatter, and before any company or claim had been put on the land in that vicinity, and soon after the Indians had left for Canada.† After this, little hostility was experienced from the Indians. The tribe that annoyed this vicinity was the Pennacooks, considered the most cruel and savage on the continent. We are unable to state the year Major Gregg came to Peterbor-

---

* History Londonderry, p. 274.
† Letter Samuel Gregg, June 5, 1873.

ough, only that it was some years previous to the incorporation of the town in 1760. Major Gregg enlisted in the British army before he was twenty years old, as a sergeant, was in the war between the French and English in 1759, and also in the battle in the Plains of Abraham under the brave Gen. Wolfe. When the Revolution broke out, he was offered a commission in the King's service, but refused, and risked all in the cause of his country.

At the commencement of the Revolution he was appointed a major in the Continental service, and was with the regiment formed in Peterborough and vicinity, which was summoned.to Charlestown at the time of the battle of Bunker Hill. As soon as possible he enlisted two hundred men and started for Charlestown, seventy miles distant, and by marching day and night he arrived the day after the battle. After a few days they returned home. The Major shared all the hardships of the expedition with the soldiers, by footing it with them.

By his own and his wife's energy and industry, they accumulated considerable property, and erected a good and comfortable dwelling-house, out-houses, and barns. He was a mechanic, and manufactured foot-wheels for spinning flax, and big-wheels, so called, for spinning wool and tow, which he peddled through the country. In those days the women had to manufacture the clothing for the family, or they had to go without it. Samuel Gregg, son of Hugh Gregg, and grandson of Major Gregg, to whom we are indebted for many of the facts in this account, says in a letter to us: "I have worn many a suit that was never out of the house until it went out on my back, and have worn many a tow shirt, all carded and spun at home. A girl was not considered marriageable until she understood the making of cloth. My grandfather was a great economist, but his table was always loaded with the substantials of life, and no person went away from his house hungry, if known to be so." His name does not appear on the town records till 1768 as selectman, while the names of John Gregg, Sen., and John Gregg, Jr., appear a number of times. He was also selectman in 1771, and perhaps for 1770; the record of that year is missing. He was one of the Committee of Safety in 1779. He m. Agnes Smiley, of Londonderry.; b. 1743; d. at Peterborough, Feb. 2, 1803, æ. 60 yrs. He was b. 1738; d. Dec. 10, 1808, æ. 70 yrs.

2 *John*, b. Feb. 23, 1764. Went West.
3 *Hugh*, b. Nov. 22, 1765; m. Sarah Holmes; d.
4 *Sarah*, b. Nov. 7, 1769; m. Gen. David Steele.

5 | *Samuel*, b. Oct. 25, 1772 ; r. Boston.
6 | *George*, b. March 15, 1775 ; m. Sally Moore, dau. Wm. Moore.
7 | *Anne*, b. Nov. 14, 1778 ; m. —— Gregg, Londonderry.
8 | *Mary*, b. Jan. 27, 1782 ; m. Asa Gibbs ; d. Feb. 24, 1813, æ. 31 yrs.
9 | *Elizabeth*, b. Dec. 21, 1785 ; m. Wm. Hutchins, Boston, Feb. 6, 1806.

---

10 | JOHN GREGG (Lieut.), we suppose the son of John Gregg, brother of the above, and grandson of Capt. James Gregg, one of the first settlers of Londonderry. He came to town about 1759, and settled on the south part of Farm C, having sixty-three rods of the south part of the same deeded to him by John Gregg, of Londonderry, Oct. 8, 1765, the father receiving a deed of the same lot C from John Hill, one of the proprietors, Dec. 6, 1743. He occupied the farm since owned and improved by his son, James Gregg. The place directly north, also a part of farm C, was begun and occupied by Major Samuel Gregg. There were other John Greggs in town, and he was designated, we know not why, as black John Gregg; m., 1st w., unknown, by whom he had six ch., to 1768 ; 2d w., Elizabeth, widow of William Stuart, and dau. of Patrick White. She d. Nov. 2, 1803, æ. 59 yrs. He d. Feb. 24, 1798, æ. 70 yrs. ; 1st w., six ch. ; 2d w., five ch.

---

11 | *Agnes*, b. April 6, 1760. (12) *Mary*, b. Feb. 27, 1762.
13 | *Jenne*, b. May 3, 1764. (14) *Benjamin*, b. May 13, 1766.
15 | *Ebenezer*, b. April 24, 1768.
16 | *William*, b. June 12, 1770.
17 | *Betsey*, b. Sept. 1, 1774 ; unm. ; d. Feb. 9, 1846, æ. 72 yrs.
18 | *Jane*, b. Dec. 22, 1776 ; unm. ; d. July 2, 1805, æ. 28 yrs.
19 | *John*, b. Aug. 10, 1779 ; unm. ; d. young.
20 | *Fanny*, b. May 8, 1782 ; unm. ; d. Aug. 9, 1866, æ. 84 yrs., 3 mos.
21 | †*James*, b. Aug. 19, 1785 ; m. Jane Miller.

10–21 | JAMES GREGG settled on the homestead, and lived there till his death. He m. Jane Miller, dau. of Samuel Miller, May 15, 1817. She d. March 28, 1845, æ. 56 yrs. He d. Feb. 28, 1842, æ. 56 yrs.

---

22 | †*John R.*, b. April 27, 1818 ; m., May 20, 1847, Sarah E. Fletcher.
23 | *Sarah A.*, b. 1822 ; m. Ervin Nelson, of Sutton ; d. March 2, 1870, æ. 48 yrs. ; three ch.

24 | *Fanny Jane*, b. 1826; m. John Nelson, of Sutton; d. April 13, 1871, æ. 45 yrs.; two ch.

21– 22 | JOHN R. GREGG succeeded his father on the home farm, but afterwards, on account of poor health, was obliged to sell the same. He subsequently bought the Adam Penniman farm, where he d. April 16, 1873, æ. 55 yrs. He m. Sarah E. Fletcher, of Antrim, May 20, 1847.

25 | *Anna Jane*, b. March 23, 1848; m. Wiley J. Macy, of Munfordville, Ky.
26 | *Sarah E.*, b. April 24, 1851; m. Frank Wright; r. Harrisville.
27 | *Hattie L.*, b. Nov. 21, 1860.

HUGH GREGG. We do not know whether this is a distinct family from the above or not. His wife's name is unknown, only the Christian name of Jean. He d. March 21, 1791, æ. 90 yrs.

28 | *Adams*, b. Sept. 23, 1745. (29) *William*, b. July 1, 1748.
30 | *Hugh*, b. Sept. 5, 1754. (31) *Jacob*, b. March 19, 1757.

JOHN GREGG, JR. We are uncertain in regard to this family. His wife's name was Jane; and on the town records we have these births. His name appears as selectman in 1767, and that of John Gregg, Sen., in 1762 and '63. I think John Gregg, Jr., is son of John Gregg, Londonderry, and brother of Major Samuel Gregg. But who is this John Gregg, Sen. ?

32 | *Robert*, b. Dec. 8, 1758.
33 | *Margaret*, b. March 19, 1762.
34 | *Jane*, b. July 26, 1764.

JOHN GREGG, whose wife's name is Rachel, is found on the town records. We do not know of what race he is, nor anything of his descendants.

35 | *Hugh*, b. Dec. 12, 1787. (36) *Rachel*, b. Jan. 8, 1789.

THE GRIMES FAMILY.

1 | AARON GRIMES was b. at Windham, Dec. 12, 1769. He came to Peterborough about 1787. He then went to Jaffrey for three years to learn his trade, that of a carpenter. He bought the Milliken place, and lived there a few years, and at various other places in town, till he removed to Lowell in 1839, where he remained till his death. He was esteemed an excellent workman

at his trade. He m. Polly Milliken, dau. of William Milliken, Nov. 1, 1804; b. at Peterborough, Oct. 18, 1784. He d. Sept. 8, 1853, æ. 83 yrs., 8 mos.

---

2   *Mary A.*, b. Oct. 25, 1805 ; unm.; r. Lowell.
3   † *William M.*, b. Dec. 6, 1807 ; m. Betsey Fairbanks.
4   *Katherine S.*, b. Nov. 10, 1809 ; m. Henry Wade ; ch., Sarah, b. March 27, 1845 ; m. E. J. Milton ; ch., George, b. May 14, 1869. Mrs. Wade d. in Lowell, Dec. 9, 1852, æ. 43 yrs.
5   *Louisa E.*, b. March 16, 1812 ; m. William Wilson, Bennington. He d. at Lowell, November, 1839 ; 2d hus., Ebenezer Crane ; three ch.
6   *John H.*, b. March 18, 1814 ; d. Burlington, Ia., May 11, 1854, æ. 40 yrs.
7   *Aaron A.*, b. Aug. 20, 1815 ; unm. ; suppose d. at sea.
8   *Frederick*, b. July 2, 1817 ; m. Margaret Wade ; ch., William and Belle.
9   *Sarah A.*, b. March 31, 1819 ; d. Aug. 25, 1844, at Lowell, æ. 25 yrs., 4 mos.
10 *Jane B.*, b. April 1, 1823 ; m. John L. Ordway, Dec. 21, 1846 ; ch., Jeannie Eliza, b. Oct. 15, 1847.
11 *Caroline J.*, b. March 17, 1829 ; unm.; r. Newton, Mass.

1– 3   WILLIAM M. GRIMES. He has always lived in town. A carpenter by trade. He m. Betsey Fairbanks, dau. of Ebenezer Fairbanks, Dec. 6, 1837.

---

12 *Caroline E.*, b. July 3, 1840 ; m. Frederick Newman, Sept. 21, 1867 ; r. Fitchburg, Mass.
13 *Kate M.*, b. April 19, 1843 ; m. George W. Wilson, Sept. 21, 1867 ; d. July 7, 1876, æ. 33 yrs.
14 *Ann*, b. June 9, 1848. (15) *Helen*, b. June 2, 1850.
16 *Alfred*, b. May 24, 1852.
17 *Frank*, b. Sept. 30, 1855 ; m., 1876, Hattie E. Lovejoy.

THE HADLEY FAMILY.

1   EBENEZER HADLEY, the son of Thomas and Ruth Lawrence Hadley, was b. May 5, 1757, and m., May 11, 1779, Phebe Winship, b. July 23, 1755, both being natives and residents of Lexington, Mass. He, with his father, Thomas Hadley, and his brother Samuel, were all members of Capt. John Parker's company, and stood on the Lexington Common on the morning of April 19, 1775, when the British troops came up and commanded them to disperse and to lay down their arms. On their refusal to obey, no doubt also with a defiant look, and a bold and menacing aspect, the British fired on them,

killing nine of these patriots ; Samuel Hadley, brother to
Ebenezer, being among the slain. Their blood was first
shed for the cause of freedom in America. Capt. Parker's company was on active duty all the day, and had
ample scope for vengeance, especially in watching and
harassing the enemy on their retreat. Both father and
son, no doubt, were among the number of this company
in that day's work. That they were bold and defiant,
the considerable loss sustained by the American force
would seem to indicate — forty-nine having been killed,
thirty-nine wounded, and five missing ; in all ninety-
three ! Ebenezer Hadley's name is among the number
of Capt. Parker's company called to Cambridge, May 6
to 10, 1775 ; also among those called to Cambridge,
June 17 and 18, 1775, while the name of the father does
not appear. Ebenezer Hadley was not in the battle of
Bunker Hill. Capt. Parker's company was detained at
Cambridge, and thereby deprived of the honor of par-
ticipating in this ever-memorable battle, from the apprehension that the British might cross the river and attack
the camp, while so many were engaged in the battle at
Charlestown. In the "History of Lexington," p. 387,
we find the services of Ebenezer Hadley rated at £9 for
five months' service at Ticonderoga in 1775, and also his
name, p. 391, among those who enlisted for three years or
during the war in 1780. Whether he rendered any other
service we have no means of knowing. His widow
received a pension of $10 per month from the time it was
given to the Revolutionary soldiers to her death.

All the sons of Ebenezer Hadley were brickmakers
by trade, and worked at it in Massachusetts till they
came to Peterborough to buy farms. It may be that
they came before their father. He moved to town in
1804. These brothers have made nearly all the brick
manufactured in town for the last seventy years. Mr.
Hadley d. from an accident. He fell from his horse,
one foot remaining in the stirrup, by which he was
dragged some distance on the ground, and was so
injured that he d. the next day. He d. June 15, 1810,
æ. 59 yrs. She d. Aug. 25, 1849, æ. 94 yrs. All the ch.
of Ebenezer Hadley were b. in Lexington.

————

2 †*Thomas*, b. June 13, 1782 ; m., 1st w., Mary Symonds ;
2d w., Martha Barber.
3 †*Isaac*, b. Aug. 9, 1784 ; m., Feb. 9, 1813, Sarah Howe.
4 †*Ebenezer*, b. May 1, 1787 ; m. Amy Howe.
5 †*Ethan*, b. April 7, 1791 ; m., 1st w., Eliza Faxon ; 2d
w., Betsey Persons.

6   *Martha*, b. March 23, 1792; unm.; d. Nov. 15, 1869, æ. 77 yrs.

7   *Jonas*, b. May 3, 1795; d. July 17, 1814, æ. 19 yrs.

1– 2   THOMAS HADLEY occupied the farm west of and adjoining the Hunt place. He m., 1st w., Mary Symonds, of Lexington, who was the mother of all his ch. She was b. March 4, 1788; d. at Peterborough, Nov. 2, 1828, æ. 40 yrs. He m., 2d, w. Martha Barber, dau. Silas Barber; d. Feb. 6, 1860, æ. 71. He d. April 3, 1856, æ. 73 yrs.

8   *Mary Ann*, b. Dec. 22, 1811; d. Dec. 30, 1811, æ. 8 dys.

9   *George W.*, b. Sept. 13, 1813; m., 1st w., Melinda Corey, April 1, 1849. She d. March 18, 1865, æ. 58 yrs.; 2d w., Sept. 21, 1865, Mrs. Sally Taylor, of Francestown; b. in Temple, Aug. 31, 1809.

10   *Jonas*, b. April 4, 1816; d. Sept. 5, 1818, æ. 2 yrs., 6 mos.

11   *Abigail S.*, b. Sept. 7, 1821; m. Moses A. Fairbanks, Dublin.

12   †*Thomas, Jr.*, b. March 16, 1824; m., 1st w., Asenath Dyer; 2d w., Maria A. Crosby.

1– 3   ISAAC HADLEY. He lived on the old George Duncan place. He was captain of the artillery. He m., Feb. 9, 1813, Sarah Howe. She d. Sept. 27, 1855, æ. 68 yrs., 6 mos. He d. June 25, 1843, æ. 59 yrs.

13   *Sarah Ann*, b. Sept. 17, 1813; m., Oct. 25, 1842, Charles W. Brown; r. California. She d. in Oakland, Cal., July 6, 1867, æ. 53 yrs.; c.

14   †*Isaac, Jr.*, b. April 17, 1816; m., Nov. 27, 1862, E. Maria Corey, Dublin.

15   †*Samuel*, b. July 12, 1818; m., Sept. 4, 1849, Mary F. Twist, b. Sept. 9, 1828.

16   *Martha*, b. March 8, 1821; d. Aug. 19, 1826, æ. 5 yrs., 6 mos.

17   *John*, b. May 30, 1824; d. April 27, 1825, æ. 11 mos.

18   *Martha*, b. July 27, 1826; m. Joseph Davis, Sept. 23, 1847; ch., (1) Charles B., b. July 8, 1850; (2) Frank J., b. Aug. 14, 1861; Charles B. m. Clara Ames, June 11, 1871; one ch., Willie B., b. May 7, 1872.

1– 4   EBENEZER HADLEY. He was a farmer, and lived on a farm south of the old homestead, now occupied by his descendants. He m., Dec. 23, 1817, Amy Howe. She d. Jan. 11, 1874, æ. 76 yrs., 4 mos. He d. June 20, 1859, æ. 72 yrs.

19   *Joel*, b. Jan. 28, 1820; unm. An invalid from his youth.
20   *Jonas*, b. Oct. 23, 1823; m. Dorothy P. Gove, Winchendon, Mass.; ch., Ida E., b. in Stoddard, April 4, 1859.
21   †*William H.*, b. Sept. 16, 1829; m., July 1, 1858, Sarah
M. Draper.

1– 5   ETHAN HADLEY. He m., 1822, Eliza Faxon, dau.
Dea. Jona. Faxon, who was mother of the first two ch.
She d. July 25, 1825, æ. 25 yrs.; 2d w., Feb. 14, 1826,
Betsey Persons, dau. Bartholomew Persons. He was a
brickmaker, and devoted much of his time to this business. He d. Aug. 24, 1872, æ. 81 yrs. In the last years
of his life he occupied his father's old farm, and d. there;
1st w., two ch.; 2d w., twelve ch.

22   *Phebe*, b. Nov. 21, 1823; m., Sept. 25, 1845, Charles B.
Carter.

23   *Charles F.*, b. July 23, 1825; m., Dec. 21, 1847, Harriet
Perkins; r. Lowell.

24   *Ira P.*, b. Dec. 13, 1826; m., Nov. 9, 1851, Harriet J.
Conant; r. Charlestown, Mass.

25   *Ethan, Jr.*, b. April 5, 1828; m., 1850, Mary L. Youngman; r. Chicopee, Mass.

26   *Eliza F.*, b. Feb. 28, 1830; d. June 22, 1834, æ. 4 yrs., 4
mos.

27   *Addison*, b. Oct. 13, 1831; m., Jan. 19, 1853, Eveline
Parker; r. Lowell.

28   *Charlotte*, b. April 3, 1833; m., Sept. 3, 1855, George
Stowers; r. Revere, Mass.

29   †*Harvey*, b. April 10, 1835; m., May 11, 1856, Maria
Fisk.

30   *Florentine*, b. Jan. 7, 1837; d. Dec. 30, 1837, æ. 1 yr.

31   *George W.*, b. Nov. 7, 1838; m., August, 1861, Mary
Ann Cross; r. Chicopee.

32   *Darius*, b. Aug. 13, 1841; m., May 25, 1870, Annie
Howland. She d. 1871. One ch., Everett, E. H., b.
1871; m., 2d w., Dec. 25, 1875, Emma Snow, a teacher
in the public schools, Charlestown, Mass.

33   *Hannah Eliza*, b. July 31, 1843.
34   *Albert S.*, b. Dec. 22, 1845; d. Jan. 7, 1848, æ. 2 yrs.
35   *Albert A.*, b. Nov. 13, 1847.

2– 12   THOMAS HADLEY, Jr. He m., 1st w., Asenath Dyer,
b. Nov. 25, 1826. She d. Aug. 29, 1855, æ. 29 yrs.; 2d
w., Maria A. Crosby, dau. of Benj. Crosby, May 28,
1856. He now r. in Hancock; 1st w., three ch.; 2d w.,
one ch.

---

36   *Mary E.*, b. July 16, 1851.
37   *Alfred G.*, b. Aug. 5, 1853.

14

38 | *Ellen A.*, b. Aug. 29, 1855.
39 | *Arthur Leslie*, b. June 6, 1862.

3– 14 | ISAAC HADLEY, Jr. He succeeded his father on the homestead. He devotes himself principally to farming, though he occasionally makes brick, agreeable to the bent of the family. He has held important offices in town, — selectman 1847, '48 '49, '51, '52, '61, '62, '63, and Representative to the State Legislature 1853. He m. E. Maria Corey, dau. Charles Corey, of Dublin, Nov. 27, 1862.

40 | *Jennie E.*, b. March 7, 1864.
41 | *Genta Maria*, b. Sept. 4, 1865.
42 | *John Osro*, b. Jan. 14, 1867.
43 | *Martha F.*, b. Dec. 5, 1869.

3– 15 | SAMUEL HADLEY. He served in the war of the Rebellion ; m. Mary F. Twist, dau. Peter Twist, Sept. 4, 1849. She was b. Sept. 9, 1828. He is a paper-maker by trade.

44 | *Luella E.*, b. March 29, 1850.
45 | *Milton L.*, b. Nov. 27, 1851 ; m.
46 | *Harriet O.*, b. July 6, 1853 ; d. Oct. 5, 1853, æ. 3 mos.
47 | *Sarah A.*, b. March 6, 1855.
48 | *Delila M.*, b. Oct. 22, 1856.
49 | *Hattie M.*, b. Oct. 22, 1861.

4– 21 | WILLIAM HOWE HADLEY. He succeeded his father on the home farm ; m., July 1, 1858, Sarah M. Draper, of Greenfield.

50 | *Elmer W.*, b. June 14, 1863.
51 | *Nettie Syrena*, b. Jan. 10, 1867.
52 | *James M.*, b. June 25, 1871.

5– 29 | HARVEY HADLEY m., May 11, 1856, Maria Fisk ; r. in town.

53 | *Eva M.*, b. May 4, 1857. (54) *Flora B.*, b. June 6, 1863.
55 | *Frank J.*, b. Nov. 28, 1866.

1 | JOHN HADLEY was of a race entirely distinct from the above. He was b. in Sterling, Mass., Aug. 22, 1796, and came to Peterborough in November, 1822. He was a clothier by trade. He lived in various parts of the town, and most of the children were born in Peterborough. He d. at Antrim, Aug. 8, 1850, æ. 54 yrs. He m. Ruthy Ames, dau. of Timothy and Sarah Kneeland Ames, May 1, 1821.

2   *John A.*, b. in Shirley, Mass., Feb. 22, 1822 ; m. Hannah B. Taggart, Sharon, Nov. 3, 1845 ; three ch.

3   *Timothy R.*, b. in Temple, May 8, 1823 ; d. Jan. 26, 1841 æ. 17 yrs.

4   *Alvah A.*, b. Dec. 5, 1824 ; m. Sarah J. Smith, Nov. 9, 1849 ; ch., (1) Fred. O.; (2) Alvah ; d. ; r. E. Cambridge, Mass.

5   *Harvey C.*, b. Aug. 3, 1826 ; m. Henrietta D. Richardson, of Antrim, Jan. 26, 1851 ; ch., (1) Charles H.; (2) Herbert O. ; (3) Helen M. ; r. Temple.

6   *Cynthia M.*, b. Aug. 10, 1828 ; m. Samuel Aiken, of Fisherville, Aug. 9, 1853 ; two ch. She d. June 25, 1858, æ. 29 yrs., 10 mos.

7   *Hepzibeth A.*, b. Oct. 28, 1830 ; m. Ephraim Slade, Oct. 16, 1851 ; ch., (1) Ella A.; (2) Walter E.; (3) Frank W. ; r. Fitchburg, Mass.

8   *Abby R.*, b. March 30, 1834 ; m. Manly Colburn, Nov. 14, 1854 ; ch., (1) Charles A.; d.; (2) Edward M.; d.; (3) Henry A. ; r. Fitchburg.

9   *Mary E.*, b. July 8, 1837 ; d. May 29, 1844, æ. 6 yrs., 10 mos.

10   *Eliza M.*, b. April 3, 1844 ; r. Fitchburg ; has always been an invalid.

11   *Granville H.*, b. March 29, 1847 ; d. Aug. 17, 1847, æ. 4 mos.

THE HAGGETT FAMILY.

1   ABNER HAGGETT came to Peterborough in 1781, and lived on the place near the late Deacon Samuel Miller's farm, where he remained until his death, it being a part of the original Hugh Wilson farm. He came from some place near Boston, the town not known. He was one of the earliest Baptists in town. He was one of the remonstrants to Mr. Dunbar's settlement in 1799, and Mr. Dunbar makes a note opposite to his name in the church records, "Turned Baptist, 1807." He was b. 1759 ; d. Jan. 12, 1844, æ. 85 yrs. He m. Mary Tuttle. She was b. 1762 ; d. Dec. 26, 1840, æ. 78 yrs.

2   *William*, b. 1780 ; unm. ; re. to Vermont, and d. 1853, æ. 73 yrs.

3   *Polly*, b. 1784 ; m. Nathan Gould, 1803 ; r. Greenfield ; d. 1838, æ. 54 yrs.

4   *John T.*, b. 1788 ; m., 1816, Lucinda Brigham ; r. Plymouth, Vt., and d. there, 1866, æ. 78 yrs.

5   *Susan*, b. 1792 ; m. Nathan Wait, 1813 ; d. 1869, æ. 77 yrs.

6   *Lucinda*, b. 1796 ; m. Wm. Diamond, Nov. 18, 1824.

7 | *Harriet*, b. 1800; m. Peter Twiss, 1821; d. 1861, æ. 61 yrs.

THE HALE FAMILY.

1 | PAUL HALE. He m. Sarah Cuningham, dau. James Cuningham.

2 | *James*, b. 1793; d. at sea.
3 | *Harriet*, b. ——; m. William Weston Hancock; d. May 9, 1831.
4 | *Thomas*, b. ——; m. in Canada.
5 | *Mary L.*, b. Aug. 26, 1806; m. Ebenezer T. Lakeman. She d. Dublin, March 26, 1876, æ. 69 yrs., 7 mos.
6 | *Caroline*, b. ——; unm.
7 | *Louisa*, b. ——; m. Ebenezer T. Lakeman, April 11, 1833. He d. Jan. 11, 1843, æ. 40 yrs. She d. Sept. 3, 1835, æ. 23 yrs., 11 mos.

THE HAMMILL FAMILY.

All we know of the Hammill family is revealed in the town records and the gravestones in the old cemetery. Joseph Hammill appears often in the town records as a man of considerable importance. He began on the land adjoining the mills long known as "Holmes' Mills," and afterwards as "Bowers' Mill," and built a saw-mill in 1778, and a grist-mill in 1781. The Holmeses bought the saw-mill of Joseph Hammill, and the grist-mill came into possession of Patrick White, who gave it to his son David, who carried on the same for some years, when he sold to Abraham Holmes, Sen. Robert Holmes owned the saw-mill before his father's death. Joseph Hammill was on a committee with Capt. Wm. Alld, Samuel Cuningham, Jeremiah Smith, and James Cuningham to propose amendments to the plan of government sent out by the Legislature in 1782. There is a double gravestone with this Latin motto: "*Moriendum est omnibus*," and then the deaths of Neal Hammill and Elizabeth, his wife. He d. Aug. 15, 1790, æ. 88 yrs. She d. Aug. 2, 1769, æ. 75 yrs.; and then a stone for Martha, dau. of above, d. April 8, 1798, æ. 67 yrs.; and then the stones for Joseph Hammill and his wife Anna. He d. Sept. 30, 1796, æ. 68 yrs. She d. March 19, 1796, æ. 70 yrs. Farther than this we have no record or tradition of this family.

THE HANNAFORD FAMILY.

1 | JAMES HANNAFORD moved to Peterborough in 1822, from Northfield, and remained here till his death, Sept.

2, 1839, æ. 66 yrs. He was b. June 6, 1773. He m. Lydia Russell, Nov. 18, 1793, b. April 1, 1773. She m., 2d hus., Aug. 9, 1849, Luther Adams. She d. April 30, 1853, æ. 80 yrs.

---

2 *Mary*, b. June 6, 1794; m., 1st hus., Nathaniel Danforth; 2d hus., James Glines; eleven ch.

3 *William S.*, b. Feb. 17, 1796; m. Rhoda Prescott; r. Sanbornton; six ch.

4 *Jesse M.*, b. Feb. 17, 1796; m. Susan Quimby; r. Sanbornton; seven ch.

5 *Margaret C.*, b. June 22, 1798; m. Isaac Childs; r. Groton; 2d hus., Wm. McGuire; nine ch.

6 *Nancy W. S.*, b. April 6, 1800; m. Samuel Prescott, of Sanbornton; re. to Peterborough, 1829; six ch.

7 *Guy*, b. Feb. 13, 1802; m. Elizabeth Tilton, of Sanbornton; re. to Peterborough; ten ch.

8 *Lydia R.*, b. July 25, 1804; m. Anson Wyman; r. Stockbridge, Vt.; nine ch.

9 † *James, Jr.*, b. Aug. 29, 1806; m., 1st w., Rebecca Bennet; 2d w., R. C. Roby.

10 *Hannah R.*, b. Oct. 4, 1808; m. Paul Boyce; r. New Ipswich; eight ch.

11 *Lavina S.*, b. Oct. 24, 1810; m. John Wells; r. Winchendon, Mass.; ten ch.

12 *Martha C.*, b. Aug. 15, 1812; m. Justin M. Wyman; r. Illinois; four ch.

13 *Phebe G.*, b. June 17, 1814; m. Luke Tarbox; r. Harrisville; three ch.

14 *Lucy R.*, b. Nov. 17, 1817; m. Daniel Felch; r. Greenville; nine ch.

1– 9 JAMES HANNAFORD, Jr., m., 1st w., Rebecca C. Bennet. She d. Oct. 2, 1867, æ. 58 yrs. He m., 2d w., R. C. Roby. He. r. many years in Lowell. Returned to town and erected a suite of buildings near Briggs' Manufactory, where he now resides.

---

15 *Harriet M.*, b. April 29, 1830; d. May 12, 1830, æ. 13 dys.

16 †*Albert B.*, b. Oct. 11, 1831; m., 1st w., Anna Gray; 2d w., Mary J. Swan.

17 † *James M.*, b. Aug. 25, 1833; m. Jane M. Chandler, April 25, 1858.

18 *Hezekiah N.*, b. Aug. 2, 1839; d. Aug. 31, 1840, æ. 1 yr.

19 *Sarah B.*, b. Oct. 17, 1840; m. George Wilder, April 16, 1862.

20 *Alonzo M.*, b. July 1, 1842; m., 1st w., Salome Moore, March 16, 1863; 2d w., Mary A. Swan, Feb. 5, 1868, dau. of Charles A. Swan.

9 –16 | ALBERT B. HANNAFORD. He m., 1st w., Oct 6, 1852, Anna Gray; 2d wife, Mary J. Swan, Dec. 14, 1859; r. Norwalk, O.

21 | *Albert S.*, b. Dec. 13, 1860.

9 –17 | JAMES M. HANNAFORD. He m. Jane M. Chandler, April 25, 1858.

THE HILL FAMILY.

1 | JOB HILL was the son of Ralph Hill, and was b. in Ashby, Mass., July 7, 1780. He m., March 3, 1808, Betsey Perry, of Rindge, b. in Lincoln, Mass., Sept. 9, 1782. They re. to Vermont in 1811, and remained there till 1825, when they came to Peterborough. In 1831 he built a brick cottage on Summer Street, which was the first dwelling erected on that street. Mr. Hill owned in part and managed the grist-mill in this village from 1829 to 1839, when he sold out, and the stone building was erected.

2 | *Selinda A.*, b. May 26, 1809; m.. December, 1837, Ephraim Holt, Greenfield, b. Dec. 12, 1803. He d. Aug. 26, 1867, æ. 64 yrs.

3 | *Betsey P.*, b. Aug. 30, 1811; d. June 20, 1821, æ. 9 yrs., 9 mos.

4 | *Mary*, b. March 29, 1813; d. Sept. 24, 1874, æ. 61 yrs.

5 | *Abigail H.*, b. March 19, 1815; m. Samuel Wilson Wheeler, New Ipswich, Nov. 7, 1838; r. in Peterborough; ch., (1) Lydia Frances, b. June 25, 1842; m. George T. Russell; 3 ch., Mabel F.; d. 1866; Lillian B.; Edith F. (2) Mary Florence, b. Sept. 25, 1845; m. Charles E. Abbot, 1865; 2 ch., Jessie M.; Charles W. (3) Harriet Caroline, b. June 2, 1856.

6 | *Caroline*, b. Nov. 15, 1816; m., Sept. 19, 1843, Rev. Levi L. Fay, of Lawrence, O. She d. Oct. 8, 1854, æ. 37 yrs., 10 mos.; ch., (1) Levi L.; (2) Albert H.; (3) Caroline E.; (4) Selinda H.; (5) Augusta D.

7 | *Charles Albert*, b. May 15, 1819; d. Aug. 11, 1842, æ. 23 yrs.

THE HOLMES FAMILY.

1 | NATHANIEL HOLMES (Dea.) was the ninth of twelve ch. of his parents, Nathaniel and Elizabeth Moore Holmes. His father was b. in Coleraine, Ireland; d., 1764, at Londonderry, N. H. He came to this country in 1740. His mother's name was Elizabeth Moore, of Londonderry, but of what family of Moores we are

uncertain. His grandfather, Nathaniel Holmes, and grandmother, Jane Hunter, lived in Coleraine, Antrim County, Ireland, and d. there. They left a family of five sons, of whom Dea. Holmes' father was the fourth. A sister of Dea. Holmes, Jane, m. William Moore, and another sister, Elizabeth, m. Dea. Robert Morison, both of Peterborough. Dea. Nathaniel Holmes was b. in Londonderry, Sept. 5, 1759, and d. in Peterborough, Sept. 10, 1832, æ. 73 yrs. He m. Catharine Allison, dau. of Samuel and Janet McFarland Allison. Samuel Allison was b. in Londonderry, 1743, and d., 1809, at Weathersfield, Vt., where he then r., æ. 66 yrs. His wife was also b. in Londonderry, and d. April 29, 1831, æ. 71 yrs. Dea. Holmes came to Peterborough to live in 1784, soon after his marriage, and they lived on the same place, next to the Dea. Thomas Davison place, the remainder of their lives. He was a deacon in the Presbyterian church. Dea. Holmes, when quite young, rendered much service in the war of the Revolution. We cannot determine just how much. He first went, in 1775, as a waiter to Lieut. Henry Ferguson, to Cambridge, and after that, as a waiter to his (Holmes') father-in-law, Maj. Duncan, of Londonderry. He was urged, in September, 1776, to enlist in Capt. Finley's company, by his brother-in-law, William Moore, who offered to make his wages equal to $10 per month. He declined on the plea that his clothes were all worn out. His sister, Mrs. Moore, hearing the conversation, said: " Billy, you furnish the shoes, and I will furnish the clothes." It was a great mystery how she could do it, as there were only two pounds of wool in the house. The next morning all their sheep were brought to the barn, and four early lambs were robbed of their fleeces; and the wool was colored, spun, woven, and made into clothing within twenty days, and when Capt. Finley came through the town on his way to Saratoga, the young soldier was ready to join the company. He was afterwards at the battle of White Plains. He returned safe, whether to Peterborough or Londonderry we do not know, and Mr. Moore fulfilled his engagement of making his pay as good as $10 per month.

2   *Jane*, b. Feb. 24, 1786; d. March 2, 1786; æ. 6 dys.

3   †*Nathaniel*, b. May 4, 1787; m. Sally Hoar, June 11, 1809,

4   †*Samuel*, b. Dec. 19, 1789; m., 1st w., Mary Annan; 2d w., Mrs. Fanny M. Priest.

5   *Jane*, b. July 14, 1792; m. Bernard Whittemore, Dec. 25, 1815.

6 | †*Andrew*, b. Nov. 29, 1794; m. Jane Taggart, Feb. 12, 1818.

7 | *Betsey*, b. March 20, 1797; m. Daniel Adams, Jaffrey; d.

8 | *Enos*, b. Dec. 14, 1799; m. Louisa Adams; r. Michigan; d.

9 | *John*, b. May 8, 1802; m., 1st w., Hepzibeth Cutter; 2d w., Emmeline Cutter; 3d w., Sybil Gates; d. Springfield, Vt.

10 | *Katharine*, b. June 18, 1804; d. March 11, 1807; æ. 2 yrs., 8 mos.

11 | *Jonathan*, b. June 8, 1807; m., 1st w., Jane T. Moore; 2d w., Mary Taggart, widow of Cicero Robbe.

1- 3 | NATHANIEL HOLMES, Jr. He was a machinist by trade, and devoted a large portion of his life to this business. He was employed in preparing the machinery for the South Factory, and in company with Artemas Lawrence he built and put in operation the Cheshire Cotton Mill in Jaffrey. He re. from Peterborough to Meredith in 1823, and subsequently to Tilton, where he built a factory for making cotton yarn, twine, and batting. He was town clerk for 1821–22, and made his record on the town books in a chirography rarely equalled for finish or beauty. In early life he was very popular as a teacher in our common schools. He was an eminently worthy and useful man. He was m. to Sally Hoar, b. June 24, 1787, of New Ipswich, dau. of Maj. Jotham Hoar and Mary Davison, dau. of Dea. Thomas Davison, June 11, 1809. He d. Jan. 23, 1840, æ. 53 yrs., 8 mos. Mrs. Holmes m., April 17, 1847, 2d hus., William Moore, of Moorsville, Mich., who d. Dec. 4, 1850, æ. 63 yrs.; and she now survives and r. with her dau., Mrs. Swasey, at Belvidere, Ill., and is enjoying a healthy, active, and sprightly old age.

12 | *Catharine A.*, b. Oct. 1, 1809; m. Zenas Clement, Nov. 5, 1835. He d. She resides in Stamford, Conn.

13 | *Mary*, b. July 15, 1811; d. Dec. 25, 1811, æ. 5 mos.

14 | *Artemas L.*, b. July 9, 1814; m. Mary M. Bloomer. He graduated at Dartmouth College, 1835. Educated a lawyer, and practised for a short time in town. Afterwards he went to St. Louis, where he remained fifteen years, and acquired a large fortune. In consequence of ill health he was obliged to relinquish all business, and re. to New York. He d. Nov. 29, 1871, æ. 57 yrs.

15 | *Abigail*, b. Oct. 22, 1816; m. E. A. Adams; d. in St. Louis, Aug. 30, 1857, æ. 40 yrs., 10 mos.

16 | *Sarah*, b. March 20, 1819; d. March 22, 1819, æ. 2 dys.

17 | *Edith A.*, b. Nov. 9, 1820; m. S. Swasey, a lawyer, Speaker of the House of Representatives, N. H., 1842; r. Belvidere, Ill.

Nathaniel Holmes

18 | *Nathaniel M.*, b. Feb. 20, 1823 ; d. May 2, 1828, æ. 5 yrs.
19 | *Henry G.*, b. Sanbornton, Jan. 11, 1834 ; m. ——
Keehn ; r. New York City.

1– 4 | SAMUEL HOLMES. He first settled on the Samuel Spear place, which he purchased ; then he removed to Springfield, Vt., and engaged in the manufacturing of cotton. He subsequently returned to Peterborough, where he remained till his death. He m., 1st w., Mary Annan, dau. Rev. David Annan, March 31, 1813. She d. at Springfield, Vt., Feb. 9, 1828, æ. 38 yrs., 5 mos. He m., 2d w., Mrs. Fanny Moore Priest, widow of Dr. J. B. Priest, Oct. 20, 1828. She d. Jan. 6, 1875, æ. 85 yrs. He d. July 8, 1868, æ. 78 yrs., 6 mos.

20 | *Nathaniel*, b. July 2, 1814. The following sketch of his life was furnished by Judge Holmes at my request : —
"He lived with his parents on a farm in Peterborough until seven years of age, and then, until fourteen, at Springfield, Vt., where his father carried on a machine-shop and a cotton factory. He attended the common schools in these places, and had some experience in the shop and factory. When about ten, he began the study of Latin under the Rev. Addison Brown, at Peterborough, and continued the same for a time at the academy in Chester, Vt., under the Rev. Uriah Burnap. After the death of his mother, in 1828, he returned with his father to the farm in Peterborough, where he attended the common school in the winter season, and worked on the farm or in a machine-shop at other times ; and in the fall of 1830 he pursued English studies at the Appleton Academy in New Ipswich. In the summer of 1831 he was sent to Phillips (Exeter) Academy, to fit for college, and was entered a freshman, in 1833, at Harvard College, Cambridge, where he graduated in the class of 1837, and took the degree of Master of Arts in 1859. While pursuing his studies he kept a common school one winter in Milford, N. H., one winter in Billerica, Mass., and another in Leominster, Mass., and in the winter of his senior year taught Latin and Greek in Weld's School at Jamaica Plain. He was a member of several college societies, and at the end of his junior year became a member of the Phi Beta Kappa Society.
"On leaving college, Mr. Holmes was employed, on the recommendation of President Quincy, as a private tutor in the family of the Hon. John N. Steele, near Vienna, on the eastern shore of Maryland, where he began the study of law. At the end of one year he returned to Cambridge, and continued his legal studies in the Law School of Harvard University, and in the office of Henry

15

H. Fuller, Esq., of Boston. On being admitted to the
bar, in Boston, in September, 1839, he went directly to
St. Louis, Mo., and there commenced the practice of law.
He opened an office alone, at first, but in 1841 formed a
partnership with Thomas B. Hudson, Esq., which continued for two years ; and from 1846 to 1853 he was in
partnership with his younger brother, Samuel A. Holmes,
Esq. In 1846, he was appointed Circuit Attorney for
the County of St. Louis, by Gov. John C. Edwards, and
held the place for about one year. From 1853 to 1855
he held by election the office of Counsellor of the Board
of St. Louis Public Schools, and from 1862 to 1865 that
of Counsellor of the North Missouri Railroad Company;
and in June, 1865, he was appointed one of the judges of
the Supreme Court of the State of Missouri, by Gov.
Thomas C. Fletcher, under the new Constitution. In
1868, he resigned this office to accept the Royall Professorship of Law in Harvard University. Upon his resignation of the professorship, in 1872, he returned to the
practice of law at St. Louis.

"In 1856, he took part in organizing the Academy of
Science of St. Louis, of which he has been at times a
vice-president and the corresponding secretary, and has
assisted in the editing of its published transactions. He
has been a Fellow of the American Academy of Arts
and Sciences since 1870. In 1866, he published a book
entitled, 'The Authorship of Shakespeare,' of which a
third edition, with an 'Appendix of Additional Matters,' was issued in 1875. His judicial opinions are
contained in volumes XXXVI. to XLII. (inclusive) of
the Missouri Reports."

Judge Holmes is a sound, learned, and philosophical
man, and probably stands among the leading jurists of
our country.

21 | *David A.*, b. April 1, 1815 ; m. Nancy Taggart ; d. Jan.
7, 1868, at Bronson, Mich., æ. 53 yrs.

22 | *Mary*, b. June 2, 1818 ; d. April 23, 1819, æ. 11 mos.

23 | *Elizabeth*, b. 1820 ; m. John Leach ; d. Aug. 31, 1861, æ.
41 yrs.

24 | *Samuel*, b. Feb. 23, 1823. Lieut. of Vols. in Mexican
war. Col. of Vols. in the war of the Rebellion. Is
a lawyer in St. Louis, Mo.

25 | *Sarah Smith*, b. Sept. 5, 1825 ; m. Horatio Kimball,
Sept. 15, 1847 ; r. Keene.

26 | *Frances Sophia*, b. Oct. 20, 1829 ; d. February, 1831, æ. 15
mos.

1- 6 | ANDREW HOLMES. In adult life he had the misfort-
une to lose one of his arms. He m., 1st w., Jane Tag-

gart, of Sharon, b. May 20, 1798, dau. of James Taggart (Wolf), Feb. 12, 1818. She d. He m., 2d w., Abigail Phillips, of Derry. He has spent most of his life in peddling light fancy articles for his livelihood.

---

27 *Caroline*, b. Oct. 28, 1818, in Jaffrey ; m. Joel Bruce ; he d. ——— ; r. Mason ; two ch.

28 *Stephen*, b. Dec. 2, 1820 ; m. Calista Dustan ; one ch., Charles D.

29 *Margaret*, b. March 6, 1823 ; m. George Dickey ; both dead ; one son.

30 *Jane*, b. Dec. 29, 1825 ; m. Urick A. Hall, Derry ; he d. ; one ch.

31 *Mary Ann*, b. Aug. 11, 1828 ; d. April 16, 1846, æ. 17 yrs., 8 mos., at Nashua.

32 *Nathaniel*, b. July 30, 1830 ; m. Angelis S. W. Mower, Jaffrey, Jan. 2, 1854 ; three ch. ; r. Turner's Falls, Mass.

33 *Andrew J.*, b. Oct. 28, 1834 ; m. Carrie Currier, of Manchester ; r. Manchester.

34 *Catharine W.*, b. Oct. 8, 1838 ; m. Frederick Griffin, of Derry.

---

1 ABRAHAM HOLMES was the son of John Holmes, of Londonderry, who was long an elder in the Presbyterian Church, in Londonderry.. His father, John Holmes, was ten years old when his father, Abraham Holmes, came from Ireland with his children, in 1719, and joined the settlement at Londonderry, having previously m. Mary Morrison for his second wife. He was an elder in the First Presbyterian Church. He d. in 1753, at the age of 70 yrs. We do not know whether there was any connection or not between this family and that of Dea. Nathaniel Holmes, though both came from Londonderry. He m. Elizabeth Russell, Oct. 11, 1764, and removed to Peterborough about 1765. He lived in the north part of the town, on the farm now occupied by Horace Whittemore. He was b. May 18, 1738 ; d. Nov. 18, 1815, æ. 77 yrs., 6 mos. She was b. June 16, 1743 ; d. Aug. 5, 1827, æ. 84 yrs. He was a pious and exemplary man.

---

2 *Sarah*, b. Aug. 12, 1765 ; m. Hugh Gregg.

3 *John*, b. Nov. 4, 1767 ; re. to Montpelier, Vt., and d. there.

4 *Betsey*, b. Aug. 17, 1769 ; d. Jan. 25, 1795, æ. 26 yrs.

5 *William*, b. March 25, 1772 ; d. May 20, 1813, æ. 41 yrs.

6 *Robert*, b. Jan. 22, 1774 ; r. New Boston.

7 *Grace*, b. March 9, 1776 ; m. William Miller, April 15, 1828.

8 †*David*, b. March 29, 1778 ; m. Elizabeth White, Oct. 12, 1800.

9	†*Abraham*, b. July 3, 1780; m., 1st w., Mary Cavender; 2d w., Mary Dickey.
10	*Jonathan*, b. Jan. 21, 1783; m. Annis Cavender; d.
11	*Thomas*, b. July 9, 1785; m. Betsey Ramsey; d. Nashua.
12	*Jacob*, b. Sept. 9, 1787; d. July 22, 1814, at Amherst, æ. 26 yrs., 10 mos.

1- 8   DAVID HOLMES resided in Amherst, where all his children were born. He was many years the cashier of the old Hillsboro Bank, at Amherst. After its failure, he engaged in the card-making business, at the same place, and continued in it until the newly invented labor-saving machines revolutionized the business. He was a deacon in the Congregational Church at Amherst, under the late Dr. Lord, but withdrew from the society in consequence of embracing the Unitarian views of Christianity. He published a pamphlet vindicating his course, which we have never been able to obtain. He m., 1st w., Elizabeth White, dau. John White, Jr., Oct. 12, 1800. She d. at Bath, Me., March 16, 1846, æ. 65 yrs., 7 mos.; 2d w., Dec. 22, 1846, Sophia Sawyer. He d. at Bath, Me., Nov. 1, 1867, æ. 89 yrs.

13	*Stephen R.*, b. Feb. 22, 1801; d. Jan. 11, 1830, æ. 29 yrs. Graduated at Harvard University, 1822. Professor of Spanish at St. Mary's College, Baltimore, Md.
14	*Asahel C.*, b. April 12, 1803; d. at New Orleans, of yellow fever, September, 1842, æ. 39 yrs.
15	*David, Jr.*, b. Oct. 18, 1805; d. in Georgia.
16	*Elizabeth*, b. Aug. 18, 1808; m. B. F. Aiken; five ch.; one only living. She d. Oct. 12, 1856, æ. 48.
17	*Mary S.*, b. June 3, 1811; d. at Bath, Me., Dec. 6, 1862, æ. 51 yrs.
18	*Charles W.*, b. June 27, 1816; m. Sarah J. Harding; three ch.
19	*Charlotte W.*, b. Nov. 21, 1823; m. Jacob S. Sewall, of Bath, Me.; two ch.

1- 6   ABRAHAM HOLMES, Jr. He always lived in town, and was usually engaged in the lumbering business. He began a set of mills, saw and grist-mill, in the north-east part of the town, known as "Holmes' Mills," and d. there. He m., 1st w., Mary Cavender, dau. of John Cavender, Greenfield, January, 1807; she d.; m., 2d w., Mary Dickey, May, 1828. She d. Oct. 5, 1860, æ. 77 yrs. He d. Feb. 3, 1858, æ. 77 yrs., 7 mos.; 1st w., four ch.; 2d w., three ch.

| 20 | *Eleanor*, b. Dec. 7, 1807; d. Nov. 28, 1826, æ. 19 yrs. |
| 21 | *Gracy*, b. June 2, 1809; m. Zalmon Smith; r. Milford. |

22 | *James*, b. Aug. 27, 1811 ; m. Mary Ann Grimes, of Greenfield.
23 | *Mary*, b. Aug. 2, 1818 ; m. Hubbard Newton ; d.
24 | † *John Dickey*, b. April 13, 1829 ; m. Sarah T. Morrison ; r. Alstead.
25 | *Elizabeth R.*, b. Sept. 27, 1830 ; m. George F. Livingston, May 20, 1858.
26 | *Sarah Jane*, b. Dec. 23, 1831 ; d. Aug. 27, 1856, æ. 24 yrs., 8 mos.

9– 24 | JOHN DICKEY HOLMES. For some years he carried on the mills erected by his father, but sold out and removed to the village, and subsequently to Alstead, where he now resides, and is engaged in the lumber and grain business, under the firm of Holmes & Buxton. He m. Sarah T. Morrison, dau. of Josiah S. Morrison, July 4, 1854.

27 | *James M.*, b. Sept. 26, 1855 ; d. Nov. 10, 1856, æ 1 yr., 1 mo.
28 | *Frederick A.*, b. April 6, 1857.
29 | *Ella J.*, b. Sept. 6, 1858.
30 | *George E.*, b. July 16, 1864.
31 | *William M.*, b. Aug. 27, 1868 ; d. March 18, 1874, æ. 5 yrs., 6 mos.

THE HOLT FAMILY.

1 | TIMOTHY HOLT, son of Joshua and Phebe Holt, was born in Andover, Mass., April 1, 1767. He m. Lydia Holt, of Andover, Nov. 7, 1793, and removed to Peterborough the 15th of the same month. She d. at Peterborough, Nov. 22, 1825, æ. 58 yrs. He m., 2d w., March 11, 1830, Charity Savage. She d. Feb. 28, 1846, æ. 67 yrs., 9 mos. He was a deacon in the Congregational Church, in Greenfield, where he always worshipped. He lived on the East Mountain, on one of the farms situated on the Greenfield line, and d. there, Oct. 20, 1856, æ. 89 yrs., 6 mos.

2 | *Lydia*, b. April 19, 1795 ; unm. ; lived in town ; d. Nov. 5, 1867, æ. 72 yrs.
3 | *Chloe*, b. March 30, 1797 ; m. Ziba Baldwin, of Greenfield, in 1834 ; d., Peterborough, 1876, æ. 79 yrs.
4 | *Talitha*, b. Sept. 16, 1799 ; unm. ; d. Jan. 22, 1855, æ. 55 yrs., 4 mos.
5 | *Timothy*, b. May 16, 1802 ; m. Mary Jackman, 1825 ; d. Fisherville.
6 | † *Joseph*, b. April 4, 1804 ; m. Mary I. Miller, dau. Adams Miller.

7 | *Joshua*, b. March 17, 1807 ; d. July 9, 1811, æ. 4 yrs., 3 mos.
8 | *Ruth*, b. Feb. 8, 1810; d. July 18, 1811, æ. 1 yr., 5 mos.
9 | *Ruth*, b. May 11, 1812 ; m. Timothy L. Hovey.

1– 6 | JOSEPH HOLT.   He remained on the homestead.   He m. Mary I. Miller, dau. Adams Miller, Jan. 17, 1832. He d. Dec. 13, 1861, æ. 58 yrs.   She d. July 16, 1870, æ. 64 yrs.

---

10 | *Lydia Ann*, b. April 18, 1833 ; m. Edwin J. Smith, July 5, 1854. He died Dec. 28, 1872, æ. 41 yrs. ; r. Nashua.
11 | *George A.*, b. Jan. 26, 1835 ; m., Oct. 5, 1856, Celestia M. Benham ; r. Morrisburg, Canada West.
12 | *James A.*, b. May 28, 1837 ; d. Aug. 3, 1860, æ. 23 yrs., 2 mos.
13 | *Mary E.*, b. Aug 8, 1839 ; m. Orlando H. Dodge ; r. Lowell.
14 | *Hannah M.*, b. Sept 28, 1844 ; m. John S. Rines ; r. Lowell.

THE HOVEY FAMILY.

1 | RICHARD HOVEY and his brother David bought their farms together in 1782, situated in the north-east part of the town, and then divided them, Richard taking the east part, now occupied by his descendants, and David the west part. David sold his farm and moved to Acworth in 1802, where he d. Sept. 3, 1838, æ. 80 yrs.
Richard Hovey was b. in Boxford, Mass., Feb 4, 1761. He was out in the Revolutionary War three months, he being very young, and happened to be at West Point at the time the traitor Arnold attempted to deliver up the American forces there to the British. He m., 1st w., Rebecca Roberts, in 1789 ; 2d w., May 29, 1811, widow A. Hall, of Francestown, maiden name, Asenath Baxter, b. in Methuen, Nov. 10, 1769, by whom he had one child, Timothy L. The rest of the children were by the first wife. He d. May 10, 1842, æ 81 yrs. 1st w. d. May 25, 1807, æ. 37 yrs., 6 mos. ; 2d w. d. Nov. 26, 1853, æ. 85 yrs.

---

2 | *Sarah*, b. Dec. 10, 1790 ; m. Thomas Carter in 1810 ; r. Windham.   Eight ch.
3 | *Stephen*, b. June 19, 1794 ; m. Martha Ferson, of Francestown ; d. in Lancaster, March 15, 1849, æ. 54 yrs., 8 mos.   Seven ch.
4 | *Joseph*, b. Oct. 19, 1800 ; m., 1827, Dolly Shattuck ; r. Pepperell, Mass.   Four ch.

5   *Jonathan*, b. July 10, 1803 ; m., 1828, Betsey Persons, of Acworth ; d. in Lancaster, June 5, 1851, æ. 47 yrs., 10 mos.

6   *Robert*,   b. May 17, 1807 ; m., 1834, Elizabeth Smiley, dau. Francis Smiley ; r. Swanzey ; twelve ch.

7   *Rebecca*,   b. May 17, 1807 ; m. Isaac Clark ; r. Barnstead ; d. Sept. 17, 1845, æ. 38 yrs., 4 mos. ; three ch.

The sons of Robert Hovey enlisted in the late war of the Rebellion, and contracted diseases in the same, which brought on consumption, of which they all d. soon after their return home.

8   †*Timothy L.*, b. Aug. 9, 1813 ; m. Ruth Holt, Nov. 17, 1836. She d. 1874.

1– 8   Timothy L. Hovey succeeded his father on the homestead, where he now lives. He m., Nov. 17, 1836, Ruth Holt, dau. of Dea. Timothy Holt ; she d. July 29, 1874, æ. 62 yrs. ; m., 2d w., Mrs. Hutchinson.

9   *Lydia Jane*, b. June 2, 1838 ; d. Sept. 18, 1854, æ. 16 yrs., 3 mos.

10   *Asenath B.*, b. Oct. 20, 1840 ; m. George W. Marden, Sept. 3, 1862 ; ch., (1) Cora A., b. Aug. 9, 1863 ; (2) Jennie S., b. Sept. 21, 1865 ; (3) Walter H., b. May 30, 1867.

11   *John A.*, b. March 19, 1845 ; m., Oct. 24, 1869, Julia Senter, of Lyndeboro ; r. on the home farm.

12   *Almon T.*, b. Sept. 17, 1846 ; m., June 5, 1870, Mary A. Senter, of Lyndeboro.

13   *Josephine*, b. Sept. 22, 1849 ; m., Nov. 1, 1871, Albert O. Smith ; a trader in town.

DAVID HOVEY, Jr. He was b. Feb. 28, 1785, and succeeded his father on the farm when he removed to Acworth. He m. Betsey Gregg, of Jaffrey, b. July 9, 1791. He remained in town eighteen years, till 1832, after his father's removal, and then he bought a farm, and removed to Francestown. His children were all b. in Peterborough. He d. at North Lyndeboro, May 5, 1868, æ. 83 yrs. His wife d. June, 1869, æ. 78 yrs.

14   *Sarah*, b. April 12, 1814 ; m. Sylvester Proctor, North Lyndeboro ; four ch.

15   *Eliza A.*, b. Aug. 24, 1818 ; m. Franklin Senter, North Lyndeboro ; one ch.

16   *Phebe F.*, b. March 19, 1825 ; m. Josiah Swinerton ; r. Lyndeboro ; five ch.

THE HOWE FAMILY.

1 SAMUEL HOWE came from Amherst to Peterborough about 1790. He lived on the place subsequently owned and occupied by his son James, who built a large house a short distance south of the old one occupied by his father. He m., June 8, 1780, Agnes Templeton, dau. of James and Janet Templeton, b. Sept. 24, 1758. He d. April 28, 1818, æ. 67 yrs. She d. Jan. 1, 1823, æ. 64 yrs., 3 mos. The first four children were born in Amherst.

2 *Jane T.*, b. July 19, 1782 ; m. J. McIntire ; d. March 21, 1854, æ. 72 yrs.

3 †*James*, b. Oct. 24, 1784 ; m., 1st w., Martha Craige ; 2d w., Eliza Gould ; 3d w., Nancy Witt.

4 *Sarah*, b. Feb. 1, 1787 ; m. Isaac Hadley.

5 *Annie*, b. April 23, 1789 ; m. Matthew Gray, Sept. 15, 1816 ; d. July 1, 1834, æ. 45 yrs.

6 †*Samuel*, b. June 6, 1791 ; m. Rachel Twiss, May 1, 1823 ; d. Sept. 18, 1872, æ. 81 yrs.

7 *William*, b. Dec. 30, 1793 ; d. Jan. 22, 1794, æ. 24 dys.

8 †*Charles*, b. April 2, 1795 ; m. Betsey Powers.

9 *Amy*, b. Aug. 26, 1797 ; m. Ebenezer Hadley ; d. Jan. 11, 1874, æ. 76 yrs.

10 *Nancy*, b. June 17, 1800 ; m. William Puffer.

11 *Asahel*, b. July 19, 1802 ; m. Fanny Spofford ; re. Nauvoo, and d. Aug. 13, 1844, æ. 42 yrs.

12 *William*, b. Feb. 26, 1805 ; m. Caroline Stone ; d. April 17, 1873, æ. 68 yrs.

1- 3 JAMES HOWE. He erected, in addition to his other buildings, a saw-mill, on a little brook running through his farm, in which he did a good deal of business for some years. Two or three years before his death he removed to Jaffrey, where he d. March 25, 1863, æ. 79 yrs. He m., 1st w., Martha Craige, Oct. 22, 1815 ; she d. Dec. 9, 1830, æ. 38 yrs ; m., 2 w., Eliza Gould, 1832 ; she d. Aug. 16, 1847, æ. 42 yrs. ; m., 3d w., Nancy Witt, of Jaffrey, March 6, 1849 ; 1st w., seven ch. ; 2d w., six ch. ; 3d w., two ch.

13 *Eleanor*, b. June 26, 1816 ; m. Nathan Leathers ; d. Dec. 9, 1861, æ. 45 yrs.

14 *Jonathan*, b. Oct. 3, 1817 ; d. Dec. 17, 1852, æ. 33 yrs.

15 *James*, b. July 23, 1819 ; m. Mary Ann Whiting, Jan. 21, 1846 ; d. Oct. 16, 1850, æ. 30 yrs.

16 *J. Samuel*, b. July 20, 1821 ; unm. ; r. California.

17 | *Montgomery*, b. Sept. 8, 1823 ; m. Lizzie Shenck ; r. California.

18 | *Martha*, b. Nov. 28, 1825 ; m. Joseph Boardman ; r. California.

19 | *Sarah Jane*, b. Feb. 25, 1828 ; m. Albion P. Dresser ; 2d hus., John Sanderson, Springfield, Mass.

20 | †*Elbridge*, b. Sept. 6, 1833 ; m. Henrietta Felch, Oct. 3, 1859.

21 | *Elizabeth Minerva*, b. Dec. 23, 1834 ; m. Jackson Clement ; one ch., Freddie A.

22 | *Alfred*, b. April 13, 1837 ; m. Georgianna Thomas ; two ch. ; r. Dracut, Mass.

23 | †*Allison G.*, b. April 16, 1839 ; m. Sarah Haskell.

24 | *Francis*, b. Aug. 14, 1841 ; d. March 24, 1843, æ. 1 yr., 7 mos.

25 | *Francis*, b. Sept. 26, 1843. Suppose killed at Fair Oaks, in 1863, æ. 20 yrs.

26 | *Louis*, b. June 7, 1850.

27 | *Elton*, b. April 19, 1854 ; d. 1875.

1— 6 | SAMUEL HOWE. He m. Rachel Twiss, May 1, 1823. She d. Jan. 22, 1852, æ. 65 yrs. He d. Sept. 18, 1872, æ. 81 yrs.

---

28 | *Samuel R.*, b. July 31, 1824.

29 | *George*, b. Feb. 5, 1828 ; m., Oct. 9, 1851, Sarah J. Wilkins ; she d. May 4, 1860 ; 1 ch., Katie Jane, b. Dec. 8, 1856 ; m., 2d w., Sept. 10, 1863, Abbie Brown, of Lynn ; r. Lynn, Mass.

1— 8 | CHARLES HOWE. He re. to Lowell after all his children were born. He m. Betsey M. Powers, dau. Whitcomb and Miriam Bond Powers, Dec. 11, 1823. He d. at Lowell, April 1, 1866, æ. 71 yrs.

---

30 | *Mary A.*, b. Oct. 10, 1824 ; m. George W. Haines, Lowell, March 7, 1846.

31 | *Charles G.*, b. April 10, 1826 ; d. Sept. 11, 1828, æ. 2 yrs., 5 mos.

32 | *Lydia E.*, b. May 27, 1828 ; m. Josephus Emery, Nashua, Jan. 13, 1862.

33 | *Charlotte A.*, b. July 4, 1830 ; m., April 14, 1849, Ira Bickford, Lowell.

34 | *Amanda J.*, b. March 20, 1832 ; m., March 10, 1855, Samuel Easter, Lowell. She d. in Lowell, Aug. 12, 1867, æ. 35 yrs., 4 mos.

35 | *Charles H.*, b. March 21, 1834.

36 | *Edwin G.*, b. May 12, 1836 ; m., May 18, 1857, Jane Howe, Lowell.

16

37 | *Miriam B.*, b. Nov. 11, 1839; m., Jan. 2, 1858, Edward Hosmer, Lowell.

3– 20 | ELBRIDGE HOWE. A mechanic, and is engaged extensively in the truss-making business in the village. He m. Henrietta Felch, Oct. 3, 1859.

38 | *Albion P.*, b. March 5, 1860.
39 | *J. Everett*, b. Sept. 7, 1869.
40 | *Dana Burdett*, b. October, 1873.

3– 23 | ALLISON G. HOWE. Early in the late Rebellion he enlisted, and remained in service till he lost his health, and came home with little hope of ever overcoming a very unpromising pulmonary disease. But by the aid of a good constitution he partially recovered, so as to learn the principles of dentistry, and prepare himself in the art, to practice the same for a livelihood. He continued the same for some years, and very acceptably to the people, and established a good character for integrity and manliness. Being attacked with a severe pneumonia, he was soon overcome with the disease from the weakened condition of his lungs. He died much regretted and lamented. He m. Sarah Haskell, of Troy, b. June 12, 1839. He d. March 3, 1872, æ. 32 yrs.

41 | *Nellie*, b. Aug. 28, 1871.

THE HOWDEN FAMILY.

1 | WILLIAM HOWDEN was born in England, and came to this country as a British soldier at the commencement of the Revolutionary War. He soon deserted the British army, and was among the patriots at the battle of Bunker Hill. He m. Sarah Barnard, of Lyman, Mass., and settled at Salem as a tailor, where all his children but one were born. He moved to Peterborough in 1790, and lived on the south part of William Smith's farm many years, and followed his trade. Left Peterborough, in 1816, for Bristol, Vt., where he d. in 1829. His w. d. at Hinesburg, Vt.

2 | *William*, b. Nov. 4, 1779.
3 | *John*, b. June 6, 1781; r. Bristol, Vt.; d. about 1858.
4 | *Sally*, b. Oct. 19, 1783.
5 | *Polly*, b. May 12, 1785; m. James Nay; re. to Vermont.
6 | *Thomas*, b. Feb. 14, 1787.
7 | *Betsey*, b. March 28, 1789; m. Girdon Mansell, Chardon, O.; d.

8 | *Henry*, b. in Peterborough, June 18, 1792; r. Hume, N. Y.

THE HUNT FAMILY.

1 | EBER HUNT was a descendant, in the fifth generation, from Enoch Hunt, an Englishman, who was one of the first settlers of Weymouth, Mass. He was the son of Ebenezer Hunt. He came to Peterborough in 1784 or '5, from Weymouth, with five ch., and at first rented the Dunbar place. He d. at an early age, Jan. 26, 1787, æ. 49 yrs., leaving his wife and family poor. Timothy, the eldest, took the principal care of the family for a year or two, when his brother Eli came to his relief. They bought the Warren farm together, now ownèd and occupied by the descendants of Timothy, and afterwards added to it the Swan farm adjoining. The brothers divided their land, and Eli took the Swan portion, while Timothy the part now occupied by his family. He m. Abigail Nash, of Weymouth, who d. Jan. 25, 1825, at Peterborough, æ. 84 yrs.

2 | *Salome*, b. Sept. 12, 1762; m. Vincent Tirrell, Weymouth, Mass.
3 | †*Eli*, b. Feb. 24, 1765; m. Lydia Rideout.
4 | † *Timothy*, b. May 3, 1767; m. Nancy Wade.
5 | *Abigail*, b. April 17, 1772; m. William Davison; d. Feb. 29, 1796, æ. 24 yrs.
6 | *Eber*, b. June 28, 1776; unm.; d. May 8, 1804, æ. 27 yrs., 10 mos.
7 | *Lucy*, b. June 5, 1780; unm.; d. Aug. 30, 1804; æ. 24 yrs.
8 | *Lydia*, b. Aug. 31, 1785; unm.; d. Feb. 7, 1810, æ. 24 yrs., 5 mos.

1– 3 | ELI HUNT. During the last years of his life lived opposite the house of James Wilson, Esq., and traded, the place now remaining in the hands of one of his descendants, Mrs. John Little. He m. Lydia Rideout, of Hollis, Dec. 1, 1805, who d. Dec. 7, 1852, æ. 65 yrs. He d. May 27, 1833, æ. 68 yrs.

9 | †*Eli S.*, b. May 25, 1807; m. Mary Goddard, of Swanzey, Feb. 11, 1835.
10 | *Mary R.*, b. Aug. 12, 1809; m. John Little.
11 | *Jane*, b. June 21, 1811; d. young.
12 | *Jane B.*, b. Oct. 7, 1813; m. Kimball W. Brown, Nashua; d. March 16, 1851, æ. 37 yrs., 5 mos.
13 | *Lydia Lucretia*, b. March 21, 1816; m. Joseph Brackett, Oct 1, 1846.

14 | *Elizabeth*, b. April 18, 1818 ; m. Francis W. G. Powers.
She d. May 23, 1870, æ. 52 yrs., 5 mos.; c.

15 | *Charles*, b. March 19, 1820; d. Sept. 19, 1836, æ. 16 yrs.,
6 mos.

16 | *Sarah B.*, b. April 21, 1822; m. John McCoy, Sharon.
He d. Oct 7, 1871 ; c.

17 | *Lucy Caroline*, b. Nov. 20, 1824; m. John S. Bellis,
Waltham, Nov. 16, 1848 ; ch., (1) George P. ; m. Jane
D. Farnsworth, Groton; ch., George A. ; (2) Albert
H. ; (3) William S.

18 | *James Albert*, b. July 24, 1827 ; m. Ann Vinal, Waltham ;
d. March 10, 1872, æ. 45 yrs., 7 mos. ; ch., (1) Clara
Ann ; (2) Lydia M. ; (3) James H. ; (4) John E.

1- 4 | TIMOTHY HUNT (Dea.) came to town with his father's
family when he was about seventeen or eighteen years
old — 1784 or '5. By the early death of his father the
principal support of the family devolved on him and his
elder brother at an early age. He was successful in life,
and reared up a large, respectable family, and d. honored
and respected in an extreme old age. He first erected
a saw and grist mill near his residence, and carried it on
many years. He was a deacon in the Presbyterian
church in town. He m. Nancy Wade, who d. Aug. 30,
1861, æ. 93 yrs. He d. March 11, 1857, æ. 90 yrs.

---

19 | *Nancy*, b. Sept. 21, 1794; m. John Dennis, March 11,
1817 ; r. Hancock. He d. at Quincy, Ill., January,
1874.

20 | *Abigail*, b. April 11, 1798 ; m. Richard T. Bass., Jr.,
March 7, 1826 ; d. Oct. 12, 1839, æ. 40 yrs., 6 mos.

21 | †*Norton*, b. March 27, 1800 ; m., 1st w., Mary Cum-
mings ; 2d w., Mrs. Rebecca Tufts.

22 | *Juliana*, b. March 14, 1802 ; m. Dea. John Vose, May 4,
1829 ; r. Antrim ; d. Dec. 23, 1831, æ. 29 yrs., 9 mos.

23 | *Lucy*, b. July 30, 1804 ; d. March 17, 1829, æ. 24 yrs., 7
mos.

24 | *Bethiah*, b. June 3, 1807 ; m. Dea. Nathaniel H. Moore,
Dec. 1, 1831.

25 | *Elizabeth*, b. Oct. 25, 1809 ; d. June 17, 1829, æ. 19 yrs.

26 | *Louisa*, b. Oct. 11, 1812 ; m. S. F. Safford, Hamilton, Ill.
He d. 1859 ; ch., (1) Sarah L. ; d. 1839 ; (2) Abby L. ;
(3) George B. ; (4) Charles C. ; (5) Stephen Henry ;
(6) Mary A. ; (7) John T.

3- 9 | ELI S. HUNT. He was many years engaged in manu-
facturing cotton goods at the North Cotton Factory,
until the works were suspended. The last part of his
life was devoted to farming. He was selectman four

years, 1861, '2, '3, '4. He m., Feb. 11, 1835, Mary God-
dard, of Swanzey. He d. Jan. 29, 1870, æ. 63 yrs., 8
mos.

---

27   *Ellen A.*, b. May 2, 1836 ; m. J. Hamilton Spofford, Nov.
25, 1858 ; d. Oct. 27, 1875, æ. 39 yrs., 6 mos. ; ch.,
Louis H. ; r. Dublin.

28   *Charles A.*, b. Aug. 30, 1838 ; m. Hattie Bryant, June,
1867 ; one ch., Charles C. ; she d. September, 1869.

29   *George E.*, b. July 27, 1843 ; m. Frances M. Richardson,
Greenfield, Nov. 24, 1868.

4– 21   NORTON HUNT (Col.) succeeded his father on the
homestead. He was Colonel of the 22d Regiment of
the N. H. Militia. He represented the town in the
State Legislature in 1847. He m., 1st w., Mary Cummings, of Hancock, who was the mother of all the children ; she d. Jan. 18, 1860, æ. 53 yrs. He m., 2d w.,
Mrs. Rebecca B. Tufts, March 14, 1861.

30   †*George A.*, b. Feb. 14, 1828 ; m. Elizabeth Curtis.

31   *Mary Jane*, b. Sept. 5, 1832 ; unm.

32   *Nancy A.*, b. July 26, 1839 ; d. May 20, 1869, æ. 29 yrs.,
9 mos.

33   †*Timothy Norton*, b. Aug. 30, 1841 ; m. Elsie Wilder.

21– 30   GEORGE A. HUNT. He graduated at Dartmouth College, 1852. Studied law, and settled at Quincy, Ill.,
where he practised his profession a few years until the
failure of his health. He stood high in the profession,
and gave promise of a high degree of eminence, but was
cut off by consumption at an early age. He d. March
24, 1867, æ. 39 yrs. He m. Elizabeth Curtis, of Hanover, Sept. 6, 1853, and left no children living. In an
obituary notice of Mr. Hunt, in the Peterborough *Transcript* of April 13, 1867, it says : " Mr. Hunt was a good
scholar, a man of a highly cultivated intellect, and had
the reputation of great culture. He was always a growing man, and, had his life been spared, would no doubt
have acquired a wide-spread reputation in his adopted
State. He was an honor to his native town, and his
memory should be cherished among those sons who have
well sustained the honor and character of the old home."
The Adams County bar, Quincy, Ill., March 26, 1867,
passed the following resolution, *viz.: " Resolved*, That
in the character of George A. Hunt we recognize all the
elements of material greatness, talent, industry, and
energy ; and in his death the bar has lost an able representative, the profession a genial companion, and the
world a fearless and honest man."

21- 33 | TIMOTHY N. HUNT. He is the third generation on the old homestead, devoting himself to farming. He m. Elsie E. Wilder, Dec. 13, 1870.

34 | *Emma W.*, b. Sept. 30, 1871.
35 | *George A.*, b. Sept. 16, 1873 ; d. 1876.
36 | *John Norton*, b. Sept. 27, 1875.

THE INGALLS FAMILY.

1 | NATHANIEL INGALLS was a native of Andover, Mass., and was born in 1752. He emigrated to Rindge with his father's family, in 1764, when twelve years of age. He removed to Peterborough with his family in 1803. He was first a miller at the Morison mill, at the South Factory Village, and subsequently, for two years or more, at the mill under the first Peterborough cotton factory. He. m., June 5, 1787, Sarah Hale, b. in Rindge, Feb. 7, 1765 ; she d. Sept. 18, 1844, æ. 79 yrs., 7 mos. He d. March 9, 1814, æ. 62 yrs.

2 | *Tabitha*, b. in Rindge, Feb. 27, 1789 ; m. Amos Woolson, Jan. 8, 1809 ; d. Jan. 14, 1812, æ. 23 yrs.
3 | *Sally*, b. May 31, 1791 ; m. Robert White, April 30, 1837 ; d. March 25, 1845, æ. 54 yrs.
4 | *Betsey*, b. Oct. 2, 1793 ; unm. ; d. Feb. 15, 1845, æ. 51 yrs.
5 | †*Cyrus*, b. Feb. 7, 1797 ; m. Mary Louisa Dakin.
6 | *Sabra*, b. October, 1799 ; unm. ; d. Feb. 6, 1860, æ. 60 yrs.
7 | *Almira*, b. Aug. 14, 1803 ; m. Charles Carter, May 8, 1827 ; r. Leominster.
8 | †*George H.*, b. March 21, 1805 ; m. Betsey Loring, 1831.
9 | *Hannah M.*, b. 1810 ; d. Jan. 21, 1812, æ. 2 yrs.

1- 5 | CYRUS INGALLS. He has resided in various places, mostly in Peterborough and Leominster, Mass. He left Peterborough in 1833. He followed the mercantile business when in town. Was town clerk, 1829, '30, '31, '32. He m. Mary Louisa Dakin, Sept. 13, 1830 ; she d. at Leominster ; r. Leominster, Mass.

10 | *Frederick Cyrus*, b. Sept. 12, 1832 ; r. Chicago ; is a lawyer.
11 | *Helen S.*, b. July 20, 1835 ; d. February, 1856, æ. 21 yrs.
12 | *Charles E.*, b. March 29, 1839.

1- 8 | GEORGE HANDEL INGALLS (Dr.). He was first engaged in mercantile business in Lowell, but afterwards studied medicine, and took his medical degree in the Berkshire Institution, Pittsfield, Mass., in 1837. He located himself at Proctorsville, Vt., as a physician, in 1838, and remained in a very successful practice until 1848, when his health failed, and he returned to Peterborough, and d. of consumption, May 26, 1849, æ. 44 yrs. He was a worthy man, and highly esteemed as a useful and skilful physician. He m. Betsey Loring, of Sterling, May 28, 1831; she d. at Proctorsville, Vt., June 30, 1842.

13   *Sarah Elisa*, b. Lowell, Feb. 13, 1834; d. Peterborough, Nov. 28, 1852, æ. 18 yrs.

14   *Mary B.*, b. Sterling, Oct. 1, 1835; d. Feb. 1, 1852, æ. 17 yrs.

15   *George F.*, b. Proctorsville, Aug. 3, 1838; m. Ellen A. Merril; r. Danbury, Conn.

16   *Betsey L.*, b. Proctorsville, April 6, 1842; r. Leominster.

THE JEWETT FAMILY.

1   JOHN JEWETT was the son of Joseph and Rebecca Abbot Jewett, of Westford, Mass. He moved to Peterborough in 1797. His father came in 1808, and d. here, Aug. 25, 1814, æ. 74 yrs. He m. Elizabeth Cummings, of Westford; she d. May 10, 1798, æ. 29 yrs. He m., 2d w., Margaret Moore, dau. Dea. Samuel Moore; she d. Jan. 6, 1850, æ. 83 yrs. He was b. in Littleton, Mass., May 30, 1766, and d. at Peterborough, Feb. 6, 1851, æ. 84 yrs., 8 mos. He first settled on Windy Row, near the factories, where he remained till 1817, when he re. to Sharon, where he remained some years, but ultimately returned to Peterborough; 1st w., four ch.; 2d w., four ch.

2   *John*, b. Dec. 1, 1786. He was ten yrs. old when his father moved to Peterborough. When he came of age he went to New York City, where, by industry and perseverance, he was eminently successful in business, and acquired a fortune. He was highly respected as an honorable, honest, and upright man. He had two wives; the last one survived him. His ch. are established in New York in the same business pursued by himself. He retired from business some years before his death, and d. at his country-seat, Orange, N. J., Dec. 23, 1867, æ. 81 yrs.

3   *Jonathan*, b. Aug. 11, 1788; d. in Mobile, Ala., 1839, æ. 51 yrs.

4   †*Ahimaz*, b. Jan. 19, 1794; m. Eliza Scott.

5   *Rebecca*, b. Dec. 30, 1795; unm.; d. in Peterborough, Aug. 18, 1848, æ. 53 yrs.

6 | *Samuel*, b. Feb. 22, 1802 ; m. Elizabeth Taggart, Sharon.
7 | *Elizabeth*, b. Oct. 22, 1803 ; m. Ira Felt, April 28, 1825.
8 | *Mary*, b. June 22, 1805 ; m., Sept. 8, 1825, Moses Gowing.
9 | *Margaret*, b. Feb. 22, 1808 ; m. John Hoyt ; r. Manchester.
10 | *Joseph*, b. Aug. 11, 1809 ; m. ; d. Albion, N. Y., March, 1867, æ. 57 yrs.

1– 4 | AHIMAZ JEWETT. He m. Eliza Scott, dau. John Scott, Esq., Feb. 17, 1821 ; she d. Oct. 12, 1842, æ. 43 yrs., 4 mos. He d. Nov. 2, 1860, æ. 66 yrs., 9 mos.

11 | *Elizabeth*, b. Jan. 17, 1822 ; m., 1st hus., Samuel C. Clement ; 2d hus., Wm. B. Hale, of Savannah, Ga. ; ch., (1) William G., b. in Savannah, Ga., Feb. 9, 1849. Fitted for college at Exeter Academy, and graduated at Harvard University, Cambridge, 1870. Was a tutor in Harvard College, and is now pursuing his studies in Germany ; (2) Gertrude E., b. Jan. 3, 1853, in Savannah. Is now a teacher in Cambridgeport ; educated at Bridgewater Normal School ; (3) Charles P., b. at Peterborough, Aug. 4, 1857 ; d. May 22, 1859, æ. 1 yr., 9 mos.
12 | †*George A.*, b. March 5, 1825 ; m., 1st w., Hannah B. Brown ; 2d w., Martha S. Fay.
13 | †*Charles*, b. Oct. 23, 1827 ; m. Mrs. Martha S. Jewett.
14 | *Sarah S.*, b. Feb. 16, 1830 ; m. Charles N. Thayer, Nov. 21, 1848 ; 2d hus., Charles B. Ford, April 3, 1872 ; r. St. Louis, Mo.
15 | *John*, b. Feb. 17, 1833 ; r. Hanover, Mass.
16 | *Henry*, b. —— ; d. Dwight, Ill., Oct. 8, 1861.
17 | *Mary*, b. July 5, 1842 ; m., Feb. 13, 1859, Rev. H. P. Satchwell, Methodist clergyman ; r. Minnesota.

4– 12 | GEORGE A. JEWETT was a deacon in the Congregational Church in town. He m., 1st w., Aug. 7, 1851, Hannah B. Brown, b. Feb. 12, 1822 ; she d. July 23, 1859, æ. 37 yrs., 5 mos. ; m., 2d w., Sept. 25, 1860, Martha S. Fay, dau. Dea. Joel Fay, b. Dec. 17, 1831. He d. Jan. 29, 1861, æ. 35 yrs., 10 mos. 1st w., three ch. ; 2d w., one ch. The following obituary appeared in the Peterborough *Transcript* at the time of his death : "We record with sadness the death of our worthy and esteemed fellow-citizen, Dea. George A. Jewett. His life was one of strict integrity and good morals, and his chief aim was, both by precept and example, that his virtues might be diffused throughout the entire community. His death, just in the prime of life, is a public loss. His obituary can be written in a few words ; he was a good man and a Christian."

18   *Joel A.*, b. Aug. 23, 1852 ; m.
19   *Mary H.*, b. July 27, 1854 ; m. —— Taft.
20   *George H.*, b. Dec. 15, 1858.
21   *Albert E.*, b. Aug. 4, 1861.

4– 13   CHARLES JEWETT m. Mrs. Martha S. Jewett, widow of Dea. George A. Jewett, April 19, 1865. He is a black-smith by trade.

22   *Fannie M.*, b. June 13, 1867.

THE KIMBALL FAMILY.

1   ELIJAH B. KIMBALL came to Peterborough in 1816, and carried on the clothing business in company with Jefferson Butler, in Samuel Smith's fulling mill, stand-ing on the spot where Brennan's large shop now stands. He afterwards removed to Dublin, and pursued the same business there for twelve years, and then returned to Peterborough, and purchased the place near the South Factory Village begun by George McCrillis, and after-wards owned by Dea. Thomas Wilson, where he now r. He m. Achsah Buss, May 6, 1819, dau. of Richard T. and Betsey Ballard Buss. She d. Jan. 24, 1869, æ. 72 yrs. He was b. in Weare, May 8, 1794.

2   *Ann A.*, b. Sept. 21, 1820; d. Feb. 8, 1862, æ. 42 yrs.
3   *Imri B.*, b. April 3, 1822 ; r. Missouri.
4   *Jane B.*, b. Dublin, March 24, 1824; m., Dec. 3, 1846, Granville P. Felt.
5   *Elizabeth S.*, b. Dublin, April 27, 1825 ; d. June 29, 1861, æ. 36 yrs.
6   †*Henry A.*, b. May 24, 1827 ; m. Sarah B. Derby.
7   *Abby B.*, b. April 15, 1829 ; m., Nov. 13, 1851, George Bruce ; d. Aug. 15, 1856, æ. 27 yrs.
8   *Mary Ellen*, b. Feb. 3, 1832 ; unm.
9   *Sarah M.*, b. Peterborough, July 6, 1834 ; m., June 1, 1854, George H. Longley.
10   *Carrie C.*, b. April 7, 1841 ; d. Nov. 25, 1872, æ. 31 yrs.

1– 6   HENRY A. KIMBALL. He is a clothier; and succeeded his father in business. He also cards wool. He m., Nov. 25, 1852, Sarah B. Derby, of Fitchburg, Mass., b. Sept. 18, 1832. His manufactory was destroyed by fire, 1873.

11   *Richard H.*, b. Sept. 15, 1853.

17

12 | *William H.*, b. June 18, 1855.
13 | *Robert B.*, b. Oct. 31, 1857.
14 | *Charles A.*, b. May 16, 1859.
15 | *Edgar B.*, b. June 26, 1861.
16 | *Frank W.*, b. March 1, 1865.
17 | *Daniel C.*, b. March 19, 1867.   A seventh son. .

1 | WILLIAM B. KIMBALL, son of Isaac Kimball and Sarah Cutter Kimball, of New Ipswich, b. May 24, 1801, at New Andover, Vt. He has lived ·successively at Jaffrey, Mason, and New Ipswich, and removed to Peterborough, Nov. 1, 1830. He is a mechanic, a superior pattern-maker, and also the author of many mechanical and patented inventions. Built his house, situated on Pine Street, in 1836, where he now r. Has been County Commissioner three years, from 1856 to '59. selectman 1852, '53 ; m. Mary Ann A. Pierce, Nov. 22, 1826, a native of Hillsboro, b. Sept. 29, 1803 ; d. Feb. 5, 1849 ; m., 2d w., Oct. 25, 1851, Louisa Goddard Oliver, b. at Swanzey, Feb. 4, 1806 ; 1st w., two ch.

2 | *Mary Ann Thursa*, b. New Ipswich, Aug. 31, 1827. She is a homœopathic physician. Was educated to the profession at the New York Medical College for Women, and the New England Female Medical College, Boston (now the Boston University). Received degree of M. D. at this institution, and commenced practice in Peterborough, April, 1870, where she now r.

3 | *Sarah Elizabeth*, b. New Ipswich, Sept. 17, 1830.

THE LAWS FAMILY.

1 | THOMAS LAWS was b. in Billerica, Mass., July 9, 1761. He first settled in Westminster, Mass., and, March 26, 1801, he moved to Peterborough, having purchased of Uriah Buss a farm situated on the East Mountain and on the east border of the town. He m., Sept. 4, 1787, Mary Locke, of Rindge, b. Nov. 2, 1761 ; d. Dec 21, 1838, æ. 77 yrs. He d. April 4, 1844, æ. 83 yrs.

2 | *Amos*, b. Jan. 14, 1790 ; d. March 12, 1795, æ. 5 yrs.
3 | *Samson*, b. Oct 22, 1791 ; d. Feb. 27, 1795, æ. 3 yrs., 4 mos.
4 | *Amos*, b. June 14, 1795 ; d. Sept. 5, 1797, æ. 2 yrs., 2 mos.
5 | †*Thomas*, b. May 11, 1797 ; m., 1st w., Abigail Atkinson ; 2d w., Mrs. Bean ; 3d w., Clarissa Melvin.
6 | *Mary*, b. Jan. 19, 1799 ; m. James Child, Temple, 1827. The above were b. in Westminster, Mass.

7   †*Nathaniel F.*, b. May 1, 1801 ; m. Polly Child, Temple, May 17, 1825.

8   *Ebenezer*, b. May 1, 1803 ; m. Belinda Wooley ; r. Washington.

9   *Solomon*, b. Nov. 13, 1806 ; m. Olive Johnson, Chester, Vt., a graduate of Dartmouth College, 1836. Studied divinity, joining the Universalist denomination. He preached some years at Temple, then removed to Marlboro, and more recently to Ohio.

1- 5   THOMAS LAWS. He m., 1st w., Abigail Atkinson, of Washington ; 2d w., Mrs. —— Bean ; 3d w., Clarissa Melvin, of Peterborough. He resided many years in Washington, engaged in mechanical business, but a few years before his death he returned to Peterborough, where he d. June 2, 1853, æ. 56 yrs.

10   *Alfred*, b. —— ; graduated Dartmouth College, 1858.

11   *Thomas Marshall*, b. ——. (12) *Mary*, b. ——.

13   *Harriet*, b. ——.

1- 7   NATHANIEL FORD LAWS. He always resided in town ; succeeded his father on the homestead. He now resides in village ; m., May 17, 1825, Polly Child, of Temple.

14   *Martha C.*, b. July 28, 1827 ; m., Nov. 5, 1846, Wm. C. Tuttle, Wilton. She d. Oct. 11, 1853, in Amherst, æ. 26 yrs.

15   *A. Frances*, b. May 16, 1832 ; m. William E. Dadman, Jan. 6, 1859 ; r. Peterborough.

16   *Albert D.*, b. Feb. 4, 1836 ; m. Sarah E. Robbe, Dublin, Jan. 7, 1863 ; re. to Bridgeport, Conn., where he now lives.

THE LEATHERS FAMILY.

1   JOHN LEATHERS, Sen., came to town with his wife, Martha, from Lee, early in 1801, and occupied the farm known as the Nathan Leathers farm, and d. there. He d. April 13, 1805, æ. 52 yrs. She d. June 2, 1816, æ. 63 yrs.

2   † *John*, b. in Lee, July 24, 1780 ; m. Emily Mitchell.

3   †*Nathan*, b. in Lee, April 15, 1782 ; m., 1st w., Mary McCoy ; 2d w., Mary Washburn.

4   *Isaac*, b. in Lee, 1789 ; killed by falling from a tree May 19, 1801, æ. 12 yrs.

5   *Sally*, b. ——. (6) *Abigail*, b. ——. (7) *Jane*, b. ——.

1– 2 | JOHN LEATHERS, Jr. He lived on the East Mountain, on the Wm. McCoy farm. He m. Emily Mitchell. He d. Dec. 22, 1860, æ. 80 yrs. She d. Dec. 3, 1858, æ. 80 yrs.

---

8 | † *John*, b. Sept. 26, 1810; m. Mrs. Susan Davis, Sept. 8, 1853.

9 | *Oliver C.*, b. March 30, 1812; d. April 19, 1812, æ. 19 dys.

10 | *Franklin*, b. May 23, 1813; d. Dec. 26, 1845, æ. 32 yrs., 7 mos.

11 | *George R.*, b. May 10, 1815; d. Nov. 13, 1843, æ. 28 yrs.; Lowell.

12 | *Mary Ann*, b. Dec. 25, 1817; d. Oct. 16, 1851, æ. 33 yrs., 10 mos.

13 | *Isaac Milton*, b. Feb. 10, 1820; m. ——; r. Lowell, Mass.

1– 3 | NATHAN LEATHERS. He succeeded his father on the homestead. He m., 1st w., Mary McCoy, Dec. 5, 1810. She d. April 17, 1827, æ. 37 yrs.; m., 2d w., Mary Washburn, dau. Calvin Washburn, Dec. 31, 1827. He d. Dec. 4, 1843, æ. 61 yrs.; 1st w., eight ch.; 2d w., two ch.

---

14 | *Robert*, b. Dec. 30, 1811; d. Nov. 18, 1848, æ. 36 yrs., 10 mos.

15 | *Mary B.*, b. Aug. 30, 1813; unm.; d. April 22, 1865, æ. 51 yrs.

16 | *Nathan*, b. July 14, 1815; m. Eleanor Howe. She d. Dec. 9, 1861, æ. 46 yrs. One son, George; r. Lowell.

17 | *Edward B.*, b. Aug. 24, 1817; m. Elizabeth Cudworth; d. Oct. 26, 1849, æ. 32 yrs. Two ch., Albert and Edward Newton.

18 | *Samuel*, b. Sept. 2, 1819; m. Rosanna Goodell, Sept. 28, 1843; r. Lowell.

19 | *Martha*, b. Oct. 9, 1821; unm.; d. May 18, 1844, æ. 22 yrs.

20 | *Jane*, b. Dec. 9, 1823; unm.; d. April 5, 1863, æ. 39 yrs.

21 | *Emily*, b. Oct. 6, 1825; unm.

22 | *Calvin W.*, b. May 9, 1830; unm.; d. April 9, 1874, æ. 43 yrs., 11 mos.

23 | *Isaac N.*, b. May 21, 1834; m. Hannah A. Foland, Nov. 14, 1855. One ch., Mary Addie, b. Aug. 30, 1857.

2– 8 | JOHN LEATHERS, 3d. He remained on the homestead. He enlisted in the United States service in the Rebellion, and d. in the army, March, 1865, æ. 54 yrs., 6 mos. He m. Mrs. Susan Davis, Sept. 8, 1853.

---

24 | *Clara F.*, b. June 27, 1855; d. Aug. 23, 1869, æ. 14 yrs.

25 | *John E.*, b. May 22, 1861.

THE LITTLE FAMILY.

1 | THOMAS LITTLE. We are uncertain when he came to Peterborough, but think it must have been not far from 1764, after the birth of Thomas, Jr., who was b. in Lunenburg in 1763. He lived on a farm out east from the John Little farm. He m. Susanna Wallace, dau. of William and Elizabeth Wallace, who are both buried by her side in the old cemetery, and also her grandmother, Elizabeth Clayland, according to the gravestone there erected. He was b. 1726, and d. on a visit to Shirley, Mass., and was buried there, June 6, 1808, æ. 82 yrs. She d. March 6, 1822, æ. 88 yrs.

2 | *William*, b. in Shirley, Oct. 20, 1753. Was a physician. Studied medicine with Dr. Young. He was settled as a physician at Hillsboro, and was drowned in the Contoocook River. He had two ch., Dea. William Little, of Antrim, and a daughter unm.

3 | *Betsey*, b. in Shirley, Nov. 19, 1756; m. William Blair, Dec. 2, 1787.

4 | *Sally*, b. in Shirley, 1758; m. John Livingston; r. Walpole. Four ch.

5 | *Joseph*, b. in Shirley, Jan. 22, 1761; re. East.

6 | †*Thomas, Jr.*, b. Lunenburg, May 11, 1763; m., April, 1793, Relief White.

7 | *John*, b. 1764; m. Lucinda Longley, of Shirley.

8 | *Walter*, b. in Peterborough, 1766. A graduate of Dartmouth College, 1796. He was a clergyman, and was settled as the first minister in Antrim, in 1800; remained till 1804, when he changed his surname to Fullerton, and subsequently went to the State of Maryland, where he d. in 1815. He did not sustain his good character to the last, as I have learned of those who knew a little of him; but both he and his errors are now consigned to oblivion.

1- 6 | THOMAS LITTLE, Jr. His father's family came to town from. Lunenburg, about 1764, after the birth of Thomas, 1763. He (son) re. to Belmont, Me., and remained there a few years, where a number of his ch. were born. He returned to Peterborough, and spent his last days in town. He m. Relief White, of Leominster, April, 1793; she was b. July 4, 1776; d. Sept. 21, 1839, æ. 63 yrs. He d. Oct. 19, 1847, æ. 84 yrs., 7 mos.

9 | *Relief*, b. Dec. 3, 1800; m., 1858, Oliver Heald, Esq.; b. Oct. 1, 1790; d. Oct. 5, 1867, æ. 77 yrs.

10 | *Betsey*, b. Belmont, May 10, 1803 ; m. Alvah Ames, May 21, 1828 ; d. March 27, 1872, æ. 68 yrs.

11 | *Jane*, b. Belmont, April 3, 1804 ; m., March 30, 1826, Willard Youngman. He d. Nov. 29, 1833, æ. 29. She m., 2d hus., Benj. Read, Newport, November, 1834 ; she d. Feb. 12, 1866, æ. 61 yrs.

12 | *Harriet*, b. Belmont, April 14, 1806 ; d. Dec. 10, 1833, æ. 28 yrs.

13 | †*Thomas, 3d*, b. Sept. 22, 1808 ; m., Sept. 3, 1832, Lucretia Munson ; 2d w., Mary W. Leathers.

14 | *Mary*, b. Sept. 14, 1810 ; m., Jan. 3, 1834, Frederick Loring ; r. Carthage, Ill. ; d. February, 1848, æ. 38 yrs.

15 | *John Wallace*, b. Feb. 28, 1812 ; m., Oct. 26, 1837, Clarissa Parker. He d. Sept. 23, 1867, æ. 55 yrs.

16 | *Jesse C.*, b. Sept. 26, 1815 ; m., Sept. 29, 1840, Eliza G. French, dau. of Whitcomb French ; re., 1852, to Salt Lake City. He is a professed Mormon, and has a number of additional wives. He has held important offices in this community, and is now one of the leading men.

1– 7 | JOHN LITTLE. He lived on the old homestead till he built a new house on the Street Road, about 1804 (which was burnt the winter of 1876), where he lived till his death. He m., in 1809, Lucinda Longley, of Shirley. He d. Sept. 19, 1850, æ. 85 yrs. She d. Sept. 13, 1850, æ. 66 yrs.

17 | †*John, Jr.*, b. Aug. 7, 1810 ; m. Mary Hunt.

18 | †*Joshua L.*, b. Sept. 8, 1812 ; m. Dorothy Carter.

19 | *Lucinda*, b. Sept. 16, 1814 ; m. Ezra Peavey, April 14, 1836 ; she d. March 12, 1847, æ. 32 yrs., 5 mos. ; ch., (1) John, b. Dec. 12, 1837 ; (2) Henry, b. August, 1839 ; (3) Wallace, b. 1841.

6– 13 | THOMAS LITTLE, 3d, resided many years in Munsonville, engaged in the cotton manufacture, when he returned to Peterborough, and has here been engaged many years in agricultural pursuits. Selectman, 1856, '64, '65 ; also overseer of the poor, 1869, '70. He is a trustee in the Peterborough Savings Bank, and director in the First Peterborough National Bank ; m., 1st w., Lucretia Munson ; she d. Nov. 2, 1874, æ. 68 yrs. ; m., 2d w., Mrs. Mary W. Leathers, East Jaffrey, Dec. 5, 1875.

20 | *Louisa W.*, b. Aug. 19, 1833 ; d. March 20, 1834, æ. 7 mos.

21 | *Thomas J.*, b. May 29, 1835 ; m., Feb. 20, 1834, Louisa A. Stearns, Greenfield.

22 *Louisa W.*, b. Aug. 14, 1837; m., April 1, 1858, Lieut. Timothy K. Ames, 2d, 1st Lieut., Co. K, 6th Reg. N. H. Vols. He was killed in the second Bull Run battle, Aug. 29, 1862, æ. 33 yrs.; 2d hus., —— Peaslee, 1875.

7– 17 JOHN LITTLE, Jr. He m. Mary R. Hunt, Dec. 1, 1837. Was Colonel of the 22d Reg. N. H. Militia. He now lives on the Eli Hunt place.

23 *Mary Lucinda*, b. Oct. 19, 1838; d. Aug. 10, 1865, æ. 26 yrs., 9 mos.

24 *Ann Maria*, b. Jan. 30, 1840; d. July 1, 1869, æ. 29 yrs., 6 mos.

25 *Lydia Carloener*, b. Nov. 28, 1841; d. Nov. 28, 1862, æ 21 yrs.

26 *Lucretia Jane*, b. Aug. 22, 1846; d. June 3, 1849, æ. 2 yrs., 9 mos.

27 *John*, b. May 21, 1848; d. April 13, 1866, æ. 18 yrs.

28 *Carrie Wallace*, b. March 7, 1851; died Aug. 8, 1865, æ. 14 yrs., 5 mos.
All the above d. of consumption, but Lucretia Jane.

7– 18 JOSHUA L. LITTLE m. Dorothy Carter, April 27, 1837. She was b. in Leominster, Mass., Jan. 30, 1814. He d. at West Wilton, Sept. 8, 1846, æ. 34 yrs. He was a tanner, and built a large tannery near his father's residence, and carried on the business a number of years before his death.*

29 † *John L.*, b. March 3, 1838; m. Ann Lakin, Aug. 6, 1862.

30 † *Charles C.*, b. May 12, 1843; m. Mary W. Lakin, Oct. 18, 1860.

18– 29 JOHN L. LITTLE. He m. Ann Lakin, Aug. 6, 1862. He has resided in Hancock; re. to California.

31 *William L.*, b. in Hancock, March 19, 1864.

18– 30 CHARLES C. LITTLE. He m. Mary W. Lakin, Oct. 18, 1860; r. Hancock.

32 *Minnie M.*, b. in Hancock, March 21, 1861; d. July 25, 1861, æ. 4 mos.

33 *Annie M.*, b. April 14, 1864.

34 *Ellen D.*, b. Oct. 26, 1867.

THE LIVINGSTON FAMILY.

1 FREDERICK LIVINGSTON is the son of William and Elizabeth Saunders Livingston, and was b. in Town-

* Mrs. Dorothy Little m. Joshua Foster, Hancock, Oct. 10, 1851; one ch., Elwyn C., b. in Hancock, Oct. 23, 1852. Joshua Foster d. March 18, 1867.

send, Mass., Oct. 23, 1801. He came to Sharon with his parents when he was three years of age. His parents were honest people, but very poor, and unable to do much for their ch. They lived in an obscure neighborhood in Sharon, where the ch. had little advantage of schooling; were also far from the short schools they had, and often lacked suitable clothing to appear among their companions at school. Even as early as thirteen years of age he started out himself to seek employment, and to better his condition. He first entered the employment of Benjamin Chamberlain, who then owned and carried on . the saw and grist mill at the South Factory Village, and he was principally employed in the same while he remained with Mr. Chamberlain. During this time he attended four winter schools, from 1813 to 1817, which comprises the amount of his school privileges. He then apprenticed himself to Zadoc Chapman to learn the brick and stone mason trade. He continued with him seven years, working for wages after the trade was acquired. He attained the greatest perfection in this business, so that he was sought for and trusted with the best business in his calling. His motto was always to do his best. While a mason he was engaged in erecting the Water Loom Factory, High Bridge, New Ipswich; the Phœnix, in this town; the Cheshire, in Jaffrey; the Union Mill, No. 1, West Peterborough; also in laying the brick in that nice work, the front of the Congregational (Unitarian) Meeting-house; besides many dwelling-houses in this vicinity.

He began his career as a manufacturer in 1826, at the urgent request and by the personal influence of Gov. J. H. Steele, who gave him employment and good opportunities in the Union Mill, West Peterborough, of learning the art of manufacturing. He continued in his employ till 1834, when he took charge of the Bell Factory, so called, and the subsequent year he was appointed superintendent of the Phœnix Factory. He relinquished the charge of the Bell Factory in 1835, and was succeeded by his brother, Jonas Livingston. In addition to the charge of the Phœnix, he also took the superintendence of the Union Mills, in 1845, and retained it till 1857, after the erection of the new mill, No. 2.

On the removal of his brother to Claremont, he again took charge of the Bell Factory, which he retained till 1865, when he resigned and sold out all his interest in the same. He resigned the charge of the Phœnix in 1860, and in 1865 he entirely retired from the manufacturing business, having been engaged in the same nearly forty years.

F. Livingston

Mr. Livingston has been connected with both of the banks in town, the First National Bank of Peterborough and the Peterborough Savings Bank, from their commencement. He has been a director in the first mentioned bank from its beginning, and president since 1865, which office he now holds. He is also a trustee in the Savings Bank. He has been an entirely self-educated and self-made man. He acquired such a competent knowledge of mechanics, by his own efforts, as to be ready for any of the complicated calculations required in the building of machinery of various kinds employed in town. We have often heard Mr. Livingston modestly and gratefully acknowledge his obligation to three men in particular who had much to do, by their advice and encouragement, in promoting his success in life, *viz.*, Charles Barrett, Esq., New Ipswich; Hon. Samuel Smith, and Gov. John H. Steele, of Peterborough. To the aid and counsel of these men, just as he was starting out in life, he ascribes, in a great degree, his present standing in society, both as to respectability and property. He m., May 14, 1832, Lucy Law, of Sharon, b. April 12, 1806.

2   † *George F.*, b. Oct. 30, 1834; m., May 20, 1858, Elizabeth R. Holmes.

3   *Ariana C.*, b. June 1, 1837; d. Oct. 30, 1838, æ. 1 yr., 5 mos.

4   † *William G.*, b. Feb. 26, 1840; m., May 26, 1863, Ellen J. Cummings.

5   *Mary Ella*, b. June 30, 1848; m., Jan. 2, 1871, Harry H. Templeton, b. Oct. 8, 1845.

1– 2   GEORGE F. LIVINGSTON. He m., May 20, 1858, Elizabeth R. Holmes, dau. Abraham and Mary Dickey Holmes; she d. Nov. 1, 1875, æ. 45 yrs.

6   *Helen*, b. March 19, 1859.
7   *Frank W.*, b. Jan. 10, 1861.
8   *Lucy A.*, b. Aug. 13, 1865.

1– 4   WILLIAM G. LIVINGSTON m., May 26, 1863, Ellen J. Cummings, dau. John Cummings, b. Sept. 6, 1841. He is a trader in the village, and was for some years cashier of the First National Bank in Peterborough, which he was obliged to relinquish on account of his health.

9   *Fred. G.*, b. Aug. 17, 1867.
10   *Wait L.*, b. Sept. 9, 1870.
11   *Alice*, b. July 18, 1874.

18

JONAS LIVINGSTON, son of William and Elizabeth Saunders Livingston, and brother of the above, was b. in Sharon, Dec. 13, 1806. He incurred all the difficulties that attended the early life of his brother — poverty, limited advantages of education and all social privileges. He was early thrown on his own resources, and surmounted all these obstacles to success by his strong will, industry, and perseverance. He also acquired the trade of brick and stone mason early in life, and became an excellent workman. He, however, gave up the business, and went into the cotton mills in Peterborough, and was in 1838 appointed superintendent of the first Peterborough cotton factory (or Bell Factory). He removed to Claremont in 1845, and took charge of the Monadnock Mills there for nineteen years, when he returned to Peterborough, and bought out a majority of the stock in the Phœnix Factory, which he now controls and manages. He is also president of the Monadnock Railroad, which he did more than any other man to establish. He represented the town of Claremont in the Legislature when he resided there, and has served, since his return to Peterborough, as Senator for the 8th Senatorial District. He m., 1st w., Angelina Morse, Aug. 27, 1832. She was the mother of all his ch.; b. April 30, 1808; d. in Peterborough, June 15, 1867, æ. 59 yrs. He m., 2d w., Susan Robbe, dau. Samuel and Betsey Scott Robbe.

12 *Sherman E.*, b. July 7, 1833; m. Zilpha Keith, of Pomfret, Vt., July 11, 1854; ch., (1) Loyd L., b. Oct. 31, 1858; (2) Northman C., b. Jan. 2, 1862.

13 *Chancellor G.*, b. Oct. 11, 1835; d. Feb. 26, 1857, æ. 21 yrs., 4 mos.

14 *Northman C.*, b. April 23, 1839; d. April 18, 1860, æ. 20 yrs., 11 mos.

15 *Viola F.*, b. May 30, 1844; m. Elbert O. Stone, May 11, 1871.

16 *Alfonso J.*, b. April 12, 1850; d. April 12, 1867, æ. 17 yrs. All the above deaths occurred at Claremont; the remains were removed to town.

THE LONGLEY FAMILY.

1 JACOB LONGLEY is a native of Shirley, Mass. When quite young he went to Stoddard and lived many years in the family of Samuel Morrison, and when they re. to Peterborough he came with them. He has since resided in town, and devoted himself successfully to agriculture. He was b. July 1, 1801. He m., March 10, 1831, Hepzibeth Ames, dau. of Timothy and Sarah K. Ames; she d. Sept. 13, 1871, æ. 68 yrs. He is a

justice of the peace. He lives on the David Robbe place, near the old Johnny Morrison farm, now abandoned.

---

2 † *George H.*, b. April 4, 1832 ; m. Sarah M. Kimball.
3 † *William Hiram*, b. June 7, 1834; m. Mary White.
4 † *Timothy M.*, b. May 9, 1837 ; m. Emma Converse.
5 †*Stillman P.*, b. April 8, 1841 ; m. Sarah S. Converse.

1– 2 GEORGE H. LONGLEY. He lives near Briggs' manufactory of piano-stools. He is engaged in the baking business. He m. Sarah M. Kimball, June 1, 1854.

6 *George Wason*, b. March 23, 1855.
7 *Fred Kimball*, b. Aug. 31, 1856.
8 *Jacob W.*, b. Feb. 13, 1862.

1– 3 WILLIAM H. LONGLEY has generally been engaged in the butchering business in town. He m. Mary White, dau. James G. and Sarah Gibbs White, Dec. 11, 1856.

9 *Frank White*, b. May 20, 1858 ; d. Sept. 29, 1858, æ. 4 mos.
10 *William H. C.*, b. Sept. 20, 1862.
11 *Samuel P.*, b. Oct. 20, 1864.
12 *Henry C.*, b. June 20, 1867.

1– 4 TIMOTHY MORRISON LONGLEY. He m. Emma Converse, dau. of Samuel and Elizabeth T. Converse, Feb. 28, 1860 ; r. Royalston, Mass.

13 *Edith*, b. Jan. 6, 1861.   (14) *Arthur*, b. Aug. 20, 1863.
15 *Maurice*, b. April 9, 1865.

1– 5 STILLMAN PARKER LONGLEY. He lives in the village. He m. Sarah S. Converse, 1867.

16 *Frank*, b. March 13, 1869.   (17) *Albert*, b. Oct. 12, 1871.

THE LORING FAMILY.

1 JONAS LORING came to town in 1798 or '99 ; was a hatter by trade, and carried on the business many years at Carter's Corner, so called, where he lived. He built here a large brick house, in which he r. till he re. to Ohio. He left town about 1838 for Medina, O. He m. Mary White, dau. John White, Jr., Aug. 11, 1801. He was b. March 17, 1775; d. at Medina, O., March 16, 1856, æ. 81 yrs. She d. Nov. 15, 1852, æ. 74 yrs.

2 *Amarette*, b. March 26, 1802 ; d. July 4, 1837, æ. 35 yrs.

3 | *Lorenzo*, b. Jan. 2, 1804; d., New Orleans, June 10, 1835, æ. 31 yrs., 5 mos.

4 | *John*, b. July 21, 1805; m. Mary Merrit, of Pennfield, N. Y.; r. Michigan.

5 | *Ashley*, b. April 21, 1807; m., June 29, 1821, Elizabeth Wheelock; d. in Ohio, Jan. 28, 1849, æ. 41 yrs., 9 mos.

6 | *Frederick*, b. Feb. 12, 1809; m., Jan. 3, 1834, Mary Little; she d. February, 1848, æ. 38 yrs.; r. Carthage, Ill.

7 | *Sally*, b. Sept. 6, 1811; m., Oct. 5, 1820, Jefferson Nay; r. Ohio.

8 | *Elizabeth*, b. Oct. 21, 1815; m., 1839, John Lozedder; d., 1847, in Illinois.

9 | *Mary*, b. Aug. 14, 1819; m., Sept. 11, 1845, Chester T. Hills; r. Medina, O.

THE McALISTER FAMILY.

1 | RANDALL McALISTER lived in the east part of the town, on land north and embracing part of the William Field farm. We have no means of determining when he came to town, only that it was before the Revolution. He came from Scotland as a soldier in the British army, and deserted at Boston a short time before the battle of Bunker Hill. He was among the Americans in this memorable battle, and was badly wounded in the mouth and side of the neck, the ball having entered the mouth and come out, one half in the back of the neck, the other in the mouth. A comrade, who knew the circumstances of his desertion, and the danger of his falling into the hands of the enemy, took him on his back and carried him over Charlestown Neck to a place of safety. He served all through the Revolutionary war. He was b. in Scotland, Sept. 21, 1744, and d. in Peterborough, May 23, 1819, æ. 75 yrs. He m. Mary Blair, dau. William Blair, Sen., b. March 4, 1749; d. Oct. 14, 1833, æ. 84 yrs.

2 | *Mary*, b. Nov. 26, 1785; m. William Field.

THE McCOY FAMILY.

1 | WILLIAM McCoy must have been an early settler, probably about 1752 or '53. He began the place afterwards owned and occupied by John Leathers. He d. there March 4, 1794, æ. 67 yrs. His wife, Mary, d. March 22, 1791, æ. 62 yrs.

2 | *Andrew*, b. July 2, 1753. (3) *Elizabeth*, b. May 13, 1755.

4 | *Martha*, b. Oct. 10, 1757; m. Dr. Gale, Dracut, Mass.; 2d hus., Col. Varnum; r. Dracut, Mass.

5 | *Mary*, b. Aug. 10, 1759 ; unm. ; d. Dec. 27, 1839, æ. 81 yrs.
6 | †*Charles*, b. Feb. 17, 1761 ; m. Jane Templeton.
7 | *Sarah*, b. 1762 ; unm. ; d. June 29, 1834, æ. 72 yrs.
8 | *Samuel*, b. 1767 ; unm. ; d. June 29, 1801 ; killed by a horse.
9 | *William*, b. 1768 ; unm. ; d. April 13, 1834, æ. 66 yrs. ; insane.

1- 6· | CHARLES McCoy. He lived on a farm adjoining his father's, which was afterwards occupied by his son, William McCoy. He m. Jane Templeton, dau. James Templeton. She d. Aug. 20, 1849, æ. 83 yrs. He d. Feb. 10, 1828, æ. 67 yrs. In the Revolution he served in Rhode Island, 1778, in Col. Enoch Hale's Reg. He also went to Bennington in 1777.

10 | *Mary*, b. 1790 ; m. Nathan Leathers.
11 | *Jane*, b. 1791 ; unm. ; d. Aug. 5, 1863, æ. 72 yrs.
12 | *Martha*, b. 1794 ; m. Parker Varnum.
13 · | †*Samuel*, b. Sept. 11, 1797 ; m. Elizabeth Bailey.
14 | *Sally*, b. 1799 ; unm. ; d. June 25, 1861, æ. 62 yrs.
15 | † *William*, b. June 2, 1802 ; m. Mrs. Carrie Cudworth.
16 | *James*, b. 1808 ; unm. ; d. Nov. 3, 1875, æ. 67 yrs.
17 | *Susan*, b. 1810 ; m. Joseph True ; d. June 20, 1845, æ. 35 yrs.

6- 13 | SAMUEL McCoy. He settled on a farm directly north of his father's farm. He was a farmer. He m. Elizabeth Bailey. He d. Sept. 4, 1871, æ. 75 yrs.

18 | *Elisabeth*, b. Jan. 16, 1823 ; d. May 28, 1864, æ. 41 yrs.
19 | †*Hiram*, b. Nov. 16, 1825 ; m. Ruth Smiley.
20 | †*Charles*, b. Sept. 28, 1827 ; m. M. C. Hildreth, Lowell.
21 | *John*, b. Sept. 1, 1835 ; m. Harriet Davis ; r. Lowell.
Then follow the births of four ch. ; all d. young.

6- 15 | WILLIAM McCoy. He lived on the homestead. He m. Mrs. Carrie Cudworth. He d. May —.

22 | *Albert*, b. April 1, 1849 ; d. Aug. 25, 1854, æ. 5 yrs., 4 mos.
23 | *Jane*, b. May 1, 1854 ; d.
24 | *William Henry*, b. March 2, 1859.

13- 19 | HIRAM McCoy. He lives on the James Howe place. He m. Ruth Smiley, dau. Francis Smiley, April 7, 1864 ; b. Dec. 4, 1823.

25 | *Willie H.*, b. Sept. 9, 1865.
26 | *Perley S.*, b. March 6, 1868.

13- 20 | CHARLES McCOY. He is a moulder by trade; r. Lowell; m. M. C. Hildreth, of Lowell, April 30, 1853.

27 | *Charles*, b. Peterborough, 1853; d. at Lowell, 1854.
28 | *Franklin*, b. Nov. 20, 1855.
29 | *George*, b. Oct. 20, 1859; d. November, 1874, æ. 15 yrs.
30 | *Alvin*, b. Sept. 4, 1861. (31) *Edward C.*, b. March 4, 1863.
32 | *Mary C.*, b. Sept. 4, 1866.

THE McCLOUD FAMILY.

1 | THOMAS McCLOUD m. Elizabeth ———. We know little of this family, only that such a family lived in town, and the following record was entered on the town books.

2 | *Charles*, b. Sept. 2, 1769. (3) *Margaret*, b. May 9, 1772.
4 | *Thomas*, b. April 25, 1775. (5) *William*, b. Nov. 29, 1776.
6 | *Elizabeth*, b. June 1, 1779. (7) *Esther*, b. Feb. 7, 1781.
8 | *Polly*, b. June 23, 1783. (9) *John*, b. July 29, 1785.

THE McCLOURGE FAMILY.

1 | GEORGE McCLOURGE, son of Charles and Esther McClourge, b. in Londonderry, May 18, 1728. He was one of the family with Robert, b. Aug. 18, 1726, Mary, b. June 5, 1730, and John, b. Sept. 5, 1734. He m. Ann ———. In regard to his residence in town we know nothing. We find the names of George and Robert McCloud, which we think should be McClourge, were enlisted in the Revolution, 1776, to serve five mos. each, probably sons of George McClourge.

2 | *Elizabeth*, b. Aug. 22, 1752. (3) *John*, b. ———.
4 | *Robert*, b. Feb. 13, 1755. (5) *Samuel*, b. Sept. 13, 1757.
6 | *Sarah*, b. March 29, 1759. (7) *George*, b. Jan. 10, 1760.

THE McKEAN FAMILY.

1 | JAMES McKEAN began the David Blanchard place about 1765, and d. at an early age. He was b. in Londonderry, June 15, 1739, and d. in Peterborough, Feb. 26, 1776, æ. 37 yrs. He m. Mary Cuningham, dau. of Thomas Cuningham, b. in Townsend, Mass., Sept. 6, 1746. After his death she m. Samuel Treadwell, and d. Aug. 27, 1833, æ. 87 yrs. A son of McKean's, when in his minority, sold the place to the Chubbucks, and they again to Elihu Penniman. Young McKean sued Penniman for posses-

sion, on account of the illegality of the sale in his
minority, but Penniman was sustained by the courts,
and held the land.

———

2 | *Levi*, b. Oct. 22, 1768 ; re. to Poughkeepsie, N. Y.

THE MAYNARD FAMILY.

1 | SAMUEL MAYNARD m., 1st w., Nancy C. Gibbs, wid.
of Abel Gibbs, and dau. James Porter. She d. April 2,
1849, æ. 62 yrs. ; m., 2d w., Mrs. —— Hayden, of Temple. He d. Nov. 18, 1863, æ. 67 yrs. He was chosen
deacon in the Presbyterian church, June 8, 1836. He
r. near Hunt's Corner, occupying, in part, the old Porter
farm.

2 | *Hannah Curtis*, b. March 20, 1824 ; d. Oct. 15, 1850, æ.
26 yrs., 6 mos.
3 | *Samuel F.*, b. April 14, 1827 ; d. in Iowa.
4 | *Israel F.*, b. June 29, 1829.
5 | *Elisa*, b. July 17, 1832 ; d. Jan. 17, 1862, æ. 29 yrs., 6
mos.

THE MEARS FAMILY.

1 | FRANKLIN MEARS, accompanied by his parents, Oliver
and Eunice Perry Mears, came to Peterborough from
Goffstown, in 1837, and purchased T. K. Ames' farm,
originally the William Powers place, and a part of the
Thomas Morison place. Oliver Mears was b. in Easton,
Mass., Nov. 26, 1777, and d. in Peterborough, June 23,
1857, æ. 80 yrs. His w. was b. in Woburn, Mass., Nov.
26, 1780, and d. in Peterborough, May 31, 1851, æ. 70
yrs. They were m. in Greenfield, Dec. 10, 1801.
Franklin Mears was b. in Greenfield, Oct. 31, 1802 ; m.,
1st w., Eliza Haseltine, b. in Amherst, Feb. 16, 1808 ;
d. Jan. 20, 1846, æ. 37 yrs., 11 mos.; m., 2d w., Sarah
McCoy, b. in Sharon, March 4, 1810 ; 1st w., two ch. ;
2d w., two ch. A farmer.

2 | † *John Milton*, b. in Goffstown, Sept. 10, 1833 ; m., 1st
w., Betsey B. Buswell ; 2d w., S. Almeda Upton.
3 | *Henry F.*, b. Oct. 4, 1845 ; m. Cyntha Frost, June, 1876.
4 | *Sarah E.*, b. July 4, 1848 ; m. Charles Farmer, 1875.
5 | *Eunice E.*, b. April 19, 1854.

1– 2 | JOHN MILTON MEARS m., 1st w., Betsey B. Buswell,
Nov. 2, 1854 ; she d. Jan. 1, 1865, æ. 35 yrs. ; m., 2d w.,
S. Almeda Upton, dau. Thomas and Lydia Snow Upton ;

1st w., three children. A carpenter by trade. He lives on the homestead.

---

6 *Ellie C.*, b. Dec. 27, 1856.
7 *George M.*, b. Nov. 19, 1858.
8 *Frank Elmer*, b. Sept. 4, 1862.

THE MELVIN FAMILY.

1 · REUBEN MELVIN was the son of Reuben Melvin, of Pelham; b. in Pelham, Feb. 27, 1768; re. to Peterborough in 1805. He m. Sarah Marshall, b. Sept. 5, 1765; she d. March 18, 1841, æ. 75 yrs. He d. June 6, 1835, æ. 67 yrs. He lived in the north part of the town.

---

2 *Reuben*, b. Oct. 29, 1794; d. September, 1818, æ. 24 yrs.
3 *Diocletian*, b. Feb. 26, 1796; m. Frances Smith; she d. Feb. 25, 1864, æ. 57 yrs.; he d. July 26, 1862, æ. 66 yrs.
4 *Sarah*, b. July 10, 1797; m. Alexander Smith; r. Londonderry.
5 *Chloe*, b. March 15, 1799; d. Nov. 25, 1815, æ. 16 yrs.
6 *Daniel*, b. June 12, 1800; m. Harriet Gregg; r. Eden, Vt.; d. Sept. 29, 1847, æ. 47 yrs.
7 *Florensa*, b. Feb. 25, 1802; m. Abram Smith; r. Eden, Vt.; d. Sept. 11, 1871, æ. 69 yrs.
8 *Clarissa*, b. Dec. 29, 1804; m. Thomas Laws; d. May 16, 1855, æ. 51 yrs.
9 *Mary*, b. Oct. 22, 1806; m. Joseph H. Ames, Aug. 28, 1832.
10 *Nancy*, b. Feb. 20, 1811; m. John Richey; r. Plattsmouth, Neb.

THE MILLER FAMILY.

1 We have had great perplexity in tracing out the origin of this family. By a record made by * S. Smith, in his Manuscript Note, it would appear that a certain Dea. Miller, of Londonderry, purchased certain lots of land in the north-east part of the town for his sons. We are not able to determine that he was a deacon, but that his Christian name was Samuel, and that he was the son of Robert Miller, one of the first settlers of Londonderry. His name appears on a tax-list of Nov. 9, 1750, for £2, 13s. 5d. for the support of preaching.† His name also appears on the Association Test, with that of his son, Matthew, April, 1776. He is reported to have purchased four hundred acres of land in town for his sons,

---

* Manuscript Note by Hon. S. Smith.
† History Londonderry, pp. 328, 332, 335.

Matthew, John, William, and James, which was bought with the proceeds of linen cloth, thread, etc., manufactured by his thrifty and industrious wife. He first provided for Matthew by a lot embracing the Parker place and that next east of it, which was sold by him to Samuel Miller, a brother, and then to young Samuel, probably the son of James, and by him to Robert Clark and Timothy Ames. And then he gave William and James lots just east; James on the south side of the road, and William on the north side. These brothers carried on their farms in common till their families had grown up. And lastly, he provided for his son John by buying land situated east of the lots of William and James. Of the father, Samuel Miller, we know very little. It is uncertain whether he ever lived in town much. He probably continued his residence in Londonderry, and d. there. His w. d. in New Boston, with her dau., Mrs. Patterson; date unknown. Matthew withdrew from town on the sale of his farm, and settled in Pomfret, Vt., late in life. The following are all the data we can obtain of Samuel Miller's family.

---

2 † *Matthew*, b. June 15, 1730; m. Mary Morrison, b. Oct. 8, 1736. He d. in Pomfret, Vt., May 30, 1824, æ. 94 yrs.

3 † *James*, ⎫
4 † *William*, ⎬ b. 1738; m. Catharine Gregg. m. Jane Todd, dau. Col. Andrew Todd.

5 *Samuel*, b. ——.   (6) *John*, b. ——.
7 *Susanna*, b. ——; m. Dea. —— Patterson; r. New Boston.

1- 2 MATTHEW MILLER. After selling his farm he returned to Londonderry, and remained there through the Revolution, and served frequently as a minute-man, and for short periods. His name is on the Association Test in Londonderry, in 1776. He subsequently re. to Pomfret, Vt., where he d. May 30, 1824, æ. 94 yrs. He m. Mary Morrison, b. Oct. 8, 1736, who d. in Rockingham, Vt., May 21, 1815, æ. 78 yrs., 7 mos.

---

8 *Mary*, b. in Peterborough, April 28, 1757; m. —— Burns; d. Pomfret, March 31, 1824, æ. 74 yrs.
9 *Samuel*, b. in Peterborough, Feb. 1, 1759; d. Rockingham, Vt., Feb. 16, 1819, æ. 60 yrs.
10 *James*, b. in Peterborough, June 24, 1761; d. in Chester, Vt., Jan. 9, 1826, æ. 64 yrs., 6 mos.
11 *William*, b. in Peterborough, Sept. 2, 1763; d. Merrimack, Jan. 14, 1818, æ. 54 yrs., 4 mos.

19

12 *Nancy*, b. in Peterborough, Dec. 29, 1765; m. ——
    Campbell; d. Acworth, Aug. 19, 1819, æ. 53 yrs., 7
    mos.

13 *Susanna*, b. in Peterborough, April 2, 1768; m. ——
    Vickery; d. in Chester, Vt., 1860, æ. 92 yrs.

14 *John*, b. in Peterborough, Sept. 15, 1770; d. in Pomfret,
    Jan. 31, 1856, æ. 85 yrs., 4 mos.

15 *Matthew*, b. Londonderry, Sept. 16, 1773; d. in Rock-
    ingham, Dec. 6, 1831, æ. 58 yrs.

16 *Jane*, b. Londonderry, August, 1776; m. —— Johnson;
    2d hus., —— Mead; d. in Cavendish, Vt., Sept. 12,
    1850, æ. 80 yrs.

17 *Anna*, b. Londonderry, May 5, 1779; m. —— Ship-
    man; d. Walpole, Jan. 8, 1821, æ. 41 yrs.

1- 3 JAMES MILLER. He occupied the place given him by
his father, and here reared up his large and important
family. He m. Catharine Gregg, who d. May 23, 1833,
æ. 89 yrs. He d. Nov. 21, 1825, æ. 87 yrs. He came from
Londonderry, but we are uncertain in regard to the time.
It is supposed that he was quite young, and that he was
a twin brother of James, as both are found to be born
the same year, 1738.

---

18 †*Hugh*, b. October, 1768; m. Anna Templeton.
19 *Samuel*, b. 1772; m. Sylvia Keep; re. to Dummerstown,
    Vt.
20 *Jenny*, b. 1774; m. Samuel Templeton.
21 †*James*, b. April 25, 1776; m., 1st w., Martha Ferguson;
    2d w., Ruth Flint, Lincoln, Mass.
22 *Polly*, b. 1777; d. Dec. 28, 1796, æ. 19 yrs.
23 *Catharine*, b. ——; m. Daniel McFarland; r. Antrim,
    and d. there.
24 *Jacob*, b. ——; m. Jane Hopkins; he d. in Arkansas, 1822.
25 *William*, b. ——.

1- 4 WILLIAM MILLER. He settled on the lot given him
by his father, opposite to his brother James' farm, which
was afterwards occupied by his son Andrew. It is
probable that he came to town at the same time his
brother did. He m. Jane Todd, dau. of Col. Andrew
and Beatrix Todd, of Londonderry. Col. Todd came
to Peterborough in 1776, and lived with his dau. till
his death, 1777. She d. Nov. 5, 1796, æ. 60 yrs. He
d. April 11, 1796, æ. 58 yrs.

---

26 *Samuel*, b. 1767; d. Oct. 15, 1793, æ. 26 yrs.
27 *Betsey*, b. 1769; m. David White.

28 †*Andrew*, b. March 18, 1774; m. Jane Ames.
29 † *William*, b. March 18, 1774; m. Ruth Ames; 2d w., Gracy Holmes.
30 *John*, b. 1778; d. Aug. 6, 1796, æ. 18 yrs.
31 *Sarah*, b. ——; m. —— Duncan; 2d hus., James Todd.

3– 18   HUGH MILLER always resided in town, occupying a farm directly south of his father's farm. He m. Jane Templeton, dau. of Matthew Templeton, in 1795, who d. June 9, 1845, æ. 71 yrs. He d. Dec. 10, 1847, æ. 79 yrs. He was always an influential man in town. In all those Sunday noon discussions under the beech trees on the meeting-house hill, he always held a conspicuous part. He was a man of ripe and sound judgment, and just views. He was honored by the town as hardly any other man ever was. He was chosen selectman for twenty-four years in succession after 1805, and also represented the town in the Legislature for ten years, from 1815 to 1832.

32 †*Samuel*, b. Jan. 5, 1796; m. Ruth Bowers, Aug. 9, 1831.
33 *James*, b. March 15, 1798; d. at Fort Smith, Arkansas, Aug. 15, 1822, æ. 24 yrs.
34 *Jane*, b. February, 1800; m. Moody Davis; d. Sept. 27, 1856, æ. 56 yrs. One ch.
35 *Rodney*, b. June 14, 1802; d. in Maine, Feb. 4, 1854, æ. 52 yrs.

3– 21   JAMES MILLER (Gen.) was a native of Peterborough, b. April 25, 1776, and son of James Miller, of this town, who was of Scotch-Irish descent, his ancestors having emigrated from the north of Ireland. They were among the first settlers of Londonderry. In early life, like all the descendants of our first settlers, he was made hardy by labor, and insured a strong, vigorous constitution by the hard discipline on the farm. While young, he received the common school education, which was exceedingly meagre at this time. He afterwards pursued his studies at the academy at Amherst, and for a time was a member of Williams College, Williamstown, Mass. He studied law with James Wilson, Sen., Esq., of Peterborough. Having finished his course of study, he was admitted to the bar of his native County of Hillsboro, in 1803. About this time he settled in the neighboring town of Greenfield, in the practice of his profession, where he was soon in command of the company of artillery attached to the 26th Regiment of the New Hampshire Militia.* His military bearing, aptitude,

* Adjutant-General's Report New Hampshire, for 1868.

and skill in manœuvering and drill, attracted the attention of Gen. Benjamin Pierce, and at his earnest recommendation Capt. Miller was appointed Major of the 4th Regiment of United States Infantry, commanded by Col. John P. Boyd, and then stationed at Fort Independence, in the harbor of Boston. His commission bears date March 3, 1809, taking rank from 8th of July, 1808. This regiment contained many officers and men from New Hampshire, and after Major Miller's appointment to it, many more joined the regiment from the interior of the State.

He remained at Fort Independence till 1811, when the 4th Regiment was ordered to Vincennes, Ind., to join the army of Gen. Harrison in the war with the Indians. Col. Boyd was ordered on in advance of his regiment, and the command devolved on Col. Miller. He proceeded to his destination by way of Philadelphia, Pittsburg, and three hundred miles down the Ohio, and one hundred and seventy miles up the Wabash in boats, — a long journey, all before the days of steamboats or railroad transportation. While at Fort Harrison, he was attacked by a fever, and was deterred thereby from taking a part in the disastrous battle of Tippecanoe, occasioned by the treachery of the Indians, in which the troops were barely victors, after a hard struggle in which the 4th Regiment took a conspicuous part.

In May, 1812, the 4th Regiment, under Col. Miller's command, was ordered to join Gen. Hull's army, at Urbana, O., where they met Gen. Hull and his army, and marched together to Detroit. Soon after June 18, 1812, war was declared against Great Britain, and preparations were made to invade Canada. In a letter to his wife, July 14, 1812, he says that he had the command in effecting a passage of the army over the river to Sandwich, Upper Canada, and also had the honor and gratification of planting with his own hands, assisted by Gen. Cass, the first United States standard on the pleasant banks of the Detroit River, in King George's dominion, Province of Upper Canada.

He was in Hull's army but a short time before it surrendered. On the 9th of August there was quite a severe encounter with the British and Indians, at Maguaga or Brownstown, his first battle, in which he had the command of six hundred men, which was quite successful. In this engagement a superior force of British and Indians was compelled to fly, and the famous Indian chief, Tecumseh, was wounded in the neck. In his letters he always expresses a confidence in the army's being able to sustain itself with proper management, and was strongly opposed to a surrender which Gen. Hull made without any consultation of his officers. He did not know that Gen. Hull had any intention of surrendering till it was accomplished.

In a letter of Aug. 27, 1812, he says: "Only one week after, I with six hundred men completely conquered almost the whole force which they then had. They came and took Fort Detroit, and made two thousand of us prisoners on Sunday, the 16th inst." He was soon patrolled and came home, but was not exchanged, so that he did no more military duty that year. He was exchanged for Lord Dacres early the next year, and he writes home from Sackett's Harbor as early as May 1, 1813. He was constantly engaged through the unsuccessful campaign of 1813 without being in many battles. He took an active and perilous part in the battle of Fort George, which continued three hours, in which the American arms were successful in capturing the fort and a large quantity of military stores. In his letter of May 27, he says: "I escaped unhurt, and hope to feel suitably thankful to that All-ruling Power who preserved me." In his letter of June 13, 1813, after speaking of the great neglect of the sick, and the want of everything to make them comfortable, he says: "I found thirty of my regiment wounded, at Sackett's Harbor, who had been brought in from the battle of York. They were as ragged as bears and lousy as cattle, and no clothing to change them. I ordered India cotton to be bought to make each a shirt, and hired them made." He says, June 24, 1813, that in consequence of the capture of Gens. Winder and Chandler the command of six regiments devolved on him, and that "Gen. Boyd is the only acting general we have." He felt great dissatisfaction through all the campaign with the management of the war. He was confident that with good generalship and persevering action, the Americans would not only be able to keep their ground, but even to drive the enemy out of the province. But the military operations of the year closed without having effected anything of importance.

In his letter, from French Mills, of Nov. 9, 1813, he says: "We have ended, in my opinion, another disgraceful campaign, much to the dishonor of the American arms. It appears to me that the termination of this campaign will have a worse effect on the public mind than even Hull's itself, and will shake the government to its centre; and could this solemn lesson teach the government to make more judicious appointments of general officers, we might yet retrieve our reputation as soldiers." The campaign of 1814 was vastly more active and successful than those of the former years. It still lacked competent generals, as in the Rebellion it took time to bring forward men qualified to conduct and command our armies; they had to be educated and trained in service, at the great peril of the nation, before they acquired or deserved the confidence of the troops or of the people. It was during this year that he saw much fighting, and was in several memorable battles, and still, as heretofore, he had the good fortune to escape unhurt. It was at the battle of Niagara, or Lundy's Lane, that occurred that memorable feat of coolness and intrepidity that has immortalized his name. When, in the course of the battle, it was necessary that a certain British battery should be carried, Gen. Brown, addressing Col. Miller, said, "Colonel, take your regiment, storm that work and take it." "I'll try, sir," responded the brave Miller promptly, and immediately moved forward to the perilous task.* The following letter gives a graphic description of this adventure:

"FORT ERIE, July 28, 1814.

"*My Beloved Ruth*,—I have great reason to thank God for his continued mercies and protection. On the 25th inst., at the Falls of Niagara, we met the enemy, and had, I believe, one of the most desperately fought actions ever experienced in America. It continued for three hours, stubbornly on both sides, when about ten o'clock at night we succeeded in driving them from their strong position. Our loss was very severe in killed and wounded. I have lost from my regiment, in killed and wounded and missing, *one hundred and twenty-six*. The enemy had got their artillery posted on a height, in a very commanding position, where they could rake our columns in any part of the field, and prevented their advancing. Maj. McRee, the chief engineer, told Gen. Brown he could do no good until that height was carried and those cannon taken or driven from their position. It was then night, but moonlight. Gen. Brown turned to me and said, 'Col. Miller, take your regiment, and storm that work and take it.' I had short of three hundred men with me, as my regiment had been much weakened by the numerous details made from it during the day. I, however, immediately obeyed the order. We could see all their slow matches and port-fires burning and ready. I did not know what side of the work was most favorable to approach, but happened to hit upon a very favorable place, notwithstanding we advanced upon the mouths of their cannon. It hap-

---

* Pictorial Field Book of War of 1812, p. 819.

pened that there was an old rail-fence on the side where
we approached, with a small growth of shrubbery by the
fence and within less than two rods of the cannon's
mouth, undiscovered by the enemy. I then very cau-
tiously ordered my men to rest across the fence, take
good aim, fire, and rush, which was done in style. Not
one man at the cannon was left to put fire to them. We
got into the centre of their park before they had time to
oppose us. A British line was formed, and lying in a
strong position to protect their artillery. The moment
we got to the centre, they opened a most destructive
flank fire on us, killed a great many, and attempted to
charge with their bayonets. We returned the fire so
warmly they were compelled to stand ; we fought hand
to hand for some time, so close that the blaze of our
guns crossed each other ; but we compelled them to
abandon their whole artillery, ammunition-wagons and
all, amounting to seven pieces of elegant brass cannon,
one of which was a twenty-four-pounder, with eight
horses and harness, though some of the horses were
killed. The British made two more attempts to charge
us at close quarters, both of which we repulsed before I
was reinforced, after which the 1st and 23d Regs. came
to my relief. And even after that, the British charged
with their whole line there several times, and after getting
within half pistol-shot of us were compelled to give way.
I took, with my regiment, between thirty and forty prisoners, while taking and defending the artillery. . . . After
Generals Brown, Scott, and others were wounded, we
were ordered to return back to our camp, about three
miles, and preparations had not been made for taking off
the cannon, as it was impossible for me to defend them
and make preparations for that too, and they were all left
on the ground except one beautiful six-pounder, which
was presented to my regiment in testimony of their distinguished gallantry. The officers of this army all say, who
saw it, that it was one of the most desperate and gallant
acts ever known ; the British officers whom we have
prisoners say it was the most desperate thing they ever
saw or heard of. Gen. Brown told me, the moment he
saw me, that I had immortalized myself. 'But,' said he,
'my dear fellow, my heart ached for you when I gave
you the order, but I knew that it was the only thing that
would save us.'"

I must not omit one other severe trial of Gen. Miller
during this year, at the sortie of Fort Erie, Sept. 17,
1814, which, after one of the sharpest and most bloody
of the battles of the war, was entirely successful. In
this engagement he had the command of one of the

divisions, consisting of the ninth, eleventh, and nineteenth regiments, and acquitted himself with his usual bravery and discretion, well sustaining the enviable reputation he had acquired a short time previous at the battle of Niagara. This was a fierce and desperate encounter, in which the officers were killed in a large proportion to the soldiery; for he says in a letter: "Our loss was betwixt four and five hundred — killed, wounded, and prisoners. We took three hundred and eighty-five prisoners, besides what we killed and wounded. Since I came into Canada this time every major save one, every lieutenant-colonel, every colonel that was here when I came and has remained here, has been killed or wounded, and I am now the only general officer out of seven that has escaped."

Gen. Miller continued in active service to the close of the war, and as an acknowledgment for his personal bravery and untiring devotion to his country, the State of New York presented him a beautiful sword, with the following inscription: "Presented by His Excellency Daniel D. Tompkins, Governor of the State of New York, pursuant to resolutions of the Senate and Assembly of the said State, to Brigadier-General James Miller, as a testimony of gratitude for his services and admiration of his gallant conduct." And Congress awarded him a gold medal, bearing the following inscription, together with a representation of the scene of the charge on the battery at the battle of Niagara: "Battle of Chippewa, July 5, 1814; Niagara, July 25, 1814; Erie, Sept. 17, 1814." He was promoted as follows: In August, 1812, he was brevetted a colonel for distinguished services, probably the battle of Brownstown or Maguaga, and in March, 1814, he was appointed Colonel of the 21st Reg. of Infantry, and subsequently brevetted Brigadier-general, for his courage and gallantry at Lundy's Lane, battle of Niagara.

In 1819, receiving the appointment of Governor of the Territory of Arkansas, he resigned his commission in the army. It was an act he always afterwards regretted. The military had engaged so long a period of his life, and had so absorbed the whole man, that he could not easily transfer his powers to any other kind of business with any satisfaction to himself. The climate of Arkansas disagreeing with his health, he returned to New Hampshire an invalid in 1823, and in 1824 he was elected a Representative to Congress in the district in which he resided; but having, in the meantime, received the appointment of Collector of Customs for the district of Salem and Beverly, he concluded to accept it, and consequently never took his seat in Congress. He retained the office of Collector of Salem twenty-four years, and until his health had become enfeebled by paralysis, when he resigned and was succeeded by his youngest son, who also held the office eight years. He then removed to his farm in Temple, where his daughters now reside. He had a second stroke of paralysis on the morning of the 4th of July, 1851, and died on the 7th at the age of seventy-five years.* His remains now repose beside those of his wife and two daughters, in the beautiful cemetery of Harmony Grove, in Salem, Mass.†

No one ever questioned the courage and military character of Gen. Miller. Hawthorne speaks of him as "New England's most distinguished soldier."‡ He was always competent to every undertaking that fell to his lot. He cheerfully submitted to all the exactions and severe discipline of military life, and required the same of others under his command. He strove faithfully and conscientiously, in·every respect, to do his whole duty. It was with great regret and sorrow he saw how miserably the military affairs, both by the government and by incompetent generals, were conducted during the first part of the war.

He possessed, in an eminent degree, all the elements of a soldier,— true honor, capacity, courage, decision, patience, and hardihood, and no doubt merited a higher rank in the war of 1812 than he held; but he gained honor enough, for few came out of that war with such a harvest of fame as he did. He bore his honors with a modesty and discretion that won for him a general esteem. He was universally respected and honored through the country. He did nothing to mar his good name, but rather to increase it, so that no one could say that it was mere chance or good-luck that had made him so famous. It was the intrinsic virtues of the man, his resolute determination to do his duty under all circumstances, be that duty what it might.

He was a man of the kindliest affections. His autograph letters to his wife during his military service on the Canada frontiers are models of good sense, sincerity, and affection, rarely met with under such circumstances. In reading these letters we are often surprised at the sagacity evinced in his views so freely expressed here. Notwithstanding all these discouragements, he never failed in his own duty; he was always ready to

* Pictorial Field Book of War of 1812, p. 820.

† History of Temple, p. 237.

‡ Scarlet Letter, p. 12.

20

carry out any order, even such as that of storming the battery at Lundy's Lane.

Gen. Miller was always respected for his virtues and sterling integrity in all the relations of life.

In his personal appearance he was highly blessed by nature. He was of a large frame, erect and graceful in his movements, and a noble specimen of manly dignity and strength, with a pleasant and agreeable countenance, and a gentle and smooth speech that always impressed strangers favorably.

His talents were of that useful kind that were aided and wonderfully elicited by good common-sense and a sound judgment. He was always a cultivated and re- fined man, making himself equally the companion and friend of the first men of the nation.

Gen. Lewis Cass, in a letter to the daughters of Gen. Miller, says (Washington City, July 8, 1858), "I knew your lamented father well. A more gallant soldier or a purer patriot it has never been my fortune to meet. He devoted the best years of his life to the service of his country, and his exertions and exposures shattered his constitution, and ultimately carried him to the grave."

He attended the centennial celebration of Peter- borough, Oct. 24, 1839, and was called out by the fol- lowing toast: "Gen. James Miller. A brave man never to be forgotten by his country or native town."

He made a brief speech, expressing his satisfaction in being present on this occasion, and meeting so many of his old friends, and thanking them for so flattering a notice, and closed with the following beautiful and exquisite sentiment: "May we encourage literature, revere religion, and love one another."

He m., 1st w., Martha Ferguson, dau. of Henry Fer- guson. She d. at Greenfield, May 12, 1805, æ. 23 yrs. He m., 2d w., Ruth Flint, of Lincoln, Mass. She d. May 20, 1830; 1st w., two ch.; 2d w., five ch.

---

36   *Mary*, b. March 13, 1803, at Greenfield; m. Capt. Jona- than M. Ropes; r. Elizabeth Port, N. J.

37   *James F.*, (Commodore) b. April 28, 1805; m. Emily Fox, New Ipswich; m., 2d w., Caroline Fox, of New Ipswich. He d. July 11, 1868, æ. 63 yrs.

38   *Ephraim*, b. October, 1808; m. Catharine Seymour. Eight years collector of customs, Salem, Mass.; r. Salem.

39   *Catharine*, b. August, 1810; d. Sept. 6, 1836, æ. 26 yrs.

40   *Rebecca*, b. Sept. 7, 1813.

41 | *Ruth,* b. January, 1815; d. Sept. 24, 1822, æ. 6 yrs., 8 mos.

42 | *Augusta,* b. April 17, 1818.

4— 28 | ANDREW MILLER. He remained on the old homestead. He m. Jane Ames, b. July 6, 1778, of Hancock; she d. Sept. 10, 1865, æ. 87 yrs. He d. April 27, 1848, æ. 75 yrs.

43 | † *William,* b. Sept. 13, 1799; m. Mary Gray, Aug. 24, 1824.

44 | *Mark,* b. Nov. 10, 1809; m., 1st w., Abby A. Abbot; 2d w., Susanna S. Pierce. He d. April 9, 1874, æ. 64 yrs., 5 mos.

Mark Miller's early life was spent on the farm. He enjoyed only the ordinary means of education. After ten years of age, being useful on the farm, he only attended the short winter term of the district school. At eighteen he attended for one or two terms an academy, kept one or two district schools, and then went to Lowell, and served the usual time in the printing business. He commenced his editorial labors in his native town, when he was twenty-three years of age, but soon moved to Fitchburg to edit a weekly paper. While here he was appointed Postmaster of Fitchburg, which office he held till he removed to Albany, 1834. He there engaged in wood and copper engraving, which occupation he followed in that city, and at Rochester, for many years. In 1848 he removed to Racine, Wis., where he issued the first number of the *Wisconsin Farmer,* which he published till 1854. He removed to Des Moines in 1862, and here started the *Homestead.* He was principally editor of this paper till 1870, when he established a monthly journal entitled the *Western Pomologist,* which he conducted till his death. In an obituary notice of his death, the editor of the *Daily State Register,* Iowa, thus speaks of him :—

"As a horticultural editor, and as a practical horticulturist, Mr. Miller had, perhaps, no superior in the country. He was not only a clear and fluent writer, and versed in practical knowledge in everything whereof he wrote, but he was also of eminent reputation as an engraver on copper and wood. He was, therefore, able to illustrate as well as write, and this he always did, which gave to his contributions to the literature of horticulture an especial value. It is not for us to award to Mr. Miller his real rank in the profession and labor he loved so well and served so devotedly. Nor may we tell in such eulogy as will be just the tribute

his life and labors deserve. . . . Meantime, it will suffice,
perhaps, to say that for the home of his later years, for
the State of Iowa, in whose development he took such
an interest, he has done much, both in journalism and in
the practical field of horticulture and agriculture. . . . He
has left his enduring monument on thousands of Iowa
farms and Iowa homes, and under the broad, kind shelter of trees and orchards and groves that his hands or
his advice helped to plant, and helped to make successful verities, a grateful people will, for long years to
come, talk kindly of the name of Mark Miller, and treasure gratefully his memory." He left five children, four
sons and one daughter. His two oldest sons are settled
near Palatka, in Florida, the others are in Des Moines.
It says further, " Mark Miller left the world much better
for his having lived in it ; and those who will mourn his
death sincerely as that of a·true friend, and a kind man,
always will be many." " The remains were laid at rest
with the head resting at the foot of a favorite apple-tree,
in a place selected by Mr. Miller a few days before he
died. There, surrounded by the objects that he loved,
and in a place that he had made beautiful and attractive,
let him sleep."

45   *Luke,* b. Aug. 18, 1815 ;. m., 1st w., Abby D. Lovell ; she
d. Sept. 12, 1865 ; 2d w., Hannah Dane, of Peterborough ; r. Lanesville, Minn.

Luke Miller by his own unaided exertions was enabled to acquire a good education. He was educated
to be a practical printer till his declining health induced
him to turn his attention to other pursuits. He now
attended the academy at Hancock, and prepared himself to enter Norwich University, where he graduated in
1841. He was attracted to the medical profession, and
studied it principally with Professor Albert Smith and
Wm. Follansbee, M.D., of Peterborough, and took his medical degree at Woodstock, Vt., in 1844. Before he left
Peterborough, he represented the town in the Legislature
for 1845, '46. He first located himself as a physician in
Troy, where he was eminently successful, and also
acquired much reputation as a surgeon. He removed to
Chatfield, Minn., in 1857, where he was soon again
engaged in a laborious practice, in which surgery had a
special prominence. His operations were numerous,
especially in the threshing seasons, when so many accidents occur with these ponderous machines. He was
elected in 1862, and for eight successive years, a Senator to the Minnesota Legislature. He was appointed by
the Governor, in 1864, as State agent to look after the
sick and wounded soldiers of Minnesota, which office he

Saml Miller

held till his health failed in 1866. Subsequently, when an insane asylum was established in Minnesota, he was appointed one of the first board of trustees, which office he held until the institution was in successful operation. He has also held important offices in the Northern Minnesota Railroad, which he has of late declined. He again changed his residence, removing to Lanesboro, Fillmore County, Minn., where he now resides. He has two children living, Luke Lovell, b. May 7, 1849, Jennie Abby, b. Nov. 28, 1852.

46   *John*, b. March 30, 1822 ; m. Harriet L. Brayton. He d. Nov. 26, 1863, æ. 41 yrs., 7 mos. ; r. Rochester, N. Y. He left town when he was eighteen years of age. He first learned the cabinet trade, but, not satisfied with it, subsequently devoted himself to engraving on wood and copper, and took up his permanent residence in Rochester, N. Y., where he d. Nov. 26, 1863, æ. 41 yrs., 7 mos. He was highly respected in the community in which he lived, for his honesty, integrity, and Christian virtues. He had only one son, Charles Andrew, who d. June 12, 1874, æ. 23 yrs.

4- 29   WILLIAM MILLER. He lived in the north-east part of the town, his farm adjoining to the Hovey lot. He m., 1st w., Ruth Ames, of Hancock, b. Nov. 8, 1780 ; she d. Sept. 24, 1815, æ. 35 yrs. ; m., 2d w., Gratia Holmes, dau. Abraham Holmes ; she d. June 11, 1855, æ. 79 yrs. He d. May 22, 1855, æ. 81 yrs.

47   *Samuel*, b. March 26, 1800. He m. Sarah Blood, of Pepperell, Oct. 16, 1825 ; ch., (1) Sarah E. ; (2) Mary Frances ; (3) Martha ; (4) Louise. He d. June 30, 1872, æ. 72 yrs. ; r. Pepperell.

48   †*David*, b. May 12, 1802 ; m., 1st w., Mary Ames, Pepperell ; 2d w., Rebecca Colburn, of Nashua.

49   *Stephen*, b. June 13, 1804 ; m. Eliza Beaverstock ; r. Cambridge, Mass. He was a pulpit and pew builder, — a first-class workman. Three ch. He d. Oct. 18, 1873, æ. 69 yrs., 4 mos. She d. April 10, 1858.

50   *Sally*, b. April 12, 1806 ; m. Moses Wilkins. She d. Feb. 15, 1852, æ. 46 yrs.
  John, b. April 20, 1808 ; d. July 19, 1811, æ. 3 yrs., 2 mos.

51   *Jacob*, b. May 27, 1811 ; m. Caroline Williams ; r. Pepperell ; a carpenter ; two ch. living, Charles H. and
52   Ellen A. Ellen A. m. Arnold F. Minor, Pepperell.
53   *Ruth*, b. April 24, 1814 ; d. Aug. 5, 1836, æ. 22 yrs.

18- 32   SAMUEL MILLER. He lived in north part of the town, on the Thomas White farm. He was a farmer. For many years he was a deacon in the Congregational (Unitarian) church in Peterborough. He was a substantial and worthy man, honest and upright in all his dealings, and reverent and devout in his feelings, a faithful and true Christian. He held many offices of trust and importance in town — selectman 1850, '51, and representative to the General Court 1851, '52. He m. Ruth Bowers, dau. of Capt. Francis Bowers, Aug. 9, 1831. He d. May 9, 1872, æ. 76 yrs.

54   † *James R.*, b. June 21, 1833; m. Carrie M. Chandler, of Westford.

55   *Frank B.*, b. June 4, 1836; m. Callie Clark; he d. May 30, 1871, æ. 35 yrs.

28– 43   WILLIAM MILLER. He lived on the homestead. He m. Mary Gray, dau. Matthew Gray, Aug. 24, 1824; she afterwards m. William S. Smith. He d. Dec. 29, 1848, æ. 49 yrs.

56   *Mary Jane*, b. Aug. 13, 1831; m. A. C. B. Phelps; d. Jan. 13, 1852, æ. 20 yrs.

29– 48   DAVID MILLER. He r. on the homestead many years, and then re. to Pepperell, where he now lives. He m. Mary Ames, of Pepperell, Nov. 28, 1836; she d. April 1, 1856; m., 2d w., Rebecca Colburn, of Nashua, June 10, 1857; 1st w., three ch.

57   *William A.*, b. Peterborough, July 20, 1838; m. Mary Dwight, of Rockford, Ill., March 6, 1867; r. Ogle Co., Ill. A carpenter.

58   *Thirza Jane*, b. Peterborough, Sept. 4, 1841; r. Pepperell. Music teacher and organist.

59   *Elijah A.*, b. Aug. 10, 1846; r. Pepperell. A carpenter.

32– 54   JAMES R. MILLER m. Carrie M. Chandler, of Westford, b. Jan. 2, 1835; r. Lowell.

60   *Mabel R.*, b. Feb. 15, 1869.

61   *Frank Perley*, b. April 14, 1873.

1   SAMUEL MILLER is of a race entirely distinct from the above, or only remotely related to it. He came from Londonderry as the other family did, and a majority of his children were b. there. We do not know the surname of his wife. He d. March 27, 1791, æ. 75 yrs. Name spelled on gravestone, Old Cemetery, Millow. His w., Margaret, d. Oct. 8, 1806, æ. 78 yrs. He lived on

farm east and opposite to William Smith, Esq. The first eight ch. were b. in Londonderry, the others in Peterborough. It is related that when the youngest of this large family was twenty-five years old, the whole family, with their wives, husbands, and children, all assembled and ate supper at the old gentleman's house.

2   *Jenny*, b. ——; m. Charles McCoy; 2d hus., Thomas Turner.

3   *Mary*, b. ——; m. Alexander Thompson, Shelburne, Mass.

4   *Elizabeth*, b. 1741; m. Moses Cuningham; d. May 13, 1819, æ. 78 yrs.

5* *Margaret*, b. ——; m. Robert Taggart.   •

6   *Sarah*, b. 1744; unm.; d. Dec. 4, 1821, æ. 77 yrs.

7   *Nancy*, b. ——; m. James Taggart (Sprawly); frozen to death on Temple Mountain.

8   *Hannah*, b. 1748; m. John White (Pond); d. Dec. 23, 1825, æ. 77 yrs.

9   †*Samuel*, b. 1752; m. Sally Adams, of Hollis, Dec. 26, 1782.

10 *Ann*, b. ——; unm.; d. in Sharon.

11 *Joseph*, b. 1756; m. Ann Wire; re. to Sharon and then to Maine.

12 *Abigail*, b. 1758; m. William Gowing; d. Feb. 23, 1830, æ. 72 yrs.

13 *Rebecca*, b. ——; m. Samuel Clark; r. Sharon.

1- 9 SAMUEL MILLER, Jr. He bought and begun a new place of two hundred acres on the East Mountain, east of the Carley place. It has within a few years been abandoned as a farm. He m. Sarah Adams, of Hollis, who d. July 9, 1835, æ. 82 yrs. He d. Jan. 17, 1834, æ. 82 yrs.

14 †*Adams*, b. Jan. 1, 1783; m. Anna Robinson.

15 *Fanny*, b. Jan. 12, 1785; unm.; d. Aug. 3, 1865, æ. 80 yrs.

16 *David*, b. July 1, 1787; m. Clarissa Haskins; d. Aug. 8, 1872, æ. 85 yrs.; she d. July 21, 1848, æ. 56 yrs.

17 *Jane*, b. May 3, 1789; m. James Gregg, May 15, 1817.

18 †*Jesse*, b. July 6, 1791; m. Asenath Bonner, of Hancock.

19 *Rhoda*, b. July 12, 1793; unm.; d. May 29, 1869, æ. 76 yrs.

9- 14 ADAMS MILLER. He lived in east part of the town, on the lot south of Hugh Miller's. He m., Nov. 28, 1805, Anna Robinson, of Londonderry, b. July 25, 1783; she d. June 1, 1856, æ. 73 yrs. He d. Dec. 27, 1859, æ. 77 yrs.

20 †*Samuel R.*, b. Dec. 11, 1809; m. Elizabeth Carter, October, 1835.

21 *Mary*, b. Feb. 1, 1807; m. Joseph Holt, Jan. 17, 1832.

22 *Lucinda*, b. Aug. 31, 1811; m. Oliver Sanderson; seven ch.

9- 18 JESSE MILLER r. many years on a mountain farm near his father's old farm, when he re. to the village, where he now lives. He m. Asenath Bonner, b. May 31, 1797; d. March 10, 1868, æ. 71 yrs.

23 †*John R.*, b. Nov. 6, 1828; m., 1st w., Allura A. Moore; 2d w., Ellen A. Townsend.

24 †*Charles A.*, b. June 2, 1830; m. Sarah A. Ames.

14- 20 SAMUEL R. MILLER r. in Lowell some years, and then returned to Peterborough, where he now lives; m. Elizabeth Carter, Oct. 1, 1835.   Selectman 1859, '60.

25 *Frances A.*, b. Sept. 7, 1836; m. W. W. H. Wilder, August, 1862.

26 *Sarah E.*, b. June 10, 1841; d. Jan. 6, 1844, æ. 2 yrs., 6 mos.

27 *Abbie A.*, b. Dec. 4, 1843; m. Wallace Scott, Nov. 13, 1865.

28 *Sarah L.*, b. Lowell, May 31, 1848; d. Nov. 18, 1865, æ. 17 yrs., 5 mos.

29 *Nettie F.*, b. Dec. 14, 1857; d. Nov. 30, 1859, æ. 1 yr., 11 mos.

18- 23 JOHN R. MILLER. He learned the printer's trade at Concord, in the office of A. C. Blodgett, publisher and editor of the *New Hampshire Courier*. He returned to Peterborough in 1847, and worked for S. P. Brown. Subsequently he associated himself with Kendall C. Scott, whom he taught the printer's trade, in the job printing business. They issued the first number of the Contoocook *Transcript*, May 27, 1849, which they continued two years, when Miller sold out to his partner, who continued the paper, with the changed name of *The Peterboro' Transcript*, and it is now in a flourishing condition. In December, 1851, he purchased the stock of drugs and medicines of the late Franklin Kendall, and by diligence and care has made himself a good apothecary, which business he now continues in the village. He was appointed postmaster, Aug. 17, 1861, and has held the office by reappointments ever since. He was appointed a justice of the peace, Sept. 10, 1863, and justice of the peace and quorum throughout the State,

Sept. 10, 1868, and now does most of the trial justice business of the town. He m., 1st w., Nov. 24, 1851, Allura A. Moore, of Sharon, b. Feb. 19, 1831. She d. July 8, 1858, æ. 27 yrs., 4 mos.; m., 2d w., Jan. 11, 1860, Ellen A. Townsend, b. July 30, 1838; 1st. w., two ch.; 2d w., two ch.

30	*Edward E.*, b. Aug. 24, 1853.
31	*Frances A.*, b. June 17, 1858; d. July 25, 1858, æ. 38 dys.
32	*Arthur H.*, b. Jan. 5, 1863.
33	*Harry E.*, b. June 10, 1867.

18– 24   CHARLES A. MILLER m. Sarah A. Ames, dau. of Alvah Ames, June 7, 1854. He is a machinist. He re. to West Meriden, Conn., where he now r.

34	*Lizzie M.*, b. Peterborough, June 2, 1856.
35	*Freddie M.*, b. Peterborough, Oct. 8, 1860.
36	*Frank E.*, b. West Meriden, Ct., May 5, 1866; d. Sept. 16, 1866, æ. 4 mos.

THE MITCHELL FAMILY.

1   SAMUEL MITCHELL (Dea.) came to Peterborough in 1759 from Londonderry. He owned the mills where the first Peterborough cotton factory now stands, and carried them on several years. These were built by Jonathan Morison in 1751, and were the first mills built in town. When the property came into the hands of Dea. Mitchell, it was found that a mortgage existed given by Jonathan Morison to Gordon and Hugh Wilson, which was not known. It was thought that Mitchell would lose his property, but it turned out that the mortgage deed was not put on record till after the deed to Mitchell had been recorded, so he sustained no loss.* We do not know just what time he sold out to Asa Evans, probably not far from 1784 or '85, about the time Evans removed to town.

In the first meeting of the town after incorporation, he was appointed, with Alexander Robbe and William Smith, to "*recon*" with the old committee. He was selectman in 1762–66, and town clerk thirteen years, from 1767. His record is a very good one, in plain, legible writing, and in good English. He appears to have been an influential man, both in the church and town. At a meeting of the town, Jan. 3, 1769, under his own record occurs the following vote: "Voted, That

---

* Manuscript Notes of S. Smith, p. 157.

21

Esq. Hugh Wilson and Samuel Mitchell be brought to an account of the money that they received when the sacraments were held in this town." "Voted" (under the same head), "Thomas Morison, William Smith, Samuel Moore, John Gregg, Sen., and David Steele should be a committee to settle with said Wilson and Mitchell, and collect the money due from them to the town, and appropriate the said money to the use which it was intended for, *vis.:* to buy utensils for serving the sacrament." It is supposed that the utensils so long in use in the Congregational Church (Unitarian), *vis.:* two tankards, four cups, and two platters, were those purchased, in part, with this money. These vessels were in constant use more than a century, when Mrs. Ruth Miller, widow of Dea. Samuel Miller, presented to the society and church a full set of beautiful silver-plated utensils for the sacramental table, *vis.:* two tankards, four goblets, two platters, a baptismal basin, and an ice-pitcher and goblet for the pulpit. He m. Janet Morison, dau. John and Margaret Wallace Morison, b. 1721. She d. Nov. 11, 1791, æ. 70 yrs. He d. May 3, 1798, æ. 76 yrs.; b. in 1722.

2　　*John*, b. Sept. 23, 1749; re. to St. Albans, Vt., and d. there.

3　　*Margaret*, b. Aug. 3, 1751; m. David Ames; r. Hancock, and d. there.

4　　†*Samuel*, b. April 22, 1753; m. Peggy Swan; r. Manchester, Vt.

5　　†*Benjamin*, b. Jan 9, 1755; m. Martha Steele.
6　　*Ann*, b. Feb. 24, 1757; m. —— Swan; re. to Manchester, Vt.

7　　*Hannah*, b. Feb. 2, 1759; m. —— Putnam, June, 1805; r. Vermont.

8　　*Janet*, b. April 27, 1761; m. Samuel Whitcomb; r. Hancock.

1– 4　　SAMUEL MITCHELL, Jr. We know but little of this family. He rendered a good deal of service in the Revolution. He was at Cambridge in 1775. He was mustered into continental service, April, 1777, being one of twenty-two men then required. He also served at Bennington and Saratoga. He removed to Manchester, Vt., the time unknown. He m. Peggy Swan.

9　　*Janet*, b. Dec. 19, 1781.
10　　*Margaret*, b. Sept. 5, 1784.
11　　*Jeremiah*, b. Dec. 31, 1786.
12　　*Samuel*, b. Aug. 15, 1789. (13) *Harry*, b. ——.
14　　*Sally*, b. ——.

1- 5 | BENJAMIN MITCHELL. He first lived on the lot south of the Charles Stuart farm, the same that was appropriated by the proprietors as the ministerial lot. Late in life he re. to the Dea. Samuel Moore place. He resided a short time in Temple, before his death. He was among those who marched to Lexington on the alarm, April 19, 1775; was also mustered into service for two mos., Sept. 20, 1776; marched to Bennington, 1777, in service from July 19 to Sept. 26. He was present at the centennial celebration of the town, 1839, and was one of three survivors present of those who signed the Association Test, or Declaration of Independence, June 17, 1776. The other two were Thomas Steele and Capt. William Robbe. He m. Martha Steele, dau. of Capt. David Steele, 1779. She d. Feb. 9, 1853, æ. 90 yrs. He d. at Temple, Sept. 24, 1840, æ. 85 yrs.

15 | *Stephen*, b. March 29, 1780; m. Sally Mills, Durham. A graduate of Williams College, Williamstown, Mass., 1801. Studied law with Judge Steele in Durham, and practised his profession there.* Mr. Mitchell was esteemed a good lawyer. He was a man of talents and standing. He had quite a literary turn, and used often to write for newspapers. When Lafayette visited Durham, in 1825, Mr. Mitchell was selected to address him in behalf of the town, which he did in a very handsome and appropriate manner. He d. Feb. 15, 1833, æ. 53 yrs.; c.

16 | *David*, b. May 31, 1782; m. Ruth Hoyt, Bradford. He studied medicine with Dr. Howe, of Jaffrey; attended medical lectures at Hanover; lived and d. in Bradford. He d. suddenly of an affection of the heart, Jan. 21, 1821, æ. 39 yrs. Two ch., Nancy and Margaret.

17 | *Margaret*, b. Sept. 6, 1784; m. Peter Bachelder; 2d hus., Dea. Stephen Holt. She taught a high school for young ladies in New Ipswich before her first marriage, and was considered highly accomplished. One ch. by 1st hus., Jane, who m. Robert Bradford, Francestown. After her second marriage, she spent her last days in Greenfield; d. Aug. 17, 1867, æ. 83 yrs.

18 | *Jonathan*, b. Jan. 21, 1787; m., March 13, 1817, Sally White; re. to Preble, N. Y., 1840. Four ch., Susan, Frances, Emily, and Stephen, all b. in Peterborough. He d. at Belvidere, N. Y., Sept. 1, 1853, æ. 66 yrs., 7 mos. She d. at same place, 1861, æ. 74 yrs.

19 | *Frederick A.*, b. July 15, 1789; m. Lucy Aiken; 2d w., Rhoda Johnson. He studied medicine with Dr. Starr,

* Letter David Steele, Esq., Dover.

of this town, and Howe, of Jaffrey, and attended medical lectures at Hanover ; practised his profession at Chester and Bradford. He relinquished the practice some years before his death. He d. in Manchester, July 28, 1869, æ. 80 yrs.   Seven ch.

20   *Elizabeth*, b. May 6, 1793 ; m. Isaac Edes, April 24, 1823.

21   *John*, b. March 22, 1795 ; m. Lucretia Mason ; re. to New York State. A hatter by trade. Two ch., sons ; d. in Ohio.

22   *Charlotte*, b. July 21, 1798 ; m. Samuel Gates, Oct. 26, 1824.

23   *Jane*, b. Feb. 21, 1803 ; d. Sept. 28, 1805, æ. 19 mos.

24   *Samuel*, b. March 4, 1807 ; m. Harriet Childs ; d. Aug. 21, 1850, æ. 43 yrs.

ISAAC MITCHELL, suppose related to the above. We know nothing more, only this record of this family on the town books.   His wife's name was Jemima.

---

25   *John*, b. Dec. 7, 1766.   (26) *Isaac*, b. Jan. 24, 1769.

27   *Martha*, b. Nov. 20, 1770.

28   *William*, b. March 7, 1773.

29   *Margaret*, b. March 31, 1775.   (30) *James*, b. May 1, 1779.

JOHN MITCHELL, probably of the same family. His wife's name was Beersheba ; this record only is found.

---

31   *John*, b. Nov. 30, 1779.

THE MOORE FAMILY.

The ancestors of this important family can be traced back to Scotland. In the Revolution of 1688, it was sometime before all the Scottish chiefs submitted and took the oath of allegiance to the new government. In 1691, King William issued a proclamation offering amnesty to all the chiefs and their clans who would take the oath of allegiance before December 31. All of them submitted within the prescribed time, except the aged MacIan, or MacDonald, of Glencoe. On the 31st he appeared at Fort William to take the oath, but the officer in command not being a magistrate, he could not administer it. MacDonald made his way as speedily as the travelling and the condition of the country would admit to Iveray, where he took the oath, Jan. 6, 1692. His allegiance happened a few days later than the time required by the proclamation, and he was represented by three great Scottish chiefs, who had been his hereditary enemies, and who were determined to avail themselves of this unintentional delay for the destruction of the tribe of MacDonald, to William as not having submitted, and dwelling in a valley with a tribe no better than a band of robbers, and as being the only remaining obstacle to a complete pacification of the highlands. An order was issued for their extirpation. It was executed with horrible treachery and cruelty. A body of one hundred and twenty soldiers was sent, Feb. 1, 1692, commanded by Campbell, of Glenlyon, to occupy Glencoe. They came professing peace and friendship, and were received with the kindest hospitality, and for a fortnight lived at free quarters in the utmost familiarity with the people. On the evening of the 12th February, after the kindest entertainment at the MacDonald house, the playing cards with him and his family, an attack was made upon the chieftain ; he was shot through the head, his family murdered, and the inhabitants of all ages cruelly massacred, with the intention, no doubt, to slaughter the whole tribe. Forty were actually murdered. The inclemency of the weather was such that the detachment of soldiers sent to guard the outlets of the valley did not arrive in season, so that most of the inhabitants, alarmed by the report of fire-arms, made their escape, not without many perishing with cold and hunger. No punishment was inflicted on the author of this crime.

A graphic account of the massacre of Glencoe is given by Macaulay in his *History of England*, Vol. 4, and Campbell has made it a subject of a poem, "The Pilgrim of Glencoe." A writer in *Blackwood's Magazine*, July, 1859, accuses Macaulay of partiality in his account of Glencoe, and charges the responsibility of the massacre on William III., acquitting him, however, of any intention of sanctioning treachery and breach of hospitality.[*]

In this infamous massacre of Glencoe, John Moore, the progenitor of the race that came to this town, was shot dead in his garden. He was the father of two daughters, whose lives were saved by a servant who took care of them, and safely re. them from the country. One of them, Beatrix Moore, married Col. Andrew Todd, afterwards so famous in our colonial history. Mrs. Moore, finding her husband dead, after covering his body with a sheet, fled to a malt-kiln for safety, and during that night was delivered of a son, the John Moore who was one of the first settlers of Londonderry. She subsequently escaped safely, and took up her resi-

[*] New American Cyclopedia, Vol. 8, p. 297. Art. " Britain" Encyclopedia Brittanica.

dence in or near Londonderry, Ireland, and here for-
tuitously met with her two daughters. In 1718 John
Moore, her son, was among the emigrants in the five
ships that came to America this year. He was with
those under the charge of Rev. Mr. McGregor, who,
with one of the ships, entered Casco Bay, intending to
settle in that region, but who, having endured the hardships of a very severe winter, and not being satisfied
with the land on the appearance of spring, they returned
to Haverhill, and from thence made their first settlement
in Nutfield, or Londonderry. He m. Janet Cochran,
and left a family of four sons and three daughters:
Robert, Samuel, William, John, and Agnes, Mary, and
Ann. Of these, Samuel and William re. to Peterborough, and were patriotic and loyal men; while John
and Robert remained in Londonderry, and were both
reported as refusing to sign the Association Test, in
April, 1776. John became a professed Tory, and Robert
remained and d. in Londonderry. The old house is still
standing in which John Moore lived, situated on the
turnpike, about two miles south of the village of Derry;
also the old well, and a huge elm planted by his own
hands. For a time he was the king's surveyor of the
town. He d. early in 1741, æ. 49 yrs.

I   SAMUEL MOORE (Dea.) came to town from Londonderry about 1751 or '52, in company with Samuel Todd,
and they fixed upon a plot of land situated in the west
part of the town, lying on the Dublin line, extending
over the river and embracing the meadows. They purchased the same of the proprietors, John Fowle, John
Hill, and William Gridley for a crown an acre.* By
deed of Nov. 15, 1753, they held it in common ten
years before they divided. When the division was made,
Dea. Moore took the westerly part, and Samuel Todd
the easterly, which occurred but a short time before
Todd was killed by the falling of a tree. Dea. Moore
lived on what was afterwards known as the "Spring
place." He built a house here, long since demolished,
and the site deserted. In 1779, he sold this place to Dr.
Marshall Spring, and then began a new one just east of
the Todd farm, since occupied by Benjamin and Jonathan Mitchell, where both he and his wife died.

After the birth of his first child, John Moore, Nov. 5,
1753, probably on account of apprehended danger of the

* See Waverley Novels. Chronicles of Canongate, p. 121. "Go put your
head under the belt of one of the race of Dermid, whose children murdered,
yes," she added, with a wild shriek, "murdered your mothers, fathers, in their
peaceful dwellings in Glencoe."

* Manuscript Notes of S. Smith.

French and Indian war, he removed with his family to
Londonderry, where he remained till after 1760. He
returned sometime before 1763, being absent about six
years, for he is elected one of the selectmen of this year.
He was chosen as a representative to a meeting held at
Exeter, Dec. 21, 1775, and was the first man to represent the town in any free meeting after the commencement of the Revolution. He was an influential man in
town. Moderator in 1771, and also selectman, tithing-
man, surveyor of highways at various times to 1783. He
was a deacon in the Presbyterian church. He m. Margaret Morison, dau. John and Margaret Wallace Morison, Dec. 31, 1751, the same day that William Smith m.
Elizabeth Morison, her sister.* It is reported that the
same night in which William Smith and Elizabeth Morison were married, Samuel Moore and Margaret Morison,
who were present at the wedding in Londonderry, after
all the ceremonies were over, mounted their horses and
rode to Chester, where they were married by Justice
Flagg, by a license.

This good man was a slave-holder, owning two slaves,
Baker and Rose. He could not be esteemed a very
hard master, as he sold his freedom to Baker, for which
he never received any remuneration, and he provided for
Rose in the following clause in his last will of Aug. 31,
1790: "And I do give and bequeath unto my said wife
during her life my negro slave, Rose, and it is my will
that my son Ebenezer shall maintain her as long as she
lives." He d. Jan. 28, 1793, æ. 66 yrs.; b. Aug. 30,
1727. She d. April 29, 1811, æ. 84.

2	† *John*, b. Nov. 5, 1753; m. Margaret Stuart.
3	*William*, b. ——; re. to Frankfort, Me.
4	†*Samuel*, b. June 10, 1756; m. Jenny Thompson.
5	*Ann*, b. 1760; m. Thomas Steele.
6	†*Ebenezer*, b. Nov. 5, 1764; m. Rosanna Duncan.
7	*Margaret*, b. Feb. 26, 1767; m. John Jewett.

1— 2   JOHN MOORE always lived in town, occupying a farm
south of Reuben Washburn's farm, and north of the
Carley place. He m. Margaret Stuart, dau. of Charles
and Esther Ferguson Stuart. She m., 2d hus., Asa
Evans, July 13, 1809; 3d hus., Richard Gilchrist, Sept.
15, 1816. She d. Aug. 7, 1818, æ. 50 yrs., 8 mos. He
d. at Cambridge, N. Y., and was buried there, on his
return from Saratoga Springs, where he had been for his
health, July 7, 1800, æ. 46 yrs., 8 mos. He was a man

* Manuscript Notes of S. Smith.

of excellent character, and highly esteemed by all who knew him.

———

8   *Fanny*, b. Oct. 15, 1789 ; m. Dr. Jabez B. Priest, April 4, 1820 ; 2d hus., Samuel Holmes ; d. Jan. 6, 1875, æ. 85 yrs.

9   *Sophia*, b. April 25, 1790 ; unm. ; d. Earlville, Ill., November, 1866, æ. 74 yrs.

10   *John*, b. March 10, 1794 ; went West ; nothing known of him.

11   *Samuel Morison*, b. Oct. 25, 1796 ; m. Mary Smith ; ch., John and S. Anna. S. Anna m. Hon. P. C. Cheney ; d. Jan. 7, 1858, æ. 27 yrs. ; r. Bronson, Mich.

12   *Charles*, b. May 26, 1798 ; d. at Peterborough, Dec. 2, 1835, æ. 36 yrs., 6 mos.

13   *Joseph Henry*, b. Aug. 25, 1800 ; m. Esther Pellet, Norwich, N. Y. ; he d. February, 1858, æ. 58 yrs.

———

1– 4   SAMUEL MOORE, Jr. He lived in the north-west part of the town, on farm adjoining Reuben Washburn's. He was mustered in the alarm at Lexington, April 19, 1775 ; also served at Cambridge in 1775. He m. Jenny Thompson, dau. Dea. Robert Thompson, in Londonderry, July 24, 1784. He d. Feb. 5, 1844, æ. 87 yrs. She was b. in Bridgewater, Mass., Aug. 8, 1759 ; d. Dec. 13, 1831, æ. 72 yrs.

———

14   *Mary*, b. June 10, 1785 ; unm. ; d. Oct. 3, 1852, æ. 67 yrs.

15   *Robert*, b. May 30, 1787 ; m., 1813, Avis Stearns, Waltham, Mass. ; d. New Orleans, July, 1820, æ. 33 yrs.

16   *Margaret*, b. May 2, 1789 ; unm. ; d. Nov. 23, 1860, æ. 71 yrs.

17   *Samuel J.*, b. July 13, 1791 ; m. Mary M. Talen, Liberty, Miss. ; d. at Alexandria, La. ; date unknown.

18   *Jane*, b. Sept. 28, 1793 ; m., Jan. 31, 1815, Harvey Lancaster, Acworth ; d. Dec. 13, 1821, æ. 28 yrs.

19   *John*, b. Dec. 31, 1795 ; m. Mehitable Foster, of Unity, May, 1824 ; d. at Acworth, Sept. 3, 1834, æ. 39 yrs.

20   *Ira*, b. Dec. 22, 1797 ; d. Lebanon, Ky., Oct. 12, 1825, æ. 28 yrs.

21   *Anson*, b. Sept. 16, 1800 ; m., 1825, Sarah Mattoon ; 2d w., Olive Tenney ; 3d w., Mrs. Esther Fairbanks. He d. in Edinburg, N. Y., Nov. 28, 1863, æ. 63 yrs., 2 mos.

22   *William*, b. Dec. 13, 1802 ; d. in infancy.

23   *Jesse*, b. Aug. 8, 1804 ; m., 1836, Nancy McGinty, Troy, N. Y. ; d. Jan. 29, 1866, æ. 62 yrs. ; r. Troy, N. Y.

24   *Sarah T.*, b. Jan. 8, 1807 ; unm.

1- 6   EBENEZER MOORE. He succeeded his father on the
homestead. In 1813 he re. to Preble, N. Y., where he
lived till his death. He m. Rosanna Duncan, dau.
George Duncan, Sen. She d. in Preble, Sept. 30, 1842,
æ. 77 yrs. He d. at Preble, April, 1851, æ. 86 yrs., 5 mos.

.25   *Samuel*, b. 1793 ; d. Oct. 24, 1800, æ. 7 yrs.
26   *Adeliza*, b. 1794 ; m. Dr. Samuel Taggart ; r. Byron, N. Y.
27   *George*, b. Feb. 9, 1797 ; m. Polly Cummings ; r. Belvidere, Ill. Two ch.
28   *Margaret*, b. 1800 ; m. Abraham Woodward ; r. Belvidere, Ill.
29   *Ebenezer*, b. 1802 ; m. Sally Cummings ; r. Preble ; d. in
Belvidere, Ill., 1870, æ. 68 yrs.
30   *Samuel*, b. May 5, 1806 ; m. Mary Ann Steele ; 2 w.,
Mary Bennie ; 3d w., Belle Thayer ; r. Belvidere, Ill.
One ch.

WILLIAM MOORE was a brother of Dea. Samuel Moore,
and son of John and Jean Moore, b. Sept. 26, 1731,* in
Londonderry. He settled in south part of the town, on
the farm now occupied by Dea. Nathaniel H. Moore and
his son William. We find in the register office for Rockingham County, Exeter, a deed recorded from John Hill
to Halbert Morison, No. 37, two divisions of two hundred
and three acres, dated July 5, 1753, and of the same
date, Lot No. 33, two divisions of two hundred and forty-
five acres, to Thomas Morison. We suppose the farm
was deeded to Wm. Moore by Halbert Morison. William Moore m. Jane Holmes, dau. of Nathaniel and
Elizabeth Holmes, and sister of Dea. Nathaniel Holmes,
in Londonderry, Dec. 13, 1763. She was b. Jan. 16,
1744, and d. Aug. 22, 1831, æ. 87 yrs., 7 mos. He d.
Sept. 7, 1818, æ. 87 yrs. It is supposed that he came to
town about the time of his marriage, 1763. He was
made selectman in 1769, and perhaps in 1770. The
record of this year is missing.

The following singular incident and coincidence is
worthy of notice, as having occurred in the experience of
Mrs. Moore. Great reliance, in our early settlements,
was placed on the household manufactures, for thrift and
success in life. The new country was well adapted to
the flax culture, and they brought such skill and industry
to its manufacture that they afforded the best and the
most perfect linen fabrics.

When a family had accumulated some two hundred
yards of linen cloth, the woman of the house took the
same on horseback, and started for a market, all alone

* Town Records, Londonderry.

22

and unprotected. Such a thing as an insult or a robbery of these unprotected females was never heard of. Having sold her cloth, and received for the same such necessaries as they needed, a part in money to pay mortgages or educate their children abroad, she returned home. It is related by George W. Moore, Esq., a grandson, as follows: My grandmother (about 1786 or '88) went to Boston with a load of cloth, and on entering a public house in Cambridgeport, she found her mother, Mrs. Duncan, of Londonderry, who had married Maj. Duncan for her second husband. After the usual friendly greetings and inquiries concerning friends, a third person entered the room, who proved to be my grandmother's daughter, Anna, who had married Daniel Moore, and lived in Bradford, Vt. Here three generations unexpectedly met, without any knowledge of each other's being there. The next day, the daughter, mother, and grandmother pursued their journey home together to Peterborough.

Mr. Moore served in the French and Indian wars before he came to Peterborough. He was a drummer; and subsequently in Peterborough he was a lieutenant in the militia under Capt. Alexander Robbe. He did not render much military service during the Revolution, having been in feeble health in consequence of an injury received in early life. But his whole heart and soul were in the enterprise, and he made every effort in his power in its behalf.

The following anecdote is furnished me by George W. Moore, Esq., a grandson of William Moore: —

"My grandfather Moore was a firm supporter of the war of the Revolution, and a great admirer of Washington. The name of Washington was a new name in New England, and was considered a very awkward one, until the war made it famous throughout the land. On the birth of his first son after the war commenced, my grandfather decided that his name should be Washington; but the mother was opposed to the name, and mentioned the names of William, Samuel, and Robert as much more appropriate. The time came when the child was to be baptized, and, as usual on such occasions, the ladies gathered round the door of the church to see the baby.

"Granny Duncan asked what they were going to call him, and my grandmother told her, that his name was to be Washington. Mrs. Duncan said it was a pity to spoil so fine a baby with such a terribly awkward name. My grandmother decided to make one more effort to prevent his name being Washington; and as they were about to enter the door of the church, she put on one of her pleasantest smiles, and placing her hand very affectionately upon his arm, she said: 'Billy, ye will not call the baby Washington, will you?' 'Indeed, I will! If I had forty children to be baptized here to-day, I would call them all Washington.'"

He bought his farm of Halbert Morison, and for more than one hundred and twelve years, it has been deeded from sire to son, through four generations, and yet remains in the family. The first house was built on the highest knoll west of the railroad, in the interval or meadow belonging to the farm. Mrs. Moore was a notable and eminently Christian woman, and has impressed her virtues on a long line of descendants. No drunkenness, immorality, or profanity has ever appeared in the race. The religious element has largely abounded, and the influence of the family is everywhere moral and good.

---

31 *Ann,* b. Oct. 1, 1764; m. Daniel Moore; r. Bradford, Vt.; d. May 24, 1824, æ. 59 yrs., 7 mos.

32 *Betsey,* b. Aug. 10, 1766; m. John Coughran; r. Attica, N. Y.; d. Aug. 16, 1847, æ. 81 yrs.

33 †*John,* b. May 10, 1768; m. Belinda Bardwell; r. Whately, Mass.

34 †*Nathaniel,* b. March 28, 1770; m. Sarah Ferguson.

35 *Euphamia,* b. May 11, 1772; m. Orange Bardwell; r. Whately; d. June 26, 1847, æ. 75 yrs.

36 *Jenny,* born June 3, 1774; m. William Smith.

37 *Sally,* b. July 5, 1776; m. George Gregg; re. to New York; d. Nov. 23, 1838, æ. 62 yrs.

38 *Washington,* b. Sept. 25, 1778; m. Susanna Rice, of Conway; re. to Michigan; d. May 25, 1856, æ. 78 yrs.

39 *Nancy,* b. Aug. 19, 1780; d. March 6, 1801, æ. 21 yrs.

40 *Mary,* b. Aug. 22, 1782; d. May 20, 1785, æ. 2 yrs., 8 mos.

41 *Mary,* b. May 6, 1785; m. Wirling Gregg; r. Sharon; d. Dec. 3, 1857, æ. 72 yrs.

42 *William,* b. April 9, 1787; m. Lucy Rice, Nov. 7, 1806; 2d w., Mrs. Sally Holmes, wid. of Nathaniel Holmes, Jr., April 17, 1847; r. Moorsville, Mich.; ten ch.; d. Dec. 4, 1850, æ. 63 yrs.

2– 33 JOHN MOORE. He early re. to Whately, Mass. He m. Belinda Bardwell. She d. Sept. 6, 1851, æ. 80 yrs., 6 mos. He d. Nov. 7, 1803, æ. 35 yrs., 6 mos.

43 *Polly,* b. Dec. 1, 1793, at Whately; m., July 17, 1810, Thomas Dinsmore, Jaffrey; d. February, 1875, æ. 81 yrs.

`44 | *Electa*, b. Feb. 9, 1795, at Whately ; m. Cephas Boyden, Conway, Mass ; d. June 15, 1855, æ. 60 yrs.

45 | *Lucy*, b. June 24, 1796 ; m. —— Wood, South Hadley, Mass. ; d.

46 | *Jane*, b. Aug. 12, 1797 ; m. Gov. John H. Steele ; d. July 30, 1831, æ. 34 yrs.

47 | *William*, b. April 23, 1799 ; m. Sarepta Rodgers ; d. Bulford Centre, Mich., Sept. 30, 1871, æ. 72 yrs.

48 | *Nancy*, b. May 8, 1801 ; m. Gov. John H. Steele.

49 | *Alinda*, b. Oct. 5, 1803 ; m. William Turner ; d. April 6, 1865, æ. 61 yrs.

2- 34 | NATHANIEL MOORE (Dea.). He succeeded his father on the homestead. He was chosen deacon in the Presbyterian Church in town, May 22, 1830. He was selectman eight years in succession, from 1819 to 1827. He was a worthy and upright man, and was universally respected. He m. Sarah Ferguson, dau. Henry Ferguson, March 14, 1800. She d. April 10, 1850, æ. 74 yrs. He d. Oct. 27, 1853, æ. 83 yrs.

50 | †*Henry*, b. Jan. 21, 1801 ; m. Charlotte Spaulding, Aug. 21, 1822.

51 | †*William*, b. July 15, 1802 ; m., 1st w., Caroline Robbe ; 2d w., Rachel P. Robbe.

52 | *John*, b. Jan. 20, 1804 ; m. Sabrina Beard ; r. Gillionsville, S. C. ; d. May 15, 1871, æ. 67 yrs.

53 | †*Nathaniel H.*, b. Nov. 18, 1805 ; m., Dec. 1, 1831, Bethiah Hunt.

54 | *James*, b. Feb. 3, 1808 ; unm. ; d. at sea, July 27, 1827, æ. 19 yrs.

55 | *Jane F.*, b. Feb. 8, 1810 ; m., Feb. 4, 1830, Jonathan Holmes ; d. April 19, 1831, æ. 21 yrs.

56 | *Sarah*, b. Feb. 12, 1812 ; m., May 5, 1836, John Smith ; 2d hus., ——.

57 | †*George W.*, b. April 3, 1814 ; m., 1st w., Caroline Morison ; 2d w., Harriet P. Bigelow.

58 | *Martha F.*, b. April 22, 1817 ; d. Sept. 28, 1818, æ. 1 yr., 5 mos.

59 | *Thomas F.*, b. Oct. 2, 1819 ; m., May 27, 1840, Rachel Todd ; r. Adrian, Mich.

34- 50 | HENRY MOORE. He m. Charlotte Spaulding, dau. Jeremiah Spaulding. In 1833 he re. from town, his first three ch. being b. in Peterborough, and the other three at Griffin's Mills, N. Y., where he now lives.

60 | *Jeremiah*, b. July 9, 1823.

61 | *Henry F.*, b. Nov. 19, 1826.

Geo. W. Moore

62 | *James*, b. May 8, 1832 ; d. Sept. 13, 1852, æ. 20 yrs.
63 | *Sarah Jane*, b. June 20, 1838.
64 | *Charles N.,* } b. Feb. 22, 1842.
65 | *Lottie E.,* }

34- 51 | WILLIAM MOORE. He was a machinist, and carried on a large and extensive machine-shop in town for many years. He was a worthy and exemplary man. He was deacon in the Congregational Church (Unitarian) ; he also held many important town offices. He was treasurer of the town for five years from 1838, and represented the town in the Legislature in 1838, '39. He m., 1st w., Caroline Robbe, dau. of Capt. Alexander Robbe, April 16, 1829 ; she d. Dec. 6, 1839, æ. 31 yrs. ; m., 2d w., May 14, 1840, Rachel P. Robbe, dau. of above. He d. of consumption, Nov. 11, 1848, æ. 46 yrs.

66 | *Sarah. C.*, b. June 1, 1830 ; d. Dec. 3, 1852, æ. 22 yrs.
67 | *Jane M.*, b. July 3, 1832 ; m., June 11, 1856, Parker W. Burnham ; ch., (1) Sarah C., b. Nov. 4, 1859 ; (2) William H., b. Sept. 28, 1863 ; (3) Edward M., b. April 21, 1871 ; r. Adrian, Mich.
68 | *William H.*, b. Feb. 22, 1835 ; d. Jan. 23, 1840, æ. 4 yrs., 11 mos.
69 | *Ellen*, b. June 30, 1838 ; d. Aug. 19, 1839, æ. 1 yr.

34- 53 | NATHANIEL H. MOORE succeeded his father on the homestead. Is a successful farmer. A deacon in the Union Evangelical Church in town ; has held many important offices in town ; Representative to the Legislature in 1865, '66. He m. Bethiah Hunt, dau. of Dea. Timothy Hunt, Dec. 1, 1831.

70 | *Julia*, b. March 6, 1835 ; m. Rev. Cyrus Jordan ; d. March, 1874, æ. 39 yrs.
71 | *Henry*, b. May 6, 1838 ; d. June 27, 1863, at Milliken's Bend, La., æ. 25 yrs. He belonged to Co. C, 118th Regt. Ill. Vols., U. S. service.
72 | *George*, b. Feb. 12, 1842 ; d. at Cincinnati, O., May 5, 1867, æ. 25 yrs. He graduated at Dartmouth College, 1866 ; was engaged in teaching.
73 | *William*, b. April 24, 1844 ; m. Ellen E. Mower, of Jaffrey, Dec. 31, 1874, and occupies the homestead.

34- 57 | GEORGE WASHINGTON MOORE. He r. in Medina, Mich. ; m., Aug. 29, 1837, Caroline Morison, dau. of Capt. Nathaniel Morison ; she d. March 17, 1849, æ. 35 yrs., 8 mos. ; m. 2d w., Harriet P. Bigelow ; 1st w., three ch. ; 2d w., two ch. He has furnished much information in relation to the early history of the town, which has been embodied in this work.

---

74 † *William C.*, b. Nov. 1, 1841; d. May 7, 1866, æ. 25 yrs.

75 *Nathaniel M.*, b. April 18, 1843; d. April 5, 1850, æ. 7 yrs.

76 *Emily C.*, b. Nov. 20, 1845; m. George A. Phelps; one ch.

77 *George D.*, b. Feb. 27, 1853.

78 *Harriet S.*, b. March 10, 1860.

57-74   WILLIAM C. MOORE enlisted in the First Regiment of Michigan Volunteers in May, 1861; was wounded and captured at the first battle of Bull Run, July 21, 1861; was maltreated and starved in the Libby Prison at Richmond; was exchanged in the spring of 1862; immediately enlisted again, was made captain, and served in the West till the close of the war. He was drowned in crossing a stream in the Indian Territory, while taking a drove of cattle from Texas to Kansas.

THE MORISON FAMILY.

The Morisons of Peterborough are all descendants of Samuel Morison, who lived in the North of Ireland, and was driven with his family under the walls of Londonderry in that famous siege of 1688, '89, by the infamous order of the French General Rosen, for the purpose of inducing the city to surrender. His son John, if indeed not all the family, were admitted within the walls. He had a family of eight children, as follows: —

I. John, b. 1678, in Ireland; d. in Peterborough, June 14, 1776, æ. 98 yrs.

II. Martha, b. in Ireland; d. June, 1738, in Londonderry; m. Thomas Steele, father of Capt. David Steele. Issue, four sons and two daughters.

III. James, b. in Ireland; d. in Londonderry; m. Janette Steele. Issue, three sons and two daughters.

IV. Halbert, b. in Ireland; d. in Londonderry; m. —— Steele. Had children by 3d wife.

V. Samuel, b. in Ireland; d. in Londonderry; m. Catharine Allison. Issue, three sons.

VI. Joseph, b. in Ireland; d. in Londonderry; m. Mary Holmes.

VII. Hannah, b. in Ireland; d. in Chester; m. Andrew Mack.

VIII. Mary, b. in Ireland; d. in Londonderry; m. Wm. Clendenin.

It is supposed that the parents, Samuel Morison and wife, did not leave Ireland, though all their children emigrated to America, and were among the first settlers of Londonderry.

---

1 JOHN MORISON, above, was one of the first settlers of Londonderry, and was the father of Jonathan Morison, the first male child born in that town. After living in Londonderry some thirty years, he removed to Peterborough in 1750 or '51, with his family, and was one of the early settlers of this town. He was seventy-one or seventy-two years old when he came to town. It is said of him in the sketch of Peterborough,* "Mr. Morison retained his faculties till within a short time of his death. He was remarkably intelligent, and his memory very retentive. He, with his parents and family, was in the city, and his age ten years, at the famous siege of Londonderry. The trying scenes he witnessed in youth, a peculiar native eloquence, his pleasing urbanity of manners, venerable age, and correctness and respectability of character, rendered his society interesting and instructive."† It is not strange that he emigrated to Peterborough so late in life, since he was preceded by nearly all his family. He m. Margaret Wallace. She d. April 18, 1769, æ. 82 yrs. By a plan of the town, it is ascertained that John Morison occupied the place where his grandson, Dea. Robert Morison lived; and he d. here June 14, 1776, æ. 98 yrs., the oldest man ever known in the town.

---

2 † Thomas, b. in Ireland, 1710; m. Mary Smith, b. 1720, dau. Robert and Elizabeth Smith.

3 Jonathan, b. in Londonderry, Sept. 18, 1719; m. Nancy Tufts, a match not particularly favorable to his peace, happiness, or respectability. He was a highly gifted man, with great ingenuity, generous in the extreme, but .unfortunately possessed of what is too often the curse of superior endowments, a violent temper and a want of self-control, which sometimes led to intemperance (see Centennial Address). For a considerable time, he was the only mechanic in town. He could turn his hand to any trade or mechanical art. The first saw and grist mill in town was built by Jonathan Morison, in 1751, on the spot where the first Peterborough cotton factory now stands. He is reported to have been one of the best extempore speakers in the town meetings in Londonderry, before he left that town; and on these occasions he was always sure to be pitted against

* Historical Account of Peterborough, by Rev. Elijah Dunbar, 1822.
† For further account of John Morison, see Centennial Address.

Capt. Samuel Allison, who was an equally good talker and fluent speaker. He was the first male child born in Londonderry, and removed to Peterborough among the first emigrants in 1749 or '50. We are uncertain as to the time and place of his death.

4 *Jane*, b. April 6, 1721; m. Dea. Samuel Mitchell; d. Nov. 11, 1791, æ. 70 yrs.

5 *Elisabeth*, b. June 11, 1723; m. Wm. Smith, Dec. 31, 1751.

6 *John*, b. Sept. 20, 1725; m. Mary Anderson. He emigrated to Nova Scotia after beginning the farm afterwards occupied by Dea. Robert Smith.

7 *Margaret*, b. Feb. 13, 1727; m. Dea. Samuel Moore.

8 *Hannah*, b. April 10, 1730; m. Samuel Todd.

9 *Moses*, b. June 7, 1732; m. Rachel Todd. Tradition has handed down any amount of the sayings, queer exaggerations, and humor of this strange man. It is for this only that his memory has survived him. It grew into a habit with the people to say, when extravagant expressions and statements were heard, "Like Uncle Mosey," so peculiar were the witticisms and the strange fun with which he always abounded. He lived near the Half Moon Pond, in Hancock, and died there. The place is now abandoned, and all the buildings have been demolished. He left a family, but we know of no one who could furnish a record of his descendants.

1-2 THOMAS MORISON (Capt.), the eldest son of John Morison, was b. in Ireland in 1710, and was quite young when his parents emigrated to America. He first settled in Londonderry, and probably was married at that time, as it is said that two of the children, John and Elizabeth, were born there, and that Robert, Margaret, and Jonathan were born in Lunenburg, and the rest in Peterborough. He removed to Lunenburg between 1744 and '45. We have no authentic record when he first came to Peterborough, but suppose he came from Lunenburg, and cleared land and returned again. It was not till 1743 or '44 that he came with a Mr. Russell, and they began the farm afterwards occupied by him, and built there a camp, about twenty rods north of where the long barn on Samuel McCoy's farm stood, against a large boulder, having a perpendicular side on the east, of six or seven feet height, against which the camp was constructed and the camp-fire built. They came from Lunenburg, on foot, with axes, packs of provisions, and cooking utensils on their backs, threading their way through the unfrequented forests, guided by blazed trees. The large boulder served, with its vertical face, to shelter and support the camp, and furnished it with a fire-place and chimney.

It is related in a manuscript account of this affair, by the late Samuel Smith, Esq., that when they went out one morning they perceived two Indian men, a squaw, and a small Indian. They intended to be friendly, and spoke to them, and invited them to take breakfast with them, which they did. After the departure of the Indians they went out to their work, but when they returned for dinner they found that the Indians had stolen every mouthful of their eatables and disappeared. They immediately set out for Townsend, not being able to obtain the least sustenance till they reached that place. They came again to work in the fall or winter, at which time all the inhabitants were frightened away, and left the town till 1749. This year, 1749, Morison came back again, and built a house of hard pine logs ten inches square, and moved his family here in the fall of 1750. He resided on his farm till his death, Nov. 23, 1797, æ. 87 yrs.

The bridge across the Contoocook at the South Village was built in 1765. The house occupied by Simeon Forbush and Betty and Sally Morison was built the same year. It was the second two-story house built in town. He erected his first saw-mill in 1759, which was burnt and not rebuilt till 1767. This was the second saw-mill in town. At the first meeting of the town after incorporation, he was elected one of the selectmen, with Hugh Wilson, Jonathan Morison, Joseph Caldwell, and John Swan, Jr. He was subsequently elected, in the years 1765, '66, and 1773, to the same office. He m. Mary Smith, dau. Robert and Elizabeth Smith, at Lunenburg, Mass., Oct. 2, 1739. She was b. in Ireland, and d. in Peterborough, Dec. 29, 1799, æ. 87 yrs.

10   † *John*, b. Londonderry, July 8, 1740; m. Agnes Hogg; 2d w., Lydia Mason; 3d w., Jenny Gray.

11   *Elisabeth*, b. Londonderry, Aug. 8, 1742; unm.; d. Jan. 15, 1831, æ. 88 yrs.

12   †*Robert*, b. Lunenburg, Nov. 29, 1744; m. Elizabeth Holmes.

13   *Margaret*, b. Lunenburg, Nov. 10, 1746; m. Matthew Wallace; r. Vermont.

14   *Jonathan*, b. Lunenburg, March 16, 1749; unm.

15   *Thomas*, b. Peterborough, April 20, 1751; m. Jerusha Field; re. to Buxton, Me.

16   *Sally*, b. Peterborough, Dec. 22, 1756; unm.; d. Oct. 12, 1840, æ 84 yrs.

23

17	†*Samuel*, b. Peterborough, April 16, 1758 ; m. Elizabeth Smith.
18	*Mary*, b. Peterborough, May 14, 1760; unm.; d. Aug. 20, 1819, æ. 59 yrs. "Aunt Polly."
19	*Ezekiel*, b. Peterborough, June 27, 1762 ; m. Hannah Ames, sister to Isabel and Sally Ames, wives of Robert and James Smith.

| 2– 10 | JOHN MORISON. He lived in the south-west part of the town. He m., 1st w., Agnes Hogg ; d. April 27, 1777, æ. 27 yrs. ; m., 2d w., Lydia Mason ; 3d w., Jenny Gray. He d. May 25, 1818, æ. 78 yrs. |

20	*Joseph*, b. April 30, 1773.
21	*Thomas*, b. April 21, 1775 ; d. Feb. 23, 1801, æ. 26 yrs.
22	*John*, b. ——; drowned in the Nubanusit in the meadows above the factories, July 10, 1828, æ. 31 yrs.
23	*Jonathan*, b. ——; d. ——.
24	*Jane*, b. ——; m., April 20, 1824, Matthew Hale, of Hollis.
25	*Thomas*, b. ——; d. at Dea. J. Field's, Oct. 31, 1825, æ. 22 yrs.
26	*Matthew*, b. ——. (27) *Mary*, b. ——.

| 2– 12 | ROBERT MORISON (Dea.). He lived on the place begun by his grandfather, John Morison, and which is yet in the family. He was a deacon in the Presbyterian Church, but when elected we cannot ascertain, as the church records were burnt in the conflagration of his house, in 1791. At a meeting of the town, Sept. 30, 1793, it was voted to pay Robert Morison seventeen dollars, with interest till paid, that amount of money belonging to the town having been lost in his house when burnt. In 1791, he built on a new site the house now owned by the family of Horace Morison, the old house having stood in the field a few rods east of the road. He m. Elizabeth Holmes, sister of Dea. Nathaniel Holmes. She was b. June 23, 1754, and d. May 17, 1808, æ. 55 yrs. He d. Feb. 13, 1826, æ: 82 yrs. He was chosen a deacon in Mr. Dunbar's church, Nov. 28, 1799, being associated in this office with William Smith, William McNay, Jonathan Smith, and Nathaniel Holmes. |

28	*Thomas*, b. Dec. 25, 1774 ; d March 26, 1775, æ. 3 mos.
29	*Mary*, b. March 26, 1776 ; d. April 12, 1776, æ. 17 dys.
30	*Stephen*, b. Nov. 8, 1777 ; d. Oct. 9, 1778, æ. 11 mos.
31	†*Nathaniel*, b. Oct. 9, 1779 ; m., Sept. 13, 1804, Mary Ann Hopkins, of Londonderry ; d. Sept. 11, 1819.

32 | *Jonathan,* ⎫
   | ⎬ b. March 11, 1782 ;
33 | *David,* ⎭

m. Rebecca Rockwood; he d. April 11, 1832, æ. 50 yrs.; r. Greenfield.

d. May 6, 1782, æ. 56 dys.

34 | †*Robert,* b. May 8, 1784 ; m. Betsey Spring.
35 | *Smith,* b. Aug. 16, 1786 ; d. Dec. 20, 1786, æ. 4 mos.
36 | *Betsey,* b. Nov. 8, 1787 ; m. William Graham, May 13, 1806. She d. Oct. 30, 1843, æ. 56 yrs.
37 | *Ezekiel,* b. Nov. 16, 1792 ; d. Sept. 11, 1823, at Greenville, Miss., æ. 30 yrs., 10 mos.

2– 17 | SAMUEL MORISON. He occupied a place in the south part of the town, begun by Gustavus Swan, and afterwards owned by Matthew Wallace, and next came into the hands of Samuel Morison. He lived here till his death. He m. Elizabeth Smith, dau. of William Smith, Esq.; all their ch. but the son, who d. at 7 yrs. of age, were born *deaf-mutes.* He d. Nov. 24, 1837, æ. 79 yrs. She d. May 21, 1833, æ. 75 yrs. The daughters were educated at the Deaf and Dumb Asylum, at Hartford, Conn.

38 | *Elizabeth,* b. 1789 ; d. Sept. 22, 1791, æ 2 yrs.
39 | *Mary,* b. June 28, 1791 ; d. Nov. 15, 1854, æ. 63 yrs.
40 | *Hannah,* b. 1793 ; d. March 16, 1809, æ. 16 yrs.
41 | *Samuel,* b. March 10, 1795 ; d. Oct. 26, 1802, æ. 7 yrs., 7 mos.
42 | *Sarah,* b. Oct. 26, 1799 ; d. Sept. 15, 1868, æ. 69 yrs.
43 | *Eliza,* b. July 1, 1801 ; d. March 13, 1875, æ. 73 yrs., 8 mos.

12– 31 | NATHANIEL MORISON. He succeeded his father on the homestead; m. Mary Ann Hopkins, of Londonderry, Sept. 13, 1804. He d. at Natchez, Miss., Sept. 11, 1819, æ. 39 yrs., 11 mos. She d. at Medina, Mich., Aug. 27, 1848, æ. 69 yrs.

For the following interesting account of the family of Mr. Morison, I am indebted to Rev. John H. Morison, D.D., one of the sons : —

"Of my ancestors on my father's side beyond John Morison, my grandfather's grandfather, I know nothing. He lived to be ninety-eight years old. For many years he was looked up to with great respect by the younger members of the family. From what I could learn, I have inferred that he was a man of sound judgment, of a mild disposition, and a natural dignity of character,— a man to command the confidence of others. The account which I gave of him in the centennial was taken from the recollections of his two grandchildren, Jeremiah Smith and Sally Morison, both of whom had very distinct and pleasant recollections of him as, more than any one else, the patriarch of the town.

"His son, Capt. Thomas Morison, was a more enterprising and ambitious man, with greater activity of mind and greater force of character. These more efficient traits were ascribed to his mother, Margaret Wallace, who wished her house, if it must be a log-house, to be a log higher than any other in the place. During the active period of his life he was, I suppose, one of the five or six leading men in Peterborough.

"His sons were none of them remarkable men. Three of his daughters, Polly, Sally, and Mrs. Wallace, were uncommonly intelligent. My grandfather, Robert Morison, was a man of good sense, but of moderate ability. He was a very devout man. I have seen many of his letters to my father that were marked by a degree of practical good judgment which I fear he did not know how to apply to his own affairs; for he was always in debt, and always appealing to my father for pecuniary assistance.

"My father, Nathaniel Morison, was the only one of his children who had more than ordinary ability. Ezekiel, his youngest son, was a man of correct and industrious habits. He died young in Mississippi. Nathaniel was born Oct. 11, 1779. In 1802, he went with an invoice of chairs to some place in the West Indies; but finding no market for them there, he took them to Wilmington, N. C. After disposing of them, he went to Fayetteville, in the same State, and entered into the business of making carriages. In 1804, he came to New England, and married Mary Ann Hopkins, who was born in that part of Londonderry which is now Windham, and returned to his business in Fayetteville, with his wife, where he remained till 1807. Then, at the urgent solicitation of his father, he came back to Peterborough, and settled down with his wife and daughter, having bought his father's farm. He brought with him five thousand dollars in specie, and there were still considerable sums of money due to him at the South. In five years he had laid up between six and seven thousand dollars. He was not fitted to be a farmer. The success of a more extended enterprise, and the habits formed in a different sphere, made him restless under its slow and limited operations. In 1811, I believe, he returned to Fayetteville, to settle up his affairs there, and when he returned he brought with him John H.

Steele, a young man whom he had found there, and considered a very ingenious and capable mechanic, and who afterwards filled so important a place in Peterborough. Three or four years more passed by, when he purchased for $10,000 what was then called the South Factory, and devoted all his energies to that and kindred enterprises. He put up a building for the manufacture of fine linen, particularly table-cloths. The women in Peterborough and the neighboring towns were famous for their labors at the distaff. The object of this new undertaking was to weave, by improved processes, the linen yarn that was spun in the vicinity. The looms were worked by hand, but with what was called a spring shuttle, then a new invention. In connection with these factories, my father, now a militia captain, opened a small store, and he had upon his hands all that he could attend to.

"But he had chosen an unfortunate time for these investments. The war with England was soon over. The country was flooded with foreign goods. There was no sale for our domestic products. The factories were closed. His little competence melted away. He was embarrassed with debts. His farm and factory property were heavily mortgaged. For all industrial enterprises, the term from 1815 to 1820 was a period of greater depression than any other period of five years during the present century. After struggling in vain with adverse events, and with embarrassments which were constantly increasing, he went to Mississippi, in the fall of 1817, to collect a considerable debt that was due him there. He carried out with him a few cases of axes and shoes, which he disposed of at a good profit. He collected his debt so as to reach home in the spring of 1818.

"While he was in Natchez, he became acquainted with several gentlemen of large fortunes, and made a contract with them to supply the city with water by means of lead pipes, for $30,000. On reaching home, he engaged a competent man in New Hampshire to lay the pipes, and in the autumn of 1818, he went out with a larger supply of axes, ploughs, and shoes. But the boat which carried a part of his merchandise struck a snag and sunk in the Mississippi. And when he reached Natchez, and had made all his arrangements and got his men and materials there to supply the city with water, the Southern gentlemen repudiated the contract which he supposed they had made, and the whole enterprise, with consequences ruinous to all his hopes, was thrown back upon him. He had recourse again to his old occupation, and endeavored to gain a little money by working as a wheelwright

and carriage-maker. But disappointment, anxiety, and
the hot, malarious, summer climate there were too much
for him. He was taken down by the yellow fever, and
after a few days of severe suffering, in which he was
carefully attended by his brother Ezekiel, and his townsman, John Scott, Jr., he died on the 11th day of September, 1819, just before he had completed his fortieth year.
Rumors of his death had already reached us, when, on a
cold, cloudy, November Saturday afternoon, I, then a
boy of eleven, walked to the village to see if any letter
had come by the mail. On entering your father's store
just before dark, I heard the people talking of the report,
and, as they did not know me, they kept on with their
conversation till I had received the letter. I had a sad
journey home in the dark night, and the burst of grief
with which the first line of the letter was greeted was
more than I could bear. The next morning, my grandfather called us all together to prayers, as the custom
was of a Sunday morning, and I shall never forget the
solemnity and pathos with which the old man, with
trembling hands and a voice broken with emotion, read
the third chapter of Lamentations. ' I am the man that
hath seen affliction by the rod of his wrath. He hath
led me, and brought me into darkness, but not into
light.'

"A month or two before, when news of the falling
through of the Natchez enterprise had reached this part
of the country, the sheriff had come to our house and
taken possession of everything that the law allowed him
to take. The sharpest pang that I felt at that time was
in witnessing my mother's anguish, and, next to that,
was when I saw the officers of the law drive away a pair
of young steers that I had watched over and tended and
fondled ever since they were born. I did not see them
again for three years, and it was very painful to me
then to find that I could not get from them any sign
of affection or recognition. They had entirely forgotten me. After my father's death, we remained in
the old homestead through the winter, till March
or April, 1820. My mother had for her portion a
shell of a house near the South Factory, and eight
hundred dollars. It required half the money to convert
the old 'weaving-shop' into a tolerable residence. I
remember well the earnest gaze and the deep sigh with
which, on leaving our early home, where all her children
but one had been born, she looked back upon it, with a
baby on each arm, and then turned slowly away towards
her new home. She had been left alone in the fall of
1818 with seven children, the oldest thirteen years, and

the two youngest four months, old. All her means of support consisted in a half-finished house, two cows, and four or five hundred dollars. She had a most delicate, sensitive nature, but a force of will and an amount of executive energy such as I have never seen surpassed. In my remembrance of her, as she was during the early period of her widowhood, I always think of her sitting at her loom, working and weeping. She diu not stop to indulge in discouraging apprehensions, but emphasized her grief by driving her shuttle with increased promptness and vehemence. With a resolution that almost broke her heart, she put her two oldest boys, one eleven and the other nine years old, into farmers' families to work for their living. Lessons of honest industry and helpfulness and self-dependence were thus learned. If there was a great deal of suffering on their part and on hers, caused by severe labor and a divided household, habits were formed which contributed largely to whatever measure of usefulness or success they may have attained. The heaviest burden rested upon our oldest sister, whose ability and willingness to help all the rest shut her out from the advantages of education which the others enjoyed.

"My father was endowed with abilities ill-adapted to his calling, and very much beyond what was required by the sphere in which he lived. He read the best books with a keen delight. The few letters of his which I have seen showed marks of a mental strength and culture superior to what we usually find in the correspondence even of the city merchants who lived at that time. Your uncle John, who was his teacher one winter, spoke to his brother Jeremiah of his mind and his ingenuous, truthful qualities with a sort of enthusiastic admiration. If he could have had the educational advantages which his sons enjoyed, I have no doubt that he would have been one of the most distinguished among all the natives of Peterborough. As it was, his lot was a very hard one, and his life very sad. He was a man of delicate sensibilities and generous impulses. He was fitted for intellectual pursuits, and would have made an admirable lawyer. But he had no special aptness for mechanical employments, or for trade. His thoughts moved in a different sphere. I have heard his social and conversational qualities very highly spoken of. But he had no special aptitude or taste for the sort of life that was put upon him. After the success of his early days, which certainly indicated no common ability even in uncongenial pursuits, he failed in almost everything that he undertook. His plan for introducing improved methods of manufacturing linen cloth showed originality of mind and no lack of judgment. Nor could any one, situated as he was, be likely to anticipate the disastrous effects of peace on our domestic industries. And no honorable man would suspect the arbitrary repudiation of a contract like that which he had made in Natchez. But the disappointment was not, on that account, any the less severe to him. He became disheartened and unhappy. He was never, I think, according to the ideas then prevailing, an intemperate man, but amid his disappointments and trials he probably fell in too much with the habits of those around him. Indeed, when I look at his ledger, and see what quantities of rum and toddy almost everybody drank in those days, I·wonder how it was that any one could have been saved from being a drunkard. My mother was so impressed with a sense of the evils and perils in this direction, and warned her children against them with such intensity of feeling, that I have no doubt she had seen in her home influences and dangers which we were not old enough to understand. In common with almost every woman around her, she used snuff, but, from her own experience and what she saw in others of the misery of such a bondage, she had a violent antipathy to it, and brought up her children with such a feeling against it, that not one of her five sons has ever, I believe, used an ounce of tobacco.

"My mother's father, John Hopkins, was a farmer. He was a·man of an easy, happy temperament, who, it was said, would sit at work on his·shoe-maker's bench, in winter, and sing Scotch songs all day long, without repeating a single song. His wife, however, Isabella Reid, was of a very different temperament, and belonged to a family of very marked and powerful characteristics. She was a woman of strong convictions, and of great energy of mind and body. She, like her daughter, Mary Ann, could do two or three days' work in one, and had no patience with the idleness or inefficiency of other people. She probably did for the Hopkinses what Margaret Wallace had done for the Morisons three generations before, and introduced into the race a much more energetic type of character. She lived to a great age, with her son, James Hopkins, in Antrim. I remember her prompt and decisive interference on two or three occasions at my father's. Once, when I was a very young boy, I took a small amount of honey from one of our bee-hives, and escaped without injury. But when the same experiment was tried a second time, it seemed to me as if the whole swarm of bees, with their stings in active exercise, had settled down on my head. In-

stantly, on hearing the cries sent out by the child, my
grandmother appeared with a bowl of water, and quickly
drove away my offended avengers of their rights. Not
long before her death I saw her in Antrim. She was
very feeble and very kind. Just before I left her, she
unlocked a private drawer, and took from it two silver
half-dollars which she asked me to give to my mother.
I was greatly affected by her kindness, for it was probably nearly all the money that she had.

"Here is a very slight sketch of those who have gone
before us, and whose lives are transmitted through our
veins to those who shall come after us. I believe in inherited qualities, but it is difficult to reconcile with this
belief the very different qualities of those who inherit
the same blood. For example, your grandfather, William Smith, and his wife, Elizabeth Morison, were the
brother and sister of my great-grandmother, Mary Smith,
and her husband, Thomas Morison. The blood in the
two families was the same, and the circumstances under
which they entered life were substantially the same. Yet
every one of the six sons of William Smith was a man
of marked ability, and not one of the sons of Thomas
Morison was much, if at all, above mediocrity. Samuel
was a shrewd, thrifty man. But that was all. Three of
the daughters of Thomas Morison, however, were uncommon women. Mary — the Aunt Polly who was so
long in your father's store — was, I suppose, one of the
most brilliant women ever born in Peterborough. Her
sister Sally was, as Judge Smith used to say, a born lady.
Her intellectual and moral qualities, and delicate, wom-
anly susceptibilities, were admirably harmonized. She
took snuff and smoked a pipe, and yet no one could
meet her or talk with her without feeling that she was a
refined and delicate woman. Margaret, the wife of Matthew Wallace, was said to be a woman of uncommon
ability.

"We sometimes seem to recognize different ancestors
in our different moods and feelings at different times.
When I am indulging in the thought of projects vastly
beyond my ability to carry out, I feel my great-great-
grandmother, the ambitious Margaret Wallace, stirring
my blood, and call to mind my grandfather's caution to
his son to remember that his name was Morison, and
not undertake more than he could do. When I feel very
much fixed in any decision, and unwilling to be reasoned
out of it, right or wrong, I feel something of the Holmes
obstinacy rising up within my veins. When I am in an
easy, indolent mood, and disposed to let the day go by
without effort in pleasant dreams, I think of my grand-

24

father Hopkins, whose name I bear, and his Scotch
songs. If I ever succeed in stripping off its surround-
ings, and looking calmly and clearly into a difficult and
important subject, without prejudice on either side, I
rejoice to feel that I have in me something of the mild,
unbiased good sense which has come down from the
Smiths as they were before they were united with the
Morisons. In this way I lead different lives, and feel
myself swayed by widely different impulses, and brought
under the influence of different ancestors, according to
the mood that happens to be uppermost. Sometimes I
feel as if I were my father, looking out from his eyes
and walking in his gait, and then I detect the mother in
the earnestness with which I find myself gazing on some
person before me, as your uncle, Judge Smith, seemed
to see his sister Betty when he put on her cap and
looked at himself in the glass."

44   *Eliza Holmes*, b. Fayetteville, N. C., July 10, 1805; m.,
Sept. 18, 1845, Stephen Felt; d. Aug. 14, 1867.

45   †*John Hopkins*, b. July 25, 1808; m., Oct. 21, 1841,
Emily Hurd Rogers.

46   †*Horace*, b. Sept. 13, 1810; m., July 27, 1841, Mary E.
Lord; d. Aug. 5, 1870.

47   *Caroline*, b. June 20, 1813; m., Aug. 29, 1837, George
W. Moore, Medina, Mich.; d. March 17, 1849.

48   †*Nathaniel Holmes*, b. Dec. 14, 1815; m., Dec. 22, 1842,
Sidney B. Brown; r. Baltimore, Md.

49   †*Samuel A.*,   m., Nov. 9, 1847, Ellen Smith; r. San Francisco, Cal.

   b. June 20, 1818;

50   †*James*,   m., 1st w., Jan. 29, 1857, Mary Lydia Sanford, of Boston; 2d w., June 16, 1868, Ellen Wheeler, of Keene.

31– 45   JOHN HOPKINS MORISON. The following autobiography was furnished at my request: —

"I was born in Peterborough, July 25, 1808, and was
the second child and oldest son of Nathaniel and Mary
Ann Morison. I remained at home till April 15, 1820.
At the age of three I began to attend school in the summer, but after I was six years old my services on the
farm were thought too valuable to be dispensed with,
and from that time forth till I was sixteen I went to
school only in the winter, from eight to twelve weeks in

a year. In the autumn of 1819, my father died, and his
family was left in great affliction, and in very straitened
circumstances. From 1820 to 1824, I lived with different farmers in the town, working hard, faring as well
as they did, and receiving but scanty wages, never, I
think, more than fifty dollars a year, even when I did
nearly a man's work. I look back upon those four years
as the most unhappy period of my life. The change
from our own home to a place with strangers was a painful one, not because I was treated unkindly, but from a
feeling that I was fatherless and homeless, and from a
longing for a better companionship and better means of
education. My principal solace was to spend the Sunday, once in a month or two, at my mother's house. My
greatest happiness, intellectually, was in reading, often by
fire-light with my head in a perilously hot place. The
books which I enjoyed most were the Bible, Rollin's
ancient history, Gibbon's Rome, and an odd volume or
two of Josephus. The little Social Library kept by Mr.
Daniel Abbot was a great resource to me.

"In October, 1824, I went to Exeter and lived there with
Mr. Joseph Smith Gilman, 'tending' in a small grocery
store, and doing what a boy might be expected to do
about the place, for ten months. The position and most
of its duties were distasteful to me. I made some ludi-
crous and embarrassing mistakes. I was not good at a
bargain, and my heart was not in my work. I was more
homesick than I had ever been. I wondered then, and
have not ceased to wonder yet, at Mr. Gilman's forbearance. He and his family were very kind to me, and I
shall never think of them otherwise than with profound
gratitude. But the young people whom I was thrown in
with were more ignorant and had lower tastes and aims
in life than any persons I ever knew; but I had a good
deal of time for reading and plenty of books. Before
leaving Peterborough I had, for six weeks, attended a
private school kept by Mr. Addison Brown, then a student in Harvard College. He had very rare gifts as a
teacher. I felt that my intellectual nature was then for
the first time waked up, and life assumed for me a new
meaning. During the winter, in Exeter, I attended an
evening school taught by Mr. Richard Hildreth, a man
of fine genius, who took great interest in my studies.
My progress with him was such that he and Mr. Gilman, the next summer, called the attention of Dr.
Abbot, the noble principal of Phillips (Exeter) Academy,
to my case, and without any application on my part, I
was allowed to take a place among the beneficiaries of the
school. Here a new world was opening before me. Every

branch of study seemed to offer a new delight. Even the primary elements of Latin and Greek had for me a singular fascination, and every step was an advance into a sort of fairy-land. I shall never forget the sensations of keen enjoyment with which I read the *Odes* of Horace, the *Iliad* of Homer, the *Bucolics* of Virgil and of Theocritus, or the utter absorption of mind with which I went through the higher branches of Agebra and Geometry, and, most of all, the Conic Sections. I remained in the academy four years, three as a scholar, and one mostly as a teacher, pursuing my sophomore studies by myself. I owe a great debt of gratitude to the teachers there, especially to Dr. Abbot and Dr. Soule.

"In 1827, '28 I had become acquainted with William Smith, a gifted, accomplished, generous young man. He introduced me to his father, the Hon. Jeremiah Smith, who, in brilliancy and strength of mind, in accuracy and extent of learning, and the higher qualities of his character, was fitted to take, as he did, an honorable place among the ablest of our distinguished men. In August, 1828, he invited me to become a member of his family, and I remained there a year, during which time his daughter died, and her death was followed by that of his son the next winter. Their illness and departure, especially the rapid and fatal decline of his daughter, a most lovely and interesting woman, took me through a wholly new experience. This life could never again be to me what it had been before. The light of worlds beyond had been let in upon it.

"In August, 1829, I was admitted to the Junior Class in Harvard College. Of the hundred dollars which I had saved from my earnings during the previous year, I was required to pay ninety for instruction which I had not been able to receive during the Freshman and Sophomore years of my class. But, notwithstanding this exaction which always seemed to me unjust, I have every reason to speak of my Alma Mater with grateful affection and respect. The last generation of American statesmen numbered among its distinguished men no grander example of a faithful, disinterested, able public man than Josiah Quincy, then President of Harvard University. He was kind to me from the beginning, and his kindness continued down to the last year of his useful and honored life. I taught school during six of the twenty-four months of my college course, so that I was really in college a little less than a year and a half. I earned what little I could, and practised a pretty severe economy. My expenses were small, and Judge Smith had generously and very judiciously so arranged matters, that

I never felt any great anxiety in regard to my immediate wants. I began life with nothing. I never have asked pecuniary assistance for myself. And yet I have never been unable to meet my engagements. Sometimes I could not see a month beforehand how the means could be procured, but they always came, and sometimes from the most unexpected sources.

"On graduating in 1831, I concluded to study law, having engaged to pursue my studies with a very learned lawyer of Baltimore, and to meet my expenses by instructing his two children. On account of this engagement I declined several advantageous offers of employment as a teacher. After waiting several weeks, when the time for such offers had passed by, the gentleman sent me word that he had engaged another young man and would not need my services. This was a very great disappointment to me. It left me without occupation, and without means of support, but it taught me a lesson as to the sacredness of engagements that has always been of great service to me. I remained in Cambridge through the fall and winter, teaching a few pupils, and attending some of the lectures of the Divinity School. At that time I became acquainted with Henry Ware, Jr., and his wife, and had a room in their house. In a social and religious point of view that season was a very profitable one to me. It gave me time to reconsider my choice of a profession, and enabled me to approach the subject with different feelings and a better understanding.

"In March, 1832, I began to teach a small private school for young ladies in New Bedford, and remained there a year. That year was perhaps the most important in my life. I was then for the first time a man among men. I had leisure for study, and devoted myself to it with the utmost intensity and enthusiasm. I read Cicero's philosophical writings, Cousin, Pascal, Madame de Staël, Dante, some of the old English prose writers, Wordsworth, and, above all in its influence on my mind, Coleridge, especially his *Friend* and *Biographia Literaria*. In the winter I gave a course of seven lectures on literary subjects to a very intelligent audience of perhaps a hundred persons. This was a new and exciting experience. It made me feel the responsibility of acting on the minds of others. But I had overworked during the winter, and from the middle of March till the last of August, 1833, spent most of the time in Peterborough, in a state of physical exhaustion which I did not understand. Among the great advantages which I enjoyed at New Bedford, especially in the society of very intelligent people, that which I valued above all the rest was the privilege of hearing Dr. Dewey preach. It was the most quickening and uplifting preaching that I have ever heard, and of itself made an epoch in my life.

"At the beginning of the academical year 1833 I joined the middle class at the Cambridge Divinity School, which was then under the able and conscientious charge of John Gorham Palfrey and the Henry Wares, father and son. There was an extraordinary degree of vitality and enthusiasm in the school at that time, especially in regard to philanthropical movements. I entered very heartily into these subjects, and took an earnest part in the preparation of elaborate papers, and in the debates. Both my moral convictions and my philosophy went much deeper, and looked to a much more thorough and radical reform than was usually contemplated in the social movements of the day. I was, perhaps, considered too conservative, because I was in fact too radical to be satisfied with the superficial measures that were suggested by the most zealous reformers. The labor question, which is just beginning to cast its portentous shadows before it now, was one on which I prepared a report that cost a vast amount of labor, and which came to conclusions that are now beginning to engage the attention of thoughtful men. During a temporary vacancy in the department I taught political economy to the senior class of undergraduates, and read nearly everything that had then been published on that great but still incomplete science. I prepared two lectures for the Exeter Lyceum, and did not slight my studies in the Divinity School. In this way I overtasked my physical powers. In May, 1834, I had a slight attack of typhoid fever, with a determination of blood to the head. After two or three weeks I went to my mother's in Peterborough. But the disease did not leave me. I spent nearly a year in a dark room, unable to sit up, or to bear the presence even of a near friend. A strong constitution was seriously broken. For thirty years afterwards I was not able to do more than one-third the amount of mental labor which had once been a healthful and happy exercise. This was a constantly recurring grief and disappointment.

"For five years I was able to do very little hard work. I preached but seldom, and was not a candidate for settlement as a minister. I supported myself as a private teacher, in New Bedford, and was very happy in the home that was opened to me. In May, 1838, I was settled as associate pastor with Rev. Ephraim Peabody, over the First Congregational Society in New Bedford.

My relation to him and to the society was a happy one. I could not have been associated with a better man. He had a lofty ideal of intellectual, moral, and religious culture. He was of a most generous and guileless nature, and was as much interested in my success as in his own. The five years of my New Bedford ministry were years of great enjoyment and improvement. During that time, in October, 1841, I was married to Miss Emily Hurd Rogers, of Salem, and in December of the following year, my eldest son, George S. Morison, was born.

"In September, 1843, I gave up my salary, and asked leave of absence for an indefinite time. This I did partly because I thought Mr. Peabody's health was then such as to enable him to go on with his work alone, and partly in the hope that change of scene and entire freedom from professional care for a year or two might reëstablish my own health. During this vacation I prepared the *Life* of my early benefactor and kinsman, Jeremiah Smith.* In the autumn of 1845, I resigned my office in New Bedford, and in January, 1846, became the pastor of the First Congregational Parish in Milton, Mass., where I have continued to this day. The society is small. The duties of the place have not been oppressive. The people have been very indulgent. Among them I have found men and women whom it has been a great joy and privilege to know as friends. I could ask for no higher or more exciting employment than to do everything in my power for their instruction and improvement. If there has been little to feed or gratify any lower ambition, there has been a great deal to cherish the best affections. The highest thought that I have been able to reach has always found a hospitable welcome. My one aim in life has been to prove myself in all things a faithful minister of Christ, and even in the apparently narrow sphere in which my lot has been cast I have found abundant opportunity for the exercise of all my faculties. I have written and published a commentary on the Gospel of St. Matthew,† and had hoped to extend the work so as to include the other evangelists. At different times I have edited the *Christian Register*, and the *Religious Magazine* or *Unitarian Review*. But the work of an editor was never to my taste. The pulpit, the parochial labors, and, above all, the studies, of a Christian minister have had for me greater attractions

* Life of the Hon. Jeremiah Smith, LL. D., Member of Congress during Washington's Administration. Judge of the United States Circuit Court, Chief Justice of New Hampshire, etc. Boston, 1845.

† Disquisitions and Notes of the Gospels. Matthew. Boston, 1860.

than any other office or calling. They have been to me always a sufficient stimulus and reward. When drawn away from them for a season by failing health it has been an unspeakable happiness to come back to them again.

"In 1870, I asked for a colleague, that I might be able to complete my work on the Gospels. But other duties providentially put upon me filled up my time. After nearly three years of faithful and intelligent labor in his profession, my dear friend and associate, Francis Tucker Washburn, whose short ministry had revealed to me rare qualities of mind and heart, was taken from us, and with a sense of bereavement and loss I again took up the work which had fallen from his hands. I never engaged in my profession with a deeper sense of personal responsibility, or entered with a more living interest or a keener sense of enjoyment into the great and solemn scenes which it presents. But I have reached an age when such a strain upon the faculties cannot long be continued with safety. I have therefore again asked to be relieved from my parish duties, and as the only effectual way of accomplishing this, I am now spending a year in Europe.

"My life has been marked by few events of any special interest. I have shrunk from prominent positions, and have been very happy in the secluded labors of my profession, in the means of usefulness which it has given, in the literary studies and pursuits which are closely connected with it, and in the intimate and lasting friendships which it has helped me to form with some of the best people in the world. I hope still to live among the people with whom I have lived, giving and receiving such services as lie within our reach to smooth the pathway of life, and enable us to look forward with a stronger faith and a more fitting preparation for what lies beyond. With every new year I have had a richer experience of God's goodness and of his universal care, and it would indicate no small degree of intellectual and moral obtuseness, as well as ingratitude, if I had any fears for what is to come. I am not without hope that I may yet prepare a small work on the study of the Gospels, better than anything I have yet done. Most of it is in my mind, the result of many years of thought and study. It is very pleasant to think of the occupation which it may give, and thus to indulge the desire, perhaps more than the hope, to be still of some service to my fellow-men. All my studies and all my experience go to strengthen my faith in the substantial truthfulness of the Gospel narrative, and in the unspeakable value of the life and the truth which are revealed in them.

"I have had many disappointments. But, as I look back, the predominant feeling in my mind is one of thankfulness. My life has been full of satisfactions and enjoyment. I have not attained to heights which I had once hoped to reach, in intellectual or spiritual culture. But in many ways life has been a rich and beneficent gift, especially in my home, which has had its trials and shadows; but no heart-rending grief has ever entered it. My children, two sons and a daughter, and my wife, have been spared thus far, so that I close this brief outline with devout gratitude and praise.

"JOHN H. MORISON.
"ROME, Feb. 16, 1876."

51　*George Shattuck*, b. Dec. 19, 1842; graduate Harvard University, 1863, LL.B., Harvard Law School, 1866; admitted to bar in New York, 1866; civil engineer, 1867; engaged in building Kansas City Railroad Bridge, 1867–9; built iron viaduct, two hundred and thirty-four feet high, for Erie Railway, at Portage, N.Y., 1875. Has published important papers on bridges and other professional subjects; owns the Samuel Morison place, in the southern part of the town; r. in New York.

52　*Robert Swain*, b. Oct. 13, 1847; graduate Harvard University, 1869, and at Divinity School (B.D.), 1872; studied in Berlin and Tubingen, Germany, 1872, '73; ordained, 1874; settled at Meadville, Pa., 1874.

53　*Mary*, b. April 30, 1851.

31– 46　HORACE MORISON in his youth experienced similar hardships with his brothers, and was made early to earn his own support. On the death of his father he went to live with Thomas Steele, Esq., with whom he remained five years, till he was fourteen, performing such service on the farm as a boy of his age was capable of doing. After three years of employment at other places, he began, when he was seventeen years old, to learn the trade of a cabinet-maker, with Moses Dodge, at the North Factory Village, where he remained till he was twenty-one, serving out his full apprenticeship.

During this time he had shown a fondness for books, had attended regularly the town schools in winter, had been one term to the academy at New Ipswich, and had taught school one winter in Temple.

He entered Phillips (Exeter) Academy in September, 1831, to prepare himself for college, and remained there till August, 1834, when he entered the Sophomore Class of Harvard College. In college he took a high rank as

25

a scholar, gained the highest Bowdoin prize for English composition, belonged to the best college societies, became a member of the Phi Beta Kappa Society, and graduated, in 1837, the eighth scholar in his class.

From college he went directly to Baltimore, where he had been appointed an instructor in mathematics in the University of Maryland, which, with the charter of a college, was in reality only a superior high school. The next year, 1838, he was appointed Professor of Mathematics in the same institution. He held this professorship till July, 1841, when he was chosen President of the Academical Department of the University. He remained in office till July, 1854, when he resigned, and returned to Peterborough, to live upon the old homestead of the family, which he had purchased in 1852. In 1841, he m. Mary Elizabeth Lord, dau. of Samuel Lord, of Portsmouth, and niece of Nathan Lord, late President of Dartmouth College.

In 1856, after a rest of two years on his farm, he returned to Baltimore and opened a girls' school, which he continued to teach till July, 1866. When his brother Nathaniel gave up his school, in 1867, he took charge of it; and he remained in Baltimore till February, 1869, when infirm health compelled him to seek relief from all serious labor. A paralytic affection had made itself felt in his limbs as early as 1856. By careful attention and active remedies, he had succeeded in retarding the progress of the disease; but he never got entirely rid of it. He returned to his farm in Peterborough in 1869, where for a time he seemed to improve, and where he d. Aug. 5, 1870, æ. 59 yrs., 11 mos.

Mr. Morison was an excellent scholar, especially in mathematics; and he had a great fondness for the natural sciences, — which he taught unusually well. Few teachers ever surpassed him in easy, lucid, and familiar explanations of natural phenomena.

Like all good teachers, he had an analytical mind; and the boy must have been dull indeed whom he could not make understand the subjects ordinarily taught in school. He was one of nature's own teachers, peculiarly fitted to impart knowledge to the young, and fond of doing so; but the government of a school was always an irksome task to him, and this rendered him less fond of his profession than he otherwise would have been. In 1851, he published a book for children, called *Pebbles from the Sea Shore.*

---

54   *Elizabeth Whitridge,* b. Baltimore, Dec. 8, 1842; r. Portsmouth.

N. H. Morison

55   *Mary Ann*, b. Oct. 24, 1844 ; r. Portsmouth.
56   *Caroline Augusta*, b. Sept. 20, 1847 ; r. Portsmouth.
57   *Samuel Lord*, b. Oct. 28, 1851 ; graduate Harvard University, 1873 ; m., Nov. 18, 1875, Nancy O. Williams ; r. Boston.

31– 48   NATHANIEL HOLMES MORISON. When he was three years old his father suddenly died of yellow fever, at Natchez, Miss., where he had a contract for introducing a supply of water into that city. At the time of his father's death, the works had not been begun, but heavy expenses had been incurred in taking men and materials to that distant place, and the family property was swallowed up by the claims of creditors ; his mother's dowry in the farm, which had descended from his great-great-grandfather, John Morison, being nearly all that was left for the support and education of seven children — five sons and two daughters, — the oldest but fourteen years of age, and the two youngest twins of a single year. His mother was a woman of uncommon intelligence and of great force of character, but her energy was taxed to the utmost to supply the wants of her large family, and provide them with the education which it was her fixed purpose to give them. Her ambition did not rise to the idea of securing a college education for her sons, but she sought to give them the best instruction which the country schools afforded, and to provide them all with trades. Few women have begun their widowhood under more discouraging circumstances, and fewer still have met the exigencies of that position with a more determined purpose to train up their children in the way they wished them to go. Her ambition and her courage fired theirs. The children caught the inspiration of the mother, but their ideas of what their education should be were soon far beyond hers.

Nathaniel spent his childhood, till he was eight years old, with his mother in the South Village, attending the school, and performing such small services at home as lay within the range of his capacity and his years. In the spring of 1825, when he was nine years old, he went to live with his father's uncle, Dea. Nathaniel Holmes, after whom he had been named. He remained with his uncle, where he was very happy, "doing chores," and working on the farm in such ways as a boy of his age could work, till December, 1828. In August, 1831, after more than two years of employment elsewhere — one summer on a farm with Peter Davis, in Dublin, and nearly two years in the woollen mill of Henry F. Cogswell, — he entered the machine-shop of Moore & Colby, where he spent two years and a half in learning the trade of a machinist.

During these nine years, he attended regularly the district school at the South Village in winter; and he spent most of his leisure hours, during the rest of the year, in reading or study, without instruction and without guidance. Besides reading numerous histories, he studied natural philosophy, astronomy, arithmetic, and algebra, entirely by himself. He was at work for an entire year on a single problem in Colburn's Algebra which arrested his progress. At that time there was not a person in town who could render him the assistance he required; and had there been such a person, it is not at all probable that he would have accepted his aid. The trait which this anecdote illustrates is probably the most prominent one in his character; and, though it may at times have given some trouble to his friends, in the more repulsive form which many call obstinacy, it has done him good service on many important occasions in life, in that other form, so essential to all successful living, — tenacity of purpose. One day, in Baltimore, several years after this, when he was dragging through the weary days of spring and early summer with a school of *two pupils*, and between the classes reading Dante's *Inferno*, in Italian, by way of recreation, Dr. Burnap, with whom he was studying divinity, asked him if he proposed to keep on with his school, under so much discouragement. Receiving in reply an unhesitating "Yes," the doctor jumped from his chair, and, swinging his hand above his head, shouted with full lungs, "Hurrah for New Hampshire!" Dr. Burnap was himself a New Hampshire man, from Merrimack, and his hearty enthusiasm on this occasion certainly had no tendency to weaken the resolution of his pupil.

On the first of January, 1834, he entered Phillips (Exeter) Academy, where he remained till August, 1836, when he was admitted into the Sophomore Class of Harvard College, having prepared himself for this advanced standing in two years and seven months.

At that time eight young men, all from the southern side of the town, and interconnected by blood relationship, were seeking a collegiate education at school or college. These were Nathaniel Holmes, Horace and Nathaniel H. Morison, Barnard B. Whittemore, James and George Walker, James Smith, and Joseph Addison White. John H. Morison, whose example had probably more or less influenced them all in their desire to secure a liberal education, had a little before completed his collegiate course, and James Morison followed immediately after. All these young men, with a single exception, graduated, — some of them with distinguished honors, all with a reputation for scholarship which was creditable to their talents and their industry. James Walker was cut off by consumption before he had finished his college course. He was a young man of fair abilities and good scholarship. He had a large head and a bright eye, but his tall, thin figure gave early indications of weakness and disease. Addison White was an earnest, persevering student, to whom learning did not come as an easy task ; but he was faithful and true to every duty, and graduated at Harvard, in 1840, with an honorable rank in his class. From college he went to Middletown, Pa., to take charge of a school. There he was married, and there he died, in 1843, leaving behind him nothing to indicate to his friends the character of the work he was doing.

These young men furnished to each other, at the most susceptible period of life, when the heart most craves sympathy, a delightful companionship. In their close intimacy at school, in their journeyings to and from Exeter, often on foot, in parties of from two to four, and in their vacations at home, even after they had separated for college, they experienced all those social and moral pleasures which came from a fellowship of young and ardent minds, having a common origin, common sentiments, common pursuits, and a common purpose in life. Like all persons from mountainous districts, they felt a strong, patriotic attachment to their old home among the hills. In their frequent foot-journeys to Exeter, they never failed to stop on the top of the East Mountain to take a farewell view of the Monadnock, before it passed out of their sight ; and in returning, as they ascended the last mountain-slope from the east, foot-sore and weary as they always were from their long journey of sixty miles, they were never too weary for a race to the top, to see who should first catch a glimpse of the grand old mountain, which rose before them firm, majestic, and impassable, like a faithful sentinel guarding the homes of their childhood.

Nathaniel Morison was placed in relations of peculiar intimacy with most of these young men. His brother Horace was his chum at Exeter, and for a year in college ; James Walker was his chum at Exeter ; Bernard Whittemore was his classmate both at Exeter and in college ; and James Smith was his chum for two years' at Exeter, and they had been companions and intimate friends from their earliest childhood up.

" For they were nursed upon the self-same hill,
 Fed the same flock by fountain, shade, and rill;
 Together both, ere the high lawns appeared
 Under the opening eyelids of the morn,
 They drove afield; and both together heard
 What time the gray-fly winds her sultry horn;
 Battening their flocks with the fresh dews of night,
 Oft till the star, that rose at evening bright,
 Towards heaven's descent had sloped her westering wheel."

As a student, young Morison was obliged to practise the most rigid economy in all his expenses — in dress, in board, in books, and in travelling. He once walked on the frozen ground, in December, from Peterborough to Exeter, the entire journey costing but the two cents paid for crossing the Merrimack at Thornton's Ferry. He carried a lunch in his pocket, and spent the night at the Rev. Jacob Abbot's, in Windham. Like most country boys of the period, he sought to increase his scanty means by teaching school in winter. He began his career as a school-master during his Sophomore year, in the brick school-house on High Street, afterwards remodelled and occupied as a dwelling by Samuel Holmes. During the next winter he taught the village school in Grafton, Mass.; and in 1838–9 he had charge of the High School at Scituate Harbor. His life at school and college was a laborious one; but it was extremely pleasant. He was on terms of easy and agreeable intercourse with all his schoolmates and classmates, joining most of their societies and social gatherings. He was a member of the Golden Branch at Exeter; and in college he joined the Institute of 1770, the Harvard Union, the Hasty Pudding Club, and the Phi Beta Kappa Society. Very early in life he had shown a fondness for poetic composition, and he was chosen by his schoolmates to write the ode for the Exhibition at Exeter in 1835, and a song for the celebration of the Fourth of July by the students in 1836. At the annual exhibition of the academy in 1835, he was appointed to deliver an original English poem, and in 1836 an original Latin poem. In college he was chosen by his classmates to write the song for the class supper at the end of their Sophomore year, and the ode for class-day at the end of their Senior year. He also delivered the poem before the Hasty Pudding Club, in 1838; and he gained one of the Bowdoin prizes for English composition the same year. He graduated in 1839, the third scholar in his class, having one of the orations for his part at Commencement.

Immediately after graduating, he went to Baltimore, to become the principal teacher in a fashionable girls' school which had just been opened in that city; and he remained in this position for nearly two years. In May, 1841, he opened a girls' school on his own account. In 1840, he, with his brother Horace, began the study of divinity with the Rev. Dr. G. W. Burnap, an accomplished biblical scholar and critic, under whom he continued until he had completed the full course of three years in theology. He was licensed to preach by the Cheshire Pastoral Association, which met at Keene, in the summer of 1843. On the 22d of December, 1842, he married Sidney Buchanan Brown, of Baltimore. She belonged to the same Scotch-Irish race from which he was descended, her ancestors having settled near Carlisle, Penn.

His school, which for an entire term consisted of two pupils, soon became so prosperous that he gradually gave up all idea of devoting himself to the ministry. He had preached only a few times and at irregular intervals. In a few years his school became the largest in the city, numbering at one time a hundred and forty pupils. For twenty years, including the war, when there was a great falling off in pupils, the average number of his scholars was a hundred and ten — the largest private girls' school ever kept in the city for so long a period. Nearly a thousand ladies from the most intelligent families of Baltimore have received their education from him; and five of its private schools, among them its leading girls' school, are now (1875) taught by his pupils. His school had the reputation of being unusually strict in its government, and rigorous in its requirements of serious study from its pupils. It therefore attracted few of those who were not disposed to learn. He was fond of his profession, and devoted to it all his energy and all the best powers of his mind; and he was amply rewarded and cheered by constant manifestations of the respect and affection of his pupils, among whom he has found some of the warmest friendships of his life.

In 1867, he was invited to take charge of the Peabody Institute, of Baltimore, which had been founded by George Peabody, of London, in 1857, and which has received from him an endowment of $1,240,000. His school was still in the full tide of success, and he long hesitated before he accepted this important but wholly unsolicited charge. He received his appointment as provost of the institute in April, and entered upon his new duties in September, 1867. He devoted himself at once to the library, which then consisted of about 15,000 volumes of miscellaneous books, among which

were very few of the great works which such a library
should contain. Under his administration more than
$150,000 have been spent in the purchase of books.
The library now contains over 60,000 volumes, and is
everywhere, among scholars, regarded as one of the best
reference libraries in the country.

Dr. Morison has for many years been a trustee of the
First Independent Church of Baltimore. For twenty-
seven years he was a member, and most of that time the
superintendent, of its Sunday-school. He is one of the
board of governors and visitors of St. John's College, at
Annapolis, from which, in 1871, he received the honorary degree of LL.D. When a volume, beautifully
printed and illustrated, was issued, in 1871, describing
the representative men of Baltimore, he was selected
as the "representative teacher" of the city, and a short
sketch of his life, with a portrait, was placed in the book.

In 1857, he purchased in Peterborough the place now
known as Bleakhouse, and fitted it up for a summer
residence. The house was built by John White in 1792,
and was the old homestead of the White family down to
1846, when Robert White died, and his farm was divided
and sold. His affection for his old home drew him back
to the place of his birth, and for nineteen years he and
his family have spent at least three months of each
summer amid the scenes so familiar and dear to his boyhood. When, in 1872, he gave up all interest in the
school which he had established in Baltimore, and over
which he had presided for a quarter of a century, he
sent all his philosophical apparatus, which cost originally about $2,000, as a gift to the high school of his
native town.

He has been too busy with the practical work of his
profession to have had much leisure for other literary
employments.

In 1843, he published *Three Thousand Questions in
Geography*, which passed through three editions, and is
still used by some of the best schools in Baltimore. He
also published a small book on *Punctuation and Solecisms*,
of which an enlarged edition was printed in 1867, under
the title of *A School Manual*. In 1871, he wrote a pamphlet on the management and objects of the Peabody
Institute. Besides these, he has written nine annual
reports to the trustees of the Peabody Institute, which
have been printed for distribution among similar institutions elsewhere.

———

58　*Frank*, b. March 18, 1844; m., Oct. 10, 1865, Lucy Ann
　　Fisk, of Boston, b. June 25, 1843; d. May 25, 1866,

at Florence, Italy. He studied law, and is now practising his profession in Boston.

59 *George Brown*, b. Jan. 5, 1846; d. May 11, 1850.
60 *Ernest Nathaniel*, b. Nov. 14, 1848 ; graduate Harvard
University, 1870; m., Oct. 31, 1871, Priscilla Ridgely
White, of Baltimore, b. Dec. '13, 1850; ch., (1)
Nathaniel H., b. Sept. 24, 1872 ; (2) Charles R. W., b.
Jan. 21, 1874 ; (3) Sidney B., b. Dec. 16, 1875. He
is engaged in business in Baltimore.
61 *Robert Brown*, b. March 13, 1851; M.D., University of
Maryland, 1874. He entered Harvard College in
1869, but left in the middle of his Sophomore year,
and went to Germany, where he remained three years.
He spent a year each at the universities of Göttingen
and Berlin, in the study of his profession. He is now
settled in Baltimore as a physician.
62 *William George*, b. May 31, 1853 ; d. very suddenly at
Exeter, where he was fitting for college, Oct. 30, 1869,
æ. 16 yrs.
63 *John Holmes*, b. Jan. 21, 1856; now a member of Harvard College.
64 *Alice Sidney*, b. Jan. 24, 1859.
65 *George Burnap*, b. May 9, 1861.

31- 49 SAMUEL ADAMS MORISON. He moved to San Francisco in 1849, where he now resides. He ,m., Nov. 9,
1847, Ellen Smith, of Bodega, Cal., b. June 6, 1820.

66 *James Henry*, b. Jan. 20, 1851.
67 *William C.*, b. Jan. 11, 1855.
68 *Wallace*, b..Dec. 29, 1861.

31- 50 JAMES MORISON, M.D. After the death of his father
when hardly a year old, he remained with his mother till
he was ten years of age; he then lived for nearly four
years as a farmer's boy in the families of Samuel Fisk
and Ivory Perry, of Dublin. He received for his services his board and clothing, and had the privilege of
going to school two or three months in the winter. He
was employed for three years, from the spring of 1833,
in the woollen factory of Henry F. Cogswell, in the
South Factory Village. In the autumn of 1836, he
entered Phillips (Exeter) Academy. In the spring of
1839, illness compelled him to suspend his studies at the
academy. He returned to Peterborough, and began the
study of medicine in the office of Drs. Follansbee &
Smith. He soon, however, regained his health, and
returned to Exeter, where he remained until 1841, when
he was admitted to the Sophomore class of Harvard

26

University. He graduated in 1844, and left immediately for Baltimore, where he resumed the study of medicine, and received his medical degree from the University of Maryland, in 1846. He received the appointment of resident physician of the Baltimore Infirmary, a position which he retained until he left for California, in the latter part of 1849. He went to California in a British steamship, by way of the Straits of Magellan, arriving at San Francisco early in the summer of 1850, where he remained in the practice of his profession until the spring of 1854, when he returned to the Eastern States, and went to Europe in the following October. He remained abroad until the summer of 1856. He spent most of his time in Paris, where he attended medical lectures and the clinics of the hospitals.

He m. Mary S. Sanford, of Boston, Jan. 29, 1857, the dau. of Philo and Martha (Druce) Sanford, b. March 8, 1821. He returned to San Francisco in the following spring. His w. d. Jan. 17, 1866, æ. 44 yrs., 10 mos., leaving two children. He returned to New England in 1867, and m. Ellen Wheeler, of Keene, June 16, 1868, dau. of Sumner and Catharine (Vose) Wheeler, b. June 18, 1837.

In 1858 he assisted in the organization of the first medical school established on the Pacific coast, under the charter of the University of the Pacific. He was appointed professor of the theory and practice of medicine and pathology in this school, a position which he held for five years. He was for several years one of the trustees of the University of the Pacific, and in 1869 vice-president of the California Medical Society. He has been an active member of the following medical and scientific societies and associations: California Medical Society, California Academy of Natural Sciences, Franco-American Medical Society, Paris, Massachusetts Medical Society, Norfolk District Medical Society, Dorchester Medical Club, and American Medical Association. In June, 1869, he removed to Quincy, Mass., where he now resides, in the practice of his profession.

---

69 | *Sanford*, b. Oct. 26, 1859, at San Francisco.
70 | *Emily*, b. Jan. 20, 1864, at San Francisco.

12- 34 | ROBERT MORISON, Jr. He m. Betsey Spring, dau. of Josiah C. Spring, Sept. 12, 1805. He d. April 25, 1861, æ. 77 yrs. Lived many years in Hancock, but returned and d. in town.

	Samuel S., b. Feb. 19, 1806; d. Oct. 21, 1825, æ. 19 yrs.
71	†*Josiah S.*, b. Jan. 12, 1808; m. Phebe V. Knight.
72	†*Robert H.*, b. March 19, 1810; m. Emily Johnson.
73	†*Nathaniel* b. May 6, 1812; m. Mary Knight.
74	*Elizabeth A.*, b. Dec. 23, 1814; m. Goodyear Bassett.
75	*Mary Ann*, b. April 20, 1817; m. George Wilcox, April
76	18, 1848.
	David, b. July 31, 1819; m. ——.
77	*Sarah*, b. Jan. 18, 1823; d. Oct. 29, 1825, æ. 2 yrs., 9
78	mos.

34– 72   JOSIAH S. MORISON now resides in South Acworth, and with his son Robert is engaged in the grain and lumber business. He has held important offices in town, — Representative 1845, '48, selectman 1849, '50.

He has been for a large portion of his life engaged in building machinery, and when the Cotton Mill, No. 2, of the Union Manufacturing Company was built, from his long experience and knowledge of machinery, he was employed to make all the calculations necessary to adapt the power to the machinery to be propelled, and to arrange all matters required to secure a successful operation of the same. Little or no change has ever been made in these arrangements. He m., Sept. 4, 1831, Phebe Knight, b. June 19, 1807.

79	*Sarah T.*, b. Lowell, Aug. 5, 1832; m. John D. Holmes; r. Alstead.
80	*Lizzie M.*, b. March 23, 1836; m. Melville S. Buxton; r. Alstead.
81	*Ellen*, b. June 29, 1840; m. Moses B. Wells; r. Bellows Falls, Vt.
82	*Sylva S.*, b. Dec. 8, 1842; d. Sept. 13, 1844, æ. 1 yr., 9 mos.
83	*Robert S.*, b. Oct. 25, 1845; m. Sarah A. Washburn; r. South Acworth.
84	*Edgar K.*, b. May 6, 1848; graduate of Bridgewater Normal School. Now a teacher.
85	*Phebe*, b. March 2, 1852; d. April 13, 1852, æ. 41 dys.

34– 73   ROBERT HOLMES MORISON. He lived many years in Lowell, when he returned to Peterborough and bought the James Gregg place, where he how lives. He m., June 27, 1855, Emily Johnson, b. Nov. 4, 1819.

86	*Elmer Leland*, b. June 20, 1857.
87	*Hermon R.*, b. Sept. 25, 1859.
88	*Stella Edwina*, b. Nov. 25, 1863.

34- 74   NATHANIEL MORISON. He lived many years in Lowell, and then re. to Peterborough, but subsequently bought a farm in Greenfield, where he now r. He m. Mary Knight, b. Oct. 18, 1815. •

89   *Edgar D.*, b. Jan. 17, 1842 ; d. Aug. 16, 1843, æ. 1 yr., 7 mos.

90   *Henry B.*, b. Nov. 18, 1845 ; m. Abby M. Weston ; one ch., Dora Mabel.

91   *Willie Aldo*, b. May 10, 1855 ; d. Oct. 9, 1856, æ. 1 yr., 5 mos.

92   *Myro Almon*, b. June 21, 1857.

1   JOHN MORRISON (Rev.) is of a race entirely distinct from the early settlers of this town who bore the same name. He was b. in Pathfoot, in Scotland, May 22, 1743. He was graduated at the University of Edinburgh in 1765. He arrived in Boston the May following, and was ordained at Peterborough, Nov. 26, 1766. He was the first settled minister of the town. He was a man of more than ordinary talents, but soon proved to be intemperate and licentious. His conduct became so scandalous that a presbyterial meeting was held, and he was for a time suspended from his office. He relinquished his connection with the society in March, 1772. In the meanwhile he visited South Carolina, but returned ; and, after the battle of Bunker Hill, he deserted to the British, and remained in their service till his death. He d. suddenly (as is supposed) at Charleston, S. C., while a commissary in the British service, May 26 or 27, 1782, æ. 49 yrs. He m. Sarah Ferguson, dau. John Ferguson, Jan. 8, 1767. He never returned to town after he deserted the cause of the colonists. His family were left in a destitute condition, and in 1776 he informed his wife that if some one would come to New York, to a place designated by him, he would send money to her. Her brother, Henry Ferguson, accordingly went, and is supposed to have been on this very service when the Association Test, or Declaration of Independence, was signed by the eighty-three in town, as his name is not found among them. He received a certain amount, some say a pound, of gold ; others, some three or four hundred dollars. In his absence he incurred the suspicion of having gone over to the British, — but never a truer man or patriot! Bad as Morrison has been represented, and bad as his conduct appears, his wife never lost her faith in him. This transaction was greatly to his credit. She d. Nov. 28, 1824, æ. 84 yrs. Her last days were tenderly and care-

fully watched over by Maria Stevens, an adopted daughter, who afterwards m. Abel Phelps, of Boston, and d. at Watertown.

2 *John*, b. 1768 ; d. Nov. 15, 1794, æ. 26 yrs.

Quite a romantic incident connected with John Morrison, the eldest son, deserves to be recorded; it is communicated in a letter from Rev. John H. Morison, D.D. : —

"He had two sons, John and James. John was educated at Phillips (Exeter) Academy, and was still remembered with great affection and respect by prominent citizens of Exeter, when I went there in 1824. The following story was told me more than thirty years ago, by Mrs. Phelps, the adopted daughter of Mrs. Morrison, and was written down by me at that time. Mrs. Phelps will be remembered by our older inhabitants by her maiden name of Maria Stevens. She faithfully cared for and watched over Mrs. Morrison as long as she lived. John Morrison, the minister's son, while in Exeter, probably somewhere near 1790 to 1792 or '93, was engaged to be married to a Miss Tilton, a very interesting young lady, afterwards Mrs. Sleeper, the mother of Capt. J. S. Sleeper, of the Boston *Journal*. A year or two before his death Mr. Morrison went to one of the West India Islands. While there he sent a letter to Miss Tilton, by his brother James, who was going to Peterborough, with a request that he would himself deliver it to her in Exeter. He accordingly went to Exeter for that purpose, but on reaching the town, he fell in with persons who disliked or were jealous of Miss Tilton, and was by them persuaded not to deliver the letter. He saw the lady, who inquired about his brother John, but as she received no communication from her former lover, she supposed that he had lost his interest in her, and she did not write to him. He thereupon, hearing nothing from her in reply to the letter, which he took for granted had been delivered, supposed that her feelings towards him had changed. Sometime after, he came home to his mother in Peterborough, far gone in consumption, and then learned why Miss Tilton had not written to him. But he had now no hope of living, and when his mother advised him to write to the lady, explaining the reasons of his apparent neglect, he said, ' No, I think she will feel my death less, if she continues to suppose that I had lost my interest in her.' A few days before he died, he took from his bosom some little keepsake, which she had given him, and threw it into the fire, saying, 'It is all over now. I have given up, and am ready to go.' I have no doubt that this account is substantially true. It was told to Mrs. Phelps by his mother. It has always seemed to me a very unselfish and touching act on his part, and reminds one of Shakespeare's beautiful sonnet: —

> "'Nay, if you read this line, remember not
> The hand that writ it; for I love you so
> That I in your sweet thoughts would be forgot,
> If thinking on me then should make you woe.'

"This is almost the only romantic incident that I find in connection with our early history. It may be well to preserve it, as an offset to the unfavorable view of the father's life and character, which we are obliged to take. The mother was a woman of rare excellence of character."

3　*Polly*, b. 1770; d. April 1, 1812, æ. 42 yrs.
4　† *William*, b. 1772.　　　　(5) *James*, b. ———.

1– 4　　WILLIAM MORRISON was b. about 1772, and lived with Henry Ferguson till he was twenty-one years of age. He remained in town till after the famous nocturnal visit to Rev. David Annan, in which he and James Miller (Gen.) were selected by the party to seize Mr. Annan as soon as he came to the door, and place him on the pole. Mr. Annan recognized William Morrison in his disguise, and reported him to his uncle, Henry Ferguson. He did not approve of the conduct of William, and his disapprobation, and the fear of prosecution and trial, were so very humiliating to him, that he resolved at once to leave Peterborough, which occurred probably about 1800.

But little has been known of him since. He at one time lived near Pittsburg, Penn. He has visited Peterborough once, in 1826 or '27, and also at the same time visited Gen. Miller's family at Salem. Nothing has been heard of him since 1829 or '30.

1　　ABRAHAM PERKINS MORRISON, a race entirely distinct from those of that name who had been the early settlers of the town, was b. in Sanbornton, Oct. 5, 1807. He was the son of Jonathan and Esther Perkins Morrison. His grandfather, Bradbury Morrison, who was also b. in Sanbornton, was the youngest but one of twelve children. After receiving the ordinary education of the district schools, which was very meagre, he was apprenticed when young to the trade of paper-making, before the advent of machines for making paper. He worked some time at his trade in Franklin, when, in company with

John Hoyt and A. C. Blodgett, he came to Peterborough in August, 1831, they having purchased the paper-mill formerly built and owned by W. S. & J. Smith. He continued in the same business till his death, having become sole owner of the premises. Mr. Morrison became a highly useful and respectable citizen. He was a good business man, safe in his judgments, and honorable and upright in all his dealings; he was benevolent and kind to those who were needy and in distress, forbearing and charitable to the errors and faults of others. He was never harsh and severe in his judgment of men and things. He was universally respected, and his death was a great loss to the community. Such men's places are not easily supplied.

He was Representative in 1848, '62, '63. He moved to the village in the autumn of 1866, having purchased the house formerly owned and occupied by Stephen P. Steele, Esq. He d. here, Sept. 15, 1870, æ. 61 yrs., 10 mos. He m., Aug. 19, 1833, Mary, dau. of James and Margaret Taggart Robbe, of Dublin.

2   †*Mortier L.*, b. July 2, 1836; m., 1st w., Susan M. Gates; 2d w., Caroline Brooks.

3   *Helen M.*, b. Nov. 1, 1838; m., Nov. 18, 1856, J. Madison Nay. She d. Dec. 23, 1865, æ. 27 yrs.

1— 2   MORTIER L. MORRISON. He was prevented in early life from attending school as he wished, by ill health, which continued to his manhood. He had to acquire his education principally by himself. · Subsequent to a severe necrosis of the tibia, which had continued for a number of years, he was attacked with a dangerous typhoid fever, when about eighteen or nineteen years old, from which, when he recovered, he found himself in better health; so that he was able to pursue and attain his trade of paper-making.

He enlisted in the war of the Rebellion, Aug. 31, 1862, and was mustered into service as Quarter Master's Sergeant, 13th N. H. Vols., Sept. 26, 1862, and as Quarter Master, Aug. 12, 1863. He remained in service to the close of the war, and was discharged in the summer of 1865. He sold the paper-mill to Adams & Nay, June, 1870. Selectman in 1868, '69, '70. Was chosen treasurer of the Peterborough Savings Bank, April 18, 1873, which position he now occupies. He m., 1st w., Aug. 9, 1861, Susan M. Gates, dau. of Samuel and Charlotte Gates. She d. May 1, 1862, æ. 27 yrs.; one ch.; m., 2d w., Caroline Brooks, dau. Charles H. Brooks, March 5, 1866; two ch.

4   *Alice Gates*, b. April 2, 1862.
5   *Mary Brooks*, b. March 8, 1868.
6   *Abraham Perkins*, b. July 7, 1870.

THE MUSSEY FAMILY.

1

JOHN MUSSEY (Dr.), b. in Kingston, Sept. 11, 1745, was the son of Reuben Mussey, one of the first selectmen of Amherst, and representative to the General Court, 1778. He studied his profession with Dr. Moses Nichols, of Amherst, and at the age of twenty-one commenced his medical practice in Pelham, where he continued twenty-five years, till 1791, when he re. to Amherst. In 1800, he bought a part of the old Hugh Wilson lot, of the heirs of Patrick White, and re. to Peterborough. We do not learn that he practised his profession after he came to Peterborough, nor, indeed, after he left Pelham. He was a devotedly religious man, and a Presbyterian of the strictest sect; he would only partake of the communion service when the bread was *unleavened*, and was compelled, in fidelity to his views, to ride to Antrim to take the sacrament.* In his old age, his son operated on his eyes for a cataract. He d. Jan. 17, 1831, of a cancer on the lower lip, æ. 85 yrs., 4 mos. He m., 1st w., Beulah Butler, of Pelham; she d. at Peterborough, Dec. 13, 1805, æ. 59 yrs.; m., 2d w., Rhoda Bartlett, of Epsom, in 1807.

---

2   *John*, b. 1778; m. Sally Robbe, dau. Lieut. William Robbe, Dec. 3, 1821. He d. Dec. 3, 1842, æ. 64 yrs. She d. Aug. 27, 1840, æ. 61 yrs.

3   *Reuben Dimond*, b. in Pelham, June 23, 1780.
He was twenty years old when his father re. to Peterborough. Determined to have an education, although too poor to attain it, he labored on a farm in the summer, and taught school during the winter, for this purpose. This he continued to do, still making all preparation in his power, until he had fitted himself to enter the Junior class in Dartmouth College, in the year 1801. He continued to teach for his support while in college, and paid all his expenses by his own exertions, except a small sum received from his father, of one hundred and thirty-three dollars. With all his difficulties, he acquitted himself creditably in college as a scholar, being reckoned in the first third of his class. He graduated in 1803, having for classmates Gov. Henry Hubbard, Frederick Hall, LL.D., George C. Shattuck, M.D., LL.D., Nathan Weston, Chief Justice

* Letter of Professor William H. Mussey, Cincinnati, O.

Engraved by J. B. Hunt. London

Yours truly

R D Mussey

Superior Court of Maine, and Edmund Parker. On graduating he immediately became a pupil of Dr. Nathan Smith, the founder of the Dartmouth Medical College, "a name ever to be mentioned in New Hampshire with veneration and respect."* The following year, 1804, he taught the academy in Peterborough, and studied with Dr. Howe, of Jaffrey. He probably taught school only a part of this year, as we find he attended lectures, and took the degree of Bachelor of Medicine in 1805; and in September of that year he commenced practice in Ipswich, Mass. He subsequently settled in Salem, Mass., where he distinguished himself for his scientific attainments, as well as his skill as a surgeon and physician. He afterwards pursued his studies in Philadelphia, where he made several interesting and novel experiments, in one of which he proved conclusively the theory of "absorption by the skin," in direct opposition to a former theory of the celebrated Dr. Rush. This was the subject of his thesis at his second graduation, in Philadelphia. In the autumn of 1814, he was appointed to the chair of theory and practice and obstetrics in the medical department of Dartmouth College, Hanover, and he gave in addition a course of lectures on chemistry.

At various periods, from 1814 to 1837, he filled all the professorships of the Dartmouth Medical College, and at the time of his resignation was lecturing in the distinct departments of anatomy, surgery, and obstetrics; and all this, in addition to a large practice, embracing all the important surgical cases in that region. He filled the chair of anatomy and surgery for four years, at Bowdoin College, and also lectured on surgery in the Medical College at Fairfield, N.Y., in 1837. Being invited, in 1837, to a professorship in Cincinnati, O., in the Ohio Medical College, he accepted the same, where he removed in 1838, and for fourteen years was the leading man in that institution. He then founded the Miami Medical College, and labored assiduously for its good six years, when he retired from active professional life, though still retaining all his ardor and enthusiasm for his chosen profession.† At the close of his professional duties, in 1858, being now seventy-eight years of age, he removed to Boston, where he spent the remainder of his life in the family of one of his daughters, and d. there, from the infirmities of age, June 21, 1866, æ. 86 yrs. This retirement was not to a life of entire ease. He

* Commemorative Address, Prof. A. B. Crosby, p. 5, to which we are indebted for many of the facts in this sketch.

† Commemorative Address, Prof. A. B. Crosby, p. 7.

27

wrote a very useful book during this period, entitled *Health ; its Friends and its Foes.* It must have cost him much labor and investigation. It embodies very much that should be again and again impressed on the public mind. Dr. Mussey, both as an operative and scientific surgeon, attained a national reputation, and was respected all through New Hampshire as one of her most distinguished sons. He performed all the capital operations in surgery, having operated for lithotomy forty-nine times, and all recovered but four ; and for strangulated hernia forty times, with only eight fatal cases. He was the first to perform the operation of tying both the carotid arteries in the same person, with entire success. "This operation gave him great *éclat*, both at home and abroad."

" As a surgeon, he was bold and fearless, and ever willing to assume any legitimate responsibility, though it took him into the undiscovered country of experiment." He lectured in medical colleges forty-four years, and was always respected and beloved by his students. He was always an impressive lecturer, and his manner was simple and earnest. He was ever, from his youth, a consistent and devout Christian, and his record is without spot or blemish. He was a good man and a great man, and few have lived such a life of usefulness as he did. During his professional life, he twice visited Europe for the purpose of medical and scientific improvement.

We are proud to recognize him among our inhabitants, as this was his only home for several years. He m., 1st w., Mary Sewall, of Ipswich, Mass., who survived the marriage only six months ; he m., 2d w., Hitty Osgood, dau. Dr. Joseph Osgood, of Salem, Mass. ; she d. May 14, 1866. He left a large family.

William H. Mussey, M.D., one of his sons, holds the professorship of surgery in the Miami Medical College, which his father founded, to whom I am indebted for many facts relating to the family.

Francis B. Mussey, M.D., another son, is practising his profession in Portsmouth, O.

4   *Jonathan,* b. 1810 ; d. Oct. 17, 1829, æ. 19 yrs. He accidentally shot himself, as was supposed.

THE NAHOR FAMILY.

1   LEONARD NAHOR, son of David and Esther Nahor, b. in Hancock, Dec. 8, 1806, m., April 6, 1837, Morindia Tenney, dau. of Stephen and Lucy Tenney, b. in Hancock, May 4, 1812 ; re. to Peterborough, April 6,

- 1837, and settled on the William Ballard farm, in the north part of the town, on the road to Hancock, where they now live.

---

2   *Susie F.*, b. April 25, 1838; m. Henry Mason, of Andover, Mass., June 2, 1862; d. Jan. 20, 1863, æ. 24 yrs., 8 mos.

3   *David J.*, b. July 22, 1839; d. Oct. 11, 1848, æ. 9 yrs.

4   *Stephen M.*, b. Aug. 9, 1841.

5   *Mary E.*, b. April 26, 1843; d. Oct. 11, 1848, æ. 5 yrs., 5 mos.

6   *Ellen M.*, b. July 26, 1849.

7   *Emma J.*, b. June 25, 1854.

THE NAY OR McNEE FAMILY.

1   WILLIAM McNEE (Dea.) was one of the early settlers of Peterborough. In the year 1745 or '46, William McNee, in company with John Taggart and William Ritchie, looked out a place in town to settle, and selected lots on the south part of the farm subsequently known as the Shedd farm, and the adjoining lands. Here they cut a strip of woods twenty rods wide, cutting out the small growth and girdling the large trees, and then left it, and did not return till 1752 with their families. This chopping had been burnt over by hunters or Indians, and was in good order for corn or rye. They had, in consequence, an abundant crop that year. Dea. McNee m., 1st w., in Ireland, Mary Eckless Brownley, by whom he had all his ch. She d. in Peterborough, October, 1759, æ. 48 yrs. He m., 2d w., wid. Sarah Smith Bell, a dau. of Robert Smith, and sister of William Smith, Esq., who d. Jan. 31, 1814, æ. 98 yrs. He was b. in Ireland, 1711, and d. in Peterborough, Dec. 23, 1789, æ. 78 yrs. We are not perfectly certain as to Dea. McNee's residence before he removed to town, but suppose it was Roxbury. The descendants of Dea. McNee to the present time, 1873, have reached the seventh generation, and the whole amount of his posterity, as nearly as could be ascertained by a careful inquiry, is one thousand one hundred and fourteen, and yet by no means embracing them all.

---

2   *Robert*, b. 1735; killed at Fort George, in Rodgers' Fight, March 13, 1757.

3   † *William*, b. 1740; m. Betsey Russell.

4   *James*, b. ——; m. Patty Swan; re. to Milton, Vt., 1802; thirteen ch.

5 *Mary*, b. 1745; m. James Cuningham.
6 *Rebecca*, b. ——; unm.; d. May 25, 1785, æ. 31 yrs.
7 *Elizabeth*, b. ——; m. Lieut. James Taggart; re. to Dublin, 1788.
8 *Mariam*, b. 1751; m. Wm. Milliken; 2d w.; d. Nov. 21, 1811, æ. 60 yrs.
9 *Agnes*, b. Aug. 14, 1758; m. John Swan; d. June 16, 1816, æ. 58 yrs.; four ch.*

1- 3 WILLIAM McNEE (Dea.). He was young when his father moved to Peterborough; m. Betsey Russell. After his marriage he removed to Dublin, about 1760, and remained there some four or five years; and his son Robert was b. there, and was the first male child b. in Dublin. He lived on or near the spot afterwards owned and occupied by Cyrus Piper. His name is found in a list of persons who worked on the roads in 1761, '62, '64, and '65. He is then supposed, in 1765 or '66, to have returned to town and succeeded his father on the homestead. He was elected a deacon in Mr. Dunbar's church, Nov. 28, 1799, with Wm. Smith, Jonathan Smith, Robert Morison, and Nathaniel Holmes. He d. April 13, 1810, æ. 70 yrs.; she d. 1815.

10 †*Robert*, b. Dublin, 1761; m. Elizabeth Swan, dau. John Swan.
11 †*William*, b. March, 1763; m. Lydia Sawyer.
12 †*John*, b. 1765; m. Betsey Puffer.
13 *Polly*, b. ——; m. David Upton; re. to Sharon.
14 *Betsey*, b. ——; m. Ephraim Weston.
15 *Samuel*, b. 1769; unm.; d. July 6,.1798, æ. 29 yrs.
16 *George*, b. 1772; m. Sally Clary; two ch., Cynthia and Betsey. He d. Sept. 7, 1798, æ. 26 yrs. Cynthia d. Dec. 6, 1798, æ. 2 yrs. Betsey m. Jonathan Bowers.
17 *David*, b. 1775; m. Martha Brown; one ch., David, Jr.; d. September, 1803, æ. 28 yrs.
18 *James*, b. 1779; unm.; d. June 3, 1798, æ. 19 yrs.

3- 10 ROBERT NAY (Lieut.) m. Elizabeth Swan, dau. John Swan, 3d. He d. Oct. 2, 1824, æ. 63 yrs.

19 *Fanny*, b.——; m. John Milliken; re. to New York; seven ch.
20 *Sally*, b. ——; m. Alexander Milliken; re. to New York; four ch.
21 *Betsey*, b. ——; m. Robert Milliken; re. to Sharon; one ch., Addison, a *non compos.*

* In Manuscript Notes of S. S., he says Nanny Nay m. John Swan. Agnes must have been thirty-eight or forty years younger than Lieut. John Swan.

22 | *Barbara*, b. ——; m. John Taggart; re. to Pennsylvania; eight ch.

23 • | *Sylvia*, b. ——; m. John Davison; re. to Michigan; seven ch.

24 | *Pitman*, b. ——; m. Sally Taggart; re. to Nebraska; four ch.

25 | *Samuel*, b. ——; m. Jane Turner; re. to New York; three ch.

26 | *Clarissa*, b. ——; m. Capt. Thomas Turner; re. to New York; four ch.

27 | *Rachel*, b. ——; m. Shepherd Miller; re. to New York; two ch.

3– 11 | WILLIAM NAY, 3D. He m. Lydia Sawyer. He d. June 1, 1813, æ. 50 yrs. She d. Aug. 28, 1850, æ. 82 yrs.

---

28 | *William, 4th*, b. 1788; m. Rebecca Foster; re. to Indiana; twelve ch.

29 | *Lydia*, b. July 15, 1791; m. Walter Gilbert; re. to New York; d. 1856, æ. 65 yrs.

30 | †*Samuel*, b. Feb. 24, 1794; m. Mary Felt; 2d w., Elizabeth F. Gray.

31 | *Asdal*, b. March 12, 1797; m. Polly Milliken; re. to New York; d. October, 1830, æ. 33 yrs.

32 | *Cyntha*, b. Feb. 5, 1799; m. Cyrus Frost; r. Dublin.

33 | *Gardner*, b. Aug. 9, 1801; m. Amelia Symonds; re. to Illinois.

34 | *Arvilla*, b. Nov. 28, 1804; m. N. B. Buss.

35 | *Jefferson*, b. May 26, 1808; m. Sally Loring; he d. 1837, æ. 31 yrs.

•3– 12 | JOHN NAY. He had the misfortune, in early life, to lose one of his legs by falling from a frame he was assisting in raising in Concord, Mass. He substituted a wooden leg of soft white pine, of his own manufacture, which answered a good purpose all his life. He learned the trade of cabinet-making, after the accident. He was a man of great natural abilities, and but for his intemperate habits might have attained to a high position in society. .He became most thoroughly reformed before his death, and gave unmistakable evidence of the Christian character, in his humble, meek, and loving spirit to all those around him. He m. Betsey Puffer, dau. Elijah Puffer; she d. March, 1858, æ. 89 yrs., 6 mos. He d. Sept. 29, 1843, æ. 78 yrs.

---

36 | *Russell*, b. Feb. 17, 1793; re. to Tennessee; six ch.

37 | *Mary*, b. Dec. 13, 1794 ; m. Elisha Wood, June 2, 1811 ; re. to Vermont ; twelve ch.

38 | *Betsey*, b. June 21, 1796 ; m. Joseph Felt, May 5, 1816 ; d. October, 1852, æ. 56 yrs. ; c.

39 | *Esther*, b. Feb. 4, 1798 ; m. James Cross, Jan. 13, 1818.

40 | †*James*, b. Oct. 30, 1799 ; m. Jane Farnsworth ; b. March 10, 1800.

41 | †*George*, b. April 22, 1802 ; m. Mary Persons.

42 | *John, Jr.*, b. April 17, 1804 ; m. Angeline Hale ; re. to Utah ; twelve ch.

43 | *William*, b. Dec. 28, 1807 ; m. Deidamia Cram ; three ch.

44 | *Matilda*, b. May 12, 1806 ; m. Timothy Weston ; 2d hus., Abisha Tubbs.

45 | †*B. Allen*, b. April 10, 1810 ; m. Syrena Chandler ; three ch.

11– 30 | SAMUEL NAY (Maj.).   He lived in Sharon till within a few years, and most of his ch. were born there. He has held many important offices of trust and honor in Sharon ; he has been moderator, town clerk, selectman many years, representative to the General Court for six years, and a member of the Constitutional Convention for 1850 ; also county commissioner for two years. He m., 1st w., Mary Felt, dau. of Oliver Felt, April 13, 1815 ; she d. Dec. 24, 1861, æ. 69 yrs.   He m., 2d w., Mrs. Elizabeth F. Gray, April 2, 1863.   Since his last marriage he has resided permanently in town.

---

46 | *Harriet*, b. Dec. 24, 1815 ; m. Horatio N. Porter ; 2d hus., John Bullard.

47 | †*Samuel*, b. May 19, 1818 ; m. Nancy Vose ; r. Antrim.

48 | *Mary*, b. July 10, 1820 ; m. Samuel Jaquith ; ch., (1) Emma J., b. Sept. 17, 1845 ; (2) Ella S., b. Feb. 13, 1856 ; d. at Wilton, May 29, 1864, æ. 8 yrs ; r. Vineland, N. J.

49 | †*Marshall*, b. April 2, 1823 ; m. Sarah Wells.

50 | *Sarah*, b. June 20, 1827 ; m. Samuel I. Vose ; d. Oct. 25, 1875, æ. 48 yrs., 4 mos.

51 | *Henry H.*, b. Sept. 4, 1832 ; m. Mary J. Shedd ; d. Aug. 23, 1858, æ. 26 yrs.   She d. March 6, 1867, æ. 28 yrs.

12– 40 | JAMES NAY.   He m. Jane Farnsworth, of Dublin, b. March 10, 1800.   She d. March 9, 1871, æ. 71 yrs.   He d. July 7, 1867, æ. 68 yrs.

---

52 | *George W.*, b. April 6, 1830 ; m. Mary E. Cromwell ; r. Rochester, N. Y.

53 | *Matilda*, b. April 13, 1832 ; m. Samuel Adams, Jr., April 21, 1853.

54 | †*James M.*, b. Dec. 25, 1833; m., 1st w., Helen Morrison; 2d w., Sarah Vose.
55 | *Esther M.*, b. Nov. 27, 1835; d. Aug. 2, 1846, æ. 11 yrs.
56 | *William A.*, b. Dec. 7, 1838; m. Emily F. Dinsmore, Sept. 26, 1859; r. Rochester, N. Y.; ch., (1) Maurice A.; (2) Frank A.
57 | *Fidelia E.*, b. Dec. 9, 1840; d. Aug. 10, 1872, æ. 32 yrs.
58 | *Helen M.*, b. June 2, 1843; m. Frank F. Young, June 2, 1873.

12– 41 | GEORGE NAY. He occupies the farm north of the Charles Stuart or Faxon place, known as the Asahel Going farm. He m. Mary Persons, dau. Bartholomew Persons.

59 | *Maria H.*, b. March 19, 1833; m. Mason H. Balch; r. Francestown.
60 | *Melora E.*, b. Feb. 17, 1835; m. Josiah C. Nay; d. May 8, 1869, æ. 34 yrs., 2 mos.; one ch., Edson O., b. Dec. 26, 1855.
61 | †*John Oscar*, b. Jan. 30, 1837; m. Carrie E. McCoy, May 2, 1861.
• 62 | *Sarah J.*, b. Sept. 2, 1842; m. Orrin J. Balch; r. Goffstown; three ch.

12– 45 | B. ALLEN NAY. He m. Syrena Chandler, March 6, 1832. He d. Feb. 22, 1839, æ. 39 yrs. She m., 2d hus., William Puffer.

63 | *Fidelia*, b. Sept. 30, 1833; d. Sept 30, 1834, æ. 1 yr.
64 | *Mary E.*, b. Feb. 26, 1835; m. Joseph Perkins; d., Wisconsin, January, 1871, æ. 36 yrs.
65 | *Syrena J.*, b. April 5, 1838; d. July 10, 1840, æ. 2 yrs.

30– 47 | SAMUEL NAY, Jr., m., May 13, 1845, Nancy B. Vose, of Antrim; b. April 12, 1828; lived in Antrim many years, then re. to Peterborough; returned to Antrim, 1873, where he now lives.

66 | *Fred. L.*, b. Sept. 5, 1848; m., Jan. 13, 1870, Maggy Palfrey, of Weare, b. Jan. 4, 1850; one ch., Harry E., b. Aug. 6, 1872.
67 | *Charles P.*, b. Sept. 3, 1853.
68 | *Morris E.*, b. May 7, 1864.
69 | *Samuel V.*, b. April 6, 1866; d. Aug. 20, 1872, æ. 6 yrs. The first child b. in Sharon, the other three in Antrim.

30– 49 | MARSHALL NAY. He m., Nov. 10, 1853, Sarah J. Wells; b. May 23, 1834. He keeps a hat, cap, and clothing store in the village.

70 | *Dora A.*, b. Dec. 16, 1854 ; d. October, 1873, æ. 19 yrs.
71 | *Delia W.*, b. Sept. 8, 1856.
72 | *Henry M.*, b. Dec. 20, 1860.
73 | *Clifford W.*, b. July 17, 1875.

40- 54 | JAMES M. NAY. He is a paper manufacturer, and under the firm of Adams & Nay, owning and carrying on the business in the paper-mill of the late A. P. Morrison. He m., 1st w., Helen Morrison, Nov. 18, 1856. She d. Dec. 23, 1865, æ. 27 yrs. ; m., 2d w., Sarah Vose, Oct. 28, 1867 ; 1st w., one ch. ; 2d w., one ch.

74 | *Mabel*, b. June 22, 1864.
75 | *Hattie M.*, b. March 30, 1872.

41- 61 | JOHN OSCAR NAY m., May 2, 1861, Carrie E. McCoy, b. Aug. 6, 1843. He r. on the homestead.

76 | *George S.*, b. Jan. 21, 1864.

THE NELSON FAMILY.

1 | HORATIO NELSON, son of Paul Nelson, of Dublin, came to town with his parents, who moved here when he was quite young. He was b. March 4, 1816. He is a house-painter. He m. Harriet Gray, dau. of William and Harriet Scott Gray.

2 | *Clarissa*, b. May 23, 1839 ; d. June 5, 1839, æ. 12 dys.
3 | *Mary E.*, b. March 4, 1841 ; m. George J. Munroe, Nov. 24, 1859.
4 | *Louisa H.*, b. March 12, 1843 ; m. Henry B. Dyer, April 15, 1869 ; r. Fitchburg.
5 | *Sarah P.*, b. Dec. 6, 1845 ; m. Edwin M. Brooks, Jan. 15, 1871 ; r. in Bedford.
6 | *Clementine*, b. Feb. 13, 1847 ; d. March 13, 1847, æ. 1 mo.
7 | *Myra M.*, b. Sept. 13, 1848 ; m. Henry A. Bacon, June 23, 1867 ; r. in Bedford, Mass.
8 | *David F.*, b. June 3, 1851.
9 | *Delia M.*, b. Aug. 19, 1853.
10 | *Ida J.*, b. July 27, 1855.
11 | *Charlie P.*, b. April 12, 1858.

THE OSGOOD FAMILY.

1 | KENDALL OSGOOD (Dr.), the son of Isaac and Betsey Flint Osgood, re. to Peterborough, from Atkinson, in 1788, and bought land just east of John Scott's farm, where he continued to live till his death, Aug. 19, 1801, æ. 45 yrs. He was born in Andover, Mass., in 1757. It was in the door of his father's house that the celebrat-

ed James Otis was struck dead with lightning. Of Dr. Osgood's early or professional education, little is known. Soon after acquiring his profession, he went out as a surgeon, in a privateer, during the last part of the Revolutionary war, by which he acquired considerable wealth. The first we know of him, he was settled as a physician at Atkinson, in 1785, at which place he remained till 1788, when he re. to Peterborough. We have no means of ascertaining whether he did much business then or not, but, by his removing so soon, presume he was not successful. During his residence at Atkinson he was among nineteen of the leading physicians of the State of New Hampshire, who petitioned the Legislature for the charter of the New Hampshire Medical Society, which was granted Feb. 11, 1791. This society is now in successful operation, having attained its eighty-fifth year, and I trust has been of great benefit to the profession in the State. Its annual meeting is held in June of every year at Concord. There is generally an attendance of sixty to eighty physicians from all parts of the State.

When Dr. Osgood first came to Peterborough he seems to have made no very favorable impression on the good people of the town. He was exquisitely clothed in the gorgeous and imposing style of the times, and contrasted strangely with the people clad in the coarse, home-spun materials of their own raising and manufacture. He was dressed in a red broadcloth coat, buff vest, and buckskin breeches, with silver knee-buckles, silk stockings, a wig, and a cocked hat, — a sight unusual, indeed, to our fathers. They had no respect for anything of the kind. They were a bold, independent, and somewhat impudent race, and without any hesitation, clothed in their plainest attire, they would have put themselves upon an equality, and addressed without the slightest embarrassment, the greatest personage of the land. The red broadcloth coat and cocked hat inspired no respect among this shrewd, outspoken people, who regarded the exterior as merely the shell of the man. I have no doubt they scanned him well. There was on the stage at this time in Peterborough an exceedingly shrewd and talented race of men, who were never slow to strip off all the disguises thrown round any one, friend or foe, and show up the *bona fide* man. The doctor did not bear this scrutiny well, for he soon gave up all pretensions to practice, and spent the remainder of his life in agriculture and the management of his own affairs. I have no means of judging of his professional acquirements, but

28

suppose they were respectable. Unless he had possessed considerable merit as a physician, it is not at all probable that his name would have been associated with some of the most eminent medical men in New Hampshire, in petitioning the Legislature for a charter for the New Hampshire Medical Society. He was m. to Louisa Peabody, of Boxford, Mass. They had two ch. Isaac P. Osgood, b. Feb. 20, 1793, became a lawyer, and till within a few years his sign was seen in Court Street, Boston, where he practised his profession all his life. He died within a few years, and in his will he remembered the place of his birth by a donation of a thousand dollars, the interest of which was to be annually distributed to the worthy poor of the town. The town accepted his gift, and have endeavored to comply with the requisites of the donation, in making such an annual distribution of the interest as they thought best.

2 *Isaac Peabody,*[*] b. in Peterborough, Feb. 20, 1793.

"Isaac Peabody and his sister Elizabeth, after the death of their father, went to live at Andover with their uncle Jacob, who was appointed their guardian by their father in his will; one item in his will was, that his son should work on the farm a certain length of time, and then fit for college. He fitted for college with Rev. Mr. Coggswell, of Tewksbury, and at Phillips Academy, Andover. He graduated at Harvard College, in the class of 1814. Among his classmates were some of the most distinguished men of New England. He studied law at the Harvard Law School, and also with Judge Fay, of Cambridge. He opened an office in Boston, No. 90 Court Street, about 1819, where he remained until 1827, when he took the office No. 5 Court Street, where he continued the remainder of his life. He was an excellent office-lawyer, considered a thoroughly upright practitioner, never a pleader, but good in examining witnesses and looking up cases. Like all his race, he married late in life. Aug. 3, 1841, he married Mrs. Mary Ann Valentine, widow of Lawson Valentine, of Boston. Mr. Osgood resided in Boston until 1846, when he removed to Roxbury, continuing his office in Court Street, going in at 8 A.M., returning at 2 P.M., as regular as the sun, unless sickness prevented, up to within three days of his death. In 1847, he accidentally discovered that he had lost the sight of one of his eyes; he was examined by an oculist, who found a cataract wholly formed on the blind eye, and one just

[*] Letter of Mrs. Frances E. Weston, Putnam Street, Boston Highlands, to which we are indebted for this interesting account of the family of Dr. Osgood.

beginning to form on the other. He submitted to an operation for the cataract on the first eye, which was an entire success, but never had nerve enough to have the other operated on.

"He was very methodical in his habits, so much so that one could always tell the time of day by his movements. He always went in and came out of town at just such a moment; did just such things after entering the house; walked so many times around Dr. Putnam's church grounds at a certain hour in the afternoon, unless prevented by severe storm or illness; went to bed at a certain hour; rose in the morning at such a moment, etc. Every article he used must be in the precise spot, and not moved; and so he continued to the day of his death. Perhaps this methodical system prolonged his life.

"He always had a dread of consumption, the disease of which his mother and sister died; and yet for ten years before his death he was in consumption, but never thought that was the case with him. After the trouble with his eyes, he gave up active practice, merely retaining a few of his oldest clients. On Wednesday, the 9th of January, he came home as well as he had been all winter, was taken suddenly ill in the night, and died on Saturday, the 12th of January, 1867, æ. 73 yrs., 10 mos. He never appeared to have his senses, from the moment he was taken until he ceased to breathe.

"By his will, he provided a resting-place for his remains at Mount Auburn, a monument to his memory, and a fund to be applied to keep the whole in order during all time. Perhaps the reminiscence of not having provided gravestones for his parents before their graves had been forgotten entirely was the cause of his being so particular about his own. I know that he went twice to Peterborough to ascertain where his parents were buried, in order to place stones to their memory, but both times he failed, and it may be that the bequest to the town of Peterborough was as much to perpetuate the name of his father as his own, on the town records, and in the memory of the town's people. Mrs. Osgood survived her husband, and now resides in Putnam Street, Boston Highlands, in a ripe and vigorous old age."

3 *Elizabeth*, b. Peterborough, March 20, 1796. She d. at Andover, in autumn of 1821, æ. 25 yrs.

"She left Peterborough when about five years of age, and ever after resided in Andover. She was said to have been a very beautiful and attractive girl, beside possessing a large fortune for that period. She became engaged to Robert Means, a lawyer of Boston, brother to Mrs. Amos Lawrence, and uncle to President Franklin Pierce's wife. All the preparations were made for her marriage, which was soon to take place, when she took a severe cold, and died of a rapid consumption in less than six weeks. She divided her property between her brother and lover, after paying out certain small legacies to her cousins and friends."

1

THE PARKER FAMILY.

ABEL PARKER, son of John and Mary Parker. He lived in the east part of the town, on land that is embraced in the farm of the late Capt. Samuel McCoy. He m. Sarah Parker, b. 1735, and d. April 16, 1817, æ. 82 yrs., 10 mos. He d. April 29, 1791, æ. 67 yrs. He was an early settler, but we cannot fix the time. In Revolutionary service, from July 7 to Oct. 21, 1780.

2   *Abiel*, b. ——.
3   † *Gideon*, b. —— ; m. Abigail Matthews.
4   *Timothy*, b. ——.
5   *Sewall*, b. —— ; d. Nov. 2, 1834, æ. 70 yrs.
6   *Sarah*, b. —— ; unm.   (7) *Sybel*, b. —— ; unm.
8   *Abigail*, b. ——.   (9) *Hannah*, b. ——.

1– 3   GIDEON PARKER m. Abigail Matthews. He began the farm, in 1787, where Dea. Timothy Holt lived. He was a carpenter by trade.

10   *John*, b. —— ; d. young.
11   † *James*, b. Feb. 29, 1791 ; m. Sarah White.
12   *Gideon*, b. April 1, 1793 ; d. April 22, 1821, æ. 28 yrs.

3– 11   JAMES PARKER. He m. Sarah White, dau. of David White, Nov. 6, 1817. He d. Dec. 9, 1826, æ. 35 yrs. A carpenter by trade. She d. November, 1875, æ. 82 yrs., 8 mos.

13   † *John Gideon*, b. July 2, 1818 ; m. Isabel E. Hurd, of Lempster.
14   † *James*, b. June 13, 1820 ; m. Eliza Watson, Nov. 16, 1848.
15   *Eliza*, b. April 24, 1822 ; unm. ; d. Aug. 31, 1838, æ. 16 yrs.
16   *Mary Jane*, b. Nov. 15, 1824 ; unm. ; d. Dec. 28, 1871, æ. 47 yrs.

11– 13   JOHN GIDEON PARKER, M.D. He m. Isabel E. Hurd, of Lempster, May 17, 1853. Dr. Parker was a very worthy and useful man. He graduated at Norwich University, Vt., 1847, with honor, and subsequently, in connection with much school-teaching, he studied the medical profession with Albert Smith, M.D., of Peterborough; attended medical lectures at Woodstock and Dartmouth schools, and took his medical degree at the latter in 1852. He first commenced his practice at Dublin, Aug. 12, 1852, and remained here till 1865, when he re. to Warner, where, after long suffering, he d. of a cancerous affection of his bowels, Sept. 12, 1869, æ. 51 yrs. He sustained a high reputation for skill and knowledge in the profession.

17 | *James Frederick*, b. April, 1854.

11– 14 | JAMES PARKER. He m. Eliza Watson, Nov. 16, 1848. She d. Aug. 31, 1861. He d. March 20, 1868, æ. 47 yrs. He r. in Lowell when he d.

18 | *Sarah Jane*, b. Aug. 23, 1850.
19 | *Frank*, b. Feb. 27, 1854.

THE PAYSON FAMILY.

1 | THOMAS PAYSON was b. in Boston, Oct. 28, 1764. He was fitted for college in Andover, and graduated at Cambridge in 1784, and immediately entered upon an engagement as preceptor of Leicester Academy. While here, he studied theology, and was licensed to preach, but only preached occasionally, choosing rather to devote himself to other pursuits. Leaving Leicester, he removed to Worcester, where he was employed two years in teaching, and afterwards, for several years, he was engaged in trade in that place. From Worcester he removed to Charlestown, where, in 1797, he again resumed the business of teaching, as preceptor of Russel Academy. He relinquished this business, however, and from 1801 to 1809 was in trade again, when he was appointed master of the Franklin Grammar School, Boston, which place he held fourteen years. In 1827, he removed to Peterborough, where he resided till his death, April 20, 1844, æ. 79 yrs., 5 mos.

"He was a man of liberal sentiments, kindly feelings, and ready sympathies. Being a good scholar, with a taste and tact for instruction, he could hardly fail to be a successful and acceptable instructor. He had, too, a frown and a manner that awed the disorderly or disobedient, as well as a cheerful look of encouragement and sunny smile that won the favor and affection of the young, and qualified him for what he so long was — a teacher."

He was much respected in the town of his adoption by all classes of the people. He never seemed to grow old. He was always fresh and lively in his feeling as ever in his life. He made himself eminently useful in town, by the attention and aid given to the common schools, and his assistance in sustaining all lyceums and other means of advancing and improving the young. He retained his mental powers in a remarkable degree to the last. He m., 1784, Mary Thatcher, of Cambridge. She d. Aug. 28, 1805, æ. ——; m., 2d w., Sarah Hennessey, of Sharon. She d. April 25, 1844, æ. 59 yrs.; 1st w., six ch.; 2d w., eight ch.

---

2   *Mary Phillips*, b. Feb. 21, 1786. After a thorough education, she devoted herself to teaching for life. She taught for a few years in Portsmouth, and, in 1817, went to Nashville, Tenn., where she was associate-principal of the Nashville Female Academy for eight years. Her health failing, she gave up her occupation, and came to Peterborough to reside. In many of her last years, she was affected with a partial insanity, and d. after a long illness, March 26, 1867, æ. 81 yrs.

3   *Caroline P.*, b. Aug. 1, 1791; d. in infancy.

4   *Caroline Eliza*, b. April 19, 1793; m., 1815, John Wheelright, a merchant in Alexandria, D.C. She became insane a few months after her marriage, and d. at the Insane Asylum in Charlestown, July 22, 1827, æ. 34 yrs.

5   *Catharine Putnam*, b. March 24, 1795; d. of consumption, 1814, æ. 19 yrs.

6   *Thomas Russel*, b. Aug. 8, 1798. Went into mercantile business in New Orleans. He lost his health from the effects of the climate, and d. on a visit to Boston, July 21, 1829, æ. 30 yrs., 10 mos.

7   *John Phillips*, b. Oct. 13, 1800. He was in mercantile business in New Orleans, in partnership with his brother, and was drowned about three months after the death of his brother, by the upsetting of a sail-boat, in which he and others had gone out upon the river. He d. 1829, æ. 29 yrs. He left a widow, the dau. of James Hall, of Boston.

8   *George Alfred*, b. Oct. 14, 1809. After fitting for Harvard College, he served an apprenticeship with David L. Mayo, with whom he continued many years. After Mr. Mayo's failure in business, he became a clerk of

Almy, Patterson & Co.; m. Anne Rowe, of Milton, Mass. Left one dau., Ann Rowe. He d. at Milton, June 19, 1874, æ. 64 yrs., 8 mos.

9   *Louisa Clifford*, b. July 10, 1811. She was educated for a teacher, and taught for a year or two in Andover, Mass. She m. Rev. M. E. White, of Ashfield, Mass., May 3, 1832, and d. 1842, æ. 31 yrs.; two ch., Catharine P. and John Phillips Payson, who is now a practising physician in New York City.

10   *Henry P.*, b. May 4, 1815; d. in infancy.

11   *Anne Catharine*, b. Nov. 23, 1817; r. Peterborough.

12   *Charles H.*, b. March 28, 1819; became a machinist. Is now a farmer, and resides in Loudon; m. Mrs. Sarah Bennet; ch., (1) Henrietta; (2) Mary P.; (3) Thomas R.; (4) John P.; (5) Charles H.

13   *Sarah Hennessey*, b. Dec. 25, 1821; d. in infancy.

14   *Joseph Rowe*, b. Nov. 26, 1823. He has been secretary to various insurance companies in Cincinnati and Chicago. He now resides in Chicago. He m. Henrietta Robbins; ch. (1) Charles P.; (2) William B.; (3) Edward E.; (4) Edith; (5) Joseph R.; (6) George A.

15   *Sarah Elizabeth*, b. June 1, 1826; d. in Milton, Mass., March 26, 1867, æ. 41 yrs. She d. on the same day as her sister Mary.

THE PEABODY FAMILY.

1   EBENEZER PEABODY, son of Ebenezer Peabody, of Boxford, Mass., was b. Feb. 13, 1767, and in early life went to Gorham, Me., and here m., March 2, 1792, Sarah Lewis, b. Jan. 13, 1766, dau. George Lewis, and re. to Peterborough about 1802. They lived on the farm of Dr. Kendall Osgood, now occupied by Thomas Little, till his death, July 26, 1816, æ. 49 yrs., 5 mos. She d., Sept. 12, 1849, at Franklin, where she re. in 1817, æ. 83 yrs.

---

2   *Kendall Osgood*, b. in Gorham, Me., Dec. 20, 1792; m., 1st w., 1821, Alice Blanchard, of Franklin; d. 1832; m., 2d w., 1833, Betsey Austin; she d. Dec. 19, 1869. He d. Jan. 23, 1855, æ. 62 yrs. Only one ch. survives, Sarah, w. of Moses B. Goodwin, of Franklin. Mr. Peabody spent most of his life in Franklin, after his boyhood, and was a successful and enterprising business man. He was at one time extensively engaged in the baking business, and subsequently in the manufacture of paper, at Franklin. He always sustained a good character for honesty and integrity, and was esteemed a useful and valuable man.

3   *Ebenezer*, b. Gorham, Sept. 3, 1794; m. Rebecca Robertson, of Franklin. He d. 1847, æ. 53 yrs. Three ch. living; r. Franklin. Was a blacksmith.

4   *Louise*, b. Gorham, Aug. 10, 1796; m. Charles M. Davis, Sept. 4, 1822; d. April 5, 1858, æ. 61 yrs., 7 mos.

5   *Caroline*, b. Gorham, July 9, 1798; m. Dexter Baldwin, May 27, 1824; she d. in Mount Vernon, Me., July 6, 1827, æ. 28 yrs., 11 mos. One son survives, George D. Baldwin, who is in business in Boston.

6   *William Henry*, b. Gorham, Jan. 20, 1801; m., Sept. 9, 1828, Hannah March, b. Dec. 9, 1804; now living in Cincinnati, O. After acquiring a good academic education, he studied the medical profession at Hanover, and took his medical degree at Dartmouth College in 1826. He established himself as a physician at Gorham, Me., and continued in practice sixteen years, till his death, March 2, 1843, æ. 42 yrs. They had seven ch., three only surviving, *viz.:* Caroline B., wife of Orland Smith, of Cincinnati, William Wirt, Superintendent of the Marietta & Cincinnati Railroad, and Sargeant Prentiss, of Cincinnati. Dr. Peabody was esteemed a skilful practitioner of medicine, and had few superiors among the medical fraternity where he was located. He was ardently devoted to his calling, and carefully kept pace with all its progress and advance by an assiduous culture. He united the character of the Christian with the physician, and was in the truest sense a Christian gentleman. His early death was a great loss to his friends and numerous patrons.

7   *James L.*, b. July 25, 1803; m., Dec. 22, 1831, Sarah J. Blake, of Chichester. Mr. Peabody was a long time in partnership with his brother, K. O. Peabody, both in the bakery and the paper-manufacture, and was considered a very efficient business man. Only one child survives, James, who now r. Chicago. He d. Aug. 7, 1866, æ. 63 yrs.; r. Franklin.

8   *Betsey K.*, b. May 5, 1805; m., Dec. 25, 1827, Ebenezer Robinson, Portland, Me. She d. April 8, 1832, æ. 26 yrs., 11 mos. One son survives, Charles D. Robinson.

9   *Sarah Lewis*, b. March 29, 1807; m., Aug. 30, 1832, Ira Greeley; r. Franklin; five ch; only two living.

THE PENNIMAN FAMILY.

1   ELIHU PENNIMAN. His wife's name is not known. He lived on the David Blanchard place, having bought it after James McKean, who began the same.

2 | *Adam,* b. 1779; m., Feb. 26, 1801, Phebe Gray. He d. April 21, 1860, æ. 81 yrs. She d. Jan. 21, 1863, æ. 84 yrs.; three ch.; d. in infancy.

3 | *Ruth,* b. ——; m. —— Potter.

4 | *Sarah,* b. ——; unm.; d.

5 | *Betsey,* b. ——; unm.; d. in Fitzwilliam.

6 | *Susan,* b. ——; m. —— Damon.

7 | *Elihu,* b. ——; m., March 10, 1808, Sarah Thayer, dau. of Dea. Christopher Thayer.

8 | *William,* b. Aug. 5, 1793; d. December, 1872, æ. 79 yrs., 4 mos.

The following is from the *Pioneer History of Orleans County, N. Y.:* "Judge Penniman was b. in Peterborough, Hillsborough County, N. H., Aug. 5, 1793. After obtaining a good common school education in his native State, he emigrated to Ontario County, N. Y., in September, 1816, and from thence to Shelby, Ontario County, in October, 1820. He took up land in that town, on which he resided eight years; he then removed to Albion, remaining there more than two years. Finally settled on a farm in Barre, near Eagle Harbor, where he has ever since resided.

"In 1825, Mr. Penniman was appointed Judge of the Court of Common Pleas for Orleans County, then lately organized, and one of the first bench judges which composed that court, which office he held five years. In 1831, he was elected justice of the peace, of Barre, and served in that office until he removed to Eagle Harbor, when he resigned. In 1846, he represented Orleans County as a member of the convention to revise the Constitution of the State of New York.

"Judge Penniman was a celebrated school-teacher for many years after he came to Orleans County, having taught school fourteen winters and seven summers. He always took a lively interest in the subject of common schools, was commissioner and town inspector each of the eight years he resided in Shelby, and served as town superintendent of schools in Barre three years, while that system was the law.

"He was a popular justice of the peace. As a judge he was firm, upright and impartial, aiming to sustain the right in his decisions, and in all his official and social relations he sustained a character marked for sound views of men and things — honest, faithful, sagacious, and true, — and now in his old age and retirement enjoys the respect of all who knew him."

THE PIERCE FAMILY.

1   STEPHEN PIERCE was b. in New Ipswich in 1770, and d. in Peterborough, April 21, 1850, æ. 80 yrs. He m. Hannah Gordon, dau. Samuel Gordon, May 12, 1801. She d. in Hancock, March 15, 1811, æ. 39 yrs.; m., 2d w., Mrs. Sally Walker, May 20, 1815. She d. March 14, 1864, æ. 73 yrs. After his second marriage he re. from Hancock, in 1816, to Peterborough, and bought the John Jewett place ; 1st w., seven ch. ; 2d w., seven ch.

---

2   *Franklin*, b. 1801 ; d. in Florida, about 1828.
3   *Stephen*, b. Feb. 23, 1803 ; d. Jan. 6, 1804, æ. 1 yr.
4   *Samuel G.*, b. Oct. 6, 1804 ; m. Mary Brackett ; r. Belfast, Me.
5   *Stephen*, b. Aug. 4, 1806 ; d. Feb. 20, 1807, æ. 6 mos.
6   *Ellen*, b. Jan. 13, 1808 ; m. Elisha Gledden ; re. Maine.
7   *Hannah*,   m. Charles Moore ; r. Belfast.
          } b. March 11, 1811 ;
8   †*Joseph B.*,   m., March 31, 1842, Lucinda J. White.
9   *Sarah*, b. Nov. 17, 1817 ; m. George Davis ; d. May 13, 1842, æ. 24 yrs., 6 mos.
10   *Lucinda*, b. Nov. 2, 1819 ; m. Amaziah Fairbanks ; d. Aug. 17, 1841, æ. 21 yrs., 9 mos.
11   *Mary W.*, b. Aug. 20, 1821 ; m. Samuel Bowker, Keene ; d. Sept. 6, 1863, æ. 42 yrs.
12   *Cyrus*, b. May 14, 1823 ; re. Canada.
13   *Wesley*, b. May 17, 1825 ; r. Massachusetts.
14   *Elbridge*, b. Aug. 13, 1827 ; m. Henrietta Reed ; r. Keene.
15   *Persina*, b. June 23, 1830 ; d. Aug. 29, 1831, æ. 14 mos.

1- 8   JOSEPH B. PIERCE now owns and occupies the John Jewett farm, having recently erected a new house on the same. He m., March 31, 1842, Lucinda J. White, dau. Wm. L. White.

---

16   *Sarah J.*, b. June 22, 1843 ; m. Walter J. Haywood, July 5, 1866.
17   *Charles S.*, b. March 29, 1845 ; m., January, 1873, Julia C. Campbell, Putney, Vt.
18   *Frank Gordon*, b. May 4, 1854.

THE PORTER FAMILY.

1   JAMES PORTER, the son of Benjamin and Eunice Nourse Porter, of Danvers, Mass., came to town about 1776. His eldest child was b. in town in 1777. He

was a tailor by trade, and for a time he lived at the Morrison House, near the old meeting-house, and then re. to the Street Road near to Hunt's Corner. He was a well-informed and quiet man. He was a great reader, and patron of all the libraries. He followed his trade in town. He m. Hannah Curtis, b. November, 1748, and d. Nov. 4, 1805, æ. 57 yrs. He was b. Jan. 13, 1755; d. Dec. 2, 1843, æ. 88 yrs.

---

2   *Peter*, b. Dec. 5, 1777; d. March 2, 1802, æ. 25 yrs.
3   *Hannah*, b. Feb. 9, 1779; m. James Cuningham.
4   *Zaccheus*, b. Oct. 25, 1780; m. Rachel Cuningham; r. Belfast, Me., and d. there, November, 1824, æ. 44 yrs. He was a lawyer in good standing.
5   *Sally*, b. Oct. 28, 1782; m. Asa Gibbs.
6   *James*, b. June 18, 1785. A graduate of Williams College, 1810. Studied divinity in Belfast. Was settled as minister in Pomfret, Conn., and continued in that relation for twenty-five yrs.; he d. June, 1856, æ. 71 yrs.
7   *Nancy Curtis*, b. April 7, 1787; m. Abel Gibbs; 2d hus., Samuel Maynard.
8   *Roxanna*, b. Aug. 18, 1792; unm.; d. June, 1874, æ. 82 yrs.

---

1   HORATIO N. PORTER, a race distinct from the above, was b. March 8, 1811; m. Harriet Nay, dau. of Maj. Samuel Nay, of Sharon, March 31, 1835. He d. Sept. 9, 1852, æ. 41 yrs. He was engaged in staging and carrying the United States mail for some years, up to the time of his death.

---

2   †*Samuel Nay*, b. March 7, 1837; m. Jane H. Steele, March 20, 1861.

1- 2   SAMUEL N. PORTER. He m. Jane H. Steele, dau. of Edwin Steele, March 20, 1861. He is a dentist, and took the degree of D.D.S., conferred by the Dental College at Philadelphia, and now practises his profession in town. Chosen town clerk in 1869; town treasurer, 1873, '74, '75, '76.

---

3   *Frank Irving*, b. Dec. 12, 1861; d. Aug. 8, 1862, æ. 8 mos.
4   *Fred Howard*, b. Sept. 29, 1864.

THE POWERS FAMILY.

1   Of WILLIAM POWERS we know very little, only that he came to town quite early and bought his place, being a

part of Capt. Thomas Morison's mill-farm, on which he built a house and erected clothing-works, and lived here, doing more or less work at his trade for twenty-five years. But he became very poor, and gave up his farm to the town for his support, which was sold to T. K. Ames, in 1815, and afterwards by him to Franklin Mears. Of his family we know little or nothing; no one living remembers anything of them; they must have left town early in the century. Mr. Powers was a clothier by trade, and the first in town. We do not know whether he died here or not, nor when. It is a family entirely distinct from the one which follows.

1   WHITCOMB POWERS was b. in Hollis, April 17, 1756, and d. in Peterborough, Nov. 19, 1826, æ. 70 yrs., 7 mos. He m., 1st w., Feb. 24, 1780, Keziah Loring, b. in Lexington, April 19, 1761. All the ch. by first w. d. young. She d. March 16, 1790, æ. 28 yrs., 10 mos.; m., 2d w., April 21, 1791, Miriam Bond, Dublin, b. July 6, 1768; d. Dec. 20, 1839, æ. 71 yrs., 5 mos.

2   *Polly*, b. July 6, 1792; d. Oct. 15, 1792, æ. 9 mos.
3   *Polly D.*, b. Jaffrey, June 29, 1793; m. Riley Goodridge, Nov. 8, 1830.
4   *Miriam B.*, b. Nov. 17, 1795; m. Collins H. Jaquith, Sept. 17, 1816; ch., (1) Ziba C.; (2) Mary O.; (3) Edwin F.; (4) Jonas H.; (5) Elbridge A.; (6) Amelia M.; (7) Sarah M.; (8) Alfred; (9) Frederick P.; (10) Addison B.; (11) Sanford A.; r. Keene; now Oakfield, N. J.
5   *Nabby*, b. May 22, 1798; d. Nov. 9, 1800, æ. 2 yrs., 5 mos.
6   *Betsey M.*, b. June 21, 1800; m. Charles M. Howe, Dec. 11, 1823.
7   *Mehitable B.*, b. Sept. 2, 1802; unm.; d. Nov. 25, 1873, æ. 71 yrs.
8   *Lydia A.*, b. April 28, 1805; m. Hugh Smith, September, 1837; he d. 1843; m., 2d hus., James Williams, October, 1855.
9   *Francis W. G.*, b. June 27, 1808; m. Elizabeth Hunt, Oct. 22, 1855; d. May 30, 1871, æ. 63 yrs. She d. May 23, 1870, æ. 52 yrs.
10   *William M.*, b. July 23, 1811; m. Mary Clark, Sept. 10, 1838; r. Council Bluffs, Ia.
11   *Stephen F.*, b. July 11, 1814; d. April 20, 1815, æ. 9 mos.

THE PRENTICE FAMILY.

1   NATHANIEL PRENTICE, a clothier by trade, was the son of William H. and Sarah Edes Prentice, b. Dec. 15,

1755, in Boston. He re. to New Ipswich in 1778, and commenced his business there; was the first clothier in town. He m. Anna, dau. of Benjamin Hoar, the third settler in New Ipswich, b. Feb. 25, 1760. He d. in Peterborough, March 15, 1825, æ. 70 yrs. She d. in Peterborough, Nov. 8, 1824, æ. 64 yrs. He came to town early in the century, and carried on the clothing business in Samuel Smith's shop.

2   *William H.*, b. New Ipswich, Jan. 22, 1781; m. Sally Whipple; r. Boston.

3   *Nancy*, b. New Ipswich, Feb. 22, 1783; m. Isaac Packard, Stoughton, Mass.

4   *Polly*, b. New Ipswich, May 12, 1785; m. Aaron Salter, paper-maker; ch., (1) William; (2) Sarah Jane; (3) Mary Ann; d. May 26, 1826, æ. 41 yrs.

5   *Nathaniel*, b. April 2, 1787.

6   *Alfred*, b. Sept. 2, 1789; d. Jan. 18, 1790.

7   *John*, b. Feb. 18, 1791; d. Nov. 21, 1802, æ. 11 yrs.

8   *Alfred*, b. May 5, 1793.

9   *Patty*, b. Sept. 27, 1795; d. April 15, 1838, æ. 43 yrs.

10   *Sumner*, b. April 28, 1798; d. Sept. 18, 1843, æ. 45 yrs.

11   *Lona*, b. Sept. 18, 1800; m. James Perham, March 6, 1825; re. to Indianapolis, Ind., 1834. She d. June 18, 1846, æ. 46 yrs. He d. 1862. He left a large family. All settled in the West.

12   *Lucy*, b. June 20, 1803; d. August, 1806, æ. 3 yrs.

THE PRIEST FAMILY.

1   JABEZ B. PRIEST (Dr.) came to town as a practitioner of medicine, in 1816, and continued in the same till his death, Aug. 17, 1826, by the epidemic dysentery of that year; æ. 36 yrs. He attained a large business, and was quite successful as a physician. He m. Fanny Moore, dau. of John Moore, April 4, 1820.

2   *Charles B.*, b. Jan. 25, 1821; d. Aug. 29, 1826, æ. 5 yrs.

3   *John M.*, b. April 26, 1825; d. Aug. 22, 1826, æ. 1 yr., 3 mos.

THE PUFFER FAMILY.

1   ELIJAH PUFFER was b. in Norton, Mass., Aug. 18, 1738, and d. at Peterborough, Feb. 28, 1816, æ. 78 yrs. He m., May 20, 1764, Elizabeth Jackson, b. in Abington, Mass., June 19, 1744; d. in Peterborough, April 7, 1822, æ. 78 yrs. They probably came to Peterborough ·

soon after their·marriage in 1764. They first lived on a place north of Gen. David Steele's. In 1786, he exchanged this farm for the farm now occupied by the family, in the north-west part of the town. Elijah Puffer was one of a family of twelve children. He was out in the French war, and at one time was stationed at Fort Cumberland.

———

2   *Matilda*, b. Jan. 26, 1765 ; d. Feb. 28, 1771, æ. 6 yrs.
3   *Polly*, b. Aug. 25, 1766 ; d. Nov. 30, 1790, æ. 24 yrs.
4   *Betsey*, b. Aug. 11, 1768 ; m. John Nay.
5   *Esther*, b. Dec. 18, 1770 ; d. Feb. 27, 1801, æ. 31 yrs.
6   *Elijah*, b. Feb. 25, 1773 ; d. July 29, 1777, æ. 4 yrs., 6 mos.
7   *Samuel*, b. Jan. 13, 1777 ; d. ; æ. 12 dys.
8   *Matilda*, b. April 3, 1778 ; d. ; æ. 14 dys.
9   *Elijah*, b. July 16, 1779 ; m., March 29, 1802, Betsey Wares ; r. Colchester, Vt., and d. there.
10   †*William*, b. April 15, 1781 ; m., 1st w., Nancy Howe ; 2d w., Mrs. Syrena C. Nay.
11   *Sally*, b. Jan. 10, 1783 ; unm. ; d. November, 1868, æ. 85 yrs.
12   *John*, b. Nov. 3, 1786 ; d. May 1, 1787, æ. 6 mos.
13   *John*, b. March 13, 1791 ; m., April 9, 1818, Susan Moors ; d., February, 1862, at Indiana ; ch., (1) John ; (2) Susan.

———

1– 10   WILLIAM PUFFER. He succeeded his father on the homestead. He m., 1st w., Nancy Howe, dau. Samuel Howe, Dec. 29, 1818. She d. Feb. 18, 1845, æ. 44 yrs., 8 mos. ; m., 2d w., Mrs. Syrena C. Nay, wid. of B. Allen Nay, Oct. 18, 1845. He d. March 1, 1870, æ. 88 yrs.

———

14   *Elizabeth Ann*, b. May 7, 1821 ; m. John Averill, Nov. 5, 1845.
15   *Edwin*, b. March 17, 1823 ; unm. ; r. North Weare.
16   *William W.*, b. Dec. 12, 1827 ; unm. ; r. California.
17   †*Alvah*, b. Jan. 8, 1837 ; m. Delle E. Parker.

———

10– 17   ALVAH PUFFER. He occupies the homestead. He m. Delle E. Parker, dau. John Parker, June 6, 1861.

———

18   *Mary E.*, b. Dec. 2, 1867.
19   *Myra L.*, b. Aug. 14, 1869 ; d. Aug. 7, 1870, æ. 1 yr.
20   *Minnie F.*, b. April 8, 1871 ; d. Nov. 10, 1872, æ. 1 yr., 7 mos.
21   *Grace L.*, b. March 6, 1874.

THE RICHARDSON FAMILY.

1   SAMUEL RICHARDSON (Dr.), son of Ebenezer and Rhoda Coolidge Richardson, was b. in Newton, Mass., Jan. 13, 1795. He studied medicine with Drs. Kidder, of Townsend, Mass., and Spaulding, of Amherst, and attended medical lectures at Dartmouth Medical College, Hanover. He commenced his practice in Peterborough, 1820, and after practising here about twenty years, he removed, about 1839, to Watertown, Mass., where he now resides. He m. Mary Kidder. She was b. in Townsend, and d. in Watertown, Oct. 9, 1861; m., 2d w., Sarah M: Barnard, June 23, 1873.

2   *Ebenezer Coolidge*, b. April 25, 1821; m. Clara R. Hartwell, Nov. 5, 1847; ch., (1) Mari Aneta, b. Feb. 4, 1849; m. Marshal O. West, Sept. 4, 1873; r. Danbury, Ct.; (2) Carrie V., b. Sept. 19, 1852; m. E. Howard Baker, June 19, 1873; r. Ware, Mass.; (3) Harriet G., b. Nov. 3, 1854; (4) Lottie H., b. March 29, 1857; (5) Mattie R., b. July 11, 1861; (6) Edward C., b. July 2, 1870; d. May 22, 1872, æ. 1 yr., 10 .mos. He studied the medical profession, and took his degree at Harvard University Medical Department, 1842, and is now a practising physician in Ware, Mass., in high standing in the community.

3   *Harriet C.*, b. May 18, 1823; m. Symmes Gardner, Boston, December, 1842; ch., (1) Frank, b. June 13, 1846; d. April 6, 1850, æ. 3 yrs., 9 mos.; (2) Charles Bartlett, b. March 31, 1850; m. Abbie Walker, June 6, 1872. Mrs. Gardner d. in Paris, France, March 4, 1870, æ. 46 yrs., 9 mos. Symmes Gardner d. Sept. 6, 1873.

4   *Sarah E.*, b. April 1, 1829; d. July 29, 1834, æ. 5 yrs.

1   REUEL RICHARDSON, son of Abijah and Elizabeth Richardson, of Dublin, a race distinct from the above, was b. in Peterborough, Sept. 2, 1793, and d. in town, Aug. 4, 1873, æ. 79 yrs., 11 mos. He came to Peterborough to live in 1820, and bought a farm in the northwest part of the town, where he remained till his death. He m. Betsey Davis, b. April 6, 1798, of Hancock, May 31, 1821.

2   *Jane*, b. April 22, 1822.

3   *Betsey*, b. Nov. 26, 1823; d. May 13, 1828, æ. 4 yrs., 5 mos.

4   †*Charles R.*, b. July 10, 1827; m., Sept. 10, 1850, Mary Eliza Fay.

5	*Mary E.*, b. July 31, 1829.
6	*Nancy D.*, b. June 11, 1832 ; d. April 9, 1874, æ. 41 yrs., 9 mos.
7	*Emeline L.*, b. Feb. 19, 1834.
8	† *Joshua*, b. Nov. 20, 1837 ; m., Oct. 6, 1858, Almeda L. Bullard.

1– 4	CHARLES R. RICHARDSON. He resides in north-west part of town, near Barker's paper-mill. He m., Sept. 10, 1850, Mary Eliza Fay.

9	*Alfaretta*, b. Aug. 2, 1851.
10	*Clara E.*, b. April 22, 1853.
11	*Fred*, b. Feb. 13, 1855.
12	*Emmagene L.,* ⎫
13	*Emegine,* ⎬ b. Jan. 1, 1860.
14	*Josephine M.*, b. Sept. 27, 1862.
15	*Fannie J.*, b. October, 1868.

1– 8	JOSHUA RICHARDSON. He resides on the homestead. He m., Oct. 6, 1858, Almeda L. Bullard, b. Oct. 21 1832.

16	*Flora F.*, b. Sept. 27, 1861.

THE RITCHIE FAMILY.

1	WILLIAM RITCHIE,* William McNee, and John Taggart were among the earliest permanent settlers in town. William ·Ritchie and his wife, Mary Waugh, came to Peterborough for a permanent residence, probably in 1749 or '50, and perhaps a little earlier. He took up his residence in the south part of the town. His son John, b. Feb. 11, 1750, was the first child b. in town. William Ritchie was b. 1728 ; d. at Peterborough, June 1, 1767, æ. 59 yrs. His wid. d. Jan. 16, 1793, æ. 69 yrs.

2	*John*, b. Feb. 11, 1750, was the first child b. in Peterborough. The date is, according to the town record, "John, b. Feb. 11, in 1750." He was a six weeks' man in the service of the colonies, in the winter of ·1776, and d. at Cambridge during this period, æ. 26 yrs. The proprietors of the town, at a meeting of the same in Peterborough, at the house of Alexander Scott, Sept. 27, 1753, "Voted, That there be granted unto John Ritchie, son of William Ritchie, Lot No. 19,

* This name was spelled by the early settlers Richey, but has of late been changed to Ritchie, which spelling has been generally adopted by the descendants.

containing fifty acres, to him, his heirs and assigns forever." Then follow the bounds of the lot. It does not designate why this grant is made. This note is made by Judge Smith: "First child born in Peterborough."

3   *Mary*, b. Nov. 24, 1752; m. Capt. —— Wilson, Coleraine, Mass.

4   † *James*, b. March 10, 1754; m. Sarah Dunlap.

5   *Jenny*, b. 1756; d. Oct. 1, 1758, æ. 2 yrs.

6   *Martha*, b. Aug. 12, 1759; m. Thomas Smith; 2d hus., George W. Miller, Coleraine.

7   †*Robert*, b. Dec. 3, 1763; m. Mehitable Putnam.

There was a garrison near the Ritchie place, for resort in case of danger.

1– 4   JAMES RITCHIE. He lived and d. on what is called the "Ritchie place," in the south part of the town. Mr. Dunbar says, in the church records, in recording his death, "A pious man." He d. March 6, 1806, æ. 51 yrs. He m., April 20, 1780, Sarah Dunlap, b. Aug. 30, 1759; she d. Aug. 4, 1832, æ. 73 yrs.

---

8   *William*, b. March 25, 1781. He m. Clarissa Kimball. She d. at Needham; four ch., William, James, Sophia, and Kimball. He graduated at Dartmouth College, 1804, studied divinity, and was settled in the ministry in Canton, July 1, 1807. Mr. Dunbar preached the ordination sermon, text, Luke ix., 60. He removed from Canton to Needham, where he preached many years, and where he d. Feb. 22, 1842, æ. 60 yrs. He was present at the centennial celebration of Peterborough, 1839, and responded to a sentiment, which speech is published, and also took part in the devotional exercises of the occasion.

9   *John*, b. Aug. 22, 1782; unm.; d. April 17, 1845, æ. 63 yrs.

10   *Margaret*, b. March 27, 1784; m. Leonard Cragin; r. Westminster, Vt.; d. June 13, 1870, æ. 86 yrs.

11   † *James*, b. Jan. 20, 1789; m. Rebecca Fletcher.

12   *Sally*, b. April 22, 1793; m., Sept. 30, 1819, John D. Barry; d. Chicago, June, 1870, æ. 77 yrs.; two ch.

13   †*Robert*, b. July 27, 1798; m. Mary Hutchinson; r. East Jaffrey.

14   *Polly*, b. Aug. 1, 1787; d. Dec. 22, 1795, æ. 8 yrs.

1– 7   ROBERT RITCHIE. He m. Mehitable Putnam, of Lyndeboro. She d. Jan. 5, 1860, æ. 87 yrs. He d. Nov. 23, 1832, æ. 69 yrs. He lived upon a farm on the mountain, in the south-east part of the town. He received, in the distribution of his father's property, the land given by the proprietors to his brother John, for his birthright, Lot No. 19, situated on Temple line, in south-east part of the town.

15 | *Mary*, b. Sept. 17, 1804; unm.; has been blind some years.

4- 11 | JAMES RITCHIE. He first lived on the George Duncan place, or the Capt. Isaac Hadley farm. He exchanged this for a farm north of Silas Barber's, where he d. He m. Rebecca Fletcher, Sept. 16, 1810; she d. Feb. 21, 1872; he d. April 13, 1849, æ. 60 yrs., 2 mos.

16 | † *John*, b. Dec. 6, 1810; m. Nancy Melvin.
17 | *James*, b. Aug. 25, 1813; d. Nov. 3, 1815, æ. 2 yrs.
18 | *Joseph F.*, b. Nov. 9, 1816; m. Sarah R. Thorning; d. Sept. 9, 1853, æ. 36 yrs., 10 mos.
19 | *James*, b. Feb. 9, 1819; d. March 9, 1819, æ. 1 mo.
20 | *Charlotte*, b. May 31, 1822; m. George Flanders; r. Prairie du Sac, Sauk Co., Wis.; one dau., Ella Jane.
21 | *Charles F.*, b. July 18, 1827; r. Sumpter, Wis.
22 | *Louisa J.*, b. Nov. 29, 1832; d. April 15, 1853, æ. 20 yrs., 4 mos.

4- 13 | ROBERT RITCHIE lived in Peterborough till 1835, when he re. to Jaffrey, and purchased the Pope farm, so called; has now sold his farm and r. in the village. He m. Mary Hutchinson, of Wilton, March 4, 1823; b. March 20, 1802.

23 | *James*, b. Jan. 11, 1824; went West; residence unknown.
24 | *Samuel*, b. July 19, 1825; m. Caroline Jackson; r. Charlestown, Mass.
25 | *John*, b. June 21, 1827; unm.
26 | *Wm. Robert*, b. April 16, 1829; unm.; re. to California.
27 | *George C.*, b. May 5, 1831; unm.
28 | *Mary Jane*, b. Jan. 20, 1833; m. W. H. Pratt; he d. in the war of the Rebellion. One ch., William H., b. Sept. 1, 1860.
29 | *Alvin*, b. Feb. 24, 1835. Suppose d. in war; unheard of; enlisted in Illinois.
30 | *Darius*, b. Jaffrey, Aug. 12, 1836; d. at Buffalo, Aug. 25, 1863, of sickness, on his way home; a soldier in the war of the Rebellion.
31 | *Henry*, b. Nov. 7, 1837; unm.; killed in battle, Sept. 30, 1864.

32 | *Edmund F.*, b. Dec. 10, 1839 ; d. in hospital in Philadelphia, Nov. 26, 1862 ; a soldier in the war of 1861.
33 | *Sarah M.*, b. May 27, 1842 ; unm.
34 | *Adelbert*, b. Feb. 13, 1846.

11– 16 | JOHN RITCHIE lived some years after his marriage in Peterborough, then re. to Lowell. He now r. in Plattsmouth, Nebraska. He m. Nancy Melvin, dau. of Reuben Melvin, b. Feb. 26, 1811.

35 | *James Clinton*, b. Nov. 24, 1845.
36 | *Clara Maria*, b. Lowell, July 24, 1850 ; d. Lowell, Jan. 7, 1857, æ. 6 yrs., 5 mos.

THE ROBBE FAMILY.

1 | WILLIAM ROBBE, by all accounts, was one of the earliest settlers in Peterborough. There is, however, much uncertainty in regard to his history. He was b. in Tyrone County, Ireland, in 1692. From the town records of Lunenburg, which are in a perfect state of preservation, and from the records of the church of that ancient town, by the careful examination of George A. Cunningham, Esq., of that town, who has kindly furnished us with these facts, we are enabled to give the following account : —

"William Robbe had two wives, both m. in Ireland. His first wife's name was Elizabeth ——, by whom he had one daughter, Margaret, b. Aug. 10, 1717 ; after this followed seven sons in succession, and whether this woman or his last wife, Agnes Patterson, was the mother of these sons we are uncertain. We incline to believe that his first wife died soon after the birth of Margaret, and that he soon m. Agnes Patterson, and that she was the mother of the seven sons, of whom William, the seventh, was born in 1730, and that the family emigrated to America between 1730 and '33, and during this period Mr. Robbe took up his residence in Lunenburg, for by the church records he and his wife, Agnes, were admitted to full communion, July 29, 1733, and that their daughter, Elizabeth, b. Oct. 2, was baptized Oct. 14, 1733."

This view of the case would seem to correspond with the representation given by Mr. Dunbar in his sketch of Peterborough, 1822, probably received by him from friends then living who knew the facts.

He says, "the first fruit of Mr. Robbe's marriage was a daughter, then seven sons in succession, then another daughter." All this family but the youngest, Elizabeth, was b. in Ireland. Of three of the sons we know nothing ; they may have died early in Ireland. We have a record of the four who came to town, John, James, Alexander, and William. All the race in town are descendants of Alexander and William. John and James left town early, and we know little or nothing of their descendants. Of the two daughters we know nothing. In an old Bible, in the possession of Mrs. A. P. Morrison, we find written the name of William Robbe, Townsend, April 14, 1747, and on another leaf that of Alexander Robbe, Jan. 29, 1748–9, Townsend. This would lead us to conjecture that before emigrating to Peterborough they removed to Townsend. The last tax against the family in Lunenburg is a poll-tax of John Robbe, 1743. William Robbe took up his land west of the John Little farm, constituting what was known as the Mitchell and Bailey farms, the latter of which he gave to his son John, and to William the former.

At a town meeting held March 29, 1763, it was voted "That William Robbe, called in the warrant 'Old William Robbe,' be permitted to build a seat for himself, at his own expense, at the left hand of the pulpit, and he may sit on it as long as he pleases." He m. Agnes Patterson, in Ireland, b. 1685, who d. in Peterborough, Sept. 8, 1762, æ. 77 yrs. He was b. 1692, and d. Peterborough, Dec. 5, 1769, æ. 77 yrs. They are both buried in the Little Cemetery on the meeting-house hill.

---

2 *Margaret*, b. Ireland, Aug. 10, 1717.
3 † *John*, b. Ireland, ——. (4) † *James*, b. Ireland, ——.
5 † *Alexander*, b. Ireland, 1726 ; m. Elizabeth Cuningham.
6 † *William*, b. Sudbury, Mass., Nov. 22, 1730 ; m. Eleanor Craton.
7 *Elizabeth*, b. Lunenburg, Oct 2, 1733.

1– 3 JOHN ROBBE. He was highway surveyor for 1760, '61, '62, '68, '69, and constable for 1772, after which his name does not appear on the town records. He probably left town before the American Revolution. His father gave him land on the west side of the river, constituting what was long known as the Bailey farm. We find by the town records that his wife's name was Elizabeth ——, and the births of the following ch. are recorded.

---

8 *David*, b. Oct. 13, 1752. (9) *Agnes*, b. May 2, 1754.
10 *Eleanor*, b. March 21, 1757. (11) *Andrew*, b. Oct. 3, 1761.

1- 4 | JAMES ROBBE. We know even less of him than of John. He was present at the first meeting of the town after incorporation, and was chosen a selectman for 1760, and also the succeeding year, and his name appears as a constable in 1774, after which his name does not appear. His wife's name was Jean ——.

12 | *Samuel*, b. Oct. 11, 1760.
13 | *William*, b. April 14, 1762.
14 | *James*, b. April 2, 1764.

1- 5 | ALEXANDER ROBBE. He came to town with his father's family about 1750, from Townsend, probably, and began the place where he lived and died, known as the Daniel Robbe farm, now owned by Samuel Adams. He was a captain in the military of that day, and commanded in an alarm, in 1777, of five days; was also mustered by Col. Enoch Hale to serve five months, 1776. He held the office of selectman seven years, *viz.:* 1763, '69, '71, '83, '84, '85, '86. He m. Elizabeth Cuningham, dau. of Thomas and Jenny Craton Cuningham, July 9, 1754. She d. Aug. 28, 1798, æ. 64 yrs. He d. Feb. 3, 1806, æ. 80 yrs. In the church records, Mr. Dunbar says: " Feb. 5, 1806, attended funeral of Capt. Alexander Robbe, æ. 80 yrs. Rev. Mr. Sprague offered prayers."

15 | † *William*, b. June 19, 1755; m. Polly Taggart.
16 | *Elizabeth*, b. Jan. 10, 1757; d. Nov. 29, 1757, æ. 10 mos.
17 | *Alexander*, b. July 6, 1761; d. April 17, 1778, æ. 17 yrs.
18 | *Susannah*, b. Dec. 4, 1765; m. Samuel Morrison (son of Plato), who was in the Revolutionary service seven years, for which he received a pension granted till his death. She d. Oct. 27, 1848, æ. 82 yrs., 10 mos. He d. Oct. 22, 1842, æ. 81 yrs.; c.
19 | *Thomas*, b. April 2, 1768; d. Feb. 22, 1793, æ. 25 yrs.
20 | †*Samuel*, b. July 5, 1770; m. Betsey Scott.
21 | † *James*, b. Nov. 6, 1772; m. Margaret Taggart, September, 1793.
22 | †*Daniel*, b. April 29, 1775; m. Betsey Torrey.
23 | *David*, b. Oct. 1, 1777; m. Betsey Chapman.
24 | *Elizabeth*, b. April 25, 1759; m. Ensign John Taggart, Dublin.
25 | *Agnes*, b. Sept. 21, 1763; m. Nathan Whittemore; c.

1- 6 | WILLIAM ROBBE (Lieut.). He was a seventh son in succession, and according to popular belief was endowed with peculiar powers to cure the king's evil, or scrofula. Mr. Robbe appears to have been an influential man in the early records of the town. We find that he was selectman for eight years, 1762, '66, '74, '75, '77, '78, '85, '86, and was one year, 1776, on that most important in the town's history of all its committees, "The Committee of Safety." He held other unimportant offices as tithing-man, pound-keeper, and deer-keeper. He lived on the farm directly west of the Annan farm, so-called, it being a part of farm A, or Gridley lot.

Mr. Robbe was not conscious of possessing any powers beyond those of other men, but from the circumstance of his birth, being the seventh son in regular succession, he was in these times esteemed a gifted person, who should use his supposed powers for the good of mankind. So to his great disadvantage he devoted himself to this business ; for the cure would not come if a fee was paid. He had rather to give his patients a small silver coin — the smallest then known, a fourpence half-penny — to be worn on their necks. If Providence so favored them that they got well, they could then reward him ; but it is. rare to all medical experience that such remembrances come to those who have attained health by any of the aids of the healing art! So the good man lost his money, lost his time, and spent his life in the practice of the most nonsensical mummery in the world. He presented the strange paradox of a good man practising deception as long as he lived. At one time Mr. Robbe was so oppressed by callers, and interrupted in his labor, that he removed to Stoddard. But he could not evade the sufferers who had faith in his powers, and followed him to his retreat, and annoyed him as much as ever; and then he fancied that things did not go well with him, because he was desirous of shirking duties that Divine Providence had laid upon him ; so he returned to Peter-borough, and faithfully devoted himself to the sick and suffering for the remainder of his long life.

His powers were held in universal belief and respect. All classes resorted to him and respected him, and with-held from the delusions all that scathing sarcasm so common to the men then on the stage, with which they were accustomed to put down other follies and absurdi-ties. This delusion has never been reasoned out, never driven out by ridicule alone, but it has been done away by the progress of the times, which have outgrown it, and left it a harmless and innocent folly in which no one now has the least faith.

Mr. Dunbar* says of Mr. Robbe, in his history of the town : "He was a man of a very amiable, disinterested disposition, of modest, unassuming manners, and of in-

* Collections, Topographical, &c., relating to New Hampshire, Vol. I., No. 3, p. 136.

flexible uprightness. When questioned as to his extraordinary powers, though he acknowledged the undeniable effects which in many cases almost immediately followed the application of his hand, he would by no means pretend to assign the reason, saying that he knew no more about it than others." He m. Eleanor Craton, dau. of Jenny Cuningham by a former husband, and w. of Thomas Cuningham. She d. July 11, 1826, æ. 84 yrs. He d. June 8, 1815, æ. 85 yrs.

26 ——, b. —— ; m. Lieut. Josiah Allen.
27 *Elizabeth*, b. March 1, 1772; m. Timothy Farnsworth; d. Oct. 27, 1812, æ. 40 yrs.
28 *Sally*, b. 1779; m. John Mussey; d. Aug. 27, 1840, æ. 61 yrs. He d. Dec. 3, 1842, æ. 64 yrs.
29 *Jenny*, b. —— ; m. Jesse White.
30 *Reuben*, b. —— ; m. Sally Templeton; 2d w., —— Robbins, dau. Joseph Robbins; 3d w., Wid. —— Dean, Jaffrey.

5– 15 | WILLIAM ROBBE (Capt.). He began the place in the west part of the town, where he always lived, and the same is in the family now. He m. Mary Taggart, b. October, 1764, and d. July 6, 1838, æ. 73 yrs., 10 mos. He d. Nov. 15, 1846, æ. 91 yrs. He was present at the centennial celebration of the town in 1839, and was one of the three survivors of the eighty-three who signed the Association Test, or Declaration of Independence, in 1776.

31 †*Alexander*, b. July 2, 1784; m. Sally Hildreth, Dublin.
32 *Elizabeth*, b. March 10, 1786; m. Otis Redding; d. Sept. 24, 1855, æ. 69 yrs.
33 *James*, b. Feb. 19, 1788; d. 1813, æ. 25 yrs.
34 *Mary*, b. Sept. 27, 1790; m. Joshua Chapman; d. Elmira, N. Y., 1862, æ. 72 yrs.
35 *William*, b. Nov. 28, 1792; m. Louisa Davison; r. Indiana; d.
36 *Harriet*, b. Oct. 30, 1794; unm.

5– 20 | SAMUEL ROBBE. He began the place where he always lived, and where he died. It was the lot next east of the Annan farm, being a part of the Gridley lot, or farm A, laid out in the original survey of the town. It was given him by his father, and was one of the most valuable lots in town. He was in service in the Revolution, at Saratoga, from Sept. 28 to Oct. 25, 1777; also from Sept. 19 to Nov. 27, 1781, in other service. He m. Betsey Scott,

1797, dau. Maj. Wm. Scott. She d. May 25, 1856, æ. 81 yrs., 9 mos. He d. July 1, 1856, æ. 86 yrs.

---

37 | *Lewis*, b. July 5, 1798 ; m. Harriet French; she d. Jan. 7, 1838 ; m., 2d w., Melinda Ober, of Hancock. He d. March 13, 1857, æ. 58 yrs., 8 mos. ; ch., (1) Sarah M. ; (2) Maria Louisa ; (3) Elizabeth C. ; (4) Charles A. ; (5) Mary Frances.

38 | *Alexander*, b. May 31, 1800; m., September, 1867, Melinda Wilson ; r. Hancock from early manhood ; d. Jan. 23, 1869, æ. 68 yrs., 7 mos.

39 | *Samuel*, b. April 14, 1802 ; d. May 15, 1805, æ. 3 yrs.

40 | *Alfred*, b. Sept. 14, 1804; m. Maria Griswold, Riley, Ill.; ch., (1) George Alfred ; (2) Catharine ; (3) Charles ; (4) Carrie ; (5) Harriet ; (6) Newton.

41 | *Samuel*, b. Aug. 11, 1806 ; m., Oct. 29, 1835, Hannah Hall ; r. Van Buren, Mich.; ch., (1) Alexander ; (2) Anna ; (3) Cicero Frank ; (4) Benjamin ; (5) Nellie.

42 | *Elisabeth*, b. Nov. 13, 1808 ; d. May 20, 1830, æ. 21 yrs., 6 mos.

43 | *Catharine*, b. Jan. 15, 1811 ; m., May 31, 1853, Asa F. Gowing.

44 | *William*, b. April 17, 1813 ; m. Rowena Whittemore ; 2d w., Jane Barber ; r. Huntley Grove, Ill.; ch., (1) Frances Marion ; (2) Harriet R.; (3) William Delos ; (4) Walter C.; (5) 2d m., Frederick.

45 | *Agnes*, b. June 12, 1815 ; m., Dec. 2, 1845, Asa F. Gowing She d. May 20, 1852, æ. 37 yrs.

46 | *Susan*, b. Aug. 23, 1817 ; m., July 22, 1868, Jonas Livingston.

47 | †*Stephen D.*, b. May 17, 1821 ; m. Nancy Warren.

5- 21 | **JAMES ROBBE.** He lived in the east part of Dublin, his farm being on the east line of the town. He m. Margaret Taggart, September, 1793. She d. Nov. 21, 1863, æ. 86 yrs. He d. Aug. 8, 1836, æ. 63 yrs., 9 mos.

---

48 | *Relief*, b. Aug. 26, 1796 ; unm.; d. Feb. 2, 1864, æ. 68 yrs.

49 | *James*, b. Sept. 15, 1798 ; m. Mary Powers ; d. Nov. 19, 1839, æ. 41 yrs. She d. March 8, 1857, æ. 52 yrs.

50 | *Thomas*, b. Aug. 25, 1800 ; m. Mary A. Nelson ; d. Feb. 22, 1863, æ. 62 yrs. She d. March 19, 1866, æ. 55 yrs.

51 | *Agnes*, b. Feb. 28, 1803 ; unm.; d. May 17, 1866, æ. 63 yrs.

52 | *Elisa*, b. March 1, 1805 ; unm.

53 | *Joseph W.*, b. Oct. 18, 1807 ; m. Maria Pierce ; r. Holley Village, N. Y.

54 | *Mary*, b. March 7, 1810 ; m. Abraham P. Morrison.

5– 22 | DANIEL ROBBE. He was a man of good talents and considerable culture, and was a strong partisan in the political questions of his day. He succeeded his father on the old homestead, but late in life sold his farm and re. to Norwich, Vt., and after a residence here of two years he again re. to Milton, N. Y., in 1837, where he d. April 1, 1867, æ. 82 yrs. He m. Betsey Torrey, b. Sept. 27, 1780; d. at Peterborough, Oct. 8, 1831, æ. 51 yrs.

55 | Cicero, b. May 7, 1805; m. Mary Taggart, Dublin. He d. March 8, 1829, æ. 24 yrs.
56 | Betsey, b. June 1, 1806; d. July 17, 1809, æ. 3 yrs.
57 | Mary T., b. Nov. 3, 1808; d. Nov. 28, 1835, æ. 27 yrs.
58 | Emeline M., b. July 5, 1812; m. Darius J. Hewitt, M.D., of Milton, N.Y., who d. at Saratoga Springs, April 24, 1874, æ. 62 yrs.
59 | Andrew J., b. Feb. 3, 1816; d. July 20, 1822, æ. 6 yrs.
60 | Samuel M., b. March 15, 1818; m. Harriet N. Paul, of Galway, N.Y. He d. Feb. 25, 1860, æ. 42 yrs.; r. Milton, N.Y.
61 | Elisa C., b. Aug. 31, 1821; d. Feb. 28, 1822, æ. 1 yr.

15– 31 | ALEXANDER ROBBE (Capt.). He succeeded his father on the home farm, where he lived till his death. He held many important offices in town; was selectman for nine years; Representative 1835, '36, '43, '44. He held the office of captain in the New Hampshire militia. He m. Sally Hildreth, of Dublin, April 23, 1807, b. April 7, 1782; d. Feb. 29, 1856, æ. 73 yrs. He d. Feb. 13, 1861, æ. 76 yrs.

62 | Caroline, b. Feb. 12, 1808; m. Dea. William Moore.
63 | Sarah Jane, b. Feb. 23, 1810; d. Feb. 1, 1831, æ. 21 yrs.
64 | Rachel Pitts, b. Nov. 14, 1812; m. Dea. William Moore; 2d hus., Dr. William Follansbee.
65 | †Franklin, b. Feb. 21, 1817; m. Lydia Boyden.
66 | †Edward A., b. Dec. 17, 1819; m. Martha J. Davis.

20– 47 | STEPHEN D. ROBBE. He lives on the homestead; m. Nancy Warren, dau. of Capt. John Warren, of Dublin, May 3, 1846; b. Aug. 19, 1823.

67 | William A., b. Dec. 9, 1849.
68 | Frederick G., b. March 11, 1852; m., 1876, Helen S. Shedd.
69 | John Warren, b. July 29, 1864.

31– 65   FRANKLIN ROBBE. He is a machinist by trade ; m. Lydia Boyden, May 6, 1840; b. Oct. 22, 1822.

    70   *Abbie Ann*, b. March 7, 1842 ; d. Aug. 29, 1843, æ. 1 yr., 5 mos.

    71   *Frank A.*, b. Nov. 14, 1844 ; m. Katie M. Hahn, Sept. 4, 1871.

    72   *Charles A.*, b. June 17, 1854 ; m.

31– 66   EDWARD A. ROBBE. He succeeded his father on the homestead ; m. Martha Jane Davis, of Temple, b. Sept. 10, 1826. He d. April 8, 1873, æ. 53 yrs., 4 mos.

    73   *Carrie J.*, b. Dec. 4, 1850 ; m., Jan. 18, 1872, John C. Swallow.

    74   *Abbie C.*, b. Sept. 22, 1853.

    75   *Harriet A.*, b. Nov. 5, 1855.

    76   *Minnie Hays*, b. Jan. 14, 1859.

    I

THE SAWYER FAMILY.

ABIAL SAWYER was directly descended from the Scotch-Irish. His grandfather, Josiah Sawyer, with his wife, emigrated from the north of Ireland, the precise time not known. He first lived in Andover, Mass., and then removed to Milford, and in 1770 to Sharon, where he lived and d., with the exception of a few years spent in Hancock. He was b. in Ireland, in 1721, and d. in Sharon, in 1813, æ. 92 yrs. His wife was b. in Ireland in 1726, and d. in Sharon, 1807, æ. 81 yrs. His son, Josiah (father to Abial), was b. in Milford, Sept. 7, 1744, and d. in Sharon, Oct. 2, 1829, æ. 85 yrs. He m. Lydia Downing, b. 1746, and d. in Sharon, Feb. 10, 1829, æ. 83 yrs. They had a large family. Among them were: Lydia, b. 1768 ; m. William Nay, and d. in Peterborough, Aug. 28, 1850, æ. 82 yrs. Moses, who lived in Sharon, b. 1774 ; d. 1851, æ. 77 yrs. Alice, b. 1781 ; m. George Shedd, in 1801, and d. Sept. 4, 1849, æ. 68 yrs. Rebecca, b. 1783 ; m. William Pettengill ; d. Dec. 24, 1869, æ. 85 yrs. Abial, b. April 25, 1784 ; raised his family in Sharon, and moved to Peterborough in 1837, and lived there till his death. He erected a house and other buildings on Grove Street in 1837. He was selectman a number of years in Sharon, and also represented the town in the General Court for the years 1835, '36, '37. He was a highly respected and worthy man. He m. Sybil Buss, b. Jan. 16, 1787. She d. Feb. 26, 1866, æ. 79 yrs. He d. Oct. 23, 1870, æ. 86 yrs., 5 mos.

2 | *Josiah,* b. June 25, 1808 ; m. Harriet Bates ; r. Tremont, Ill. ; ch., (1) Abial B. ; (2) Josiah M.

3 | †*Silas,* b. June 8, 1810 ; m., 1st w., Harriet N. Bacon ; 2d w., Mrs. A. Lawrence.

4 | *Joseph A.,* b. April 12, 1812 ; m. Martha Richmond ; 2d w., Almeda Wells ; ch., (1)Edward F. ; (2) Emma E. ; (3) Albert ; (4) Sarah L. ; (5) Lucy A. ; (6) Laura ; (7) Ella ; (8) Henry ; r. Geneseo, Ill.

5 | *Almira,* b. Dec. 10, 1814 ; m. Wirling Gregg, March 19, 1833 ; d. Jan. 10, 1836 ; ch., (1) Nancy, b. May 30, 1834 ; d. April, 1863, æ. 28 yrs., 10 mos. ; (2) Almira, b. Jan. 8, 1836 ; r. Sharon.

6 | *Louisa,* b. Dec. 17, 1816 ; d. Aug. 24, 1867, æ. 50 yrs., 8 mos.

7 | †*Albert,* b. Aug. 16, 1819 ; m. Sophia M. Gowing, Aug. 26, 1846.

8 | *Susannah,* b. Aug. 5, 1821 ; m. Miflin Bailey, 1852 ; one ch. ; she d. Sept. 21, 1873, æ. 52 yrs. ; r. Tremont, Ill.

9 | *Anna,* b. May 25, 1825 ; m. Albert S. Scott, Nov. 25, 1851.

10 | *Andrew J.,* b. Aug. 19, 1827 ; d. Sept. 25, 1829, æ 2 yrs.

1- 3 | SILAS SAWYER. He re. to Peterborough in 1864. He was selectman in Sharon for four years, and represented the town in the Legislature in 1838, '39, '50, '51. He m., June 1, 1837, 1st w., Harriet N. Bacon, of Sharon, b. July 31, 1815 ; she d. Aug. 19, 1856, æ. 41 yrs. ; m., 2d w., Feb. 9, 1857, Mrs. Annis Lawrence, b. Dec. 30, 1808. His ch. b. in Sharon.

11 | *Stephen A.,* b. April 14, 1840 ; r. Kansas.

12 | *George A.,* b. Feb. 25, 1850 ; d. Oct. 28, 1850, æ. 8 mos.

13 | *Mary L.,* b. Aug. 11, 1856 ; d. June 16, 1869, æ. 12 yrs., 10 mos.

1- 7 | ALBERT SAWYER succeeded his father in his residence in the village. He m. Sophia M. Gowing, Aug. 26, 1846. Now deputy-sheriff.

14 | *Emma S.,* b. May 25, 1847 ; m., Dec. 13, 1870, J. P. Farnsworth ; ch., Charles A., b. Jan. 15, 1871 ; r. Fitchburg, Mass.

2 | JOSIAH SAWYER, b. 1772, son of Josiah Sawyer, of Sharon, and brother to Abial, lived in the north part of the town, on the Greenfield line, where he d. 1801, and left the following family, according to the town records. His wife's name was Patty Wyman.

15   *Mary*, b. Nov. 25, 1795 ; m. Benjamin Howard ; r. Jaffrey.

16   *Sally*, b. Aug. 14, 1797 ; m. Lot Nichols ; r. Sharon.

17   *Josiah*, b. July 7, 1800 ; m. Mary French ; r. Jaffrey.

THE SCOTT FAMILY.

1   WILLIAM SCOTT, Sen., was the son of William Scott, and emigrated to America, accompanied by his father's family, in 1736, and first lived in Hopkinton, Mass., two years, when he came to New Ipswich, and lived with Col. Kidder a part of one year, and then came to Peterborough, in 1739 or '40, and took up the place where he lived till his death. This was a swell of land just west of the James Wilson house or Hunt's Corner, so called, and on the south part of the meeting-house hill. The ground gradually descends to the south ; the situation very sightly, and one of the best early locations in town. The old cellar-hole now only marks the spot where the buildings stood. He was m. to Margaret Gregg about 1740, and they immediately came to Peterborough. They were driven off by fear of the Indians soon, and returned to Hopkinton, and while here Ellen, the first child, was b., 1742. They were supposed to have returned to Peterborough soon after her birth, but did not probably till a number of the children were b. ; as Mary, b. in 1744, Jean, b. 1746, David, b. 1749. These children were not b. in Peterborough, as the first child b. in town was John Ritchie, son of William Ritchie, b. Feb. 11, 1750. The inference is that the family did not return till after 1750, though William Scott might have been here part of the time. His family first occupied a log-cabin, which he had made temporarily for himself. He was among the very first settlers of the town. His son, William, Jr., being the youngest son, was settled at home on the old homestead, and remained there till his death. William Scott and wife were of Scotch-Irish descent, and came from Coleraine, in the north part of Ireland. He was b. 1713, and d. in Peterborough, Nov. 20, 1795, æ. 82 yrs. She was b. in 1717 ; d. in Peterborough, Oct. 3, 1797, æ. 80 yrs.

---

2   *Ellen*, b. March 2, 1742 ; unm. ; d. Feb. 12, 1833, æ. 95 yrs.

3   *Mary*, b. July 14, 1744 ; d. Jan. 24, 1812, æ. 67 yrs., 6 mos. ; a cripple from childhood.

4   *Jean*, b. Nov. 20, 1746 ; m. William Cochran for his 2d w.

5   *David*, b. June 8, 1749 ; m. Nancy Robbe ; 2d w., Isabel Moore ; r. Stoddard ; d. 1815, æ. 66 yrs.

6   *Thomas*, b. Peterborough, Aug. 18, 1752 ; m. Eunice Weekwan ; had a large family of twelve children in Nova Scotia ; served through Revolution before removing to Nova Scotia. He returned to Peterborough late in life, and d. there, May 25, 1833, æ. 81 yrs.

7   *Hannah*, b. Oct. 20, 1754 ; m. David Robbe ; went to New York, then to Ohio. She had a family of children. She was supposed to be bewitched. She d. about 1830, æ. 84 yrs.

8   † *William, Jr.*, b. Jan. 8, 1756 ; m. Catharine Ames ; 2d w., Dorcas Pulcifer.

·9   *Margaret*, b. Jan. 2, 1760 ; m. Samuel Wills ; had a family ; d. 1835, æ. 75 yrs. ; re. to Vermont.

Ellen and Mary each had a maintenance secured them in their father's farm.

1-- 8   WILLIAM SCOTT, Jr., settled on the homestead. He m., 1st w., Catharine Ames ; she d. June 5, 1808, æ. 49 yrs., and was the mother of all the ch. ; m., 2d w., Dorcas Pulcifer, April 24, 1815 ; she d. Feb. 27, 1826, æ. 51 yrs. He d. Oct. 10, 1829, æ. 73 yrs. He lost the use of his lower limbs, and was a cripple for about thirty years before his death.

---

10   *Nathan*, b. April 15, 1782 ; r. Italy Hollow, N. Y., in 1810 ; had a large family ; d. 1864, æ. 82 yrs.

11   *David*, b. March 20, 1785 ; studied law with James Wilson, Sen., Esq. ; re. to Columbus, O., in 1811 ; m. Nancy White, dau. John White, Jan. 1, 1810 ; ch., (1) William ; (2) Alexander H. ; (3) Amelia. William is a lawyer ; lives in Hillsboro, O., and is successful in his profession. Alexander H. lives in St. Joseph, Mich.

12   *Thomas*, b. Jan. 25, 1787 ; unm. ; d. Aug. 29, 1818, æ. 31 yrs.

13   *Sally*, b. Feb. 18, 1789 ; unm. ; d. May 3, 1857, æ. 68 yrs.

14   *William*, b. Feb. 16, 1791 ; unm. ; d. 1832, æ. 41 yrs.

15   *Betsey*, b. June 3, 1793 ; unm. ; d. July 11, 1827, æ. 34 yrs.

16   *Jane*, b. Nov. 29, 1795 ; m. Michael Maxfield, of Naples, N. Y. ; ch., (1) Hiram ; (2) Catharine ; (3) Elizabeth ; (4) Frances. She d. June, 1868, æ. 73 yrs.

17   *John*, b. Feb. 18, 1797 ; m. Sally Knowland, mother of the ch. ; 2d w., Jane A. Abbot, dau. of Daniel Abbot, of Peterborough ; ch., (1) John ; (2) William ; (3) David ; (4) James ; of these ch., James only survives. He d. Sept. 1, 1846, æ. 49 yrs. ; was successful and acquired a large property ; r. Detroit, Mich.

18   † *James*, b. Feb. 17, 1807 ; m. Sarah Ann Wilson, dau. Capt. William Wilson.

8– 18

JAMES SCOTT has always resided in town, and owns and lives on a portion of the old farm of his fathers, it being the north-west corner of the same. From his house the old lot extended on the present highway to "Carter's Corner," so called, thence on the north side of the road leading to "Hunt's Corner," where Col. John Little now lives, then north far enough to make one hundred acres. The old house was located on the hill, between Carter's and Hunt's Corners. An old cellar-hole now only marks the spot. Mr. Scott has held many offices of trust and honor, both in county and town; has been a road commissioner for six years; was many years deputy sheriff. In town has been selectman six years, 1847, '48, '50, '56, '57, '65; Representative 1849, '50, and many minor offices. He has been a director of the National Monadnock Bank, East Jaffrey, nineteen years, and president twelve years. He is now president of the Peterborough Railroad.

In early life he became the chief stay of the family. His father having lost the use of his limbs for nearly thirty years became, in his old age, very helpless and needy; and his uncle, Thomas Scott, came from Nova Scotia in indigent circumstances. Both required to be supported on the slender means of the small farm they occupied. This heavy burden was shared with him by his sister Sally, who was always untiring in her devotion to her friends. By these cares and labors, James was prevented, in some degree, from enjoying all the opportunities of even a common-school education. This he had to make up by himself, or go hopelessly ignorant: and he has done it so effectually as to enable him to meet and discharge faithfully and acceptably all the duties that have devolved on him in all and every station in life in which he has been placed. To this he has added an unusually accurate knowledge of mankind, and an extensive acquaintance with every form of common business in the community. His integrity and common-sense, combined with these qualifications, render him a very valuable member of society; and his advice and counsel are much sought by those who are experiencing perplexities and difficulties in their business.

This early discipline was not lost upon Mr. Scott. He learned the significance of economy and temperance, which he has followed through life; and it has prepared him to easily and naturally acquire a competence, even a fortune with us, by slow and sure means, and with rarely any failure of judgment in any of his financial operations. Few men evince such a judgment and knowledge of men and things, or apply such a power to a better use.

James Scott

He m., May 28, 1840, Sarah Ann Wilson, dau. of Capt. Wm. Wilson.

---

19   *William*, b. Sept. 1, 1841 ; d. Aug. 24, 1842, æ. 11 mos.
20   *Catharine*, b. Dec. 30, 1842 ; m. Maj. John A. Cummings, Dec. 1, 1861. She d. Aug. 13, 1862 ; drowned by the sinking of the steamer "West Point," coming in collision with the "George Peabody," while going up the Potomac River to Washington, from Fortress Monroe.
21   *Franklin*, b. July 15, 1848 ; d. Aug. 19, 1848, æ. 1 mo.
22   *Frederick*, b. June 13, 1854 ; d. same day.
23   *Jennie*, b. March 9, 1857.

---

1   ALEXANDER SCOTT is represented in Mr. Dunbar's history as being one of the first five who made any attempt at settlement as early as 1739. They may not have stayed more than a single season. Another account does not include his name among the very first pioneers. He no doubt came early, but just the time we have no means of knowing. He was probably b. in Ireland, and came over with the other emigrants of the same name, William Scott and family, in 1736, with whom there was, no doubt, a relationship, but of what kind we do not know. It is evident that he re. here from Townsend, for the births of two of his children are found recorded in Townsend, David, b. Aug. 16, 1742, and John, b. April 16, 1749. It is probable that the family moved to Peterborough in 1749 or '50. In this record they are the children of Alexander and Margaret Scott. The first we hear of Alexander Scott in town he is keeping a tavern, on the spot where Major Robert Wilson succeeded him, and a meeting of the proprietors was held at his house, September, 1753. He is next living on a lot east of the old graveyard, just where we do not know. He afterwards re. to Dublin. No record of the death of either himself or his wife can be found.

---

2   † *William*, b. 1742 ; d. Litchfield, N.Y., Sept. 19, 1796, æ. 54 yrs.
3   *David*, b. Townsend, Aug. 16, 1744.
4   †*Alexander*, b. —— ; m. Betsey Taylor.
5   *John*, b. Townsend, April 16, 1749.
    Of David and John above we know nothing more, only that they were mustered into Continental service, April, 1777, by Col. Enoch Hale. They probably removed from town.

1– 2 | WILLIAM SCOTT (Maj.) was young when his father re. from Townsend to Peterborough, not more than eight or nine years of age. In the history of Dublin, it appears that Alexander Scott resided in that town, on the lot where Thaddeus Morse now lives, between 1750 and '60, probably after he gave up his tavern in Peterborough, and kept a tavern here, or furnished entertainment to those persons, especially soldiers, who passed from Peterborough to Keene. William Scott, son of Alexander, lived on the farm (Lot 13, Range 6) now owned by John Gleason. The Hon. John Scott, son of William, was born here.* "He was heard to say that he well remembered, when quite young, playing with his brothers on the shore of the pond (Monadnock Lake); that occasionally the play was pushing one another from the fallen trees or slippery logs into the water." We do not know of any other residence of Wm. Scott, though it is probable that the family re. to Peterborough, and resided there, during his absence in the Continental service, and subsequent to the war. The name of his wife is also unknown. He received a captain's commission, Jan. 1, 1777, in Col. Henley's Regiment, Mass. line, afterwards Col. Henry Jackson's. According to the *Historical Collections*, Vol. I., p. 28, three battalions were raised in New Hampshire in 1776. In the battalion commanded by Col. Joseph Cilley, of Nottingham, are the names of James Taggart, of Peterborough, Lieut. of Co. 1, and William Scott, of Peterborough, Capt. of Co. 8. He saw much military service, and with his two sons remained in the army till he resigned, in 1781. After this he entered the naval service on board of the frigate "Dane," and served in that and other ships until peace was proclaimed. His son David died in the sixth year of his service. For a more particular account of Maj. Scott, I refer to the Centennial Address. He appears to have been a man of noble character, and a great honor to his adopted town. It is a matter of great regret that there is so little historic account of this man, or that tradition has handed down so little concerning him. We know little of him beside what is related in the Centennial Address, and no descendant, or older inhabitant, can add anything more. He d. at Litchfield, N. Y., Sept. 19, 1796, æ. 54 yrs.; b. 1742.

6 | † *John*, b. Dublin, March 23, 1765; m. Bethiah Ames.
7 | *Polly*, b. ——; m. —— Ramsey; re. to Litchfield.
8 | *Phebe*, b. ——; m. Abel Whitney; r. Tunbridge, Vt.

* History of Dublin, p. 131.

9 | *William*, b. ——; unm.; d. Presque Isle, N. Y.
10 | *James*, b. ——; unm.; d.
11 | *Betsey*, b. 1775; m. Samuel Robbe.
12 | *Agnes*, b. ——; m. —— Lincoln; d. of cancer.
13 | *Sally*, b. Oct. 23, 1780; m., Nov. 1, 1810, Ashbel Loomis; d. in Alstead, Sept. 10, 1841, æ. 60 yrs., 10 mos.; r. Alstead.
14 | *David*, b. ——; m. Anna Lyon, Hudson, N. Y.; d. in 1819; ch., (1) William; d.; (2) Anna Maria, b. May 19, 1810; m. Richard James, New York City; (3) Jane, b. Dec. 18, 1811; m., 1st hus., —— McCoy; 2d hus., Stephen P. Steele.

1- 4 | ALEXANDER SCOTT. He had a club foot (*talipes varus*), and was consequently lame all his life. He m. Betsey Taylor, dau. Isaiah Taylor. We have been able to get very little information of this man. He was a shoemaker by trade, and lived on the cross-road from Windy Row to the Faxon place; house now demolished. Cannot ascertain when or where either he or his wife d. If our early recollections of this man are correct, no great loss is sustained by the scanty reminiscences that remain of him.

15 | †*I. Taylor*, b. Feb. 13, 1795; m., May 20, 1828, Hannah Stickney.

2- 6 | JOHN SCOTT (Hon.) was b. in Dublin. When very young he accompanied his father, Major Scott, in the war of the Revolution, and was out several years, when he was from thirteen to sixteen years of age. He was always through his life an ardent patriot and a staunch supporter of his government. In the division of parties, which took place in the early stage of our government, he took the Democratic side, to which he adhered through life. He was selectman eight years, 1810, '11, '12, '14, '15, '16, '17, '18. He was one of the presidential electors for 1840. He was deeply interested in all the municipal affairs of the town, and was always one of the most influential debaters in the town meetings. He lived on a farm directly west of the Osgood place, and his farm included eighty acres of the Gridley lot, or farm A, extending down to the Nubanusit River. Late in life he sold his farm and re. to the village, and built a house in which he lived till his death. He m. Bethiah Ames, of Groton, Mass., b. Nov. 30, 1770, who d. Feb. 16, 1852, æ. 81 yrs. He d. Dec. 27, 1847, æ. 82 yrs., 9 mos.

32

16 | *Sally*, b. Dec. 22, 1789; m. James Scott; r. Stoddard.
17 | *Harriet*, b. July 30, 1792; m. William Gray.
18 | *John*, b. June 20, 1794; m. Susan Mabin, Natchez, Miss.; d. Barre, Mass., March 19, 1836, æ. 44 yrs.
19 | *Clarissa*, b. Nov. 26, 1795; unm.; d. Sept. 22, 1872, æ. 75 yrs.
20 | *Nancy*, b. April 20, 1797; m. Samuel Bullard; 2d hus., —— Cobb; now a widow, and blind; r. Hancock.
21 | *Eliza*, b. June 11, 1799; m. Ahimaz Jewett.
22 | †*William*, b. Feb. 19, 1801; m. Phylinda Crossfield; 2d w., Malinda Ward.
23 | *Mary*, b. Jan. 5, 1806; m. Charles Fuller; d. Nov. 17, 1842, æ. 36 yrs., 10 mos.; ch., (1) Charles L.; (2) Mary Sophia. Both were lost in the war of the Rebellion. He was a lieutenant in the N. H. Vols., and was killed in the second Bull Run battle, Aug. 30, 1862. She, being on her return from a visit to her husband, Col. Charles Scott, was drowned by the collision, on the Potomac River, of the "West Point" steamer with the "George Peabody," by which the former boat was sunk and most of the persons on board were drowned, Aug. 13, 1862.
24 | *Charles*, b. Jan. 26, 1808; d. Oct. 2, 1826, æ. 18 yrs.

4– 15 | ISAIAH TAYLOR SCOTT. He was a shoemaker. He m. Hannah Stickney, May 20, 1828. He d. May 5, 1858, æ. 63 yrs. She d. ——, 1875, æ. 72 yrs.

---

25 | *Mary Ann*, b. June 18, 1829; m. Alonzo Bowers, April 12, 1853; c.; r. Waltham, Mass.
26 | *Alfred*, b. April 2, 1832; d. Jan. 17, 1851, æ. 18 yrs., 9 mos.
27 | *George*, b. July 18, 1833; d. June 8, 1856, æ. 22 yrs., 10 mos.
28 | *Edson*, b. Sept. 28, 1837; d. May 8, 1838, æ. 7 mos.
29 | *Wallace*, b. Oct. 20, 1746; m., Dec. 13, 1865, Abbie Miller, dau. S. R. Miller; divorced in May, 1872; r. Haverhill, Mass.

6– 22 | WILLIAM SCOTT. He succeeded his father on the homestead. He was a worthy and useful man. Any enterprise for the good of society always had his hearty coöperation and support. He was kind-hearted, well-informed, and a live man, and his loss was sincerely and deeply felt. He was universally respected, and the memory of his useful, and unselfish, and disinterested life still freshly survives him. He was cut off in the full maturity of his powers, by a typhoid fever that pre-

Albert S. Scott

vailed extensively during that season. He d. Sept. 24, 1846, æ. 45 yrs.; he m., Jan. 19, 1823, Phylinda Crossfield, of Keene, b. April 9, 1798; she d. May 23, 1839, æ. 41 yrs.; m., 2d w., Malinda Ward, b. Jan. 18, 1807; she d. Sept. 13, 1862, æ. 55 yrs. He was selectman for five years, 1836, '37, '38, '42, '45.

30

31   *John*, b. June 2, 1823; d. Jan. 19, 1827, æ. 3 yrs., 7 mos.

  †*Albert S.*, b. May 8, 1824; m. Anna Sawyer, Nov. 25,
32   1851.

  Susan A., b. July 4, 1825; m. Robert Orr, Oct. 16,
    1851; ch., (1) William S., b. Sept. 14, 1853; d. April
    23, 1854, æ. 7 mos.; (2) Addie P. S., b. March 19,
    1856; d. Oct. 5, 1863, æ. 7 yrs., 6 mos.; (3) C. W.
    Wallace, b. Jan. 29, 1858; r. in Corinth, Vt.

33   *William H.*, b. July 30, 1826; m., June 1, 1856, Maria
    D. Farnum, b. June 10, 1825.

34   *Sophronia D.*, b. June 25, 1827; m. John Allyn, June 2,
    1861; r. Washington Territory.

35   †*Charles*, b. April 14, 1829; m., 1st w., Mary S. Fuller;
    2d w., Charlotte M. Wilkins.

36   *Kendall C.*, b. April 26, 1830; m., Oct. 9, 1851, Lucy A.
    Clark, b. May 6, 1830. Editor for many years of the
    Peterborough *Transcript*, and owner of the book-store
    and news-depot in town. He sold out and re. to
    Keene to engage in the sash and blind business; on
    account of his health he was obliged to retire, and
    finally, after a long-continued consumption, he d. at
    Keene, Jan. 3, 1875, æ. 44 yrs., 8 mos. He was
    town clerk of Peterborough, 1867. He also repre-
    sented the town of Keene in the Legislature.

37   *Phylinda*, b. Oct. 29, 1832; m. S. G. Blanchard; r.
    Spring Vale, Iowa.

38   † *Walter*, b. Sept. 23, 1835; m. Laura M. Day, Oct. 13,
    1859.

39   *Mary*, b. Nov. 11, 1841; m. George H. Clark, b. Oct.
    15, 1836; ch., (1) George H., b. Nov. 5, 1862; (2)
    Lucinda S., b. Feb. 22, 1865; (3) Willie E., b. Dec. 4,
    1867; (4) John B., b. March 21, 1869; (5) Lottie A.,
    b. Jan. 31, 1870.

40   † *John*, b. Sept. 9, 1844; m. Lucinda C. Forbush.

22– 31   ALBERT SMITH SCOTT was b. on the Senter place, so called, where Mrs. Wilcox now lives. When he was four years of age, his father removed to the old homestead, the farm of his father, the late Hon. John Scott, where he spent the remainder of his life. This farm was subdued by Hon. John Scott from its primitive state, who cut down the timber, rolled away the logs, and built the house now standing on the same.

Mr. Scott's earliest attendance at school was in District No. 9, and subsequently at the Peterborough Academy for several terms. He was fitted for college at the "Hancock Literary and Scientific Institute," and the Phillips (Exeter) Academy, and entered the class of 1848 in Dartmouth College, in the spring of 1845. In consequence of his limited means, and the death of his father, which occurred about this time, he was obliged to leave college at the close of his Sophomore year, and was employed for a time as assistant-teacher under Horace Morison, in Baltimore College, Md. On his return to Peterborough he commenced the study of medicine with Prof. Albert Smith, and after attending one course of Medical Lectures at the "New Hampshire Medical Institution," Dartmouth College, he abandoned the profession as not congenial to his tastes, and commenced the study of law in the office of Dearborn & Cheney, then practising attorneys in Peterborough. He was admitted to the Hillsborough County bar, N. H., in 1859. During all this period of his preparation for a profession, he supported himself by teaching, and while thus engaged he was principal in the Peterborough Academy for several years.

He was an excellent teacher, and aided many individuals, through his thorough and systematic instruction, to become useful and successful teachers. He taught his first school in Wilton, before he was fifteen years of age, at $12 per month, and "boarded round."

It must not be omitted to mention that at this period of his life, he had an attack of *hæmoptysis*, from which, by a judicious use of cod-liver oil, proper exercise and regimen, he recovered; but never to a state that gave him sure and perfect health. He has always to be careful, both as to body and mind. He entered upon the practice of his profession in Peterborough, soon after being admitted to the bar, and has continued in the profession since, with the exception of three years, when he became cashier of the First National Bank, in Peterborough.

He served for many years, with great efficiency and acceptance, on the superintending school committee, and rendered great service to the educational interests of the town; he also did efficient work in the organization of the high school, and as chairman of the high school committee, during the first two years succeeding its organization.

He now stands at the very head of his profession,

and has a brilliant future of success, if his health will permit.

He represented the town in the years 1855, '57, and 1866, '67, and was elected Councillor for his district in 1875, '76. The degree of A.M. was conferred on him by Dartmouth College, 1868.

41	*Charles A.*, b. June 9, 1855 ; d. Sept. 9, 1855, æ. 3 mos.
42	*William A.*, b. Dec. 8, 1856.
43	*Edward W.*, b. July 22, 1861.

22– 35   CHARLES SCOTT (Col.). He has always resided in town. He was Lieut.-Colonel in the Sixth Reg., N. H. Vols., and did some service early in the war, but in consequence of the failure of his health he was obliged to resign. He was appointed high-sheriff for the County of Hillsborough, July, 1865, and held the office till 1874, when the Democrats attained the accession of power in the State. He was reappointed to same office again in June, 1876, which he now holds. He has been many years moderator in town, for 1860, '66, '67, '68, '69, '70, '71, '72, '73, '74, '75, '76. He m., 1st w., July 25, 1848, Mary S. Fuller, dau. Charles and Mary Scott Fuller. She was drowned on board "West Point" steamer, on River Potomac, Aug. 13, 1862 ; m., 2d w., Charlotte M. Wilkins, Sept. 7, 1863 ; 1st w., two ch. ; 2d w., two ch.

44	*Charles Albert*, b. Jan. 17, 1854 ; d. Aug. 17, 1854, æ. 7 mos.
45	*Ella Sophia*, b. July 19, 1857 ; d. Oct. 19, 1857, æ. 3 mos.
46	*Mary Luena*, b. May 13, 1865.
47	*Katie Sophia*, b. July 2, 1870.

22– 38   WALTER SCOTT m., Oct. 1, 1859, Laura M. Day, b. March 17, 1841.

48	*Laura E.*, b. July 7, 1861 ; d. Oct. 5, 1861, æ. 3 mos.
49	*Freddie*, b. Aug. 21, 1862. (50) *Charles*, b. July 1, 1864.

22– 40   JOHN SCOTT is a printer by trade ; a member of the firm of Farnum & Scott, in job printing, &c., in town ; also one of the editors of the Peterborough *Transcript;* m., May 1, 1866, Lucinda A. Forbush, b. June 26, 1846.

51	*Harry F.*, b. Nov. 2, 1869 ; d. Jan. 1, 1870, æ. 2 mos.
52	*Mabel M.*, b. Aug. 1, 1872.

THE SENTER FAMILY.

1   GEORGE W. SENTER came to Peterborough in 1817. When he first came to town he was engaged in trade at the South Factory Village, but subsequently in manufacturing at the North Cotton Factory, and still later he became a mail-contractor, and was extensively engaged in staging. He obtained the mail-contract that for the first time secured to the town a regular and permanent stage-route to Keene, and a frequent mail. He was selectman for 1832, '33. He m. Mary Steele, dau. of Gen. John Steele, Aug. 23, 1821. He was b. May 20, 1790, and d. Sept. 6, 1850, æ. 60 yrs.

2   *George*, b. Nov. 3, 1822 ; r. California.
3   *John*, b. Dec. 15, 1823 ; r. Eagle River, Lake Superior.
4   *Henry*, b. Jan. 25, 1825 ; r. St. Louis, Mo.
5   *Mary Antoinette*, b. Sept. 7, 1829 ; m. Samuel Mandlebaum ; one ch., Mary ; r. Detroit, Mich.
6   *Albert W.*, b. April 8, 1832 ; d. Dec. 13, 1865, æ. 33 yrs.

THE SHEDD FAMILY.

1   GEORGE SHEDD was b. in Billerica, Mass., Feb. 2, 1777, and d. in Peterborough, Oct. 30, 1855, æ. 78 yrs. He m. Alice Sawyer, dau. Josiah Sawyer, of Sharon, Nov. 26, 1801 ; she d. Sept. 4, 1849, æ. 68 yrs. He came to town in 1806, or '7. His parents re. from Billerica to Sharon not far from 1790. After his marriage he moved to Stockbridge, Vt., and from thence to Peterborough, in 1807 or '8, and bought the farm which George Shedd, Jr., now occupies, and remained till a few years before the close of his life, when he sold the farm, and lived with his children.

2   *Sullivan*, b. Aug. 18, 1803 ; m., Dec. 10, 1833, Phebe S. Dodge, of Stoddard.
3   *Alice*, b. June 3, 1805 ; d. Oct. 17, 1806, æ. 1 yr., 4 mos.
4   *John D.*, b. July 20, 1807 ; d. October, 1871, æ. 64 yrs.; r. Jamestown, N. Y.
5   *Alice*, b. March 27, 1810 ; m., March 1, 1832, Joseph McCoy ; d. Aug. 9, 1849, æ. 39 yrs.
6   *Hannah*, b. July 14, 1811 ; m. Samuel Ryan ; r. East Jaffrey.
7   †*George, Jr.*, b. Nov. 4, 1812 ; m. Mary Dodge, of Stoddard.
8   *Mary*, b. April 3, 1814 ; d. April 14, 1817, æ. 3 yrs.
9   *Phylinda F.*, b. May 23, 1817 ; m. James Taggart ; r. Winchendon, Mass.

10 | †*Daniel*, b. April 25, 1826; m. Jane M. Nelson, Sept. 20, 1848.

1- 7 | GEORGE SHEDD, Jr. He lives on the homestead; is a farmer; m. Mary Dodge, of Stoddard, March 28, 1837, b. Nov. 24, 1812. She d. Sept. 26, 1875, æ. 62 yrs., 10 mos.

---

11 | *Mary Jane*, b. March 14, 1838; m. Henry Nay, Feb. 26, 1857. She d. March 6, 1867, æ. 28 yrs., 11 mos. He d. Aug. 27, 1858, æ. 26 yrs.

12 | *Ellen*, b. Aug. 23, 1840; d. Aug. 27, 1842, æ. 2 yrs.

13 | *Jerome B.*, b. Nov. 17, 1844; d. July 16, 1845, æ. 8 mos.

14 | *Francis J.*, b. Jan. 30, 1847; m., Oct. 9, 1870, Sarah J. Preston, b. April 14, 1844; two ch.

15 | *Albert G.*, b. July 29, 1852; m. —— Gould.

16 | *Jerome B.*, b. Oct. 27, 1854.

1- 10 | DANIEL SHEDD m. Jane M. Nelson, dau. Paul Nelson, Sept. 20, 1848, b. May 28, 1829. He lives in the village, and has been much engaged in the beef business.

---

17 | *Clara A.*, b. Aug. 1, 1851; m. William Dane, Nov. 28, 1872.

18 | *Alice M.*, b. Sept. 8, 1854; m. John A. Peasley, September, 1872; r. Fitchburg, Mass.

19 | *Hannah J.*, b. Feb. 14, 1856; d. Jan. 18, 1874, æ. 17 yrs., 11 mos.

20 | *Helen S.*, b. May 12, 1858; m., 1876, Frederick G. Robbe.

21 | *Lena M.*, b. Dec. 10, 1869.

THE SMILEY FAMILY.

1 | DAVID SMILEY (DR.). The following extract is from the history of Haverhill, Mass.: —

"Dr. David Smiley was born in Haverhill, Mass., April 10, 1760; at an early age, he was bound an apprentice to a Mr. Hale in this town, a shoemaker. He continued to work with his master till his seventeenth year, when he enlisted in the American army. He was stationed at Winter Hill for three months, the period of his enlistment, when he returned home. He afterward enlisted again, and was at Stillwater, West Point, and in New Jersey. He was finally placed in command of a small guard on Fishkill Mountains, where he remained until his term of service expired. He returned to Haverhill, and walked, in company with five others, sixty miles in one day, and spent the greater part of his wages, in the depreciated currency of the country, for his day's food. In 1782, he married Rachel Johnson, of the East Parish of this town, and in the same year removed to Peterborough, N. H., where he worked at his trade for about two years. In 1784, he removed to Alstead, N. H. Two years later, he purchased a small farm in the north-east part of Peterborough, where he immediately moved. In 1793, he began the study of medicine with Dr. Stephen Jewett, of Rindge, N. H. His practice commenced almost simultaneously with his studies, and for many years he had a large practice. His ride extended into all the neighboring towns, and not unfrequently into more distant towns in other counties. Though not a regularly educated physician, he enjoyed the confidence of many of the most intelligent families, and commanded the respect of all who knew him. He resided on his own farm until the death of his wife in 1842, when he went to live with his son in the village of the same town. He gave up the laborious duties of his profession only when compelled to do so by the infirmities of age. He d. at the same place, Oct. 3, 1855, æ. 95 yrs., and nearly 6 mos."

Dr. Smiley was a Baptist, and a licensed preacher of that denomination, and an earnest and devoted Christian. He preached in Bennington a number of years, and also, at different times, in Hillsboro and in this town. He was a conscientious, worthy, and useful man. From his imperfect education and the difficulties of acquiring medical knowledge in those times, he was never able to take such a standing in the profession as his talents would seem to have warranted; or it may be that his attempt to sustain two professions at once rendered success in either of them an impossibility. He was always highly respected in town. He was present at the centennial celebration of the town in 1839, and was one of the vice-presidents on that occasion.

Dr. Smiley was the son of John Smiley, who emigrated from the north of Ireland and settled in Haverhill, Mass., and d. there, Nov. 12, 1774, æ. 54 yrs., 3 mos. He had nine children, of whom David was the eighth.

Rachel Johnson, the wife of Dr. Smiley, was the dau. of Elias Johnson, of English descent, who was b. in 1734. Her mother, Elizabeth Bixby, was b. April 17, 1738. Rachel was the oldest of six children. Olive Johnson, her sister, unm., b. Sept. 29, 1767, lived in Peterborough, and d. here, Jan. 5, 1845, æ. 77 yrs., 3 mos. Dr. Smiley was b. in Haverhill, April 10, 1760, and d. in Peterborough, Oct. 3, 1855, æ. 95 yrs., 5 mos. He m. Rachel Johnson, Aug. 22, 1782, b. May 22, 1761; d.

Sept. 24, 1842, æ. 81 yrs., 4 mos. He received the pension awarded to the Revolutionary soldiers by the government.

———

2   *Elias*, b. July 10, 1783 ; m. Betsey Bowers, of Rindge ; r. Jaffrey ; d. November, 1866, æ. 83 yrs.

3   *Elisabeth*, b. Aug. 7, 1785 ; m. Benjamin Skinner ; r. Wakefield ; d. Feb. 1, 1826, æ. 41 yrs.

4   †*Francis*, b. Sept. 9, 1787 ; m., March 4, 1810, Sally Ames, Andover, Mass.

5   *John*, b. Dec. 14, 1789 ; m. Priscilla Chase ; r. Wakefield ; d. June 4, 1853, æ. 63 yrs.

6   *William*, b. June 6, 1792 ; d. July 4, 1792, æ. 1 mo.

7   *Mary*, b. Sept. 21, 1793 ; m. Benjamin V. Miller ; r. Nashua.

8   *Ruth*, b. Oct. 12, 1798 ; d. Sept. 6, 1800, æ. 1 yr., 11 mos.

9   †*David, Jr.*, b. Dec. 28, 1800 ; m., 1st w., Harriet C. Farnum ; 2d w., Harriet Page, of Manchester, July 14, 1867.

10   *James*, b. Dec. 13, 1802 ; d. Dec. 31, 1802, æ. 18 dys.

———

1– 4   FRANCIS SMILEY. He was a carpenter by trade. He lived in the north-east part of the town, east of the Andrew Miller place, and near his father's residence, the same farm now occupied by his son James. He m., March 4, 1810, Sally Ames, of Andover, Mass., b. Aug. 14, 1790. He d. Feb. 19, 1867, æ. 79 yrs., 5 mos.

———

11   *John*, b. May 14, 1811 ; m. Lydia Ham, of Great Falls ; r. Lowell.

12   *Elisabeth*, b. May 22, 1813 ; m. Robert Hovey ; r. Swanzey ; ch. living, I. Ida J., Ruth C., and Emma J.

13   *Sally*, b. April 2, 1815 ; m. William Parker, Jr. ; r. New Boston ; ch. living, (1) Sarah M. ; (2) Ellen M. ; (3) Laura R. ; (4) Hermon H.

14   †*Benjamin F.*, b. April 21, 1819 ; m., 1st w., Mary L. Howard ; 2d w., Martha Kidder.

15   *Ruth*, b. Dec. 4, 1823 ; m. Hiram McCoy.

16   *David*, b. Sept. 9, 1827 ; d. Oct. 10, 1852, æ. 25 yrs.

17   †*James*, b. Nov. 15, 1829 ; m. Abby Woodward, of Marlboro.

———

1– 9   DAVID SMILEY. He is a watch-maker and jeweller, and has carried on this business over forty years in this village. His skill and great mechanical ingenuity have given him great success in his business. He m., 1st w., Harriet C. Farnum, Sept. 2, 1826 ; she d. May 1, 1864, æ. 61 yrs.; m., 2d w., July 14, 1867, Harriet Page, of Manchester; she d. 1875. .

18   *Harriet Maria*, b. April 7, 1830; m. George W. Wilson.
19   *Sarah Almira*, b. March 2, 1840; m. John G. Leonard, Jr., of Boston; r. Bangor, Me.; ch., (1) Mary E.; (2) Hattie F.

4- 14   BENJAMIN FRANKLIN SMILEY. He owns and occupies the old farm of Dr. Smiley. A farmer. M., 1st w., Mary L. Howard, of Jamaica, Vt.; d. Nov. 21, 1864, æ. 39 yrs.; m., 2d w., Martha Kidder, of New Boston; 1st w., two ch.; 2d w., one ch.

20   *Sarah A.*, b. Jan. 21, 1855.
21   *Melissa E.*, b. Dec. 22, 1859.
22   *Johnnie F.*, b. Feb. 9, 1867.

4- 17   JAMES SMILEY succeeded his father; is a farmer; m. Abby Woodward, of Marlboro.

23   *Emma N.*, b. Dec. 14, 1861.
24   *Charlie W.*, b. June 4, 1868.

THE SMITH FAMILY.

MEMORIAL OF THE SMITH FAMILY, BY J. H. MORISON, D. D.

During the first and second generations after the settlement of the town, the leading families in Peterborough were the Davisons, the Robbes, the Moores, the Fergusons, the Cuninghams, the Steeles, the Wilsons, the Millers, the Scotts, the Smiths, and the Morisons. I can speak only of those whom I happen to know something about. The three most prominent families, in the second generation, were, undoubtedly, the Steeles, the Wilsons, and the Smiths. They were closely connected by marriage, but had their social rivalships, and often took different sides in the public questions of the day. There were strong men among them, and the debates, so vividly described by Gen. Wilson, in front of the old meeting-house and at the town meetings, furnished a useful stimulus and exercise for the youths who listened to them, and who learned from them valuable lessons of wisdom as well us the use of language.

The sons of William Smith were all men of uncommon mind and character. Robert, the first-born of many brethren, died before my remembrance. In the

family, he was thought to be the least gifted. His letters which I have read showed good sense and an
earnest purpose. He was a very devout man, and at
one time proposed to become a Presbyterian minister.
Of his children, Jesse was a most able and accomplished
physician, and his early death was regarded as a great
public loss to the city of Cincinnati. His daughter
Fanny was a woman of decided ability. She was a devoted Calvinist, and in her theological encounters with
the ablest of her uncles, they did not always come off
triumphant. When I was a child of nine or ten, she used
to walk from Rindge to Peterborough, on Saturdays, to
take the entire charge of two Sunday-schools, one in the
village at the centre of the town, and the other in an
old, uninhabited house near my father's. I was one of
her scholars, and recited to her from memory nearly the
whole of the Gospel of Matthew. Her devotional services, when she knelt down and prayed in the school,
were very impressive. She did, in this way, a great
deal of good. Wherever she was, she endeavored, and
usually with success, to induce the people around her to
study the Bible. Later in life, she became deeply interested in the anti-slavery movement, and I cannot read
without deep emotion the remarkable and prophetic inscription which she prepared for her monument.

John Smith was regarded by his brother Jeremiah as
the ablest of his father's children. He was a man of
vast proportions, — great in body, in voice, in mind, and
in heart. He was usually overflowing with wit and mirth.
He could not bear with any unreasonable pretension or
conceit, and was full of expedients to put it down. A
young man at a public place was boasting of the speed of
his colt. Squire Smith told him that he had a pair of
steers that would outrun him. A race was agreed upon.
The animals were got ready to start. As a signal for
starting a dry cowhide was rattled near them, which so
disconcerted the colt, and drove the steers away so
rapidly, that the colt was entirely distanced, amid the
shouts and laughter of the by-standers. Practical jokes
of this sort not unfrequently contributed to the merriment of those days, when log-rolling bees, house-raisings,
huskings, trainings, brought the young men of the town
together, and gave them some little variety and relaxation amid their hard and continuous labors. John Smith
entered into these things with the hilarity of a strong and
healthy child overflowing with animal spirits. He was
a man of boundless wit and humor. A joke was not
spoiled for relation's sake. He was an earnest Federalist. When Jefferson was President, at some large

gathering he met a family connection who was a Democrat, and who asked him if there was any news. "Yes," he said, "very important news. The President has established a new office here in Peterborough, and has decided to put you at the head of it. I understand that he is going to make you keeper of the geese in Cuningham's pond."

Much, however, as Squire John (that was the name he went by) loved a joke, it would be doing him great injustice to speak of that as the leading quality of his mind. It was only the natural effervescence of a great, joyous, healthy nature. He was a man of generous impulses and a tender heart. His whole soul reached out towards a child, and folded itself round him like the atmosphere of a pleasant summer's day. I shall never forget the kindliness of his greeting to me in my earliest years. If there was something terrible in his denunciation of meanness or dishonesty, his severity was entirely disarmed by suffering or misfortune. For many years he held some of the most important offices in Peterborough, and, with or without office, he always exercised a great influence in the town. He had a commanding personal presence. He dressed in the plain, homespun garments common among our farmers. But no one could meet him, even for a few minutes, without feeling that he was a man of power. There probably never was a deeper sensation of grief among all the inhabitants of the town than was caused by his sudden and violent death, in the summer of 1821. His oldest son, John, who died while still young, was greatly beloved. He had a beautiful voice, and led the singing in the church. His countenance was as beautiful as his voice, and gave the impression of great sweetness and purity of heart. I never have been more moved by sacred music, or felt more strongly its power to awaken the best emotions of our nature, than during the time when he was the leader of the church choir. His brother Robert was a man of talent and of a large and liberal nature. He studied the law, I think, rather late in life, and served three or more terms in Congress, as a member of the House of Representatives from Illinois. His two remaining brothers, James and William, successful and beneficent merchants in St. Louis, are still living. Of the three sisters, Louisa only is now living. Harriet died very young. Jane, the wife of John Cavender, deserves, with her husband, a longer and better notice than I can give. During the latter part of their lives their one object seemed to be to do good, and their days were probably shortened by the exertions which they made for

the relief of the suffering in the dark days of our civil war.

James Smith, who spent most of his life in Cavendish, Vt., was also a man of mark, holding always a post of honor and influence in the community where he lived. He was a man of clear intellectual convictions, and of the most kindly affections. He was happy in his children. One of them, Sarah, wife of James Walker, filled an important place in the town of Peterborough, as a most unselfish woman, taking a leading part in every good word and work. In this respect she was said to be like her only surviving brother, William, of Cavendish.

Of Jeremiah Smith, lawyer, Governor, Judge of the U. S; District Court, and Chief-Justice of the Superior Court of N. H., I have written elsewhere, and therefore need say but little here. He would have been recognized as a leading man anywhere. As a wit or a scholar, as a statesman or a jurist, as an advocate at the bar or a judge on the bench, as a genial companion or a brilliant talker, he would have been received, indeed he was received, as their peer by the ablest and most accomplished men in the land.

Jonathan Smith, the deacon, as he was called, was a modest, clear-headed, upright man, who read, and thought, and formed his opinions for himself, and lived and died true to his own convictions, finding his happiness in faithful and devout living. He was a leading man in the town, and in the discussions before the old meeting-house, but not to the same extent as his brothers, John and Samuel, were. His oldest son, Jonathan, was an eminent lawyer in the northern part of New Hampshire, and died while still a young man. His son William, a man of great intelligence and widely-extended information, lived for many years and died in the State of Illinois. His brother John still lives in Peterborough, holding in the church the office which his father held so modestly and blamelessly. Jeremiah lives in La Harpe, Ill. Of the three sisters, one, Charlotte, died in early youth; Nancy m. Dr. John H. Foster, and lives in Chicago; and Caroline m. James Reynolds, and d. at La Harpe, Ill., July, 1875, æ. 63 yrs.

Samuel Smith, the youngest son of William Smith, was, in some respects, the most remarkable man among them. He was the most enterprising of them all. He had the bearing and manners of an accomplished gentleman. He would have been anywhere a man of mark. He was born to take the lead. For many years he was moderator in the town meetings, and the choice of the people was hardly needed to give him the place. He early saw the advantages for manufacturing purposes, which its superior water-powers gave to our locality, and set himself to improve them. He built a paper-mill, which was the admiration of the neighboring country. His store became the central point of the town, taking the place which Wilson's tavern had held a generation before, where the people were drawn together informally for animated talks and the discussion of public or private measures. When he was not present himself his part was ably sustained by his cousin, Polly Morison, who took care of the store, and who was quite a match in wit and swiftness of repartee for any persons who were bold enough to measure their strength with hers.

Samuel Smith was chosen a member of Congress in 1813, and would undoubtedly have distinguished himself there, but he could not leave his private business, and therefore resigned his seat. It is rightly inscribed upon his monument that he was "the founder of this village." It used to be called "Smith's Village." And well it might be, for his was the enterprise and the controlling mind which prepared the way for its enlargement and prosperity. His enthusiasm and strength gave an impulse to the whole town, and did not a little to keep the minds of the people awake, and to increase their material prosperity, while nothing that was mean or underhanded or dishonest could ever find a shelter near him. He failed at last, not so much from lack of judgment as because he had undertaken more than his limited resources would enable him to carry out. He felt painfully the want of active enterprise and employment. They who saw him only in his latter days could, from what they saw then, form no conception of the dignified, animated, energetic leader who once had such a commanding influence among men.

His son, Frederick, who died at an early age, was a young man of a very uncommon mechanical genius. His son, Jeremiah, was distinguished for his rapidity and skill as a penman and mercantile accountant. He was for many years a merchant in New York City, and died there in 1860. The third son, Samuel G., had a great aptitude and taste for mechanics and natural science. He was a man without guile, of a most genial, kindly disposition. He was engaged in manufacturing, as the agent, successively, in different companies, and died in 1842. Hamilton, the fifth son, was considered one of the brightest and happiest young men in Peterborough. But ill-health prematurely weakened his energies, and caused his death in 1858. Of the other sons,

Albert only is living. Sidney d. Sept. 26, 1875, æ. 72
yrs. Of the daughters, the oldest, Elizabeth, the wife
of Rev. Levi W. Leonard, D.D., d. in 1848, greatly beloved by those who knew her. Mary died while yet a
child, and two, Mrs. Sarah Blanchard and Mrs. Ellen
Smith, yet survive.

I have just given a slight and inadequate account of a
very remarkable family of men. They, most of them,
lived in a narrow sphere, but they were men of large
ideas. They were led by generous impulses. If they
sometimes "failed to bear with fools gladly, seeing they
themselves were wise," and sometimes made merry, too
boisterously, over the weaknesses and absurdities of
others, they were always very tender and compassionate
towards the needy and the helpless. No poor man was
ever made poorer by their taking advantage of his necessities. The widow and the fatherless have reason to bless
them. Gov. Steele, in his Centennial Address, spoke
with a warmth which was honorable alike to his heart
and his head, of the encouragement which he, an unknown youth, had received from one member of the
family. The same might be said of every one of them, by
young men who were encouraged and helped by them to
advantages of education, or posts of usefulness and emolu-
ment, beyond anything which they had been permitted to
enjoy for themselves. Grand times they used to have
when they came together, as they sometimes did, in their
mature years, and made the old house, where their father
had lived, ring with loud voices and sounds of laughter,
as they "tauld their queerest stories," or with assault and
repartee met one another in keen encounters of pleasantry and wit. Nor were the sisters inferior to the men
in the use of the same weapons. The judge was a very
handsome man, "the handsomest old man," said Prof.
Bowen, "the wittiest wise man, and the wisest witty man,
that I ever knew." His sister, Mrs. Samuel Morison, was
as homely as he was handsome. In a playful humor, at
her house, when she was old and very infirm, the judge
put on her nightcap, and going to the looking-glass exclaimed, "Why, Betty, I thought it was you that I saw
in the glass." "Yes," said she, with an air of disdain,
"they always told me that I looked like you, and it
mortified me almost to death." Well, they have passed
away. They believed in God and in the religion of
Jesus. They felt more than they expressed. With them,
faithful, upright, Christian living was more than any professions could be. When, in talking with Fanny, the
most Calvinistic and Antinomian of them all, I once said,
" I had not supposed that I should ever have to impress

on *you* the importance of faith," as quick as a flash she answered, "Show me thy faith *without* thy works, and I will show thee my faith *by* my works." They have gone. But their spirit is not dead. They have not lived in vain. The people of Peterborough to-day are a better and nobler race because of the virtue which has gone out from these grand specimens of our humanity. In an age of intemperance, I never heard the charge of drinking too much brought against any one of them, nor did any suspicion of dishonesty ever sully their good name.

They were all men of mind, and had a great influence in Peterborough. And whatever influence they had was always exercised on the side of truth, and uprightness, and fair-dealing between man and man. In the consciousness of superior strength they may sometimes have been overbearing and impatient. They sometimes used very plain language. A conscientious Presbyterian, who could not stay in the meeting with a bass-viol, which he considered an instrument of Satan, consulted Jeremiah Smith as to the legality of certain steps which might be taken in order to defraud his neighbor of a piece of land. The young lawyer could not help exclaiming : " You want, then, to *cheat* him out of it ! " " No," said the pious man, "not cheat him. I wad na cheat him out of it for the world ; but I thought that perhaps I might kind of *work* him out of it." He had asked advice from the wrong man. These Smiths were above all such arts and tricks as that. Wherever their power was felt, it was on the side of open-handed justice and honor. There was no double-dealing about them. What they thought they said very distinctly, and sometimes, perhaps, in louder tones than were necessary. They were in favor of a liberal policy in education, and in whatever might elevate the standard of morals, while they always, by precept and example, favored what the Apostle James calls " pure religion and undefiled, before God and the Father."

I have written these few paragraphs in the midst of ancient Rome, with the memories and associations of a history reaching through five-and-twenty centuries, and moulding the policy and the fortunes of the world, pressing upon me. And I cannot but see that the principles and habits which contribute to the well-being and happiness of my native town among the mountains of New Hampshire are the same as those which once placed this city at the head of the world's civilization. As long as it preserved its pristine honor and virtue, and its habits of industry, frugality, and simple living, it went on prospering and happy ; but when it left these principles and habits behind, and became the seat of all the worst crimes that disgrace our humanity, its day of doom came swiftly and fatally upon it. It is pleasant to turn away from this mournful history, and the decaying monuments which I see around me, to the still youthful and hopeful land of my birth, and to bring vividly before me some of the truthful, hard-working, intelligent men, who helped to form the character and secure the prosperity of that humble settlement.

ROME, Feb. 22, 1876.

For most of the facts and details under this name we are indebted to a genealogy of the family of William Smith, prepared in 1852 by Rev. L. W. Leonard, D.D., and Rev. Samuel Abbot Smith.

1   ROBERT SMITH, of Moneymore, variously spelled Munnehaugh, Moneymar and Moneymore, in the County of Londonderry, and north of Ireland, near the Lough Neah, was the son of James Smith, of Ireland, and came to this country with a number of families in the autumn of 1736, and spent the following winter in Lexington, Mass. He was a tanner, and brought with him considerable property. Some of his brothers settled in Virginia, and though considerable inquiry has been made, yet no trace of the family has ever been discovered. Most of this company made a settlement in Lunenburg, Mass. Four children came with him and settled in Peterborough. His wife, Elizabeth, was a daughter of James Smith, of England, who was a son of James Smith, of Scotland. She d. in Lunenburg, Sept. 28, 1757, æ. 74 yrs. It appears that Robert Smith came to Peterborough to live soon after the death of his wife in 1757, and d. Jan. 14, 1766, æ. 85 yrs. It is said that he put down four tan-vats, now in a good state of preservation, in the tan-yard of the late Deacon John Field, now Deacon A. A. Farnsworth; and probably, as old as he was, he did some little business in tanning. The necessities of the people probably required it. The children who came with Robert and Elizabeth Smith to this coun-try were as follows.

2   † *John*, b. in Ireland, 1715; m. Mary Harkness.
3   *Sarah*, b. in Ireland, 1716; m., 1st hus., James Bell, the ancestor of Samuel and John Bell, of Hooksett; 2d hus., Deacon William McNee, by whom she had no children. She d. Jan. 31, 1814, æ. 98 yrs., some supposed 100 yrs.

34

4 | *Mary*, b. in Ireland, 1720; m. Capt. Thomas Morison; d. Dec. 29, 1799, æ. 79 yrs. In the church records, Dec. 31, 1799, Mr. Dunbar makes this entry: "Attended the funeral of the aged Widow Mary Morison, relict of the late Capt. Thomas Morison, and sister of William Smith, Esq. She died yesterday morning, after a long confinement and a total loss of bodily strength and of all her mental powers."

5 | † *William*, b. in Ireland, 1723; m. Elizabeth Morison, dau. of John Morison.

1-2 | JOHN SMITH was b. in Ireland, and was twenty-one years old when his father emigrated to America. He m. Mary Hartness or Harkness, of Lunenburg, and came to Peterborough some time before 1754, when his first child was b. He began the place in the south part of the town, where his descendants lived so long, and raised a large family. He was selectman in 1761 and '73, and his name occurs often on the town records, as surveyor and also on committees and in the frequent legislation about roads. He d. Jan. 28, 1801, æ. 86 yrs. In the church records, Jan. 29, 1801, Mr. Dunbar says: "Attended the funeral of the aged Mr. John Smith (æ. 86), brother to William Smith, Esq., a native of Ireland, and came to New England sixty-three years ago. He survived his mental powers." She d. May 14, 1822, æ. 87 yrs.

---

6 | *Elizabeth*, b. June 14, 1754; m. John White, Jr.

7 | *Thomas*, b. June 8, 1756; m. Martha Ritchie; two ch., Thomas and Mary; d. 1825.

8 | *Mary*, b. Nov. 6, 1757; unm.; d. Dec. 5, 1796, æ. 39 yrs.; always an invalid.

9 | *Robert*, b. April 29, 1759; m. Louis Kidder. He practised medicine in various places, as Durham, Milford, Petersham, Bristol, and Addison, Vt., at which latter place he d.; ch., (1) Frederick; (2) Charles; (3) Henry; (4) Fanny; (5) Nancy.

10 | *Sarah*, b. April 29, 1761; m., 1st hus., Rev. David Annan; 2d hus., John Todd.

11 | *Hannah*, b. Aug. 29, 1763; m. Thomas Dunshee; r. Bristol, Vt.; eight ch.

12 | *Margaret*, b. April 29, 1765; m. Thomas Fletcher; r. New Ipswich; d. 1845; two ch.

13 | *John*, b. June 18, 1767; d. Sept. 25, 1778, æ. 11 yrs.

14 | *Jenny*, b. 1769; unm.; had a son by David Smiley; David Smith, her son, was in Dartmouth College three years, and then studied divinity, and the last heard of him he was preaching in Michigan. His mother d. with him.

15   *Nancy*, b. November, 1772 ; m. Dea. Jonathan Smith.
16   † *William*, b. July 3, 1773 ; m.,. 1st w., Jane Moore ; 2d w., Olive Gray ; 3d w., Nancy Sheppherd.
17   *James*, b. ——; d. 1778.
18   *Naomi*, b. 1775 ; m. William Burns ; r. Bristol, Vt. ·

2— 16   WILLIAM SMITH succeeded his father on the homestead. Late in life he sold his farm, and spent a few years before his death with his daughter, Mrs. Russell, of Jaffrey. He d. June 23, 1875, at Jaffrey, æ. 96 yrs. He m., 1st w., Jane Moore, Dec. 25, 1800 ; d. Feb. 7, 1803, æ. 29 yrs. ; m., 2d w., Olive Gray, April 22, 1806 ; she d. Nov. 28, 1820, æ. 38 yrs. ; m., 3d w., Nancy Sheppherd, February, 1822 ; 1st w., two ch. ; 2d w., nine ch. ; 3d w., two ch.

19   *John*, b. Aug. 20, 1801 ; d. Sept. 10, 1802, æ. 1 yr.
20   *William M.*, b. Jan. 18, 1803 ; m. Levina Hardy ; ch., (1) Charles ; (2) Justin ; (3) James ; (4) Clarissa ; (5) Levina ; r. Lowell.
21   *Jane*, b. March 11, 1807 ; m. George McCrillis ; ch., May Jane and Henrietta.
22   *Mary*, b. Oct. 18, 1808 ; m. Andreas Emery, Jaffrey ; ch., (1) George ; (2) Lucy ; (3) Charles.
23   *Sarah*, b. Nov. 21, 1809 ; m., 1st hus., Joseph H. Findley ; m., 2d hus., —— Whiting ; ch., (1) Charles ; (2) George ; (3) Emma.
24   *John*, b. Nov. 7, 1811 ; m. Sarah Moore ; ch., (1) James ; (2) Sarah ; (3) Ellen ; r. Hudson, Mich. ; d.
25   *Dexter*, b. Jan. 20, 1813 ; m. Almira Stearns ; ch., (1) George ; (2) William ; r. Michigan ; d.
26   *Margaret*, b. Sept. 5, 1814 ; m. Luke Pierce ; one ch., Sarah ; r. and d. in Michigan.
27   *James*, b. Jan. 13, 1816.*
"He graduated at Yale College, in 1840, studied law at Harvard, and settled in New Orleans, 1843. He was a young man of superior talents and excellent scholarship, possessing a proud nature and a towering ambition, guided and controlled, however, by noble and generous impulses. He began the practice of law in the great Southern city which he had selected for his home, with every prospect of success. Friends, who had been his classmates in college and at the law-school, gave him a favorable introduction ; and business grew upon him more rapidly than he had any reason to expect, or than is usual with young lawyers. He loved his profession, and devoted himself to it with a single-

* Letter Nathaniel H. Morison, LL.D.

ness of purpose which is sure to win success. He
examined his own mental powers with calmness and
impartiality, and decided that they promised a more
distinguished career on the bench than at the bar.
After this conclusion was reached, it became his highest
ambition to qualify himself for filling the office of a
great judge. He had probably made a correct diagnosis
of his case; but the high esteem in which his great
relative, Judge Smith, of Exeter, was held in the State,
and his own admiration for him, may not have been
without influence on his judgment. In the midst of his
plans, and his dreams of the greatness that lay before
him, he was struck down by that insidious disease, consumption, which has destroyed so many of his family.
One damp evening, on riding out rather late to his
lodgings, which were a few miles from the city, he felt
an unusual chill, and took a cold bath, thinking that the
reaction which should follow would restore the proper
temperature. He was not aware of having taken cold;
but in the bath he was seized with a violent hemorrhage.
No one was in the house, except the negro servants, who
waited upon him, and no physician was near. He perceived at once the full significance of what had occurred,
and he knew too well the destiny that awaited him. In
a few days, however, he had so far recovered as to be
able to attend to his business again; but other attacks
soon followed which weakened his constitution, naturally
strong, and destroyed all hope of a permanent recovery.
He then quietly arranged his business affairs, took leave
of the lady to whom he had become engaged, and bid-
ding farewell to his other friends, came back to his old
home with the full consciousness that he must die.

" To but one friend did he ever reveal the keen disappointment, the utter desolation, which he felt when he
found that all his hopes had been blasted, and that the
future to which he had looked so confidently was to be
for him a mere blank. But he uttered no complaint to
any one, not even to the sister who was dearest to him,
and who watched over him lovingly to the last. His
family were not aware of his marriage engagement, as he
never talked of his personal affairs, and destroyed all the
letters which he received from the South. He bore his
sufferings, mental and physical, with stoical fortitude,
and died as he had lived, the loftiest, proudest spirit in
that little band of ardent, aspiring young men, who had
started in life together (at Exeter Academy). He
breathed his last at his father's house, in the South Village, just as the clock struck the midnight hour which
ushered in the new year, 1847, æ. 31 yrs."

28 *Charles,* b. April 23, 1817 ; d. May 20, 1820, æ. 3 yrs.
29 *Olive,* b. June 13, 1820 ; m. Sylvester Russell ; r. Jaffrey.
30 *Henry,* b. Jan. 22, 1823 ; m. Harriet Frost ; r. Lowell ; killed on railroad.
31 *Nancy,* b. June 9, 1824 ; d. May 10, 1854, æ. 30 yrs.

1- 5   WILLIAM SMITH. We suppose that he took up his residence in town about the time of his marriage, Dec. 31, 1751, no doubt having been here more or less for some time previous, in preparing for the support and shelter of a family. He was considered one of the best informed of the early settlers, was justice of the peace many years, delegate to the Provincial Congress, 1774, deacon of the church, "was a man of singular discretion, modesty, and goodness," a useful citizen, and much employed in the business of the town. He held various offices in town. At the first meeting after incorporation he was chosen one of a committee to settle with the "old committee," and subsequently he was moderator, selectman, tithing-man, treasurer, etc., at various times. He m. Elizabeth Morison, dau. of John and Margaret Wallace Morison, Dec. 31, 1751. She was b. in Londonderry, and was distinguished for industry, economy, and energy. She d. Sept. 15, 1808, æ. 85 yrs. He d. Jan. 31, 1808, æ. 85 yrs.

32 †*Robert,* b. Feb. 15, 1753 ; m., 1st w., Agnes Smiley ; 2d w., Isabel Ames.
33 † *John,* b. April 10, 1754 ; m. Margaret Steele.
34 † *James,* b. Jan. 29, 1756 ; m. Sally Ames.
35 *William,* b. March 14, 1757 ; d. Jan. 31, 1776, æ. 19 yrs.
36 *Elizabeth,* b. July 28, 1758 ; m. Samuel Morison.
37 † *Jeremiah,* b. Nov. 29, 1759 ; m., 1st w., Eliza Ross ; 2d w., Elizabeth Hale.
38 *Hannah,* b. May 18, 1761 ; m., Dec. 7, 1795, John Barker ; r. Rindge ; ch., (1) Hannah, b. April 24, 1801 ; (2) John, b. Nov. 28, 1804.
39 † *Jonathan,* b. April 11, 1763 ; m. Nancy Smith.
40 †*Samuel,* b. Nov. 11, 1765 ; m. Sally Garfield.

5- 32   ROBERT SMITH. He was a deacon in the Presbyterian Church, and very much respected for his good sense and Christian character. He lived on a farm in the south part of the town, originally deeded by Jeremiah Gridley, John Hill, and John Towle to Halbert Morison, July 5, 1753, and by him to William Smith, June 2, 1761, and by him to his son Robert. He d. early, in consequence of an injury to his knee. He m., May 25, 1778, Agnes Smiley, dau. of William Smiley. She d. Oct. 10,

1791, æ. 36 yrs.; m., 2d w., May, 1792, Isabel Ames, who m., for 2d hus., Shubael Hurd, of Lempster. She d. August, 1847, æ. 84 yrs. He d. Dec. 31, 1795, æ. 43 yrs.; 1st w., two ch.; 2d w., three ch.

41   *William*, b. May 16, 1779; unm.; d. Aug. 31, 1840, æ. 61 yrs. He was subject to epilepsy, which greatly impaired his mental powers.

42   *Fanny*, b. Sept. 4, 1780; unm. She d. July 10, 1858, æ. 78 yrs. She was a talented but eccentric woman. She very early espoused the anti-slavery cause, but was not permitted, as many of her associates were, to see such a glorious realization of all her hopes. She ordered the marble obelisk which stands over her grave, and dictated the inscription in 1858: "This side is dedicated to the glorious cause of emancipation. May God prosper it, and all the people say, Amen."

43   † *Jesse*,   m. Eliza Bailey.

                 b. March, 1793; m.; had three wives; r. Buffalo, N. Y. All his ch.
44   *Stephen*,   deceased. He d. in 1867, æ. 74 yrs.

45   †*Robert*, b. Aug. 8, 1795; m., Nov. 18, 1818, Nancy Nesmith.

32–43   JESSE SMITH, M.D., graduated at Dartmouth College, 1814. He concluded to study the medical profession, but having expended all his means, and more too, and having incurred debts for his collegiate education, he was obliged to teach a few years while pursuing his medical studies, and did not receive his degree till 1819, when he graduated in the medical class of that year, in Harvard University. In 1820, he was appointed to lecture on anatomy, in the Dartmouth Medical College, where he acquitted himself so creditably that he was invited to the Professorship of Anatomy and Surgery, in the Ohio Medical College, Cincinnati, which he accepted, and held to the time of his death. He became eminent as a surgeon, standing at the very head of the profession in the Western States. He operated thirteen times for stone in the bladder. He was an independent and strong-minded man, with an indomitable will that overcame all obstacles, and with a wide culture in his profession which rendered him an interesting and instructive lecturer. He m. Eliza Bailey, dau. of Jonathan Bailey, of Charlestown, who m., 2d hus., Rev. John Wright, of Cincinnati.

They had seven children, all deceased but one, Mary Elizabeth, b. March 7, 1830; m. John R. Wright; have six ch. Prof. Smith d. of cholera, July, 1833, after fourteen hours' sickness, a victim to his professional zeal and ability, during the prevalence of cholera in that city. See Centennial Appendix.

32– 45 | ROBERT SMITH, b. Aug. 8, 1795; m., November, 1818, Nancy Nesmith. He went south early in life, and taught school some years in Mississippi, when he removed to Simmsport, La., where he owned and carried on a plantation. He had several children, of whom Samuel only survived, and now lives in Louisiana. He d.

5– 33 | JOHN SMITH. I am indebted to his daughter, Mrs. Louisa Fifield, now residing in Alton, Ill., for the following graphic sketch of her father, as well as for many of the ideas in the remaining part. She says:—
" Her father when twenty-one years of age could read the Bible, and knew a little of arithmetic. His first use of his freedom was to raise a crop of rye, from the proceeds of which he supported himself at school, at Exeter, some six months, and gained, with other acquisitions, the rudiments of Latin. With this scanty provision of education, he began his life's work, supplemented by diligent reading of the Bible, which he loved, and by the thorough perusal of such works as Edmund Burke's speeches, Hume's *History of England*, Boswell's *Life of Johnson*, Blair's sermons, and, above all, Burns' poems, in which he greatly delighted. He was liberally educated, in a higher and better sense than that of the thoughtless graduates of our colleges. The town library, the weekly newspaper, and an occasional book loaned by a friend, were the scanty, but sufficient, means of culture. A strong mind that used its opportunities made him an influential and leading citizen. He was early made a justice of the peace, and did most of the justice business in town for many years. He was always deeply interested in town affairs, and held all the offices of trust except that of selectman. He was moderator 1793, '97, '98, '99, 1801; representative to the General Court twelve years, from 1791 to 1803, and much employed in committees on all important business. Speaking evil of no one, and judging all men kindly as he would himself be judged, he exercised a kindly and genial, as well as a strong, influence over his fellow-men.
" His influence, said the Hon. John H. Steele, in his centennial speech, 1839, contributed much towards giving a distinct character to the town. But where now is

the man who never lets a human being pass him unheeded ; whose ever active mind and ready talent can
draw forth alike the budding powers of childhood or
those of ripened age ; who is ever ready to aid, counsel,
or direct, with wisdom, purse, or hand his fellow-man ?
Such a man was John Smith."

His sudden death spread a gloom over the town
hardly ever felt before, and the words added to the record of his death in the church-book by Mr. Dunbar tes-
tified to the universal esteem in which he was held : —

"*Ast eheu quantum benevolentiæ, quantum integritatis
e terris convolavit.*"

The question arises how such men as Mr. Smith acquired such funds of knowledge and wisdom in those
times, when the means of cultivation were so limited,
books so scarce, and periodicals and newspapers almost
unknown. We can only partially account for the fact.
He inherited more than a common share of talent, and
in his early life of hardship, in which his physical powers
were fully developed and strengthened, his constant association with men of a superior character for strength
and purity tended to a constant elevation of his moral
as well as his intellectual powers. His means of early
education were exceedingly limited, but it was effective ;
for such men only need to be started ; an ardent thirst
for knowledge and a keen observation of men and things
would open the way to any acquisition. Perhaps I
should not omit to mention, as one of the elements of
his success, his great moderation in eating, and an entire abstinence from all luxuries ; his sustenance was
upon a plain, nourishing diet, which insured the greatest
share of health. The books read were few, but they
were read thoroughly, and the contents, with much re-
flection and conversation, made his own. His associates
were thinking men, men who had large, expanded views,
and were able to grapple with almost any subject, without extraneous aid. But we never cease to wonder how
such men as the subject of this notice could have arisen
without more means of culture and improvement. Were
it not that other instances of native greatness were often
exhibited in this town, that a race almost came forth with
shrewdness, knowledge, and wisdom unprecedented, we
should have said that this was merely one of those exceptions of individual excellence that spring up now and
then, no one knows how. He settled on the Street Road
near to and north of his father's residence. He m.,
Dec. 1, 1791, Margaret Steele, dau. Capt. David Steele.
She d. at Franklin, Sept. 30, 1830, æ. 73 yrs., 8 mos.

Robert Smith

He met his death by a fall from a load of hay, Aug. 7, 1821, æ. 67 yrs., 3 mos.

---

46   *Harriet*, b. Nov. 3, 1792 ; d. May 17, 1818, æ. 25 yrs., 6 mos.

47   *Louisa*, b. May 9, 1795 ; m., Sept. 18, 1827, Joshua Fifield, Franklin ; he d. at Alton, Ill., Nov. 27, 1840 ; ch., Mary Mansfield, the only child living, b. Feb. 8, 1835 ; m. George Kellenberger, who d. Jan. 4, 1866 ; two ch., Anna and Edith ; r. Alton, Ill.

48   *John, Jr.*, b. April 16, 1797. He lived in town till 1822, when he went to Northfield, and associated himself with Thomas Baker and John Cavender, for the purpose of building a cotton factory. While earnestly laboring in this enterprise, he sickened and d., Oct. 8 of the same year, 1822, æ. 25 yrs. He was a young man of much promise.

49   *Jane*, b. March 14, 1800 ; m., Jan. 26, 1823, John Cavender, a trader in Peterborough many years ; a manufacturer of Franklin from 1822 to 1836, and then a merchant in St. Louis, Mo., one of the firm of Smith Brothers & Co. He d. at St. Louis, Jan. 5, 1863, æ. 69 yrs. She d. at St. Louis, Dec. 5, 1858, æ. 58 yrs., 8 mos. ; two ch., John S. and Robert.

50   *Robert*, b. June 12, 1802.

He spent his early years at home in labor on his father's farm, on which he worked steadily till he was nineteen years of age, only enjoying the winter district-schools, with a term of three months at Daniel M. Christie's school in the autumn of 1820, and three months at the New Ipswich academy, as all his advantages of education. In the spring of 1820, he went into the machine-shop of his Uncle Samuel to learn the trade of making machinery, where he remained till the death of his brother John in 1821, when he took his place in the Smithville Manufacturing Company, with John Cavender and Thomas Baker, in building a cotton-factory in Northfield, near the point where the Winnipiseogee and Pemigewasset unite.

He remained here, sedulously employed in the manufacturing and mercantile interests of the company, till 1832, when he emigrated to the State of Illinois, pitching his tent in the town of Alton, "near which was a traders' post of some note, called St. Louis." (How strange! now a mighty city.) He rose to distinction in political life by his own ardent and unaided efforts, overcoming all the obstacles that his want of early discipline and training presented. He was chosen to the twenty-eighth Congress in the district in which he lived, for three terms, or six years, from 1843 to '49.

"His general course in the national councils has been guided by those democratic principles and doctrines upon which he was originally elected. He here sustained the administration of Mr. Polk in all its cardinal features of its policy, excepting as to appropriations for rivers and harbors. These he has always broadly and liberally advocated." *

He was appointed paymaster in the late civil war, in which office he did faithful service, till ill-health compelled him to resign. He was a man of very genial nature, and of the strictest integrity. He possessed uncommonly popular talents,.and few men ever held such a power over the popular will. He m., Nov. 3, 1828, Sarah P. Bingham, of Lempster; ch., (1) Robert Bingham, b. July 31, 1838 ; (2) Sarah Bingham, b. May 27, 1843. He d. at Alton, Ill., Dec. 21, 1867, æ. 65 yrs.

51 *James*, b. Oct. 28, 1804; m., May. 15, 1832, Persis Garland, of Franklin; c. After spending some five years in business in New York, he formed a copartnership with his brother, William H. Smith, and their brother-in-law, John Cavender, under the firm of Smith Brothers & Co., and commenced business in St. Louis, May, 1833, which was successful under his untiring energy and cautious, prudent management, till the "big fire of 1849," when the old firm dissolved, showing a prosperous business, in spite of losses by the disastrous fire. In 1851, a new copartnership was formed, in which George Partridge was associated with James and William H. Smith, under the style of Partridge & Co., the Smiths only to render such service in the business as suited their inclinations. It is but justice to say that the continued prosperity of the new firm was quite as much due to the cautious, prudent counsel and management of James Smith as in the old company. The Smiths withdrew from this copartnership in 1863. James Smith, after an unremitting service of more than thirty years, retired to wisely consider how he could best discharge the "trust of a beneficent Providence," in the disposition of his earnings and savings. If report be true, he has chosen the sensible plan of becoming his own executor, to which the Washington University and kindred institutions of the city of his adoption bear ample testimony as to the wisdom or folly of his example.

* History Congress, Biographical and Political. Henry G. Wheeler. Harper & Brothers. 1848.

Truly
James Smith

very truly Wm H Smith

52   *Jeremiah*, b. Oct. 1, 1806 ; d. April 6, 1816, æ. 9 yrs., 6 mos.

53   *William H.*, b. Dec. 26, 1808 ; m., Nov. 5, 1837, Lydia Pettengill, of Salisbury; she d. at St. Louis, Feb. 10, 1841, æ. 29 yrs. He m., 2d w., Sept. 13, 1843, Ellen Smith, dau. Samuel and Sally G. Smith. Of their four ch. only one survives, William Eliot, b. Dec. 31, 1844 ; m. Alice Cole, of Alton, 1873. When Wm. H. Smith retired from business in St. Louis, in 1863, he took up his residence in Alton, and here bought a farm, erected a suite of buildings, and adapted the farm to the fruit culture.

5- 34   JAMES SMITH. He settled in Cavendish, Vt., in 1790. He was here highly respected, and held various offices of trust and honor. He was many years justice of the peace ; a Representative in the Legislature of Vermont for thirteen successive years, and much employed in town business. He was said to be second to none of his family in talents or intelligence. He m., Dec. 31, 1791, Sally Ames, b. May 6, 1769; she d. May 16, 1833, æ. 64 yrs.; he d. Aug. 11, 1842, æ. 86 yrs., 6 mos.

---

54   *Sally*, b. Sept. 1, 1795 ; m. James Walker, Esq., of Peterborough.

55   *James*, b. Nov. 13, 1797 ; m. Betsey Brown, of Plymouth, Vt. He represented Cavendish in the Legislature ; afterwards re. to Schoolcraft, Mich., May, 1833, where he d. Feb. 4, 1842. She d. May 11, 1841. Three of his large family only survive, *viz.*: Betsey, Sarah and Marcia.

56   *William*, b. July 31, 1800 ; m., Oct. 6, 1828, Rhoda Bates, of Cavendish. She d. Aug. 8, 1844 ; m., 2d w., Aug. 20, 1845, Mrs. Isabel Page, dau. of John Proctor, b. July 4, 1823. Of his children, Rhoda, who m. Franklin Rice, of Boston, and Ellen and William survive. He has represented Cavendish in the Legislature of the State, and been much employed in municipal and probate business in the town. At one time he was extensively engaged in the woollen manufacture at Proctorsville, Vt., but sold out his interest in the same, and has now for many years devoted himself to agriculture.

57   *Joseph Addison*, b. March 31, 1806 ; m., Oct. 8, 1835, Sarah M. Proctor, b. Jan. 16, 1819. He d. at Proctorsville, Vt., Feb. 28, 1851. One ch. only survived of his family, John P.

58 | *John*, b. Aug. 31, 1812; m., Feb. 25, 1836, Nancy Willard. He d. April 20, 1839, æ. 26 yrs., 7 mos, ; r. St. Joseph, Mich.

5- 37 | JEREMIAH SMITH. Judge Smith is the representative man of the race and of the town. He was among the most eminent men that New Hampshire has ever produced. If, as has been said in relation to an early period of New Hampshire history, " there were giants in those days," he was certainly among these giants. He was an eminently great and good man. All his efforts were exerted for the honor and benefit of his State ; and few men have accomplished so much as he did in elevating his profession, the law, then in a low condition, to a true and honorable basis — even to a high standard. His memory will be long cherished as one of the public benefactors of New Hampshire.

He commenced the practice of law in Peterborough, in 1787, where he remained ten years. During this time he represented the town in the Legislature in 1788, '89, '90; was a member of the convention that formed the present Constitution in 1791, '92. He took an active and important part in the deliberations of that body. His vote was cast for expunging that clause of the Constitution by which " no person can be capable of being elected a Senator or Representative who is not of the Protestant religion," an article which is still in the Constitution.

In 1790, he was chosen a Representative to the second Congress, and was continued for three successive terms. He here formed an acquaintance with all the great men of that period, and was upon terms of intimacy with that remarkable man, Fisher Ames, which continued through his life. In 1797, he removed to Exeter, and was that year appointed U. S. Attorney for the District of New Hampshire, and at the same time he resigned his office as member of Congress. In 1800, he was appointed Judge of Probate for the County of Rockingham, and held the office about two years. In February, 1801, he was appointed a Judge of the U. S. District Court, but on the repeal of the " Judiciary Law," in March, 1802, his office was abolished ; but in May, of the same year, he was appointed Chief-Justice of the Superior Court of Judicature in New Hampshire. He held this office till 1809, when he was chosen Governor of the State ; but failing of a reëlection, he returned to the bar. Under a new judiciary act in 1813, Mr. Smith was reluctantly induced to accept the office of chief-justice, which office he held till 1816, when the judiciary act was rescinded by the Legislature, and he once more returned to the practice of law.

In 1820, at the age of sixty-one, he withdrew from active business, having acquired an ample fortune by the fruits of his industry and judicious economy. To those who wish to know more of this remarkable man, we would refer them to an excellent Life of Judge Smith, written by John H. Morison, D. D., and published in 1845. He received the honorary degree of LL.D. from Dartmouth, 1804, from Cambridge in 1807. He m., 1st w., March 8, 1797, Eliza Ross, of Prince George County, Md. She d. June 19, 1827, æ. 59 yrs.; m., 2d w., Sept. 20, 1831, Elizabeth Hale, dau. of Hon. William Hale, of Dover. He d. Sept. 21, 1842, æ. 82 yrs., 9 mos.

59 *Ariana*, b. Dec. 28, 1797; unm.; d. June 20, 1829, æ. 31 yrs., 6 mos.

60 *William*, b. Aug. 31, 1799; unm.; d. at Centreville, Miss., March 29, 1830, æ. 30 yrs., 6 mos., where he had gone for his health. He was graduated at Harvard University in 1817. He studied law, and practised his profession in Portsmouth, the last two or three years of his life, till his health failed. He represented the town of Exeter in the General Court in 1821, '22, '23.

61 *Jeremiah*, b. Aug. 20, 1802; drowned Sept. 26, 1808, æ. 6 yrs.

62 *Jeremiah*, b. July 14, 1837; m. Hannah Webster, of Dover. Was graduated at Harvard University, 1856; studied law, and was appointed, Oct. 16, 1867, one of the Justices of the Supreme Court in New Hampshire, which office he resigned in consequence of the failure of his health, January, 1874.

5- 39 JONATHAN SMITH remained on the old homestead, and spent his life there. The farm was deeded to him, May 5, 1791, for which he was to support the parents, and also to see that John Scott was taken care of in a comfortable manner, and pay within a year after his decease twenty pounds to Elizabeth Morison, and also the same sum to Hannah Barker. The sons, John, James, Jeremiah, and Samuel, were cut off in his will with one dollar each. He was a deacon in the church, long a leader of the choir. He was selectman six years, 1799, 1800, '1, '2, '3, '4; representative to the General Court eight years, 1821, '22, '23, '24, '25, '26, '27, '28.

He was a man of a strong mind, which had been long maturing, and he felt very little of the withering effects of age, although he had nearly reached eighty years. His knowledge was not very general, though he was a great reader ; but on some subjects he was exceedingly well informed. His reading had taken a theological turn, and but few persons possessed his knowledge on these matters. He was a strong *Unitarian*, and was ready to give any man a reason for his faith. He was a man of kind affections and feelings, yet strong in his prejudices, and rather more ready to forgive an injury than to forget it. His life was a useful one, he having at various times held all the offices in the gift of the town ; but it was mostly spent in the retirement of his own home, and in the management of his own affairs. He was a modest man. Those who remember him at the centennial will recollect with how much diffidence he presided on that occasion. The responsibility of the important trust of presiding disturbed his sleep for many nights. He, nevertheless, performed all the duties of the occasion well when the time came, which added very much to the success of the celebration.

He was a good man, — good without ostentation and without pretension ; his life showed forth the man, for it was a living and preaching illustration of Jesus. He lived and died on the same spot on which he was born. He went down to his grave like a shock of corn fully ripe, with so pure and upright a character as falls to the lot of but few mortals here below. He m., August, 1792, Nancy Smith, dau. of John Smith. She d. May 13, 1847, æ. 74 yrs., 6 mos. He d. Aug. 29, 1842, æ. 79 yrs., 4 mos.

---

63   *Betsey*, b. Feb. 3, 1795 ; m., Dec. 30, 1819, John Gordon ; re. to Montebello, Ill., 1831 ; she d. in Hamilton, Ill., Aug. 12, 1845, æ. 50 yrs.

64   † *Jonathan*, b. Aug. 15, 1797 ; m. Hannah Payson.

65   *Mary*, b. May 17, 1799 ; m., Dec. 3, 1818, Timothy Fox ; re. to Denmark, Iowa, in 1836. He d. and she d. Only one of their large family survived.

66   *William*, b. July 8, 1801 ; m., Oct. 9, 1838, Elizabeth, dau. John Stearns, of Jaffrey ; r. La Harpe, Ill., where he d., Oct. 25, 1873, æ. 72 yrs. ; four ch. survive, *viz.*, William H., Jonathan, Albert, Elizabeth.

67   † *John*, b. April 17, 1803 ; m. Susan Stearns.

68   *Nancy*, b. 1805 ; d. Aug. 23, 1808, æ. 3 yrs., 6 mos.

69   *Charlotte*, b. 1806 ; d. Sept. 9, 1808, æ. 2 yrs.

70   *Nancy*, b. Aug. 5, 1808 ; m., Sept. 21, 1840, Dr. John H. Foster, b. March 8, 1796, at Hillsboro. He received

the degree of M. D. from the New Hampshire Medical Institution, 1821, and practised his profession first at New London, then Ashby, and at Dublin from 1828 to 1833. He then re. to Chicago, and relinquished his profession, and after that acquired an immense fortune. Three ch. living, (1) Clara, b. Jan. 1, 1844; m. Perkins Bass, Esq., of Chicago; (2) Julia, b. Aug. 22, 1846; m. Rev. Mr. Porter, of Racine, Wis.; (3) Adele, b. Aug. 31, 1851; m. George Adams, Esq., of Chicago. Dr. Foster d. from an injury received in being thrown from his carriage, May 17, 1874, æ. 78 yrs.

71 *Charlotte*, b. 1810; d. Aug. 10, 1825, æ. 15 yrs.

72 *Caroline*, b. Nov. 13, 1812; m. James Reynolds. He d. at Hannibal, Mo., 1873; ch., Anna, b. March 24, 1853; d. in Hannibal, 1873, æ. 20 yrs. She d. at La Harpe, Ill., July, 1875, æ. 62 yrs.

73 *Jeremiah*, b. Sept. 15, 1815; m. Sarah Oatman; 2d w., ——; lives in La Harpe, Ill.

5- 40 SAMUEL SMITH. His early opportunities for education were probably better than of most of the young men of his day. In addition to the common advantages at home, he enjoyed longer or shorter periods of schooling at the academies at Exeter and Andover, and thereby fitted himself to become an accomplished talker, a ready debater on almost any topic, and a man of vastly more than common intelligence. When we add to this his courteous manners and gentlemanly deportment, and his great knowledge of mankind, together with a physique of fine proportions, and commanding and pleasant mien, we have altogether a man that does honor to our common nature.

He was a man of a strong and highly cultivated intellect, with exceedingly active and energetic powers, of quick perception and ready judgment. He was particularly distinguished for his colloquial powers, which were remarkable, and his conversation was always rich and instructive, and his ideas were clothed in singularly accurate and appropriate language.

It is not too much to say that, in the height of his prosperity, he exerted over the community an elevating and enlightening influence; that he was by his character and intelligence a public educator, and raised and sustained the tone of public sentiment in town. He was always particularly posted up in all the topics of the day, beside his extensive general reading. He delighted in politics, and had devoted much attention and study to it, never wishing to be known by any other title than that of a Federalist of the old school, with all the unmerited reproach attached to the name. Of course he was much involved in the bitter controversies that so much prevailed in the first organization of the Democratic and Federal parties in our country, and did strong and effective service for his party. He was chosen to represent his district in Congress in 1813–15, but on account of the press of his private business, he resigned his seat, after attending the first session and a part of the second.

He possessed great business talents, and could accomplish a great undertaking with singular despatch and success; but he scorned little things, and all care and economy of these he entirely ignored. He was in his element with fifty workmen at his beck, and with a great job of a dam or wall or embankment; and no man could manage them more pleasantly and kindly than he, and yet accomplish such an immense amount of work; and after all he was not an economical manager of these great enterprises; the little things, so important in every undertaking, always more than counterbalanced the rapid progress of any work. He was persevering in the object which engaged his attention, but did not look to the end. He often seemed visionary, and many of his plans and projects came to an end half-completed. He was fair and honorable and upright in all his business transactions. Though he took great pride in making good bargains and profitable contracts, it was not so much through the love of gain, as exhibiting shrewdness, judgment, and talent. He was never very scrupulous if the bargain was not fulfilled to the letter, only so be it that he had made a good bargain. The consequence of all this was, that he never had things well done, however shrewdly projected.

He always had a nice sense of right. There are very few acts of his long business life on which you can lay your hand, and say that they were the result of any moral obliquity. He was kind, benevolent, and forbearing, in an eminent degree, with those who were dependent on him.

He was a man of uncommon equanimity of temper, and this followed him to the very last. He has been often heard to say that this equanimity of temper was the result of his own efforts; that he began business with being fractious and irritable, but seeing the evils of it, and the difficulties and perplexities it occasioned, he schooled himself to this equable state of mind that followed him through all his life.

He had great faith in mankind; he was never heard,

with all his hard experience in life, to rail at our race. He had acquired a great knowledge of mankind, and did not lose his respect for them by an extensive intercourse.

He began business as a trader in Peterborough in 1788, when he was twenty-three years of age, and was some years located at what was called "Carter's Corner," having there built a house and store, afterwards occupied by Oliver Carter. He built his mill in 1794, a building two hundred feet long, and two stories high, which was the wonder and admiration of the whole country. In the south end of this great structure he finished off a commodious dwelling into which he moved, Jan. 1, 1795, where he continued to live till 1805, when he removed to his new house on the east side of the river. He carried on, in this building, for many years, the business of paper-making, and had also at the same time in operation a saw-mill, a clothier's shop, a trip-hammer shop, a wool-carding machine, and an oil-mill, in addition to his trading and farming. All this occurred before the cotton manufacture commenced. He then engaged in this business, and the paper-manufacture was given up, and his great building was converted to this purpose.

It is what now constitutes the Phœnix Factory. A part of this factory was burned, Dec. 18, 1828, and Mr. Smith, having a large interest in the same, and having permitted his insurance to run out, lost so much by this fire that he was obliged to close his business, and all his property in the village was divided into small portions and sold at auction. He never engaged in business after this, but devoted himself to hunting up files of the political papers of our early times, as preparatory to writing a political history of the early days of our government. But age crept on him too rapidly to admit of any such undertaking. All these valuable papers are now safely deposited in the Dartmouth College Library, and owned by the Northern Academy of Sciences.

He always took a deep interest in the municipal affairs of the town, and was a leading actor in the same. He was moderator for seventeen years, beginning in 1794 and ending in 1829. He may justly be considered the founder of the village, where not one single object exists to perpetuate his name.

He m. Sally Garfield, of Fitchburg, Mass., dau. of Elijah and Jane Nichols Garfield, Nov. 10, 1793, b. Oct. 21, 1771. She d. Sept. 1, 1856, æ. 85 yrs. He d. April 25, 1842, æ. 76 yrs.

74   *Jeremiah*, b. Nov. 23, 1794. He was fitted for college in early life, but his services were so necessary to his father's business that he could not be spared. He became a superior clerk, having specially improved his handwriting, so that few could equal his chirography. He retained his literary tastes all his life; became an extensive reader, and a fine classical scholar. He re. to New York in 1825, and was for some years engaged in the commission business in the firms of Nesmith, Smith & Co., Smith, Wheeler & Fairbanks, and Smith & Wheeler. After relinquishing this business he became the chief clerk of the New York & New Haven Railroad, which office he held at the time of his death. He d. in New York, May 16, 1860, æ. 65 yrs., 5 mos., by a railroad accident; a street-car ran over him, as he stepped from one car to another without being aware of its approach, which accident he survived only two days. He m., May 22, 1832, Emeline Van Nortwick, of New York City.

William Bruce, b. New York, May 7, 1834; m., June 19, 1872, Margaret L. Norton; r. Baldwin, Queen Co., L. I.

Cornelia Luqueer, b. New York, Oct. 18, 1835; m., Sept. 16, 1857, Edward J. Kilbourne; ch., David Wells, Alanson Jermaine, Cornelia Edna; r. New York City.

Elizabeth M., b. July 5, 1838; m., June 17, 1872, Elbert Floyd-Jones, So. Oyster Bay, L. I.

Jeremiah, b. May 30, 1843; d.

Francis T. L., b. Jan. 24, 1845; d. Oct. 9, 1848, æ. 3 yrs., 8 mos.

Frederick Augustus, b. Nov. 7, 1847; d. in New York, Jan. 20, 1875, æ. 24 yrs.

Clarence Beverly, b. Dec. 8, 1850; r. New York City.

75   *Frederick A.*, b. Feb. 8, 1796; d. June 29, 1818, æ. 22 yrs. He was a skilful machinist. The following anecdote deserves to be recorded in relation to him: When he had been sent to see the weaving of cotton cloth by the water-loom, at Waltham, Mass., and had gained admission, by a permit from Patrick Jackson, one of the *employés* at the factory, who showed him the new works, said to Mr. Jackson, "Don't send such young men to inspect our machinery, if you do not want all our processes mastered and adopted elsewhere."

76   *Maria*, b. March 30, 1797; d. June 15, 1798, æ. 1 yr., 2 mos.

77   †*Samuel G.*, b. Aug. 23, 1799; m., 1st w., Sarah D. Abbot; 2d w., Elizabeth Dow.

78 †*Albert*, b. June 18, 1801; m., Feb. 26, 1828, Fidelia Stearns.

79 † *William S.*, b. Dec. 14, 1802; m., 1st w., Margaret Stearns; 2d w., Mary Miller.

80 *Alexander H.*, b. Aug. 5, 1804; m. Sophronia Bailey, Charlestown, Mass.; five ch.; only two survive, Jonathan, who lives in St. Louis, Mo., and Eliza, in Cincinnati, O. She d. in Cincinnati, O., July 15, 1848, æ. 43 yrs., 2 mos. He d. at St. Louis, Mo., November, 1858, æ. 54 yrs.

81 *Elizabeth M.*, b. Aug. 8, 1806; m., Sept. 8, 1830, Rev. L. W. Leonard, D.D., of Dublin; ch., (1) William S.; (2) Ellen E. She d. Sept. 13, 1848, æ. 42 yrs. He m., 2d w., Mrs. Elizabeth D. Smith, Exeter, wid. of Samuel G. Smith, March 25, 1851. He d. at Exeter, Dec. 12, 1864, æ. 74 yrs.

82 *Sarah Jane*, b. Sept. 16, 1808; m., 1843, Abraham W. Blanchard, of Boston; one ch., Catharine Ellen. He d.

83 *Maria*, b. Aug. 30, 1810; d. May 19, 1812, æ. 1 yr., 8 mos.

84 *Mary Soley*, b. Sept. 11, 1812; d. Aug. 14, 1822, æ. 10 yrs.

85 *Ellen*, b. Jan. 23, 1815; m. William H. Smith, Sept. 13, 1843.

39– 64 JONATHAN SMITH, Jr. He was graduated at Harvard University in 1819, studied law with Hon. Levi Lincoln, Worcester, and settled in Bath, N. H. He soon became a prominent man. He represented the town in the Legislature. He was a promising and rising man at the time of his death, and had already attained a high legal standing in the State. Always slender in health, a pulmonary disease became fastened upon him, which a winter's residence in the warm climate of the West Indies failed to remove or alleviate; he d. Aug. 10, 1840, æ. 42 yrs., 11 mos. He m. Hannah P. Payson, dau. of Moses P. Payson, Esq., of Bath. She d. May 18, 1838, æ. 28 yrs.

---

86 *Ariana E.*, b. May 29, 1831; d. Sept. 20, 1837, æ. 6 yrs., 3 mos.

87 *Moses Payson*, b. May 29, 1833; m., Dec. 6, 1869, Catharine Smith, dau. of Dr. Albert and Fidelia Smith; have r. in Marion and Montezuma, Ind., and Tuscola, Ill.; now in Newark, O.; three ch., Anna Perley, b. Sept. 19, 1871, at Marion; Albert, b. at Tuscola, Ill., March 3, 1873; Edith Payson, b. in Newark, O., March 16, 1876; d. Aug. 4, 1876, æ. 4 mos., 18 dys.

88 *Henry*, b. Sept. 18, 1835; d. at Chicago.

89 | *William H.*, b. Aug. 29, 1837; d. July 27, 1845, æ. 7 · yrs., 10 mos.

39– 67 | JOHN SMITH. He succeeded his father on the homestead. He has held important offices in town, — was selectman 1838, '39, '40, and Representative in 1859, '60. He is one of the deacons in the Congregational (Unitarian) Church. He sold his farm in 1873, and removed to the village, where he now lives. He m., Sept. 2, 1834, Susan, dau. John Stearns, of Jaffrey, b. May 30, 1809. She d. Jan. 9, 1870, æ. 60 yrs.

90 | *Mary Frances*, b. Jan. 7, 1836; r. Chicago.
91 | *John S.*, b. Nov. 27, 1837; m. ——; r. Chicago.
92 | *Jonathan*, b. May 26, 1840; d. July 30, 1841, æ. 1 yr., 2 mos.
93 | *Jonathan*, b. Oct. 21, 1842; graduate Dartmouth College, 1870. Studied law, and is now practising in Manchester.
94 | *Susan P.*, b. Oct. 13, 1844; m., 1873, Eugene Lewis; r. Moline, Ill.
95 | *Caroline*, b. March 3, 1847; teacher in public schools in Chicago.
96 | *Jeremiah*, b. July 2, 1852.

40– 77 | SAMUEL G. SMITH. He was first the agent of the Phœnix Cotton Factory in Peterborough, afterwards of a factory at Warren, Md., and lastly at South Berwick, Me., where his health entirely failed. He d. at Peterborough, Sept. 9, 1842, æ. 43 yrs., of a bronchial consumption, in the very vigor of his manhood. He had been absent from Peterborough some twelve or fourteen years, and returned on a visit but a few weeks before the dread summons came. Most of his life had been spent in the manufacture of cotton, in which business he is said to have acquired great skill, and to have equalled the best manufacturers of his day. He was a self-made man; his early opportunities for an education had been limited, and had there been no self-culture, there would have been no man. By his own, and almost unaided, efforts, he made himself a mathematician, became a great and general reader, and had acquired a large fund of knowledge. He was a man of rare excellence of character, of great purity of life, — the very soul of honor and integrity. His memory is embalmed in many hearts that will not soon forget him. He bore his last sickness, which was long, with great fortitude, and died calmly, in the firm hope of a better state of existence hereafter.

Saml Abbot Smith

He m., 1st w., Sarah D. Abbot, dau. of Rev. Abiel
Abbot, D.D., b. June 22, 1801. She d. June 11, 1831,
æ. 30 yrs. He m., 2d w., Elizabeth Dow, dau. of Jeremiah Dow, of Exeter, who survived him, and m., 2d hus.,
Rev. L. W. Leonard, D.D., of Dublin, March 25, 1851.

97 | *Samuel Abbot*, b. April 18, 1829.
He was graduated at Harvard University in 1849,
and was prepared for the ministry at the Cambridge
Divinity School, and settled over the Unitarian society
in Arlington, June 27, 1854, where he remained till his
death. He d. of a malarious fever contracted at Norfolk,
Va., where he had gone on missionary service to the
army. He returned with the fever upon him, and d.
May 20, 1865, æ. 36 yrs.
He was a man of rare excellence of character, and
was greatly esteemed as an able and sympathizing pastor. His people manifested the most sincere sorrow and
regret at his death, and look back to him as one of the
sainted ones of the earth. He was cut off in his prime
and in the midst of his greatest usefulness. Soon after
his death, a beautiful volume, entitled *Christian Lessons
and a Christian Life*, containing an extended biography
and numerous extracts from his writings, was published
by Prof. E. J. Young.
He m., June 27, 1854, Maria Edes, dau. of Samuel
and Maria Edes; ch., (1) Abbot E., b. Sept. 20, 1855;
(2) Maria Ellen, b. Feb. 13, 1857; (3) George A., b. Oct.
15, 1861; (4) Samuel H., b. April 5, 1864.

98 | *Ellen Parker*, b. July 12, 1837; d. at Exeter.
99 | *Sarah Abbot*, b. July. 7, 1839; m. John L. Dearborn; r.
St. Louis.
100 | *Ednah Dow*, b. May 12, 1841; m. Knight Cheney; r.
South Manchester, Ct.

40- 78 | ALBERT SMITH, M.D., LL.D. He was fitted for col-
lege at Groton Academy, from twelve to fifteen years of
age, and, returning home, there was such a depression
of business succeeding the war of 1812 that his father
could not then send him to college, and he went to work
in his cotton-factory, where he continued five years to
superintend the spinning. In September, 1821, he entered Dartmouth College, having kept up his studies as
well as he could by himself during this interval, without
any additional schooling. He was graduated in 1825,
having assigned to him in the commencement exercises
an oration on the "Navigation of the Connecticut River."
For a few years, he was clerk of the Phœnix Factory,

and assisted in his father's business till his failure in 1829, when he decided to study the medical profession. He attended medical lectures at Bowdoin Medical School, at the College of Physicians and Surgeons, New York, and at the Dartmouth Medical College, and took his degree at the latter institution in 1833. He first commenced business in Leominster, Mass., where he remained from 1833 to 1838, and then removed to Peterborough, where he continued his practice as long as his strength permitted. He was appointed Professor of Materia Medica and Therapeutics in the Dartmouth Medical College in 1849, where he continued to lecture annually till his resignation in 1870. He has since been appointed professor *emeritus* of the same branch. In 1857, he delivered his course of lectures before the Vermont Medical College, Castleton, Vt., and also the same course at Bowdoin Medical School in 1859. The honorary degree of LL.D. was conferred on him by Dartmouth College in 1870, and also an honorary M. D. by the Rush Medical College, Chicago, in 1875. He has also been elected an honorary member of the New York Medical Society. He has published a lecture on Hippocrates, also one on Paracelsus and a commemorative discourse upon the death of Dr. Amos Twitchell, besides various articles in the medical journals from time to time, and the transactions of the New Hampshire Medical Society. He m., Feb. 26, 1828, Fidelia Stearns, dau. of John and Chloe Stearns, of Jaffrey, b. Oct. 25, 1799.

_____

101 *Frederick Augustus*, b. June 18, 1830. He was fitted for college at New Hampton Academy, and was graduated at Dartmouth College in 1852. His habits and tastes leading him to the medical profession, he pursued it with much zeal and earnestness, attending his medical lectures at the Dartmouth Medical College and the College of Physicians and Surgeons of New York, and taking his degree at the former institution. He subsequently spent one year at the hospitals on Blackwell's Island as an assistant, by which he had well prepared himself for his profession. He located himself at Leominster, Mass., in August, 1856, and d. there suddenly of an affection of the heart, Dec. 20, 1856, æ. 26 yrs. He was a highly cultivated, refined, and promising young man, and bade fair to make his mark in the world. He m. Frances Gregg, of Belleville, N.J., June 18, 1856.

102 *Susan S.*, b. Feb. 4, 1832; d. at Leominster, April 20, 1836, æ. 4 yrs.

103 *Catharine*, b. Dec. 5, 1837; m., Dec. 6, 1869, M. Payson Smith; ch., (1) Anna Perley, b. Sept. 19, 1871, at Marion, Ind.; (2) Albert, b. March 3, 1873, at Tuscola, Ill.; (3) Edith, b. Newark, O., March 16, 1876; d. Aug. 4, 1876, æ. 4 mos., 18 dys; r. Newark, O.

40- 79 WILLIAM SYDNEY SMITH, a paper-maker at Peterborough, and in 1829 at Belleville, Canada West. He returned to Peterborough, and has remained here since. All his children were b. in Canada. He m., 1st w., Nov. 18, 1834, Margaret Stearns, b. March 18, 1805. She d. in Belleville, March 20, 1851, æ. 46 yrs.; m., 2d w., in Peterborough, Mary Miller, dau. of Matthew Gray. He d. at Peterborough, Sept. 26, 1875, æ. 72 yrs.

104 *William A.*, b. in Belleville, Feb. 9, 1836; m. Augusta Frances Ames, dau. of Joseph H. and Mary Melvin Ames, Oct. 9, 1865. He d. by an accidental discharge of a musket, in Nebraska, Feb. 24, 1870, æ. 34 yrs.; ch., (1) Margaret Ellen, b. Oct. 3, 1866; (2) Frederick W., b. Feb. 23, 1869.

105 *Samuel G.*, b. Belleville, April, 20, 1838; m. Dora Bascom, of Jaffrey. A jeweller and watch-maker in Boston; two ch., Kate and Dexter.

106 *Josiah P.*, b. Belleville, Oct. 20, 1840. Killed in battle at Fort Hudson, 1863, æ. 23 yrs.

107 *Sydney S.*, b. Belleville, Feb. 8, 1843; d. at Alton, Ill., July 9, 1871, æ. 28 yrs., 5 mos.

108 *Elizabeth Ellen*, b. Belleville, May 19, 1845; m. Samuel Reeder; r. Topeka, Kansas.

THE SPALDING FAMILY.

1 JEREMIAH SPALDING came to town in 1799; m. Mehitable Pearly, September, 1799. He was a blacksmith. He settled on Sharon line, south of the Shedd farm. His dwelling-house was in Peterborough, and his shop in Sharon. He did a great business at his trade for some years, and in 1832 he removed to Griffin's Mills, N. Y., and d. there. He d. March 31, 1858, æ. 83 yrs. She d. Feb. 5, 1854, æ. 75 yrs.

———

2 *Betsey*, b. Sept. 3, 1800; d. Nov. 8, 1821, æ. 21 yrs.

3 *Charlotte*, b. Feb. 8, 1803; m. Henry Moore, Aug. 21, 1822; r. Griffin's Mills, N. Y., 1832.

4 *Jeremiah*, b. May 2, 1806; d. Griffin's Mills, Sept. 2, 1849, æ. 43 yrs., 8 mos.

5	*John Milton,*	d. in Wisconsin, March, 1855, æ. 45 yrs.
		b. Sept. 6, 1810;
6	*Benjamin Franklin,*	d. at Peterborough, April 4, 1828, æ. 18 yrs.

THE SPOFFORD FAMILY.

IRA and JOHN SPOFFORD were sons of Amos and Mary Taggart Spofford, of Sharon, and grandsons of Abijah Spofford, who re. to Sharon late in life, about 1780. He probably lived with his son Samuel, whose farm was in the north-east part of the town, on very high land, which has long since been abandoned as a residence.

1 IRA SPOFFORD was b. in Sharon, Sept. 11, 1797 ; m., 1820, Marion Atwood. He lived in various places in town. He was a stone-mason. He d. March 7, 1869, æ. 71 yrs., 5 mos. She d. Jan. 15, 1875, æ. 74 yrs.

2 *William W.*, b. Nov. 8, 1820 ; m. Sarah Barnes ; r. Boston.

3 *Nancy,* b. Oct. 24, 1822 ; m., 1st hus., John Challis ; 2d hus., Thomas Upton.

4 *Ira A.,* b. Aug. 15, 1824 ; m. Sabrina Twitchell, of Dublin.

5 *Nathan Henry,* b. Oct. 3, 1826 ; m. M. A. Buckingham ; r. Boston.

6 *M. Augusta,* b. April 12, 1829 ; m. Fred Farwell.

7 *George W.,* b. Aug. 9, 1831 ; m. Hannah Morrison. He was educated at Exeter Academy ; was superintendent of the Foster School, Chicago, fourteen years, and on retiring he became a real estate dealer, under the firm of Spofford, Byrne & Drake, Real Estate Dealers, in which business he is now engaged. He continues to r. in Chicago ; one ch. living.

8 *John L.,* b. Sept. 22, 1834 ; d. March 18, 1862, æ. 27 yrs., 5 mos.

9 *Elizabeth,* b. Aug. 15, 1836 ; m. Joseph Alexander. He d. 1873.

10	*Albert,*	d. March 28, 1839, æ. 3 mos.
		b. Dec. 18, 1838 ;
11	*Alvah A.,*	m. Ada Luthers ; d. Providence, R. I., April, 1869, æ. 30 yrs.

JOHN T. SPOFFORD, b. in Sharon, May 28, 1807 ; m. Submit Barnes, dau. of Asa Barnes, of Sharon, April 5,

1828, b. in Sharon, Jan. 4, 1808. He lived on the Boynton place, near the Samuel Morison farm. He d. March 7, 1869, æ. 61 yrs., 9 mos.

12 | *John W.*, b. July 28, 1829 ; d. April 12, 1830, æ. 8 mos.
13 | *Caroline A.*, b. April 5, 1831 ; m. Charles Emery, of Jaffrey, Sept. 1, 1861 ; she d. Dec. 23, 1867, æ. 36 yrs., 8 mos. ; r. Jaffrey.
14 | *Joseph H.*, b. March 13, 1833 ; m. Ellen A. Hunt, Nov. 25, 1858 ; r. Dublin. She d. Oct. 27, 1875, æ 39 yrs., 6 mos.
15 | *William C. B.*, b. April 21, 1835 ; m. Alice E. Sanderson, of Bridgewater, Vt., Sept. 17, 1862 ; r. Harrisville.
16 | *James S.*, b. Jan. 23, 1837 ; m., Dec. 10, 1861, Sarah W. Stacy. He d. Aug. 31, 1864, æ. 27 yrs., 7 mos. She d. in childbirth, Feb. 16, 1865.
17 | *John W.*, b. May 3, 1839 ; d. in the army, Sept. 5, 1862.
18 | *Longley J.*, b. Aug. 30, 1841 ; m., July 3, 1872, Edith Creighton.
19 | *Melissa M.*, b. Aug. 31, 1843 ; m., July, 1864, Lorin B. Kendall, of Westminster, Mass. ; r. Clinton, Mass.
20 | *Harriet E.*, b. July 18, 1845 ; m., Nov. 10, 1866, Charles Lombard, Westminster, Mass. ; r. Westminster.
21 | *Marcellus E.*, b. Dec. 13, 1847 ; m., Dec. 13, 1872, Abbie E. Robbins, of Harrisville ; r. Harrisville.
22 | *Charles H.*, b. Nov. 5, 1850 ; m., May 1, 1872, Clara Raymond, of Keene ; r. Conklingville, N. Y.

THE SPRING FAMILY.

1 | Converse Spring was brother to Dr. Marshall Spring, of Watertown, who bought his farm for him about 1780, at which time Converse re. to town. It was the farm begun and long occupied by Deacon Samuel Moore. His wife's name was Mary, the surname unknown. He d. April 13, 1812, æ. 77 yrs. She d. May 23, 1804, æ. 60 yrs.

2 | † *Josiah Converse*, b. June 29, 1764 ; m. Betsey Clark.
3 | †*Silas*, b. Aug. 13, 1766 ; m. Margaret Stuart.

1– 2 | Josiah C. Spring. He succeeded his father on the homestead. He m., 1784, Betsey Clark, b. Aug. 10, 1764. He d. and she d.

4 | *Liba G.*, b. April 17, 1785 ; d. Feb. 24, 1870, in Penn.
5 | *Betsey*, b. June 28, 1787 ; m. Robert Morison.
6 | *Alpheus*, b. Sept. 12, 1789.

7 | *Converse M.*, b. Sept. 11, 1791.
8 | *Sarah G.*, b. July 16, 1796; m., Oct. 12, 1824, Daniel Bickford.
9 | *Mary Ann*, b. June 9, 1799; m., Sept. 23, 1823, Jona. Persons; d. April 19, 1870, æ. 70 yrs., 10 mos.
10 | *Horace B.*, b. Sept. 14, 1802.
11 | *John C.*, b. July 16, 1804; d. Feb. 6, 1854, at Wilton, æ. 50 yrs.
12 | *Amelia M.*, b. Dec. 12, 1809; m. George Smith.

1-3 | SILAS SPRING. He lived on the East Mountain, where he began a new place. He m. Margaret Stuart, dau. of Thomas Stuart. She d. May 27, 1858, æ. 87 yrs. He. d. Nov. 16, 1839, æ. 73 yrs. He began with nothing and left a good estate.

13 | *Thomas*, b. Feb. 20, 1795; m. Mary A. Sprague, Sept. 18, 1818. Two ch., Jane A. and George M. He d. at Goffstown, Aug. 25, 1864, æ. 69 yrs.
14 | *Sally*, b. Oct. 27, 1797; unm.
15 | *Mary*, b. Dec. 21, 1799; m. Joshua Bailey, March 2, 1824.
16 | *Eliza*, b. July 3, 1806; d. April 9, 1829, æ. 22 yrs., 9 mos.

THE STEELE FAMILY.

1 | THOMAS STEELE was the progenitor of the Steele family. He was b. in Ireland about 1694, m., in 1715, Martha Morison, dau. of Samuel Morison, and sister to John Morison, the progenitor of the Peterborough Morisons. He emigrated to this country in 1718, and settled in Londonderry in 1719, and was one of the first settlers of that town.
He d. in Londonderry. She d. in Londonderry, June, 1738. They had four sons and two daughters. We have been able to account for the sons, but know nothing of the daughters.

2 | *Thomas*, b. Londonderry, Dec. 25, 1721.
3 | *James*, b. Londonderry, March 25, 1724; re. to Antrim, and d. 1818 or '19, æ. 102 yrs.
4 | *John*, b. Londonderry; re. to Western New York.
5 | †*David*, b. Londonderry, Jan. 30, 1727; m. Janet Little, in 1751.

1-5 | DAVID STEELE (Capt.). He came to Peterborough, probably, about 1763; his name occurs first on the town records in 1765, as selectman, which office he held six years, to 1780, and was moderator in 1786, '87. He was on the Committee of Safety two years, 1776 and '78, which is a full endorsement of his patriotism in those times. He began his place in town, the " Gen. John Steele farm," and raised a large and influential family. * He m. Janet Little, sister of Thomas Little, Sen. ; † she was b. in Ireland in 1729; first resided in Lunenburg, 1738, and then, on marriage, removed to Londonderry and lived there ten years ; then, after the birth of three or four children, they removed to Peterborough, 1763.

He d. July 19, 1809, æ. 82 yrs.; she d. Sept. 30, 1816, æ. 87 yrs.

---

6   † *Thomas*, b. Londonderry, March 5, 1754; m. Ann Moore.

7   *Jane*, b. Londonderry, September, 1756 ; m. Samuel Gregg, Sharon ; d. Aug. 15, 1850, æ. 94 yrs.

8   † *David*, b. Londonderry, 1758 ; m., 1st w., Lucy Powers ; 2d w., Sarah Gregg.

9   *Jonathan*, b. Sept. 3, 1760.

A lawyer of much eminence. He studied his profession with Gen. John Sullivan, after obtaining such an academic education as he could, and settled in Durham, where he continued to reside till his death. He was a popular advocate, and took a leading rank at the bar. His friends thought him too sensitively modest to claim his proper place in society. Judge Smith spoke of him as an eloquent pleader at the bar, and thought that no one could easily surpass him. He was appointed Judge of the Superior Court, by Gov. Jeremiah Smith, and after retaining the office two years resigned in 1812, and returned to his private practice. It is supposed that he could not afford to retain the office any longer, the salaries then being so very low.‡ "He gradually lost his interest in town affairs, and became unsocial in disposition, and very retiring in his habits, owing, perhaps, to some domestic infelicities. In the latter part of his life, he became interested in religious matters, and paid liberally towards the support of religious societies" ; m., Jan. 23, 1788, Lydia, dau. Gen. John Sullivan, b. March, 1763 ; she d. April 9, 1842, æ. 79 yrs. He d. Sept. 3, 1824, æ. 64 yrs.

They had two children who came to maturity, (1) Janet, b. June 14, 1791 ; d. Durham, 1870, æ. 79 yrs. ; (2) Rich-

* Records of Londonderry.
† Records of Londonderry.
‡ Letter of J. A. Richardson, Durham, Oct. 9, 1875.

ard, b. Jan. 6, 1797; educated a physician; graduated Dartmouth College, 1815, and M.D. 1825; a bright and intelligent man, but ruined by intemperance; d. at Durham, 1870, æ. 73 yrs.

10   *Martha*, b. 1763; m. Benjamin Mitchell.
11   *Elizabeth*, b. Peterborough, 1767; m. James Wilson.
12   *Margaret*, b. Jan. 3, 1766; m. John Smith.
13   † *John*, b. February, 1773; m. Polly Wilson; 2d w., Hepzibeth Hammond.

5- 6   THOMAS STEELE. He began the place where he lived, his farm being a part of the farm B, laid out in the north part of the town. He was one of the best and most useful men of that day in our municipal affairs. He was a man of rare judgment and good common-sense, and his literary attainments were very creditable for his meagre opportunities. He was selectman eighteen years, from 1786 to 1804; town clerk nineteen years, from 1787 to 1813. No town clerk, through all its history, has presented, as to penmanship or clearness of expression, the proceedings of the town, in a record superior to his. The early settlers, in the first years of their municipal government, were very prone to change their town officers, and down to the time of Mr. Steele there was no permanency in any office in town. He spent his last years in the village, and yet to the last retained his interest in town affairs, and was always a debater in town meetings. He m. Ann Moore, dau. of Deacon Samuel Moore, and raised a large family. He d. Nov. 11, 1847, æ. 94 yrs. She d. April 29, 1838, æ. 78 yrs.

14   *Ann*, b. June 5, 1786; unm.; d. April 29, 1858, æ. 72 yrs.
15   † *Jeremiah S.*, b. Feb. 29, 1788; m. Irene Felt.
16   *Margaret*, b. April, 1790; unm.; d. Feb. 4, 1824, æ. 34 yrs.
17   *Jonathan*, b. Feb. 8, 1792.

A graduate of Williams College, Mass., in 1811. He was a student at law with his uncle, Judge Steele, of Durham, where he completed his studies, and located himself as a lawyer at Epsom, where he resided the rest of his life. He was a modest man, and did not push forward as much as his abilities would warrant. He had talent for great success in his profession. Judge Nesmith,* who was well acquainted with him, says: "He had many of the qualifications of a good lawyer; he had good common-sense, was pretty accurate in his judgment of men and things, had a quick perception of every-

* Letter from Judge G. W. Nesmith, Oct. 1, 1875.

thing humorous, had a fine, musical voice and a tolerable knowledge of the law. I heard him occasionally argue his cases with considerable ability. His good memory enabled him to state evidence with accuracy and clearness. He and George Sullivan were engaged for the plaintiff in the case in which Ezekiel Webster fell dead, while arguing for the defendant. This occurred in April, 1829. Nothing prevented Jonathan Steele from being eminent in his profession except his appetite for intoxicating drinks." Judge Smith used to say that Jonathan Steele's pleading was -beyond any music he ever heard. He m. Elizabeth McClary; ch., (1) Charles; (2) John; (3) Michael M.; (4) Thomas; (5) Elizabeth. He d. September, 1858, æ. 66 yrs.

18 *David*, b. Nov. 27, 1793; educated a lawyer, and settled in New Durham, where he practised his profession to 1867, when he removed to Dover, where he now r. He m. Lydia Burnham; ch., (1) Thomas; (2) George. The latter d. in the war of the Rebellion.

19 *Janet*, b. Nov. 27, 1795; m., Oct. 1, 1829, Dr. John Ramsey, of Greenfield.

20 *Samuel*, b. Sept. 1, 1797; m. in Montebello, Ill., and d. November, 1860, æ. 63 yrs.

21 *Betsey*, b. Aug. 6, 1799; unm.

5- 8 DAVID STEELE (Gen.). His farm lay just north of his father's. He m., 1st w., Lucy Powers, of Hollis, 1784. She d. Jan. 27, 1795, æ. 36 yrs.; m., 2d w., Sarah Gregg, dau. of Maj. Samuel Gregg. She d. Jan. 15, 1822, æ. 52 yrs. He rose to be a major-general in the New Hampshire Militia, and also held important town offices; moderator seven years to 1817. He d. March 19, 1836, æ. 78 yrs.

22 †*Stephen Powers*, b. July 26, 1784; m. Jane McCoy.

23 *David*, b. Sept. 30, 1787; m., 1838, Catharine Kendall; A graduate of Williams College, 1810; studied law; was settled at Hillsboro Bridge many years. * He was a modest, retiring man. He seemed to have a strong aversion to professional labor at the bar. He seldom spoke in court. He was considered a man of integrity, and was useful and much respected in the community where he lived. He d. Dec. 10, 1866, æ. 79 yrs.; c.

24 *Janet*, b. May 24, 1790; m. Samuel Swan.

* Letter Judge G. W. Nesmith, Oct. 1, 1875.

5– 13 | JOHN STEELE (Gen.). He was well-educated for the times. He kept school much in early life, and was accustomed to survey land as his services were needed in the town. He was a remarkably genial and agreeable man. He possessed colloquial powers of the highest order, and abounded with a fund of anecdotes which no man could tell better. In the war of 1812, he went to Portsmouth as a volunteer with his regiment, being then a colonel, where he remained about twelve weeks. He was subsequently a major-general in the New Hampshire Militia.

He held the office of selectman seven years, and was town clerk fourteen years, from 1805 to 1820. He succeeded his father on the homestead. He was engaged subsequently in manufacturing, being concerned in the North Cotton Factory in Peterborough. He m., 1st w., Polly Wilson, dau. of Maj. Robert Wilson. She d. Feb. 9, 1819, æ. 43 yrs.; m., 2d w., Mrs. Hepzibeth Hammond, of Swanzey. She d. April 22, 1836, æ. 58 yrs. He d. Aug. 10, 1845, æ. 72 yrs.

25 | *David*, b. Dec. 2, 1795; m., 1st w., Sally Adams, October, 1821; she d. March 5, 1838; m., 2d w., Isabella A. Nesmith, of Derry. He was graduated at Dartmouth College, 1815. Studied law and settled at Goffstown, where he remained till his death. He was a lawyer in high standing, and a man of excellent character. He was President of the Hillsboro County Bar; d. Oct. 1, 1875, æ. 79 yrs., 10 mos.; ch., (1) John, b. Nov. 4, 1839; d.; (2) James, b. June 5, 1842; m. —— Farwell, and lives in Chicago, Ill.

26 | *Mary*, b. July 12, 1797; m. George W. Senter.
27 | *Thomas*, b. Aug. 1, 1799; d. 1826, æ. 27 yrs.
28 | *James*, b. Dec. 22, 1802; d. 1804, æ. 2 yrs.
29 | *Jane*, b. June 13, 1805; d. 1810, æ. 5 yrs.
30 | *Jonathan*, b. Feb. 27, 1810; d. at Chicopee, 1852, æ. 42 yrs.

31 | *Martha*, b. June 13, 1812; m. Rev. Isaac Willey; r. Pembroke; ch., (1) Albert S., b. May 10, 1850; (2) Martha A., b. Dec. 11, 1852.

6– 15 | JEREMIAH S. STEELE. He lived on the farm directly north of his father's place. He m., April 29, 1823, Irene Felt, dau. Oliver Felt; she d. May 19, 1868, æ. 71 yrs. He d. Sept. 30, 1856, æ. 68 yrs., 7 mos.

32 | *James*, b. Feb. 9, 1824; m. Mary J. Lindsay, Nov. 7, 1854; r. Chester, Ill.

33 | *Samuel M.*, b. Nov. 17, 1825 ; m. Lizzie Montroy, April, 1866 ; r. Hamilton, Ill. ; d. 1874, æ. 49 yrs.

34 | *Margaret*, b. Oct. 6, 1827 ; d. June 11, 1828, æ. 8 mos.

35 | *Cyrus Felt*, b. May 21, 1829 ; m. Susan Cochran, May, 1856 ; r. Carthage, Ill.

36 | *Mary Ann*, b. March 13, 1831 ; unm.; d. Feb. 5, 1858, æ. 26 yrs., 10 mos.

37 | *Charlotte J.*, b. April 22, 1833 ; m. Harrison A. Rice, June 18, 1868 ; r. Henniker.

38 | *George*, b. July 11, 1836.

39 | *Charles E.*, b. July 23, 1838 ; m. Mary E. Smith, October, 1859, of Norwich, Vt. ; 2d w., Alma Fletcher, November, 1870.

8– 22 | STEPHEN P. STEELE, a graduate of Williams College, Williamstown, Mass., 1808. He studied law, and practised his profession in town. He held many offices of trust ; was town clerk six years, from 1823 to 1829 ; representative to the General Court, 1841, '42 ; a delegate to the Constitutional Convention in 1850. He m. Mrs. Jane McCoy. He d. July 22, 1857, æ. 73 yrs.

---

40 | *David Powers*, b. June 14, 1850 ; vocalist, Boston.

---

1 | JOHN H. STEELE (Gov.), of a race entirely distinct from the preceding, was born in Salisbury, in the County of Rowan, N. C., Jan. 4, 1789. His father was a native of the north of Ireland, but came to this country early in life, and established himself as a brick-mason in Salisbury. Gov. Steele was left an orphan at an early age, having neither father nor mother, brother nor sister, to watch over him, and to rejoice in his ultimate success in life. His early advantages for an education were limited. At the age of fourteen he was apprenticed to what was called the "chair-making business," which consisted in making Windsor chairs, gigs, and sulkies. Having heard of the progress of mechanical skill and enterprise in this town, from Capt. Nathaniel Morison, who was about this time temporarily residing in Fayetteville, N. C., he came to Peterborough in May, 1811, which was his home during the remainder of his life. Without funds and without friends, he at first worked for Capt. Morison at carriage-making, afterwards at machinery, at $13 per month. This opened the way for the development of his mechanical skill and genius. He was soon himself a manufacturer, and in 1817 he put in operation the first power-looms in New Hampshire. In 1824, he commenced the erection of a new and extensive cotton-mill in West Peterborough, which he finished and super-

intended till 1845. He was chosen Representative to the Legislature for 1829, and for the years 1840 and '41 he was elected Councillor for the old Hillsboro District. In 1842, partly on account of his health and partly for the purpose of examining the improvements in machinery for manufacturing, he visited England, and also the oppressed country from which his father emigrated so many years before.

He was elected Governor of the State in 1844, and also the succeeding year, 1845. After retiring from manufacturing business, he returned to his farm, not merely to guide and direct, but to lead, in a course of skilful and scientific husbandry. The course did not prove remunerative, and he abandoned it before his death, and took up his residence in the village. He held in town, besides the office of Representative, that of moderator for six years, from 1830 to 1838, selectman 1846. He always had great influence in town, and it was generally exercised for its best interests and welfare.

He m., 1st. w., Jane Moore, dau. John Moore, Nov. 5, 1816. She d. July 30, 1831, æ. 34 yrs.; 2d w., Nancy Moore, dau. of John Moore, Jan. 8, 1833. She d. Feb. 26, 1870, æ. 68 yrs., 8 mos. He d. July 3, 1865, æ. 76 yrs., 6 mos.

2	†*Edwin*, b. May 12, 1817 ; m. Abigail M. Warren.
3	*John*, b. Dec. 26, 1819 ; unm.; an imbecile.
4	†*Henry*, b. July 6, 1822 ; m. Mary Ann Chapman.
5	†*George*, b. July 26, 1828 ; m. Charlotte W. Low.
6	*Hardy*, b. July 20, 1831 ; d. Oct. 30, 1832, æ. 1 yr., 3 mos.
7	†*Charles*, b. Jan. 2, 1834 ; m. Maria J. Swan.

1– 2   EDWIN STEELE. He was selectman 1851 ; m. Abigail M. Warren, of Dublin, May 22, 1838. He d. Nov 10, 1862, æ. 45 yrs.

8	*Jane H.*, b. Dec. 2, 1839 ; m. Samuel N. Porter, D.D.S.
9	*Mary C.*, b. March 22, 1842 ; d. Sept. 20, 1844, æ. 2 yrs., 5 mos.
10	†*John Henry*, b. July 24, 1845 ; m. Anna S. Follansbee.

1– 4   HENRY STEELE, a machinist by trade. Devoted his last years to trading in town. He was town treasurer for six years, from 1849 to 1855. He m., Aug. 6, 1846, Mary Ann Chapman, b. Dec. 12, 1823. He d. Feb. 21, 1865, æ. 42 yrs., 7 mos.

11   *Isadore M.*, b. April 30, 1851 ; d. Feb. 28, 1870; æ. 18
yrs., 9 mos.

12   *Alice E.*, b. July 14, 1854 ; d. July 18, 1870, æ. 16 yrs.

13   *Franklin P.*, b. Nov. 9, 1856.

14   *Nilla J.*, b. March 2, 1858.

1- 5   GEORGE STEELE. Worked many years at the paper-manufactory of A. P. Morrison & Co., till he removed with his family to Pleasant Valley, Wis., in 1868. He m., Aug. 12, 1852, Charlotte W. Low, dau. of William Low, and granddaughter of Dr. Peter Tuttle, late of Hancock, b. Sept. 19, 1831.

15   *Charles Hardy*, b. May 29, 1853.

16   *William Low*, b. Oct. 26, 1858.

17   *Henry Tuttle*, b. May 3, 1861.

1- 7   CHARLES STEELE. He resided many years in Norwalk, O., engaged in the business of railroading, but has recently re. to Toledo, and is now master of the yard on the Lake Shore & Michigan Southern Railway. He m., Nov. 6, 1853, Maria J. Swan, dau. of Capt. William A. Swan, of Peterborough.

18   *Anna J.*, b. in Norwalk, O., Nov. 21, 1855.

19   *J. Henry*, b. in Norwalk, O., May 16, 1857 ; d. March, 1858, æ. 9 mos.

20   *Emma E.*, b. in Norwalk, O., Feb. 28, 1859.

21   *Charles F.*, b. in Norwalk, O., March 13, 1865 ; d. September, 1869, æ. 4 yrs.

22   *Fred. Ames*, b. in Norwalk, O., April 2, 1873.

2- 10   JOHN HENRY STEELE, stationer and bookseller in Peterborough ; town clerk 1871, '2, '3, '4, '5, '6, which office he now holds ; m., Nov. 6, 1867, Anna S. Follansbee, dau. of George F. Follansbee.

23   *Mary Abbie*, b. Jan. 28, 1869 ; d. Aug. 24, 1869, æ. 7 mos.

24   *Harrie Leon*, b. Aug. 22, 1872.

25   *Katie*, b. Dec. 28, 1874.

THE STEVENS FAMILY.

1   EPHRAIM STEVENS came to town from Townsend in 1797, to work at blacksmithing for Samuel Smith, and continued in his employ many years. He was b. in Townsend, Jan. 10, 1771 ; d. March 4, 1853, æ. 82 yrs. He m. Jerusha Chapman, b. in Ipswich, Mass., March 4, 1773 ; d. Nov. 3, 1871, æ. 98 yrs., 7 mos.

38

2 | *Jerusha*, b. Townsend, Dec. 4, 1793; m. Nehemiah Woods; d. April 25, 1875, æ. 81 yrs.

3 | *Ephraim*, b. Townsend, April 9, 1796; d. March 11, 1802, æ. 6 yrs.

4 | † *Joshua*, b. Peterborough, Dec. 5, 1798; m., 1st w., Lydia Peavey; 2d w., Mrs. Sarah D. Goss.

5 | *Betsey*, b. Peterborough, June 22, 1806; m. Benjamin Fessenden; r. Townsend; one ch.

6 | *Lucy*, b. Peterborough, Dec. 8, 1812; m. Hamar Lewis; r. Townsend; four ch.

1- 4 | JOSHUA STEVENS is a machinist by trade. He has worked at the various factories in town many years. He now resides in the village. He m., 1st w., Lydia Peavey, June 29, 1826, b. in Greenfield, Nov. 12, 1803. She d. Jan. 26, 1856, æ. 52 yrs., 2 mos.; m., 2d w., Mrs. Sarah D. Goss, of Temple, Sept. 24, 1868.

7 | *Lydia Ann*, b. Oct. 24, 1827; m. Charles S. Gray.

8 | *Louisa C.*, b. Jan. 22, 1830; m. George W. Brown, June 23, 1864; r. Townsend.

9 | *Albert*, b. Jan. 23, 1837; m. Jennie Abbot, June 5, 1862; one ch., Ida.

10 | *Charles*, b. Nov. 24, 1839; d. Jan. 7, 1849, æ. 9 yrs., 1 mo.

11 | *George Eddie*, b. Nov. 28, 1852.

THE STUART FAMILY.

The name of this family is spelled differently by the branches of the same family, — Stuart and Stewart. We adopt the former spelling.

1 | WILLIAM STUART, son of Solomon and Martha Stuart, b. 1700, came to Peterborough from Lunenburg about 1750, and settled on land south of the "Smith farm." He m. Margaret Sanderson. He d. March 15, 1753, æ. 53 yrs. He was the first man that d. in town. He was buried in the little cemetery on meeting-house hill. She d. March 8, 1795, æ. 87 yrs.

---

2 | *John*, b. Lunenburg, Aug. 28, 1737; killed in Rodgers' fight, March 13, 1757.

3 | † *William*, b. Lunenburg, Nov. 5, 1740; m. Elizabeth White.

4 | † *Thomas*, b. Lunenburg, May 3, 1743; m. Elizabeth Stinson.

5 | † *Charles*, b. Lunenburg, Oct. 8, 1745; m. Esther Ferguson.

6 | *Elizabeth*, b. Lunenburg, April 8, 1748; m. Gilbert Mc-Coy.

1– 3 | WILLIAM STUART. He m. Elizabeth, dau. of Patrick White. He d. Oct. 25, 1771, æ. 31 yrs. Was buried in little cemetery on meeting-house hill. His wid. m. John Gregg. She d. Nov. 2, 1803, æ. 59 yrs.

7 | *John*, b. 1769; d. at Charles Stuart's, March 17, 1795, æ. 26 yrs.

8 | *William*, b. 1771; m. Rachel Cram. He lived with Patrick White till he bought his farm, where George Steele now lives. He d. May 25, 1822, æ. 51 yrs.; one ch., John, b. March 25, 1800; m., June 1, 1826, Elizabeth Lacy, of Hillsboro. He d. Aug. 30, 1874, æ. 74 yrs., 5 mos.

1– 4 | THOMAS STUART. He was seven years old when his father moved to town. He lived in the east part of the town. He m. Elizabeth Stinson. He d. Nov. 7, 1833, æ. 90 yrs. She d. Sept. 28, 1787, æ. 47 yrs.

9 | *John*, b. ——; m. in Maine, and then went West, but where unknown.
10 | *Margaret*, b. Aug. 30, 1770; m. Silas Spring.
11 | *Jane*, b. 1772; unm.; d. June 10, 1822, æ. 49 yrs.
12 | *William*, b. 1774; m. Abigail Palmer; one ch., Elizabeth; m. J. C. Stickney, and re. to Utah. He d. Sept. 7, 1863, æ. 89 yrs. She d. June 30, 1859, æ. 81 yrs.
13 | *Elizabeth*, b. 1776; m. John Brackett.
14 | *Thomas*, b. 1779; unm.; d. Nov. 17, 1829, æ. 50 yrs.
15 | *Mary*, b. 1781; m. Josiah Brackett.

1– 5 | CHARLES STUART settled on a lot given to his wife by her father, John Ferguson, now known as the "Faxon farm," where he lived till his death. He held various offices of trust in town; was selectman ten years, from 1781 to 1798; was on the Committee of Safety for 1779, and held other minor offices. He m., Aug. 27, 1766, Esther Ferguson, dau. of John Ferguson, b. at Groton, Mass., March 31, 1747. She d. Aug. 22, 1826, æ. 79 yrs., 4 mos. He d. Oct. 13, 1802, æ. 57 yrs.

16 | *Margaret*, b. Dec. 7, 1767; m., 1st hus., Lieut. John Moore; 2d hus., Asa Evans; 3d hus., Richard Gilchrist. She d. Aug. 7, 1818, æ. 51 yrs.
17 | *Sarah*, b. Nov. 2, 1769; m. Asahel Going; ch., (1) George; d.; æ. 18 yrs.; (2) Charles, d. early. She d. June 10, 1834, æ. 65 yrs. He d. at Lancaster, March 13, 1843, æ. 72 yrs.

18 | *Elizabeth*, b. Sept. 4, 1771 ; m. Samuel Turner.
19 | *Mary*, b. Dec. 12, 1773 ; d. April 10, 1858 ; one ch., Sarah Ferguson, m. Samuel Gates.
20 | *Jenny*, b. Oct. 19, 1775 ; m. Oliver Carter ; 2d hus., Capt. Thomas Sherwin.
21 | *Esther*, b. March 17, 1780 ; m. —— Moore, Northumberland ; d. June 15, 1846, æ. 66 yrs.
22 | *John*, b. Sept. 5, 1782 ; m. Sally Brazier, of Groton ; d. 1848, æ. 65 yrs.
23 | *Martha*, b. Aug. 15, 1785 ; m. John Evans, Boston ; d. Sept. 3, 1871, æ. 86 yrs.
24 | *Charles Jesse*, b. Sept. 20, 1788 ; m. Eliza Austin ; d. in Lancaster, May 17, 1836, æ. 46 yrs. ; ch., (1) Charles ; d. ; æ. 20 yrs. ; (2) Arabella, m. Prof. F. Bowen, Harvard University, Cambridge.

THE SWAN FAMILY.

1 | JOHN SWAN, called "Old John," came to Peterborough from Lunenburg. He was the progenitor of all the Swans in town. His son, Gustavus, having begun the Samuel Morison place, went to New York to make brick, and his father, John Swan, came from Lunenburg to Peterborough to live, and d. on this farm. He planted the first apple-tree in town on this farm. He m., in Ireland, 1st w., Peggy McCrossin ; 2d w., Mrs. Jane Wilson, mother to Maj. Robert Wilson ; her maiden name was Jane Bell ; 3d w., Mary Glaney, originally Mary Alld, aunt to Capt. William Alld. Dates of death unknown.

2 | † *Gustavus*, b. 1717 ; m. Isabel Wilson.
3 | † *John* (Lieut.), b. —— ; m. Agnes Nay, dau. Deacon William McNee, Sen.
4 | *William*, b. —— ; m. Mary Russell ; d. in French war, and his wid. m. Moses Adams, of Dublin, and had nine children.
5 | *Jeremiah*, b. about 1736 ; m. Nabby Stuart, or Saunders. He was lost in the French war, 1758 or '59.
6 | † *Alexander*, b. —— ; m. Elizabeth Pitman ; 2d w., Lizzie Stiles, of Lunenburg ; deserted by her former husband.

1-2 | GUSTAVUS SWAN. He m. Isabel Wilson, of Townsend, Nov. 4, 1747. He d. Jan. 8, 1769, æ. 52 yrs. She d.

7 | † *Willam*, b. March 17, 1747 ; m., 1st w., Annas Wood ; 2d w., Abigail Colburn.
8 | † *Robert*, b. Sept. 16, 1752 ; m. Jane Alld.

9　*Jean*, b. March 9, 1755 ; m. —— Stimson ; r. Maine.
10　*Elizabeth*, b. July 24, 1759 ; m. —— Parker ; r. Stoddard.
11　*Susey*, b. June 30, 1761 ; m. Frank Stuart ; r. Grand Isle, Vt.
12　† *Jeremiah*, b. April 25, 1764 ; m. Anna Wilson ; d. Jan. 3, 1828, æ. 65 yrs.

1- 3　JOHN SWAN (Lieut.). He m. Agnes Nay, dau. of Dea. Wm. McNee, Sen. Dates of their deaths unknown.

13　*Mary*, b. Aug. 14, 1758 ; m. Richard Gilchrist, Dublin ; d. Jan. 16, 1816, æ. 57 yrs., 5 mos. ; ten ch.
14　*Agnes*, b. March 26, 1760 ; m. Ezra Morse, Dublin, 1779 ; d. Aug. 22, 1815, æ. 55 yrs. ; five ch.
15　*Elizabeth*, b. March 5, 1762 ; m., April 2, 1782, John Caldwell ; re. to Coleraine, Mass.
16　*Margaret*, b. March 14, 1764 ; m. a French doctor, near Poughkeepsie, N. Y.
17　*Jeremiah*, b. March 6, 1766.
18　*John, Jr.*, b. 1768 ; m. Agnes Nay ; re. to Ohio.
19　*Aaron*, b. 1770 ; m. Azuba Bullard, Feb. 6, 1790 ; one ch.

1- 6　ALEXANDER SWAN. He m. Elizabeth Pitman ; 2d w., Lizzie Stiles, of Lunenburg.

20　† *John*, b. —— ; m. Sarah Taggart.
21　*Gustavus*, b. —— ; m. —— Montgomery. He was drowned in the Penobscot River.
22　·*Alexander*, b. —— ; killed by fall of a joist.

2- 7　WILLIAM SWAN. He m. Annas Wood, by whom he had seven ch., all probably b. in Peterborough ; m., 2d w., Abigail Colburn, by whom he had his two last ch. He re. to St. Albans, Vt. He was drowned in Lake Champlain, Christmas, 1799, by the breaking of the ice, on his way to Montreal, and was buried Jan. 1, 1800, æ. 53 yrs.

23　*Martha*, b. Jan. 23, 1771 ; m. Samuel Alld.
24　*Sarah*, b. May 22, 1773 ; m. Silas Gears, of Durham, Canada.
25　*Gustavus*, b. April 8, 1776 ; m. Polly M. Wood, of North Island, Vt. ; re. to Canada.
26　*William*, b. May 12, 1778 ; d. young.
27　*Jenny*, b. May 30, 1780 ; m. William Gears, Durham, Canada.
28　*Joseph*, b. Sept. 27, 1782.
29　*Nathan*, b. Sept. 8, 1784.
30　† *William Alld*, b. Dec. 4, 1798, at St. Albans, Vt. ; m., 1st w., Judith Jackman ; 2d w., 1831, Tamazon Stone.

31 *Bethiah*, b. March 24, 1800; m. Enoch Sawyer, Dec. 7, 1816; seven ch.; she d. May 10, 1876, æ. 76 yrs.

2- 8 ROBERT SWAN. He lived in the east part of the town. In presenting the following sketch of Mr. Swan, we indicate the methods by which the early settlers, with their slender opportunities, became such intelligent men. He came up in the early days of the town, when all was comparatively a wilderness, and when they were surrounded by all kinds of trials and hardships, when even they could hardly answer the imperious demands of nature, as to what they should eat and as to what they should wear. With all these natural wants to supply, it could not be expected that these early settlers could do much towards affording an education to their children, and they, of course, came up with little school training. There was also a dearth of books, no newspapers, and not the least attempt at anything like periodical literature. The Bible was almost their only book, and this they read and understood far in advance of this generation, which, having so much to read, let this volume, too often, be a sealed book to them. Capt. Swan, in early life, enjoyed no school advantages; he had no special culture, beyond the teachings of the Bible and the routine of the farming of those days. Under such circumstances, we know not how it was that he made such intellectual improvement, that he acquired such a very general knowledge of passing events, and also so much of history and politics. He possessed great natural powers, and gathered up knowledge by intuition, as it were; he only needed to have a thing repeated to him before he incorporated it into his own mind, and made it his own. He did not read much; he had no opportunity to do so; but he was an acute observer, a ready listener, and a deep thinker; and contrived, by his accurate observation and the careful hearing and digesting of all his information, to be always posted among the foremost on all foreign and domestic affairs. He was much respected by the best people in town, for his judgment, his extensive information, and excellent common-sense. In town affairs he was often employed on important committees, and always found to be a safe and judicious counsellor in all exigencies. He was a good talker, not a whit behind the best of the men of that day, and his expressions are repeated to this time,— "By the Lord!" "By the Lord!" with which he interlarded much of his talk, and especially when he was in any degree under the inspiration of liquor.

It is always a wonder how such men happen to know so much. We can hardly estimate how much may be learned by observation and listening alone, by an eager and inquisitive mind, when all the facts and material thus taken in are all well digested and laid up for use, till we see an example of this kind. Books he had none, nor did he read any; he read the book of life and experience, till he became a strong man. I am told that he gathered up much knowledge from his associations with the late James Wilson, Esq., and other educated men in town. He was always sure to be found with a docile and teachable spirit among those who could impart instruction. Dea. Samuel Weston suggests that he was most aided in his efforts in acquiring knowledge, by his frequent visits to the counting-room of Samuel Smith, Esq., where all topics were considered and all subjects freely discussed, which were led off by Mr. Smith, who was gifted with extraordinary conversational powers. This place became a kind of an educator of the people; it was resorted to by a large class of the people, and especially by the politicians of all parties in the town, in which it greatly abounded some fifty years ago. Mr. Smith, being a well-educated, progressive, and reading man, and posted thoroughly in all the affairs of the day, a ready talker, and a man who loved to communicate what he knew, freely distributed his stores of knowledge, and exercised a very perceptible effect in the improvement of the whole community. Swan knew and appreciated these advantages, and richly gathered up knowledge and made it his own, without the labor of reading or studying. But for his intemperate habits, which grew upon him in his old age, he must have been one of the very first men of Peterborough, and in those times, too, when it took rare qualities to stand upon a level with the best men of that day.

This is a striking illustration how much a man can improve and educate himself under the most forbidding circumstances, if he will only arouse himself and apply all his powers in the acquisition of knowledge. This was the great and almost only culture of our fathers; and how successfully, without books, except that Book of books which they all read and revered, without teachers or schools, did they make themselves men of such a heroic stamp! He m. Jane Alld, dau. of Capt. William Alld. She d. April 10, 1846, æ. 84 yrs. He d. May 25, 1835, æ. 83 yrs.

31   *Polly*, b. June 20, 1780; m. ——— Butters; re. to Houlton, Me.; d. 1850, æ. 70 yrs.

32 | *Robert*, b. Oct. 20, 1781 ; m. Margaret Scofield, of Maryland ; d. there 1846, æ. 63 yrs.
33 | *Jane*, b. 1783 ; unm. ; d. Nov. 13, 1849, æ. 66 yrs.
34 | *Lettuce*, b. Jan. 15, 1784 ; m. Hugh Graham ; d. in St. Louis, Mo., 1852, æ. 67 yrs.
35 | *James*, b. —— ; d. in Maryland, on a visit to his brother.
36 | †*Samuel*, b. June 16, 1791 ; m. Janet Steele.
37 | *Sally*, b. 1796 ; m. Zadoc Chamberlain, New York ; d. 1836, æ. 40 yrs.
38 | *William*, b. 1802 ; m. Louisa Fletcher. He d. 1865, æ. 63 yrs. She d. 1856, æ. 45 yrs.

2– 12 | JEREMIAH SWAN. He m. Anna Wilson, dau. Major Robert Wilson. She d. in Montreal. He d. Jan. 3, 1828, æ. 65 yrs.

39 | *William Wilson*, b. 1790 ; d. Feb. 14, 1793, æ. 3 yrs.
40 | †*James W.*, b. Feb. 14, 1792 ; m. Agnes Nancy Blair.

6– 20 | JOHN SWAN (Lieut.). He always resided in town till late in life, when he went to reside with his children in New York, where he d. He m., 1764, Sarah Taggart, dau. of John Taggart, one of the first settlers in town. They lived in the marriage relation over seventy years. She d. Dec. 30, 1834, æ. 90 yrs. He survived her a few years. He d. about 1836.

41 | *Elisabeth*, b. —— ; m. Robert Nay.
42 | *John, 4th*, b. —— ; m. Sally Learned ; re. to New York State.
43 | *Jonathan*, b. —— ; m. —— ; re. to New York State.
44 | *Sarah*, b. —— ; m. —— Breighton, New York.
45 | *James*, b. New York.
46 | *Rachel*, b. —— ; m. Enoch Hoyt ; r. Vermont.
47 | *Gustavus*, b. —— ; m. —— ; r. Columbus, O. ; a lawyer ; became a judge in Ohio ; a man of talents and influence. He became very wealthy. He left town 1810 ; d.

7– 29 | WILLIAM ALLD SWAN. He was three years old when he came to town to live with Samuel Alld, whose first w. was half-sister to him, and was brought up by him. He resided a few years in Lowell, but returned to Peterborough, where he resided many years before his death. He m., 1st w., Judith P. Jackman. She d. Oct. 17, 1829, æ. 31 yrs. ; m., 2d w., Mrs. Tamazon Stone, 1831, b. Feb. 22, 1798 ; d. June 6, 1858, æ. 60 yrs. He d. Dec. 26, 1860, æ. 62 yrs. ; 1st w., three ch. ; 2d w., five ch.

48   †*Charles A.*, b. May, 1823 ; m., 1849, Maria L. Hill, Charlestown, N. H.

49   *Maria,*   ⎫ were drowned together in the Canal at Low-
           ⎬ ell, in 1831, at the ages of 4 and 2 yrs., re-
50   *Isabella,* ⎭ spectively.

51   *Maria J.*, b. in Lowell, May 6, 1832 ; m. Charles Steele ; r. Toledo, O.

52   *Harriet A.*, b. in Lowell, Oct. 14, 1833; m., June 29, 1863, John H. F. Wiers ; ch., (1) Carrie A., b. June 27, 1864; (2) Edgar S., b. Meadville, Pa., May 15, 1873 ; r. Meadville, Pa.

53   *William H.*, b. in Lowell, Oct. 21, 1835 ; was killed by the cars at Grafton, O., Dec. 29, 1858, æ. 23 yrs.

54   *Mary J.*, b. in Lowell, Dec. 5, 1839 ; m. Albert B. Hannaford.

55   *Sarah E.*, b. in Peterborough, Sept. 25, 1843 ; m. John J. Moore, April 6, 1863 ; ch., (1) Ella M., b. Nov. 20, 1865 ; (2) Frank S., b. Oct. 17, 1872 ; r. Meadville, Pa.

8–.36   SAMUEL SWAN. He resided many years on his farm, on East Mountain, when he purchased the Gen. David Steele farm, where he lived some years till his death. He m. Janet Steele, dau. Gen. David Steele, Sept. 7, 1817. He d. Sept. 17, 1854, æ. 63 yrs.

---

56   *David S.*, b. May 21, 1818 ; m. Charlotte Moore, 1844 ; she d. Nov. 8, 1866. One son, Albert M. ; m., 1866, Helen Churchill. He d. February, 1874, æ. 56 yrs. ; r. Lawrence, Mass.

57   *Elizabeth S.*, b. Jan. 11, 1820.

58   *Lucy Ann*, b. Aug. 9, 1823 ; m. Charles F. Mitchell, 1848 ; one son, George ; r. Lawrence, Mass. ; she d. June 7, 1858, æ. 34 yrs. ; he d. Jan. 8, 1851, æ. 33 yrs.

59   *Albert*, b. Nov. 4, 1826 ; d. Aug. 26, 1845, æ. 18 yrs., 9 mos.

60   *George*, b. June 19, 1829 ; m. Abbie Mott, Nov. 3, 1851 ; ch., (1) Eva ; (2) Ithamar ; (3) Charlotte ; re. to Pennsylvania.

61   *Janet*, b. Oct. 24, 1831 ; m. Edward S. Cutter, May 21, 1850 ; r. Amherst ; she d. 1873, æ. 42 yrs.

12– 40   JAMES W. SWAN. He lived and d. on a farm north of the Gen. David Steele place. He m. Agnes Nancy Blair, April 6, 1815 ; she d. April 7, 1845, æ. 56 yrs. He d. Dec. 30, 1824, æ. 32 yrs.

---

62   *William*, b. Dec. 6, 1815 ; m. Frances Kemp, Sept. 26, 1844 ; d. June 5, 1866, æ. 50 yrs., 6 mos.

39

63 | †*James*, b. July 9, 1816; m., 1st w., Elizabeth P. White; 2d w., Mary W. Grant.
64 | *Anna*, b. 1821; d. Jan. 10, 1853, æ. 32 yrs.
65 | *Mary*, b. ——; m. John Kelso White; r. Hanover, Ill.

29- 48 | CHARLES A. SWAN m. Maria L. Hill, Charlestown, N. H. She d. Jacksonville, Ill., Oct. 31, 1871.

66 | *Mary A.*, b. Charlestown, Nov. 12, 1849; m. Alonzo M. Hannaford, Feb. 20, 1868.
67 | *Maria L.*, b. Charlestown, April 21, 1851.
68 | *Charles A.*, b. Charlestown, Jan. 2, 1854.
69 | *Carrie J.*, b. Norwalk, O., Nov. 22, 1855.
70 | *Arabella F.*, b. Norwalk, O., Aug. 14, 1857.
71 | *William H.*, b. Cleveland, O., September, 1859.

40- 63 | JAMES SWAN m., 1st w., Elizabeth P. White, dau. of John S. White, March 17, 1846; she d. Oct. 14, 1856, æ. 39 yrs., 3 mos.; m., 2d w., Mary W. Grant, Jan. 30, 1862. He re. to Hanover, Ill., in 1867 or '68; 1st w., three ch.; 2d w., one ch.

72 | *James W.*, b. Jan. 18, 1849; d. Sept. 12, 1850, æ. 1 yr.
73 | *Anna J.*, b. April 30, 1853; d. April 10, 1863, æ. 10 yrs.
74 | *Elizabeth P.*, b. June 5, 1856.
75 | *Nancy L.*, b. Nov. 26, 1862.

THE TAGGART FAMILY.

1 | JOHN TAGGART came to town with Deacon William McNee and William Ritchie, with his family, about May 1, 1752, and occupied the place purchased of Joseph Caldwell, "the George Shedd farm." He came from Roxbury, Mass., his first five ch. being b. there. He m. Barbara ——; he d. 1813, æ. 92 or 93 yrs.

2 | *Margaret*, b. Sept. 17, 1740; m. William McClary; r. New Ipswich.
3 | *James*, b. May 11, 1742; m. Elizabeth Nay; re. to Dublin, 1788; ch., (1) Barbara; (2) William; (3) Elizabeth; (4) Margaret; (5) Rebecca; (6) James; (7) John; (8) Washington.
4 | *Sarah*, b. Feb. 26, 1745; m. John Swan.
5 | *Catharine*, b. June 14, 1747; m. Daniel Cleary; r. New Ipswich.
6 | *John* (Ensign), b. Feb. 11, 1750; m. Anna Eames; re. to Dublin, 1797; ch., (1) Jacob; (2) David; (3) John; (4) Sally; d. Nov. 15, 1832, æ. 82 yrs., 9 mos.

7   *Mary*, b. June 23, 1752 ; m. Samuel Hogg, name changed to Shepherd.

8   *Rachel*, b. in Peterborough, Feb. 26, 1755 ; m. Hugh Gregg.

9   *Esther*, b. in Peterborough, May 23, 1759 ; m. William Milliken ; d. March 28, 1790, æ. 31 yrs.

10   *William*, b. in Peterborough, Dec. 28, 1761 ; m. Hannah Barnes ; ch., (1) William ; (2) John ; (3) Abner ; (4) Sally ; (5) Hannah ; (6) Betsey. He d. March 9, 1844, æ. 82 yrs., 2 mos. She d. Oct. 13, 1857, æ. 91 yrs. ; r. Sharon.

ALBERT TAGGART, son of Washington Taggart, of Sharon, b. Nov. 30, 1828 ; m. Mary E. Gowing, dau. of Moses and Mary J. Gowing, July 30, 1849.

---

11   *Florence M.*, b. April 19, 1850 ; a teacher in Maryland ; m., July 25, 1876, John Doyen ; r. Winona, Minn.

12   *Sophia Adelia*, b. June 6, 1856.

THE TAYLOR FAMILY.

1   ISAIAH TAYLOR lived on the Jabez Carley farm, which he purchased of George Duncan, Sen., of Londonderry, in 1778, and probably came to town to live about that time. He m. Mary ———. He d. Nov. 1, 1801, æ. 74 yrs. ; she d. July 7, 1803, æ. 74 yrs.

2   *Betsey*, b. ——— ; m. Alexander Scott.

3   *Polly*, b. ——— ; m. James Smith ; they lived on the same farm of (Isaiah Taylor) many years ; re. to New Ipswich.

4   *Charles*, b. 1762 ; m. Betsey Whittemore ; ch., (1) Joseph ; (2) Charles ; he d. Nov. 20, 1800, æ. 38 yrs.

5   *Nabby*, b. ——— ; m. James Stroud, Canada.

THE TEMPLETON FAMILY.

1   MATTHEW TEMPLETON and his brother James came to America from Ireland when young. They came to Peterborough from———, where Matthew m. Jennie Harkness, at precisely what time we cannot determine. It was probably as early as 1770, near the time of his marriage, for we find that he was chosen tithing-man in 1771, treasurer in 1776, and one of the Committee of Safety in 1778. He began his farm in the east part of the town, the same now owned by Caleb Wilder. Here he lived and died.

Matthew Templeton was one of the striking characters among our early settlers. He made a deep impression upon the people of his time, and I well recollect in my early years that no name was more frequently on the lips of his descendants and successors than his. His eccentricities and peculiarities have come down to us, marking a strong-minded, wilful, and obstinate man. He was most notorious for his hostility to any — the least — innovation in the mode of public worship. He was eminently a religious man, but stern and austere, reminding one of the old Scotch Covenanters, who feared neither man, flesh, nor the devil. Many of the old Presbyterians of that day were as fixed in their religious notions as the Medes and Persians, — they knew no change.

This is somewhat facetiously, but well, illustrated in the prayer of the Scotch elder, who besought the Lord that he might always be right, adding, "for thou knowest, Lord, that I am very hard to turn," or as expressed in the Scottish dialect, "ye ken, Lord, that I am unco hard to turn."

They had no idea that there could be any true worship but what was similar to theirs; what they did not understand, they took on assumption, taking care always to believe enough, — living and showing to the world more of the type of a Jewish than a Christian community. It is very little we know of the domestic character of Mr. Templeton; his family government must have been patriarchal and after the model of the old Testament; kind in his way, but little amenable to the teachings of the new dispensation, in which love, forbearance, kindness, and forgiveness are so prominent. He was esteemed a pious man, and no doubt that family and daily worship was set up in his house, the Scripture read and explained, his children catechised, and all with great sincerity and propriety; and if music was ever introduced, it was only of the voice that was tolerated; for though David played on the harp, and stringed instruments were used in the worship of the Jews, yet Mr. Templeton considered all instrumental music as coming from the devil. It was a great trial and abomination to him when a bass-viol was carried into the meeting-house, and he is said to have gone out, with great indignation against those who would bring in Dagon for the worship of God. The following anecdote, has been furnished me by Deacon Samuel Weston: He was displeased with their using musical instruments in the church, so that on one Sabbath he thought he would go to Greenfield to meeting, where he should not be annoyed with Dagon; but to use his own words, he says: "When I got in sight of the meeting-house, there was a man with a goon (bassoon), and Dagon was there too, and I jist got on to mee ould meer and cum home." He even indulged in a spite against so innocent and necessary an instrument as the pitch-pipe; and it is related that on one occasion, when the singers did not get the right pitch on the tune, the old gentleman, who had a seat just back of the singers, cried out audibly, so as to be heard all over the house, "Try the whostle agen."

When Mr. Dunbar was settled, Mr. Templeton was among the remonstrants on that occasion; and always adhered to his Presbyterianism; and yet I suppose that he used to go to meeting. I imagine that he entertained no personal hostility to Mr. Dunbar. He makes a record on the church-book as follows, June 2, 1809: "Attended the funeral of Mr. Matthew Templeton, aged seventy-four years; a member of the Presbyterian communion, who died after a long decline and much distress and darkness, but. I hope is gone to a better world. Though opposed to my settlement, he exhibited many proofs of friendship to me of late years, and called for me to visit him in his sickness."

He d. May 30, 1809, æ. 73 yrs. She d. Nov. 9, 1780, æ. 43 yrs.

---

2   *Betsey*, b. 1770; m. John Holmes; re. to Montpelier, Vt.
3   †*Samuel*, b. March 30, 1772; m. Jane Miller.
4   *Anna*, b. 1774; m. Hugh Miller.
5   *Sally*, b. 1776; m. Reuben Robbe; never lived with him.
6   *Jennie*, b. 1778; unm.; d. Feb. 19, 1849, æ. 71 yrs.

1- 3   SAMUEL TEMPLETON succeeded his father on the homestead. He m. Jane Miller, dau. of James Miller. He d. Oct. 8, 1832, æ. 60 yrs. She d. June 18, 1840, æ. 66 yrs.

---

7   *John*,   d. Oct. 8, 1806, æ. 14 dys.
     b. Sept. 24, 1806;
8   *Harkness*,   d. May 30, 1818, æ. 12 yrs.
9   *Catharine*, b. Oct. 22, 1811; m. Caleb F. Wilder.

JAMES TEMPLETON was a brother to Matthew Templeton, and came at the same time to town with him, and occupied a farm adjoining his, now constituting the Edes farm and that of William S. Treadwell. He re. to Montpelier in 1800, and d. there in 1807. He m. Jennet

10 | *Agnes*, b. Sept. 24, 1758.   (11) *Mary*, b. April 10, 1760.
12 | *William*, b. Oct. 24, 1762 ; m. Mary Moore, of Sharon.
13 | *John*, b. Nov. 14, 1764.
14 | *Jenny*, b. 1766 ; m. Charles McCoy.

THE THAYER FAMILY.

1 | CHRISTOPHER THAYER (Dea.) was the son of Christopher and Mary Morse Thayer, and grandson to Ephraim and Sarah Bass Thayer, of Braintree, Mass.; the wife of Ephraim Thayer, his grandmother, was a third descendant direct from John Alden, the pilgrim.   One of Deacon Thayer's sisters, Ruth, b. July 1, 1752, m. John Field, who came to town at the same time he did.   Her father, Christopher Thayer, came late in life to Peterborough, and d. here, Dec. 10, 1787, æ. 84 yrs.   Mr. Thayer was out in the French war when he was sixteen years of age, and was at Cape Breton in 1757.   He subsequently served in the Revolutionary War, but when and where we have no means of determining.   He lived on a farm north of the Gordon place, which had been improved some years when he came to town.   He emigrated here from Braintree in 1786.

He m. Bethiah Hunt, and the children were all born before he moved to town.   He was b. in Braintree, April 27, 1741 ; d. at Peterborough, Sept. 28, 1823, æ. 82 yrs. She was b. Nov. 30, 1744 ; d. Feb. 28, 1817, æ. 73 yrs. He was a deacon in the Presbyterian Church.

2 | †*William*, b. Nov. 25, 1767 ; m. Abigail Wyman, of Ashby, Mass.
3 | *Mary*, b. July 8. 1771 ; d. in infancy.
4 | †*Eber*, b. Aug. 17, 1773; m., 1st w., Elizabeth Jaquith ; 2d w., Sarah Everett.
5 | *Christopher*, b. Dec. 28, 1776 ; an imbecile ; d. May 12, 1818, æ. 41 yrs., 4 mos.
6 | *Sarah*, b. Feb. 12, 1779 ; m. Elihu Penniman, Jr. ; d. March 10, 1807, æ. 28 yrs.
7 | *Joseph A.*, b. May 18, 1781; d. Aug. 18, 1803, æ. 22 yrs.
8 | †*Elihu*, b. May 1, 1783 ; m. Susan Everett.

1– 2 | WILLIAM THAYER.   He died suddenly at Amherst, of injuries received in a playful and innocent scuffle with Mr. Cushing, editor of the *Farmer's Cabinet.*   He then carried the mail, on contract, from Brattleboro, Vt., to Portsmouth, once every week, and was on his return when the accident occurred.   He was the first mail-contractor in town.   His routes were made on horseback,

the roads being too rough for any kind of a carriage.
His successor, Mr. Gibbs, also carried the mail in this
manner many years. It is singular that both of these
early contractors for carrying the mail should have
come to a violent death. It will be remembered that
Mr. Gibbs lost his life by being thrown off the great
bridge in 1824. He m. Abigail Wyman, of Ashby, b.
Sept. 6, 1774. She d. July 11, 1818, æ. 43 yrs., 10 mos.
He d. Aug. 6, 1807, æ. 39 yrs., 8 mos.

9 | *Abijah Wyman*, b. Jan. 5, 1796 ; m. Susan Bradley.
10 | *Cephas P.*, b. Sept. 6, 1797 ; m. —— ; r. Cambridge ; is a
printer.
11 | *Stephen Wyman*, b. Aug. 1, 1801 ; m. —— ; r. Clyde,
N. Y.
12 | *Elizabeth S.*, b. March 23, 1803 ; d. Jan. 18, 1817, æ. 13
yrs.
13 | *Abigail S.*, b. Dec. 3, 1804 ; m. Royal B. Hancock, June,
1832 ; went as a missionary to Burmah and d. on her
return passage.
14 | *Sarah W.*, b. July 6, 1806 ; d. Jan. 22, 1807, æ. 5 mos.

1- 4 | EBER THAYER. He m., 1st w., Elizabeth Jaquith, of
Washington, b. April 25, 1780 ; she d. Oct. 30, 1805, æ.
25 yrs. ; m., 2d w., Sarah Everett, May 8, 1817 ; b. May
21, 1785 ; she d. Dec. 8, 1866, æ. 82 yrs. He d. Jan. 23,
1849, æ. 75 yrs.

15 | *Maria Everett*, b. March 10, 1818 ; d. Feb. 11, 1839, æ.
21 yrs.
16 | *Joseph A.*, b. Nov. 25, 1819 ; m. —— Messer ; r. Jaf-
frey.
17 | *Elizabeth J.*, b. Oct. 21, 1822 ; m. Abner Haggett, June
24, 1845.
18 | *Abigail*, b. July 27, 1824 ; d. July 12, 1850, æ. 26 yrs.

1- 8 | ELIHU THAYER. He succeeded his father on the
home place. Mr. Thayer is a lineal descendant, on the
paternal side in the sixth generation, from John Alden,
one of the pilgrim fathers. John Alden's youngest dau.
m. John Bass, of Braintree, now Quincy, and Sarah, dau.
of John Bass, m. Ephraim Thayer, and Christopher,
father of Deacon Christopher Thayer, of Peterborough,
and father of Elihu, was one of fourteen children of his
family. He has always resided in town, a chair-maker
and painter by trade. He now survives, at the age of 93
yrs. He m., April 11, 1813, Susan Everett, b. Nov. 3,
1783 ; d. Sept. 20, 1855, æ. 71 yrs.

19 | *Eliza Ann*, b. Nov. 4, 1813 ; m. Mark Wilder.
20 | *William*, b. March 4, 1815 ; m., 1st w., Sarah Allison ; d. June 18, 1846, æ. 29 yrs., 10 mos. ; m., 2d w., Clarissa Osgood, of Lawrence ; r. Haverhill, Mass.
21 | *Susan*, b. April 1, 1816 ; m. Lyman Baker ; r. Northampton, Mass.
22 | † *John N.*, b. Aug. 5, 1817 ; m. Loretta H. Thayer.
23 | *Sarah P.*, b. Oct. 10, 1818 ; d. Oct. 2, 1826, æ. 8 yrs.
24 | *Martha E.*, b. July 8, 1821 ; m., Nov. 25, 1847, Allen Buckminster ; ch., (1) Susan A., b. Sept. 24, 1848 ; m., Jan. 15, 1872, Charles W. Holt ; r. Springfield, Mass. ; (2) Mary Emma, b. Sept. 18, 1856 ; (3) Julia M., b. July 25, 1859.
25 | *Mary J.*, b. Aug. 10, 1822 ; unm. ; r. Manchester.
26 | *Charles*, b. May 18, 1824 ; d. Sept. 4, 1826, æ. 2 yrs.
27 | *Nancy Hunt*, b. March 3, 1826 ; d. July 15, 1829, æ. 3 yrs.
28 | *George*, b. Feb. 16, 1828 ; m. Malvina Kidder ; r. Haverhill, Mass.

2– 9   ABIJAH WYMAN THAYER. His early youth was spent in town, where he enjoyed the limited means of education afforded by the common schools, till he was fourteen years of age, when he was apprenticed to Lincoln & Edmunds, of Boston, to learn the printer's trade. Being drafted during his apprenticeship, in the war of 1812, he served three months as a soldier in the fort in Boston Harbor. He was first employed in the book printing-office of Flagg & Gould, of Andover, Mass., but soon bought an interest in the Concord (N. H.) *Gazette*, when he began his editorial labors. After two years, he removed to Portland, Me., where till 1826 he was editor of the *Independent Statesman*, the only paper of extended circulation which at that time advocated the election of John Quincy Adams to the presidency. He conducted the canvass with great spirit and sagacity, and was mainly instrumental in securing the vote of the State to his candidate. In 1826, Mr. Thayer removed to Haverhill, Mass., to become the editor of the Haverhill *Gazette*, which he soon purchased and changed the name to that of *Essex Gazette*.

The *History of Haverhill*, published in 1861, makes frequent allusions to Mr. Thayer, and says of him: " From October, 1826, to July, 1835, Mr. Thayer resided in this town, during which time he was one of our most active, useful, and respected citizens. He was one of the first to enlist in the temperance movement ; was the secretary of the first meeting and the first secretary of the first society when organized, in which office he continued until he removed from town. He early advocated the cause in his paper, but such was the opposition that in a short time he lost about four hundred subscribers. His *Gazette* was the first *political paper* that ever came out in advocacy of total abstinence from intoxicating liquors, and the *second of any kind in America, or in the world*. When the movement was commenced in Haverhill, there were twenty-nine places in town where liquors were sold; but in five years from that time there was not a single place where it was openly sold, and but one where it was supposed to be sold clandestinely. As a political paper, the *Gazette* was at this time classed among the very first in the county and State."

With the exception of six months in 1830, from January 1st to July 10th, when John G. Whittier occupied the editorial chair, Mr. Thayer was sole editor, publisher, and proprietor of the *Essex Gazette* from the time mentioned before till 1835. In that year, he sold out the establishment and removed from town. He has since been connected with various papers in Philadelphia, Worcester, and Northampton. In 1841, he removed to Northampton, and engaged once more in editorial labor. He continued to reside here till his death in 1864. During the latter years of his life he did business as a broker and insurance and United States claim agent, though he always kept up his habit of occasional writing for the newspapers. Mr. Thayer was a sagacious, enlightened, and public-spirited man, with a kind and generous heart.

The Northampton *Free Press* in a notice of his death says: "In clearness of style as a writer, Mr. Thayer had few superiors; he never failed to make his points strongly, and his articles always commanded attention and respect. While editor of the *Essex Gazette* he exercised much influence in the politics of Eastern Massachusetts, and was an intelligent and honorable supporter of the Whig party. His knowledge of political history was unsurpassed, and few occupying a similar position had so extensive acquaintance with the distinguished men of the country.

"In 1827, while editor of the *Essex Gazette*, he came out boldly in favor of the temperance cause, and fought the battle of temperance from that time onward with unwearied courage and vigor, often at the risk of great personal danger and pecuniary loss. He was also, as editor of the *Gazette*, one of the earliest advocates of the anti-slavery cause. He maintained to the last his early convictions of the evils of intemperance and slavery, and died regretting that he could not see the war ended,

40

and the abolition of slavery finally and completely accomplished."

Mr. Thayer m., Nov. 9, 1824, Susan Bradley, dau. Jonathan Bradley, of Andover, Mass., who survives him, and resides in Northampton. He d. 1867, æ. 71 yrs.

29   *Sarah Smith*, b. at Haverhill, Oct. 6, 1827 ; r. Northampton, Mass.

30   *William Sidney*, b. at Haverhill, April 15, 1829.

He entered the Sophomore Class at Harvard College in 1847, having prepared himself without the aid of a tutor, and graduated in 1850. After leaving college, he was engaged for some two years in teaching private pupils and reading law at Milton, Mass. But the profession of journalism was more to his taste than that of law, and in 1853 he went to New York City and joined the staff of the New York *Evening Post*, becoming in a few years its chief officer and editor, and "imparting to its columns" (it was said by a contemporary journal) "an interest and ability never before or since surpassed." The duties of his profession were arduous, and his health became greatly impaired ; and when, in 1861, he received the appointment of Consul-General for Egypt, he gladly availed himself of the opportunity it offered of residence in a milder climate, and entered at once upon the duties of his office, which he discharged with energy and ability. At his instance the rebel flag was excluded from the Egyptian ports, and an abuse inflicted upon the agent of a Christian missionary was not only instantly redressed through his intervention, but was made the occasion of securing for the future a larger toleration for the Christian faith, a service for which he received the marked approval of his own government, and the thanks of large bodies of Christians in England and America.

He was industrious in gathering and transmitting information touching the resources of Egypt, the culture of cotton, and other subjects of interest to the commercial world ; and the value of his services in these respects was shown in the early publication by the State department of portions of his despatches to the government. His health for a year or two steadily improved, but in the summer of 1863 he was prostrated by severe illness, from the effects of which he never recovered, and he d. at Alexandria, April 10, 1864, æ. 35 yrs.

In a notice of his death, one of many which the event called forth, the Springfield *Republican* said : "He was a man of rare accomplishments, of wise and various culture, refined tastes and habits, wise without dogmatism, earnest without coarseness, witty without vulgarity, practical and poetical alike, a model journalist and a lovable man."

31   *James Bradley*, b. in Haverhill, Jan. 15, 1831.

He entered Harvard College in 1848, having prepared himself mainly without help, and graduated the ninth scholar in his class, in 1852. After leaving college, he taught a private school in Milton, Mass., two years, reading law at the same time; and in 1854 entered the Law School, at Cambridge, where he remained two years, and received the degree of LL.B., securing also the first prize of his class for an essay on the "Law of Eminent Domain," which was afterwards printed in the *Law Reporter* of that year.

In 1857, he began business in Boston, in partnership with Hon. William J. Hubbard, a connection which he maintained until the death of Mr. Hubbard, in 1864, when by appointment of. Gov. Andrew he succeeded Mr. Hubbard as one of the Masters in Chancery for Suffolk County. In 1865, he became a partner with Hon. Peleg W. Chandler, in the land firm of Chandler, Shattuck & Thayer, and afterwards Chandler, Thayer & Hudson, and in 1873 he was chosen Royal Professor of Law in the Law School at Cambridge, entering upon the duties of the office in 1874. He resided in Cambridge from 1854 until 1861. In April of that year he m. Miss Sophia Bradford Ripley, of Concord, Mass., and removed to Milton, where he remained until the autumn of 1874, when he returned to Cambridge to undertake the duties of the office which he now holds. He has four children. We are in part indebted to an account of Prof. Thayer published in the *Harvard Book*, from which we have also taken the following paragraph: —

"Mr. Thayer has been a frequent contributor to the columns of the Boston *Daily Advertiser*, and in former years to those of the New York *Evening Post*. He has also been a writer in Bouries' *Law Dictionary*, and in the *American Law Review*, and other periodicals. He was entrusted with the editing of the twelfth edition of Kent's *Commentaries*, and had throughout the sole responsibility for that work. His happy selection of an associate, however, resulted in reducing his own labors mainly to those of simple revision, and the work appears without the addition of his name."

32   *Susan Bradley*, b. in Haverhill, Oct. 7, 1833; m. John C. Alexander; r. New York City.

8– 22   JOHN N. THAYER. He has always resided in town; is a stone-mason; m., Oct. 15, 1844, Loretta H. Thayer, b. Nov. 10, 1823, of Mansfield, Mass.

33 | *Clara*, b. May 2, 1849; m. Henry M. Shepard, Aug. 12, 1875; r. Boston.
34 | *Nellie*, b. June 27, 1853; m., Dec. 8, 1874, L. C. Taylor, dentist; r. Hartford, Conn.
35 | *Abbie*, b. Dec. 19, 1857.

BARTHOLOMEW THAYER, b. July 15, 1757, was son of Dea. Peter Thayer, son of Ephraim Thayer, and brother of Christopher Thayer, father of Dea. Christopher Thayer, of Peterborough. Dea. Peter Thayer d. in Peterborough, 1799, æ. 90 yrs. Bartholomew Thayer came to Peterborough about 1786, and lived on the John Little place while in town. He m. Elizabeth Blanchard, of Braintree, in 1789. Late in life he re. to Ohio, and both he and his w. d. there. He was tithing-man in 1788, '93, 1801, '2. Left town 1802.

---

37 | *Ephraim*, b. ——; r. Ohio.
38 | *Jabez*, b. ——; d. in childhood.

THE TODD FAMILY.

1 | ANDREW TODD (Col.). His genealogy does not strictly belong to this town, but his family is so intimately connected with many of our early settlers that we have thought best to introduce it here. Col. Todd was b. in Ireland in 1697, and came to Londonderry in 1720, being among the first settlers of that town, and became a leading man. He represented the town in the Provincial Legislature, held a commission in the French war of 1744, and in 1755 he held the rank of colonel in the provincial levies. He was a marked man in those times, having gained a high reputation in these wars. He m. Beatrix Moore, dau. of John Moore, murdered at the massacre of Glencoe, in 1692. He re. to Peterborough toward the close of his life, 1776, to live with his dau., w. of William Miller, Sen., where he d., Sept. 15, 1777, æ. 80 yrs. He was buried in the Old Cemetery. *Vide* gravestone, Old Cemetery.

---

2 | †*Samuel*, b. in Londonderry, June 3, 1726; m. Hannah Morison; 2d w., Ann Cochran.
3 | *Rachel*, b. Londonderry, April 14, 1733; m. Moses Morison; r. Hancock.
4 | *John*, b. 1730; was drowned at Amoskeag Falls, 1754, æ. 24 yrs.
5 | *James*, b. ——. He succeeded his father on the Aiken Range, and d. of hemorrhage of the lungs.*

* John Todd, Jr., thinks he d. at Worcester, Mass.

6   *Jane*, b. 1736 ; m. William Miller, and moved to Peterborough.

•7   *Alexander*, b. Jan. 2, 1731 ; m. a dau. of Deacon George Duncan, Londonderry, and had several ch. He lived in Hooksett on what is now known as the Todd farm, but returned again to Londonderry. He was a captain in the French war, and was taken a prisoner by the Indians. They stripped off his clothes to burn him, as the custom was in those times, and in putting his shirt over his head he made a strong effort, and tore one sleeve out at the shoulder, and ran about forty rods. Two Indians who were behind a tree caught him by that sleeve which was fastened around his wrist by a crystal button. He unbuttoned it with his other hand and got away. He was three days and nights naked before he got into camp. He d. in Londonderry, æ. about 70 yrs.

8   *Andrew*, b. 1739; unm. Many anecdotes are told of this man, who led a useless and vagabond kind of a life. Uncle Andrew Todd, as he was called, labored at two kinds of work: to use his own language, "Thrashing grain with a flail and scratching lint," or, in Yankee phrase, dressing flax. Uncle Andrew stayed over night with a Mr. Duncan in Hancock, and in the morning he went out where Duncan was chopping, with his jug of rum, and laid down to sleep a few rods from where Duncan was at work. A large hemlock tree fell over where Andrew was sleeping with his jug near his head. Duncan ran, and, pulling him out from under the tree, said, "Uncle Andrew, are you killed?" "I don't know, Sam; but hand us the jug; we will na part with dry lips." He survived this incident some years, and d. at Deacon Timothy Hunt's, April 15, 1808, æ. 69 yrs.

1– 2   SAMUEL TODD. We refer to the account given of the beginning of the Todd farm in the article on Deacon Samuel Moore,—they taking up the land in common first, till they divided, only a short time before the death of Todd. Samuel Todd began what is called the Todd place and endured many hardships in the first settlement. There was no grist-mill in town till 1751, and he carried his grain on his back to Townsend to have it ground. The Indians came to his camp one day when he was gone to mill, and stole what provisions he had, but did no other damage. He had buried most of his provisions back in the woods. The camp was on the hill, south side of the old road to Dublin, south of the house built by Deacon Samuel Moore, and afterwards occupied by Jonah C. Spring, and now owned by the heirs of Reuel Richardson. He came to town for a permanent residence not far from 1750. He was killed on the same farm by the falling of a tree, March 30, 1765, æ. 39 yrs. He m., 1st w., Hannah Morison, dau. John Morison, and sister of w. of William Smith, Esq., by whom he had two ch., Betty and John. She d. November, 1760, æ. 30 yrs. He m., 2d w., 1762, Ann Cochran. She d.; 1st w., two ch.; 2d w., two ch.

9 | *Betty*, b. 1754; unm.; d. Aug. 24, 1826, æ. 72 yrs.
10 | †*John*, b. April 9, 1757; m., 1st w., Rachel Duncan; 2d w., wid. Sarah Annan.
11 | *Jane*, b. ——; m. John Morison; r. Hancock.
12 | *James*, b. ——; m. —— Page, Goffstown; 2d w., wid. Sarah Duncan, her maiden name Sarah Miller, dau. of William Miller, Sen.; he d. in Francestown.

2– 10 | JOHN TODD. On the death of his father, 1765, then being eight years old, he went to Londonderry and lived with John Bell, until the commencement of the Revolutionary War. He enlisted as a volunteer under Gen. Stark, was in the battle of Bennington, and several others in the valley of the Hudson, also at the surrender of Gen. Burgoyne. After the war he returned home, and moved on to his father's farm in Peterborough, 1783, and remained there the rest of his life. He m. Rachel Duncan, in 1783, dau. of Dea. George Duncan; she d. April 26, 1815, æ. 56 yrs. He m., 2d w., Sarah Annan, Jan. 1, 1817, wid. of Rev. David Annan: She d. April 6, 1846, æ. 85 yrs. He d. Oct. 27, 1846, æ. 89 yrs., 5 mos.

13 | *Hannah*, b. Nov. 14, 1783; m. Dr. Robert Taggart, of Coleraine; d. Nov. 8, 1867, æ. 84 yrs.
14 | *Samuel*, b. Oct. 24, 1785; d. Adrian, Mich., Feb. 19, 1867, æ. 82 yrs.
15 | *James B.*, b. Nov. 25, 1787; m. Sarah Appleton, 1816; d. May 29, 1863, æ. 75 yrs., 6 mos.
16 | *Mary*, b. Oct. 29, 1789; d. Sept. 14, 1790, æ. 1 yr.
17 | *Daniel*, b. Aug. 14, 1791; m. Mary Taggart. One son, Samuel John, b. in Preble, N. Y. He is now a lawyer in extensive practice, and with a good reputation, in Beloit, Wis. Mr. Todd d. in Preble, N. Y., Aug. 18, 1826, æ. 35 yrs.
18 | *John*, b. Nov. 17, 1793; d. Oct. 25, 1800, æ. 7 yrs.
19 | *Esther*, b. Nov. 11, 1795; d. Oct. 16, 1800, æ. 5 yrs.

20 | *Mary*, b. May 12, 1798; d. Oct. 6, 1800; æ. 2 yrs.
21 | † *John, Jr.*, b. June 12, 1800; m., Dec. 4, 1828, Mary Taggart, wid. of Daniel Todd.

10– 21 | JOHN TODD, Jr. He went out to New York for a few years, after attaining his majority, but returned to Peterborough in 1829, to take care of his parents after the removal of his brother James to the West. Soon after the death of his father, 1846 or '47, he removed to Wiscoy, N. Y., where he now resides. He held various offices of trust in town; selectman three years, 1839, '40, '41, and Representative for 1838, '39. His w. d. Jan 14, 1869, æ. 76 yrs. He was a deacon in the Presbyterian Church.

22 | *Frances*, b. March 19, 1833; m. Chancey S. Brown, Wiscoy, N. Y., Nov. 26, 1856; one ch., John C., b. Sept. 1, 1857.

THE TREADWELL FAMILY.

1 | SAMUEL TREADWELL came to town about 1777, from Portsmouth, where he was b. Oct. 4, 1741. He first lived for a few years where David Blanchard now lives, then moved to the east part of the town where Capt Samuel McCoy lived the few last years of his life, a farm between the Robert Swan and the McCoy farms, and d. here. He m., April 10, 1764, Mary Stoodley, b. March 31, 1741. She d. Oct. 4, 1771, æ. 26 yrs.; m. 2d w., Mary McKean, wid. of James McKean, May 1, 1777. She d. Aug. 27, 1833, æ. 87 yrs.; 1st w., three ch.; 2d w., five ch. He d. Dec. 13, 1819, æ. 78 yrs.

2 | *Daniel*, b. Portsmouth, Jan. 28, 1766.
3 | *Mary*, b. Portsmouth, Feb. 20, 1768.
4 | *Sarah*, b. Portsmouth, Nov. 20, 1770.
5 | *Elizabeth*, b. Peterborough, Feb. 15, 1778; m. Abel Weston.
6 | † *William Earl*, b. Feb. 6, 1780; m. Elizabeth Secomb, of Amherst.
7 | *Anna*, b. Feb. 24, 1782; m. —— Buss; re. to Maine.
8 | *Susanna*, b. May 3, 1784; m. —— Mansur; r. Temple.
9 | *Frances*, b. June 18, 1786; unm.; d. Feb. 7, 1849, æ. 63 yrs.

1– 6 | WILLIAM E. TREADWELL. He lived on a part of the James Templeton farm, near the Edes place. He m., Jan. 21, 1810, Elizabeth Secomb, of Amherst, b. April 24, 1785. She d. April 1, 1863, æ. 78 yrs. He d. July 11, 1847, æ. 67 yrs.

10 | *John S.*, b. Nov. 20, 1818 ; m. Lucy Kendall, of Temple, 1848 ; c.
11 | *William S.*, b. Sept. 30, 1821 ; m. H. Jane Clark, of Lyndeboro, May 1, 1849 ; c.

THE TURNER FAMILY.

1 | THOMAS TURNER, the son of Joseph and Rachel Turner, was b. in Ireland in 1725. He was accompanied by his parents when he emigrated to America, and also by two brothers, Joseph, who lived on the Sanders place, and William, on the Jewett place, both in Jaffrey. Their father and mother both d. in Peterborough. Joseph Turner, Sen., d. June 10, 1783, æ. 77 yrs. Rachel, his w., d. Dec. 23, 1787, æ. 87 yrs. Thomas Turner began the settlement on his farm. It is not certain when he came to town ; it was early. He was here Sept. 26, 1753, according to the Proprietors' records, in which the Proprietors grant him fifty acres, or Lot No. 92, adjoining his Lot No. 29, in consideration of his relinquishing to them Lot No. 7 of fifty acres. He m. Jenny McCoy, wid. of Charles McCoy, and dau. of Samuel and Margaret Miller. She d. June 19, 1812, æ. 77 yrs. He d. April 14, 1802, æ. 77 yrs.

2 | *John*, b. 1763 ; m. Mary —— ; r. Jaffrey. He d. May 22, 1844, æ. 81 yrs. ; she d. Nov. 29, 1836, æ. 67 yrs.
3 | †*Samuel*, b. June 16, 1764 ; m. Betsey Stuart, Dec. 7, 1802.
4 | † *Thomas*, b. —— : m. Polly McClary.
5 | † *Joseph*, b. —— ; m. Polly Watts.
6 | *Jenny*, b. —— ; m. Elijah Welman ; r. Jaffrey.
7 | *Rachel*, b. —— ; m. Samuel Sanders ; r. Jaffrey.
8 | *Peggy*, b. 1775 ; unm. ; d. Jaffrey, Dec. 29, 1867, æ. 92 yrs.

1– 3 | SAMUEL TURNER. He settled in the north-west part of the town. He m. Betsey Stuart, dau. of Charles Stuart, Dec. 7, 1802 ; she d. May 4, 1845, æ. 74 yrs. ; he d. Feb. 1, 1839, æ. 76 yrs., 7 mos.

9 | *Esther*, b. Oct. 18, 1803 ; m., Sept. 3, 1850, Joshua Shedd, Pepperell ; d. Oct. 12, 1853, æ. 50 yrs.
10 | *Elizabeth*, b. July 24, 1807 ; m. Samuel Converse.
11 | *Harriet*, b. December 19, 1809 ; m. Warren Nichols, Nov. 4, 1846 ; ch., (1) Samuel, b. Nov. 4, 1847 ; (2) Clark R., b. Nov. 4, 1850.
12 | *Sarah S.*, b. March 15, 1812 ; m. Rodney Goodhue, March 3, 1853.

| 1- 4 | THOMAS TURNER m. Mary McClary, of New Ipswich, Nov. 25, 1802. He d. 1846, æ. 75 yrs.; she d. in Clarendon, N.Y., 1863, æ. 82 yrs. |

13 *Thomas*, b. ——; d. 1826, æ. 21 yrs.
14 *Daniel*, b. ——; m. ——; d. in Michigan, 1863.
15 *John*, b. 1806; unm; d. July 3, 1874, æ. 68 yrs.
16 *Bernard*, b. ——; d. about 1840; an imbecile.
17 *William*, b. 1810; r. Clarendon, N. Y.
18 *Mary Ann*, b. 1815; m. Abel Nutting, of Jaffrey; d. Aug. 8, 1847, æ. 32 yrs.
19 *Margaret*, b. 1819; unm.
20 *Catharine*, b. March 30, 1821; m. Samuel Taggart, December, 1845; one son, Frank Eugene, b. Dec. 14, 1851; m. Alice Lovejoy; one ch., Katie M., b. March 3, 1875.

| 1- 5 | JOSEPH TURNER m. Polly Watts. |

21 *Betsey*, b. ——; m. Peter Davis, Dublin.
22 *Thomas*, b. ——; m., July 3, 1828, Clarissa Nay, dau. of Robert Nay.
23 *Luke*, b. ——; m. Sarah A. Warren, Dublin, Oct. 8, 1835; d. at Clarendon, N. Y., Oct. 21, 1875, æ. 67 yrs.
24 *Margaret*, b. ——; m. John Preston, Clarendon, N. Y.
25 *Joseph*, b. ——; m. Lydia Townsend, of Dublin; r. Clarendon.
26 *Jane*, b. ——; m. Samuel Nay; r. Clarendon.
27 *Louisa*, b. ——; m. —— Dewey; r. Clarendon.

THE TUBBS FAMILY.

1   JOSEPH TUBBS, son of Capt. Joseph and Rhoda Henry Tubbs, was born in Marlow, Jan. 23, 1789. He served an apprenticeship at paper-making in Paper Mill Village, Alstead, and on completing it came to Peterborough in 1811, and worked in the mill of Hon. Samuel Smith. In 1814, in company with Thomas Baker, he purchased the Eagle Factory, which was located on the spot where Felt's machine-shop now stands, where they manufactured cotton yarns, battings, candle wicking, etc. They continued business some years, when Mr. Baker retired, and Joseph Tubbs associated with him his brother Abisha, under the firm of J. & A. Tubbs. They continued in business until the invention of the power-loom, which necessitated an entire change of machinery. The machinery of the factory being much worn, they did not deem it advisable to add looms, but sold the mill and site to Moore & Colby, March 30, 1833, who converted

the same into a machine-shop. Mr. Tubbs remained in town two years—till 1839,—when he removed to Hancock, and subsequently to Marlboro, and returned to Peterborough in 1857, where he d., May 22, 1859, æ. 70 yrs., 3 mos. He m. Azubah, dau. of Dr. Joseph and Azubah Henry Monroe, b. in Hillsboro, March 7, 1795, and d. in Hancock, Jan. 16, 1871, æ. 75 yrs., 8 mos. Dr. Joseph Monroe, her father, was "the second physician of Hillsboro, was a good physician, and an amiable and upright man." He d. Feb. 24, 1798, æ. 41 yrs.

2 *Thomas Baker*, b. Feb. 24, 1815; r. Hancock.
3 *Maria*, b. Sept. 22, 1817; m., March 15, 1849, Ambrose C. Blood, of Hancock, who d. Nov. 26, 1873.
4 †*Elijah Monroe*, b. March 21, 1823; m. Sarah Merriam.
5 *Sarah Wallace*, b. April 12, 1826; m., June 26, 1851, Benj. F. Merriam; now r. in Marlboro. They have three surviving ch., *vis.:* Frank Irving, b. Aug. 3, 1852; Joseph Sumner, b. March 17, 1854; Henry Zadock, b. July 14, 1865.
6 *Louisa*, b. July 25, 1828; r. Hancock.
7 *Henry L.*, b. Feb. 24, 1831; a dentist; m., Dec. 25, 1865, Mary Ann Rogers; two ch., Annie L., b. Aug. 3, 1868; Gertie M., b. Oct. 27, 1874; r. in Newport.

1- 4 ELIJAH MONROE TUBBS. He received his academical education at the Hancock and Phillips (Exeter) Academies, and studied dentistry with Dr. Luke Miller, at Peterborough, and Dr. S. Hanson, of Boston. He located himself at Peterborough in 1845, where he remained in the practice of his profession twenty-one years. During this period he established the first regular drug-store in Peterborough in company with Franklin Kendall, to whom he soon disposed of his interest in the same. He was also for a time engaged in daguerrotyping. He published a small work entitled *The New Hampshire Kitchen, Fruit, and Floral Gardner.* He was for several years a member of the Superintending School Committee, also of the Library Committee, and one of a committee to give a full report of the doings of the Peterborough soldiers in the war of the Rebellion. He made an elaborate report on this subject, which was entered on the town records, and has furnished all the data needed for this history. He represented the town in the Legislature in the years 1864, '65. He was also appointed a justice of the peace and quorum.

In 1864, in company with J. G. Fish, he commenced the manufacture of a hair preparation, "Ring's Vegetable Ambrosia." Mr. Fish sold out his interest to Hon. P. C. Cheney, of Peterborough, now of Manchester. They have had associated with them for a time P. Ring, of Wilton, and Ira Cross, of Manchester, both of whom have retired from the firm. Of this preparation they have sold nearly seven hundred thousand dollars' worth. He is also a member of the firm of P. C. Cheney & Co., and is associated with others in the ownership of large paper-mills in Hanniker, Goffstown, and Manchester. He removed to Manchester in 1868. He m., in 1848, Sarah, dau. of Zadock and Sally Snow Merriam, who was b. at Goshen, Aug. 7, 1828.

8   *Sarah*, b. Feb. 17, 1849 ; m., Jan. 5, 1872, George E. Hersey, M. D. ; one ch., Everett Monroe, b. April 11, 1875 ; r. Manchester.

9   *Annabelle*, b. June 17, 1851 ; m., Feb. 25, 1874, Charles H. Thayer, of Manchester. She d. at Rye Beach, July 20, 1874, æ. 23 yrs.

10   *Monroe*, b. July 13, 1853 ; r. Manchester.

ABISHA TUBBS, a brother of Joseph, and son of Capt. Joseph and Rhoda Henry Tubbs, was b. in Marlow, May 21, 1791. He came to Peterborough in 1815, and has resided here since. He m., 1st w., Belinda Fisk, of Dunstable, now Nashua, February, 1823. She d. Oct. 23, 1846, æ. 44 yrs. He m., 2d w., Sept. 22, 1859, Matilda Weston, wid. of Timothy Weston, of Hancock.

11   *Cemira*, b. March 30, 1824 ; m., Nov. 24, 1852, Amos Sawyer, who d. May, 1863 ; ch., Alice, b. Dec. 2, 1861 ; r. Marlow.

12   *Justina M.*, b. April 22, 1827 ; m., Sept. 28, 1847, James B. Tubbs ; of six ch. only one survives, Flora J., b. Oct. 31, 1862.

THE TWISS FAMILY.

1   PETER TWISS m. Harriet Haggett, dau. of Abner Haggett. They lived two years in New Boston, then re. to Vermont and remained there till 1833, when they returned to Peterborough, and occupied the old farm of Abner Haggett. He d. 1853, æ. 58 yrs. She d. 1861, æ. 61 yrs.

2   *Mary F.*, b. Sept. 9, 1828 ; m., Sept. 4, 1849, Samuel Hadley ; ch., (1) Milton ; m. Amanda Corey ; r. Fitchburg ; (2) Ada S. ; m. W. W. Richardson ; r. Sullivan

(3) Luella E.; m. Frank O. Emerson; r. Fisherville;
(4) Delila M.; (5) Hattie Maria.

3   *Samuel Bartlett*, b. Nov. 4, 1829; r. West.

4   *Abner H.*, b. 1832.

5   *Hattie S.*, b. 1834; m., 1st hus., George Stearns; 2d
    hus., George Richardson; ch., (1) Herman G.; (2)
    Frank Twiss; r. Lowell. .

6   *Martha S.*, b. 1839; m. William Broodry; r. Lowell; c.

THE UPTON FAMILY.

The Uptons * of Peterborough and Sharon were descendants of John Upton, who is the ancestor of all in
this country who bear the name of Upton.

1   JOHN UPTON, fourth generation, came to Sharon from
    Middleton, Mass., about 1790. He m. Mary South-
    wick, 1756. When he re. to Sharon he was accompanied
    by four sons, John, Joseph, Jacob, and David, all of
    whom purchased farms. He d. in 1805.

2   *John*, 1758; m. Dorcas Upton; 2d w., Atta F. Upton,
    wid. of Thomas Upton, of Peterborough; ch., (1)
    Betsey, b. Aug. 31, 1786; m. Eli Upton; d.; (2) Lucy,
    b. Aug. 31, 1791; m. Eli Upton,—his fifth w.; d.

3   *Joseph*, b. 1763; m. Betsey McCoy; ch., (1) Joseph, b.
    Nov. 11, 1805; m. Hannah Evans; 2d w., Lucy
    Ann Evans; (2) Jesse, b. Jan. 22, 1808; unm.; now
    living' in South Village; (3) Emily, b. June 2, 1813;
    unm.; now living in South Village.

4   *Jacob*, b. 1766; re. to Stoddard in 1804.

5   †*David*, b. May 19, 1775; m. Polly Nay, dau. Dea. Wm.
    Nay, 2d. He passed most of his life in Sharon; sold
    his farm, and came late in life to Peterborough, and
    d. there, Oct. 9, 1860, æ. 85 yrs., 4 mos.; she d.

1- 5   DAVID UPTON, m. Polly Nay; d. in Peterborough,
    Oct 9, 1860, æ. 85 yrs.

6   *David*, b. Oct. 30, 1798; m. Mary Scripture.

7   *Mary*, b. Aug. 1, 1800; m. Eli Upton; d. May 14, 1875,
    æ. 75 yrs.

8   *Martha*, b. May 31, 1803; unm.; d. March 19, 1822, æ.
    18 yrs., 9 mos.

9   †*John*, b. May 20, 1805; m. Elizabeth Baker.

10   *Jeremiah*, b. Jan. 8, 1807; m. Eliza Vosburg; r. Den-
    ver, Colorado.

11   *Jane*, b. June 26, 1809; unm.; d. June 8, 1858, æ. 48
    yrs., 11 mos.

* The Upton Memorial. 1874.

12 | *Louisa*, b. Sept. 13, 1811; unm.; d. January, 1831, æ. 20 yrs.

13 | *Lucinda*, b. May 14, 1813; unm.; d. March, 1829, æ. 16 yrs.

14 | *Melinda*, b. Sept. 14, 1814.

15 | *Sarah*, b. Feb. 26, 1817; m. John Smith; ch., (1) Sarah Jane; m. Alvin Bailey; (2) Jeremiah; m. Jennie Crampton, of Greece, N. Y.; (3) Emerson R.; m. Anna Keyes, of New Ipswich; (4) George C.; (5) Elmore; (6) Elizabeth Edna; (7) Ella Idella.

16 | *Harriet*, b. Nov. 18, 1818; m. Samuel K. Upton; d. July 6, 1860, æ. 41 yrs., 7 mos.

3- 17 | JOSEPH UPTON, son of Joseph Upton. He lived on the Dea. William Nay place, south part of town; m., 1st w., Hannah Evans; d. April 1, 1853, æ. 42 yrs., 7 mos.; m., 2d w., Lucy Ann Evans. He d. Sept. 1, 1872, æ. 66 yrs., 9 mos.; 1st w., eight ch.; 2d w., two ch.

18 | *Joseph H.*, b. Sept. 18, 1836; d. Aug. 11, 1838, æ. 1 yr., 10 mos.

19 | *Hannah E.*, b. June 3, 1838; d. Jan. 14, 1844, æ. 5 yrs., 7 mos.

20 | *Almira J.*, b. March 20, 1840; m., July 5, 1866, Alfred J. Morse, of Mason; ch., (1) Ida M., b. June 8, 1868; (2) Joseph A., b. Sept. 22, 1870.

21 | *Emily Ann*, b. Feb. 22, 1842.

22 | *Clarissa L.*, b. Jan. 12, 1844; m., Dec. 26, 1867, Lyman A. Hall; ch., (1) Arthur L., b. Oct. 26, 1871.

23 | *Elizabeth E.*, b. Feb. 2, 1846; d. Sept. 2, 1847, æ. 1 yr., 7 mos.

24 | *Susan M.*, b. Dec. 29, 1847; d. Oct. 4, 1848, æ. 9 mos.

25 | *Sarah F.*, b. Oct. 18, 1849.

26 | *Abby Jennette*, ⎱ b. Nov. 9, 1857. He d. April 4, 1858,

27 | *Albert Jesse*, ⎰ æ. 4 mos.

5- 9 | JOHN UPTON m. Elizabeth Baker, of Nashua. Now lives at South Village, in town; is a machinist by trade.

28 | *Eldro*, b. in Denver, Colorado, Aug. 8, 1849; r. Arvada, Col.

29 | *Emma Frances*, b. Feb. 9, 1851; d. Oct. 16, 1867, æ. 16 yrs., 8 mos.

1 | THOMAS UPTON, like the above, is a descendant of John Upton, though remotely related to this branch of the family. He lived many years in Marblehead. About the year 1801 or '2, after living in Andover awhile, he settled on a farm in Peterborough, formerly owned by

Dea. Robert Smith, and begun by Halbert Morison. He m., June 20, 1782, Atta Frost, b. 1761, in Andover, Mass. He d. Oct. 24, 1809, æ. 47 yrs. His wid. m. John Upton, of Sharon, and after his death returned to Peterborough, and d. June 9, 1843, æ. 82 yrs.

2 †*Eli*, b. Jan. 16, 1785; m., 1st w., Rebecca Watts; 2d w., Mary Upton.

3 †*Thomas*, b. Jan. 13, 1787; m. Lydia Snow.

4 *Atta D.*, b. Jan. 25, 1789; unm.; d. Marblehead, Mass.

5 *Polly*, b. 1790; unm.; d. March 26, 1806, æ. 15 yrs.

6 *William*, b. Dec. 31, 1792; m. Mary Taggart, dau. James Taggart, Sharon; ch., (1) William, b. June 7, 1820; m. Sally Upton; one ch., James, b. Nov. 20, 1858; (2) Mary Ann, b. Oct. 24, 1829; m. Luke Nutting, Jaffrey; (3) Priscilla R., b. Nov. 23, 1837; m. Charles Corser; r. Fitchburg. He lived in Jaffrey, midway between the village of East Jaffrey and Peterborough. where he owned a farm and saw-mill, near where his son William now lives. He d. June 2, 1862, æ. 70 yrs. She d. June 17, 1867.

7 *Nathan*, b. Oct. 1, 1796; m., 1st w., Mercy Colburn; 2d w., Mary Hayden. He lived some years in Rindge, then re. West, and now lives at Effingham, Ill.

8 *Joseph*, b. 1798; unm.; d. October, 1827, æ. 29 yrs.

9 *Joshua*, b. in Peterborough, Jan. 3, 1801; m. Priscilla Taggart; re. to Pennsylvania.

10 *Benjamin*, b. March 3, 1803; m. Susan F. Dawson; re. to Virginia.

1– 2 ELI UPTON. He inherited half of his father's farm, which was divided between himself and his brother Thomas. It was the same purchased by his father of the heirs of Deacon Robert Smith. He followed teaming goods from Boston many years till his health failed. He d. of consumption, May 29, 1829, æ. 44 yrs. He m., 1st w., Rebecca Watts. She d. Dec. 11, 1824, æ. 35 yrs.; m., 2d w., Mary Upton, b. Aug. 1, 1800. She d. May 14, 1875, æ. 75 yrs.; 1st w., five ch.; 2d w., one ch.

11 *Nathaniel W.*, b. July 3, 1812; m. Sarah Ann Hathaway.

12 *Atta*, b. June 30, 1814; m. William Hunter.

13 *Eli*, b. Aug. 14, 1816; m. Phebe Bangham.

14 *Thomas*, b. Aug. 31, 1818; m., 1st w., Marietta Cutter, b. Jan. 25, 1820. She d. Feb. 16, 1857, æ. 37 yrs.; m., 2d w., Lucinda S. Allen; ch. by 1st w.; (1) Lucius Edwin, b. May 19, 1843; enlisted in the war of the Rebellion in 1862, and served his time out and re-

turned in safety. In April, 1864, he enlisted again for three years, and d. after a severe sickness of several weeks at Washington, Aug. 7, 1864, æ. 21 yrs.; (2) Adelia Parker, b. Jan. 14, 1851.

15   *Joshua*, b. July 10, 1820; m. Sarah M. Bangham.
16   *Mary*, b. Nov. 12, 1827; d. Oct. 30, 1846, æ. 18 yrs., 11 mos.

1– 3   THOMAS UPTON. He lived on half of his father's farm, having divided the same with his brother Eli. He sold his farm a few years before his decease, and re. to Chesterville, Me., where both he and his w. d. He m. Lydia Snow, b. April 21, 1792; she d. Oct. 20, 1868, æ. 76 yrs.; he d. May 1, 1871, æ. 84 yrs.

---

17   *Mary*, b. Feb. 4, 1811; m. Benj. S. French, of Chesterville, Me., Jan. 1, 1838.
18   *Joseph S.*, b. Nov. 18, 1812; d. Sept. 23, 1815, æ. 3 yrs.
19   *Sylvia*, b. Oct. 29, 1814; m. J. S. French; both deceased.
20   *Joseph S.*, b. Nov. 28, 1816; m. Myra Ann Gould, of Lowell; r. Lowell.
21   *Emily M.*, b. Jan. 28, 1820; m., Dec. 15, 1845, W. S. Bradford; 2d hus., William F. Carter, of Lowell.
22   *John*, b. March 29, 1822; m. Marinda Seaver; re. to California, 1868.
23   *Lydia*, b. Sept. 30, 1824; m. Charles L. Bailey; d. Sept. 16, 1846, æ. 21 yrs., 11 mos.
.24   *Martha Ann*, b. Dec. 19, 1826; m. John Langley, 1850; one ch., Lizzie; re. to Illinois, and he d. there; she m., 2d hus., John Toulson, Lyons, Ia.
25   *Thomas*, b. Feb. 27, 1829; m. Clara Houghton; r. California; has been eminently successful; is a large land owner; three ch.
26   *Lucy G.*, b. March 19, 1831; unm.; d. March 3, 1851, æ. 19 yrs., 11 mos.
27   *Almeda Sarah*, b. April 10, 1837; m. John Milton Mears, Nov. 19, 1865; c.

THE VOSE FAMILY.

1   JOHN VOSE (Dea.) removed from Antrim to Peterborough in 1835, and bought the farm of Thomas Steele, Esq., and lived there till his death. He was a deacon in the Presbyterian Church, and an estimable and worthy man. He m., May 4, 1829, 1st w., Juliana Hunt, dau. Dea. Timothy Hunt. She d. at Antrim, Dec. 23, 1831, æ. 29 yrs., 9 mos.; m., 2d w., Maria Poor, April 30, 1833. He d. June 4, 1867, æ. 65 yrs., 9 mos.; 1st w., one ch.; 2d w., three ch.

2 | *John Hazen*, b. in Antrim, Feb. 2, 1830; m. Alice Cragin.
3 | †*Samuel W.*, b. Jan. 27, 1840; m. Hannah M. Cragin.
4 | *Harriet Maria*, b. June 16, 1842; d. Oct. 29, 1852, æ. 10 yrs., 4 mos.
5 | *Mary Frances*, b. Aug. 2, 1844.

1- 3 | SAMUEL W. VOSE. He succeeded his father on the homestead; m. Hannah M. Cragin, dau. Francis Cragin, May 6, 1869.

---

6 | *Hattie C.*, b. Nov. 6, 1870.
7 | *Alice E.*, b. Nov. 22, 1872; d. March 11, 1873, æ. 3 mos.

THE VARNUM FAMILY.

1 | PARKER VARNUM moved to Peterborough in 1838, from Dracut, Mass., and occupied the farm formerly owned by Jesse Miller. He was b. 1790, and d. in Peterborough, Aug. 20, 1859, æ. 69 yrs. He m. Martha McCoy, dau. of Charles and Jane T. McCoy. She d. Aug. 11, 1858, æ. 64 yrs.

---

2 | †*John P.*, b. Jan. 17, 1828; m. Ardilla Dutton, 1857.
3 | †*Charles*, b. June 8, 1837; m. Mary J. Davis.

1- 2 | JOHN P. VARNUM. He purchased and lived on the Capt. Robert Swan farm. He m. Ardilla Dutton, 1857. He d. July 13, 1871, æ. 43 yrs.

---

4 | *Frederick F.*, b. April 19, 1857.
5 | *George A.*, b. Oct. 25, 1858.

1- 3 | CHARLES VARNUM. He succeeded his father on the home place, where he now lives. He m. Mary J. Davis, Sept. 23, 1858.

---

6 | *Charles E.*, b. July 25, 1861.

THE WALKER FAMILY.

1 | JAMES WALKER was the son of Joshua and Mary Walker, b. in Rindge, March 10, 1784, and d. in Peterborough, Dec. 31, 1854, æ. 70 yrs. He graduated at Dartmouth College, 1804; a lawyer by profession. He came to Peterborough in 1814, and practised his profession, with the exception of a few years, until his death. He was an eminent lawyer, and a man of talent and in-

tegrity. He m., 1st w., Sally Smith, dau. James and Sally Ames Smith, of Cavendish, Vt., May 31, 1819. She d. Aug. 26, 1842, æ. 47 yrs.; m., 2d w., Mary Ann Abbot, dau. Rev. Jacob Abbot, of Windham, Feb. 22, 1844. She d. Aug. 9, 1856, æ. 38 yrs.; 1st w., three ch.; 2d w., two ch.

---

2 | *James S.*, b. July 25, 1820; d. of consumption, at Cavendish, Vt., Aug. 28, 1840, æ. 20 yrs.
3 | †*George*, b. April 1, 1824; m. Sarah Bliss.
4 | *Ariana S.*, b. Nov. 8, 1829; m., Aug. 28, 1854, Frank B. Sanborn. She d. Aug. 31, 1854, æ. 24 yrs., 9 mos.
5 | *Edith Abbot*, b. Dec. 31, 1846; d. Sept. 2, 1848, æ. 1 yr., 8 mos.
6 | *Martha*, b. May 8, 1849.

1–3 | GEORGE WALKER was fitted for college at Phillips (Exeter) Academy, and entered Yale College, but took up his connections here, and entered Dartmouth College and was graduated in 1842. Studied law at Cambridge, and commenced his practice at Chicopee, Mass., 1846, but in 1849 removed to Springfield, where he now resides. He was a member of the Massachusetts Senate for 1857, '58; of the House of Representatives for 1868; Bank Commissioner from 1860 to 1864; President of the Third National Bank, Springfield, from 1865 to 1872. In 1865, he went to Europe as agent of the Treasury Department of United States, and while abroad he published a paper on the finances of the United States, which was extensively published in the French, German, and English papers, and widely distributed, and which rendered great service to the nation in the depressed condition of its financial affairs at the close of the war. He has been a frequent writer of reviews, essays, pamphlets, and newspaper articles, chiefly on finances, down to the present time. He m. Sarah Bliss, dau. Hon. George Bliss of Springfield.

---

7 | *Louisa Dwight*, b. Nov. 8, 1850.
8 | *James S.*, b. Springfield, May 20, 1854.
9 | *Arthur*, b. Springfield, May 12, 1857; d. Feb. 8, 1858, æ. 1 yr., 2 mos.
10 | *Philip*, b. June 29, 1859.
11 | *Mary Bliss*, b. Springfield, Nov. 29, 1861; d. Sept. 21, 1870, æ. 8 yrs., 9 mos.
12 | *Ariana*, b. July 23, 1868.

THE WALLACE FAMILY.

1   MATTHEW WALLACE was b. in Londonderry, June 23, 1731; came to Peterborough, and owned the Samuel Morison place before Samuel Morison's marriage, 1789. He was town clerk in 1781; selectman 1781; and tithing-man 1785. His name does not appear on the town records after this. He re. to Vermont, and d. there. He m., 1st w., Sarah Wright, dau. of Matthew Wright, one of the first settlers of Jaffrey; m., 2d w., Margaret Morison, dau. of Capt. Thomas Morison. The dates of the deaths of himself and wives unknown, or where they died; 1st w., three ch.; 2d w., five ch.

2   *John*, b. March 4, 1767.   (3) *William*, b. Feb. 27, 1769.
4   *James*, b. April 27, 1771.
5   *Thomas*, b. Sept. 3, 1778.
6   *Mary*, b. Jan. 31, 1780; d.
7   *Sarah*, b. Oct. 8, 1781; m. —— Mitchell, Sharon, Vt.; d. in Berlin, Vt.
8   *Jonathan*, b. March 20, 1784; r. Potsdam, N. Y.; Universalist clergyman.
9   *Mary*, b. Dec. 25, 1789.

WILLIAM WALLACE, a family distinct from above. He came to Peterborough from New Boston, and worked many years in the cotton factories. He m. Mary E. Ames, dau. of T. K. Ames, Oct. 31, 1840. He d. Aug. 1, 1853, æ. 40 yrs., 9 mos.

10   *William B.*, b. Dec. 13, 1840; d. at Memphis, Tenn., in U. S. service, Sept. 16, 1863, æ. 22 yrs. He was a brave young soldier in the war of the Rebellion, having enlisted in Co. E., 6th Reg. N. H. Vols. It is inscribed on his tombstone, "Freedom is always costly."
11   *Abbie L.*, b. April 1, 1843; m. J. Frank Noone, June 28, 1864; ch., (1) Katie Eva, b. March 28, 1867; (2) Ernest W., b. Nov. 3, 1870; (3) Arthur F., b. Jan. 8, 1873; d. May 28, 1873, æ. 4 mos.
12   *George F.*, b. April 25, 1847; d. Aug. 16, 1848, æ. 1 yr.
13   *Frank A.*, b. Jan. 5, 1850; m., July 4, 1876, Effie Preston.
14   *Lottie E.*, b. Nov. 25, 1852; m., December, 1873, Daniel Spline. One ch., Willie Morris, b. Feb. 19, 1875.

THE WASHBURN FAMILY.

1   REUBEN WASHBURN was b. in Hancock, July 20, 1789. He came to Peterborough when a boy, and lived with

Samuel Spear till he was of age. He subsequently spent a few years lumbering in the British Provinces, and returned to town and purchased the old farm of Mr. Spear, and resided there till his death. Mr. Washburn was a worthy man and a good citizen. His life was governed by the strictest principles of honor, honesty, and integrity. He was highly respected in the community as a kind neighbor, as benevolent to the poor, as a staunch supporter of good order, and always liberal in sustaining the institutions of learning and religion. He m. Sally Tuttle, of Hancock, May 10, 1821. They celebrated their golden wedding, May 10, 1871. He d. Aug. 1, 1876, æ. 89 yrs.

2   *Sarah*, b. April 13, 1822; d. March 7, 1842, æ. 20 yrs.

3   *George*, b. May 15, 1823; m., Sept. 16, 1847, Abby M. Cheney, b. Dec. 21, 1823; ch., Frank Leslie, b. May 1, 1849; a graduate of Bates College, Lewiston, Me., 1875; r. Ashland.

4   *Franklin*, b. March 26, 1825; d. Sept. 21, 1826, æ. 1 yr., 5 mos.

5   *Mary*, b. Feb. 2, 1827.

6   †*Sampson*, b. Oct. 21, 1828; m. Sarah E. Clark.

7   *Leonard*, b. Jan. 7, 1831; m., Oct. 25, 1860, Sarah A. Wood; ch., (1) Nellie Gertrude, b. Aug. 26, 1864; (2) Alice M., b. May 24, 1866; r. San Francisco, Cal.

8   *Henry*, b. Sept. 1, 1832; r. San Francisco, Cal.

9   *Anna*, b. July 1, 1835; m., July 23, 1861, Milo P. Holmes; ch., Henry E., b. Nov. 20, 1865; r. San Francisco, Cal.

10   *Harriet*, b. Dec. 5, 1837.

.1– 6   SAMPSON WASHBURN. He lives on the homestead; has been much engaged in the lumbering business. He m., April 12, 1860, Sarah E. Clark, dau. of Samuel Clark.

11   *Albert Henry*, b. Dec. 25, 1864; d. Sept. 23, 1866, æ. 1 yr., 8 mos.

12   *Lizzie Clark*, b. Dec. 23, 1868.

1   WATSON WASHBURN, son of Elijah and Betsey Watson Washburn, was b. in Hancock, June 16, 1796; m., June 4, 1822, Orra Stanley, dau. of Israel and Eunice Norwood Stanley, b. in Swanzey, Nov. 11, 1804. He came to town in 1824, and first lived on the Fletcher farm till 1832, when he purchased and occupied the Alld farm, which he sold in 1848, and removed to the village, where he now resides. He was elected a deacon in the Presbyterian Church, March 18, 1840.

2   *Lorenzo S.*, b. in Hancock, Dec. 8, 1823; m. Nancy M. Dinsmore; ch., (1) Andrew; (2) Watson; (3) Angelia; r. Louisville, Ky. Is a photographer in an extensive and successful business in that city.

3   *William W.*, b. in Peterborough, Nov. 2, 1825; r. New Orleans, La. Is engaged in photography, in which he has attained much eminence and success.

4   *Leander W.*, b. June 12, 1830; was killed in Boston by the explosion of a soda-fountain, July 1, 1848, æ. 18 yrs., 6 mos.

5   *Charles H.*, b. June 19, 1837. He was also a photographer, skilful and eminent in his profession; m. Jennie M. Stanley, July 20, 1875; one ch., Charles H., b. April 25, 1876. He d. Nov. 24, 1875, æ. 38 yrs., 5 mos.; r. New Orleans.

---

1   CALVIN WASHBURN, another family with no distinct relationship to the above, was b. in Easton, Mass., Aug. 30, 1780, and d. in Peterborough, April 10, 1864, æ. 84 yrs., 7 mos. He m. Polly Straw, 1804, and lived in various places in town. She d. Jan. 20, 1865, æ. 83 yrs. He came to town about 1795.

---

2   *Elizabeth S.*, b. Sept. 23, 1805; m. Daniel Pratt, the son of Joshua Pratt, b. in Easton, Mass., in 1797; came to Peterborough in 1807, and d. at Newton, Mass., in 1861, æ. 64 yrs.; ch., (1) Franklin D., b. 1824; d. in 1825; (2) Mary W., b. 1825; m. William R. Haywood, of Easton, Oct. 15, 1844; (3) Lowell H., b. 1830; m. Susan Watkins in 1854; d. Oct. 25, 1857, æ. 27 yrs.; (4) Sylvia S., b. 1832; d. 1837, æ. 5 yrs.

3   *Mary*, b. July 16, 1807; m. Nathan Leathers, Dec. 31, 1827.

4   *Levina*, b. Jan. 1, 1811; m. Horace Evans, April 30, 1833; d. March 4, 1857, æ. 46 yrs., 2 mos.; ch., (1) Horace E., b. June 20, 1834; (2) Harrison D., b. May 2, 1836; (3) Samuel D., b. June 26, 1839; d. July 8, 1840; (4) Calvin A., b. Feb. 6, 1842; d. Feb. 7, 1843, æ. 1 yr.; (5) Mary E., b. Nov. 23, 1845; (6) Abbie L., b. July 19, 1849; d. Oct. 5, 1849, æ. 2 mos.

5   *Roansa*, b. Nov. 3, 1813; m., Nov. 27, 1835, John Holt, b. Sept. 25, 1807. He d. of a cancer of the stomach, Feb. 8, 1875, æ. 67 yrs., 4 mos.; ch., (1) Mary M., b. July 15, 1836; (2) John W., b. April 15, 1840; m. Ann M. Bemis, of Troy, Nov. 28, 1861, b. April 30, 1842. He d. March 24, 1866, æ. 25 yrs., 11 mos.

6   †*Harrison D.*, b. April 25, 1816; m. Betsey M. White.

7   *Ranseleer M.*, b. Feb. 5, 1821; d. May 16, 1821, æ. 3 mos.

8 | *Abigail S.*, b. May 22, 1824 ; m. William F. White.
9 | *Calvin Nelson*, b. Oct. 25, 1826 ; m. Sarah Cragin. She d. Feb. 24, 1875, æ. 49 yrs.

1– 6 | HARRISON D. WASHBURN m., Oct. 27, 1842, Betsey M. White, dau. of William M. White. He d. of an abscess of the liver, Feb. 2, 1862, æ. 45 yrs., 10 mos. He lived in the north part of the town on the Reuben Melvin place.

---

10 | *Sarah A.*, b. May 1, 1844 ; m., May 23, 1869, Robert S. Morrison ; r. South Acworth.
11 | *Georgiana A.*, b. Nov. 24, 1848 ; m., Dec. 31, 1868, Frederick F. Turner ; r. South Acworth.
12 | *William W.*, b. Jan. 21, 1851 ; d. Aug. 2, 1854, æ. 3 yrs., 6 mos.
13 | *Sylvia F.*, b. Dec. 18, 1853.
14 | *Clara A.*, b. Dec. 30, 1855.
15 | *Lizzie A.*, b. Sept. 29, 1858.
16 | *Elmer H.*, b. July 27, 1861.

THE WESTON FAMILY.

1 | ABEL WESTON came to town in 1794, from ——— ; b. ———. He was a shoemaker by trade. He lived in the east part of the town. He m., February, 1796, Elizabeth Treadwell, dau. of Samuel Treadwell. He d. Feb. 17, 1860, æ. 90 yrs.

2 | †*Samuel*, b. Nov. 23, 1796 ; m. Eliza Gardner.
3 | *Levi M.*, b. Aug. 3, 1798 ; m., Aug. 21, 1828, Erthen M. Knapp ; r. Newburg, N.Y.
4 | *Mary*, b. May 2, 1800 ; m., October, 1823, Joseph True ; d. March 15, 1831, æ. 31 yrs.
5 | *Helen*, b. Aug. 16, 1802 ; m. Thomas Floyd, Nov. 15, 1823 ; d. June 9, 1831, æ. 29 yrs.
6 | *Nancy*, b. May 2, 1804 ; d. Aug. 17, 1831, æ. 27 yrs.
7 | *Harriet*, b. May 6, 1806 ; m. Cyrus Brown, April, 1826 ; d. May 14, 1833, æ. 27 yrs.
8 | *Clarissa*, b. Dec. 16, 1808 ; m. Hale True, March 17, 1829 ; r. Derry.
9 | *Timothy*, b. Dec. 11, 1810 ; m. Eunice O. Cushman, July 1, 1839 ; d. April 13, 1856, æ. 46 yrs.
10 | *Amos*, b. Aug. 10, 1813 ; m. Betsey Patch, March, 1837 ; r. Wisconsin.
11 | *Cummings*, b. Jan. 15, 1816 ; m. Adaline Champion, July 3, 1842 ; d. March 27, 1870, æ. 54 yrs.

12	*Elizabeth*, b. Sept. 17, 1818; m. Hiram Wheeler, July 29, 1840; r. California.
13	*Martha*, b. Nov. 13, 1822; m., May 7, 1874, Daniel Sawyer, Greenfield.

1-2   SAMUEL WESTON m. Eliza Gardner, Sept. 19, 1822. They celebrated their golden wedding, Sept. 19, 1872. He lives on the Carley Road, so called, a mile east of Hunt's Corner. He is a deacon in the Baptist Church.

14	*Ann E.*, b. June 28, 1823; m. James Ferren, Oct. 24, 1848; ch., (1) Eliza Annie, b. Oct. 13, 1849; m. Herbert Ollis; ch., Harry Frank, b. Feb. 23, 1875; (2) Frank W., b. May 31, 1852; d. Aug. 15, 1858, æ. 6 yrs.
15	*Samuel T.*, b. March 2, 1825; m., Feb. 3, 1857, Laura S. Smiley. He d. March 3, 1876, æ. 51 yrs.
16	*Orland*, b. Nov. 18, 1826; d. Nov. 1, 1838, æ. 12 yrs.

EPHRAIM WESTON m. Betsey Nay, dau. of Deacon William Nay, 2d. He d. She d. at Hancock, May 7, 1844, æ. 70 yrs.

17	*Ephraim*, b. ——; d. in Cambridge, Mass.
18	*Betsey*, b. ——; unm.; d. Feb. 26, 1865.
19	*William*, b. April 15, 1798; m. Harriet Hale; 2d w., Wid. —— Fisher. He d. June 24, 1848, æ. 50 yrs.
20	*Harriet*, b. ——; m.
21	*John*, b. ——; m. Sarah Farwell, Washington.
22	*Timothy*, b. ——; m. Matilda Nay; d. in Hancock.
23	*Esther*, b. ——; m. —— McClure, Antrim.

THE WHITE FAMILY.

All the inhabitants in town, at the present time, by the name of White are the descendants of Patrick White. John White, his son (called Pond John), came before his father Patrick, and settled in the east part of the town, near the Cuningham pond. There are now of the descendants of John White ten voters in town, five of the third and five of the fourth generation.

It is supposed that, in the earliest settlement of the town, say from 1740 to 1750, his farm must have been a somewhat dangerous locality, from the fact, that the Indians had a trail through the notch of the mountain near where the road now is. Their course must have been by the Town Line Brook, which runs through this farm. This stream was called by them Nubanusit (little waters). Samuel White (son to John), who lived on the brook, had noticed the foundations of the Indians' wigwams on his land, and had often ploughed up Indian implements; once in particular a tomahawk, and also flint arrow-points from three to eight inches in length. James G. White, Esq., his son, to whom I am indebted for all the data relating to the White family, recollects his father showing him these foundations, and giving him a tomahawk for a plaything when a small boy.

Game was plenty at this time — wild turkeys were then common, — and the brook was well supplied with trout. It is reported on good authority that within two hundred rods of John White's house, Maj. Heald, the Nimrod of Temple, caught eleven bears in wood-traps, in one season.

No one of this race has ever been imprisoned for debt or crime, and all have been distinguished as quiet and industrious citizens and as kind, peaceable and honest men. No quarrels were known among them, no over-reaching or prevarication or insincerity. Though they took little part in the administration of the municipal affairs of the town, yet on all occasions requiring physical effort or personal skill none went before them. They were hardy and resolute. Though not strictly religious men, they nevertheless attended and supported cheerfully all the ordinances of religion; but in patriotism, in those times when all men were tried, they came up true and earnest patriots. The name of this race is found in every quota of troops furnished by the town during the Revolution.

1   PATRICK WHITE, son of John and Elizabeth White, was b. in Ireland in 1710. He was a man of education, and possessed some wealth. He studied for a Catholic priest, but renounced the doctrine and fled his country. He came first to Londonderry, and m. Jane White, Dec. 14, 1741; re. to Lunenburg, where he raised a large family. He came to Peterborough about the year 1778, and located himself on the Mussey place, so called, now occupied by Benjamin Crosby, where he d., May 10, 1792, æ. 82 yrs.; she d. Dec. 16, 1803, æ. 84 yrs.

2   † *John*, b. Dec. 5, 1742; m. Hannah Miller.

3   *Elisabeth*, b. Jan. 6, 1745; m. William Stuart; 2d hus., Lieut. John Gregg.

4   *Mary*, b. May 10, 1747; unm.; re. to Unadilla, N. Y.; d. March 21, 1840; æ. 92 yrs.

5   † *William*, b. Jan. 7, 1750; m., June 22, 1776, Betsey Shearer, of Palmer, Mass.

6   *Jane*, b. July 19, 1752; m. John Shearer, Jr., of Palmer.

7 | *Eleanor*, b. Jan. 5, 1755; m. Jacob Gregg; 2d hus., Richard Gilchrist.

8 | *James*, b. June 6, 1756; re. to Coleraine, Mass.

9 | †*David*, b. Sept. 17, 1758; m. Betsey Miller; 2d w., Sally Dutton.

10 | †*Thomas*, b. Jan. 3, 1762; m. Nancy Wiley; d. March 6, 1843, æ. 82 yrs.

---

1 – 2

JOHN WHITE (Pond), called thus to distinguish the individual from others of the same name, lived near the Cuningham Pond. He was the first of Patrick White's family, that settled in Peterborough about the year 1770. He first purchased land in Rindge, which he exchanged with a Mr. Hendricks for the farm on which he lived to the close of his life. About one acre of trees had been felled, which was all the betterment that had been made on it. It is situated in the south-east part of the town, adjoining the Cuningham Pond, being nearly the same farm now occupied by Isaac D. White. He went to work with a will, and being a strong and athletic man he soon, with hewn timber, built him a house and barn. It was to him then a howling wilderness all around him, and the forests abounded with a plenty of bears and wolves, and lesser animals. The wild turkey was then found here. In these early days, once during a hard snow-storm, the wolves broke into his barn in the night, and killed his cow, which was a severe loss.

Mr. White was a quiet, unostentatious man, a kind husband, a generous father, and always at home and at work. He is said to have been uncommonly expert with his axe, even among those who used this instrument more than all others in the early settlement. This anecdote is told of him: At one of the country stores of that day, a number of the early settlers were assembled, when those whose names were William boasted that the Williams could beat any other name in town in chopping, or in any other use of the axe. John Smith, Esq., being present, said, "No, they cannot. I will bring you a man by the name of John that can beat any man in town." "Produce your man," said they. He said they dare not take the stakes against John White; nor, indeed, did they dare. Hon. Samuel Smith being also present, said, "I will wager a certain sum that John White will hew one side of a stick of timber, in one day, reaching from the meeting-house in Peterborough to the meeting-house in Hancock, provided that it is properly laid up for this purpose." He served in the Revolution, — how much we cannot tell. It is often difficult to know which John White rendered the service. The homestead of John

White consisted of a part of the Stuart, the Samuel and William White farms, now occupied by Albert Clark, Josiah Brackett, and F. P. Condy. He m. Hannah Miller, dau. of Samuel and Margaret Miller. She d. Dec. 23, 1825, æ. 77 yrs. He d. Jan. 11, 1823, æ. 79 yrs.

11   *Jane*, b. 1776; d. 1778.
12   †*Samuel*, b. March 30, 1778; m. Thirza Gowing.
13   *Elizabeth*, b. Oct. 27, 1781; m. Nathan Cram.
14   † *James*, b. March 30, 1784; m. Milly Law.

15   *Nellie*, m. Eli Upton; d. Oct. 23, 1859, æ. 71 yrs.
16   *Sally*, b. Oct. 2, 1788; m. Joseph Cram.

1– 5.   WILLIAM WHITE. He settled on the farm now occupied by F. P. Condy, in south-east part of the town. He was a worthy, excellent man. He rendered service in the Revolution at various times; he was called out at the alarm at Lexington, April 19, 1775; was in the army at Cambridge, 1775; three months in New York, at Saratoga, 1777. He m. Betsey Shearer, of Palmer, Mass., June 12, 1777, b. Aug. 4, 1754. She d. July 14, 1836, æ. 82 yrs. He d. March 10, 1837, æ. 87 yrs,

17   † *John S.*, b. June 9, 1778; m. Jean Gray.
18   *Jane*, b. May 30, 1780; unm.; d. Dec. 22, 1849, æ. 69 yrs.
19   *Polly*, b. Sept. 24, 1783; unm.; d. Hanover, Ill., Sept. 8, 1856, æ. 73 yrs.
20   *Betsey*, b. Sept. 29, 1785; m., Nov. 17, 1808, Wm. Stearns, of Temple; d. May 7, 1818, æ. 33 yrs.
21   † *William L.*, b. April 13, 1789; m. Jane White.
22   † *Jonathan*, b. March 17, 1792; m. Sarah B. Goss, Amherst.
23   *Nellie*, b. June 16, 1797; m. Dexter D. Carley; d. Hanover, Ill., January, 1874, æ. 77 yrs.

1– 9   DAVID WHITE. He settled in the north part of the town. He m., 1st w., Betsey Miller, dau. of William Miller, Sen. She d. Sept 19, 1796, æ. 29 yrs.; m., 2d w., Sally Dutton, of Greenfield. She d. He d. Sept. 25, 1843, æ. 84 yrs. For some years he owned and carried on the grist-mill at the Holmes or Bowers Mills. He served in the Revolution, alarm at Lexington, in army at Cambridge, 1775, and three months in Rhode Island, 1778; 1st w., three ch.; 2d w., eight ch.

24   † *William M.*, b. July 12, 1788; m. Sally Law.

43

25   *Jane*, b. Sept. 12, 1790; m. William L. White.
26   *Sarah*, b. March 31, 1793; m. James Parker.
27   *Lydia*, b. Aug. 1, 1799; m. Philip Grant; r. Orleans, N.Y.
28   *Alvah*, b. May 7, 1801; m., March 25, 1828, Almira Parker, of Antrim; m., 2d w., Susan Goodwin, of Dover; lived in Lowell, and re. to Exeter, where he d. Jan. 23, 1861, æ. 59 yrs., 8 mos.

29   *Reuben*,   d. young, 1804.
          } b. July 8, 1803;
30   *Nancy*,   m., Nov. 15, 1843, William Dennis; r. Hancock.

31   *Louis*, b. Oct. 9, 1807; m., Oct. 12, 1827, Silas Farmer, of Greenfield; re. to Redfield, N.Y. She d. July 14, 1856, æ. 48 yrs., 9 mos.
32   *David*, b. Nov. 18, 1809; m., Dec. 12, 1838, Mary Ann Carr; r. Antrim.
33   *Deidamia*, b. Oct. 6, 1814; m., April 20, 1834, Franklin Perry; r. Antrim.
34   *Belinda*, b. Aug. 30, 1817; m., Dec. 22, 1842, Alfred Swain; r. Epping.

1- 10   THOMAS WHITE. He settled on the farm afterwards occupied by Deacon Samuel Miller. He re. to Unadilla, N.Y., 1824. He m., March 4, 1790, Nancy Wiley. She d. March 31, 1856, æ. 90 yrs. He d. March 6, 1843, æ. 82 yrs.

---

35   *Jane*, b. Jan. 22, 1791; unm.; d. May 19, 1862, æ. 71 yrs.
36   *John*, b. Nov. 17, 1792; m., Oct. 9, 1820, Sally Fay; five ch.; d. Sept. 9, 1872, æ. 79 yrs., 9 mos.
37   *Thomas, Jr.*, b. June 29, 1795; d. from the kick of a horse, Oct. 1, 1818, æ. 23 yrs.
38   *Samuel*, b. June 7, 1798; d. March 14, 1811, æ. 12 yrs.
39   *Daniel*, b. Feb. 22, 1801; m., June 26, 1832, Sarah Prentiss; d.
40   *Stephen S.*, b. March 17, 1807; unm.; d. May 13, 1860, æ. 53 yrs.

2- 12   SAMUEL WHITE. He went to Belfast when a young man, and assisted in laying out some townships in that section. He returned to Peterborough, and settled on land owned by his father, which he cleared, and on which built a set of buildings; which place he occupied till his death. He was a worthy, good man, always amiable, kind, and honest. He m. Thirza Gowing, dau. of James Gowing, of Dublin, b. July 3, 1775; she d.

March 18, 1851, æ. 75 yrs., 8 mos. He d. May 28, 1860, æ. 82 yrs.

---

41   *Irene*, b. Dec. 23, 1808; unm.; d. July 20, 1875, æ. 66 yrs., 6 mos.

42   † *James G.*, b. Sept. 29, 1810; m. Sarah S. Gibbs.

2— 14   JAMES WHITE (Capt.). He lived on the old homestead. He was at one time captain of the artillery. He m. Milly Law, of Sharon, Feb. 4, 1812; she d. August, 1873, æ. 82 yrs. He d. July 6, 1859, æ. 75 yrs.

---

43   †*Isaac D.*, b. April 10, 1812; m. Timnah Mansfield.

44   †*Stephen*, b. Nov. 30, 1813; m. Phebe Greenfield.

45   *Nathan C.*, b. August, 1815; m. Polly Greenfield; c.

46   † *John Milton*, b. Aug. 19, 1820; m. Mary Fitts; r. New Ipswich.

47   *Emily*, b. May 12, 1817; unm.

48   *Charlotte*, b. July 11, 1825; unm.

5— 17   JOHN SHEARER WHITE. He lived on the Maj. Samuel Gregg place in the north part of the town. He m. Jean Gray, Dec. 2, 1813; she d. Sept. 27, 1854, æ. 78 yrs. He d. Feb. 22, 1855, æ. 77 yrs.

---

49   *Elizabeth P.*, b. June 24, 1817; m. James Swan, March 17, 1846.

50   † *John Kelso*, b. July 2, 1819; m. Mary H. Swan.

5— 21   WILLIAM L. WHITE. He settled on his father's place, but not permanently; m. Jane. White, dau. of David White, June 6, 1811; she d. Aug. 8, 1846, æ. 55 yrs., 10 mos. He d.

---

51   *Sarah E.*, b. July 18, 1817; m. Thomas Upton; d. at Reading, Mass., June 3, 1840, æ. 22 yrs., 10 mos.

52   *Lucinda*, b. Sept. 28, 1819; m. Joseph B. Pierce.

5— 22   JONATHAN WHITE left Peterborough in 1812 when he was twenty years of age, and took up his residence in Amherst. Soon after, he became associated in the business of manufacturing cards for cotton and wool with David Holmes, in which he continued till 1830, when he removed to Lowell, to carry on his business by the aid of water power. He continued in the business till 1850, new inventions having entirely superseded all the old processes of manufacture, when he removed to Hanover, Ill., where he subsequently interested himself

in various pursuits, as farming, trade, etc., and was postmaster of the place till he resigned in his eightieth year.
In Lowell, he was many years a member of the Common
Council, but declined other municipal offices. He m.
Sarah B. Goss, dau. of Ephraim and 'Anah Goss, of Amherst, Jan. 1, 1817. Mrs. Goss was b. in Lunenburg, Feb.
1, 1770 ; d. March 20, 1875, æ. 105 yrs., 11 mo., 19 dys.
He had a large family of eleven ch., of whom seven are
now living.

9– 24 | WILLIAM M. WHITE. He lived on the Wiley farm,
now occupied by his son, Wm. Franklin. He held
many offices in town. Selectman 1839, '40. He m.
Sally Law, of Sharon, April 10, 1817, b. Dec. 25, 1788 ;
d. July 29, 1874, æ. 85 yrs., 7 mos. He d. June 12,
1863, æ. 74 yrs., 11 mos.

---

53 | *Betsey M.*, b. March 30, 1818 ; m. Harrison Washburn.
54 | *Reuben L.*, b. Dec. 2, 1819 ; d. Jan. 5, 1822, æ. 2 yrs., 1
mo.
55 | *Sarah J.*, b. Aug. 16, 1824 ; m. Levi W. Fisk, Harris-
ville, Feb. 26, 1857.
56 | *Wm. Franklin*, b. Nov. 18, 1822 ; m. Abby Washburn,
Dec. 31, 1850, b. May 22, 1824.

12– 42 | JAMES G. WHITE. He was absent from town nine
years after he came of age, and then returned and built
a house on School Street, where he now lives. County
commissioner 1852, '53 ; justice of the peace ; selectman 1845, '46 ; m. Sarah S. Gibbs, dau. of Asa Gibbs.

---

57 | †*Samuel G.*, b. March 3, 1842 ; m. Nancy Carter.
58 | *Mary*, b. July 14, 1838 ; m. Wm. H. Longley.
59 | *Nellie Gertrude*, b. Nov. 8, 1846 ; d. May 16, 1864, æ. 18
yrs., 6 mos.

14– 43 | ISAAC D. WHITE. He lived on the old homestead of
the family, and was the only descendant of the ancestor,
John White (Pond), that owned any of the original farm.
He m. Timnah Mansfield, Rindge, March 28, 1839. He
d. July 5, 1875, æ. 63 yrs., 2 mos.

---

60 | *Martin V. B.*, b. June 24, 1840 ; m. Melissa Hill ; one
ch., Freddie.
61 | *Daniel M.*, b. May 4, 1843 ; m. Martha Billings, Oct. 18,
1866, b. March 8, 1840.
His early life was spent on the farm. He received his
education at the district schools and the neighboring

academies, having attended the latter entirely at his own expense. In the war of the Rebellion, he enlisted in 1864 in the 1st Regiment of the New Hampshire Cavalry, and was promoted to the lieutenancy before he was discharged, July 15, 1865, at the close of the war. In 1872, he enlisted and organized a company of cavalry in town of sixty-five members, the only company of cavalry in the State. It has the name of being the best cavalry company in the New England States, and is an honor to the town and the State.

In March, 1869, he commenced reading law with Ezra M. Smith, Esq., in Peterborough, and was admitted to the Hillsborough County bar, May 12, 1874, and commenced in town the practice of law the June following.

62	*Anthony W.*, b. Sept. 21, 1845; d. Aug. 13, 1851, æ. 6 yrs.
63	*Nathan L.*, b. Feb. 18, 1848; d. July 28, 1851, æ. 3 yrs., 5 mos.
64	*Irving M.*, b. March 28, 1853.
65	*Isaac L.*, b. Aug. 5, 1855; d. Sept. 10, 1856, æ 1 yr.
66	*Herman A.*, b. March 3, 1858.
67	*Milly J.*, b. Sept. 7, 1861.

14- 44   STEPHEN WHITE m. Phebe Greenfield, Dec. 25, 1842; b. Sept. 5, 1820.

68	*Adelaide H.*, b. Jan. 23, 1844; m., Nov. 8, 1866, N. G. Whittemore; r. Fitchburg; one ch., Frank E., b. March 6, 1870.
69	*James M.*, b. Dec. 19, 1845.
70	*Clarinda M.*, b. April 2, 1848; d. Sept. 14, 1849, æ. 1 yr., 5 mos.
71	*Delia I.*, b. July 14, 1850; m. George Shattuck, Nov. 14, 1872.
72	*Clarence E.*, b. Jan. 30, 1855.

14- 46   JOHN MILTON WHITE m. Mary Fitts, of New Ipswich.

73	*Fremont*, b. ——; m. Mary Difley, New Ipswich.
74	*Josie*, b. ——. (75) *Ida*, b. ——.

17- 50   JOHN KELSO WHITE. He settled on his father's place, but upon the decease of both of his parents he re. to Hanover, Ill., where he now resides; m. Mary H. Swan, dau. of James W. Swan, Dec. 19, 1844.

75	*Agnes Jean*, b. Nov. 17, 1845; m. Arthur B. Leighton, Feb. 17, 1864. She d. at Macomb, Ill., Sept 9, 1872; four ch.

76 | *Mary Anna*, b. July 31, 1850.

42– 57 | SAMUEL G. WHITE. Is a machinist; m. Nancy Carter, Nov. 15, 1866, b. July 25, 1844.

---

77 | *M. Gertrude*, b. May 2, 1868.
78 | *Nellie C.*, b. May 26, 1870.

JOHN WHITE. This is another branch of the White family. John White was the brother of Patrick White, and son of John and Elizabeth White, of Lunenburg, where he was b. We do not know the exact date of his emigration to Peterborough, but before 1762, when Jeremiah Gridley and John Hill deeded to John White a lot of land, two hundred and sixty-eight acres, May 5, 1762. We find that he was tithing-man in 1763 and 1776; selectman 1764, '73, and on the Committee of Safety 1777, '79. He began the "White place," so called, now in possession of Nathaniel H. Morison, Esq., as a summer residence. He m., Dec. 9, 1747, Molly Wallace, b. April 3, 1724, dau. William and Elizabeth Wallace, of Lunenburg. She d. May 14, 1800, æ. 78 yrs. He d. Feb. 24, 1796, æ. 77 yrs.

---

79 | † *John*, b. at Lunenburg, Dec. 13, 1748; m. Elizabeth Smith.
80 | *Charles*, b. Feb. 5, 1749; m. Sarah Gray.
81 | *William*, b. Nov. 2, 1751; m. Esther Gray.
82 | *David*, b. Oct. 22, 1753; re. to Bristol, Vt.; owned the Plato place.
83 | *Betsey*, b. July 1, 1755; m. John Burns.
84 | *Nancy*, b. 1757; m. Benj. Alld; he d. Nov. 4, 1823, æ. 64 yrs.
85 | *Polly*, b. Nov. 4, 1759; m. ——, at Dorset, Vt.
86 | *Susan*, b. May 28, 1764; m. David Grimes.
87 | *Jonathan*, b. ——; studied medicine; was talented and capable, but ruined by intemperance; d. at Carlisle, Penn., in 1812.

2– 79 | JOHN WHITE, Jr. He succeeded his father on the homestead. He first lived over the river on what has been called the "Bruce place," until the last years of his father's life, when he removed to the old farm. He was tithing-man three years, 1777, 1801, '2; selectman 1787. He m. Elizabeth Smith, dau. of John Smith; she d. April 24, 1822, æ. 68 yrs. He d. Jan. 15, 1818, æ 70 yrs.

88 | *John*, b. July 1, 1775; M. Polly Brewer; r. Kentucky; d. on his way home. He was a saddler and harness-maker, and carried on the business till 1809 or '10, when he changed his business, and engaged in building the machinery of the first Peterborough cotton factory. He d. Sept. 10, 1822, æ. 47 yrs.

89 | †*Robert*, b. Dec. 6, 1776; m., 1st w., Ruth Burns; 2d w., Sally Ingalls.

90 | *Mary*, b. Oct. 4, 1778; m. Jonas Loring, Aug. 11, 1801; d. 1852, æ. 74 yrs.

91 | *Betsey*, b. Aug. 7, 1780; m. David Holmes; d. 1846, æ. 66 yrs.

92 | *Jesse*, b. Aug. 9, 1782; m. Jenny Robbe; re. to New York; d. 1854.

93 | *Sally*, b. April 6, 1787; m. Jonathan Mitchell; d. Jan. 26, 1861, æ. 74 yrs.

94 | *Nancy*, b. Aug. 31, 1789; m. David Scott; d. Dec. 6, 1819, æ. 30 yrs.

95 | *Charles*, b. Sept. 10, 1795. Graduated at Dartmouth College, 1816; went to Mississippi to teach, and d. on his return passage, at sea, Aug. 10, 1817, æ. 22 yrs.

96 | *Charlotte*, b. July 20, 1798; d. Jan. 1, 1821, æ. 23 yrs.

79– 89 | ROBERT WHITE. He succeeded his father on the home farm. He was a great reader, and could repeat pages of what he had read from memory. In early life he followed the sea, and had seen much of the world. He was entirely self-educated. He was selectman in 1813, and also held some minor offices in town. He m., 1st w., Ruth Burns; she d. Sept. 19, 1836, æ. 53 yrs.; m., 2d w., Sally Ingalls; she d. March 24, 1845, æ. 54 yrs. He d. March 30, 1845, æ. 69 yrs., 2 mos.

---

97 | *Charles F.*, b. Aug. 18, 1812; d. Sept. 4, 1831, æ. 19 yrs.
98 | *Nancy G.*, b. March 12, 1815; m. I. Newton Cuningham; r. Rockford, Ill. He d. Dec. 24, 1865, æ. 59 yrs., 11 mos.; ch., Ella; m. John E. Lakin; one ch.

99 | *Joseph A.*, b. June 19, 1817; m., Oct. 11, 1842, Mary Bowers. A graduate of Harvard University, 1840; d. Jan. 20, 1843, æ. 25 yrs., 7 mos.

100 | *Harriet*, b. July 11, 1819; m., July 26, 1840, John Spafford; ch., (1) Katie; (2) Alice; (3) Jennie.

101 | *Caroline*, b. April 20, 1822; d. Aug. 22, 1824, æ. 2 yrs.
102 | *Robert B.*, b, Dec. 20, 1824; d. May 10, 1827, æ. 2 yrs.
103 | *Elizabeth B.*, b. June 21, 1827; m., March 25, 1850, A. Catlin Spafford; ch., (1) Beel; (2) Nettie; (3) Jessie; (4) George.

THE WHITTEMORE FAMILY.

1   NATHANIEL WHITTEMORE, the son of Nathaniel Whittemore, who was one of five brothers who came to this country from Hitcham, County of Hertford, England, was b. in Spencer, Mass., March 9, 1756. He m.; 1st w., Lucy Harrington, at Leicester, a few months before he removed to Peterborough, probably 1778; she d. at Peterborough, July, 1793, æ. 39 yrs. He m., 2d w., Phebe Waite, of Leicester, Mass.; she d. June 3, 1834, æ. 77 yrs. He m., 3d w., Mrs. Joanna Hadley, of Dublin, Sept. 29, 1835; she d. He d. June 9, 1839, æ. 83 yrs.; 1st w., seven ch.; 2d w., four ch. He settled on the spot where he died, which was just beyond the old Alexander Robbe farm, and a short distance east from the junction of the road from West Peterborough with the old county road, as it was called. He here built a house, and subsequently kept a tavern in it. He was a carpenter by trade, and built his own house, which at first comprised but one room, and was afterwards enlarged by several additions. He probably settled there before a road was constructed in that part of the town, as when a proposition for a road was made in town-meeting, some one objected on the ground that it was not needed because only "twa Robbes, twa Hoggs, and a Whatamore" would be accommodated by it.

---

2   *Paul*, b. Dec. 8, 1780; d. April 28, 1834, æ. 53 yrs., 4 mos.

3   †*Nathaniel*, b. May 21, 1783; m. Betsey Dodge, of New Boston.

4   *James*, b. May 9, 1785; d. March 18, 1816, æ. 30 yrs., 9 mos.

5   †*Bernard*, b. Aug. 13, 1787; m. Jane Holmes.

6   *Lucy*, b. May 14, 1789; d. June 21, 1789, æ. 1 mo., 7 dys.

7   *Thomas*, b. Sept. 3, 1790; d. May 23, 1849, æ. 58 yrs., 8 mos.

8   *John*, b. April 17, 1793; d. Dec. 20, 1795; æ. 2 yrs., 8 mos.

9   *Lucy*, b. July 22, 1795; m. William Farwell, of Fitchburg, Mass., June 2, 1813; d. Plymouth, N. Y., March 13, 1818, æ. 22 yrs., 7 mos.; ch., (1) John W., b. Dec. 20, 1813; d. at Port au Prince, West India Islands, November, 1835, æ. 22 yrs.; (2) Lucy W., b. April 4, 1816; m. Daniel Spalding, of Templeton, Mass., Jan. 2, 1857; (3) Nathaniel W., b. in Plymouth, N. Y., March 9, 1818; m. Eliza Fletcher, Waltham, Mass., June 5, 1842; ch., (1) John W., b. April 17, 1843; (2)

Mary Eliza, b. Aug. 6, 1845 ; (3) Evelyn Almena, b. Jan. 23, 1848.

Mr. Nathaniel W. Farwell is among the most worthy and successful sons of Peterborough. The following sketch of his life appeared in the *Transcript* of last year : —

"He has, by his own unaided exertions, raised himself to an enviable position as to wealth and standing in society, and developed the best traits of a true manhood. He began life here a poor boy, living with his grandfather, Nathaniel Whittemore, Sen., where he was kindly cared for as circumstances would admit, but had to endure many privations that his companions knew nothing about, who often shunned him on account of the shabby appearance of his clothes. His opportunities for schooling were very limited, confined almost entirely to the short hours of the district school. Thus in early life constant labor seemed his inheritance, by which, with other circumstances, he was often reminded that he was a poor, friendless orphan. The spirit was in him, even then, to be, some day, the equal of his companions, and even more. After working some years in this town at low wages, he went to Waltham seeking employment, being then twenty-one years of age. He first applied to the superintendent of the factories there for the situation of watchman. He was gruffly repulsed with the reply, 'There is no chance, and probably won't be.' He then hired himself to a milkman in Waltham, to work eighteen hours per day for the summer. While there the superintendent before applied to, who no doubt had heard of him in this situation, sent for him, and employed him for some years as watchman. In this service he was on duty half the day and half the night, and the other half-day he sawed wood as he could find work. He here made a beginning of his fortune. Being requested to go into the bleachery as second-hand, he reluctantly consented, with the condition of having his old place if he did not like. He soon had the entire charge of the bleachery department, and acquired much skill in the art. This was the opening event of his great ultimate success. Subsequently he was engaged to plan and manage the Great Falls Bleachery, of which he and his son are now proprietors ; he also planned a bleachery in New Jersey, and the Lewiston Bleachery and Dye Works, of which he was proprietor ten years. He is now largely engaged in cotton manufacture, and is now just starting the 'Farwell Mills,' of twenty thousand spindles, at Lisbon, Me. Always being an energetic man, and with quick perception and ready judgment, his efforts have been crowned with abundant

44

success, and he has accumulated a large fortune. He
surpasses in wealth any emigrant that ever went out of
Peterborough, and could now with his own means buy
up nearly the whole town. Having little taste for
politics, and being engaged in his own extensive business, he has rarely been drawn into public life. But at
the earnest solicitation of the citizens of Lewiston he
was induced to represent the city in the Legislature, and
more recently, with an almost unanimous vote, to serve
as Mayor."

He does not forget the home of his youth, or the
associates of his early days, in his great prosperity. He
has at various times contributed largely to benevolent
objects in town, and always keeps alive a deep interest
in its prosperity. The Unitarian society are indebted to
him for a large subscription to their organ, of two hundred dollars, and his large subscription of ten thousand
dollars to the Monadnock Railroad did more than anything else to insure its completion.

10 · *Phebe Read*, b. July 29, 1797 ; m. Elisha Stetson, Medford, Mass. ; d. Oct. 8, 1870, æ. 73 yrs.

11 *Elisa Waite*, b. Oct. 10, 1799 ; m. William Simmons,
Aug. 27, 1829 ; ch., (1) Phebe W., b. Jan. 31, 1822 ;
m. Moses Ward ; d. April 13, 1849, æ. 27 yrs., 2 mos.;
(2) Betsey D., b. Jan. 23, 1825 ; d. 1826 ; (3) William
H., b. Jan. 30, 1827 ; m. Mary J. Durgin, Northwood ;
she d. Nov. 29, 1863 ; m., 2d w., ———, Feb. 24, 1872 ;
(4) Almira E., b. Nov. 6, 1829 ; d. Nov. 3, 1848, æ.
19 yrs. ; (5) Thirza M., b. Jan. 30, 1832 ; m. John S.
Blake, June 4, 1850 ; w. of Wm. Simmons d. at Templeton, Mass., Oct. 14, 1871, æ. 72 yrs.

12 *Thirza W.*, b. March 5, 1805 ; d. Dec. 24, 1855, æ. 50
yrs., 8 mos.

1- 3   NATHANIEL WHITTEMORE, Jr. He went to Boston
when twenty-one years of age, without any means, and
by his own efforts he accumulated a large property. He
re. to Peterborough in 1828, where he remained till
1842, engaged in farming. He bought the Charles
Davison farm, the same now occupied by Cyrus Frost
and son. He next re. to Rome, N.Y. He d. May,
1860, æ. 77 yrs. ; m. Betsey Dodge, of New Boston, 1808.

13 *John*, b. ——— ; m. Lucretia Glover.

14 *James*, b. ——— ; m. Jane S., dau. Thomas Whittemore ;
d. December, 1860.

15 †*Nathániel, Jr.*, b. April, 1818 ; m., 1st w., Charlotte
Ames ; 2d w., Sarah A. Damon.

16 | *Joseph*, b. ——; m., 1854, 1st w., Margaret C. Fay; 2d w., Katharine Hobby, Utica, N. Y. Educated as a lawyer; was for a time law-partner of James Nye, late Senator of Nevada, then residing in Hamilton, N. Y. He has of late years acquired much reputation as a commercial lawyer. He now resides in Detroit, Mich. Moved there in 1854.

17 | *Lizzie*, b. ——; m., 1857, Clark Moulthrop; d. 1871.

1– 5 | BERNARD WHITTEMORE. He resided some years in Boston, and afterwards removed to Peterborough, and was engaged in trading. He d. at Nashua, Aug. 8, 1846, æ. 58 yrs., 11 mos. He m. Jane Holmes, dau. of Dea. Nathaniel Holmes, Dec. 25, 1815.

18 | *Bernard Bemis*, b. in Boston, May 15, 1817. He was fitted for college at Phillips (Exeter) Academy, and graduated at Cambridge, 1839; admitted to Hillsboro County bar in August, 1842; practised. law till November, 1846, when he and his brother, F. P. Whittemore, became proprietors and publishers of the Nashua *Gazette*, and still continue to publish the same under the firm of B. B. & F. P. Whittemore. He was elected to the State Senate, in District No. 7, in 1852 and '53, and elected one of the Aldermen of the city of Nashua in 1860, and City Treasurer of the same city in 1861.

19 | *Catharine H.*, b. July 12, 1819; m., Oct. 8, 1840, Gen. Israel Hunt; ch., (1) Israel T., M.D., b. Oct. 12, 1842; (2) Frank W., b. April 26, 1849; r. Nashua. Gen. Hunt d. September, 1875.

20 | *John*, b. Sept. 18, 1821; d.

21 | *Elouisa C.*, b. Aug. 28, 1822; m., June 8, 1843, David F. McGilvray. He d. at Nashua, Aug. 30, 1871; ch., (1) Alice E., b. Jan. 26, 1845; d. in Boston, Feb. 22, 1869, æ. 24 yrs.; (2) David F., Jr., b. at Palmer, March 8, 1847; d. in infancy; (3) Jacob B., b. Nashua, Aug. 13, 1850; (4) Katharine H. W., b. Boston, May 19, 1855; (5) David F., b. Boston, Oct. 5, 1858; (6) Irene W., b. Boston, May 21, 1863; d. in infancy; (7) Dexter B., b. Boston, July 11, 1867; d. young.

22 | *Francis P.*, b. Peterborough, March 29, 1825; m., Jan. 27, 1851, Angeline H. Parks, of Palmer; ch., (1) Helen A., b. Nashua, Nov. 5, 1851; (2) Alice P., b. 1853; d. young; (3) Fred Parks, b. Nashua, Oct. 25, 1855.

23 | *Mary Jane*, b, Peterborough, July 29, 1827.

24 | *Nathaniel H.*, b. Peterborough, Jan. 22, 1830.

25 | *Ann Frances*, b. Peterborough, Aug. 16, 1834 ; m., Feb. 22, 1864, Bloomfield J. Beach, at Nashua ; d. at Rome, N.Y., Oct. 18, 1867, æ. 33 yrs., 2 mos. ; one ch., John B., b. at Rome, May 5, 1866.

3– 15 | NATHANIEL WHITTEMORE, Jr. or 3d, m., 1st w., Charlotte Ames, dau. of T. K. Ames, Esq. She d. June 2, 1850, æ. 32 yrs. ; m., 2d w., Sarah A. Damon. He has resided in various places ; first at Peterborough, then Boston, Ashby, Rome, N.Y., and Bay City, Mich., where he now lives. He has held for some years the office of Recorder in the Michigan courts ; is now an acting justice of the peace ; 1st w., five ch. ; 2d w., three ch.

26 | *Frances D.*, b. Dec. 9, 1837 ; m. Frank Johnson, Ashby, April 16, 1855.
27 | *Catharine B.*, b. April 7, 1839 ; m. Alfred Hetfield, Oct. 8, 1873 ; r. Chicago.
28 | *Walter*, b. Feb. 9, 1842 ; m., Nov. 26, 1866, Sarah Carpenter ; r. Bay City, Mich.
29 | *Joseph F.*, b. Oct. 26, 1846 ; m., Jan. 21, 1873, Jenny Hannon ; r. in Bay City, Mich.
30 | *Charles E.*, b. Dec. 12, 1849.
31 | *Francis E.*, b. April 10, 1852.
32 | *James H.*, b. May 18, 1859.
33 | *Alice R.*, b. July 17, 1869.·

THE WILDER FAMILY.

1 | MARK WILDER is the son of Abel and Deborah Perry Wilder, who lived in Dublin till late in life, when they re. to Peterborough, and d. here. Mark Wilder was b. Aug. 15, 1806. He carried on the shoe-peg business in town many years. He m. Eliza A. Thayer, dau. of Elihu Thayer, April 21, 1835; she d. Nov. 28, 1871, æ. 58 yrs.

2 | †*Charles*, b. May 13, 1836; m. Mary E. Jones, Aug. 5, 1860.
3 | *George*, b. July 31, 1837 ; m. Sarah B. Hannaford, April 16, 1862.
4 | *Elihu*, b. Sept. 26, 1838; m. Laura Moses, of Portland, Me. ; r. Manchester.
5 | *William H.*, b. July 7, 1840 ; m. Frances A. Miller, Aug. 31, 1862 ; ch., Frances Lillian, b. Jan. 16, 1871.
6 | *Ann Maria*, b. Jan. 28, 1842 ; d. Feb. 14, 1864, æ. 22 yrs.

7 | *Mark A.,* b. July 17, 1843; m. Eva S. Ramsey, June 8, 1870; ch., (1) Willie A., b. Feb. 24, 1871; (2) Edwin M., b. Dec. 12, 1872.

8 | *Irving,* b. March 13, 1846.

9 | *Ellen B.,* b. Feb. 4, 1849.

10 | *Abel J.,* b. Oct. 12, 1850; d. Galesburg, Ill., May 29, 1874, æ. 23 yrs., 7 mos.

11 | *Eliza J.,* b. Aug. 15, 1852.

12 | *John F.,* b. Oct. 15, 1855.

ABEL WILDER, Jr., brother to the above. He was b. July 27, 1808. He m., Nov. 6, 1845, Amna A. Gowing, b. March 17, 1817.

---

13 | *Luena R.,* b. Aug. 15, 1846.

14 | *Ella L.,* b. Sept. 16, 1855; d. Sept. 26, 1856, æ. 1 yr.

JOHN WILDER, a brother of the above, b. Oct. 28, 1822; m., 1st w., Diantha Royce, of Marlow, March 30, 1847. She d. Aug. 29, 1865, æ. 43 yrs.; m., 2d w., Sophia Grant, June 23, 1867; ch. by first w. He is engaged in the clothing business in the village.

---

15 | *Elsie E.,* b. March 4, 1850; m. Timothy N. Hunt.

16 | *Frank H.,* b. Sept. 28, 1854; d. May 7, 1855, æ. 7 mos.

1-2 | CHARLES WILDER obtained his education in the common schools and at the academy in town. He became a very efficient and popular teacher before he went into business, and for a time was the principal of the academy. He intended to obtain a collegiate education and fit himself for the law, but his father's circumstances becoming deranged, he felt it a duty, as the eldest of the family, to give up his own plans and take charge of the business. After following successfully the shoe-peg business for two years, he purchased the property of the North Cotton Factory, and in August, 1860, commenced in the large building of the same the manufacture of barometers and thermometers. He has struggled through the incipient stage of discouragement and uncertainty in his business, and has now established an important manufactory upon a permanent basis.

Mr. Wilder, through his enterprise and energy, has attained an eminent success in his business, and has become an influential and useful citizen in town. He is always found forward and ready in all projects for the advancement of the interests of the town, in all its literary, moral, and religious aspects, and combines with the *live man* the sincere Christian. He was Representative in 1869, '70 ; moderator 1869 ; m., Aug. 5, 1860, Mary E. Jones, of Dublin.

17 *Charles A.*, b. June 1, 1861 ; d. March 22, 1864, æ. 2 yrs., 9 mos.
18 *Frank F.*, b. April 23, 1863.
19 *Harry E.*, b. Sept. 19, 1864.
20 *Mary A.*, b. Oct. 5, 1869 ; d. Sept. 24, 1870, æ. 11 mos.
21 *John M.*, b. April 29, 1872.
22 *Grace*, b. July 7, 1873.

1 CALEB F. WILDER, a descendant of the Wilders of Leominster, Mass. He came to Peterborough early in life, and m., July 20, 1837, Catharine Templeton, dau. of Samuel Templeton, and granddaughter of Matthew Templeton. They live on the farm occupied by her father and grandfather. He is of a distinct race from the Wilders in town. He d. Jan. 28, 1876, æ. 67 yrs.

2 *Lucy Jane*, b. May 16, 1838.
3 *Martha*, b. June 25, 1840.
4 *Rodney H.*, b. June 30, 1843 ; m., March 6, 1873, Laura G. Hill, of Francestown ; r. Francestown.

THE WILSON FAMILY.

1 ROBERT WILSON (Maj.), the ancestor of the Peterborough Wilsons, born in Tyrone, Ireland, was the son of William Wilson, who came to this country in the year 1737, bringing a wife, one daughter, and his son Robert. They spent the winter of 1737-8 in West Cambridge, and then removed to Townsend. When he had attained his majority, in 1755, there being a call for soldiers for the French war then raging between the English and French, he enlisted and was among the provincial soldiers that accompanied Gen. Wolfe in his daring attempt to climb the precipitous cliffs called the Heights of Abraham, on the day and night of the 12th of September, 1759, and stood there upon the table-land on the morning of the 13th, ready for the fight. He saw his gallant commander, Gen. Wolfe, fall, mortally wounded ; but the troops fought it out, and gained a glorious victory. The result of this battle was to deprive the French of the possession of the Canadas, and in fact of all their possessions in the north-east part of the American continent.

Not long after the fall of Quebec, in September, 1759, the provincial troops were disbanded, and Robert Wilson returned to Massachusetts. In 1761 or '62, he married Mary Hodge, of West Cambridge, and they removed and settled in Peterborough. They resided on the farm now occupied in part by his grandson, James Wilson, on what used to be called the "Main Street Road," and to the business of clearing up and cultivating a farm they added that of keeping tavern to entertain strangers. They occupied a house on the west side of the road, about seventy-five or eighty rods to the south-westward of the house now occupied by James Wilson, and some forty rods north of the brick school-house. An old cellar-hole only marks the place.

He was a stout, strong, and vigorous man, about six feet in height. He was very industrious, careful, and prudent in the management of his worldly affairs. By his own hard work and the superior, skilful care and perseverance of his wife they were successful. They accumulated comparatively, for those times, a large fortune. He had a pitifully poor education. He could read and write a little, but quite clumsily. His means for an education had been very limited; but nevertheless by his experience in life he was qualified to hold some of the most important offices in town. He was selectman in 1765, '71, treasurer 1786, '87, '88, and one of the Committee of Safety in 1776.

He was a true patriot through the Revolutionary struggle. He was early elected to office in the militia in the town. He was lieutenant in 1771, a captain in 1775, and a major in 1777.* On the night preceding the 19th of April, 1775, the alarm came to town of the aggressive movements of the British at Lexington, and immediate preparation was made to respond to it, and on the 19th the company under Capt. Wilson were ready to march to Concord and Lexington by noon. "There was no little amusement" (says Gen. James Wilson, a grandson, to whom I am indebted for all the facts here stated) "among the men at the character of the arms some of them bore. Some few had fire-arms, with a meagre supply of powder and ball; some of the arms were the old, heavy, clumsy Queen's arms; some were light French pieces, called fusees. They probably almost all came out from Canada at the close of the old French war. Some of the men had pitchforks, some

---

* It is given above as represented by Gen. James Wilson in his account of his ancestor, Maj. Robert Wilson. The news of the aggressive movements of the British troops could not have reached Peterborough till sometime during the day of the 19th of April. It only reached Concord, Mass., at 3 o'clock A. M. of that day.

had good, stout shillalahs; but among them all the
most laughable was one Tom McCoy, who had brought
with him his *grain-flail*, with which to give the British a
literal thrashing. The men laughed and joked for the
oddity of his weapon to fight with, but Tom replied in
broad Scotch, 'Gath, I vow, I'll gie a Britisher a devlish
good lick o'er the head, an I get in reach of him.' They
all knew that Tom would be as good as his word, if it
came to trial. The foremost of them got as far as Groton, when they learned the result of the Lexington and
Concord fight. They were ordered back to their homes,
but to hold themselves in readiness for any further calls
that might be made upon them. In less than two months
they were ordered to join the patriotic citizens at Bunker
Hill, and were equally prompt in responding to the
call."

When the New Hampshire troops were called out to
repel the invasion by powerful armies on our Northern
frontier, Gen. Stark was appointed to the command, and
Robert Wilson was a Major in his division of militia.
He was present at the various engagements of Bennington, Saratoga, etc., and was appointed by Gen. Stark to
command a guard detailed to escort six hundred Hes-
sian prisoners of war from Bennington to Boston.

Maj. Robert Wilson d. on the 25th of December,
1790, in the fifty-seventh year of his age. His death
was sudden, and occasioned by a strangulated hernia.
An operation would probably have saved him, but no
surgeon of competent skill was near, and he d., as thousands have before, from the ignorance and incompetency
of medical attendants. Mrs. Wilson survived her husband thirty-five years. She m., 2d hus., Enos Knight, of
New Ipswich, Sept. 16, 1803. She was a widow again
many years, and resided at the old residence. She d.
Dec. 22, 1825, æ. 90 yrs.

2 | *Anne*, b. March 28, 1764; d. Aug. 16, 1771, æ. 7 yrs.
She was killed by a log falling off a fence upon her.
3 | † *James*, b. Aug. 16, 1766; m., 1st w., Elizabeth Steele;
2d w., Elizabeth Little.
4 | † *William*, b. Feb. 8, 1770; m. Dotia Smith.
5 | *Anne*, b. May 3, 1768; m. Jeremiah Swan.
6 | *Mary*, b. May 21, 1775; m. Gen. John Steele.
7 | *John*, b. Jan. 10, 1772; m. ——; d. Belfast, Me., 1848,
æ. 76 yrs. He was an eminent lawyer; a member of
Congress in 1813, '14.
8 | *Sarah*, b. 1777; m. Joseph Haynes Johnson, Nov. 6,
1803; d. in Illinois; ch., (1) Lucretia Knapp, b.
1804; educated at Cincinnati; m. John Scott Harri-

son, son of President Harrison; d. 1829, æ. 25 yrs.; (2) Susette Grafton, b. 1808; m. Josiah C. Smith; r. Mississippi. She d. 1830. (3) Joseph Haynes, b. Feb. 29, 1812; spent his early life in Montreal; went to the mines in California; made extensive travels, and returned to Lacon, Ill., where he now resides; (4) Mary Wilson, b. Jan. 8, 1811; m. Rev. Wm. N. Stinson. She d. at Amity, Ia.; (5) Caroline A.; m. Robert Brown; d. ——; (6) Charlotte Ann, b. July 4, 1817; m. Hugh T. Reed, a lawyer. She d. 1841; c.; (7) James Wilson, b. 1819; was a mechanic and natural inventor; d. of cholera, 1849; (8) Elizabeth Sarah; educated at Keene, N. H.; m. John T. Fisk, of Kentucky, who has since become an eminent lawyer. He was Lieut.-Governor of Kentucky during the rebellion, and a loyal man during the civil war.

9   *Joseph*, b. 1780; d. April 24, 1794, æ. 13 yrs.

1- 3   JAMES WILSON. His opportunities for early education were very limited in that early day in the town, when the people were obliged to make the most energetic exertions to secure for themselves a living. Young Wilson remembered very distinctly the alarm given at his father's house of the British attack on Lexington and Concord, April 19, 1775. He remembered also the great stir among the people of the town when the brave men were taking their departure to join their patriotic brethren in the battle of Bunker Hill, of the same year.

On his eleventh birthday he was aiding and assisting some Peterborough men in driving cattle from the town to Bennington, for the support of Stark's army. His father, then a Major, and almost every able-bodied man in town were among Stark's troops, and took part in the Bennington battle, Aug. 16, 1777. He remained at home with his parents, working on the farm, until the close of the Revolutionary War.

About the year 1782 or '83, he was, by the persevering efforts of his mother, as mentioned before, allowed to go to Phillips (Andover) Academy to prepare for college. He entered Harvard College in 1785. He was then a stout, strong, well-developed, muscular young man of nineteen years of age. When he entered college, he was the stoutest, most skilful, and best wrestler in the institution. Wrestling was then the test of championship, and Wilson took the badge for this feat in his Freshman year, and retained it during the whole period of his college life. There is good authority for this statement. Sixty years afterward, upon the introduction of his son, J.

45

Wilson, Jr., to the late Hon. John Quincy Adams, he said, when ascertaining his parentage, " Your father was the best wrestler in college."

James Wilson graduated at Harvard in 1789, and immediately entered the office of Judge Lincoln, of Worcester, Mass., as a student of law. He remained with Judge Lincoln, pursuing his law studies, till Dec. 25, 1790, when he was summoned home by his mother, on account of the sudden death of his father. He was united with his mother in the administration of his father's estate. He remained in Peterborough from that time, completing his legal studies in the office of Judge Smith, who was then a practising lawyer in town. Mr. Wilson was admitted to the bar in New Hampshire, in 1792, and as Judge Smith was elected to Congress from New Hampshire in 1791, and continued to hold that office for several succeeding years, and finally removed to Exeter, Mr. Wilson commenced the practice of his profession in his native town. He remained there till 1815, when he removed to Keene, where he continued the active practice of his profession until 1823, when his son was admitted to the bar, and succeeded to the business of the office and in the courts.

Mr. Wilson was a good lawyer, understood the science of the law thoroughly, was a man of quick and clear perception, vigilant in the preparation of his cases, and managed them, before the court and the jury, with distinguished ability. In that particular branch of the professional duties of a lawyer he had but few superiors and not many equals in the State.

He had an extensive practice in the Counties of Hillsboro and Cheshire, attending all the courts of both counties, and was retained as council, on one side or the other, in most of the cases that were tried.

In addition to his business in the courts, he did a large business in justice courts, in both Hillsboro and Cheshire Counties.

Mr. Wilson, while in the active practice of his profession, had many young men in his office as students of law; while at Peterborough, Gen. James Miller, John Wilson, D. Smiley, Thomas F. Goodhue, Zacheus Porter, Stephen P. Steele, David Scott, Charles J. Stuart, Matthew Perkins. After he removed to Keene, David Steele, Amos A. Parker, Amasa Edes, and J. Wilson, Jr., all studied their profession with him. He held many offices of trust and honor in town, — moderator five years, from 1800 to 1814; representative to the General Court, from 1803 to 1815. He was a member of Congress for the Hillsboro District, from 1809 to 1811, the first two years of President Madison's administration.

Mr. Wilson was all his life an out-and-out, old-fashioned Federalist of the old school. The delegation from New Hampshire to the Eleventh Congress was unanimously of the Federal party. It was changed in the next Congress, and Mr. Wilson was not in public office afterwards.

He m., 1st w., Elizabeth Steele, 1792, dau. Capt. David and Janet Little Steele; she d. Nov. 4, 1806. He m., 2d w., Elizabeth Little, dau. Wallis Little, Esq., of Shirley, Mass., in November, 1810; she d. at Keene, Sept. 30, 1830. Mr. Wilson was a good citizen, a kind, generous, noble-hearted man, a grateful, dutiful son, a good husband and a sympathetic parent, very kind to his children and to all his friends. He was industrious, just, and vigilant in all matters of business, and died universally respected and esteemed by all who knew him. He d. at Keene, the 4th of January, 1839, æ. 73 yrs.; 1st w., two ch.; 2d w., three ch.

---

10 | *Charlotte*, b. May, 1794; d. March 26, 1796; æ. 1 yr., 10 mos.

11 | † *James, Jr.*, b. March 18, 1797; m. Mary L. Richardson.

12 | *Robert*, b. Sept. 24, 1811; m. ——; c.; d. at Keene, April 8, 1870, æ. 58 yrs., 6 mos.

13 | *Elisabeth Jane*, b. September, 1815; m. William G. Hunter; c.

14 | *Sarah M. A.*, b. 1819; m. Col. Frank Lee, of Boston.

1–4 | WILLIAM WILSON. He kept a public house, situated on the east side of the Street Road, a short distance north of his father's residence, which was much patronized in the early part of the century. All the assemblies and balls in town for many years were held at his house, and most of the public meetings. There were no accommodations for this purpose elsewhere. He lived in town all his long life, but ceased to entertain travellers many years before his decease. He m. Dotia Smith, of Hadley, Mass., b. Sept. 16, 1783, and d. Sept. 12, 1871, æ. 88 yrs. He d. July 6, 1860, æ. 90 yrs.

---

15 | *Mary*, b. June 22, 1807; d. Sept. 11, 1825, æ. 18 yrs.

16 | *Eunice*, b. Dec. 1, 1808; m. William Gibbon, Marlboro, Mass., Feb. 12, 1835; three ch. living.

17 | *Joseph*, b. Sept. 1, 1810; d. June 11, 1812, æ. 16 mos.

18 | *William*, b. May 28, 1812; d. Jan. 16, 1814, æ. 19 mos.

19 | *Sarah Ann*, b. May 18, 1814; m. James Scott, Esq.

20 | *James*, b. Feb. 11, 1816; m. Sybil Stone, May 15, 1845.

21 *Charlotte G.*, b. Oct. 24, 1818; m., May 3, 1848, James Jackson; r. Cazenovia, N. Y.

22 *Harriet H.*, b. July 26, 1821; d. Aug. 13, 1821, æ. 18 dys.

23 *Jane Gregg*, b. March 14, 1823; d. Aug. 12, 1851, æ. 28 yrs.

24 *John*, b. 1826; d. April 9, 1828, æ. 2 yrs.

25 †*George W.*, b. July 7, 1828; m., 1st w., H. Maria Smiley; 2d w., Katie M. Grimes.

3-11 JAMES WILSON, Jr. The following autobiography has been kindly furnished by Gen. Wilson at my request:—

"His early life was passed in his native town, with only such educational privileges as were there to be had, which at that early day were very limited. His mother became an invalid when her son James was only two years old, and remained so during the remainder of her life, thus depriving him of that kind, maternal care and attention so indispensable to the proper development of a young mind. She departed this life when he was in the ninth year of his age.

"In the year 1807, young Wilson was sent for a few months to the academy at New Ipswich. In 1808, he was sent to Atkinson Academy, where he remained for some three or four years. In the year 1813, he attended Phillips (Exeter) Academy, at Exeter, N. H., for some six months.

"Our country was then involved in war with Great Britain, and young Wilson at sixteen years of age was desirous of joining the American army, as some of his acquaintance but little older than himself already had done. His father would not give his consent to his son's enlistment, and he was not old enough to be subject to the draft. Disappointed and vexed at being deprived of the privilege of entering upon a military career, he left Exeter, and returning to his native town went into the North Factory at Peterborough as a common hand. He continued to work in the cotton factory during the autumn of 1813, the whole of the year 1814, and until the spring of 1815, when peace between the United States and England was proclaimed. That put an end not only to the war, but also to the manufacture of cotton at the North Factory. When peace between those countries came, in 1815, the price of cotton advanced, and the price of American manufactured cotton goods immediately declined, so that the proprietors of the factory had to shut down their gates. Young Wilson went home in the spring of 1815, and worked on his father's farm as a common farm-laborer. He worked during the following summer. In the autumn of that year, as his father was about removing to Keene, the son, having '*no whither else to go,*' picked up his books and went back to his studies.

"James Wilson, Jr., entered Middlebury College in 1816, graduated from that institution in 1820, entered his father's office at Keene as a student at law, and was admitted to the bar in Cheshire County, N. H., at the fall term, 1823.

"His father, J. Wilson, Sen., retired from the active professional duties of his office on the admission of his son to the bar, and the young man, attaining his father's business, continued to practise law in Cheshire and Sullivan and Grafton and Coos Counties, until the year 1836, when by a stroke of paralysis his father became unable to attend to his own private affairs, and required his son's assistance. He then gave up the northern counties, but continued the practice of the law in Cheshire.

"On leaving college in 1820, and fixing his residence at Keene, J. Wilson, Jr., entered the military service of the State. He was elected Captain of the Keene Light Infantry on the 1st day of January, 1821, and continued in the militia, constantly doing duty, until 1839, when he resigned the office of Major-General of the Third Division of New Hampshire Militia.

"At the March election in 1825, he was chosen as one of the two Representatives from the town of Keene to the State Legislature. In 1828, he was elected Speaker of the House of Representatives of the State of New Hampshire. In that House there were several men of distinguished reputation and of prominent standing in the Whig party, such as the Hon. Ezekiel Webster, the Hon. B. M. Farley, the Hon. Joseph Bell, Hon. P. Noyes, and others from different parts of the State. From the year 1825 to the year 1840 inclusive, he represented the town of Keene in the State Legislature, every year except the years 1833, '38, and '39. The last two years, *viz.*, 1838 and '39, he was the candidate of the Whig party in the State for Governor, but was defeated by his Democratic opponent.

"The year 1840 was a year of great political awakening in this country. The Democratic party had nominated Martin Van Buren as President of the United States for a second term. The Whigs went into the political battle under the banner of 'Tippecanoe and Tyler too,' 'and with them' determined to 'beat little Van.' The Whigs succeeded. Gen. James Wilson, of New Hampshire ('*Long Jim,*' as he was then familiarly called), did a good deal of political service in that campaign. He stumped almost all the New England States, spoke several times in Pennsylvania, and gave a whole month's work, on the stump, in the State of New York (Mr. Van Buren's State). Mr. Van Buren lost New York, Pennsylvania, and most of the New England States, and was defeated.

"Gen. Harrison was elected President, and John Tyler Vice-President. They were inaugurated on the 4th of March, 1841. Gen. Harrison lived only one month after his inauguration, and Mr. Tyler succeeded to the presidency. About June, 1841, Mr. Tyler offered to Gen. Wilson the office of Surveyor-General of Public Lands in the then Territories of Wisconsin and Iowa, which office he accepted, and took possession of the Surveyor-General's office, at Dubuque, Iowa, in the early part of the summer. He continued to hold that office and to perform its duties for four years. In 1845, James K. Polk having been elected President, he was removed.

"In 1846, the voters of the town of Keene returned Gen. Wilson again, as their representative, to the General Court. That year the Whigs and a party styling themselves 'Independent Democrats' succeeded in defeating the regular *old line Democracy* in New Hampshire. The State was districted for the choice of Representatives to Congress, and the following year he was elected a Representative from the Third Congressional District to the Thirtieth Congress. He was re-elected to the Thirty-first Congress, and held his seat until the 9th day of September, 1850, when he resigned and left this Eastern country for California. He resided in California eleven years continuously, and only returned East at the breaking out of the war of the Rebellion in 1861. On meeting his old friend, Abraham Lincoln, then President of the United States, Mr. Lincoln offered him a Brigadier-General's commission in the army of the United States, which offer Gen. Wilson declined, for the reason of his advanced age and his physical infirmities. He remained East about a year and a half, giving such aid and moral support as he could to the Union cause. He returned to California in the autumn of 1862, and resided there until 1867, when he left the Pacific coast and returned to his old home in Keene, to live out the residue of his days among his old friends and acquaintances who had been so true and kind to him throughout so many, many years.

"In 1870 and '71, the voters of Keene elected him again to represent them in the General Court of the State of New Hampshire."

Gen. Wilson possessed much reputation as a lawyer,

and had his whole efforts been turned to his profession, he must have become eminent. He was drawn off by the military and by politics, so that his profession became quite neglected. But in both these departments he excelled—there were in the State very few military men his equals,—and as a politician he gained great reputation. His power of addressing and holding a great multitude in times of excitement was extraordinary. It may be said in truth that he had very few equals in that oratory required for a political campaign. His success was wonderful; he gained good opinions at all points,—almost made his opponents yield to his mode of putting the political topics handled.

He now survives, at nearly eighty years of age, in the full possession of all his faculties, and resides at his former residence in Keene. But for bodily infirmities, we know not but his efficiency would be as great as ever; mentally he seems as competent for active service as in his best days. May he be spared many years.

26 | *Mary E.*, b. Oct. 27, 1826; m. John Sherwood, New York; three ch.

27 | *James E.*, b. July 28, 1829; d. March 9, 1832, æ. 3 yrs.
28 | *William R.*, b. Nov. 22, 1830; d. March 17, 1834, æ. 4 yrs.

29 | *Annie F.*, b. Sept. 23, 1832; m. Col. Francis S. Fisk; five ch.

30 | *Charlotte J.*, b. Aug. 31, 1835; m. Frank S. Taintor; three ch.; r. New York.

31 | *James H.*, b. Dec. 31, 1837.
32 | *Daniel W.*, b. Feb. 13, 1841; d. Jan. 18, 1846, æ. 5 yrs.

4– 25 | GEORGE W. WILSON is a harness-maker by trade. He lives in village, and is employed in upholstering at Briggs' Patent Piano Stool Manufactory. He m., 1st w., March 31, 1853, H. Maria Smiley, dau. of David Smiley, Jr.; d. July 23, 1855, æ. 25 yrs.; c.; m., 2d w., Katie M. Grimes, Sept. 22, 1867; she d. July 8, 1876, æ. 33 yrs.; 2d w., three ch.

---

33 | *William F.*, b. Aug. 19, 1868.
34 | *Hattie M.*, b. Dec. 8, 1869.
35 | *Bessie*, b. May 13, 1873; d. soon after birth.

---

1 | HUGH WILSON, a race, as far as known, entirely distinct from the above. He came from Londonderry, where he was an important character. He was moderator in Londonderry in 1742 and also in 1750, and not

after. He was also a representative to the General Court in 1738, and selectman 1737, '38, '39. It is supposed that he moved to town not far from 1752 or '53, having been here for some time previous in preparing. He was authorized by the charter to call the first meeting of the town under the act of incorporation, and was chosen moderator March 17, 1760, John Ferguson, town clerk ; Hugh Wilson, Thomas Morison, Jonathan Morison, Joseph Caldwell, and John Swan, selectmen ; surveyors of highways, Hugh Wilson, Thomas Morison, Jonathan Morison, John Smith, Thomas Cuningham, and John Robbe ; tithing-men, James Robbe and Hugh Dunlap ; constable, William Robbe, Jr. He was moderator seven years, from 1760 to '73, and selectman 1760, '64, '72. His name often appears in the town records till 1774, when it is no longer found, after the following vote, Sept. 12, 1774 : " Voted, To acquit Hugh Wilson on account of his delivering up the charter of the town, and voted that Samuel Mitchell should have charge of the same charter." The inference here is, that he had shown some reluctance to give up the charter of the town, which was justly in his hands, and having consented to do it the vote was in vindication of this act.

We know nothing of what became of this important character after the above date, nor have we any trace, for the last seventy years or more, of a single member of his family. He bought three long lots a mile long, that made six hundred acres, nearly a mile square. The Pratt place was nearly the centre of it. The Mussey farm embraces a part of it, given to his son John, who sold it to Patrick White in 1777. He was also justice of the peace. He was m. when he came to town, and had four ch. by his 1st w., and according to notes of Samuel Smith he m. Hugh Gregg's sister, and then followed three more ch.

---

2 † *John*, b. Londonderry, ——— ; m. Barbara Gregg.
3 *Ann*, b. Londonderry, March 20, 1726 ; m. Joseph Hammill ; d. March 19, 1796, æ. 70 yrs.
4 *Jenny*, b. ——— ; m. (Black) John Gregg.
5 *Robert*, b. July 8, 1731.
6 *Margaret*, b. July 8, 1733 ; m. Charles Cowell.
7 *Hugh*, b. Londonderry, April 7, 1742.
8 *Samuel*, b. Londonderry, April 14, 1746 ; m. Sarah Darrah.
9 *Molly*, b. Londonderry, Oct. 11, 1748 ; m. John McDonald.
10 *James*, b. Londonderry, ——— ; m. Martha Taggart, dau.

of Heeland Taggart. He lived in various places ; d.
of small-pox in Canada, in 1798.

1- 2 | JOHN WILSON m. Barbara Gregg.

11 | *John*, b. Oct. 5, 1759.   (12) *Hugh*, b. Oct. 16, 1761.
13 | *Margaret*, b. Jan. 8, 1764. (14) *Ann*, b. April 3, 1766.

THE YOUNG FAMILY.

1   JOHN YOUNG (Dr.) was the first physician of Peterborough, of whose early life and education very little is
known. He was b. in Worcester, Mass., June 2, 1739,
and after obtaining such an education as the times afforded, he studied his profession with the elder Dr.
Green. The preparation for the profession of medicine
in those days must have been very meagre compared
with even the advantages now enjoyed, which are poor
enough. He was considered among the best read men
of his day, and our old people had a very high opinion
of his medical knowledge and skill. He commenced
his practice in Pelham, Mass., where he continued for a
short time, and during this period he married and also
buried his first wife. He now returned to Worcester,
and was m. to Elizabeth Smith, who was b. Jan. 17, 1740,
and they removed to Peterborough about 1764. We
have no means of fixing definitely the precise time when
he came to town. In his old account-books some
charges are made in 1764, but none go back of this
date. His name first appears on the town records as
moderator of a meeting held Jan. 1, 1765, and then it
occasionally occurs all alone, to 1800. He was moderator eight years, and selectman five years. He seems to
have been a prominent man with our fathers in all these
years previous to the present century. They had a large
family of ten children after they came to town, none of
whom are now living. They all left Peterborough early
but one daughter, Jane, who was unmarried, and lived
and died here. Mrs. Young survived her husband many
years, and was again married to Samuel Twitchell, Esq.,
of Dublin (father to the late Dr. Amos Twitchell, of
Keene), but again became a widow, and returned to
Peterborough and spent the residue of her life with her
daughter Jane. She d. Sept. 25, 1825, æ. 84 yrs.
    Dr. Young sustained the reputation of being one of
the best physicians of his day, and was extensively employed in all this region. The elderly people of the
town always spoke highly of his skill and judgment as a

46

physician, while they deplored his intemperate habits, which grew upon him and greatly abridged his usefulness, especially during the latter part of his life. Among a hospitable people, such as were the early settlers of this town, the temptations to intemperance were very great, particularly to the physician. He could hardly avoid falling into this vice, unless he had been a "total abstinence man," a thing unheard of in those days. The practice of medicine was attended with great hardship. The roads were poor, often little more than bridle-paths, or the course pointed out by blazed trees. All was an interminable forest yet inhabited by wild beasts. I am told by an aged inhabitant of this town, now living, Mr. Elihu Thayer, that about ninety years ago Dr. Young, on a professional visit to his father's house — Deacon Christopher Thayer's, — came into the house in great trepidation, having been followed by a wolf, which had been attracted by a quarter of beef his brother had just brought home on his saddle before him. He stayed all night, fearing to go home through the woods.

The charges for medical services were very low at this time, and also very poorly paid. The early settlers had little to pay with but the produce of their farms; and I suppose the ancient doctor then shared the same fate with his successors, — that his bill was the last to be provided for, and most easily pushed on from year to year without payment. It was the custom of the early physicians to charge so much a mile, and extra for all the medicines dispensed. Dr. Young, before the Revolution, charged eightpence per mile, but he afterwards increased it to one shilling a mile. The medicines were charged high — they were probably more expensive than at the present time, — and if our subject may be authority, they were used with a pretty liberal hand. In Dr. Young's charges there is great profuseness of medicine in some of his cases, and it would often be difficult to devise with what intention a great deal of it was prescribed. It was no doubt necessary for the reputation of the doctor, and to satisfy the patient.

Though Dr. Young continued in full practice, yet he became very poor as he grew old, probably in consequence of his intemperate habits, and was obliged to ask assistance of the town towards the support of his family. The action of the town was kind and delicate towards him; for in 1799 the following vote was passed: "Voted, To take into consideration Dr. Young's low circumstances in worldly affairs. Chose Henry Ferguson, Robert Morison, Robert Swan, a committee to make inquiry of the said Young's situation, and propose such relief as they shall think proper."

We have no account of the report of the committee, but suppose their suggestions were acted on at once, and that he was aided as much as was necessary.

One other vote of the town is found, June 5, 1805: "Voted, That the selectmen furnish Dr. Young with two cows for his use, being the town's property."

We suppose that Dr. Young was considerably above mediocrity in his profession, and he enjoyed for many years the entire confidence of a community quick to see defects, ready to sift pretensions and expose shams. He went through the ordeal successfully, and but for his intemperance would have passed off as one of the most honored and worthy of the early physicians. He d. of a cancer of the face, after long suffering, Feb. 27, 1807, æ. 68 yrs.

2   *John*, b. March 8, 1764; m. —— White, Whitestown, N. Y.
3   *William*, b. Aug. 14, 1768; m. Eunice Porter.
4   *Elizabeth*, b. Feb. 21, 1771; m. —— Earl, Chester, Vt.
5   *Jane Foster*, b. May 24, 1773; unm.; d. March 2, 1857, æ. 84 yrs.; always lived in town.
6   *Susanna*, b. Aug. 24, 1776; m. Capt. B. Carryll.
7   *David*, b. Oct. 25, 1779.
8   *Foster*, b. March 25, 1784; m. ——, Chester, Vt., and re. to Buffalo, N. Y.

THE YOUNGMAN FAMILY.

David Youngman, Sen., was the son of Jabez Youngman, who was b. in Hollis, March, 1764; was a soldier in the Revolutionary War, as were his three older brothers, the oldest of whom, Eben, was killed in battle at Bunker Hill. He m., March, 1785, Susannah Powers, b. in Hollis, Aug. 28, 1768, where they lived several years, when they removed to Lempster, and lived many years in comfortable circumstances, and where they both d. within three days of each other; he d. April 30, 1839, æ. 75 yrs.; she d. May 3, 1839, æ. 71 yrs., after living in the marriage relation fifty-four years; they were buried in the same grave.

1   DAVID YOUNGMAN was b. in Hollis, Dec. 19, 1790. Came to Peterborough about 1810; served an apprenticeship in the tanning and currying business with Dea. John Field, for whom he afterwards worked some dozen years, and identified himself with the interests of the

town. He m. Ruth Field, dau. of John Field, March 7, 1816. She d. Sept. 5, 1817, æ. 22 yrs. He removed to Franklin, Tenn., in 1821 or '22, where he engaged in tanning and currying, which he carried on successfully many years. He afterwards purchased an extensive farm, with saw and grist-mills ; became a slave-owner, and was prosperous after the Southern fashion, until the war of the Rebellion set his slaves at liberty, and, during the struggle, he was robbed by both parties — Union as well as Confederate — of his horses, mules, cattle, leather, provisions, and, in fact, of everything that soldiers could find to steal, by which he became considerably reduced in circumstances. He m., 2d w., Nancy McMahon, April, 1833 ; no ch. He is still living in Franklin, Tenn., enjoying a serene old age, now in his eighty-sixth year.

2   †*David*, b. in Peterborough, Aug. 26, 1817 ; m. Mary Ann Stone.

WILLARD YOUNGMAN was a younger brother of David, b. in Lempster, April, 1804. He came to Peterborough in early life ; m. Jane Little, dau. of Thomas Little. She m., 2d hus., Benjamin Read, of Newport, November, 1834, and had by him one son, Wallace L., b. July 22, 1842. She d. Feb. 12, 1866, æ. 61 yrs. Willard Youngman was for several years engaged in building mills and mill-dams, during those years when the Union Factory and other large mills were erected. He lived at West Peterborough, where he built a house, and where he d. Dec. 1, 1833, æ. 29 yrs., of chronic ulceration of the hip-joint, induced by his previous peculiar exposure, and was among the first persons buried in the Village Cemetery.

3   *Jane L.*, b. Feb. 9, 1827 ; m. Nathan T. Eaton ; ch., (1) Abbie Louisa, b. April 9, 1847 ; d. Sept. 6, 1849, æ. 2 yrs., 6 mos. ; (2) Eva Cariola, b. July 20, 1850 ; (3) Frank W., b. April 23, 1853 ; d. June 2, 1853 ; (4) Ella L., b. Sept. 25, 1855.

4   *Mary L.*, b. June 17, 1828 ; m. Ethan Hadley ; r. Chicopee.

5   *Addison*, b. November, 1829 ; d. Feb. 18, 1830, æ. 3 mos.
6   *Susan W.*, b. April 11, 1831 ; m. Elias Cheney ; r. Lebanon.

1– 2   DAVID YOUNGMAN, M. D. He fitted for college at New Ipswich, and graduated at Dartmouth College in 1839. He subsequently engaged in teaching at Franklin, Tenn., and at Hartford, Vt., when he returned to

David Youngman

Peterborough and taught the academy two years, 1842 and '43. He studied the medical profession with Albert Smith, M.D., at Peterborough, and with Profs. Crosby and Peaslee, at Hanover; and after attending the usual courses of lectures, one at Woodstock, Vt., and two at Hanover, he took the degree of M.D., at Dartmouth, in 1846. He settled in South Woburn, Mass., (now Winchester) in 1846; was elected the first town clerk of Winchester in 1850, which office he held six consecutive years, until he removed from town. He interested himself in educational matters, and was a member of the school committee for several years. He was always interested in the study and practice of church and social music, and taught the same in various places in New Hampshire and Vermont during his pupilage, and was for many years an efficient and popular leader of the singing in church. He removed to Boston in 1856, where he still resides in the practice of his profession, and as a specialty devotes his time largely to the examination of mental and nervous diseases. He m., Aug. 1, 1842, Mary Ann Stone, of Hartford, Vt.

7   *Albert Legrand*, b. in Peterborough, Jan. 22, 1844; d. in Peterborough, Jan. 17, 1845, æ. 1 yr.

8   *Willis Blake*, b. in Winchester, Mass., June 29, 1846; m. Alma A. Sanborn, Dec. 25, 1871. Is engaged on cabinet organs in Boston. Has recently become quite successful as an artist in stipple and crayon portraiture.

9   *Mary Ruth*, b. in Winchester, June 24, 1849; d. Jan. 2, 1852, æ. 2 yrs., 6 mos.

10   *Clara Elizabeth*, b. in Winchester, July 3, 1851; m. Walter W. Scott, Jan. 5, 1875. He is a jeweller and optician in Boston.

11   *Emma Knapp*, b. in Winchester, July 30, 1853. Is a teacher in the public schools, Boston.

INDEX.

NOTE. — Figures followed by a * refer to the Genealogical pages.